Pakistan Occupied Kashmir
Politics, Parties and Personalities

Pakistan Occupied Kashmir
Politics, Parties and Personalities

Surinder Kumar Sharma
Yaqoob ul Hassan
Ashok Behuria

INSTITUTE FOR DEFENCE STUDIES & ANALYSES
NEW DELHI

Pakistan Occupied Kashmir: Politics, Parties and Personalities
Surinder Kumar Sharma, Yaqoob ul Hassan and Ashok Behuria

First Published in 2019

Copyright © Institute for Defence Studies and Analyses, New Delhi

ISBN 978-93-86618-67-2

All rights reserved. No part of this publication may be reproduced, stored in a retrieval system, or transmitted, in any form or by any means, electronic, mechanical, photocopying, recording, or otherwise, without first obtaining written permission of the copyright owner.

Disclaimer: The views expressed in this book are those of the authors and do not necessarily reflect those of the Institute for Defence Studies and Analyses, or the Government of India.

Published by
PENTAGON PRESS LLP
206, Peacock Lane, Shahpur Jat,
New Delhi-110049
Phones: 011-64706243, 26491568
Telefax: 011-26490600
email: rajan@pentagonpress.in
website: www.pentagonpress.in

In association with
Institute for Defence Studies and Analyses
No. 1, Development Enclave,
New Delhi-110010
Phone: +91-11-26717983
Website: www.idsa.in

Printed at Aegean Offset Printers, Greater Noida, U.P.

Contents

Foreword		ix
Acknowledgements		xi
Abbreviations		xiii
About the Authors		xv
Introduction		xvii

1. 'AJK' and Pakistan: A Relationship of Disenchantment — 1
Politics of 'AJK': The Early Phase — 2
The 1970s — 7
Interim Constitution Act, 1974 — 9
Government and Politics in 'AJK': Post-1974 — 12
Politics of Representation — 14
Economy and Hydro-Energy — 25
Dissenting Voices — 27

2. Political Parties in 'AJK' — 33
All-Jammu and Kashmir Muslim Conference (AJKMC) — 34
Jammu and Kashmir Liberation Front (JKLF) — 48
Jammu and Kashmir Liberation League (JKLL) — 52
Jammu and Kashmir People's Muslim League (JKPML) — 59
United Kashmir People's National Party (UKPNP) — 61
Jammu and Kashmir National Awami Party (JKNAP) — 65
All-Parties National Alliance (APNA) — 66
AJK Pakistan People's Party (AJKPPP) — 70
AJK Pakistan People's Party Shaheed Bhutto (AJKPPPSB) — 76
AJK Pakistan Muslim League-Nawaz (AJKPML-N) — 77
AJK Muttahida Quami Movement (AJKMQM) — 84
Pakistan Tehreek-i-Insaf (PTI) — 93
Jamaat-e-Islami AJK (JIAJK) — 98
Kashmir Voice International (KVI) — 104

3. Gilgit-Baltistan: A Historical Perspective — 116
Introduction — 116
Area and Population — 116

Demography and Religion	116
Economic Conditions	118
Karakoram Highway	120
Tourism Industry	121
Political History	122
Political Structure of GBESGO	130
November 2009 Elections after the Promulgation of GBESGO	131
Legislative Assembly Elections June 2015	132
Reactions to GBESGO, 2009	135
India's Response	136
Political Developments	137
Local Government Act 2014	139
Sectarianism in Gilgit-Baltistan	139
The Diamer Bhasha Dam	141
Challenges	144
Land Scam	145
Threat to Buddhist Heritage	146

4. Political Parties in Gilgit-Baltistan 153

Pakistan People's Party Gilgit-Baltistan (PPP-GB)	153
Pakistan People's Party Shaheed Bhutto	156
Pakistan Muslim League-Nawaz-GB (PMLN-GB)	156
Pakistan Muslim League Quaid-i-Azam-GB (PMLQ-GB)	160
All-Pakistan Muslim League-GB (APML-GB)	161
Pakistan Tehreek-i-Insaf-GB (PTI-GB)	162
Islami Tehreek Pakistan (ITP)	164
Jamiat Ulema-e-Islam-Fazlur Rehman-GB (JUIF-GB)	164
Jamaat-e-Islami-GB (JI-GB)	165
Muttahida Quami Movement-GB (MQM-GB)	166
Majlis-e-Wahadat Muslimeen Gilgit Baltistan (MWM-GB)	166
Tanzeem Ahl-e-Sunnat Wal Jamaat (TASWJ)	167

Nationalist/Pressure Groups 168

Balawaristan National Front (BNF)	168
Balawaristan Students' National Organisation (BSNO)	171
Jammu and Kashmir Liberation Front (JKLF)	173
Karakorum National Movement (KNM)	174
Gilgit-Baltistan Democratic Alliance (GBDA)	175
Gilgit-Baltistan United Movement (GBUM)	176
Gilgit-Baltistan United Alliance (GBUA)	177
Gilgit-Baltistan National Alliance (GBNA)	178
Awami Workers Party (AWP)	178
Gilgit-Baltistan National Movement (GBNM)	180
Gilgit-Baltistan National Congress (GBNC)	180
Gilgit-Baltistan Thinker's Forum (GBTF)	181
Gilgit-Baltistan Bar Council (GBBC)	182
Gharib Qaumi Movement (GQM)	184

5.	**Demand for Provincial Status in Gilgit-Baltistan: Dilemmas of the Pakistan State**	190
	Earlier debates on inclusion of 'AJK'	190
	The demand for representation in G-B	191
	Self-Governance Act of 2009	192
	The Debate (2009-2017)	194
	GB Reforms Order 2018	197
6.	**China-Pakistan Economic Corridor and Gilgit-Baltistan**	202
	CPEC and Kashmir Issue	207
7.	**Profiles of Prominent Leaders of 'AJK' and Gilgit-Baltistan**	211
	(A) Prominent Leaders of 'AJK'	211
	(B) Prominent Leaders of Gilgit-Baltistan	222
	(C) Some other Leaders and the current Cabinet of Gilgit-Baltistan	227
	Conclusion	230
	Chronology of Developments in PoK with Special Focus on Gilgit-Baltistan Since July 1947	237

Appendices

I.	The Boundary Agreement Between China and Pakistan, 1963	255
II.	Karachi Agreement	259
III.	Simla Agreement, July 2, 1972	263
IV.	'AJK' Interim Constitution (Thirteenth Amendment) Act, 2018	266
V.	List of Political Parties in 'AJK' and Names of the Party Heads and General Secretaries	288
VI.	Presidents/Prime Ministers of 'AJK'	295
VII.	Members 'AJK' Legislative Assembly 2016	297
VIII.	The Northern Areas Council Legal Frame Work Order, 1994 (With Amendments)	299
IX.	Gilgit-Baltistan (Empowerment and Self-Governance) Order, 2009	325
X.	Balawaristan National Front	373
XI.	Registered Political Parties of Gilgit-Baltistan with Election Symbols	376
XII.	Electoral Rolls of Gilgit-Baltistan Election 2015	378
XIII.	Members of Gilgit-Baltistan Assembly	379
XIV	Letters Exchanged Between Yasin Malik and Nawaz Sharif	381
XV	Pakistan Supreme Court Order on Gilgit Baltistan on January 17, 2019	385
	Maps	466
	Bibliography	470
	Index	475

Foreword

Pakistan Occupied Kashmir (PoK), which includes both the so-called "Azad Jammu and Kashmir (AJK)" and Gilgit-Baltistan (GB), was legally a part of the erstwhile princely state of Jammu and Kashmir, which acceded to India in October 1947. The entire state legitimately belongs to India and its disputed status has been reiterated by India for the last 70 years. The PoK is kept under tight control of the Government of Pakistan through the Ministry of Kashmir and Gilgit-Baltistan Affairs, while at the local level in both the units, notional representative systems have been allowed to deal with local resentments. The internal affairs of these two areas do not receive too much of media attention, and therefore, there is very little in the public domain in India on the evolution of politics in this terrain, as well as on the parties, pressure groups and personalities that struggle to voice their concerns about their neglected status over the years.

The scholars at IDSA follow the events and political processes in these two regions regularly and there is a project devoted to this job in the Institute, which has been running for the last 10 years. This book is a result of research undertaken on the subject by the scholars associated with this project. It seeks to provide facts and analyses on the genesis and evolution of various political parties, interest groups, and the background and role of different personalities operating in both parts of PoK. The main aim of the publication is to help the scholars, analysts, and policy-makers to understand the dynamics of the political systems in PoK, the complex interaction of these systems with the government in Islamabad and the responses of the local leadership to their subservient status over the last 70 years.

This study is a welcome effort by the three authors, Shri S.K. Sharma, Dr. Yaqoob ul Hassan and Dr Ashok Behuria, who have consulted a variety of primary and secondary sources like government documents, books and articles published in the newspapers and journals, especially those in the vernaculars, the reports of a number of international institutions, and the websites of various political parties to gather facts pertaining to the subject.

I commend the efforts undertaken by the authors who, in spite of scarcity of material available on the theme, have been able to bring out a publication that will be useful for wider academic and strategic purposes. I take this opportunity to thank the two anonymous referees who added value to the publication by their comments and suggestions. I hope this publication will draw the attention it deserves from the strategic community in India.

September 18, 2018 **Jayant Prasad**
Director General, IDSA

Acknowledgements

We have been associated with this book project for quite some time. We have received help from a number of individuals for successful completion of this book. We owe a debt of gratitude to those individuals without whose help and contribution this book could not have been completed.

First and foremost, we record our debt to Shri Jayant Prasad, former Director General, IDSA and Deputy Director Maj Gen. Alok Deb (Retd.) for their valuable support. We are also greatly indebted Dr. Arvind Gupta for conceiving the idea of this project, when he was the Director General of the Institute.

This book would not have been the same without critical and constructive comments and suggestions from the anonymous referees. We thank the referees for their critical analysis and reviews.

The library staff of IDSA, have been very helpful. We would like to thank all the library staff for the help they extended.

Our special gratitude for Mr. Vivek Kaushik, Associate Editor, IDSA, for taking care of the editing and production process of the book. We also thank the copy editor for editing the manuscript.

Our families were steadfast in their support as always, and without their encouragement and support this project could not have been successfully completed.

Surinder Kumar Sharma
Yaqoob ul Hassan
Ashok Behuria

Abbreviations

AJK	Azad Jammu and Kashmir
AJKEC	Azad Jammu and Kashmir Election Commission
AJKMC	Azad Jammu and Kashmir Muslim Conference
AJKNC	All-Jammu and Kashmir National Conference
AJKPML-N	Azad Jammu & Kashmir Pakistan Muslim League-Nawaz
APHC	All-Parties Hurriyat Conference
APML	All-Pakistan Muslim League
APNA	All-Party National Alliance
ASSP	Anjuman Sipah-i-Sahaba Pakistan
AWP	Awami Workers Party
BLP	Boloristan Labour Party
BNF	Balawaristan National Front
BNF-H	Balawaristan National Front-Hameed
BRF	Balor Research Forum
BSNO	Balawaristan Students' National Organisation
FCR	Frontier Crimes Regulation
GB	Gilgit-Baltistan
GBC	Gilgit-Baltistan Council
GBDA	Gilgit-Baltistan Democratic Alliance
GBESGO	Gilgit-Baltistan Empowerment and Self-Governance Order
GBLA	Gilgit-Baltistan Legislative Assembly
GBLDM	Gilgit-Baltistan Ladakh Democratic Movement
GBNC	Gilgit-Baltistan National Congress
GBUM	Gilgit-Baltistan United Movement
ICG	International Crisis Group
ISI	Directorate for Inter-Services Intelligence

ITP	Islami Tehreek Pakistan
J&K	Jammu and Kashmir
JI	Jamaat-e-Islami
JKLF	Jammu and Kashmir Liberation Front
JKLL	Jammu and Kashmir Liberation League
JKNSF	Jammu and Kashmir National Students Federation
JUI	Jamiat Ulmah Islam
JKPML	Jammu and Kashmir People's Muslim League
JUI-F	Jamiat Ulema-e-Islam-Fazl
KANA	Kashmir and Northern Areas
KNM	Karakorum National Movement
KSO	Karakorum Students Organisation
LoC	Line of Control
MC	Muslim Conference
MKA	Ministry of Kashmir Affairs
MMA	Muttahida Majlis-e-Amal
MQM	Muttahida Qaumi Movement
MRD	Movement for the Restoration of Democracy
MWM-GB	Majlis-e-Wahadat Muslimeen Gilgit-Baltistan
NALC	Northern Areas Legislative Council
PML-N	Pakistan Muslim League-Nawaz
PML-Q	Pakistan Muslim League-Quaid-e-Azam
PoK	Pakistan Occupied Kashmir
PPPAJK	Pakistan Peoples Party Azad Jammu & Kashmir
PPPGB	Pakistan People's Party Gilgit-Baltistan
PTI	Pakistan Tehreek-i-Insaf
PYF	Progressive Youth Front
TASWJ	Tanzeem Ahl-e-Sunnat Wal Jamaat
TF	Thinkers Forum
UN-GBCIP	United Nations Gilgit Baltistan Commission for India and Pakistan
UNPO	Unrepresented Nations and Peoples Organisation
UKPNP	United Kashmir Peoples' National Party

About the Authors

Mr. Surinder Kumar Sharma has been attached to the Institute for Defence Studies and Analyses (IDSA) as a Consultant. He has a ring-side view on the rise of global terrorism specially surrounding India with special focus on Pakistan and Jammu and Kashmir. Besides writing regularly in the national and international newspapers, he is a co-author of the book (with Anshuman Behera) *Militant Groups in South Asia* (2014). He has held a number of important positions in the Indian security establishment, i.e. Cabinet Secretariat and the National Technical Research Organisation (NTRO), and has been decorated with the 'Outstanding Performance Award' by the National Security Adviser.

Dr Yaqoob ul Hassan is a research analyst at IDSA. He was an SAV Visiting Fellow in 2018 at the Stimson Center, Washington DC. He received his PhD from Jamia Millia Islamia in New Delhi, India and his thesis was on United States-Pakistan relations after 9/11. He was also a Post-doctoral Fellow in the Department of Political Science and International Relations at Istanbul University, Turkey. His research interests include politics and security of Pakistan and Afghanistan, Kashmir and Political Islam.

Dr Ashok Behuria is a Senior Fellow and Coordinator of the South Asia Centre at IDSA. He is a PhD from Jawaharlal Nehru University (JNU), New Delhi, India. He has worked as Assistant Director at the International Centre for Peace Studies (ICPS), New Delhi and has also been Editor of *International Studies*, the prestigious research journal published from JNU. He is on the Editorial Boards of *Journal of Peace Studies* and IDSA's flagship journal, *Strategic Analysis*. He is a recipient of the 'K Subrahmanyam Award for Excellence in Strategic Studies' for his work on Pakistan in 2009. He has published many articles on strategic issues related to Pakistan, India-Pakistan relations, Sri Lanka, Nepal and the South Asian security environment in Indian and foreign journals. He has edited books on South Asia and continues with his research on Pakistan, evolving strategic scenario in the Af-Pak region, radicalisation of religious discourse in the region, India's engagement with the neighbourhood, regional security, and inter-state cooperation.

Introduction

Pakistan Occupied Kashmir (PoK) comprises both the so-called 'Azad Jammu and Kashmir' ('AJK') and Gilgit-Baltistan (GB), which Pakistan called 'Northern Areas' till 2009. The entire PoK area occupied by Pakistan in 1947 formed the part of erstwhile princely state of Jammu and Kashmir. This region is not officially regarded as Pakistani territory. As per the figures provided by the governments of 'AJK' and Gilgit-Baltistan, the total area of the region is 90,972 square kilometres, out of which 'AJK' and Gilgit Baltistan account for 13,297 and 72,495 sq. kms respectively while the Trans-Karakoram Tract in the Shaksham valley, ceded by Pakistan to China on March 2, 1962 accounts for 5180 square kilometres.[1] The PoK's financial dependence and the unbridled interference of Pakistan in the administrative matters, through various promulgated ordinances and acts, without the people's consent define the nature of relationship between PoK ('AJK' and Gilgit-Baltistan) and the state of Pakistan. Over the years, the token representative civilian administrations in 'AJK' and Gilgit-Baltistan have been vested with little power, and they are continually under the mercy of the governments in Islamabad. According to local media reports, PoK's civilian leadership kowtows to the army and are often summoned by military to the army headquarters and prompted to conduct their affairs in a manner that conforms to the army's interests. Without any freedom of speech and expression in the region, the demand for autonomy, and even separatism, is simmering in both parts of PoK – 'AJK' and Gilgit-Baltistan.

Political parties pledging their loyalty to Pakistan, i.e., favouring accession of PoK to Pakistan, are allowed to operate in both 'AJK' and Gilgit-Baltistan. Those advocating autonomy are tolerated, while those demanding independence or genuine autonomy are barred from contesting elections. More often, they are not allowed to engage in any kind of political activism in the region. Given these limitations, local units of major Pakistan-based political parties that promote Pakistan's objectives on Kashmir (rather than representing the aspirations of the people of the area) have usually fared well in the local elections. In Gilgit-Baltistan, Pakistan-based parties have done well, while in 'AJK', both local and Pakistan-based political parties compete with one another for power.

There are groups which represent those people who question Pakistan's occupation of Kashmir and hence advocate freedom from Pakistan. They are opposed to the signing of any agreement that acknowledges Kashmir's final accession to Pakistan. Parties representing such a nationalistic outlook have been reduced to political non-entities by the Pakistani state.

Initially, Pakistan supported the Muslim Conference's rise to power in a significant part of the princely State of Jammu and Kashmir it had occupied through its invasion in 1947 and called it 'Azad' Kashmir or 'Azad Jammu and Kashmir ('AJK'). It had full faith in the loyalty of the Muslim Conference, which went on to name itself as All-Jammu and Kashmir Muslim Conference (AJKMC) whose leaders uphold Pakistan's claim to Kashmir because of the Party's allegiance to the ideology of the Muslim League. In Gilgit-Baltistan, which until 2009 was officially known as the Northern Areas, political activities were considered criminal under the special law, enacted and implemented by the British, called the Frontier Crimes Regulations (FCR), widely known as the black law. When Pakistan unlawfully assumed control of this region, it retained the FCR and other cruel British measures against the locals. After Zulfiqar Ali Bhutto came to power, this law was abolished and political activities were allowed in limited form. In 1994, then Prime Minister Benazir Bhutto's reforms allowed political party-based elections to the Northern Areas Council. That opened the flood gates for Pakistan-based political and Islamic parties to rush into Gilgit-Baltistan. They have reduced the significance of the local parties, which were firmly rooted in the nationalistic aspirations of the people, and have made deep inroads into local politics. As a consequence the mainstream political parties in Pakistan are in power today in both parts of PoK ('AJK' and Gilgit-Baltistan).

The Muslim Conference was installed in 'AJK' not because it represented a significant segment of the Kashmir opinion but because it gained the trust of the founder of Pakistan, Mohammad Ali Jinnah for having split away from the Sheikh Abdullah-led All-Jammu and Kashmir National Conference (henceforth the National Conference) and added the prefix "Muslim" to the Party's name (which was earlier dropped by Sheikh Abdullah in June 1939).

The renaming of the Muslim Conference as the National Conference with a view to opening it to non-Muslims was an antithesis of the Muslim League's two-nation theory and hence unacceptable to a cross section of leadership in the state who advocated communal politics. Jinnah had wanted Sheikh Abdullah to rename the National Conference as Muslim Conference. But he turned it down saying Jammu and Kashmir, being overwhelmingly a Muslim-majority State, did not suffer from a minority complex, which was the basis of Jinnah's two-nation theory. Jinnah was planning to use the Muslim Conference as a subsidiary of the Muslim League in Kashmir. A hint of this scheme was given by Jinnah himself when he said at a reception given in his honour by the National Conference in Srinagar that the reception was accorded to him as the leader of the Muslim League, much to the annoyance of some of the National Conference leaders, who walked out of the gathering.[2]

Interestingly, Sardar Abdul Qayyum Khan, who went on to become the supreme leader of the Muslim Conference, resisted the entry of the Muslim League into 'AJK' for many years on the plea that in the presence of the Muslim Conference, there was no need of the Muslim League in 'AJK'. Qayyum's party acted as a well-paid proxy of Pakistan whenever Pakistan needed its service.

Muslim Conference's monopoly began to crack in 1975 when the Pakistan People's Party (PPP) captured power in 'AJK' in the first elections held under the 1974 Interim Constitution. The PPP government was thrown out when General Zia-ul-Haq staged a military coup in Pakistan in July 1977. Eventually, the Muslim Conference as a proxy of Muslim League and the PPP became two main political parties which alternately 'won' elections in 'AJK' depending on who was ruling in Islamabad. When the military or the Muslim League ruled in Islamabad, the Muslim Conference won the elections in 'AJK'. When the PPP ruled in Islamabad, the PPP's 'Azad Kashmir' chapter won in 'AJK'. Thus, the people of the area seemed to gravitate towards the political parties that were ruling in Islamabad either to ensure better allocation of resources for development at the local level, or fell prey to their mobilisation tactic through use of money and administrative machinery – the trend that continues to this day.

The fact remains that neither of the mainstream national parties have cared for local needs and grievances. A clear example of this indifference was the approach of the authorities in Islamabad to the massive earthquake which struck 'AJK' on October 5, 2005, killing thousands of people and rendering a large segment of the population homeless. Foreign relief workers loaded with relief goods descended upon 'AJK' while winter was setting in, but the politicians from Pakistan did not show up for quite some time. When things returned to normal, they did not even feel the need to apologise to the people for their callousness.

The 'AJK' Muslim Conference is near extinction now. In the July 2016 elections it could win only three of the 41 seats. Its supreme leader, Sardar Abdul Qayyum, is no more. His son, Attique Ahmed Khan is struggling to lead the party that is burdened with allegations of corruption and malpractices. The second major party, the 'AJK' chapter of the PPP, which was in power during the elections, was hurt by a massive wave of anti-incumbency sentiment and was routed in the polls, securing just two seats. In the 2013 Pakistan general elections the party became a near non-entity – except in Sindh. In tune with the political trend in Pakistan, the June 2015 Legislative Assembly elections in Gilgit-Baltistan saw the decimation of the erstwhile ruling party, the PPP, which won only one seat. The party then ruling in Islamabad – the PML-N – came to power in Gilgit-Baltistan in June 2015 and in 'AJK' in July 2016. After 2018 general elections that saw Imran Khan led Pakistan Tehreek-e-Insaf (PTI) coming into power at centre. Therefore, it is more likely that the PTI's 'AJK' and Gilgit-Baltistan chapter may also win next elections in both the regions of PoK, provided, PTI completes its tenure at centre.

Both the Muslim Conference and the AJKPPP have never bothered to clear themselves of the charges of massive corruption during long years of their rules. Like the Muslim Conference, the AJKPPP too is burdened with allegations of corruption, particularly under Benazir Bhutto's and her husband, Asif Ali Zardari's leadership. Moreover, the couple's son and its present co-Chairman of the party, Bilawal Bhutto Zardari, is regarded as politically immature. Apart from the absence of the strong leadership at the local level, the PPP is also facing an ideological vacuum. The absence of any socio-economic vision that meets the contemporary requirements of the bulk of the young electorate in Pakistan has reduced to it a regional party confined to a rural vote bank of the Sindh.

The elections in 'AJK' in July 2016 posed a huge existential challenge for the AJKPPP. Nawaz Sharif's Pakistan Muslim League- Nawaz (PML-N), which then ruled Pakistan, won the elections in spectacular fashion bagging 31 out of the total 41 seats and five out of eight seats based on proportionate votes polled. The main reason for its win was not only that the people chose a party that was ruling in Islamabad, but also that being in power it was in the best position to control the resources for the elections. The regional PPP-led government, quite predictably, blamed Nawaz Sharif for using funds to rig the polls. On March 25, 2016, the then 'AJK' cabinet headed by then Prime Minister, Chaudhry Abdul Majeed, issued a statement in which it strongly condemned the 'AJK' Council for direct release of developmental funds on the basis of political affiliation to influence the voters in the elections. The cabinet declared it as pre-poll rigging.[3]

All 'AJK'-based top political parties have an uncertain future. Parties like Jamaat-i-Islami and Muttahida Quami Movement (MQM) are electoral lightweights. Imran Khan's PTI, which emerged as the largest party in 2018 general elections, is a new entrant in local politics. Its candidate, Barrister Sultan Mahmood Chaudhry, formerly with AJKPPP, opened the 'AJK' chapter of the PTI by winning a by-election in Mirpur in March 2015. Enthused by his victory, Imran Khan hoped that the PTI would sweep the Assembly elections in 2016 and form the government. However, as the turn of events proved later, Mahmood owed his victory to his own influence in Mirpur, which has been his stronghold for long. Ironically, he lost his seat in the 2016 elections following his association with PTIAJK and Imran Khan. Moreover, PTIAJK had an electoral understanding with the 'AJK' Muslim Conference. The elections were held under the supervision of army and rangers and PML-N swept the elections signalling an electoral shift towards the party in power in Islamabad.

As far as the future of political parties in Gilgit-Baltistan is concerned, the trend there is not very different from that of 'AJK'. As outlined above, in Gilgit-Baltistan (GB) too, the regional chapters of PPP and PML-N are now the main political parties, patronised by their mother parties in Pakistan. The local AJKPPP rose to power when its mother party ruled at the centre. As the ruler of Gilgit-Baltistan, the PPP allegedly indulged in corruption with no holds barred. Even when elections were coming closer, it made no efforts to mend its ways. But the AJKPPP's defeat at the hands of the PML-N in Gilgit-Baltistan cannot be blamed on its corruption alone: even without the allegation of corruption, its defeat was a foregone conclusion because the tide had turned in Islamabad and the PML-N had come to power in Pakistan. This trend is not in the interest of local politics in both the regions of PoK, because it is not the intention of the Pakistan establishment to let a viable political party system grow in these two parts of occupied Kashmir. Viable independent locally-based parties are seen as a threat to Pakistan's control. For this reason, Pakistani patrons are not seen encouraging local leadership in either 'AJK' or GB.

With the change in the geo-politics of the region post 9/11 and Pakistan's unabated internal crises, the military dispensation led by Gen. Musharraf, then ruling in Islamabad, had been forced to revisit old policies vis-à-vis India and Kashmir. There had been ostensibly a shift in Pakistan's approach towards Kashmir after the September 11, 2001 attacks on the US, when the world at large refused to buy Pakistan's theory that there was a distinction between terrorism and freedom struggle. Such change at the global level had forced Pakistan to relax its approach towards PoK and there were talks of introducing more representative administration in both parts of PoK, as intra-Kashmir connectivity and trade were promoted under persuasion from India during 2004-2007.

Moreover, with the advent of social media, the people of the region were seen to be asserting themselves politically during this period. However, the trend of politics both within Pakistan and the region since 2008 – especially after the 26/11 terror attacks in Mumbai (on November 26, 2008) – is far from encouraging. There is a clear disinclination in Islamabad to proceed with the dialogue process initiated during the rule of Gen. Musharraf and recent terror attacks on India during 2014-2018 show that there is an effort to restart insurgency and terrorism in Kashmir. This is likely to have negative impact on the political situation in both parts of PoK, while the military is likely to have an upper hand in managing the local political and security affairs in the region.

NOTES

1. See Appendix I.
2. Sheikh Mohammad Abdullah, *Atish-e-Chinar*, Gulshan Books, Srinagar, 2008, p. 222.
3. Rao Atiq ul Amin Khan, "AJK Cabinet for Increase in Hydro Power Royalty", *Pakistan Observer*, March 19, 2016, at http://pakobserver.net/2016/03/19/ajk-cabinet-for-increase-in-hydro-power-royalty/

1
'AJK' and Pakistan: A Relationship of Disenchantment

The whole of Pakistan Occupied Kashmir (PoK) remains in a state of limbo ever since it was illegally brought under the control of Pakistani security forces in October 1947. On April 28, 1949, Pakistan bifurcated the territory under its occupation into two different political entities. One of these, more populous but consisting of about 15 per cent of the occupied territory, was called 'Azad Jammu and Kashmir' (AJK), and given the notional status of an *'azad'* or independent state but in reality, it was administered *de facto* by a minister in charge of Kashmir and Northern Areas (KANA) in Islamabad till 1974, and by an executive council headed by Prime Minister of Pakistan. The other part, less populous but accounting for about 85 per cent of the territory occupied by Pakistan – consisting of Gilgit Agency and Baltistan, the vassal units of the erstwhile Jammu and Kashmir princely state – was separated from AJK and called 'Northern Areas'. The latter was made to operate as a stateless entity, under the direction of the Pakistani state with the continued application of the Frontier Crimes Regulation (FCR) the infamous colonial law invented by the British to keep the border areas on a tight leash.

During the last about 70 years, a variety of administrative reforms has been introduced in both these areas to make the dispensation more representative. But overall control remained with the government of Pakistan. Between both parts of PoK, 'AJK' is better off than Gilgit-Baltistan (GB). Moreover, common to both regions is their political-economic subjugation by the Pakistani state; a process has been institutionalised over the decades. The state apparatus in Islamabad has been used coercively to keep the region under strict control. Pakistan has dealt with PoK in a manner that is contrary to the provisions mentioned in its own constitution, which do not authorise Pakistan to administer PoK under Article 257, which clearly states, "When the people of the State of Jammu and Kashmir decide to accede to Pakistan, the relationship between Pakistan and that State shall be determined in accordance with the wishes of the people of that State."[1] The history of Pakistan's dealings with both parts of PoK, and various interim set-ups introduced with or without the consent of the people of the area reveals that 'AJK' is not even autonomous, let alone 'Azad' (which means independence or freedom), by any stretch of imagination. As elucidated by one observer from the area: "One can vaguely deduce the status of 'AJK' from the statement that Azad Kashmir is neither a sovereign state nor a province of Pakistan but rather a 'local authority' with responsibility over the areas assigned to it under the ceasefire agreement."[2] As regards Gilgit-Baltistan its status is even worse than that of the 'AJK'. It has no legal standing and is being ruled as a de-facto colony of Pakistan.

The political and legal aspects of PoK, are far from settled. The territory that is occupied by Pakistan legitimately belonged to the princely state of Jammu and Kashmir, and to India, after accession of the state by the King to the Indian Union, on October 26, 1947. In Pakistan, there is a view that control over these areas was entrusted to Pakistan by the UN. For example, Justice Manzoor Gillani (Retd.) holds that "the administration of AJ&K and Gilgit-Baltistan was entrusted to Pakistan under UN Security Council resolutions. They have since been treated in many respects as administrative units of Pakistan and are subject to most of the liabilities and obligations of a province under the Pakistan constitution"; He recognises the fact, however, that "they do not have any of the constitutional rights and powers enjoyed by the provinces".[3] Therefore, it is pertinent to go back to history and trace the developments in the region that define Pakistan's relationship with PoK.

Politics of 'AJK': The Early Phase

The paradoxical nature of PoK's status vis-à-vis Pakistan goes back to 1947-48. During that period, three important developments, according to Christopher Snedden, divided that part of Jammu and Kashmir State, occupied by Pakistan, which is now called PoK, but also confirmed that "the princely state was not deliverable in its entirety to [either] India or Pakistan".[4] The first was the anti-Maharaja uprising in Poonch around the time of partition in July-August 1947. The second was the anti-Muslim violence in Jammu. The third was the creation of the Provisional 'Azad Kashmir' Government (A.K. Government, as it was originally called) in areas occupied by Pakistan on October 24, 1947. Thereafter, two separate Karachi agreements changed the state of politics in PoK forever. On April 28, 1949, the then president of 'AJK', Muhammad (but the document spelt it as Mohummad) Ibrahim, and the President of All-Jammu and Kashmir Muslim Conference (AJKMC), Ghulam Abbas, signed away their rights over Gilgit and Baltistan in an agreement with a minister without portfolio, Government of Pakistan, M.A. Gurmani. This was months before the ceasefire agreement was signed between the military representatives of India and Pakistan on July 27, 1949, settling the line of military disengagement. This changed the complexion of politics over Jammu and Kashmir forever.[5]

After the ceasefire agreement, Pakistan, quite smartly, demobilised the so-called 'Azad Kashmir' soldiers by applying the Pakistan Army Act over 'AJK', which was notionally 'independent'. Thus, Pakistan succeeded in controlling the occupied part of the Jammu and Kashmir state without any resistance. Initially, the 'AJK' government, under Sardar Muhammad Ibrahim, who Pakistan installed as the first President, tried to be assertive in demanding recognition of the 'Provisional "Azad" Government' from Pakistan and the United Nations Commission for India and Pakistan (UNCIP) officials.[6] But this assertiveness was short-lived. Neither the UNCIP, nor Pakistan was interested in recognising the 'Provisional "Azad" Government' as a legitimate and independent government. The 'AJK' government was soon reduced to the position of a mere municipal authority without substantial power. All power was vested in a ministry called Ministry of Kashmir Affairs (MKA)—later, it became Ministry of Kashmir and Northern Affairs (KANA)— in Islamabad to rule over the occupied territory. There was opening for the 'AJK' government to raise its voice independently in any forum. Mushtaq Ahmad Gurmani, who signed on the Karachi Agreement of April 1949 as a minister without portfolio, was made the first to head the MKA. His shrewd politics of divide and rule helped him to establish strong control over the affairs of 'AJK'. By driving a wedge between the Muslim Conference President, Chaudhary Ghulam Abbas, and Sardar Ibrahim, the President of 'AJK', he ensured his tight hold over' 'AJK'. While analysing the role played by the MKA in imposing Pakistan's writ on the region, Snedden sums up:

> MKA manipulation meant that it went 'without saying' that no Azad Kashmir president could 'sanely, think of keeping himself in [the] saddle if and when the Government of Pakistan wants him to quit'. They stayed in office, or left, on MKA orders ... this Pakistani bureaucrat and his colleagues ensured that Pakistan's writ applied throughout Azad Kashmir. They also treated the Azad Kashmir president and senior Azad Kashmir Government officials as second-class citizens. It was 'quite normal' that Azad Kashmir 'chief executives'

should wait outside the office of the joint secretary, who theoretically was subordinate to the Azad Kashmiris, before they were 'called in' at his pleasure. Azad Kashmiris had to accept such belittling treatment. Their region lacked international recognition and it was dependent on Pakistan for many things, including financial, military and physical support, such as food grains and basic staples.[7]

According to the terms of the 1949 Karachi Agreement, the 'AJK' government became an adjunct of the Pakistan state. The agreement divided the functions among the three signatories – the Government of Pakistan, Azad Kashmir Government, and Muslim Conference.[8]

Matters within the Purview of Pakistan
  (i) Defence (including control over Azad Kashmir Forces)
  (ii) Negotiations with UNCIP
  (iii) Foreign Policy of Azad Kashmir Government
  (iv) Publicity in Pakistan and Foreign Countries
  (v) Coordination of arrangements for relief and rehabilitation of refugees
  (vi) Coordination of publicity and all arrangements in connection with the plebiscite
  (vii) All activities within Pakistan itself with regard to Kashmir such as procurement of food and civil supplies transport, running of refugee camps, medical arrangements, etc.
  (viii) All affairs of the Gilgit and Ladakh areas under the control of the Political Agent at Gilgit

Matters within the purview of the Azad Kashmir Government
  (i) Policy with regard to administration in Azad Kashmir
  (ii) General supervision of Administration in Azad Kashmir
  (iii) Publicity with regard to activities of the Azad Kashmir Government and its administration
  (iv) Advise to H.M. (Honourable Minister) without portfolio [who went on to become Minister MKA] with regard to negotiations with UNCIP
  (v) Development of economic resources of Azad Kashmir Area

Matters within the Purview of the Muslim Conference
  (i) Publicity with regard to plebiscite in Azad Kashmir area
  (ii) Field work and publicity in the Indian occupied area of the state
  (iii) Organisation of political activities in the Azad Kashmir area and the Indian occupied areas of the state

(iv) Preliminary arrangements in connection with plebiscite
(v) Organisation for contesting the plebiscite
(vi) Political work and publicity among Kashmir refugees in Pakistan
(vii) General guidance of Azad Kashmir Government
(viii) Advice to H.M without portfolio with regard to negotiations with UNCIP

This agreement defined 'AJK''s relationship with Pakistan. The leaders of Muslim Conference were made to lose their control over 'Gilgit and Ladakh areas' as mentioned in the agreement which was to be administered by a political agent to be appointed by the government of Pakistan. In the very beginning, instead of giving importance to representative government or democracy, priority was given to raising an army.[9] But soon after that Islamabad felt compelled to form a government in order to run the day-to-day affairs of the land occupied after the July 1949 ceasefire agreement with India.

The April 1949 Karachi agreement was, to a large extent, modelled after the rules of business enunciated to run the affairs of the provisional Azad Kashmir government. It was formed with Pakistani blessings on October 24, 1947, sans legal and constitutional framework. This government declared itself as a "War Council" with the single objective of "liberating" the parts of J&K which remained under Indian control.[10] This War Council had formalised the Rules of Business for running the administration of the region. The President was vested with both executive and legislative powers, and nominated under the Rules of Business by the pleasure of the General Council of the Muslim Conference. But both were under the control of the Chief Advisor appointed by the Government of Pakistan.[11] To run the judicial system, courts were created and laws codified, "some laws of Punjab were adopted for the state while a good body of the former Jammu and Kashmir State Code was retained".[12]

But things went wrong with the release of Chaudhary Ghulam Abbas in March 1948 by Sheikh Abdullah who became the Chief Emergency Administrator after the Maharaja acceded to India and agreed to put in place a popular administrative machinery in the state. Abbas became the supreme head of the Muslim Conference in 1949. The Working Committee of the Muslim Conference adopted a resolution on March 2, 1949 to give significant powers to the supreme head. These powers included to appoint the President and other members of the council. The Government of Pakistan did not show any hesitation in recognising the supremacy of Ghulam Abbas. Rather they found it easier to do business with Abbas than with Sardar Ibrahim.

Very soon, there was a clash of personality; Abbas and Ibrahim fell out with each other. They discovered that they differed in their political beliefs. Abbas not only dismissed Ibrahim's government in 1950 but was also vehemently against any democratic set-up in the region. According to Ershad Mahmud, "He was not in favour of establishing a democratic set-up as he thought that electoral politics would take leaders, parties and the people away from the cause of liberation. Above all, the 'AJK' politics revolved around the clan system, and Chaudhary Abbas, being from the other side of the J&K state, had no roots in the area."[13] Three distinguished personalities started controlling the politics of 'AJK'. There were three different Muslim Conferences fighting among themselves for influence, led by Ghulam Abbas, Sardar Ibrahim and Mirwaiz Yusuf Shah who was from an influential religious family in Srinagar and uncle of Mirwaiz Umar Farooq of Srinagar and leader of his faction of Hurriyat Conference in the valley today.

Taking advantage of this struggle for power in 'AJK', among different personalised factions of Muslim Conference, the Rules of Business were revised in 1952, and instead of aiming at creating a balance of power between the 'AJK' government and the Muslim Conference and empowering the people to elect their leader, the new Rules vested all powers with the MKA. Now the President was elected according to the wishes of the MKA. The revisions "weakened the grip of the Muslim Conference on state affairs".[14] It was signed by the President, Colonel Sher Ahmad Khan, who hailed from Sudhan Biradari– a powerful tribe in 'AJK'– and was politically inept. The new Rules reduced Azad Kashmir to the stature of a municipality. The MKA not only abolished the office of the Supreme Head (read President of the Muslim Conference), but under the Rules the MKA was to be consulted on almost all matters undertaken by the Azad Kashmir Government and it also had supervisory power over the Executive. The MKA was thus vested with supreme legal authority to deal with the affairs of Azad Kashmir and a Joint Secretary in the Ministry wielded disproportionate power. Snedden writes that "four years after being a belligerent anti-Indian fighting force, the Azad Kashmir movement was emasculated. It now was a supplicant, not a surrogate."[15]

The 'Rules of Business' were revised again for the third time in 1958. Under the new Rules, a Chief Advisor was introduced who replaced the Joint Secretary. Ironically, the Chief Advisor was to be selected by the Minister in charge of Kashmir Affairs (MKA), not by the Government of Azad Kashmir. This Ministry later changed its name to Ministry of Kashmir Affairs and Northern Areas (MKANA). Interestingly, even if the same Ministry continues till date with yet another change in nomenclature after 2009 as Ministry of Kashmir

Affairs and Gilgit-Baltistan, the Ministry retains 'KANA' in its internet web address (http://www.kana.gov.pk/).

After the revisions in 1958, all functions of the 'AJK' government were exercised in the name of the president, while real power was exercised by MKANA officials. The 'AJK' government was not even allowed to create any post which had a monthly salary of over Rs. 150, and was not allowed to spend over Rs. 100,000 without the permission of MKANA.[16] Thus, the Pakistani Government, through various institutions and constitutional acts, not only strengthened its hands at the cost of the 'AJK' government, but also ensured that it was in full control of 'AJK''s internal political affairs. Successive governments in 'AJK' were removed and appointed at will on the whims of the government in Islamabad. During 1947-1959, over a period of 12 years, there were eight presidents (one of them was selected twice) and the Pakistani state's suspicion regarding the political agenda of Azad Jammu and Kashmir Muslim Conference (AJKMC), often led to such frequent change of leadership in 'AJK'. Under the presidential system, during 1958-1970, the political and administrative rights granted to the 'AJK' Government were minimal.

The 1970s

After taking over power in Pakistan in October 1958 in a bloodless coup, General Ayub Khan introduced 'Basic Democracy' on the basis of party-less elections. He banned all political parties and activities in Pakistan. Initially, Ayub did not introduce 'Basic Democracy' in 'AJK', and appointed K.H. Khurshid, one time private secretary to Muhammad Ali Jinnah, as the President of 'AJK' on May 1, 1959. Ayub Khan held elections in 'AJK' in 1961. Khurshid won the elections to become the first elected president and later formed a party called Jammu and Kashmir Liberation League (JKLL) because of his differences with AJKMC. He remained in that post till 1964, when he developed differences with the establishment and had to quit.

Right from the beginning of his tenure, Khurshid was not received well by the MKA. He was branded as uncooperative and difficult to work with. Moreover, his strained relationship with AJKMC leadership, particularly with Chaudhary Ghulam Abbas, was also another issue that led to a power struggle, in which Khurshid's opponents – the MKA and AJKMC– got the better of him and the news of his resignation, "on personal grounds" was announced by the government in Islamabad on August 5, 1964. Some accounts say that a mid-level police official forced him to resign and months later he was kept in detention in Palandari and Dalai camp for some months. What hastened his removal was a strong rumour in Pakistan that he had warmed up to Sheikh Abdullah during the latter's trip (May 24-27, 1964) to 'AJK' and was planning for an independent Kashmir.

After his resignation, Khurshid struggled to keep himself and his party politically relevant, but without much success. Later, he died a pauper in a road accident on March 11, 1988, while travelling in a public transport vehicle with Rs 37/- in his pocket (*Dawn*, March 11, 2011). Ironically, Khurshid was appointed President of 'AJK' by the military and was also removed by it when he sought to move towards independence from Pakistan's control. Khurshid was replaced by Khan Abdul Hamid Khan, former Chief Justice of 'AJK' High Court, and brother of Sardar Qayyum Khan who had become President of 'AJK' for less than a year from September 8, 1956 – Apr 13, 1957. Khan Abdul Hamid Khan remained president for more than five years allowing himself to be brazenly guided and controlled by the Pakistan government and security forces. Like Khurshid, he ruled without any cabinet and tried to consolidate his position in 'AJK'.

The period following Khurshid's ouster witnessed continued marginalisation of the people, which led to a wave of agitations launched by leading 'AJK'-based political parties against the MKA. Sardar Ibrahim, and Sardar Muhammad Abdul Qayyum Khan, the successor of Ghulam Abbas, joined hands to weaken the MKA's hold on 'AJK'. They demanded elected and responsible government – an elected president and a legislature with full powers of legislation, including the budget approving power.[17]

When Ayub's regime was replaced by Gen. Yahya Khan in March 1969, 'AJK' was given some nominal degree of political autonomy. Yahya Khan appointed a retired army general, Abdul Rahman Khan, his own man, as the minister of the MKA. After consulting all the stakeholders of 'AJK', he announced that democratic rule would be introduced soon in the region. Finally, a democratic set-up was introduced in 'AJK' through the 1970 Act. Under this Act, adult franchise was introduced in 'AJK' and the President of 'AJK' was to be elected on the basis of one person-one vote. Apart from adult electorates from 'AJK', the refugees from Jammu and Kashmir settled in other areas of Pakistan were also eligible to cast their votes.

The 1970 Act introduced a directly elected 'AJK' Assembly' with 24 elected members and one nominated lady member. The assembly was granted some legislative powers while defence, foreign affairs and currency remained the preserve of the government of Pakistan.[18] It had even the power to remove the president by two-third majority. The state subject law – that bars non-Kashmiris from getting state citizenship – also became part of this act in deference to local opinion.

Interim Constitution Act, 1974

Pakistan's first elections on the basis of one-man-one-vote were organised by Gen. Yahya Khan in December 1970. These elections witnessed emergence of East Pakistan based Awami League as the majority party. However, establishment in West Pakistan was not willing to recognise these results. This led to violence in East Pakistan. The subsequent use of brutal force by the Pakistan army to suppress the Bengali-speaking population of East Pakistan leading to large-scale influx of refugees into India compelling India to get involved in a war that saw defeat and surrender of Pakistani forces on December 16, 1971. After the breakup of Pakistan in 1971, Zulfiqar Ali Bhutto became the Chief Martial Law Administrator of a truncated Pakistan and witnessed the strengthening of the civilian forces in West Pakistan for some years. The outcome of the 1971 War, although it was not fought over the issue of Kashmir, affected the politics of the region in a significant manner. The following factors played an important role in 'AJK' politics after 1971:

(i) There was a growing demand in 'AJK' for a parliamentary system of government from the local chapter of Pakistan Peoples' Party (PPP) when Zulfiqar Bhutto got a new constitution drafted which put in place a parliamentary form of government in Pakistan. The local chapter of PPP Azad Kashmir (AJKPPP) lobbied Bhutto for a similar system in 'AJK'. Therefore, presidential system of government, which had worked for about 4 years, was replaced by a parliamentary system introduced under the "AJK interim Constitution Act, 1974". This so called 'Interim' act has had a long run for more than four decades and undergone about 13 amendments till 2018. the Assembly consisted of 40 members, elected on the basis of adult franchise and two co-opted lady members. Today, the Assembly consists of 41 elected Members (29 from 'AJK' proper and 12 from among the refugees) and 8 co-opted members – 5 women, one member from Ullema-e-Din/Mushaikh, one from among the 'AJK' technocrats and other professionals, and one from amongst 'AJK' nationals residing abroad.

(ii) According to many scholars, Zulfiqar Bhutto and then Prime Minister of India, Indira Gandhi, had reached an understanding about settling the issue around the status quo – recognising the Line of Control (LoC) as the international border. Under the Simla Agreement in 1972, both sides decided to settle all outstanding issues including

Kashmir, bilaterally.[19] Confirmation of LoC as border would turn Azad Kashmir to a full-fledged province of Pakistan, "something Bhutto possibly initiated when he came to power."[20] Few even believe that Bhutto had offered to make 'AJK' a province of Pakistan.[21]

(iii) The administrative changes Bhutto brought about in Northern Areas, which is now better known as Gilgit-Baltistan (G-B or GB), almost turned the latter into the *de facto* fifth province of Pakistan. New administrative changes further integrated Gilgit-Baltistan into Pakistan.

(iv) People of the region as well as the Pakistani authorities had perhaps realised that annexing Kashmir by force was now impossible owing to India's size of military strength.

The 'AJK' Interim Constitution Act of 1974, introduced parliamentary system with a Prime Minister as the executive head and an indirectly elected President. As the executive head of 'AJK', the Prime Minister wielded restricted power because the real power was vested in a new body called 'AJK' Council chaired by the Prime Minister of Pakistan. The 'AJK' Council is vested with both legislative and executive powers.[22] Headed by the Prime Minister of Pakistan, it consists of 11 members, six of whom are elected by the 'AJK' Assembly and five are nominated by the Pakistani Prime Minister. The 1974 constitution thus took away most of the powers accorded to the 'AJK' assembly by 1970 Act and vested these in the 'AJK' Council. These included the power to appoint High Court and Supreme Court judges. The major sources of income for the 'AJK' Government, like income tax, were given away to the 'AJK' Council. The 'AJK' Government's power to appoint the Chief Election Commissioner and the Auditor General was also taken away.

The following subjects were under the 'AJK' Council:

(a) Electricity and Hydro Power Generation
(b) Tourism
(c) Population planning
(d) Banking
(e) Insurance
(f) Stock exchange
(g) Future markets, trading corporations, telecommunication
(h) Planning for economic coordination,
(i) Highways, minerals, oil and gas
(j) Development of industries, etc.

A critical analysis of the Interim Constitution Act, 1974 indicates that the Act has not only allowed the Kashmir Council to function as a parallel government but has also led to problems in governance.[23] In an email dated May 4, 2018, in response to a query from one of the authors, Jalaluddin Mughal, a senior journalist from Pakistan commented that Kashmir Council enjoyed "ambiguous status since it was established, and it was not a representative body of 'AJK' people because majority of its members were not elected by 'AJK' people. He held that the Council drew its authority not from the Interim Constitution Act of 1974, but rather from the 1949 Karachi Agreement, "which gives all powers to Pakistan government". He also pointed out that "neither the Act of 1974 nor the Karachi agreement was drafted, signed and ratified by any elected representative of the 'AJK' people". and even "now the AJK Assembly does not have the power to amend the 1974 Act without prior approval of the federal government". That is why, he concluded, "the elected leadership of 'AJK' has been demanding [review] of all the agreements with Pakistan and to amend [the 1974 constitution] to empower the local elected government rather than operate through the 'AJK' Council, [which is not entirely representative of the will of the people of 'AJK']". While the 'AJK' Government remains accountable both to the Council and the Assembly, the Council is not accountable to either the 'AJK' Government or Accountability Bureau. According to Tanveer Ahmad, a PoK-based social activist, "'AJK' is a legal anomaly and the current governance structure in 'AJK' is most certainly not a structure, which accommodates accountability and transparency of any kind."[24] Even those matters that come under the purview of the 'AJK' Government are in effect run by the bureaucrats, the government in Islamabad controls their appointment. Senior civil servants – Chief Secretary, Additional Chief Secretary, IG Police, Finance Secretary, Health Secretary, Auditor General and Accountant General – are appointed by the Pakistan government.[25] While commenting on the loopholes of the Interim Act, a Pildat report maintains:

> This generates grievance among AJ&K services group who feel their powers having been curtailed in operation of even routine affairs. Known as 'Lent Officers', and not being under the AJ&K Government's control in matters of discipline or posting, the posted officers are a strong check on the exercise of powers by the President and Cabinet of AJ&K. This system of 'Lent Officers' is a permanent feature, and has never been changed. The Government of Pakistan, therefore, always retained an extremely strong influence in AJ&K affairs.[26]

The Interim Constitution Act 1974 left the 'AJK' Government with very little power. The Act not only denied the political rights of the people by empowering the Kashmir Council more than the 'AJK' Assembly, but also marginalised the 'AJK' Government's power over the areas under its control.

On June 1, 2018, the President of 'AJK' assented to the 13th amendment passed by the joint sitting of Joint Session of 'AJK' Legislative Assembly and 'AJK' Council. This amendment seeks to transfer executive and legislative powers from 'AJK' Council to 'AJK' government, and create four more constituencies on the basis of the increased population. (For details see Appendix IV)

Government and Politics in 'AJK': Post-1974

The controlled 'democratic' system in 'AJK' was resented by local leaders, even by those who supported Kashmir's final accession to Pakistan. It has denied political rights to the people by making the Kashmir Council more powerful than the legislative assembly. Pakistan found it easy to deal with these pro-Pakistan Muslim Conference leaders and therefore, it felt itself under no pressure to allow the people the right to decision making. There has never been a serious effort to install a political system where people would have their say in policy making. On various occasions leaders of the Muslim Conference have criticised Pakistan's carrot and stick policy to woo or punish them. However, Pakistan has succeeded in patronising these leaders who advocate merging of entire Kashmir with Pakistan. However, a vocal constituency wedded to the idea of independence of entire Kashmir has also made its presence felt all along even if it has not been allowed to participate in the elections in 'AJK'.

Such policies have "stifled the development of indigenous institutions" as Pakistan is obsessed with the idea of control of 'AJK' people and disallowed the local leadership to evolve any responsive system on their own lest they would veer towards independence. Therefore, the people have always been asked to wait for the promised plebiscite to resolve things. With the mainstream political parties in Pakistan making successful entry into the political scenario in 'AJK', there has been regular emphasis on strengthening Pakistan's hold on AJK. This has shut the door on political dissent in 'AJK' and "meant that [AJK] did not develop any positive political alternatives, democratic or otherwise, to those on offer in Indian J&K".[27]

Other factors that played an equally important role in setting the dismal record of democracy in 'AJK' included the endemic factionalism within the Muslim Conference (for details, see the chapter on the Muslim Conference) and the role of the *biradari* (clan) system which divided politicians. Apart from its socio-political significance, the *biradari* system in 'AJK' is also important in that different clans have different views on what it means to be a Kashmiri.

This innate instinct of people of 'AJK' to maintain a separate identity has determined the power relationships among politicians and parties/groups.[28] Historically, the Sudhans, who are mostly concentrated in Bagh and Rawalakot, in the Poonch district, have been politically very influential. The other influential group includes people from the Rajput *biradari*. Leaders from these two *biradaris* have ruled 'AJK' ever since it came into being as a controversial political unit.[29] Along with these two clans, the Jats of Mirpur, although numerically less in number, have also emerged as yet another important group in 'AJK's politics, especially since the boom in migrant economy in the region. According to Human Rights Watch Report 2012, "Mirpur economic clout has paid political dividends, helping propel barrister Sultan Mahmood Chaudhry to power as the first Mirpur leader of Azad Kashmir in 1996."[30] While commenting on the rise of the Mirpur *biradari* in 'AJK' politics, Alexander Evans aptly states:

> The Mirpur Jats, looked down upon by Rajputs and Sudhans, gained power in the 1990s largely because of their wealth ... Valley Kashmiris view Mirpuris with much the same condescension as their Punjabi counterparts, but they also consider Mirpuris part of the former princely state of Jammu and Kashmir. They remain Kashmir state subjects – even if not ethnically Kashmiri as Valley Kashmiris would understand it.... On the Pakistani side, the southeast (Sudhan heartland) and south (Mirpur) dominate, while the north (both Muzaffarabad and the Neelum) is less influential ... but Rajputs and Sudhans remain important brokers in local politics – not least as Gujjars tend to follow the lead of local Rajput and Sudhan leaders.[31]

It is to be noted that both the Sudhans and the Mirpur Jats perceive the Kashmir conflict differently. The Sudhans still take pride in being the first ones to take up arms against Maharaja Hari Singh's forces, "aiming, as they still do, to bring the whole Kashmir into wider Pakistan – their slogan is '*Kashmir banega Pakistan*' [Kashmir will become Pakistan]".[32] On the other hand, Mirpuris stress on their "Kashmiri entity which would be entirely independent of both India and Pakistan – their slogan is '*Kashmir Azad banega*' [Kashmir will be free]".[33] According to Roger Ballard, this position adopted by the Mirpuris in contrast to that of the Sudhans is not only due to their cultural distinctiveness but also because of their sense of alienation and disillusionment about the way in which Islamabad has treated them.[34] For further understanding the *biradari's* role in 'AJK"s body politic, two political developments should be kept in mind. The first one is the famous revolt of May 1950 by the Sudhans of Poonch when Chaudhary Ghulam Abbas sacked Sardar Ibrahim, who belonged to the Sudhan *biradari*. The Sudhans took it as an insult, and rose in rebellion against Pakistan.

They also set up a parallel government during the revolt.³⁵ The rebellion was, however, crushed by the Pakistan Army. Nonetheless, Pakistan succeeded in pacifying the Sudhans later by factoring in *biradari* system in its interventions in 'AJK'. Col. (Retd.) Sher Ahmad, another Sudhan, was appointed as a cabinet minister with important portfolios of defence, education and health. It was a masterstroke by Pakistani authorities to placate the Sudhans and at the same time weaken Sardar Ibrahim's leadership.³⁶ The other development took place when Ayub Khan decided to conduct party-less elections in 1961 under the system of 'Basic Democracy'. The people defeated the purpose of a party-less election by voting openly for those who belonged to their own tribe and clan.³⁷

The *biradari* system is also used from time to time by mainstream parties of Pakistan to manipulate electoral politics in 'AJK'. According to Shams Rehman, the pro-accession-to-Pakistan, political forces have again been polarized on *biradari* lines into two main political parties of Pakistan – the local branches of Pakistan Muslim League-N (PML-N) and Pakistan People's Party (PPP). The former has become predominantly a party of the Rajas and the latter a party of the Jats. The Muslim Conference, which used to be backed by the Pakistani military establishment once upon a time, remains the only local party of "any electoral significance in the race."³⁸ Underscoring the importance of *biradari* politics, Javid Hayat states that at the internal level, ethnicity or cross-cutting cleavages based on tribes/clans (*biradri*) and region (based on Districts and Divisions) play a significant role in shaping and reshaping local politics in 'AJK'. Traditionally, politicians have encouraged such divide for their own vested interests, and thus, racial identity appears to be "an increasingly growing phenomenon for internal power-sharing and political allegiances in future."³⁹

Politics of Representation

There are 49 seats in the 'AJK' Assembly at the moment (four more were to be added if 13th amendment of June 2018 was to be implemented). Forty-one of these are elected through direct elections – 29 from constituencies based in 'AJK', and 12 seats allocated to the Kashmiri refugees (six for the people migrated from Jammu and the other six are elected by the refugees of Kashmir). Five out of the eight reserved seats are for women and one each for representatives from overseas Kashmiris, technocrats and religious leaders.

Over the years, there has been a growing concern in various segments of the people about the significance of having reserved seats for the refugees. In 2014, a petition was filed in the Supreme Court for the cancellation of the refugee seats. The petitioner claimed that having reserved seats for the refugees is nothing but a symbolic gesture and is in utter disregard of the fundamental rights of the people of 'AJK'.[40] It is also alleged that the Kashmiri refugees are over-represented, whereas those from Jammu are underrepresented.[41] 'AJK''s first free-and-fair elections were held on October 30, 1970, when the president of 'AJK' was directly elected by the people for the first time under universal suffrage. The presidential candidates were: Sardar Ibrahim (Azad Muslim Conference), K.H. Khurshid (AJK Liberation League), Sardar Qayyum (AJK Muslim Conference) and Muhammad Sharif Tariq (J&K Plebiscite Front). Sardar Qayyum of AJKMC won the elections. Most of these parties were based in 'AJK'. But after the enactment of the 1974 Interim Constitution, the mainstream political parties of Pakistan started setting up their offices in 'AJK' and through alliances with local parties as well as manipulation of political processes tried to consolidate their position there.

Electoral Politics During 1975-1996

When the first elections for Legislative Assembly under the interim constitution were held on May 18, 1975, the Pakistan People's Party founded by Bhutto raised its local affiliate in 'AJK' and announced a United Front Alliance against the AJK Muslim Conference (AJKMC) along with three other prominent local parties, i.e., AJK Liberation League (AJKLL), the Azad Muslim Conference (AMC) and a breakaway faction of the Muslim Conference led by Sardar Ibrahim – who was announced by the AJKPPP as the joint presidential candidate. The four-party alliance launched an aggressive campaign against Sardar Qayyum-led AJKMC that the party decided to boycott the elections. The then leader of PPP, Zulfiqar Ali Bhutto used the service of his confidante Hayat Muhammad Khan Tamman to secure maximum seats for the AJKPPP. Interestingly out of the 12 refugee seats, Hayat delivered as many as nine to AJKPPP.[42] The results were shock to Qayyum who expressed his anguish over the police and the military intimidating him and his party workers before and after the elections. While addressing the media, he said that the elections were a fraud, and the results had already been rigged by the Pakistan Government. He also alleged that the government had sent 20,000 police and armed civilians into 'AJK' to intimidate him and his supporters. He was even barred from entering 'AJK' and most of his key party workers were arrested.[43] The United Front Alliance jointly contested for all the 29 local seats. For the remaining seats, the alliance members were free to fight on their own. Out of the 34 seats, which the alliance finally secured, the AJKPPP won 22, the Liberation League (AJKLL) five, the Muslim Conference (Ibrahim) four, and the Azad

Muslim Conference (AMC) three. After the elections, the AJKPPP formed its own government ignoring its alliance partners. Sardar Ibrahim was elected President, and Khan Abdul Hamid Khan Prime Minister. Bhutto's political advisor, Hayat Muhammad Khan Tamman, played an important role in ensuring that the "correct people were elected. Basically, the elections were rigged".[44]

However, the AJKPPP's rule was short-lived. The Pakistan army chief Gen. Zia ul Haq's imposed martial law on July 5, 1977 and brought the occupied territory under military control by dismissing the AJKPPP government. He installed a serving military officer, Brigadier Mohammad Hayat Khan, as the president. He suspended the 1974 Constitution, and both 'AJK' Council and political parties found themselves in wilderness. Sardar Ibrahim dissolved the Legislative Assembly on August 11, 1977 and issued an order for conducting fresh elections. Major General Abdul Rehman Khan – who was earlier picked by the military government headed by Yahya Khan as president during 1969-1970 – was appointed by Ibrahim as the Chief Executive. On October 31, 1978, Zia dismissed Ibrahim invoking Article 56 of the interim constitution and appointed Brigadier Muhammad Hayat Khan, a Sudhan, as both President and Chief Executive of 'AJK', who was supposed to work towards holding elections in 'AJK'. But Zia ul Haq did not allow elections to be held as he first wanted politicians to be made more accountable. Hayat decided to form an Advisory Council, whose members would be cherry-picked by Zia. The infamous Political Parties Ordinance was promulgated in September 1979 to regulate political parties. Under this Ordinance, political parties were registered on the following conditions: A party had to: (a) publish its foundation document or constitution; (b) have periodic elections of principal officers; and (c) subscribe to the ideology of Pakistan and J&K's accession to Pakistan.[45] The AJKPPP refused to get registered, whereas Jamaat-i-Islami did register but later did not take part in elections.

After much dismay and harassment, the political leaders of 'AJK' started protesting against the delay in elections and the setting up of the Advisory Council. Hayat Khan, who continued as President till February 1983, became very unpopular and to fend off further accumulation of local resistance against him. The military brought in Abdul Rehman Khan for the second time as President. Abdul Rehman Khan continued till 1985 elections. When elections were finally announced on May 16, 1985, seven political parties entered into alliance against the AJKMC. The alliance was led by K.H. Khurshid of the Liberation League, and other parties included Tehrik-i-Amal led by Brigadier Hayat Khan, Islami-Jamhoori Party, Democratic Front, Jamaat-i-Islami AJK,

Inqilabi Mahaz and Azad Jamhoori Mahaz. Later Jamaat-i-Islami boycotted elections in protest against alleging Zia government's preferential treatment to the Muslim Conference.[46] That scepticism proved correct when election results were declared on May 16, 1985. Muslim Conference got 19 seats, Tehrik-i-Amal eight, Liberation League four, Azad Muslim Conference two and seven seats went to independent candidates, who were regarded as pro-AJKPPP, which had not registered as a political party and hence did not participate in the elections officially. Zia's favourites emerged as President and Prime Minister of 'AJK'. AJKMC leader Sardar Qayyum Khan was elected as President and Sardar Sikandar Hayat Khan became the Prime Minister.

After Zia died in a plane crash on October 17, 1988, Benazir Bhutto's PPP came to power in Pakistan. The four-party alliance in 'AJK' – AJKPPP, AJKLL, Tehrik-i-Amal and other parties demanded the removal of Qayyum's government. But Qayyum had, in the meantime, become close to then Punjab Chief Minister, Nawaz Sharif. This bonhomie between the Muslim Conference and Pakistan Muslim League helped Qayyum to complete his tenure.

The next elections for the 40 directly elected seats of the fourth 'AJK' Legislative Assembly were held on May 21, 1990. The main contest was between the AJKPPP and the AJKMC. The election results saw the AJKPPP the AJKMC both getting 16 seats each – the AJKMC's 8 of the 16 seats came from the refugee quota. The AJKMC got three, the Tehrik-e-Amal and the Liberation league one each. The Jammu and Kashmir Liberation Front (JKLF) could not contest elections because it refused to pledge mandatory support to J&K's accession to Pakistan. It stood for independence of Kashmir. Finally, Raja Mumtaz Rathore of AJKPPP won the post of prime minister by defeating the Muslim Conference candidate, Sikander Hayat Khan, by 29 votes to 15. Sardar Qayyum, as the president, refused to swear in Rathore and his 17 members calling the PPP an "anti-national and anti-Islam party".[47] However, after pressure from Islamabad, which was then ruled by PPP, the Speaker of the Assembly administered the oath of office to Rathore.

Rathore's government soon faced the heat from Sardar Qayyum who launched a campaign for his removal after then Pakistani Prime Minister Benazir Bhutto was dismissed by then President Ghulam Ishaq Khan on charges of corruption in August 1990. After the victory of PML-N in the subsequent elections, both Nawaz Sharif and the president of Pakistan assured Rathore that his government would not be destabilised. But still, Rathore felt unsafe and tried to muster help from the Pakistan army. During this time, out of frustration, he came out with statements which were critical of Pakistan. For example, he alleged that the "Pakistani rulers use the Kashmir issue for capturing and retaining power". Such pungent rhetoric from 'AJK' Prime Minister embarrassed the Pakistani leadership.[48] His relationship with Islamabad, and especially the Ministry of Kashmir Affairs (MKA) soured leading finally to the fall of Rathore government.

The trouble started after the June 29, 1991 mid-term elections, when Rathore's AJKPPP lost badly. Rathore called the elections a massive fraud and declared them null and void. He accused Islamabad of massive rigging and argued that "senior bureaucrats, in connivance with Islamabad, had ensured his defeat".[49] It is believed that Nawaz Sharif, who was at the time ruling at the centre, played it down in the beginning on the suggestions from the foreign office. But things became murkier after Rathore upped the ante by ordering fresh elections and announced that July 6 would be observed as a protest day throughout 'AJK'.[50] As a consequence, an army operation led by a Brigadier arrested the Prime Minister Rathore and took him to Islamabad where he was detained at the Simla Rest House for 30 days under the Maintenance of Public Order Ordinance. Condemning his arrest, Barrister Sultan Mahmood Chaudhry, then leader of AJKPPP, said at a press conference: "What is the difference between 'Occupied Kashmir' [he meant Indian state of Jammu and Kashmir] and the 'liberated' territory [the so called Azad Kashmir]? There, the Indian army is launching aggression against the Kashmiri freedom fighters demanding the right to vote. And here in the liberated territory, the army is arresting the prime minister."[51] Section 56 of the Interim Constitution 1974 was used by Pakistan to justify removal of Rathore.[52] The text says:

> Nothing in this Act shall derogate from the responsibilities of the government of Pakistan in relation to the matters specified in sub-section 31(3) or prevent the government of Pakistan from taking such action as it may consider necessary or expedience for the effective discharge of those responsibilities.

Section 31 (3) states:

> Neither the council nor the assembly shall have the power to make any law concerning: (a) the responsibilities of the Government of Pakistan under the U.N. resolutions, (b) the defence and security of Azad Jammu and Kashmir, (c) the current coin or the issue of any bills, notes or other paper of currency or (d) the external affairs of Azad Jammu and Kashmir, including foreign trade and foreign aid".

It was not his accusation of rigging but his announcement of marking July 6 as a protest day that upset the Pakistan government. It indicated the beginning of a struggle that would open the Pandora's Box of regular interference by successive federal governments and the army in 'AJK' politics. Astonishingly, the AJKPPP's mother organisation, led by Benazir Bhutto did not support Rathore. Benazir avoided getting into the mess Rathore had created.

The June 1991 elections were held under Rathore but the AJKMC won 28 out of the 34 seats for which results were declared. The Rathore-led AJKPPP could secure only two seats. The 'AJK' Jamhoori Ittehad got four seats. Sardar Abdul Qayyum, who until elections was the President, resigned. Sensing victory, before and during elections, he decided to run for the position of prime minister. Sahibzada Ishaq Zafar of AJKPPP was made the interim president. His tenure was short-lived spanning only nine days. He was sacked after his outburst against unabated interference of Pakistan in the internal affairs of the 'AJK'. He accused Nawaz Sharif of interfering in the internal matters and attempting to foist a one-party system upon the state.[53] Underscoring the events during the 1990s in 'AJK', Askari sums it up:

> If the developments in Azad Jammu and Kashmir proved anything at all it was that the top leadership in the state can be unbelievably childish and also that *no set up in the state can hope to function once it falls into disharmony with those who happen to be in power in Islamabad (italics by the editors)*. That is how it was under the PPP government in 1972-77, when the AJK Interim Constitution was promulgated; and that is how it is now, when the IJI and Nawaz Sharif are in power.[54]

The next five years (1991-95), AJKMC was in office. Sardar Qayyum Khan became Prime Minister after relinquishing the office of President and Sardar Sikandar Hayat Khan became President in August 1991. Nawaz Sharif, who came to power in Pakistan in November 1990, was made to quit office in July 1993. The subsequent elections in 1993 returned AJKPPP to power. Benazir Bhutto became the Prime Minister in Islamabad; but her government was dismissed by President Farooq Leghari in November 1996. Nawaz Sharif's party succeeded her and returned to power in February 1997.

The Elections of 1996 and 2001

In the June 30, 1996 elections, the AJKPPP captured power by winning 26 out of 40 seats. AJKMC could secure only eight seats. It was almost a repetition of the 1991 elections. Benazir Bhutto was in power in Islamabad during both these elections. The voters chose the party which ruled Islamabad, probably hoping for better financial benefits for the region, and this has almost become a trend in 'AJK' since a token representative system was introduced since the

1970s. The AJKPPP government completed its term in spite of Nawaz Sharif returning to power in Islamabad in February 1997. It was partly because of a divided AJKMC and also because of the fact that Nawaz government lost its popularity soon as it got enmeshed in a power struggle with the army following the army's Kargil misadventure and was overthrown in October 1999. The military government under Musharraf chose it better not to ruffle the feathers in 'AJK' in a hurry and allowed the AJKPPP government led by Barrister Sultan Mahmood Chaudhry – the first Mirpuri to be prime minister of 'AJK'– to continue and complete its term.

The July 2001 elections in 'AJK' witnessed dramatic developments. The AJKMC, known for its good relations with Nawaz Sharif's party, PML-N, secured 21 seats, while the AJKPPP won 15 seats. Pakistan was under military rule and given Musharraf's disliking for PML-N, his government was not willing to have Sardar Muhammad Abdul Qayyum Khan as the prime minister. Moreover, Qayyum's open praise of the Indian Prime Minister Atal Bihari Vajpayee for involving Hurriyat Conference in Indo-Pak talks and his criticism of the Pakistan military had offended Gen Musharraf.

Ironically, until then, the army and AJKMC had always maintained a good understanding. Moreover, AJKMC, Pakistan Muslim League and the Army had close relationship among themselves during the 1990s. However, with Qayyum favouring Nawaz and opposing the army takeover, the relationship between him and the army had deteriorated beyond repair. Thus, sensing the displeasure of the military, AJKMC chose to field Sardar Sikandar Hayat Khan as prime minister and Sardar Attique, Sardar Qayyum's son, to run for the president's post. But the Army imposed Major General Sardar Muhammad Anwar Khan as the president of 'AJK' instead. Anwar was asked to resign from the army and was rushed to Muzaffarabad, where the Assembly elected him as president on August 25, 2001. This was in violation of Section 5(2)(ix) of the 'AJK' Legislative Assembly (Elections) Ordinance, 1970, according to which the General should have retired two years before being considered for the post of president.

The incident of 9/11 which occurred days after Anwar's assumption of presidency set off a new political dynamic in Pakistan and kept Musharraf busy reshaping his government's policy towards terrorism and Kashmir. Sardar Sikandar Hayat Khan of AJKMC continued as prime minister till the next elections in July 2006.

The Elections of 2006, 2011 and 2016

The elections for the eighth (2006) and ninth (2011) Legislative Assemblies were not much different from the earlier ones. In 2006 elections (July 11), AJKMC bagged 22 seats while AJKPPP had to be content with six. Musharraf backed People's Muslim League and Muttahida Quami Movement (MQM) secured two seats each – the latter winning two refugee seats from Karachi.

After elections, aware of the need to keep the military government in good humour, the AJKMC leaders were seen to be warming up to Musharraf and since Sardar Qayyum was not acceptable to Musharraf for his pro-Nawaz Sharif leaning, his son Sardar Attique Khan was chosen as prime ministerial candidate in July 2006. Raja Zulqarnain Khan– who claimed royal ancestry as Raja of Chhib (Bhimber), earlier a confidante of K.H. Khurshid and General Secretary of Jammu and Kashmir Liberation League during the 1960s, had joined AJKMC later and served as minister on several occasions – was projected as presidential candidate and was elected president of 'AJK', in August 2006.

Backed by Musharraf, Sardar Attique's government pulled on till 2009 when it was confronted with a no-confidence motion moved by the opposition AJKPPP. In fact, Musharraf's fortunes had declined since the beginning of 2007 and in March 2008, PPP came to power in Islamabad. Under the force of circumstances, Musharraf had to resign in September 2008. It is widely believed that the PPP government in Islamabad conspired to remove the existing government blessed by Gen Musharraf and install a favourable government in place in 'AJK'. In the subsequent days, 'AJK' witnessed tremendous political instability with four prime ministers assuming office in three years.

In January 2009, a no-trust vote moved by Raja Farooq Haider, a fellow AJKMC legislator who had chosen to form a separate camp (Forward Block) within the party, allegedly with the support of another veteran 'AJK' leader, Sardar Sikander Hayat Khan, who had a bitter relationship with Attique and his father within the AJKMC for a long time. Sikander's hand, if it was there at all, was a hidden one. Farooq Haider alleged that the government led by Sardar Attique was corrupt, and he indulged in nepotism and deviated from the ideology of Muslim Conference. The motion was passed with 31 members voting in favour and 14 against with two abstentions. Exercising his constitutional prerogative, Sardar Attique chose Sardar Yaqoob Muhammad Khan – who had been denied a ticket by Attique's father to contest in the 2006 elections and had won as an independent candidate – as the prime ministerial candidate. Sardar Yaqoob, a businessman, originally from Poonch but raised in Karachi, had dabbled in politics in Sind during his student days as a member of Punjabi Pakhtun Ittehad party and was later associated with 'Tehreek-e-Amal', a party based in 'AJK', before joining AJKMC. Yaqoob was supported by AJKMC splinter group as well as other opposition parties.

Yaqoob's government continued till October 2009, when a no-confidence motion was tabled in the assembly against his government by various factions of the AJKMC reunited under the leadership of Raja Farooq Haider and nominated Haider as the alternate prime ministerial candidate. Yaqoob resigned before the motion was to be passed in the assembly, yet contested the prime ministerial election supported by a four party alliance which included the local branch of the PPP. However, Haider secured 29 votes while Yaqoob could only muster 19 votes in his favour.

Raja Farooq Haider became the prime minister while Sardar Attique continued as AJKMC party president. Haider held the post from October 23, 2009 till July 2010, when he too had to resign to avoid the humiliation of facing a trust vote. This time, the no-trust motion was moved on July 22, 2010, by two legislators, one of whom was Chaudhry Abdul Majeed Khan who had won his seat as an independent but had his sympathies for the AJKPPP. Seeing the writing on the wall, Haider resigned on July 25, one day before the motion was to be subjected to vote in the assembly.

Sardar Attique Khan, President of AJKMC who was nominated in the motion as the prime minister went on to win 39 votes in his favour – 21 from his own party, seven from AJKPPP, six from the 'Friends Group,' three from the Peoples Muslim League (PML-Q) (a de facto branch of pro-Musharraf PML-Quaid led by Barrister Sultan Mahmood) and two from MQM. Attique could manage to hold on to his position till the end of the tenure of the assembly in July 2011.

Interestingly, before resigning as prime minister, Haider had raised the issue of an assertive judiciary in 'AJK', under Chief Justice Riaz Akhtar Chaudhury, who had passed a 'controversial' judgment on March 15, 2010, challenging the jurisdiction of Pakistan Supreme Court on 'AJK', as it was an independent entity and by doing so Haider tried to warm up to the military establishment of Pakistan.[55] Moreover, the PML-N had taken note of the political roulette in 'AJK' and started siding with Haider, who was seemingly being targeted by the PPP government in cahoots with local operators, during this period.

In June 2011, the results of the elections in 'AJK', was 'unsurprising'[56] and the PPP, then in power in Islamabad, registered an easy win. Out of 41 elected constituencies, AJKPPP secured 22. The PML-N won in nine while AJKMC could secure only four. The AJKPPP found it easy to win because of the decision of the recently formed AJKPML-N, largely composed of dissenters from AJKMC, not to enter into any alliance with AJKMC and go it alone in the polls. This resulted in AJKMC splitting the votes in many constituencies making it easier for the AJKPPP to win with narrow margins. The AJKPML-N fared better (eight seats) than local AJKMC (four seats).

The AJKPPP government was headed by Chaudhry Abdul Majeed Khan, a Jat politician from Mirpur – second prime minister from Mirpur after Barrister Sultan Mahmood, and leader of opposition in 'AJK' assembly since 2006. Majeed was also president of AJKPPP during the elections and was chosen by PPP President Asif Ali Zardari as the PM candidate. He contested and won an intra-party election where his rival, Barrister Sultan Mahmood, finally voted in his favour. Chaudhry Abdul Majeed secured 35 votes while Raja Farooq Haider of AJKPML-N managed only 11 votes.

Raja Zulqarnain, then president of 'AJK', was replaced subsequently by Sardar Muhammad Yaqoob Khan, who had sensed the political wind blowing in favour of AJKPPP and joined the party ahead of the elections. On 29 July 2011, Yaqoob was elected as the president securing 40 votes while his rival Khan Bahadur Khan of the AJKPML-N obtained only 11 votes.

Majeed's government pulled on through allegations of widespread corruption and nepotism till there was a change of government in Islamabad with assumption of power by PML-N led by Nawaz Sharif on June 5, 2013. A month and a half later, on July 22, 2013, there was a revolt within AJKPPP leading to two party members tabling a no-trust motion against his government. They alleged that Chaudhry Abdul Majeed Khan's government was involved in massive corruption in developmental projects like Mirpur Greater Water Scheme, Jinnah Model Town Housing Scheme, Mirpur University of Engineering and Technology, Mirpur Development Authority and the construction of two medical colleges in the state, and it had also failed to highlight the case of Kashmir at the international fora.

The dissidents were apparently led by Barrister Sultan Mahmood who reportedly claimed[57] that he had the support of 32 candidates including the support of AJKPML-N legislators. However, three days later it was reported that, Prime Minister Nawaz Sharif "directed his party representatives in the legislature not to take part in any move to topple the AJK prime minister"[58] and the whole drama fizzled out. Barrister Mahmood nourished a grudge against both PML-N and the AJKPPP and subsequently joined Imran Khan's Pakistan Tehreek-e-Insaf (PTI).

By July 2016, when the elections were held, AJKPPP was riven with internal feud and there was a strong anti-incumbency wave sweeping 'AJK'. AJKMC was also facing revolt within as many of its erstwhile strong supporters had either joined AJKPML-N or AJKPPP. In this context, the decision of the central leadership of PPP to bank on anti-India and anti-Nawaz rhetoric backfired. When the elections were held under tight military security, the AJKPML-N won a landslide, its first-ever electoral sweep, securing 31 out of 41 directly elected seats. Both AJKMC and AJKPPP could only get three seats each, while local branch of Imran Khan's PTI led by Barrister Sultan Mahmood, who himself lost the election, could bag only two seats. Raja Farooq Haider who had been courted by Nawaz Sharif since July 2010, when the no confidence motion was tabled against him, led the local branch of PML-N to victory and was chosen as the prime minister of 'AJK'. He assumed office after being duly elected by the 'AJK' Assembly on July 30, 2016, securing 38 of the 48 votes cast, while two other contestants Chaudhry Muhammad Yaseen of AJK PPP and Ghulam Mohiuddin Dewan, jointly fielded by AJKPTI and AJKMC, received five votes each.

The new Prime Minister announced a nine member cabinet comprises two ministers each from Muzaffarabad, Bagh and Kotli districts, one each from Haveli, Sudhanoti and Bhimber district. On December 12, 2016, Farooq Haider inducted three more ministers into his cabinet raising its strength to 12. While one was from Mirpur, other two were from Pakistan-based refugee areas. Days later, the PML-N parachuted Ambassador Masood Khan, then Director General of Institute of Strategic Studies Islamabad (ISSI), as presidential candidate, who defeated AJKPPP's Chaudhry Latif Akbar with 42 votes to six on August 16, 2016, to replace outgoing president of 'AJK', Yaqoob Muhammad Khan, on August 25, 2016. Masood Khan, a former diplomat, was nominated in violation of every electoral and legal norm of the state. According to media reports, Masood Khan is originally from Rawalakot, Poonch; but he did not hold the 'state subject' certificate (that he was a resident of the State of Jammu and Kashmir) and his name was inducted in the electoral rolls recently under pressure from the government. The 'AJK' High Court was moved to challenge his qualification and an interim verdict was given in Khan's favour to legitimize his position as president of 'AJK'.

These elections show that there has been a gradual erosion of support base for the local political parties, whose influence at the local level is diminishing very fast. At another level, local political outfits have been affected by personality clashes and petty and selfish interests have weakened their position as well. The national political parties – PPP, PML-N and PTI – are expected to hold their sway over the regional political parties in 'AJK'. Thus, the writ and hold of Pakistan have now become stronger than ever. In the past, it was the Pakistan Army and the MKA that kept the dissident politics in 'AJK' in check; now the national parties through their affiliates are expected to do the same.

Economy and Hydro-Energy

A landlocked territory of insignificant size and cultivable mountainous terrain 'AJK' is dependent on Pakistan for its economy. Its northern districts (Neelum, Muzaffarabad, Hattian, Bagh, Haveli, Poonch and Sudhanoti) are mountainous, characterised by deep ravines, rugged and undulating terrain, while southern districts (Kotli, Mirpur and Bhimber) are relatively plain. 'AJK' has only 13 percent of its land cultiviable for agricultural purposes. Due to rudimentary irrigation system of the olden days, which has not been improved over the years, the land has very limited productivity.[59]

There is very little information available about the details of economy of 'AJK'. At the time of partition, the economy of 'AJK' was at the subsistence level, mostly dependent on the trade along the Jhelum Valley road. Once this road was closed after the de facto partition of the state along the ceasefire line (CFL)/Line of Control (LoC), the lifeline of the region came to an abrupt end. Through this road, large quantity of timber was transported to other parts of the state. Today, 'AJK' is an economically disadvantaged region, mainly because of its unproductive terrain. It also lacks communication infrastructure – roads, railways – to boost its economy. Moreover, Pakistan has not contributed enough to help improve the economy of 'AJK', and rather institutionalised its economic over-dependence on Islamabad in order to strengthen its hold on the territory.

However, there have been extraneous changes leading to some amelioration of the economic condition of the people of 'AJK'. In the 1960s and 1970s there was mass emigration of 'AJK' population to the UK and other western countries. Many Mirpuris migrated to the UK because their land had been either submerged or taken over for the construction of Mangla Dam. They complained that they were given neither financial compensation nor jobs in return. This emigration brought about huge remittances that significantly changed 'AJK''s old economic and social base, particularly in Mirpur and Poonch.[60]

The standard of living of the people changed accordingly. According to a socio-economic study of 'AJK', about 35 per cent of the migrants were sending to their families remittances up to PKR (Pakistani Rupees) 70,000 per year; 46.4 per cent Rs. 40,001 to Rs. 90,000 per year; 23 per cent Rs. 65,000 to

Rs. 150,000 per year; and 6 per cent above 100,000 per year.[61] It is believed that deposits from 'AJK' in Pakistani banks amounted to Rs. 2.4 trillion, which was "960 times the size of [AJK's] 1987-88 budget of Rs. 2.5 billion".[62] Ironically, the people of 'AJK' are not allowed easy access to this money, let alone invest it. Presumably, even if they could access it, there is no avenue to make a profitable investment of it. They cannot build roads and bridges. For any investment, the most essential prerequisite is the presence of efficient and effective communications network and electricity. Therefore, with no infrastructure back home to invest in, people are spending money on house constructions, hotels, sports shops, cloth markets and branches of various branded Pakistan-based outlets. Travel agencies, currency exchange, private education and healthcare are now thriving concerns in 'AJK'.[63] With UK leaving the European Union and the looming uncertainty over the post-Brexit economic situation, the remittances have fallen by 10 percent since the Brexit Referendum in June 2016.[64]

The other issue that has led to reduction in the remittances coming from the UK is the erosion of ties with their kinsmen. The young generation of immigrants do not prefer to spend their time and money in 'AJK'. There is no sense of belonging among the young generation of the Mirpuris in UK towards their ancestor's land.[65]

In the absence of a strong legal status, 'AJK' is not in a position to negotiate with foreign donors and investors. It is Pakistan which negotiates on 'AJK''s behalf and also acts as a guarantor when international consortiums invest in infrastructure development or hydroelectric power generation projects in 'AJK'.[66] An official from the Asian Development Bank (ADB) reportedly told the Brussels based International Crisis Group: "Our relationship with AJK is not very different from the one we have with other provinces in Pakistan. The federal government takes the loan and transfers the money to 'AJK' as a grant, making 'AJK' dependent on Islamabad for its development budget."[67] Talking about 'AJK''s dependence on Pakistan, a senior civil servant from Muzaffarabad in an interview to the International Crisis Group stated, "Islamabad controls us through our finances, because it is well aware that we cannot survive without its financial support."[68]

Furthermore, 'AJK''s water resources are crucial for Pakistan's irrigation and electricity supply. However, this hydroelectric potential is severely under-utilised; though having a potential of 17000 megawatts, only 34 megawatts are produced. In effect, according to the Director General of the electricity department, "we have to buy 92 per cent of our energy from Pakistan".[69] The

Pakistan Government, on its part, has identified a number of hydroelectric energy projects (see Table 1).

Table 1: Upcoming Independent Power Producers (IPPs) – Hydropower Projects (as on June 16, 2015)

Project	Sponsor/Company Name	Location	Capacity (MW)	Completion time
Patrind Hydropower Project	Star Hydropower Limited	Kunhar River KPK/AJK	147	2017
Gulpur Project	Mira Power Ltd	Poonch River/ Gulpur AJK	100	2019
Sehra Hydropower Project	Farab Energy & Water Project, Iran	Poonch River, AJK	130	2019
Azad Pattan Hydropower Project	Alamgir Power Pvt Ltd	Jehlum River/ Sudhanoti, AJK	640	2022
Chakothi-Hattian	Suhail Jute Mills Ltd	Muzaffarabad, AJK	500	2022
Kohala	China International Water & Electricity Company	Jehlum River/ Kohala, AJK	1100	2023

Source: Private Power & Infrastructure Board Government of Pakistan Ministry of Water & Power[70]

If the ownership of all these projects is handed over to the 'AJK' Government, it will lessen its economic over-dependence on Pakistan. Even the royalty received from already existing projects such as the Mangla Dam is very minimal. According to Snedden:

> Traditionally, Pakistan has taken 70 per cent of royalties; Azad Kashmir has received the rest (although these amounts did not appear in budgetary documents until recently). Even if Azad Kashmir had received all royalties, these would not have made the region financially self-sufficient, although they would have reduced its dependency on Pakistan.[71]

Dissenting Voices

The right to vote, sans the right to rule, kills the very essence of democracy. Ever since 'AJK' came under Pakistani control in 1947, the right to dissent of 'AJK' people was taken as an anti-national act by Pakistan. Even mere talking about restructuring the relationship between Islamabad and Muzaffarabad does not go down well in the power corridors of Islamabad. Pakistan does not allow political parties that do not support J&K's accession to Pakistan to contest the elections. Kashmiris who talk about Pakistan's highhandedness are thrown into jails; they are also threatened, denied travel documents and tortured.[72] The growing poverty, alienation and resentment vis-à-vis Pakistan has given birth to demands for social liberation within 'AJK'. A proto-nationalist movement is now emerging in 'AJK':

> The issue of social liberation has come to the fore within the nationalist movement. The revolutionary currents developing amongst the youth through the Jammu and Kashmir National Students Federation (JKNSF) in [AJK] are worrying the rulers in Islamabad.[73]

Voices are being raised in various quarters in 'AJK' demanding redefining of the contours of the current relationship with Pakistan based on the 1974 Act. The only issue they are facing is in terms of the strategy and the ways and means of channelising the voices of dissent.[74] Upward political mobilisation and awareness has given a fillip to the demand for autonomy. After the 18th and 19th constitutional amendments of the Pakistan Constitution which devolved the powers from federal to the provinces and to some extent reduced the central's government's role in provinces, this demand has gathered strength within 'AJK' as well.[75]

According to Javid Hayat:

> In this last decade, issues pertaining to the status of AJK, ownership of natural resources, and empowerment of the people in a truly democratic mechanism have been discussed among political parties, civil society and media. This has led to some academic intervention, conferences and panel group discussions in AJK. They found the structure unjust which left insufficient space for self-governance in this region. In addition, this has failed to address the national question including sovereign rights and fragility of governance. There is consensus amongst the political parties of AJK on redefining the current relationship with the government of Pakistan based on Act 1974. The only difference appears to be on strategy.[76]

Although there is a consensus within 'AJK' on revisiting the 1974 Act, there are divergent views on what exactly should they strive for. Most of the prominent members of the civil society (e.g. Majeed Malik, former Chief Justice of the 'AJK' High Court; Tanveer Ahmed; Sardar Aftab Ahmad Khan, a UK-based political and social activist; and other nationalist forces) are in favour of going back to the October 24, 1947 declaration restoring sovereignty with the 'AJK' Government. There are others who would want to restore the 1970 Act with a parliamentary form of government. There are still others (e.g. Manzoor Gillani, a retired Jurist) who want 'AJK' to be made something close to a province but without declaring it as a province.[77]

To further stifle the nationalist sentiments, the 'AJK' Government in March

2016, banned 16 pro-independence books on Kashmir. Two of them were written by JKLF founder Mohammad Maqbool Bhat.[78] On expected lines, separatist group and civil society on both sides of Kashmir slammed the decision. The JKLF leader Yasin Malik termed the decision of banning pro-freedom books by the Pakistan authority as the denial of the right to expression. He further said, "Whether you like the views of these writers or not, common people should be allowed to read them. It is undemocratic to ban books".[79] Therefore, Pakistan continues to maintain zero tolerance for any ideology that questions its control over 'AJK'. "It is just a matter of time that the present generation or next one may get swayed by the ideology that could start demanding actual Azadi."[80]

With contentious issues flaring up rather than being resolved, the resentment level is at an all-time high. Moreover, unending marginalisation of the people of 'AJK' suggests that "Pakistan is fast losing traditional sympathetic constituencies owing to indifferent core-periphery attitude".[81] Against this backdrop, the 13th amendment to the Interim Constitution of 1974 in June 2018, enabled by the outgoing PML-N government led by a lame-duck prime minister, Khaqan Abbasi, assumes significance.

The amendment passed by joint sitting of 'AJK' legislative assembly and legislative council and assented by the 'AJK' President aims at granting greater financial and administrative autonomy to the 'AJK' government to address chronic developmental issues like the supply of electricity, water usage charge and resource sharing. It empowers the legislative assembly to frame laws on issues of local importance and seeks to enhance the capacity and efficiency of the 'AJK' administration. With the failure of the PML-N to return to power in July 25, 2018 elections, however, the fate of this amendment remains uncertain. Moreover, the amendment does not abolish the Council which continues to retain its veto over any issue having implications for security, foreign policy and currency related issues. This connotes continued interference by Islamabad on local governance and it is likely to be resented by the 'AJK' people once the amendment gets operationalised.

NOTES

1. The Constitution of the Islamic Republic of Pakistan, at na.gov.pk/uploads/documents/1333523681_951.pdf, p. 151.
2. Ershad Mahmud, "Status of AJK in Political Milieu", *Policy Perspective*, 3 (2), at http://www.ips.org.pk/education/1115-status-of-ajk-in-political-milieu.html.
3. "Proposed Constitutional Amendments in The Constitution of Islamic Republic of Pakistan 1973, for Empowerment of Azad Jammu & Kashmir and Gilgit-Baltistan", Discussion Paper, Pakistan Institute of Legislative Development and Transparency (PILDAT), May 2011, p.10,

4. Christopher Snedden, *The Untold Story of the People of Azad Kashmir*, Hurst & Company, London, 2012, p. 37.
5. Ibid., p. 87.
6. Navnita Chadha Behera, *Demystifying Kashmir*, Pearson Longman, USA, 2007, p. 172.
7. Christopher Snedden, *The Untold Story of the People of Azad Kashmir*, p. 90.
8. See "Appendix II", *Karachi Agreement*.
9. Ershad Mahmud, "Status of AJK in Political Milieu".
10. Ibid.
11. Samuel Baid, "Azad Kashmir", Jasjit Singh (ed.), *Pakistan Occupied Kashmir: Under the Jackboot*, Cosmo Publications, New Delhi, 1995, p. 87.
12. Ershad Mahmud, "Status of AJK in Political Milieu".
13. Ibid.
14. Ibid.
15. Christopher Snedden, *The Untold Story of the People of Azad Kashmir*, p. 93.
16. Ershad Mahmud, "Status of AJK in Political Milieu".
17. Ibid.
18. For details, see: "An Appraisal of Constitutional, Financial and Administrative Arrangements between the Governments of Pakistan and Azad Jammu and Kashmir", Centre for Peace, Development and Reforms (CPDR) Azad Jammu and Kashmir, June 2011.
19. See Simla Agreement at Appendix III.
20. Christopher Snedden, *The Untold Story of the People of Azad Kashmir*, p. 101.
21. Ershad Mahmud, "Status of AJK in Political Milieu",
22. *The Azad Jammu & Kashmir Interim Constitution Act, 1974*, Amended up to date and Modified up to September 2005, Azad Govt. of the State of Jammu and Kashmir, at www.ajkassembly.gok.pk/ajkinterimconstituionact1974.pdf.
23. Javid Hayat, "Shadow Governance: Right to Vote and Rule in Azad Jammu & Kashmir-Analysis", *Eurasiareview*, July 23, 2012, at http://www.eurasiareview.com/23072012-shadow-governance-right-to-vote-and-rule-in-azad-jammu-kashmir-analysis.
24. Ibid.
25. PILDAT, "Pakistan-Azad Jammu & Kashmir Politico-Legal Conflict", PILDAT, September 2011, p. 16, at www.pildat.org.
26. Ibid.
27. Christopher Snedden, *The Untold Story of the People of Azad Kashmir*, p. 117.
28. Roger Ballard, "The Kashmir Crisis: A View from Mirpur", *Economic & Political Weekly*, 1991, p. 514.
29. "'With Friends Like These …': Human Rights Violations in Azad Kashmir", *Human Rights Watch*, 18 (12), September 2006, at http://www.hrw.org/reports/2006/pakistan0906/3.htm#_Toc14592374.
30. Ibid.
31. Alexander Evans, "Kashmir: A Tale of Two Valleys", *Asian Affairs*, XXXVI (1), March 2005.
32. Roger Ballard, "The Kashmir Crisis: A View from Mirpur", p. 2.
33. Ibid., p. 514.
34. Ibid., pp. 513-517.
35. Parvez Dewan, "A History of POK - Pakistan Occupied Kashmir", in Virendra Gupta and Alok Bansal (eds.), *Pakistan Occupied Kashmir: The Untold Story*, Manas Publications, New Delhi, 2007, p. 110.
36. Christopher Snedden, *The Untold Story of the People of Azad Kashmir*, p. 122.

37. Ibid., p. 132.
38. Shams Rehman, "Azad Kashmir: A Brief Introduction", at http://dadyal.com.pk/azad-kashmir-a-brief-introduction-by-shams-rehman/.
39. Javid Hayat, "Shadow Governance: Right to Vote and Rule in Azad Jammu & Kashmir-Analysis".
40. Mazhar Iqbal, "Fundamental Rights and the Kashmiri Refugee Vote", *Foreign Policy Journal*, September 29, 2014, at www.foreignpolicyjournal.com/2014/09/29/fundemental-rights-and-the-kashmiri-refugee-vote/.
41. Ibid.
42. Farooq Suleria, "Provincialising AJK", *The News*, September 07, 2016, at https://www.thenews.com.pk/print/148366-Provincialising-AJK
43. Samuel Baid, "Politics in 'Azad Kashmir'", Jasjit Singh (ed.) *Pakistan Occupied Kashmir: Under the Jackboot*, Cosmo Publications, New Delhi, 1995, p. 112.
44. Christopher Snedden, *The Untold Story of the People of Azad Kashmir*, p. 190
45. Ibid., p. 192
46. Samuel Baid, "Politics in 'Azad Kashmir'", p. 116.
47. Ibid., p. 119.
48. Ibid., p. 120.
49. Nasir Mallick, "Trouble in Paradise", *The Herald*, July 1991, p. 84.
50. Ibid., p. 85.
51. Ibid., p. 83.
52. See The Azad Jammu and Kashmir Interim Constitution Act, 1974, at http://www.ajkassembly.gok.pk/AJK_Interim_Constitution_Act_1974.pdf
53. M.H. Askari, "Kashmir Through the Looking Glass", *The Herald*, July 1991, p. 85.
54. Ibid., p. 86.
55. Justice Riaz Akhtar Chaudhry was appointed as judge of the AJK Supreme Court on Sept 24, 2006 and then as its Chief Justice within 25 days of his appointment. He had superseded the senior-most judge of AJK Supreme Court Justice Manzoor Hussain Gillani on October 24, 2006 by the military controlled dispensation in Islamabad. Gilani was senior to him by six years in judicial service, and two years his senior in the Supreme Court. Riaz had also functioned as a junior judge under Gillani in the high court earlier. Justice Gillani had then knocked the doors of the Supreme Court of Pakistan to seek justice. However, a three-member bench headed by Chief Justice Riaz Akhtar Chaudhury passed a judgment on March 15, 2010 that the Supreme Court of Pakistan could not go beyond the territories defined in Article 1 of the Constitution of Pakistan and that it had no jurisdiction to entertain any petition regarding appointment of judges of superior courts of AJK. Prime Minister of Pakistan from passing any notification regarding Chief Justice of AJK. The order also restrained Law, Justice and Parliamentary Affairs Department from issuing any fresh notification and the President of the AJK from administering oath to any judge for the office of the AJK CJ. See details "AJK SC challenges Pakistan SC in new row", at http://www.kalpoint.com/national-news/-ajk-sc-challenges-pakistan-sc-in-new-row.html
56. Farooq Tirmizi, *The Express Tribune*, June 27, 2011, at http://tribune.com.pk/story/197253/ajk-elections-an-unsurprising-result/
57. "Pent-up resentment: AJK premier faces revolt in house", *The Express Tribune*, July 23, 2013, at http://tribune.com.pk/story/580698/pent-up-resentment-ajk-premier-faces-revolt-in-house/ and also http://tribune.com.pk/story/581062/ajk-prime-minister-pml-n-supports-no-confidence-motion/
58. "Resolution withdrawn: AJK premier gets 'tainted' trust vote", *The Express Tribune*, July 28,

2013, at http://tribune.com.pk/story/582922/resolution-withdrawnajk-premier-gets-tainted-trust-vote/

59. For details, see: "Azad Jammu and Kashmir, at a Glance, 2013", Azad Jammu and Kashmir Planning & Development Department, Muzaffarabad.
60. For details of country-wise workers' remittances, see: State Bank of Pakistan, Statistics & DWH Department, at www.sbp.org/ecodata/Homeremit.pdf.
61. Humayun Khan et al., "Impact of Remittances on the Socio-Economic Conditions of Rural Families in District Poonch of Azad Jammu and Kashmir", *Sarhad J. Agric*, 27 (4), 2011, at www.aup.edu.pk/sj_pdf/IMPACT%20OF%20REMITANCES%20THE%20SOCIO-ECONOMIC%20CONDITIONS%20OF%20RURAL.PDF.
62. Christopher Snedden, *The Untold Story of the People of Azad Kashmir*, p. 183.
63. Shams Rehman, "Azad Kashmir: A Brief Introduction".
64. "Brexit hastens Azad Kashmir's economic break with UK", *Dawn*, October 30, 2016, at, http://www.dawn.com/news/1367221
65. Ibid.
66. International Crisis Group, "Steps Towards Peace: Putting Kashmiris First", Asia Briefing No. 106, June 3, 2010, p. 9.
67. Quoted in Ibid., p. 9.
68. Ibid., p. 9.
69. Ibid., p. 10.
70. Private Power & Infrastructure Board Government of Pakistan Ministry of Water & Power, at www.ppib.gov.pk/N_upcoming_hydel.htm.
71. Christopher Snedden, *The Untold Story of the People of Azad Kashmir*, p. 181.
72. "International Crisis Group, "Steps Towards Peace: Putting Kashmiris First", p. 8.
73. PILDAT, "Pakistan-Azad Jammu & Kashmir Politico-Legal Conflict", p. 17.
74. Javid Hayat, "Shadow Governance: Right to Vote and Rule in Azad Jammu & Kashmir-Analysis".
75. PILDAT, "Pakistan-Azad Jammu & Kashmir Politico-Legal Conflict", p. 16.
76. Javid Hayat, "Shadow Governance: Right to Vote and Rule in Azad Jammu & Kashmir-Analysis".
77. Ibid.
78. "AJK govt bans 16 books", *Dawn*, March 8, 2016, at http:// www.dawn.com/news/1244261
79. Ban on Pro-Azadi Books in Pak, Kashmir Observer, March 14, 2016, at http://kashmirobserver.net/2016/editorial/ban-pro-azadi-books-pak-4328
80. Nilofar Qurashi, No azadi in Azad Kashmir, Kashmir Images, March 27, 2016, at http:dailykashmirimages.comDetails/10528/no-azadi-in-azad-kashmir
81. PILDAT, "Pakistan-Azad Jammu & Kashmir Politico-Legal Conflict", p. 18.

2

Political Parties in 'AJK'

The 'Azad Jammu and Kashmir Election Commission (AJKEC)' lists 44 political parties who are registered with it before the election of July 2016.[1] For the July 21, 2016 elections, 727 candidates had filed their nomination papers for 41 seats of the state legislative assembly representing over 4.3 million people – 29 seats from 'AJK' and 12 seats from all over Pakistan consisting of Kashmiri refugees. The total number of electorates is 2,674,586 (1,483,747 males and 1,190,839 females; 2,235,702 from 'AJK' and 438,884 from different areas of Pakistan).[2] Out of the 727 nominations only 427 from 25 parties (after check of eligibility and withdrawals, 299 from 'AJK' and 128 from different areas of Pakistan) finally contested the elections.[3] Apart from 41 seats for which direct elections are held, eight seats are allocated to political parties on the basis of proportional representation.

The 2016 elections indicated rising levels of political participation and growing appetite for representative politics as well. However, the trajectory of 'AJK' politics shows that there is a steady incursion of mainstream political parties from Pakistan into local politics and gradual decimation of traditionally local parties. The grand old political party like Azad Jammu Kashmir Muslim Conference (AJKMC) and other important parties like Jammu Kashmir Liberation League (JKLL), Jammu and Kashmir Liberation Front (JKLF), which have not been allowed to participate in the elections because of pro-independence stance, and some others have gradually lost their appeal and reach over the years. The nationalist parties who would not subscribe to the ideology of accession of Kashmir to Pakistan, are kept out of the elections. Therefore, there has been an effort to study major political parties in the following sections.

ALL-JAMMU AND KASHMIR MUSLIM CONFERENCE (AJKMC)

Genesis and Development

The history of the 'AJK' in Pakistan occupied Kashmir (PoK) is incomplete without the mention of All-Jammu and Kashmir Muslim Conference (AJKMC) also referred to as the Muslim Conference. It was established in 1932 by Sheikh Abdullah to provide a political direction to the Muslims of Jammu and Kashmir when the entire state was ruled by Maharaja Hari Singh. There were two important developments that paved the way for the formation of the Muslim Conference. The immediate provocation for the formation of the party was the Glancy Commission report on popular rising against Hari Singh. In the backdrop of the 1931 uprising, Maharaja Hari Singh announced the appointment of a commission under the chairmanship of Sir B.J. Glancy to look into the grievances of the people, particularly the Muslims. The Kashmiri pundits however resented the establishment of the Commission. The Commission recommended constitutional reforms and also talked about providing due weightage to the educated Muslim youth.[4] The second development was the birth of a Jammu-based political organisation known as the Dogra Sabha in 1904. The Kashmiris witnessed the Jammu-based caste nationalism as communal nationalism, which was regarded as the "manifestation of the kind of sub-nationalism in one region of the state [which] eventually produced a counterpoise in the formation of Muslim Conference by Kashmiri leaders in 1932."[5]

Secularisation and Factionalism of the Party

In an atmosphere infected with the communal virus, Sheikh Abdullah took a pragmatic stand. He talked about religious harmony. In 1935, he appealed to all the communities for harmony, observing that his "fight [was] for the emancipation of [his] own country". He urged the people: "Let us all rise above petty communal bickering and work jointly for welfare of the masses. I appeal to all Hindu brethren not to entertain imaginary fears and doubts. Let us assure them that their rights shall not be jeopardised if they join hands with the Mussalmans."[6]

During the early phase of the Muslim Conference, both Sheikh Abdullah the leader of Muslim Conference and Mirwaiz Mohmmad Yousaf Shah, who belonged to the family of the prominent spiritual leader from the valley with lineage traced back to 16th century preacher from Hamadan, Iran, took recourse to religion to mobilise the Muslim masses. They used the Quranic verses literally to appeal to the masses as if they were leading a Muslim movement. Sheikh Abdullah, however, soon developed a view that the emancipation of the masses was possible only if all communities came together under one forum. This was in direct contrast to the stand taken by an influential section within Muslim Conference who continued to subscribe to a communal viewpoint and emphasised on the emancipation of the majority Muslims in the principality. Nevertheless, Sheikh Abdullah succeeded in influencing the majority in the party to subscribe to his view and even proposed a change in nomenclature of the party to signify a secular change in the party's outlook. On June 28, 1938, the working committee of the Muslim Conference met to review the nomenclature of the party. The committee passed the following resolution:

> Whereas in the opinion of the working committee the time has come when all the progressive forces in the country should be rallied under one banner to fight for the achievement of Responsible Government, the working committee recommends to the General Council that in the forthcoming annual session, the name and the Constitution of the organisation be so altered and amended that all people who wish to participate in the political struggle are enabled to become members of the Conference irrespective of their caste, creed or religion.[7]

By June 1939, Muslim Conference changed its name to National Conference. It then joined the All India States Peoples Conference, a conglomerate of popular movements taking place in princely states of India which came together in 1927, and was finally affiliated to the Congress in 1939.

The process of secularisation of Kashmiri politics helped the Muslim Conference to garner support from the Indian National Congress at its October 1939 session. The Muslim Conference, known as National Conference since 1939, not only endorsed the Congress's policy towards the Second World War but Sheikh Abdullah also followed the leadership of the Congress.

All this had inevitable impact on Muslim politics in Jammu and Kashmir. Right since the beginning, it was very difficult to bring the two opposite world-views of Sheikh Abdullah and Mirwaiz Mohammed Yousaf Shah together. There was a deep variance between the two in terms of political ideology. Sheikh Abdullah was greatly influenced by the Pundit Jawaharlal Nehru's secular credentials, while Mirwaiz Yousaf Shah was ideologically close to the Muslim League's call for a separate homeland for the Muslims and was also at odds with Sheikh Abdullah about the status of the Ahmedis.[8] The differences came out in the open when Mirwaiz accused Sheikh Abdullah in a public gathering of being an agent of the Qadianis and propagating their cause.[9]

Sheikh Abdullah renamed the party as the All Jammu and Kashmir National Conference (AJKNC) to make the party secular and open it to non-Muslims. In his autobiography, *Aatish-e-Chinar*, Sheikh Abdullah writes that renaming the Muslim Conference as National Conference was a painful act in the face of strong opposition within the party.[10] His secular ideology inclined him towards a party that is professing inclusive, secular, and democratic values. Perhaps, he wished to carve out an independent Kashmir having close ties with India. Moreover, Abdullah considered renaming the party as a prerequisite to get support from Indian National Congress in the struggle against the Maharaja. This secularisation of the Kashmir politics under AJKNC further widened the gulf between Mirwaiz and Sheikh Abdullah. Their differences were not only ideological but also personal.

The opponents of Sheikh Abdullah's political philosophy and secularisation of politics revived the Muslim Conference on June 13, 1941. There was a clear division not only at the ideological level within the state of Jammu and Kashmir but also within the support bases of the two parties. In the late 1940s it became almost impossible to thwart the communal strife striking the societal cord of the state. As Snedden writes: "[T]he support of the Hindu communal groups was unstintingly rendered to the ruling Prince and the support of the Muslim communal groups extended to those who would not accept the secular approach of the National Conference."[11] This interplay of communal politics was well marked in the Jammu region. The Muslim Conference's support base was in the Jammu region, whereas the National Conference was popular in the Kashmir valley. The Muslim Conference found much support in Jammu because of the communal divide, and therefore, exploitation of religion became a handy tool to get political dividends. In contrast, the presence of secular credentials within the society in the valley did not yield any space to politically motivated religious slogans. Christopher Snedden outlines the differences by saying that, "certainly, Kashmirness and the 'secular thinking' of Kashmiris were significant reasons why the Kashmir Valley experienced almost no communal violence during 1947. Kashmiris were more tolerant, their practice of Islam and Hinduism more liberal, and their inter-communal relationships more involved and harmonious than those in other parts of the princely state".[12] This can be further gauged from the reception Mohammad Ali Jinnah received during his visit to Kashmir on May 8, 1944. From Suchetgarh to Ramban Jinnah was greeted by the supporters of the Muslim Conference, and from Bannihal onwards it was Sheikh Abdullah's National Conference that managed the show.

The ideological barrier further widened when Jinnah-Abdullah conflict emerged on the political horizon of Kashmir. The reason was Jinnah's speech in which he praised the Muslim Conference and claimed that it was the sole representative of the Kashmiri Muslims, "99 per cent of the Muslims who met me are of the opinion that Muslim Conference alone is the representative organisation of the State Muslims."[13] An irked Sheikh Abdullah took it as an insult to him. He expressed his anger vis-à-vis Jinnah in his autobiography, *Aatish-e-Chinar*. He wrote: "At that time, Mr. Mohammad Ali Jinnah was intoxicated by power. He thought it beneath his dignity to talk to a poor and resourceless nation. When this equation of power went against him, he woke up in panic from his dream. But by this time, the snake had escaped; only its line remained."[14] Right from the beginning, the Muslim Conference was favourably disposed to changing sides, from espousing independence to joining Pakistan. However, to guard against the fears and suspicion of the minorities, it cautioned Hari Singh not to accede to India but to declare independence.[15] Finally on July 19, 1947, the Muslim Conference declared accession of Jammu and Kashmir to Pakistan as the core objective of the Kashmiris.

After the Tribal Invasion: Autocratic Leadership

The state lay divided after Pakistan occupied a large part of Jammu and Kashmir through an incursion in 1947-48. The Muslim Conference became the sole representative of the people of the Pakistan occupied Jammu and Kashmir who were anti-Maharaja, pro-Islam, and pro-Pakistan in their outlook. In anticipation of the plebiscite, the Muslim Conference did not feel it necessary to establish a participatory political system. Therefore, its only concern was, "[w]hich individual would control the party and subsequently control [the so called] Azad Kashmir".[16] The Muslim Conference being the only political party in the so called 'Azad Jammu and Kashmir' (AJK) as also its pro-Pakistan stance made it easy for Pakistan to control the affairs of the region through this party.[17] According to Snedden, not holding the plebiscite was not the only impediment in establishing a vibrant political system; the role played by the Muslim Conference leader, Chaudhry Ghulam Abbas was equally disruptive, "as he was the Supreme Head of the Azad Kashmir Movement, a position higher than the AJK President, power flowed downwards from the dictatorial Abbas".[18] The bitter rivalry between Sardar Ibrahim and Chaudhry Abbas greatly afflicted the Muslim Conference for years to come. Abbas also controlled the selection of various important positions, including the president of 'AJK'. This dictatorial tendency was followed by his successors, Sardar Ibrahim, K.H. Khurshid and Khan Abdul Hamid Khan.[19]

This autocratic tradition was not the only reason of less, rather no, democracy within the Muslim Conference; the "buy off" policy Pakistan adopted vis-à-vis 'Azad Kashmiris' was also a significant factor: "Pakistan basically bought off Muslim Conference politicians by offering them senior positions, or by getting the Ministry of Kashmir Affairs in Islamabad to pay allowances that made them dependent on Pakistan."[20] The other issue which impeded the Muslim Conference from becoming a democratic party was internal factionalism. The seeds of rivalry were sown when on July 19, 1947, a resolution on independence was discussed by the leaders of the Muslim Conference, sent by Chaudhry Abbas from his prison cell. The independence resolution was opposed, rather rejected, by Sardar Ibrahim.[21] Those who wanted to see Kashmir independent felt disheartened, and Abbas never reconciled with Sardar Ibrahim. However, for this gesture, Pakistan rewarded Sardar Ibrahim by making him the first president of the 'AJK' on October 24, 1947.[22]

After Abbas was released by Sheikh Abdullah in 1948, he became the President of the Muslim Conference, and sacked Sardar Ibrahim.[23] Under the Rules of Business, the President of 'Azad Kashmir' could stay in power as long as he enjoyed the support from the General Council of the Muslim Conference. But 'AJK' President Sardar Ibrahim was not taken well by the senior leaders within the Muslim Conference. Moreover, Ghulam Abbas could not tolerate his junior, Sardar Ibrahim, presiding over the occupied regions.[24] The rivalry between Ghulam Abbas and Sardar Ibrahim became very tense due to the latter's rise in prestige and popularity.[25] Later Sardar Ibrahim was not liked by Pakistan after he tried to establish direct access with United Nations (UN) officials, sidelining-Pakistan. Then Prime Minister of Pakistan, Liaquat Ali Khan, was also annoyed with arrogant behaviour of Sardar Ibrahim and "wanted to eliminate or at least disgrace him".[26] The differences between Abbas and Ibrahim were exploited by Sardar Qayyum to his advantage and it gave an opportunity to begin his political career. Qayyum, patronised by Abbas, opposed Ibrahim. The Muslim Conference got divided into two factions; the new faction headed by Sardar Ibrahim was called the Azad Muslim Conference. The following period only saw the frequent installation and removal of 'AJK' presidents at Pakistan's behest.

Post-1970 Politics of Limited Democratisation

The overall political development in 'AJK' has much to do with Pakistan's troubled experience with democracy. Pakistan had its first election on one-man, one-vote basis in December 1970. Gen. Yahya Khan ordered those elections under intense domestic pressure. In 'AJK', retired army Brigadier, Abdul Rehman Khan, who had been made president, was tasked to give "politically" everything that 'AJK' wanted.[27] Therefore, for the first time, 'AJK' was given internal autonomy with limited Pakistani control under the 1970 Government Act. The Act provided for a President and a 25-member Council to be elected through adult franchise. Elections held in 1970 were a watershed moment in 'AJK', breaking the jinx of Pakistan's extensive interference in elections. For the first time, the president of 'AJK' was elected directly by the people, who tasted the experience of universal suffrage. Sardar Qayyum's Muslim Conference won the Presidential elections. The breakaway faction, led by Sardar Ibrahim, lost badly. He could have lost probably also because he was seen with disdain in Islamabad as well.[28] After his defeat, Sardar Ibrahim returned to the Qayyum-led Muslim Conference. But this patch-up did not last long. Soon the differences between Qayyum and Ibrahim emerged again, first over cabinet formation and later when the centre-led Pakistan People's Party (PPP) put pressure on the 'AJK' government to oust Qayyum after the promulgation of the 1974 Interim Constitution.[29] Sardar Ibrahim moved to the PPP, and subsequently became 'AJK''s president.

Thus the stint of internal autonomy in 'AJK' was short lived. Pakistan's then Prime Minister, Zulfiqar Ali Bhutto, introduced the prime ministerial system via "Azad Jammu and Kashmir Interim Constitution Act 1974" in order to ensure Pakistan's grip over the internal politics of 'AJK'.[30] This period saw the most tumultuous years in AJK's embryonic democratic set-up. The elections held in 1975 under this Constitution Act were boycotted by the Muslim Conference. Qayyum opposed the entry of the PPP in 'AJK' arguing that this trend would defeat the very ideology of the Kashmir Movement.[31] The party complained that it was not allowed to campaign freely and situation was created by the government in Islamabad to ensure the victory of the PPP Azad Kashmir (AJKPPP)-led United Front Alliance.[32] Abdul Hamid Khan became the Prime Minister and the head of a five-member cabinet. Forty assembly members were elected directly. Sardar Ibrahim was elected President unanimously by the United Front. Sardar Ibrahim initially was in favour of a coalition government of the United Front. However, when AJKPPP got a clear majority, it decided to form the government on its own. This was taken as a breach of trust by other two allies – the AJK Liberation League and Azad Muslim Conference – Ibrahim. K.H. Khurshid, the leader of the Liberation League, felt disheartened, saying that "he had made the biggest mistake of his political career by entering into such an alliance", and that "he had not realised that the alliance would provide yet another 'cover for the perpetuation of the Punjabi bureaucrats' rule with the help of the security forces'."[33]

When Zia-ul-Haq came to power in a military coup, he said that all politicians would have to undergo the process of accountability. Qayyum felt threatened because there were lots of charges of corruption against him. He thought Zia's order was aimed at him. He, therefore, decided to become part of the anti-martial law campaign in Pakistan. This anti-Zia campaign was formed with PPP's Begum Nusrat Bhutto in the lead. However, when in March 1981, a Pakistan International Airlines (PIA) plane from Karachi en route to Peshawar was hijacked and made to land first in Kabul and then flown to Damascus by Al Zulfiqar group (formed in 1979 after Zulfiqar Ali Bhutto's execution and led by his son Murtaza Bhutto), Sardar Qayyum blamed the PPP and India for this hijacking and disbanded the MRD. That made him the army's blue-eyed boy.

Furthermore, the period of parliamentary system in 'AJK' was cut short by the military takeover in Pakistan. Gen. Zia-ul-Haq dismissed the 'AJK' government and brought back the presidential system in 'AJK'. In the next elections in 'AJK', on May 16, 1985, Zia-ul-Haq promulgated a rule that banned unregistered political parties from taking part in the elections. Thus, the PPP was kept out of the elections. That left the field open for the Muslim Conference which won the highest number of seats (16), followed by Tehrik-e-Amal party (8), the Liberation League (5), Azad Muslim Conference (Ibrahim) (2) and independents (7). The Muslim Conference secured 67.3 per cent of the total votes. Sardar Qayyum became the president and Sardar Sikander Hayat Khan was elected the prime minister. By this time, Qayyum enjoyed tremendous support from Islamabad and showed great proximity with the Pakistani Army.

When in the 1990s the anti-India insurgency was at its peak in the Kashmir Valley, there was a larger consensus both in Muzaffarabad and Islamabad to support the insurgents. Seemingly, the only big challenge for political parties in 'AJK' was how to use this anti-India sentiment for political gains.[34] This period also saw the emergence of other parties, which in later years changed the political map of 'AJK'. Anti-Qayyum parties tried hard to pursue Benazir Bhutto to topple Qayyum's government. They did not succeed because of Qayyum's relationship with both the army and the Pakistan Muslim League led by Nawaz Sharif's family. Qayyum had also developed a good rapport with the Punjab government. Qayyum thus managed to complete his tenure. When elections were held for the fourth 'AJK' Legislative Assembly on May 21, 1990, Benazir Bhutto's government was only about three months away from its removal (by then President Ghulam Ishaq Khan, who ousted her government in August 1990 on charges of corruption). Election results were as follows: the AJKPPP secured 16 seats; Sardar Ibrahim's Azad Muslim Conference got two seats, Maj Gen. (retd.) Hayat Khan's Tehrik-e-Amal Party and K.H. Khurshid's Liberation League got two seats each. Two seats were bagged by independent candidates. The pro-independence parties including the Jammu and Kashmir Liberation Front (JKLF) and Jammu and Kashmir People's National Party (PNP) were not allowed to take part in the elections because they refused to comply with the mandatory commitment from their side to Kashmir's accession to Pakistan.[35] The AJKPPP's Mumtaz Rathore became the prime minister by defeating Muslim Conference's Sardar Sikander Hayat Khan by 21 votes to 15. Qayyum, as president administered the oath of office to Rathore, after initially refusing to do so on "the specious plea that this was anti-national and anti-Islam party".[36]

The mid-term June 1991 (fifth legislative assembly) elections called by Raja Mumtaz Rathore again saw the Muslim Conference coming back to power. This time, it swept the poll by securing 31 out of 40 seats. Later, the party bagged several reserved seats as well. Rathore was sacked because he refused to accept the election results. The move was welcomed by Sardar Abdul Qayyum who resigned from office to run for the post of prime minister. Qayyum went on to compete his tenure as prime minister in July 1996. Sardar Sikandar Hayat Khan became the president during this period (August 1991-May 1996).

The sixth Legislative Assembly elections were held on June 30, 1996, three years after Benazir Bhutto returned to power in 1993, and close to her second dismissal (President Farooq Leghari dismissed Bhutto's government in November 1996 on charges of corruption). The AJKPPP had a clean sweep and secured 37 out of 48 seats, the Muslim Conference nine, the Pakistan Muslim League (Junejo) one and Jamaat-e-Islami one.[37] The AJKPPP ousted Sardar Sikander just before the elections, and after the elections selected the PPP old guard, Sardar Ibrahim, as the president who continued in office from August 1996 till August 2001.

The defeat of the Muslim Conference in the 1996 assembly elections again proved that Islamabad had a great say in installing or toppling a government in 'AJK'. With Islamabad's support, Prime Minister Barrister Sultan Mahmood Chaudhry initially did not face any problem except that Mumtaz Rathore, who had re-emerged as the leader of the AJKPPP, wanted to become the Prime Minister. Finally, his party membership was cancelled. The change in the government in Islamabad did not affect Mahmood. He was also considered harmless by the then ruling Nawaz Sharif government and carried on even after Nawaz Sharif was thrown out in a coup in October 1999. The military rule under General Musharraf allowed the government to complete its tenure in July 2001.

The next election in 2001 was quite predictably manipulated by Musharraf administration and AJKPPP lost to AJKMC led by Sardar Abdul Qayyum Khan. About 32 candidates fielded by pro-freedom parties such as All Party National Alliance (APNA) and Jammu Kashmir Liberation Front (JKLF) were disallowed to contest invoking the Art. 7(2) of the Azad Jammu and Kashmir Interim Constitution Act, 1974, which states: "No person or political party in Azad Jammu and Kashmir shall be permitted to propagate against or take part in activities prejudicial or detrimental to the ideology of the State's accession to Pakistan."

The election and formation of the government followed a high voltage drama in which the army played a leading role. Qayyum Khan was the leader of the Muslim Conference, but the army intervened and persuaded the party to choose Sardar Sikander Hayat Khan for the post of prime minister. Qayyum was taken aback, as he wanted his son, Sardar Attique Ahmad Khan, to become the prime minister. As such, Qayyum declined to stand for the post of the president,[38] and that was exactly what the army perhaps wanted. Major General Anwar Khan, who had served the army for 35 years was made to resign hurriedly from the Pakistan Army just four days before his election as president on August 1, 2001. Interestingly, he was made to retire under an ordinance issued by then President Musharraf who waived the restriction on government servants (that they could not accept any political post for a minimum of two years after their retirement). He was rushed to Muzaffarabad where Muslim Conference's Assembly members quite obligingly elected him as president. During its tenure, this Assembly also made the 11th Constitutional Amendment to provide for one more seat to raise its total strength to 49,[39] including the 41 directly elected [29 seats in 'AJK' and 12 seats for Refugees settled in various parts of Pakistan] and eight reserved or co-opted members (five seats for women and one each for Ulama/Mushaikh, Overseas Kashmiris, and Technocrat).

The internal power politics paved the way for the entry of the Pakistan Muslim League-Nawaz (PML-N) into 'AJK' politics. Attique and his father, Sardar Abdul Qayyum Khan, supported the coup by General Pervaiz Musharraf and this political opportunism affected AJKMC's traditional ties with the Sharif family and his faction of the Muslim League.[40] General Anwar Khan and Sardar Sikandar completed their tenures as president and prime minister respectively through the eventful days after 9/11 and massive earthquake in October 2005.

The elections for the eighth Assembly were held on July 11, 2006, at a time when Musharraf was firmly in saddle. He was quite favourably disposed towards changing the leadership in 'AJK' by then. Quite like the elections in 2001, the July 2006 elections barred about sixty pro-independence candidates belonging to the JKLF, APNA and other smaller groups who had filed their nominations without the required affidavit to pledge their commitment to final accession of 'AJK' to Pakistan. Contrary to expectations, despite the role played by some religious groups in providing relief works, the performance of the infamous religious conglomerate, Muttahida Majlis-e-Amal (MMA) – derisively called Mullah Military Alliance because of its linkages with the agencies – was miserable. All of its 33 candidates failed in the polls, with some losing their deposits.

However, quite predictably, the main political party backed by Islamabad, AJKMC, secured 31 out of 49 seats despite pervasive spread of anti-incumbency sentiments because of poor implementation of post-earthquake rehabilitation and reconstruction policies by the ruling AJKMC dispensation led by Sardar Sikandar Hayat. This was opportunity for Musharraf to unseat Sikandar and bring in Sardar Attique Khan as prime minister, who was in race during 2001 as well. Raja Zulqarnain of Bhimber – a lawyer-politician, from the lineage of Chib rajas of Bhimber. He was earlier associated with K.H. Khurshid's Liberation League. Zulqarnain was introduced by Musharraf administration as a loyalist of his military rule. However, Musharraf had no control over internal political dynamic within the AJKMC which came to the fore soon afterwards.

This period witnessed a whirlwind of political turmoil, in which four prime ministers were changed, shifting their loyalties from one group to another. The politics in 'AJK' took a dramatic turn when one rebel faction of the AJKMC led by Raja Farooq Haider defeated Sardar Attique Khan in a no-confidence motion on January 6, 2009 with support from the AJKPPP and the federal government, which was a democratic one led by Peoples' Party of Pakistan (PPP) which assumed office after the fall of Musharraf's military regime in early 2008. There was a strong allegation against Sardar Attique that he spent more time outside 'AJK' during the time he was in power. He was in office for 2 years 5 months and 13 days, out of which spent only 155 days in in the capital at Muzaffarabad. He spent 121 days abroad and in Islamabad, and 615 days in other places in Pakistan.[41]

On January 7, 2009, Sardar Mohmmad Yaqoob Khan was made prime minister by consensus. But once again Sardar Attique and Farooq Haider came together to throw him out on October 22, 2009. However, this development could not bridge the gap between Sardar Attique and Farooq Haider, and eventually, they came apart again. This badly hit the political development of 'AJK'. As one political analyst puts it, "In this political wrangling members of the assembly got badly discredited in the eyes of masses as they had become a selling commodity since they had ditched three prime ministers and then voted for the fourth one. How can one guarantee that they would not change their allegiance in the coming days provided they get better offer?"[42] In order to get rid of Farooq Haider, two arch-rivals, with opposing ideologies – the Muslim Conference and the AJKPPP – joined hands together, which paved the way for Sardar Attique Ahmad Khan to again become the prime minister on July 29, 2010 until July 26, 2011.

Elections in 2011: AJKMC Marginalised

The elections to the ninth Assembly were held on June 26, 2011. These elections were a big challenge for the AJKMC as it was facing the PML-N for the first time as an opponent along with the AJKPPP. For the AJKMC, that had ruled the region for much of its history, the results were very disappointing, bagging only four seats. Its leader, Sardar Attique Khan, won his seat but his son was defeated. The PML-N, which had hitherto supported the AJKMC but later abandoned the alliance, won nine seats, four of which were those representing the Kashmiri refugees in Punjab, where it was the ruling party. The AJKPPP played its cards smartly. The division of right-wing votes between the AJKMC and the PML-N helped the AJKPPP to secure 19 out of 36 seats,[43] which led to Chaudhry Majeed's election as the prime minister and Sardar Muhammad Yaqoob Khan the president. Sardar Yaqoob Khan had joined AJKPPP in December 2010 and endeared himself to the top PPP leadership and he was rewarded for this when he was offered presidency after the elections. He continued till the end of his tenure in August 2016, when retired diplomat from Poonch, Masood Khan was sent in from Islamabad to replace him as President.

Election of July 2016: Decline and Fall of AJKMC

AJKMC's hold over local politics declined further in the election of July 2016. As a party with a strong historical background and preponderant base in local politics, AJKMC found it difficult to maintain its importance, especially with the onset of democratic politics in the post-Musharraf period. Many of its leaders have, over the years, defected regularly to local branches of Pakistani political parties and found it politically profitable to operate through them. In these elections the anti-incumbency sentiments against local branch of the PPP, were tapped well by the AJKPML-N which was also led effectively by Raja Farooq Haider since he left AJKMC in 2010 and opened the 'AJK' chapter of Pakistan Muslim League-Nawaz (PML-N).

In the election AJKPML-N under Farooq Haider's leadership bagged 31 seats, followed by three each by the AJKPPP and the AJKMC, two by the Pakistan Tehreek-i-Insaf (PTI) and one by the Jammu Kashmir Peoples Party

(JKPP). The AJKPML-N won 22 out of 29 seats in 'AJK' and nine out of the 12 constituencies located in various parts of Pakistan. AJKMC secured all its three seats from 'AJK' only. All the seven seats in the Muzaffarabad division, which once used to be dominated by AJKMC went to AJKPML-N this time.[44] These elections were held under the supervision of more than 17,000 army personnel and 15,200 para-military personnel with the coordination of local civilian law enforcement agencies including the 'AJK' police, the Punjab and KP police and the Frontier Constabulary.

Changing Trend Post-2001

Positive vibes came after Gen. Musharraf ostensibly banned anti-India militant organisations under the US pressure after the 9/11 terrorist attacks on America. Sardar Qayyum, while addressing the second Intra-Jammu and Kashmir 'Heart-to-Heart' talks in Delhi said that there was need to strengthen the India-Pakistan peace process and turning the region into a "danger-free area".[45] He further said, "Terrorism should not be allowed to become an excuse for stalling the process."[46] This was the time when talks were going on between India and Pakistan. Sardar Qayyum, who was once persona non grata because of his political and pro-Pakistan ideology, was now well-received in India. There are various reasons for the change in the Muslim Conference's attitude vis-à-vis Kashmir. Firstly, epiphany within the Pakistani establishment that it was impossible to resolve Kashmir by force. The international community was no longer buying the Pakistani argument for supporting militancy in Kashmir. Secondly, his interaction with Kashmiri separatists and their appreciation for Musharraf's 'Four Point Formula' on Kashmir. Qayyum also expressed reservations about his party's policy by questioning the armed struggle in Kashmir: "There is no Jihad in Jammu and Kashmir. Terrorists are tools in the hands of vested interests. Jihad is waged to protect destitute and the downtrodden and not to kill women and children. The purpose of Jihad in Jammu and Kashmir has been defeated."[47] He further added, "Guns have no place in Jammu and Kashmir. And the blood of innocent people must not be spilled."[48] This was a huge shift not only at the party level but also on a personal level. The Muslim Conference might have realised that it was not the sole spokesperson of Kashmir. The rise of other political parties in 'AJK' has decentralised the power politics and the Muslim Conference can no longer determine the power dynamics in the region.

The death of Sardar Qayyum on July 11, 2015 at a local hospital in Rawalpindi has spelled doom for the party. His son, Sardar Attique Ahmad

Khan whom he was promoting to take his place has proved a failure. He lacks political acumen.

Sardar Attique rejected PML-N's offer to a have political alliance for the July 21, 2016 elections. However, the party entered into an alliance with PTI. The leadership of both AJKMC and PTI agreed on seat adjustment for the July 2016 elections in 'AJK'.[49] However, such political tactics did not work, the party seems to have suffered a major electoral shock.

Aims and Objectives

From its inception as a political party, the main objective of the AJKMC was its ideological focus on accession of Kashmir with Pakistan. Article 4 of the Constitution of the AJKMC deals in detail about the aims and objectives. Following are some of its objectives:

(a) Organising a freedom movement throughout the state and also to seek assistance and help from Pakistan.
(b) The State of Pakistan should be made strong and transparent so that the marooned Muslim subjects under enemy's occupation get a sigh of relief in Pakistan.
(c) The scope of party should be extended so that the Muslims all over the world can get united for further struggle so that the helpless Muslims under occupation can escape from slavery.
(d) On a strong and mental plane we should have strong religious, moral values and also raise resources so that our Islamic state stands foremost amongst the Muslim world.

Elaborating further on the socio-economic aspects, the AJKMC aspires:

(1) To separately maintain the existence of Muslims in state and protect their rights. And also to protect the rights of other communities in state. Also maintain right kind of rapport with those communities.
(2) To strongly maintain the relations with Muslims inside and outside the state and make it stable and strong.
(3) Betterment and welfare of the workers, labours, skilled workers, farmers, women, students and weak persons so that the class differences can be reduced.
(4) Protection of old Islamic schools, other religious centres and revival of education institutions.
(5) Eradication of bias among Kashmiris related to language, region, sect, position and towards non-Muslims.

(6) Improving living standard, economic conditions of the people residing in the state of Jammu and Kashmir. Encouragement to the skilled labour, measures to widen the scope of education facilities; encourage home industries, trade and commerce, economic development and betterment and to channelise all state/provincial resources for bringing happiness and prosperity to our Kashmiri brethren.
(7) Protection of religion, civilisation, language (Kashmiri, Pahari, Gojri, Sheena, Dogri, Punjabi, Ladakhi, Tibetan, Kishtewade, Khward, Broshteski and Pushtu), apart from it, the protection of Urdu, which is a common language of all the Muslims of the state have to be preserved as an asset from our ancestors. All these languages to be protected and measures will be taken for the development and propagation in the state.
(8) All possible assistance and help to deserving downtrodden, strife-torn victims and tormented for their uplift.
(9) All reforms wherein there is no opposition to Islamic values, state identity, and inter-religious solidarity should be complete with other religious and political organisations.

Leadership
President – Sardar Attique Ahmed Khan
Senior Vice President – Malik Muhammad Nawaz
Secretary General – Madam Mehrun-Nissa
Additional Secretary General – Fida Kiani
Deputy Secretary General – Tahir Tabassum – Sardar Khizar Hayat
Secretary Information – Sardar Saghir Chughati
Deputy Secretary Information – Wajid Bin Arif
Secretary Finance – Sardar Abdul Qayyum Niazi
Chairman Finance – Sardar Altaf Khan.

Current Status
After Sardar Qayyum took over, the Muslim Conference became a dynastic party. But Sardar Qayyum did not train his son Sardar Attique in politics and running the party affairs. When Sardar Qayyum handed over the party affairs to his son, he was immature. After Sardar Attique took over the reins of the party, its performance has been disappointing. It appears that party has no future.

JAMMU AND KASHMIR LIBERATION FRONT (JKLF)

The Plebiscite Front[50] (Britain) was renamed as Jammu and Kashmir Liberation Front (JKLF) by its Working Committee in Birmingham on May 29, 1977. According to Amanullah Khan, this change was made at his suggestion, but he could not become its member for nine months because of some restrictions.[51] The JKLF started launching its activities from 'AJK' in 1982 under the overall leadership of Amanullah Khan. With active support from the Inter-Services Intelligence (ISI) and the Pakistan Government, the JKLF trained thousands of Kashmiri youths from the Indian state of Jammu and Kashmir. In an interview to the *Daily Jang* in 1992, Amanullah admitted that the JKLF kicked off insurgency in Srinagar in 1988 at the behest of Pakistan intelligence agencies, but they replaced JKLF by jihadi groups soon afterwards. Amanullah does not mention this in his autobiography, *Jehad-e-Musalsal*, although it was published in February 1992.

The JKLF carried out major terrorist incidents in the Kashmir Valley between 1990 and 1992.[52] In the late 1990s, the party experienced an internal split when Yasin Malik renounced violence and decided to follow the constitutional path in his struggle for independence of Jammu and Kashmir. The JKLF flourished as an organisation with initial support from the Pakistani security forces. But despite such cooperation between Pakistani security agencies and the JKLF, each side harboured deep-rooted suspicions against each other. The JKLF's demand for an independent state of Jammu and Kashmir (J&K) clashed with Pakistan's goal of merging the entire state of J&K with it. Gradually the Pakistani Government reduced dependence on JKLF in 'AJK' for spreading militancy in J&K and began encouraging militant groups like Hizb-ul-Mujahideen and Lashkar-e-Taiba for conducting anti-India operations in J&K. The JKLF itself underwent several changes and faced enormous challenges to survive as a political entity but nevertheless it retained its limited but committed support base within entire 'AJK'. Pakistan has also not completely withdrawn its support and considers JKLF as a useful tool to highlight the Kashmir cause at international forums. It should be remembered here that Amanullah Khan, who was born in Gilgit kept emphasising independence of entire 'AJK' including Gilgit and Baltistan. The party's "aims and objectives clearly state that "[p]ending the final settlement", the JKLF would "aim to merge Gilgit/Baltistan territories with Azad-Kashmir" and "to establish therein a democratic representative government with full powers to serve as a base-camp in accordance with the objectives of the Provisional Azad (Free) Government established on 4th October 1947".[53]

Leadership and Organisational Structure

As stated earlier, the initial leadership for the JKLF in 'AJK' was provided by Amanullah Khan. Under his guidance, the party expanded its presence in different parts of PoK. In the late 1980s and 1990s, there occurred ideological splits within the JKLF. The main bone of contention within the JKLF was its insistence to promote the independence of Kashmir as the primary cause of the party. This line of thought did not go down well with the ISI who had materially and financially supported JKLF in 'AJK'. The ISI engineered a split breaking the JKLF in 'AJK' into Amanullah and Farooq Haider factions. But, in due course of time, the former faction prevailed, and thus Amanullah continued to lead the party as its Patron-in-Chief in AJK. The JKLF split again when Rauf Kashmiri formed another faction, but Amanullah-led faction remained the most talked-about and most-followed outfit that Kashmir watchers consider the original JKLF.

Currently, Advocate Sardar Saghir is the Chairman of the JKLF in 'AJK'.[54] He is followed by Dr Toqeer Gilani and Zia-ul-Haq Zia who acts as the Vice President of the party in 'AJK'. The Gilgit-Baltistan zone is being headed by Zia-ul-Haq Zia. The JKLF has a well laid out organisational structure. It consists of the 'Policy and Planning Committee', which is the supreme advisory body.[55] The Central Executive Committee remains the primary body responsible for making important decisions in the organisation.[56] Below the Central Committee is the Executive Committee consisting of 15 members. The Working Committee, consisting of different representatives from all districts of 'AJK', is the body responsible for policy implementation at the local level.[57]

The leadership of the JKLF in 'AJK' consists of Patron in Chief, President, Senior Vice President, General Secretary, Chief Organiser, several Vice Presidents, Deputy Chief Organiser, Secretary of Information, Finance and several Zonal Working Committees.[58] Despite having specific committees for different tasks, the primary decision-making power rested with Amanullah Khan in 'AJK', till his death in April 2016.[59] The JKLF also has a student's wing called the Jammu and Kashmir Students' Liberation Front (JKSLF).

Ideology, Aims and Objectives of JKLF

Like its counterpart in Kashmir, the JKLF in 'AJK' propounds a separatist ideology. The primary aims and objectives of the organisation are as follows:[60]

(a) The JKLF in 'AJK' seeks the complete reunification of the entire state and complete independence from India and Pakistan.

(b) The 'AJK' wing of the JKLF calls vehemently for the merger of Gilgit-

Baltistan areas into Azad Kashmir and creation of a 'democratic representative government' which would then serve as the base camp for future political activities.[61]

(c) In the present circumstances, the party's aim vis-à-vis the Pakistani Government is "to struggle for getting political and constitutional rights for the people of entire state especially for Gilgit Baltistan".

(d) The JKLF also calls for setting up a democratic, federal and secular government in the reunified Kashmir which will maintain cordial relations with both India and Pakistan.[62]

(e) It advocates a secular agenda and wants the inclusion of Ladakhis, Buddhists, and Kashmiri Pandits in any future independent state of J&K.

Therefore, adherence to such a secular agenda has often brought JKLF 'AJK' into conflict with Pakistan. For example, the party bitterly opposed Gen. Musharraf's four-point formula for the resolution of the Kashmir dispute and the conversion of the Line of Control (LoC) into a de facto permanent border.[63]

Activities in 'AJK'

The JKLF advocates a three-front struggle to achieve its objectives, i.e. political, diplomatic and armed struggle. At the political front, the party and its cadres resort to demonstrations, dissemination of information through pamphlets and magazines, holding of seminars/conferences and public awareness campaigns on political issues. The party's top leadership often resorts to tactics like courting arrests to highlight their political grievances. The party also opposed the Gilgit-Baltistan Empowerment and Self-governance Order 2009, introduced by the Zardari-led government.[64] When it was rumoured in 2009 that the Pakistan Government was formulating a plan to grant a province-like status to Gilgit-Baltistan, the JKLF vociferously opposed such a move, and the party even staged a long march to Islamabad with 18,000-20,000 supporters.[65] At the political level, the party has tried to contest the local elections in 'AJK' time and again, but has been denied permission as JKLF candidates refused to sign any undertaking pledging support to Kashmir's accession to Pakistan. On the diplomatic front, the party has representatives across different countries to place its demands at the international level.

The JKLF has utilised the services of its Kashmiri diaspora in countries like the UK, US and United Arab Emirates (UAE) to highlight the Kashmir cause. For example, Lord Ahmed, a prominent Kashmiri raised the issue of annexation of Gilgit-Baltistan and rejection of JKLF candidates' nomination papers in the 'AJK' assembly elections in the British Parliament.[66] Similarly, the diplomatic wing of the party also raised the issue of illegality of Gilgit-Baltistan's possible merger with Pakistan at the UK Foreign and Commonwealth Office in London.[67]

Apart from these activities, the JKLF also believes in armed struggle to achieve its objectives. The party initially received financial and military support from Pakistani security forces. With this support, the JKLF unleashed widespread violence and terrorist activities in the Kashmir Valley. For nearly two decades, Kashmiri youths were trained and indoctrinated in camps run by the JKLF in 'AJK'. But by the middle of the 1990s,[68] the JKLF shunned violence, as other groups with a pro-Pakistan agenda secured greater state support from Pakistan. However, it needs to be noted that the JKLF never resorted to violent activities against Pakistani security forces in 'AJK' and elsewhere. Despite ideological differences, the JKLF never confronted the Pakistani security forces. Instead, the JKLF now opposes the use of radical forces like the Taliban, Jamaat-ud-Dawa and Hizb-ul-Mujahideen. The JKLF and its leaders contest that use of such elements have spoiled the secular image of the Kashmiri movement.[69]

Presence in 'AJK'

The JKLF has a presence in all the districts and tehsils in both parts of PoK.[70] From open source data one can decipher that the cadre strength of the JKLF in 'AJK' could be somewhere near 20,000-22,000.[71] The party's portrayal of a secular agenda and the setting up of a federally structured government in the event of independence enables it to network with other local parties in both parts of PoK. Together with these parties, JKLF has tried to present a collective front vis-à-vis Pakistan on the issue of independence of Kashmir. The party also networked with other political parties in 'AJK' on the issue of Diamer Bhasha Dam controversy and argued in favour of the rights of Gilgit-Baltistan to its resources.

Funding Sources

The party received funding primarily from two sources in the past. Firstly, it derived major part of its financial help from the ISI and the Pakistani Government in the initial years and later from the Kashmiri diaspora abroad.[72] Due to ideological differences with Pakistan over the Kashmir issue, it can be assumed that this source of funding has gradually reduced if not dried up entirely.[73] A large number of Kashmiri expatriates have contributed financial help over time bit more so during the last decade. The party draws large share of financial contributions from the Mirpur community from 'AJK', settled abroad.[74] The party has a significant presence in the UK, UAE, and US. Hence, it can be safely assumed that the Kashmiri expatriates settled in these countries are making active monetary contributions to the JKLF. One report has emphatically suggested that the UK has been one of the major sources of funding for the JKLF. It is also suspected that sometime ago Didar Singh, who was associated with the World Sikh Organisation, helped the JKLF in raising funds.[75]

Networks and Alliances with Other Organisations

The JKLF AJK has formed alliances and contacts with different political parties, Non-Governmental Organisations (NGOs) and think-tanks within Pakistan and abroad. A report from the Canadian Information Service states that the JKLF has contacts with organisations like the Kashmir American Council, World Kashmiri Freedom Federation,[76] World Kashmir Freedom Movement, Jammu Kashmir Council For Human Rights, Kashmir Welfare Association (Kashmir Relief Fund), Council for Human Rights in Kashmir, Kashmir Study Group (KSG), Kashmir Canadian Council, Pakistan-based Kashmir Action Committee, Karachi-based Jammu Kashmir Welfare Association, UK-based Tehreek-e-Kashmir, Kashmir Council for Human Rights and Kashmir Watch.[77]

The party is also connected with local political parties in 'AJK'. At the height of militancy in J&K in the late 1980s, the JKLF had become an alliance partner of the Kashmir Liberation Alliance (KLA).[78] Surprisingly, JKLF (Amanullah faction) has not joined the All Party National Alliance (APNA), which is a conglomeration of 'AJK'-based political parties.[79] However, JKLF (Yasin Malik faction) is a member of the APNA. The JKLF is also loosely connected with local parties in Gilgit-Baltistan on an ad hoc basis on certain common and pressing issues concerning 'AJK'. For example, it maintains connections with the Gilgit-Baltistan Democratic Alliance which comprises the Balawaristan National Front, Karakorum National Movement, Gilgit-Baltistan National Movement, Gilgit-Baltistan Thinkers Forum, Baloristan Labour Party, Gilgit-Baltistan United Movement, Bolor Research Forum and Gilgit-Baltistan National Conference.[80] After the death of Amanullah Khan, the main branch of JKLF operating from PoK has not been seen to be as active as the Yasin Malik faction in Jammu and Kashmir.

JAMMU AND KASHMIR LIBERATION LEAGUE (JKLL)

Introduction

The Jammu and Kashmir Liberation League (JKLL) was formed in 1962 by

K.H. Khurshid after he left the All Jammu & and Kashmir Muslim Conference (hereafter AJKMC or Muslim Conference) in 1960 following a split in the party. Khurshid became the first elected President of the 'AJK', having defeated Sardar Abdul Qayyum Khan in the presidential election in October 1961.

Khurshid was born in Srinagar in 1924. After completing his graduation, he launched the Kashmir Students' Federation to increase political awareness among Kashmiri youth. Later, he became the personal secretary of Mohammad Ali Jinnah, who found him intelligent and articulate. He became a close confidant of Jinnah who is quoted to have said that "creation of Pakistan was made by him, his typewriter and his private secretary".[81] Khurshid had a good support base among the masses, particularly the Kashmiri refugees. With their support, the Liberation League emerged as the second-largest party in 'AJK' in 1970. It won five of the 25 seats in the Legislative Assembly elections in 1970. These five seats included one from 'AJK' and four from 12 seats allotted to the Kashmiri Refugees spread throughout Pakistan.[82] These elections were held under a new Constitution introduced by the then military ruler, General Yahya Khan, in September 1970. This Constitution provided for a president and a 25-member council to be elected on the basis of adult franchise. The JKLL President, Khurshid, was one of the four contestants along with Sardar Abdul Qayyum Khan of the AJKMC, Sardar Ibrahim of the Azad Muslim Conference, an offshoot of AJKMC, and another candidate from Plebiscite Front. Sardar Qayyum, whose party also bagged the majority of the 25 council seats, won the contest and became the president of 'AJK'.[83]

The elections in 'AJK', under the interim constitution of 1974, were held on May 18, 1975. A four-party alliance, comprising the AJKPPP, JKLL, AJKMC (Ibrahim) and Azad Muslim Conference, was formed with the aim of defeating the Muslim Conference. The alliance won 34 seats, with the JKLL winning five seats. The AJKPPP, which won an absolute majority by winning 22 seats and formed the government alone by ignoring the alliance partners. The alliance thus ended. Upset over the AJKPPP's decision to keep its electoral allies out of the government, the JKLL President admitted that by joining the alliance, he had committed the biggest mistake, and that he had not realised this alliance would provide another "cover for the perpetuation of Punjabi bureaucrats' rule with the help of the security forces".[84] The AJKPPP government had to go on July 5, 1977 when General Zia ul Haq overthrew the Bhutto government in Islamabad and sent him to jail. Martial Law was not imposed in 'AJK' but it was practically put under the military rule. The AJKPPP government was overthrown and a serving Brigadier was appointed as the President of 'AJK'. The move was criticised by the 'AJK' political parties.

The JKLL Chief, K.H. Khurshid said since there was no Martial Law in 'Azad Kashmir', there was no justification for creating a constitutional vacuum there.[85]

Khurshid was again in the limelight when under his leadership a seven-party front was formed to oppose the Muslim Conference during the May 16, 1985 elections. But Khurshid's party could get only five seats. The party could not recover from this setback. It could win only one seat in the May 1990 elections. Its worst showing was in the elections held in 1996, 2006 and 2011, when it failed to even open its account. The JKLL did not participate in the 2001 elections. It allied with the Jammu and Kashmir Pakistan Muslim League (JKPML) for the 2006 polls. Launching the alliance manifesto in Islamabad on June 29, 2006, Convenor of the JKPML and former 'AJK' prime minister, Sultan Mahmood Chaudhry termed Kashmir Liberation Movement as the topmost priority of the alliance and said that "all possible steps would be taken in consultation with All-Party Hurriyat Conference (APHC), militant organisations and other institutions which could help lead the movement to its logical conclusion".[86]

Ideology/Objectives

The JKLL stands for the freedom of the people of Jammu and Kashmir state and Kashmiris' right to self-determination to choose their own future. Although the party is committed to not compromise on this principle, it is generally not vocal against Pakistan like the Jammu and Kashmir Liberation Front (JKLF). At the time of its formation on August 11, 1962, the party announced the following as its main objectives:[87]

(a) To prepare the people of the State for the decisive moment and the final struggle for freedom and self-determination.
(b) To strive for the recognition of the Azad Government of the State of Jammu and Kashmir as the lawful government of the entire State.
(c) To strengthen and stabilise the representative system of government in Azad Kashmir with a view to protecting and defending the democratic, civic and traditional Islamic value as well as promoting close ties with Pakistan.
(d) For this purpose, to re-unify the state and organise public opinion under the banner of the party.

According to Kashmir Information Centre, the main ideology of the JKLL is:

> The government of Azad Kashmir should be accepted as an independent government and representative of the whole state. In addition to this, their motto is that the people of Kashmir should be given their basic right to

decide their future accordingly to their own choice in free and fair atmosphere. It is the choice of the people what they want, whether they want to accede with Pakistan or India or remain independent.[88]

The main and most controversial plank of the party's programme demanded Pakistan's recognition of the 'AJK' Government as the legitimate authority representing the entire state of Jammu and Kashmir.[89] The JKLL is of the view that "till the time of plebiscite or final settlement of the future of the State, the 'AJK' Government may enter into a Stand-still Agreement with the Government of Pakistan and settle that the Government of Pakistan may control the responsibilities of Defence, Foreign Affairs, Communication, Currency and Coinage of Jammu Kashmir State".[90] In order to retain coordination between Pakistan and state of Kashmir, the party proposed to constitute an Advisory Council consisting of Prime Minister of Pakistan, the President and Prime Minister of 'AJK', whose functions may be to determine policy, vis-à-vis Kashmir issue and matters of national importance.

The JKLL said that the 1974 Interim Constitution did not promote the objective of the freedom movement for which millions of people sacrificed their lives. The JKLL President Justice(retd.) Abdul Majid Malik said that 1974 Interim Constitution Act 1974 was an insult to the word constitution which "is always framed by constituent assembly and the AJK has never had a constituent assembly".

It is in this context that the JKLL proposes that "the Constitution should be federal and democratic conferring fundamental rights and civil liberties on the citizens and prescribing responsibility of the citizens towards the State and towards accomplishment of freedom of all the people living in three parts of the world".[91]

The JKLL proposed that the Parliament should consist of two Houses – People's House and Upper House – which would be constituted by representatives, elected directly on the principle of proportionate representation and size of area and population. In the proposed People's House, 60 seats will be allotted to AJK, 30 to Gilgit-Baltistan, 10 to refugees by co-option, while 100 seats will be kept vacant for Jammu & Kashmir. Similarly, in the Upper House, 15 seats have been earmarked for 'AJK', 15 for Gilgit-Baltistan, 15 for refugees, while 15 seats will be kept vacant for Jammu & Kashmir.[92]

It is notable here that the JKLL treated Gilgit-Baltistan as a part of 'AJK' or for that matter of whole state of Jammu and Kashmir. Commenting on the resolution adopted by the Gilgit-Baltistan Assembly in 2014 asking Pakistan to give provincial status to Gilgit-Baltistan, Misfar Hassan, Convenor of the

JKLL, UK, said that any change in its status would neither be in accordance with the principled and historical stand of Pakistan on Kashmir in the United Nations (UN) nor be acceptable to the people of Jammu and Kashmir.[93]

Organisational Structure and Leadership

The organisational structure of the JKLL includes a Central Executive Committee (CEC) consisting of Central President, Senior Vice President, Additional Vice President, Central General Secretary, Finance Secretary, Foreign Secretary, Information Secretary, four Senior Executive Members and Convenors for Europe, America and Gulf Zones. The CEC is the main decision-making body of the party. The headquarters, known as Central Wing of the Party is located at House No. 38, Sector B/2 Murree, 'AJK'. The central office bearers of the JKLL are as follows:[94]

Central President – Justice (retd.) Abdul Majid Malik
Sr. Vice President – Chaudhary Muhammad Suleman
Vice President – Chaudhry Shaukat Ali
Addl. Vice President – Mir Abdul Latif
Central General Secretary – Sardar Imtiaz Akbar
Finance Secretary – Sardar Imtiaz Iqbal
Foreign Secretary – Chaudhary Latif Sani Advocate
Secretary Information – Khawaja Muhammad Khalil Advocate
Senior Executive Member & President Preliminary Board – Khawaja Manzoor Qadir
Senior Executive Member & District President – Muhammad Kaleed Ul Fateh
Senior Executive Member & District President Mirpur – Shahid Majeed Mallick
Executive Member & District President Muzaffarabad – Gulshan Ahmed Butt
Executive Member – Raja Khurshid Ahmed
Executive Member & Additional Information Secretary – Muhammad Tariq Mughal
Chairman Organisation Board – Raja Muhammad Khurshid
Chairman Information Board & Executive Member – Abdul Aziz Kate
Chairman Agricultural Board – Shaikh Noor Muhammad
Convenor for US – Qazi Javed Iqbal
Convenor for UK/Europe Zone – Dr. Misfar Hassan
Convenor for Gulf Zone – Khawaja Muhammad Ramzan Butt

Cadre Strength and Funding

The exact strength of the party cadre is not known although it is active throughout 'AJK'. The membership is open to anyone, by filling a membership form. The party is, however, on the look-out for enrolling new members especially those who are in a position to raise funds for the party at the international level.[95] Most of the funding comes from donors and expatriates based in the Gulf countries, the US and Europe. In this connection, the party President regularly visits these countries.

Network and Area of Influence

The JKLL has set up political, international, educational, development, and student wings to spread its network.[96] It has opened its offices in all the districts of 'AJK' and other provinces where the Kashmiri refugees are settled. In addition to that the party has opened offices in the US, Europe and Gulf countries.

Links and Alliances with other Political Parties and Militant Groups

JKLL's President, K.H. Khurshid, during the initial years, joined hands with AJKPPP to topple Sardar Abdul Qayyum's government, in an attempt to become President of 'AJK' again. The JKLL was also part of a four-party alliance in the May 1975 elections to defeat the Muslim Conference which had complete control in 'AJK'. The JKLL also headed the seven-party front with Tehrik-i-Amal Party, Islami Jamhoori Party, Democratic Front, Jamaat-i-Islami, Inqilabi Mahaz and Azad Jamhoori Mahaz to oppose the Muslim Conference in the May 1985 elections.

On April 29, 1991 the JKLL and the AJKPPP announced that they had formed a four-party electoral alliance called the Jammu and Kashmir Democratic Alliance. Other two parties who joined the alliance were the Muslim League and People's National Party (PNP).[97]

The JKLL also joined a rally organised by 11 pro-Kashmiri parties in Lahore on October 26, 2003. The protestors raised anti-India slogans and alleged that atrocities are being committed against the Kashmiris. According to media reports, law enforcement agencies clamped down on the rally and did not allow them to read out the joint declaration.[98]

In protest against the decision taken by the military regime to bar political groups in 'AJK' not professing allegiance to Islamabad from contesting the July 2001 Assembly polls, the JKLL and other groups joined a *"chakka jam"* movement in July 2001. The call was given by the JKLF Chairman, Amanullah Khan.[99] The JKLL had also participated in a series of demonstrations over several days in October 1992, including an attempt to cross the ceasefire line. In its efforts to block similar attempts by the JKLF and other groups, Pakistan and 'AJK' authorities used force which resulted in killing of 10 people.[100]

The JKLL also joined another anti-India rally at Muzaffarabad on January 26, 2005 under the aegis of the Kashmir Liberation Cell. The rally ended at the office of the UN Military Observers near Domel, where a memorandum addressed to then UN Secretary General was delivered. The memorandum called upon the UN chief to exert pressure on India to stop unabated killings and other inhuman atrocities in Kashmir. It also urged him "to use his good offices in granting right to self-determination to Kashmiris which had been pledged to them more than five decades ago by the world body through several Security Council resolutions".[101]

Its international wing has also been organising similar rallies abroad. On February 8, 2015, the US chapter of the JKLL joined other 'AJK' parties and Kashmiri groups to observe the Kashmir Solidarity Day in North Virginia. This day is observed all over Pakistan and 'AJK' on February 5 every year. The function was chaired by Dr. Ghulam Nabi Fai, President of Kashmir American Council.[102] It also sent an appeal to the UN Secretary General on January 5, 2013 urging to resolve the Kashmir dispute according to the UN resolutions and allow the Kashmiris 'their birth right of self-determination'.[103] It may be mentioned that founder President of the JKLL had attended the Non-Aligned Summit in Harare in September 1986 where he met heads of the various delegations and also distributed 'An appeal to Members of Non-aligned Movement' on behalf of 16 million people of Jammu and Kashmir, who it alleged "continue to suffer".[104] Although the founder of the JKLL hailed from Srinagar, it has no presence in Kashmir.

Current Status

The JKLL which emerged as the second-largest party by winning five seats in the first elections held in 'AJK' in 1970, lost its support base with the death of its founder K.H. Khurshid in 1988. It failed to win even a single seat in the last three elections held in 2006, 2011 and 2016. Interestingly, it was seen making adjustments with AJKPML-N on some seats in the last elections but finally it could not win any seat.

Its present President is Chief Justice (retd.) Abdul Majid Malik who as the Chief Justice of the 'AJK' High Court had delivered the famous judgement in 1993 directing the Pakistan Government to hand over control of the Northern Areas to the 'AJK' Government. Justice Abdul Majid Malik has not able to build a strong base for his party. The party has formed a number of committees to spread its ideology. But it has not been able to consolidate its own party cadre, nor build any strong relationships with other political groups. Its students' wing is also largely ineffective, primarily due to lack of financial resources.

To keep alive the Kashmir issue, Justice Malik had said in May 1999 that Kashmiris would never allow the division of Kashmir and they expected pressure from Pakistan and the international community on India for the removal of Indian forces from Kashmir. Speaking at a press conference in Rawalpindi, he said that Pakistan should not indicate deviation from its principled stand on Kashmir. In December 2005, he urged India to accept then President Musharraf's proposal of demilitarisation and self-rule in Kashmir, which, he said would help to resolve the Kashmir dispute.[105]

Justice Abdul Majid Malik visited India in December 2014 where he categorically stated that people in his territory were peace-loving and never supported any sort of terrorism or violence in Jammu and Kashmir. He stressed the need to immediately bring an end to the status quo on the relations between the divided parts of Jammu and Kashmir by allowing free movement of people from both sides of the LoC for strengthening trust and mutual confidence. When his attention was drawn towards the continued support of Pakistan to the terrorists and the Mumbai massacre in 2008, Justice Abdul Majid Malik said, "I condemn such incidents. But why the people of undivided Jammu and Kashmir are made to suffer because of such inhuman acts. We cannot be pushed to the walls because of blasts in Mumbai or Karachi. Why cannot we be allowed to decide our fate, make good use of our available resources and strive for progress."[106]

In spite of all this, Justice Abdul Majid Malik himself has not proved equal to K.H. Khurshid, the founder of the party. Thus the party obviously needs an effective leadership.

JAMMU AND KASHMIR PEOPLE'S MUSLIM LEAGUE (JKPML)

Introduction

The Jammu and Kashmir People's Muslim League (JKPML) was formed on April 20, 2006 by former Prime Minister and the then Leader of the Opposition in the 'AJK' Legislative Assembly, Barrister Sultan Mahmood Chaudhry, following serious differences with the Pakistan People's Party (PPP) high command for ignoring his contribution and appointing Sahibzada Ishaq Zaffar as the president of AJKPPP. Launching the JKPML, Sultan Chaudhry said that he had the support of 12 members of the 'AJK' Legislative Assembly and one member of the 'AJK' Council. He further added that the new party would end the two-party system in 'AJK' which had given nothing to the people of the state. He promised to give 30 per cent representation to women in the 'AJK' Legislative Assembly, 'AJK' Council and local bodies. Terming overseas Kashmiris as the backbone of the country's economy, he said a Ministry of Overseas Kashmiris would be created after his party comes to power. He also assured that his party would woo investment and promote industrialisation in the state to end unemployment. On the Kashmir question, he said that India should withdraw "her occupation troops" from major cities of Kashmir, if it was serious about finding out a peaceful solution to the Kashmir dispute. Besides, India should "repeal all draconian laws including POTA [Prevention of Terrorism Act] and TADA [Terrorist and Disruptive Activities (Prevention) Act] to help create a conducive atmosphere for settlement of the long standing Kashmir tangle".[107]

Ideology/Manifesto/Alliance with other Political Parties

In view of the 2006 elections in 'AJK', the Jammu and Kashmir People's League, Jammu Kashmir Muslim League, led by Major General (retd.) Muhammad Hayat Khan, and Jammu and Kashmir Liberation League, headed by Chief Justice (retd.) Abdul Majid Malik, formed an alliance – the Jammu and Kashmir Pakistan Muslim League (JKPML). On June 29, 2006, Alliance convenor Sultan Chaudhry launched the election manifesto promising various relief measures for the affected people of the quake hit areas in 'AJK'. Salient features of the manifesto were as follows:[108]

(a) The residents of affected areas would be exempted from the payment of six-month utility bills. In addition, government loans payable against the people in quake-hit areas would be written off.

(b) Necessary legislation would be made to ensure the quality of reconstruction of hospitals, educational institutions and government buildings in line with the building codes developed in accordance with the seismic survey reports. Legal action would be taken against the people involved during the reconstruction process.

(c) The suspended local bodies system in the state would be reactivated, the number of seats in 'AJK' Legislative Assembly and 'AJK' Legislative Council including those reserved for women would be increased.

(d) A new Master Plan for the development of 'AJK' would be developed and administrative reforms would be introduced to improve

performance of different government departments. Rules of Business would also be amended to improve government's performance.
(e) Kashmir Liberation Movement will be considered as the top most priority of the alliance. In this connection all possible steps would be taken in consultation with the APHC, militant organisations and other institutions which could help lead the movement to its logical conclusion.
(f) Establishment of Ministry of Overseas Kashmiris which would fully benefit from the capabilities of the Kashmiri expatriates. Steps would also be taken to provide an opportunity to the Kashmiri expatriates to cast votes in the countries they are residing.
(g) All bottlenecks in the way of setting up a TV station in 'AJK' would be removed. Steps would also be taken to benefit the Kashmiri people living on the divide to benefit from the FM radio stations in 'AJK'.
(h) Construction of new airports in Mirpur and Kotli while the existing airports in Muzaffarabad and Rawalakot.
(i) Impediments in the way of setting up the dry port announced by President Musharraf would be removed.

Current Status

Inspite of the alliance, in the 2006 elections, the JKPML could win only four seats, three in the 'AJK' and one in Pakistan (refugee). The ruling Muslim Conference clinched 22 seats including seven refugee seats.[109] The AJKPPP won seven seats in 'AJK' and drew a blank in the refugee seats in Pakistan while its ally Jammu Kashmir Peoples Party grabbed one seat in Poonch.[110]

The party has no future as the founder of JKPML, Barrister Sultan Mahmood Chaudhry, joined the local branch of Pakistan Tehreek-e-Insaf on 6 February 2015 ahead of the 2016 elections. He lost his seat for the first time after 25 years in politics on 21 July 2016.

UNITED KASHMIR PEOPLE'S NATIONAL PARTY (UKPNP)

Introduction

The United Kashmir People's National Party (UKPNP) is a nationalist party. It was founded as People's National Party on April 10, 1985 and renamed the UKPNP in 1994. The name, according to the party, was changed to better support the idea of creating a state independent of India and Pakistan which would be called 'United States of Kashmir'. It was founded by Shaukat Ali Kashmiri, who is the chairman of the party. Its former Vice Chairman was

Sharif Kakad, who was arrested by local authorities in Gilgit Baltistan in 2014. The party has condemned his arrest and has appealed to all human rights organisations for his release. The UKPNP's main objective is to change the already existing narratives of the Kashmir conflict coined by Pakistan and India.[111] The party aims to struggle for an Independent Kashmir, free from India, China and Pakistan control where Kashmiri people can live in peace.

In the initial years of its formation, the UKPNP found it hard to propagate its stand because its cadres and leadership had been bearing the brunt of state repression. However, over the years, the party has succeeded to a great extent in strengthening its roots among the revolutionary sections of the Kashmiri society. The UKPNP has succeeded in garnering the attention of the general public because of its stand on socio-economic plight of the people of the region. The other important factor that helped in nurturing and shaping the political ideology of the party was the unabated exploitation of human and natural resources of the 'AJK' and Gilgit-Baltistan by Islamabad.[112] The alienation and resentment because of "political and economic marginalisation of Pakistan-controlled areas gave birth of new ideology seeking equal rights, political ownership and economic empowerment of Pakistan-controlled Kashmir." In broader Kashmir conflict UKPNP's aim has been to provide a parallel inclusive narrative that "represent all regions, its people, culture, faiths, languages and ethnicity-not only valley centric-and be equal stakeholders in shaping up its future".[113] The party is keen to establish an independent democratic society on the basis of just intra-community relations. It envisages that besides the Kashmiri nation, seven other communities (the Dogras, Ladakhis, Baltis, Gilgitis, Poonchis, Brushaski and Kishtwaris) settled in the United States of Kashmir shall have equal share in the new political set up (independent or sovereign Kashmir).

Party Structure, Leadership and Activities

Party structure consists of National Council, Centre Committee, Central Cabinet, regional organisations, and overseas zones. Its Chairman is Shaukat Ali Kashmiri. He is living in exile in Switzerland since 1999; Senior Chairperson is Naila Khaneen, Sayed Tahir Shah Gardezi, Secretary General Sardar Altaf, Deputy Secretary General, Professor Rafiqul Bhatti, Chief organizer and Nasir Aziz Khan, Central Spokesman of the party. The UKPNP in its party manifesto maintains that it is a progressive, secular and democratic organisation. The UKPNP accuses Islamabad of using the Kashmir conflict to avoid people-centric approach and also maintaining status quo by encouraging a territorial centric approach to resolve the conflict.[114] The Central committee of the party at its meeting on 30th September 2016 at Rawalpindi asked Pakistan and India to deescalate ongoing tension between the two countries on the LoC and demanded Kashmir issue be resolved through dialogue and peaceful means as per wishes and aspirations of Kashmiri people. UKPNP has expressed its deep concern over the recent announcement made by the 'AJK' government that it has decided to hand over large area of disputed Kashmir to China. It warned that party will not tolerate and allow any country to colonize "our territory and national resources."

However, the UKPNP like other nationalist parties is barred from taking part in elections in the 'AJK' because the "Interim Constitution Act 74" as well as Gilgit Baltistan Empowerment and Self Governance Order of 2009 require every political party and candidates to sign an affidavit pledging their commitment to Jammu and Kashmir's accession to Pakistan. Therefore, all nationalist parties and leaders are not allowed to contest elections. Not letting the UKPNP to take part in the political process of the region has not stopped it from mobilising the public opinion. It regularly holds conferences, issues press releases and hold demonstrations against Pakistan. It claims it has succeeded to a great extent in raising awareness about the plight of the people of PoK at various international forums.[115] On April 23, 2009, Shaukat Ali Kashmiri addressed a press conference in Geneva where he strongly urged the world community to ask the Pakistan government to guarantee the freedom of speech, assembly and freedom of thought and that all political parties should be allowed to take part in the elections and the democratic process. He also demanded that the Pakistan government should be asked to take stern action against those who are involved in the killings of political leaders and civil society activists in the region. He urged the Pakistani rulers to establish a fact-finding mission to administer social-economic, cultural, constitutional, educational, and developmental situations in 'AJK' and Gilgit-Baltistan.[116] He asked Pakistan to dismantle the terrorist infrastructure in 'AJK'. According to Shaukat Ali Kashmiri, these terrorist organisations are thriving because of the blessings of Pakistani state and its intelligence agencies. He also requested the world community to force Pakistan to stop the construction of Bhasha Dam and also halt the plundering of the natural resources of the region.[117] In an interview with the *Indian Express* on July 11, 2016, Central Spokesman of the party Nasir Aziz Khan advised Kashmiris not to pick up guns rather to join hands with secular and democratic forces of the state. He further said that "the Kashmiris should keep in mind that Pakistan has no love with Kashmiris and she is exploiting religious sentiments of the Kashmiris and is plundering their natural resources".

UKPNP has spread its network both in Europe and North America. It has an overseas committee to look after the interests of the party headed by Sardar Zahid Khan in Canada, Aftab Hasan Khan in UK, Akhlaq Baslar in USA, Mohammad Zee Mustafa in Switzerland, Sajid Abbasi in Belgium and Iftiqar Ahmad in Italy. Amjad Yousaf is the president of its network in Europe. Its branch in Canada was earlier headed by Mumtaz Khan who is living in exile since 1998. The other branch is in Switzerland where it regularly attends the biannual session of the United Nations Human Rights Council in Geneva. A resolution adopted by the party held under the chairmanship of Shaukat Kashmiri demanded that, "elements that propagate violence as a solution to the Kashmir problem be banned wherever they exist".[118] While talking to media, the UKPNP Secretary of Foreign Affairs, Khalid Perwaize stated that UKPNP is "fighting for a completely independent Kashmir". Khalid Perwaize who lives in Scotland further said that the "New State will be secular rather than a Muslim State."[119]

In March 2016, a number of exiled leaders from 'AJK' and Gilgit-Baltistan organised a protest on the sidelines of the 31st session of the UN Human Rights Council where they condemned Pakistan for its oppressive policies and human rights violations in 'AJK' and Gilgit-Baltistan.

On the eve of 2016 elections, UKPNP organised a multiparty conference titled 'Azad Jammu Kashmir elections under 'AJK' Interim Constitution and Violation of Right of Self Determination and Freedom of Expression' in Islamabad. All nationalist parties present there passed a resolution demanding immediate removal of section 4[7(2)] of 'AJK' Interim Constitution Act 1974 and allow all nationalist political parties and individuals to contest incoming elections; abolition of Kashmir Affairs ministry and Kashmir Council; call back all officers appointed by Pakistan, establish market at the local level for trade, through local traders only, between both parts of Kashmir in India and Pakistan, "consider reservations and get representation of people of Kashmir and Gilgit Baltistan on Pak-China CPEC before its implementation" and free Awami Watan Party (AWP) leader Baba Jan, Iftikhar Hussain and other political leaders from prison and withdraw all fake cases against them. Representatives from nationalist and other likeminded mainstream parties like JKLL, JK National Awami Party, JKLF, JK National Party, Balawaristan National Front, Gilgit Baltistan Action Committee, JK Peoples Party, PPP Jammu Kashmir, All Parties National Alliance, Balawaristan National Movement and other human rights organisations participated in the conference. According to media reports the leaders of the nationalist parties also denounced what they called undue

Jammu and Kashmir National Awami Party (JKNAP)

Introduction

The Jammu and Kashmir National Awami Party (JKNAP) was founded in 1996. It was carved out from the Jammu and Kashmir National Students Federation (JKNSF) formed earlier in September 1966. JKNAP is a left-wing party advocating a secular and united Kashmir. The JKNAP believes in peaceful methods to achieve political objectives. It rejects violence in any form in the political struggle. Since its inception, party has strengthened its base in 'AJK'. Rawalakot, Kotli, Bagh and Muzaffarabad are its strongholds. It has its headquarters in Muzaffarabad. Its student wing JKNSF is a largest progressive student organisation in 'AJK'. The JKNSF was the leading force in resisting Zulfiqar Ali Bhutto's attempt to turn 'AJK' into the fifth province of Pakistan. Since then JKNSF has aligned too much towards left-wing politics and despite its earlier advocacy of complete merger with Pakistan it has always come under attack from the Pakistani intelligence agencies.[121]

JKNAP and its student wing JKNSF have not only been under attack from the intelligence agencies but also from Jihadis in 'AJK'. In 2009 JKNAP protested against establishing militant camps in Muzaffarabad. After the Swat military operation in 2009, Pakistani establishment relocated Jihadis to some locations in 'AJK'. The JKNAP leadership felt threatened that these jihadists would be used against the nationalists in 'AJK'. The purpose of settling Afghan Jihadis in 'AJK' according to JKNAP had two reasons:

(a) To pressurise India to accept Pakistani version of Kashmir solution
(b) These Jihadis would be used to suppress local progressive left groups who have got more influence in the region.[122]

Another reason why JKNAP is intimidated by the Pakistani intelligence agencies is that it exposed local pro-Pakistan Kashmiri leadership, its collaboration with Pakistan and implementing anti-people policies in 'AJK'.

The JKNAP had also reservations on the Interim Constitution, 1974. According to JKNAP, the Interim Constitution Act was a colonial design of Pakistan to prolong its occupation and it was meant to deny the people of the region their fundamental rights and their legitimate rights over their resources. The main objective of the Act according to JKNAP is to "control the indigenous thoughts and struggle which represent the real interests of the people for their demand of national independence from Pakistan."[123] The Act does not empower 'AJK' Judiciary and the legislature. For JKNAP, the Act does not propose amendments which can empower and protect the fundamental rights of the state subject holders of the occupied territory.

The JKNAP has established close ties with Jammu and Kashmir National Independence Alliance (JKNIA) shortly after its establishment in 1996. The alliance is headed by Mahmood Kashmiri, who participated in the Kashmir Solidarity day in London on February 5, 2019, but he was asked by Pakistani organisers to leave the place because he and his party were considered a security risk. JKNIA is an amalgam of seven nationalist political parties which are working for the peaceful resolution of the Kashmir issue through a negotiated settlement for complete 'independence' and unification of Kashmir. The following are the member parties of JKNIA:[124]

(1) Jammu and Kashmir National Liberation Conference (JKNLC-EU)
(2) Jammu Kashmir National Awami Party (JKNAP)
(3) Jammu Kashmir Freedom Movement (KFM)
(4) Association of British Kashmiris (ABK)
(5) Kashmir Liberation Organisation (KLO)
(6) Jammu Kashmir Plebiscite Front (JKPF)
(7) Jammu Kashmir Liberation Front (JKLF).

The JKNAP is also affiliated with the All-Party National Alliance (APNA) of 'AJK' and Gilgit-Baltistan. These parties organized many protest rallies against the atrocities and brutalities committed against the people of the region. In consequence, hundreds of party workers have been arrested by security agencies. This was also highlighted in a report prepared by the Canada immigration and Refugee Board of Canada, on February 16, 2004.

Most of its leadership is living in exile in Europe. Those who stay back are often harassed and tortured by Pakistan security agencies. Its prominent leaders are Sadiq Subhani, Liaquat Hayat Khan; Prof. Mark Khalique, and Mehmood Baig. The party has also opened its branches in UK and Canada. The UK branch is headed by Sajad Raza, and Azad Raza, who is its chief organiser.

ALL-PARTIES NATIONAL ALLIANCE (APNA)

Introduction

The All-Parties National Alliance (APNA) is a conglomerate of 14 nationalist political parties and groups operating in 'AJK' and Gilgit-Baltistan. These include Jammu Kashmir National Awami Party (JKNAP), United Kashmir

Peoples National Party (UKPNP), Jammu and Kashmir Liberation Front (JKLF), Balawaristan National Front (BNF), Karakoram National Movement (KNM), Gilgit-Baltistan United Movement (GBUM). The group advocates closer ties between the peoples of these two regions.

APNA was formed in January 2001. Its main objective is to liberate Kashmir from both Pakistan and India. It wants independence and unification of the erstwhile princely state. Besides politicians, its cadre includes academicians and people from the civil society. The alliance criticises Pakistan's Kashmir policy and blames it for deliberately prolonging and complicating the Kashmir issue by proposing new formulas, such as the Chenab formula.[125] According to APNA's leader, Mirza Wajahat Hasan, "Chenab formula is not the solution of the Kashmir issue. We reject all such formulas that are against our motherland's integrity and sovereignty. Only Kashmiri nation reserves the right to decide about their motherland without complying with international pressure."[126] APNA also rejects Pakistan's claim that the tribal invasion of Kashmir in 1947 was orchestrated to liberate Kashmiri Muslims. APNA's leader, Late Arif Shahid said:

> Our brave tribal brothers attacked. It was said that we sent tribals to help Muslims of Kashmir. My brothers, my elders and my friends, in the Kashmir valley, in Muzaffarabad there are 90 to 95 per cent Muslims. Please tell me, what wrong five per cent of non-Muslims could have done to 95 per cent Muslims? What harm they could have caused? What atrocities they could have inflicted? In Jammu, 80 per cent of non-Muslims reside, in Ladakh 80 per cent of non-Muslims reside, no tribal was sent there. It is completely wrong that they helped Kashmiris, that they helped Muslims. They have not done anything like that. Then, they were trying to serve their own interests to get Srinagar then, and even now they are doing the same.[127]

Network and Influence

APNA wanted to contest elections but was barred because it did not commit itself to accession to Pakistan. During elections, its candidates, after filing their nomination papers, were not allowed by the Election Commission to contest. But one good thing that came out of their efforts was that they brought international attention to Pakistani highhandedness towards the people of 'AJK' and also popular resistance against Pakistan.[128]

APNA joined hands with the Gilgit-Baltistan Democratic Alliance (GBDA) – the nationalist alliance of Gilgit-Baltistan. According to Shaukat Kashmiri both APNA-GBDA have been holding press conferences, seminars, rallies and address foreign observers, to inform people about their fundamental rights.

These parties often hold protests against illegal arrests of their members. Together, they also periodically protest against the elections held in 'AJK'.

Apart from independence and unification of the State of Jammu and Kashmir, as it existed in 1947, these parties also call for the lifting of restrictions on trade and people-to-people contact across the Line of Control (LoC).[129] The other demands are, asking both India and Pakistan to withdraw troops from the 'occupied' land of J&K, stop cross border shelling and killing innocent people. In one of its one day conferences organised on January 11, 2010 at National Press Club, Islamabad, APNA resolved that India and Pakistan should withdraw their armies from all the three units including Gilgit-Baltistan. The nationalist leaders also condemned the "criminal negligence" of the Government of Pakistan towards Attabad, Hunza, land slide victims. The land slide led to the formation of the giant Attabad lake that submerged land and other belonging of poor people. They demanded all out support for the victims. The conference also resolved that Gilgit-Baltistan, shall be given an 'AJK' like government, instead of a provincial setup.[130] APNA observes April 29 – the day on which Karachi Agreement was signed – as black day.

Arif Shahid, prominent leader of APNA, was allegedly killed because of his nationalistic ideas. He wrote many books on Kashmir's independence, and his growing influence in the region got him in trouble with the Pakistani authorities. His name was put into the exit control list. Few months before his assassination, he was arrested and tortured in Mirpur along with two political leaders from Jammu and Kashmir who had gone to 'AJK' on a valid visa.[131] M.A. Khalique, APNA's spokesman accused the Pakistani intelligence agencies and told the media that Shahid was "the victim of targeted killing by some state actors".[132]

APNA has condemned the killing of Sardar Arif Shahid, its former chairman, allegedly by the Pakistani intelligence agency on May 13, 2013. Following this, there were large-scale demonstrations in 'AJK' where the protesters demanded that the Pakistani authorities should constitute a judicial enquiry into the murder of Arif Shahid, arrest and punish all those involved in the conspiracy and murder. They also demanded that authorities should stop harassing and intimidating the people. People of both the regions should be allowed to enjoy their fundamental human rights.[133]

The current chairman of APNA, Mirza Wajahat Hasan, along with his brother, Mirza Nadir Hasan, was expelled from Gilgit-Baltistan for two months after their arrest on October 31, 2009. They were charged for celebrating the day on November 1 on which they claim to have liberated Gilgit-Baltistan from the Dogra rule on November 1, 1947.

Both APNA and Jammu and Kashmir Liberation Front (JKLF) fielded their candidates in the 2001 and 2006 elections in 'AJK'. In 2001, they fielded 32 candidates; however, they were barred from contesting elections because they refused to support Kashmir's accession to Pakistan. According to Part 7(2) of the 'Azad Jammu and Kashmir' Interim Constitution Act 1974: "No person or political party in Azad Jammu and Kashmir shall be permitted to propagate against or take part in activities prejudicial or detrimental to the ideology of the State's."[134] In the 2006 elections, the Election Commission of 'AJK' again rejected the nomination papers of JKLF and APNA candidates for similar reasons. When the party leaders questioned the decision, the candidates were detained, harassed and tortured by the security agencies.[135]

According to Shabir Choudhry, Arif Shahid was the man of integrity and intellect. It was because of that he could easily recognize and make distinction between real and fake nationalists. He used to call fake nationalists as a 'B team' of Pakistan. Arif took it upon himself to expose those fake nationalists so that they cannot fool people further. In his book, *Dagh Dagh Ujala*, he asserts that all Kashmiri nationalists of Azad Kashmir and Pakistan (minus JKLF Amanullah Khan, which feels comfortable making alliances with pro Pakistan parties) were part of All Parties National Alliance and Yasin Malik was represented by late Dr Farooq Haider.[136]

But Arif was always suspicious about the conspiracy hatched against the APNA. His suspicions proved right. Few days after Islamabad public meeting Dr Farooq Haider invited Arif Shahid to his residence and told him that he had instructions from the JKLF Chairman Yasin Malik to leave the APNA, and they cannot work together'.[137] Although Arif tried his best to persuade Haider about the importance of this alliance, APNA, and asserted that it was imperative to make APNA effective to advance the cause of united and independent Jammu and Kashmir. Haider agreed with Arif Shahid, but expressed his helplessness as he could not defy the instructions of Yasin Malik.

Realising his predicament, Arif Shahid requested Dr Farooq Haider not to issue a public statement about leaving the alliance, as it would harm the cause of an independent Jammu and Kashmir. Dr Farooq Haider kindly agreed to that. Arif Shahid highly appreciated the services of Dr Farooq Haider. However, he did not have praiseworthy words for Yasin Malik and Amanullah Khan. This is meticulously expounded by Arif Shahid himself in his book:

> A few years after JKLF Yasin Malik's departure from the APNA, Yasin Malik visited Rawalpindi, and Dr Farooq Haider invited all Kashmiri nationalists at his residence. During the meeting Yasin Malik suggested that nationalists

of Azad Kashmir and Gilgit Baltistan should make an alliance. It was astonishing to hear this from Yasin Malik, as it was he who stabbed APNA in the back by ordering Dr Farooq Haider to leave the alliance.

In his reply to Yasin Malik, Arif Shahid said that:

> There was no need of a new alliance as APNA is already there, and it has representation from all the regions. Yasin Malik expressed his ignorance about APNA, to which he (Arif Shahid) said, if you had no knowledge of APNA then why you instructed Dr Farooq Haider to leave APNA. Yasin Malik had no reply to this and was embarrassed. Arif Shahid said you come to Pakistan, visit Pakistani cities from Rawalpindi to Karachi, but you have no time to visit Gilgit-Baltistan. The discussion continued till 1am. Yasin Malik was assigned a target to destroy APNA, and formulate a compliant alliance. He failed in that. This was a second attack from Yasin Malik, and by grace of Allah both attacks failed. Our crime was that we were fighting against Islamabad's Kashmir policy. We were not fighting a war against them. Yasin Malik is fighting for Pakistani interests in Srinagar; we are voicing against Pakistani injustice and oppression in Azad Kashmir and in Gilgit-Baltistan. This is why Pakistan and their agents are against us, but they all failed. We have shown the world the ugly face of Pakistan.[138]

AJK PAKISTAN PEOPLE'S PARTY (AJKPPP)

Introduction

AJKPPP is a local branch of PPP, one of the important mainstream political parties in Pakistan, which was launched on November 30, 1967 at a convention, held in Lahore. Zulfiqar Ali Bhutto was its first elected Chairman. The main aim for which the party was formed included, inter alia, the establishment of an "egalitarian democracy" and the "application of socialistic ideas to realise economic and social justice". A more immediate task was to fight against General Ayub Khan's dictatorship. Ayub was at the height of his power and Z.A. Bhutto, his one time confidante, had fallen out with him, when the PPP was formed.[139]

As per its official website, the party's four guiding principles are: "Islam (is our Faith); Democracy (is our politics); Socialism (is our Economy); and all power to the people."[140] The party also promised elimination of feudalism in accordance with established principles of socialism to protect and advance the interests of the underprivileged and especially the peasantry of Pakistan. Under the leadership of Zulfiqar Ali Bhutto, the party had been very active and won majority of seats in the December 1970 elections in West Pakistan on the socialist mandate of *Roti, Kapda aur Makaan* ('bread, clothes and shelter').[141] Following the loss of East Pakistan (which became Bangladesh) in 1971, Bhutto was sworn in as President and Chief Martial Law Administrator of truncated Pakistan. As promised in PPP's socialist mandate, Bhutto's government introduced significant social and economic reforms, which considerably improved the life of Pakistan's impoverished masses and also gave the country the 1973 Constitution.[142] The measures included nationalisation of large-scale industries, insurance companies and commercial banks. Besides, Bhutto also set up a number of public corporations to expand the role of the government in areas related to commerce, construction and transportation.[143] In the 1977 elections, the PPP once again came to power by winning 155 seats out of 200, as against 36 seats secured by the Pakistan National Alliance, a coalition of nine political parties. The opposition accused the PPP of large-scale rigging and violence erupted on the streets resulting in the imposition of martial law in the country by General Zia-ul-Haq on July 5, 1977.

Bhutto, who was charged with murder was sentenced to death by hanging on April 4, 1979. His daughter, Benazir Bhutto, was elected Prime Minister twice in 1988 and 1993, but her government was dismissed both times on corruption charges. Following the assassination of Benazir Bhutto on December 27, 2007, her husband and party's co-Chairman, Asif Ali Zardari, was elected the President of Pakistan in September 2008. He held the position till 2013 when the party lost elections to Nawaz Sharif's Muslim League.

The PPP opened its 'AJK' chapter, AJKPPP in 1970 and came to power after the May 1975 elections by forming a 'United Front' alliance, comprising the AJKPPP, AJK Liberation League and Azad Muslim Conference.[144] But the AJKPPP government could last only for two years as Pakistan was once again put under Martial Law on July 5, 1977. Pakistan's Army Chief General, Zia ul Haq, staged a military coup, sacked and jailed Bhutto, dissolved the National Assembly, suspended the operation of the constitution and outlawed political activities.[145] 'AJK' was not put under Martial Law, but General Zia dismissed the AJKPPP government and installed a serving army officer, Brigadier Hayat Khan as President and Chief Executive of 'AJK'.[146] In protest against the undeclared military rule in 'AJK', a campaign was launched by four parties' alliance comprising the AJKPPP, AJK Muslim Conference, Azad Muslim Conference and Plebiscite Front. The intensity of the protests was so high that the military government decided to hold elections in May 1985. However, the AJKPPP could not participate as it was not registered as a political party, as was required by the Political Parties Ordinance issued in September 1979.[147]

Although both the AJKPPP and AJK Muslim Conference won 16 seats each in the May 1990 elections, the AJKPPP nominee, Raja Mumtaz Hussain Rathore, was elected as Prime Minister by defeating AJK Muslim Conference candidate Sikandar Hayat Khan by 29 votes to 15.[148] This was not at all well-received by Sardar Qayyum, who after the dismissal of the Benazir government in August 1990, started a campaign for the removal of the Rathore government. This led to the June 29, 1991 elections in which the AJK Muslim Conference won 31 seats as against three by the AJKPPP. The results were a rude shock to Rathore who charged Islamabad with rigging and demanded the elections should be annulled.[149]

The AJKPPP received a boost by winning the 1996 elections, in which it trounced the AJKMC by winning 37 seats. The AJKMC came second by winning nine seats, the 'AJK' branches of Pakistan Muslim League-Junejo (PML-Junejo) and the Jamaat-e-Islami one each. Barrister Sultan Mahmood Chaudhry was elected Prime Minister, and Sardar Ibrahim Khan was elected President. The Assembly approved 44 bills and passed many resolutions about the Kashmir issue and matters concerning the public.

The seventh Assembly elections were held on July 5, 2001 where the AJKMC secured 31 seats and the AJKPPP 17. Sardar Hayat Khan was elected as Prime Minister and Major General (retd) Muhammad Anwar Khan as President. The ruling AJKMC retained power in the eighth Assembly elections held in July 2006. It elected Sardar Attique Ahmad Khan as Prime Minister and Raja Zulqarnain Khan as President. But the period from January 2009 to the next Assembly elections in 2011, was full of intrigue and conspiracies. During the short period of two years, 'AJK' saw three Prime Ministers – Sardar Muhammad Khan, Raja Muhammad Farooq Haider Khan and Sardar Attique Khan. The AJKPPP swept the ninth Assembly elections in June 2011, and elected Chaudhry Abdul Majeed as Prime Minister and Sardar Muhammad Yakub Khan as President. Commenting on the results and the victory of AJKPPP, Ershad Mahmud, an Islamabad-based commentator on 'AJK', says:

> The people of AJK had had enough of the rule of the Muslim Conference which could not deliver anything during its ten years stint in power. Its members were frequently switching their loyalties from one camp to another only to advance their own vested interests. Just in five years in AJK saw four prime ministers which had practically paralysed the entire administration in Muzaffarabad and eventually made the Muslim Conference a non-entity.[150]

Ideology/Objectives

The AJKPPP's ideology and objectives remain the same as that of the PPP.

According to its manifesto, the party aimed at introducing "real democracy" for which the first condition was the abolition of privileges and the transfer of power to the people. It believed that political privileges were inseparably related to economic privileges and inequalities. In calling for a socialistic solution to the country's problems, the PPP manifesto proclaimed that the only correct way to deal with them was to change (a) the exploitative capitalist structure, and (b) Pakistan's situation as an underdeveloped country within the neo-colonialist power sphere. The ultimate objective of the party's policy was the attainment of classless society which it thought was possible only through socialism.[151] By 1972 Bhutto had consolidated his power, but thereafter, as eminent Pakistani economist Dr. Akmal Hussain says, Bhutto began to shift the balance of class forces within the PPP in favour of the landlord group. Elaborating his point, Dr. Akmal Hussain says:

> After the election, Bhutto realised that if the socialist rhetoric of the left wing of the PPP was to be implemented, it could not be done through the existing State apparatus. It would involve institutionalising party links with the working class and the peasantry by building grass-roots organisations. This would soon generate a working-class leadership which would not only threaten his own position within the party but would also unleash a momentum of class conflict that would place the PPP on a collision course with the military and the bureaucracy. Given Bhutto's commitment to seek democratic reforms within the framework of the State as constituted at that time, he was unwilling to take a path that would lead to a confrontation with the State apparatus. Consequently, the socialist rhetoric of the PPP had to be toned down, its radical petit bourgeoisie elements quietened or purged from the party, the rudimentary organisational links with the working class and poor peasants broken and the landlord elements of the PPP firmly established as the dominant element within the party.[152]

This resulted the PPP workers who believed in its left-wing ideological stance leaving the party.. At the Lahore Convention held on November 30, 1967, the participants took a strong line on Kashmir issue and on relations with India. The Convention demanded that the resolution of the Kashmir issue, on the basis of the relevant United Nations (UN) resolutions, recognising the right of self-determination, should be given the top priority for normalisation of relations with India.[153] However, in its 2013 Manifesto, the party listed the normalisation of trade relations with India among some of the important achievements of its government over the last five years in integrating regional trade and commerce. But the manifesto supported the rights of the Kashmiri people and a dialogue process with India on all key issues, including Kashmir.

Adding further, "Without prejudice to UN Security Council resolutions, we support open and safe borders at the Line of Control to socially unite the Kashmiri people. We note that India and China have a border dispute and yet enjoy tension-free relations." While commenting on the June 2011 'AJK' Assembly elections, AJKPPP chief, Chaudhry Abdul Majeed said:[154]

(i) Coming elections will be of exceptional importance in view of the existing global scenario which was seeking early peaceful settlement of the Kashmir problem;

(ii) Sanctity of the territory of 'AJK' being the base camp of the Kashmir freedom struggle will be maintained in all circumstances;

(iii) India was denying Kashmiris their birth right to self-determination by staging so-called elections drama in Jammu & Kashmir.

Similarly, the Secretary General of the AJKPPP, Chaudhry Latif Akbar, said in Muzaffarabad on May 23, 2011 that the foundation of the PPP was laid to resolve the Kashmir issue, and supporting the independence movement was the part and parcel of its manifesto.[155]

Organisation, Structure and Leadership

The PPP has a well-formed organisational structure in Pakistan, 'AJK' and Gilgit-Baltistan. The highest body of the party is the Central Executive Committee (CEC), which is the decision-making body. The CEC consists of a Chairman, a Co-Chairman and Presidents and Vice-Chairmen. It coordinates activities between the Federal Council and Provisional Presidium and Secretary Generals. Below are the Federal Council and Provincial Presidents and General Secretaries. The 48-member Federal Council is headed by the Co-Chairman of the Party. There is also a women's wing called the PPP Central President Women's Organisation, and a youth wing – the PPP Youth Organisation and People's Student Federation. Both these wings are headed by Faryal Talpur, a member of the National Assembly. The Party has also set up chapters in Europe, the US, Canada and many other countries which are supervised by the Overseas Central Committee.[156]

The Party is led by Asif Ali Zardari and his son, Bilawal Zardari Bhutto who is the Co-Chairman of the Party. Its Secretary General is Sardar Muhammad Latif Khan Khosa, Central Information Secretary is Qamar Zaman Kaira and Amjad Ikhlaq is the Secretary Finance. The office bearers of its 'AJK' chapter are as follows:

Chaudhry Latif Akbar – President
Chaudhry Pervez Ashraf – Senior Vice-President

Raja Faisal Mumtaz Rathore – General Secretary
Javed Ayub – Information Secretary
Ms Shaheen Qausar Dar – Deputy Information Secretary
Zia Qamar – Youth President

Chaudhry Latif Akbar has replaced Chaudhry Abdul Majeed, the ex-prime minister of 'AJK' in the outgoing PPP-led coalition government in the region. Chaudhry Majeed was removed from the office of the AJKPPP president by the party's top leadership after its humiliating defeat in the 2016 election.

Cadre Strength and Funding

Since its entry into 'AJK' in 1970, the AJKPPP has been a major political player. While the exact cadre strength of the party is not available, the party has its members in almost all the districts of 'AJK'. Anyone who follows the party's ideology can become a member of the PPP. The party raises funds from members and donors. The funds are also collected by the party offices from Pakistanis living abroad. The party has never faced shortage of funds after its doors were open to industrialists and members of the landed elite who became members after the AJKPPP downplayed the word socialism from its manifesto for the 1970 elections.[157]

Network and Area of Influence

Since its formation, the PPP has established an effective network by capturing power in 1977, 1988, 1993 and 2008. In the 2008 elections, the PPP was the leading party of the ruling coalition at the centre with two other parties, the Awami National Party (ANP) and the Muttahida Quami Movement (MQM). It was also the first Pakistani civilian government which completed its full term in office.

The AJKPPP had swept the elections to the 'AJK' Legislative Assembly held in June 2011. It secured 21 seats, the PML-N winning nine and the Muslim Conference just four. Two seats were bagged by independent candidates.[158] The credit for this victory goes to the AJKPPP leadership who had formed a comprehensive strategy by creating "a factional rift within the Muslim Conference which caused a vertical split in the party".[159] According to Ershad Mahmud, the Federal Minister for Kashmir Affairs, Manzoor Ahmad Wattoo played his cards well to win over the former 'AJK' premiers Barrister Sultan Mahmood Chaudhry and Sardar Yaqoob Khan which gave a boost to the party. Later, the Muslim Conference tally rose to five and MQM opened its account by securing two refugee seats. The AJKPPP invited both the factions of the

Muslim Conference to join the government under the philosophy of "political reconciliation" espoused by the PPP.[160] The move was criticised by the PML-N which said that the alliances had been formed "to deny it victory in the [2013] general election".[161]

During election campaign in 'AJK', Bilawal Bhutto raked up the Kashmir issue and assured the people that he would take back the entire Kashmir from India but at the same time the party suffered a big setback as three of its ministers joined the PTI.

Current Status

In the 2013 election in Pakistan, the PML-N came to power but the AJKPPP government elected in 2011 was allowed to complete its term. But there were efforts by local branch of the PML-N to consolidate its position with leaders who had defected from AJKMC, while preparing for the next elections. Its efforts paid off in the July 2016 elections by raising up anti-incumbency sentiments in the region. The AJKPPP was routed, it got only three seats. This may not, however, be the end of AJKPPP, because the electoral politics of the region is heavily influenced by politics in Pakistan, and PPP remains a major political party with the potential to return to power in Islamabad in future. In his efforts to spread party network, PPP co-chairman, Bilawal Bhutto has appointed office bearers in all the districts of 'AJK'.

When most of analysts were predicting bleak future of the party and were terming it as a regional party confined to a one province only, the 2018 general elections in Pakistan dismissed all those notions. It got 43 National Assembly seats and 74 in Sindh Assembly. Most noticeable were the seats it secured in Punjab where it was thought that PPP has lost its support base.

AJK PAKISTAN PEOPLE'S PARTY SHAHEED BHUTTO (AJKPPPSB)

Introduction

Pakistan People's Party Shaheed Bhutto (PPPSB) is a breakaway faction of the PPP. After returning from exile, Murtaza Bhutto wanted to revive the PPP according to its founding principles. However, he faced opposition within the party particularly from his sister Benazir Bhutto. The subsequent events forced Murtaza to hand over leadership to Benazir. In September 1996, Murtaza was killed in an encounter with police. Benazir was then the prime minister of Pakistan. After her government was dismissed on the charges of corruption in

November 1996, Zardari was detained briefly for his role in Murtaza's assassination. Thereafter, in 1997, Ghinwa Bhutto, wife of Murtaza Bhutto, formed PPPSB claiming it to be the real successor of Zulfiqar Ali Bhutto's PPP.[162] However, the party has not fared well politically even in Sindh province, home to the Bhuttos. Its only politically heavyweight is Ghinwa Bhutto. After the dismal performance of the PPP in 2013 elections, PPPSB wanted to take advantage by reorganising the party before the arrival of its new leader, Zulfiqar Ali Bhutto Junior – the son of Murtaza Bhutto. It was decided that Junior Bhutto would take charge of the party, while his sister, Fatima Bhutto, would be the candidate for prime ministership in the general elections of 2018 and she would contest elections from her ancestral constituency, Larkana, from where her grandfather Zulfiqar Ali Bhutto, her aunt Benazir Bhutto and her grandmother Nusrat Bhutto were elected in the past.[163] PPPSB chalked out the strategy to open its offices throughout the country. However, in the elections on July 25, 2018, Fatima did not contest from Larkana and Bilawal Bhutto, son of Benazir won it with a comfortable margin of 34,000 votes, of course, certainly lower than what his mother and grandfather could poll earlier. Fatima's PPPSB candidate lost his deposit with just 1,652 votes.

The party has opened a chapter in 'AJK' where its president is Munir Hussain Chaudhry. The AJKPPPSB decided to field its candidates in all the constituencies of 'AJK' Legislative Assembly elections in July, 2016 elections. Munir Hussain Chaudhry underlined the meritorious services of the Bhutto family for the Kashmir cause – especially Kashmiris' right to self-determination. He said that time has come to contribute due share by the PPPSB to give an impetus to Kashmiris' indigenous struggle for freedom of the motherland from Indian control. The party, however, could not open its account in 2016 elections.[164]

AJK PAKISTAN MUSLIM LEAGUE-NAWAZ (AJKPML-N)

Introduction

The Pakistan Muslim League-Nawaz (PML-N) is the most dominant of all the successor factions of the Muslim League that had led the movement for a separate state for the Muslims of the subcontinent which culminated in the formation of Pakistan. Right since the establishment of the AJK Muslim Conference (AJKMC) as a political outfit in 'AJK', Muslim League was allied with it and partly shaped its pro-Pakistan political agenda. In fact, immediately after its formation, AJKMC passed a resolution to work towards merging entire Jammu and Kashmir with Pakistan. Ideologically, AJKMC embraced the Muslim League's two-nation theory.

Factionalism Within the Muslim League

At the time of partition, the All-India Muslim League claimed to be the sole representative of the Muslims of undivided India. It was founded at Dhaka (now in Bangladesh) on December 30, 1906 to safeguard the rights of the Muslims in British India. A number of factors played an important role in Muslim League's emergence: impact of the 1857 Mutiny on Muslims, relations with the British, and the introduction of the representative political system by the British. Initially, the Muslim League adopted a policy of loyalty towards the British, but soon after partition of Bengal in 1905, two main groups emerged: one called "conservatives" led by Sir Mohammad Shafi and the other "progressives" led by Jinnah, which criticised the conservatives' unconditional loyalty to the British.[165]

After Pakistan came into being on August 14, 1947, the All-India Muslim League came to be known as only Muslim League. It witnessed many ups and downs as a national political party. In its first party convention held in February 1948, Chaudhry Khaleequzzaman was elected chief organiser and assigned the job of reorganising the party.[166] In the process of making the party stronger, Khaleequzzaman made government officials subservient to the office bearers of the party.[167] That resulted in dual leadership with both sides wanting to get the upper hand. This was the beginning of the factionalism within the Muslim League. Moreover, factors such as the language controversy, provincialism and indecision on the part of the then Pakistani Prime Minister, Khawaja Nazimuddin, to solve the controversial issues not only complicated the affairs at hand but also sowed the seeds of dissent within the Muslim League in the provinces.[168] Most of the top leaders left the party after death of Jinnah on September 11, 1948. They either formed a new party or joined anti-Punjab Muslim League fronts. For example, H.S. Suhrawardy formed a new party known as the All Pakistan Awami Muslim League in February 1950, and Nawab of Mamdot formed the Jinnah Muslim League in 1949. Both these factions merged in 1950 and formed Jinnah Awami Muslim League which dropped 'Muslim' from its name and became Jinnah Awami League in 1953. After winning the provincial elections in East Pakistan, it shed 'Jinnah' from its name and emerged as a Bengali nationalist party named Awami League by 1956. In 1949, the left wing leaders in Muslim League walked away from the party and formed Azad Pakistan Party. It merged with some other left-leaning political groups to form National Awami Party in 1957. There were provincial Muslims Leagues too.

General Ayub Khan, after assuming power in 1958 in a coup, thought of uniting some factions of Muslim League, and in 1962, he formed Pakistan

Muslim League (PML) which later became PML-Convention. Some of the old Leaguers opposed to Ayub formed PML-Council in 1965 and fielded Jinnah's sister Ms Fatima Jinnah as their presidential candidate against Ayub Khan. By November 1967, Zulfiqar Ali Bhutto, who was a member of PML-Convention, left the party – both because he developed his differences with Ayub Khan and also because latter's political prospects were in decline – and formed Pakistan People's Party (PPP). Following PPP's spectacular win in the 1970 elections in West Pakistan (81 seats), complete routing of PML-Convention (7 seats) and PML-Council (2 seats), and loss of East Pakistan in 1971, these two prominent League factions came together to form PML-Functional (PML-F) under the initiative of Pir Pagaro in 1973. When PML-F welcomed Zia-ul-Haq's coup in 1977, this faction witnessed further divisions. Zia-ul-Haq lifted martial law in 1985 and under his patronage PML-F allied itself with other minor factions of the League to become 'united' PML in 1985. There was a leadership issue within PML after it won the 1990 elections. It elected Nawaz as prime minister. Those in the party who opposed Nawaz walked away from the party in 1993. The faction of the party under Nawaz's leadership was renamed as PML-Nawaz. During Musharraf's rule (1999-2008), several league factions were merged to form PML-Quaid which functioned as a secular political party loyal to the military dictator.

The League under Military Junta

Under military rulers in Pakistan, political parties are either banned or made use to get their rule legitimised. After Ayub Khan assumed power in 1958, he took drastic steps to keep political parties under control. He issued Election Bodies Disqualification Ordinance (EBDO) under which politicians were disqualified; introduced the Political Parties Act (PPA) to revive political parties but did not allow the politicians, banned under EBDO, to contest elections held under his Basic Democracy. After facing pressure from the National Democratic Front, Ayub formed his own political party known as the Convention Muslim League to contest the presidential elections, which he subsequently won. All those Muslim Leaguers who did not join Ayub's Convention Muslim League formed their own organisation, called the Council Muslim League.

In the 1970 elections, both Convention and Council Muslim Leagues were routed by the Awami League in East Pakistan. Soon after the elections, the Council Muslim League disintegrated when Khan Abdul Qayyum Khan broke away and formed his own party known as PML (Qayyum). With Zulfiqar Ali Bhutto's Pakistan People's Party (PPP) emerging on the political horizon of

Pakistan, Ayub's Convention Muslim League went to abyss. Following Ayub Khan, Gen. Zia-ul-Haq and Gen. Pervez Musharraf, too, got pro-military politicians together under the nomenclature "Muslim League".

General Zia-ul-Haq encouraged different factions of the Muslim League to dissolve themselves under Mohammad Khan Junejo. Junejo was made Prime Minister and Nawaz Sharif became the President of the party.[169] Differences soon emerged between Zia and Junejo which finally culminated in the dismissal of the Junejo government. Nawaz wittingly didn't condemn Zia, and for that gesture he was awarded the caretaker Chief Ministership of Punjab.[170]

After Zia's death, many groups emerged from the Muslim League: Pir Pagaro named his group as PML-Functional, Malik Mohmmad Qasim as PML-Qasim, PML-Liaquat and PML-Jinnah. Hamid Nasser Chatha, who was Secretary of the PML-Junejo, formed his own group known as PML-Chatha.

As part of the Islami-Jamhoori-Ittehad (IJI), the Muslim League did well in Punjab. Nawaz Sharif became the Chief Minister of the largest province. He remained part of the IJI till 1993 when his government at the centre was dismissed by then President Ghulam Ishaq. After Junejo was dismissed by Zia, Nawaz Sharif quit the PML and established his own party, the PML-N.[171] After developing differences with Nawaz Sharif, Zia's son Ijazul Haq broke away from Sharif and formed the PML-Zia. When Musharraf came to power, a pro-establishment leader from Lahore, Mian Azhar founded the PML (Quaid-i-Azam), or PML (Q), with Syeda Abida Hussain, Khurshid Mahmood Kasuri and Chaudhry Shujaat Hussain as its founding members. The party as supporter of President-cum Army Chief Gen. Pervaiz Musharraf became the ruling party after the 2000 general elections. In five years of its rule it changed five prime ministers. PML-Q saw another faction known as the Like Minded, although its members have yet to form political party. The unified PML seems to be impossible for years to come.

PML-Quaid suffered a big set-back in 2008 elections and PML-N reappeared on the political horizon again as a party of consequence, even if it conceded space to PPP, the party with largest number of seats, to form government in Pakistan. It showed political maturity by not indulging in conspiracies to topple the PPP government which lasted its entire term and became the first government to do so in Pakistan in recent years. The PML-N won handsomely in 2013 elections and has been in power in Pakistan ever since. Its branch in 'AJK' swept the local elections defeating the incumbent AJKPPP in July 2016.

Aims and Objectives of PML-N[172]
   (1) Protect territorial integrity and uphold the ideology of Pakistan.
   (2) Uphold and protect the constitution.
   (3) Enable the Muslims of Pakistan to live in accordance with the teachings and requirements of Islam as set out in the Quran and the Sunnah.
   (4) Establish friendly relations with other nations and to strengthen fraternal relations and solidarity with other Muslim States.
   (5) Ensure tolerance and social justice as enunciated by Islam are fully observed and enforced in Pakistan.

PML-N in 'AJK' Politics

In the political spectrum of 'AJK', Islamabad always found it easy to deal with the AJKMC because of its anti-India posture and right-wing politics. Over the years, various incarnations of PML perceived the AJKMC as their natural partner because of their ideology and stand on the overall Kashmir issue. Thus AJKMC always received support from the PML and the army.

The PML made its presence felt in 'AJK' in 1991, when a rather new political party, Tehrik-i-Amal, founded by Maj. Gen. (retd.) Muhammad Hayat Khan in 1983 converted itself into the AJK Muslim League on April 2, 1991.[173] In the 1985 elections Tehrik-i-Amal had secured eight seats with 19 per cent of the total votes cast. In the 1990 elections it secured only one seat. The PML always maintained a close relationship with the Muslim Conference. When Hayat Khan joined the IJI alliance along with the AJK Liberation League and the AJKPPP, Nawaz Sharif did not appreciate Hayat's stand and instead reiterated support for AJKMC. In a statement he even said that, "we consider Muslim Conference as Muslim League in Azad Kashmir. We supported you in the past, in future also will maintain this tradition".[174] However, the PML-N finally thought of participating more actively in 'AJK' politics in 1996 when the PML (Junejo) participated in the elections and won one seat. The PML-N's 'AJK' chapter was formally launched on December 26, 2010 by its leader Nawaz Sharif.[175]

Sharif family's bonhomie with AJKMC came to an end when the latter extended support to the military dictator Gen. Musharraf after he toppled Nawaz government in a military coup in October 1999. This was obvious from the fact when PML-N supported Raja Farooq Haider in the 'AJK' local elections against the alliance of the AJKPPP and Muslim Conference. PML-N did not take part in the elections held under Musharraf's regime. It was only in the 2011 elections when the PML-N fought on the Muslim Conference's turf. It entered into an alliance with the Jamaat-e-Islami Azad Jammu and Kashmir (JIAJK). While cautioning federal government against interfering in elections of 'AJK', Nawaz Sharif announced that PML-N would participate in the elections with the JIAJK.[176] This alliance couldn't do well in the elections but gave a clear signal to the Muslim Conference that the PML-N had got their new ally. The Emir of JIAJK termed this unity as a natural alliance and said that both shared common interests and same vision for the future.[177] Although PML-N and its 'AJK' chapter were able to mobilise the huge public rallies, but they only secured eight seats. The AJKPPP won 21.[178] The 2015 by-elections in 'AJK' saw these erstwhile opponents come together. The by-election for the seat, LA-3, Mirpur-III, had fallen vacant after Barrister Sultan Mahmood resigned from the 'AJK' Assembly and joined the Pakistan Tehreek-e-Insaf (PTI). The PPP and PML-N came together against the PTI. The PPP nominated Chaudhry Mohammad Ashraf as its candidate and requested PML-N to withdraw its candidate and vote for Mohammad Ashraf; the PML-N obliged. But Barrister Sultan Mahmood won convincingly, bagging 15,485 votes to the PPP's 12,811 votes.[179]

In the election held in July 2016, the PML-N initially decided to contest all the seats without entering into an alliance after it failed to woo Sardar Attique of the Muslim Conference. Attique refused to enter into an electoral alliance with the PML-N because the latter wanted to field in the areas which are regarded as Muslim Conference strongholds. The PML-N finally entered into a seat sharing arranged with Jamaat-e-Islami Azad Kashmir (JIAJK). Both the parties decided to keep open four seats from Rawalakot, two from Kotli and one form Mirpur, whereas, the PML-N agreed not to field its candidate against JIAJK's Noorul Bari in Khyber-Pakhtunkhwa Valley-VI constituency, where Kashmiri refugees are settled. PML-N also agreed to give a special seat to the JIAJK's Turabi as he withdrew in favour of PML-N's Mushtaq Minhas. The top leadership of the PML-N under the chairmanship of Prime Minister Nawaz Sharif constituted an 18-member parliamentary board to kick off its election campaign.

When elections were held for the 49-memeber 'AJK' Legislative Assembly on July 21, 2016, the PML-N swept the polls by winning 31 seats. The winning of PML-N in 'AJK' reaffirmed the trend that ruling party at centre in Pakistan always wins elections in the region. The PML-N nominated Raja Farooq Haider as Prime Minister of 'AJK'. Although, there were reports that journalist turned Raja Mushtaq Minhas could be the choice for prime ministership as he is seen very close to the Pakistan military establishment.

Organisation and Party Leadership
The organisational structure of the party consists of President, Senior Vice Presidents, Vice Presidents, Secretary General, Assistant Secretary Generals, Finance Secretary, Information Secretary, Overseas Organisation Secretary and Joint Secretaries. All these office bearers according to the party constitution are elected by PML-N Council. The party is supposed to hold intra-party elections at all levels after the expiry of 4 years' term from the date of previous elections at Central/Provincial/Local levels through secret ballot.

Raja Farooq Haider Khan is the president of the PML-N chapter in 'AJK'. Central Secretary General is Shah Ghulam Qadir (former speaker of the 'AJK' Assembly) and Raja Zafar ul Haq.

Cadre Strength and Funding
The PML-N is a cadre-based political party. Punjab provides most of its cadre strength. It's very difficult to know the exact strength of the party in 'AJK'. However, it does have a following within the conservative section of the society. Funding of the party has never been an issue. The PML-N at the centre is a pro-business entity. Most of its top leadership belongs to industrialists. On various occasions the PML-N has been accused of spending money to rig elections. In 2011, then Minister for Kashmir Affairs, Mian Manzoor Ahmad Wattoo, warned Nawaz Sharif that he should not use the resources of the Punjab government during the 'AJK' elections.[180]

PML-N's Take on Kashmir Issue
Like other political parties in Pakistan, the PML-N, too, stands for resolving the Kashmir issue through dialogue. After becoming Prime Minister of Pakistan in 2013, Nawaz Sharif initially maintained a positive posture vis-à-vis India. He signalled that he would not allow sanctuaries to anti-India extremist groups. He even said that he would allow transit facilities to Indian trucks. However, according to perceptions created by Pakistani media reports, the Pakistani Army did not allow Nawaz to move in that direction. The final bolt came when India cancelled the Foreign Secretary level talks with Pakistan. resenting Pakistani High Commissioner in India, Abdul Basit's meeting with separatist leaders, despite India's expression of displeasure over it.[181]

Nawaz Sharif did raise the Kashmir issue at every forum. While addressing the 69th session of the United Nations (UN) General Assembly on September 26, 2014, Nawaz emphasised on the Kashmir issue more vociferously than in the previous years. Being vocal on Kashmir at the UN General Assembly had much to do with India's cancellation of talks. On October 13, 2014 he again raised the Kashmir issue with a delegation of US Senators. Sharif told them that the "UN resolutions must form the basis for any solution for Kashmir and people of Kashmir be made part of it".[182]

He did not stop there, when the then US President Barack Obama was supposed to travel to India in January 2015, Nawaz Sharif requested him on telephone to raise the Kashmir issue with the Indian leadership. The Prime Minister's Office made this conversation public. It said, 'The Prime Minister also urged President Obama to take up the cause of Kashmir with the Indian leadership, as its early resolution would bring enduring peace, stability and economic cooperation to Asia."[183]

The above-mentioned statements give the impression that the Nawaz Sharif-led PML-N had again gone back to its position vis-à-vis Kashmir, internationalising it at every forum. However, it could have been a political gimmick to keep the right-wing forces and establishment happy. Although even Kashmir could not save Nawaz Sharif. He was finally deposed by army on corruption charges by using judiciary.

AJK MUTTAHIDA QUAMI MOVEMENT (AJKMQM)

Introduction

Politics in 'AJK' took a dramatic turn on June 10, 2006 when the Muttahida Quami Movement (MQM) announced that the party would participate in the elections for the 'AJK' Legislative Assembly in July 2006. It then issued the list of its candidates for 26 out of the 41 constituencies. The decision to participate was announced by MQM's Parliamentary Leader in the then National Assembly, Dr. Farooq Sattar, and then Minister for Housing and Works, Syed Safwanullah, at a news conference in Islamabad. Explaining the reasons for entering the election fray in 'AJK', Sattar said that the MQM was becoming a national-level party and, therefore, it had decided to take part in the elections in 'AJK' for the first time. Before making the announcement, the party had already done the ground work in 'AJK' by launching relief measures in the areas which were hit during the October 5, 2005 earthquake.

According to Dr. Sattar, the MQM supremo, Altaf Hussain, had personally donated Rs five million for relief work. In addition, the party provided goods and aid worth Rs 3.5 billion to the earthquake-affected areas. The relief goods were distributed by teams led by MQM ministers, advisers, MNAs, MPAs and Senators in the affected areas.[184] The MQM was, however, able to win only two refugee seats in Karachi where other contestants had boycotted polling following alleged rigging.[185] Most of the political parties alleged that the Musharraf government had rigged the polls in favour of the AJKMC. The MQM candidates, Malik Abdul Manan and Sardar Abdul Aziz, levelled similar allegations and demanded re-election in the refugee constituencies in Sindh.[186] According to Christopher Snedden, it is likely that President Pervez Musharraf, who himself is a Muhajir, might have helped MQM to win the two seats it had secured in its maiden attempt in 'AJK'.[187]

The MQM had participated in the June 2011 elections in 'AJK'. Addressing a big election meeting in Muzaffarabad on June 19, 2011 by telephone from London, Altaf Hussain said that future of 'AJK' and Kashmir belonged to the MQM. He said that the time was not far when there would be an MQM government in Kashmir and the Kashmir dispute lying on the backburner for the past 63 years would also be settled. He asked the Indian Government to stop military action and desist from using state power in Kashmir. He added that the Indian Army should be stopped from killing innocent Kashmiri people and from violating the Kashmiri women, and demanded that the Kashmiri people should be given the right of self-determination according to the resolutions of the United Nations. He claimed that no one could understand the sufferings of the Kashmiri people better than the MQM, adding, "We remained steadfast in the face of hardships and unending vitriolic propaganda unleashed against us. It was because of our patience that MQM had reached Kashmir."[188]

Earlier, while talking to Kashmiri workers at the International Secretariat in London on May 23, 2011, Altaf Hussain assured that if the MQM got a chance to come to power in Kashmir, it would not only resolve the Kashmir dispute but also get the people of Kashmir their legitimate rights.[189] In this election also, the MQM was able to win only two Kashmiri refugee seats of Jammu (LA-30) and Kashmir Valley-1 (LA-36) where its candidates, Muhammad Tahir Khokhar and Muhammad Salim Bhat, got elected. In all, 12 candidates contested from LA-30, while 11 contested from LA-36.

MQM, the Parent Organisation

The MQM was formed in 1984 by Altaf Hussain as Muhajir Quami Movement. It claimed to represent the interests of Muhajirs – the Urdu-speaking people who left India, after the Partition in 1947. The decision to form the party was taken after Altaf Hussain felt in the early 1980s that the Muhajirs were being discriminated against in every field by the Pakistani State and, like other nationalities in the country, should enjoy equivalent rights. For example, the Muhajir students were refused admission for higher education in various colleges and the universities of Sindh.

Keeping this in mind, Altaf Hussain formed the All-Pakistan Muhajir Students' Organisation (APMSO) at the University of Karachi on June 11, 1978, "which could help them, recognise their existence as a separate ethnic group as well as gain their legitimate rights".[190] It subsequently led to the formation of the Muhajir Quami Movement. At the time of its formation, the MQM represented only the Muhajir community but changed its name to Mutttahida (United) Quami Movement in July 1997 to attract all ethnic groups into its fold, "since the MQM was not against any nationality or institution but against the 'exploitative forces' which comprised feudal lords, waderas, corrupt government officials and bureaucrats and some corrupt generals".[191] Within a short time, its political base expanded in Sindh where it trounced other parties in the 1987 local party elections, with several of its candidates elected as mayors, and made its debut in Parliament and Sindh Assembly in 1988.[192] Since then, it has been contesting the polls as a key partner to keep its influence in every government in Pakistan.

Ideology/Objectives/Manifesto

The cherished goals of MQM are: eradication of political authoritarianism, abolition of feudal system, promotion of cultural pluralism, devolution of power to the grass-roots level and to achieve full provincial autonomy and a completely devolved local government system. The MQM believes in the induction of common man in the power structure to provide opportunity to economically and socially deprived people, "empowerment for all" for a better and safer life for today and tomorrow.[193]

Explaining his party's ideology, Altaf Hussain reiterated in 2011 that the MQM was not a party of the feudal lords, adding that it was the only political party working in the interests of the poor and middle-class people. He emphasised that MQM did not want to change the borders of the country but only wanted to change the decayed political system and empower the poor and middle-class people.[194] Elaborating his point, the party's website says:

> Ideologically speaking, MQM is not a proponent of Socialism, Communism or unbridled Capitalism. It only believes in Realism and Pragmatism. By adopting this philosophy it desires to establish an economic system based on principles of free market in accordance with the spirit of democracy. MQM seeks drastic reforms in all sectors including agriculture, industry, commerce, education, health, defence, finance judiciary. These are considered essential for the solidarity, security, progress and prosperity of the country as well as for the welfare of the common man. MQM wants to see the total elimination

of corruption, bribery, injustices, tyranny, exploitation, illiteracy, unemployment, poverty, drug trafficking and other such social evils. It aims to introduce a comprehensive program to make Pakistan prosperous and stable, and create a just society in which opportunity to progress and prosper is available to all, without discrimination.[195]

On foreign affairs, it states:

MQM wants an independent foreign policy for Pakistan and wants to promote close, friendly and honourably relations with all the countries, especially with the neighbouring countries. MQM believes in the policy of coexistence, or in simple words, live and let live. MQM believes that all the disputes and conflicts be resolved through dialogue and peaceful means. MQM wants to solve the Kashmir issue through meaningful, sincere and honourable dialogue according to the wishes of the Kashmiri people. MQM encourages confidence building measures (CBMs) and dialogue process with India and desires peace and close cooperation between the countries of South Asia, especially in economic fields so as to provide peace, progress and prosperity to one-fifth population of the world living in the region.[196]

MQM in 'AJK' Politics

Besides good governance and freedom of expression in 'AJK', the MQM promises to stand by the Kashmiri people in their struggle for 'self-determination' and their 'legitimate rights'. The salient points of the MQM's manifesto for 'AJK' elections 2011, released by Dr Farooq Sattar, Federal Minister and Deputy Convenor of MQM coordination committee, on May 20, 2011, are as follows:[197]

(i) Kashmir dispute should be resolved according to the wishes and aspirations of the people of Kashmir.
(ii) The MQM stands by the people of Kashmir in their struggle for self-determination and legitimate rights.
(iii) Able leadership for poor and middle class will be introduced and a corruption-free society will be established in Kashmir.
(iv) Two-fold education system will be abolished and free education will be given up to matriculation level.
(v) 'AJK' will get its due share in the royalty of Mangla Dam like Balochistan and Khyber Pakhtunkhwa.
(vi) Hospitals and basic health centres will be established in the districts and villages of Kashmir for providing healthcare facilities to the poor people.

(vii) Hydroelectric power projects will be started with the help of private sector.
(viii) Cottage industries will be protected. A department will be established for promoting exports of marble products, fruits and garments.
(ix) Scholarships will be given to the poor Kashmiri students to higher education.
(x) Black laws against women will be abolished and they will be given 33 per cent representation in all public institutions.
(xi) Full and transparent audit of funds collected for the reconstruction of areas hit by earthquake will be done.
(xii) Kashmiri emigrants will be given the right to vote and practical steps will be taken for the solution of Kashmiri migrants.
(xiii) Income generated from development of natural resources will be used for the uplift of Kashmiri people.
(xiv) Human rights and freedom of speech will be protected.
(xv) Good governance and system of merit will be implemented in Kashmir.

Further, in 2011, Altaf Hussain assured that the people affected by the Mangla Dam Raising Project would be given alternative land. Besides, residential colonies would be built for Kashmiri migrants, who would also be given an allowance of Rs 1,500-2,000 per month. Special attention would be given to the construction of roads, which are presently in bad shape.[198] Moreover, on its website, the MQM acknowledges the role played by the minorities of Pakistan in nation-building, the sacrifices rendered by them, and the problems and issues, faced by them. It further claims that the MQM members join the Hindus and Christians to celebrate festivals like Holi, Diwali and Christmas in Pakistan.[199]

Organisation, Structure and Leadership

The party is led by Altaf Hussain, who heads the Rabita Committee, also known as the Central Coordination Committee. The 34-member Rabita Committee (24 from Pakistan and 10 from London) formulates the party's political programme. On November 20, 2011, the MQM set up a 42-member Central Executive Council (CEC) drawn from Sindh, Punjab, Khyber Pakhtunkhwa, Balochistan, 'AJK' and Gilgit-Baltistan, with representation of people from all nationalities including the minorities. The CEC was formed to assist the Coordination Committee in structuring the party's organisation, policy issues, propagation of party policies and in the preparation of party manifesto and in holding of party programmes.[200] While making this announcement, Deputy

Convenor, Dr. Farooq Sattar said the CEC shall hold a meeting on quarterly basis under the Coordination Committee and play an active role in abolishing feudal system, corrupt political culture and elimination of dynastic politics in the light of the political philosophy espoused by the MQM Chief, and also work for creating awareness among the public for the empowerment of poor and middle-class people of the country.[201]

It is in this context that the MQM seeks drastic reforms in all sectors, including agriculture, industry, commerce, education, health, defence, finance and judiciary, which the party feels are considered essential for the solidarity, security, progress and prosperity of the country as well as for the welfare of the common man.[202] While talking to members of CEC on March 24, 2015, Altaf Hussain said that the CEC was a parliament and policy-making body of the MQM and its members were responsible of making the party's constitution.[203] The party structure is further divided into wings, zones, chapters and sector bodies to streamline the functioning of the party. The credit of MQM's achieving success in the urban areas of Sindh goes to the charismatic leadership of Altaf Hussain who went from being called "Altaf Bhai" to "the Quaid-e-Tehreek and later as Pir Sahib".[204]

The MQM had two members in the 'AJK' Legislative Assembly elected in 2011. They were Salim Butt, Minister for Youth Affairs, and Muhammad Tahir Khokhar, Transport Minister in the 'AJK' Government. Tahir Khokhar was also member of the 42-member central body the CEC which was formed in 2011.[205] He also headed the 'AJK' unit in the July 2016 elections, which did not return even a single candidate to the assembly.

Cadre Strength and Funding

The exact cadre strength of Party's members in 'AJK' is not known. However, it mainly has representation in Sindh and has made some headway in Punjab, Khyber Pakhtoonkhwa, 'AJK' and Gilgit-Baltistan. To increase the party strength, the MQM started a week-long campaign in November 2014 all over Pakistan and abroad appealing people to join the MQM. Anyone by filling a form, which costs Rs 10, can become a member. Despite a grenade attack at a camp set up for the new membership drive, hundreds of people enrolled themselves to become members. The Taliban claimed the responsibility for the grenade attack at Orangi Town in Karachi in which one person was killed and 50 injured including three members of the Sindh Assembly.[206]

The MQM funds come from members' donations. It is, however, alleged that it also raises funds through extortion, narcotics smuggling and other criminal activities.²⁰⁷ The funds are also collected by overseas branches from various charitable institutions. The MQM had also introduced the *bhatha* system (forced extraction) to collect party funds from shopkeepers, businessmen and industrialists. Refusal to pay *bhatha* could "result in torture, loss of property and even loss of life".²⁰⁸ The party was also allegedly responsible for a factory fire in the Baldia area of Karachi after failing to extort US$ 1.9 million from the factory owner. The fire killed 258 people. The allegation has, however, been denied by the MQM.²⁰⁹ The party is also accused of money-laundering activities.

Network and Area of Influence

The party continues to enjoy prominence in local politics due to muhajir vote bank. Its headquarter is in Karachi, and it has an International Secretariat located in London. Initially, the party maintained a low profile but after two years of its formation the party used street power to control Sindh. The MQM leadership dealt harshly with its opponents both within and outside the party, and did not tolerate criticism. Many journalists were threatened for writing against the MQM. During Operation 'Clean Up in the early 1990's', the Army discovered cells in Karachi that were allegedly used by the MQM "to torture and at times kill dissident members and activists from rival groups".²¹⁰ Its Supremo, Altaf Hussain, is living in exile in London after he fled Karachi in 1992 to escape arrest on charges of kidnapping and torturing an army officer.

The MQM's network covers all the urban towns of Sindh, and it has been able to show its presence by winning seats in Mirpur Khas, Sukkur, Gilgit-Baltistan, 'AJK', and two local government seats in Balochistan. The MQM has opened branches in the US, Canada, South Africa, Japan and several European nations. Its international secretariat at London regularly brings out bulletins, press releases of speeches of Altaf Hussain, activities of the party and alleged atrocities being committed by Pakistan security agencies on MQM workers. To help the poor and needy, the MQM has set up a welfare wing called the Khidmat-e-Khalq Foundation. This wing also started an ambulance service in Karachi on June 15, 2011.

Links and Alliances with other Political Parties and Militant Groups

MQM's relations with other Muhajir parties are not cordial. Its sworn enemy is the MQM (Haqiqi), which was allegedly created by the Pakistan Army/Inter-Services Intelligence (ISI) to break MQM's increasing influence. Other Muhajir groups – Muhajir Ittehad Tehriq (MIT) and Mohajir Rabita Command (MRC)

– do not approve of its violent tactics. For this reason both the parties have kept their distance from the MQM.[211] Both MIT and MRC were formed in the mid-80s, and are led by Dr Salim Haider and Maulana Wasi Mazhar Nadim, respectively.

The MQM has also been involved in frequent clashes with Pashtuns who dominate the transport business in Karachi and are prosperous.[212] The US think tank, the National Memorial Institute for Preventing Terrorism (MIPT) considers the MQM as a terrorist outfit and has bracketed it with Lashkar-e-Jhangvi, Balochistan Liberation Army, Sipah-i-Sahaba Pakistan, Lashkar-i-Taiba, Harkat-ul-Mujahideen and others.[213]

MQM's relations with the PPP can be traced to the Sindhi-Muhajir ethnic tussle which started soon after the creation of Pakistan in 1947 when Muhajirs started arriving in Karachi, Hyderabad and other parts urban parts of Sindh. They soon dominated Pakistan's political scene "with their [Muhajirs'] high levels of literacy, political and business acumen and solidarity they effected fundamental changes in the polity, economy, society and culture of Sindh".[214] The Sindhis, who had begun to feel like outcasts in their own province, found voice in the PPP which was set up in 1967 by Zulfiqar Ali Bhutto, a Sindhi wadera. Sindhis consider the PPP their bulwark against Muhajir domination. In 1984, Muhajirs too had their own political party, the MQM. Soon after, bloody clashes started between the PPP and MQM. The PPP Chairperson, Benazir Bhutto called the MQM a terrorist organisation. After Bhutto's death in December 2007, her husband, Asif Ali Zardari, who became the joint Chairperson of the PPP, tried to normalise relations with the MQM. When Zardari was elected the President of Pakistan in 2008, the Sindh Assembly gave him 100 per cent vote.[215] He brought the MQM on board by taking its nominees into the PPP government formed after the 2008 elections. However, the PPP workers were not happy with this stand, especially in the light of MQM's demand to divide Sindh into two administrative parts.

Before the MQM came into being, the Muhajirs in Karachi and Hyderabad voted for the Jamaat-e-Islami en bloc. Later, Muhajirs voted for the MQM, and the Jamaat-e-Islami almost disappeared politically from these two cities.[216] This and the MQM's secular credentials made the Jamaat hostile to it.

MQM's problems with the Awami National Party (ANP) started in the wake influx of refugees from Afghanistan and FATA. The Afghan refugees and Pakhtuns captured public transport business in Karachi as "most bus routes were allocated to Pashtuns transporters in the aftermath of 1965 election by Ayub Khan as a reward for the support of his ethnic brethren in the presidential race".[217] They were also accused of gunrunning and drug smuggling. The first violent clash took place between the Pashtuns of Sorab Goth and Muhajirs in Karachi in 1985 when a Muhajir girl, Bushra Zaidi, was run over by a Pashtun minibus driver. This led to the violent riots between the Muhajirs and Pashtuns which left 65 dead and 165 injured.[218] The second influx of Pashtuns into Karachi began after the 9/11 attacks (September 11, 2001) when Pakistan joined the US-led war against global terrorism and launched operations in tribal areas. Now Pashtuns established a number of settlements in Karachi. The Pashtun-based ANP took advantage of it and opened its Karachi branch. Many Pashtuns joined it on ethnic considerations, adding an ethnic-politicised conflict between the Muhajirs and Pashtuns in addition to the post-1947 Muhajir-Sindhi war. This has led to occasional bloody clashes between the MQM-ANP. Interestingly, both follow similar ideologies and have together supported the PPP governments in Islamabad and Karachi.

Current Status

Ever since its formation, the party has maintained a firm grip over Karachi. The party has also raised an illegal armed wing which is allegedly involved in Karachi's criminal economy of drugs, extortion and land theft.[219] The MQM however is generally opposed to the growth of extremist Islamist politics in Pakistan. It also supports the US-led war on al Qaeda.

The future of MQM in 'AJK' appears to be bleak. The military operation led by Pakistan rangers broke MQM's power strength in Karachi. It lost power and influence due to further factionalism within MQM. It got divided further into MQM-Pakistan (MQM-P) and MQM-London(MQM-L). The former is led by Dr Sattar and the later led by Altaf Hussain. The party could not win two of its seats in the July 2016 elections held in 'AJK' which it had bagged in the 2011 elections. In the general elections held in 2018, the MQM did not secure much seats. It got only six National Assembly and 16 Provincial Assembly seats. Although it entered into an alliance with PTI in centre but nevertheless it lost most of its base to the PTI in Karachi.

The recent defection from the party and allegations by senior MQM leader, Mustafa Kamal that the party is funded by the Indian Intelligence Agency, the Research and Analysis Wing (RAW), has further eroded its standing. Such allegations are not new to MQM, but this time it will surely divide the MQM vote bank.

PAKISTAN TEHREEK-I-INSAF (PTIAJK)

Introduction

Pakistan Tehreek-i-Insaf (PTI) meaning by the "Movement for Justice", is a political party in Pakistan founded on April 25, 1996, in Lahore by ex-cricketer Imran Khan. The main objective to form the party was "to make Pakistan an egalitarian, modern, Islamic democratic welfare state which upholds the fundamental rights of the people in which all citizens, regardless of gender, caste, creed or religion can live in peace, harmony and happiness".[220]

Initially, the party was not able to make a mark in Pakistani politics: in the 1997 general elections, PTI lost all the seven constituencies it contested across Pakistan. In the October 2002 elections, the PTI Chairman won only one seat from Mianwali. The party boycotted the February 2008 general elections but in the elections held in May 2013, it emerged as a close third in the National Assembly, the largest in Khyber Pakhtunkhwa Assembly and second-largest in the Punjab Assembly. The PTI also trounced the bastion of its rival, MQM, by emerging as the second-largest political force in Karachi.[221] The PTI won 34 out of 99 of the Khyber Pakhtunkhwa provincial Assembly seats, and formed a coalition government in the province with Jamaat-e-Islami (JI) and Qaumi Watan Party of Aftab Ahmed Khan Sherpao.[222] However, in the 2018 general elections PTI was able to form a coalition government at the Centre. This may help PTI to strengthen its base in PoK politics.

PTI in 'AJK' Politics

The PTI launched its 'AJK' chapter, PTI Azad Jammu and Kashmir (PTIAJK), with former Prime Minister of 'AJK', Barrister Sultan Mahmood Chaudhry as its President in 2015. The party fielded him as its candidate for the by-election to the 'AJK' Legislative Assembly from Mirpur (LA-III) on March 29, 2015. The PTI Chairman, Imran Khan, visited Mirpur to address election rally with his eye on the general elections in 'AJK' in 2016. His speech highlighted some of his party's objectives in 'AJK', which were not different from what the party promised in Pakistan:[223]

    (i) Entrusting power to the representatives of the masses at the grass-roots level
    (ii) Advocating jihad against corruption
    (iii) Providing clean administration to the people
    (iv) Empowering all people – no gender bias
    (v) Proposing 'AJK' as "Naya Azad Kashmir", with his party's broad-based programme of turning the country into a "Naya Pakistan"
    (vi) No mention of the Kashmir dispute

The Mirpur seat had fallen vacant when Barrister Sultan Mahmood Chaudhry quit the PPPAJK and resigned from the Legislative Assembly a day before joining the PTI on February 5, 2015 as its regional chief. He defeated Chaudhry Mohammad Ashraf of the AJKPPP by about 3,000 votes. The AJKPML-N candidate had withdrawn from the contest in favour of the AJKPPP candidate.[224]

Ideology/Objectives

The PTI is of the view that the creation of Pakistan was the result of relentless struggle of Muslims in India under the inspiring leadership of Quaid-e-Azam Mohammad Ali Jinnah to establish a homeland for Muslims where they could freely practise their beliefs and ideals.

However, the party deplores that his dream has not been fulfilled. Rather, it is convinced that Pakistan stands at the threshold of an "economic disaster, breakdown of institutions, collapse of governance, social disorder, desperation and disillusionment". Even, Jammu and Kashmir has remained an incomplete agenda of the Pakistan Movement. As per the party's ideology, this has happened because Pakistan fell into the hands of a ruling elite consisting of inept, corrupt and selfish politicians, civil and military bureaucrats, feudal mindset and a host of vested interests that plundered Pakistan and brought it to the brink of disaster.[225] Thus, the PTI was launched to mobilise people, extricate Pakistan from its present state of despair and set it on the path of attaining unity, solidarity, social justice and prosperity.[226]

PTI's ideology is essentially derived from Jinnah's vision of a modern Islamic republic that advocates tolerance, moderation and freedom to practice the religion of one's choice. According to the party's manifesto, the PTI is not merely a political party: it is a broad-based political movement that embraces the interests of all Pakistanis. While establishing the rule of law and ensuring protection of human rights through independent and honest judiciary, its mission is to strive for the social development and economic prosperity of citizens, especially the poor and unprivileged masses.[227] The following are the goals of the PTI, as highlighted in its manifesto:

(i) Establish Pakistan as a truly independent and sovereign state that becomes the source of pride for the people.
(ii) Strengthen state institutions to promote democracy and complete political, economic and religious freedom for the people.
(iii) Provide an accountable and efficient government that ensures the protection of life and prosperity of its citizens.

(iv) Launch an Education Revolution to promote universal literacy and raise the standard of education in our schools, colleges and universities.
(v) Ensure the availability of adequate healthcare services for all citizens.
(vi) Give the highest priority to poverty alleviation through policies aimed at creating more job opportunities and enabling ownership of assets to the poor.
(vii) Evolve a merit-based system that provides equal opportunity for employment and upward social mobility for all, especially the working classes.
(viii) Create an environment which encourages the private sector to grow and create greater wealth and employment opportunities.
(ix) End the VIP culture by setting an example in simple living and austere lifestyle.
(x) Eliminate draconian laws that give unchecked power to the Police and Agencies or which limit the rights of citizens.
(xi) Evolve a self-reliant economy which is free of dependence on foreign aid.
(xii) Promote regional peace and strengthen the relationship with friendly countries.[228]

The PTI's 2016 manifesto for 'AJK' elections maintained that the PTIAJK if comes in power will declare 'AJK' self-reliant through 74th constitutional reforms act. Education, health and industrial sector and establishing a gas company in 'AJK' was also mentioned in its manifesto.[229] Its constitution maintains that the agenda for Kashmir is "to strive for the right of self-determination for the people of the State of Jammu & Kashmir".[230]

Organisation, Structure and Leadership

The organisational structure of the PTI comprises the National Council, Central Executive Committee (CEC), Provincial Council, Regional Organisations, District Organisations, Primary Organisations, Union Council and Tehsil/Taluka/Town Organisations. The National Council is the supreme body of the party which reviews the progress of the party from time to time, and formulates programmes and policies suitable to the needs and demands of the time. The National Council consists of:[231]

(i) Office bearers of the Provincial Organisations
(ii) Presidents of the Regional Organisations
(iii) Presidents of District Organisations
(iv) 35 members, five each from the women, youth, students, labour,

farmers, minorities, lawyers and overseas organisations to be nominated by their respective organisations

(v) Technocrats and professionals in the country to be nominated by the Chairman who shall not exceed one-fourth of the total number of the members belonging to cases (i) to (iv) above

Further, the CEC is PTI's main central council. Its responsibility is to assist the Chairman to carry out day-to-day functions of the National Council, lay down the party policy, guide the party at national level and act as executive authority at the national level. The CEC consists of the Central Office bearers and 30 members nominated by the Chairman from amongst the members of the National Council, which include one member each from Christian, Hindu and Sikh, Parsi and other communities. The Presidents of Provinces are the ex-officio members of the CEC. The term of office for all the organisations at all levels is four years.

Prominent leaders of the PTI National Council are: Imran Khan, Chairman; Shah Mahmood Qureshi, Vice Chairman; Jahangir Tareen, General Secretary; Dr. Shirin Mazari, Secretary Information; Ibraul Haq, Secretary of Foreign Affairs; Naeemu Haq, Chief-of-Staff of Chairman; Zafar Anwar, Chief Organiser; and Dr. Swaran Singh, Secretary of Minorities. As mentioned earlier, Sultan Mahmood Chaudhry is the President of the PTIAJK. Raja Musadiq is the Regional Organiser of the PTIAJK chapter. Other leaders from 'AJK' include Sardar Tahir Akbar, Babar Tahir, Chaudhry Aslam, Habib Ullah Butt, Sardar Nasreen, Rashid Mughol, Asad Saleem and Azhar Rasheed Advocate.[232]

Cadre Strength and Funding

In August 2012, PTI had claimed that that its membership had exceeded 10 million members, making it the largest political party in Pakistan. But later it was found that the party had only 350,000 members who were eligible to vote in intra-party elections in November-December, 2012.[233] Its current strength in 'AJK' is not known. However with the taking over reins of party by Sultan Mahmood Chaudhry, a number of party members from the PML-N have joined the PTIAJK.[234]

According to the PTI Constitution, the party has permitted the Provincial Organisations to retain the membership fee collected from members. Moreover, the Central and Provincial Executive Committees are authorised to organise fund-raising activities to meet the financial targets, and the Chairman and Provincial Presidents form fund-raising committees for the Centre and Provinces, respectively.[235] There are reports that the party is involved in money laundering, as donations worth about over two million US dollars were received by the party from the US, allegedly from "illegal and prohibited" sources. In this connection, a petition filed before the Election Commission of Pakistan (ECP) by Akbar S. Babbar, a founding member and former information secretary of the PTI, accused the party of "committing and financial corruption and violating laws relating to collection of donations and managing them". In addition, the ECP was also requested to make PTI accountable for millions of dollars raised personally by Imran Khan during numerous fund-raising events in the US, Canada and Europe.[236]

Links and Alliances with Other Political Parties

The PTI has always questioned anti-terrorism campaigns, particularly against the Taliban. It believes that dialogue is the only way to broker peace with the Taliban. Other parties though have reservations. However, when the military operation, Zarb-i-Azb started against terrorists in North Waziristan on June 15, 2014, both the PTI and its old rival, the PML-N welcomed it, knowing very well that the target of the operation was the Taliban.

Imran Khan's dharna in Islamabad in August 2014 to protest against the alleged rigging of the 2013 elections in favour of the Nawaz Sharif's PML-N was opposed by many 'AJK' political leaders. The AJK-PML-N Chairman, Farook Haider Khan, said that Imran Khan's call for civil disobedience was not only illegal but also tantamount to treason which the government should take seriously. Similar call was made by the JI's 'AJK' former Chief, Abdur Rashid Turabi. It may be mentioned that JI is part of the PTI-led coalition government in Khyber-Pakhtoonkhwa province. However, former 'AJK' Prime Minister and Chief of AJKMC, Sardar Attique Ahmad Khan backed the *Inquilab* and *Azadi* marches, saying, "Every Pakistani and Kashmiri should support Imran Khan and Tahirul Qadri who are fighting to end hereditary politics in Pakistan."[237]

Current Status

The party's slogan for 'AJK' is "Naya Azad Kashmir". But the party's Chairman, Imran Khan, did not explain what it exactly means. He has also not elaborated on what is going to be his party's relationship with jihadi groups who want Kashmir to be ceded to Pakistan. His new Kashmir policy also does not say how it will accommodate the army and Inter-Services Intelligence policies towards Kashmir. With so much of its unexplained agenda PTI failed to impress the voters with just a slogan at the elections in 'AJK' in July 2016. Imran Khan kicked off the election campaign in 'AJK' during his visit on February 04, 2015 where he opened the PTI Secretariat and also constituted a four-member committee tasked with awarding tickets to candidates for the July 2016 elections.[238] In spite of its best efforts in the elections, however, the party, led by Barrister Sultan Mahmood Chaudhry, lost heavily and could only secure two seats. Sultan Chaudhry lost the election for the first time. The central leader of the party, Imran Khan, accepted defeat; however, Sultan Chaudhry alleged widespread rigging and refused to accept AJKPML-N's massive win (31 out of 41 seats) in the elections.

With the forming of PTI government in Islamabad, it is unlikely that the Imran led government will topple the government in 'AJK'. It seems PTI will allow the PML-N government in 'AJK' to complete its tenure. But it will make every effort to strengthen its base in the region.

JAMAAT-E-ISLAMI AJK (JIAJK)

Introduction

Jamaat-e-Islami Azad Kashmir (JIAJK) has had great significance on the political landscape of 'AJK'. Whether it is its clandestine or explicit support to the various militant groups in Jammu and Kashmir or social work – educational institutions, hospitals and social welfare programmes – the Jamaat-e-Islami (JI) AJK has emerged an important element within 'AJK''s political arena. JIAJK's stand on Kashmir is not different from its parental organisation, the JI Pakistan. JI's approach towards the Kashmir conflict has largely depended on its relationship with the military/Inter-Services Intelligence (ISI) in Pakistan.

Early Phase

During the 1930s when the concept and creation of a nation state was the buzz word, JI, in opposition to Congress's secular state and Muslim League's Muslim nationalism, came up with the concept of 'Sharia state'.[239] JI was established in Lahore on August 26, 1941 as a conservative societal set-up. Its founding father, Maulana Abul Ala Maududi, was the brain behind the organisation which was based on the revolutionary concept of Islamic ideology. Maududi was against Muslim nationalism, rather he concentrated on the Muslim Ummah at large. Once Pakistan came into being in August 1947, Maududi migrated to Pakistan and took it as an opportunity to realise his dream of an Islamic state. He wanted to make Pakistan a truly Islamic state and prove to the world that Islamic laws could coexist in the modern age. For Maududi, sovereignty belonged only to God. His argument revolved around the "Divine

Sovereignty". For him, any government in Pakistan was administering the country as His (God's) agent. In the beginning, the JI confined its role to reform the society, but the widespread anti-Ahmadi movement in 1952 gave it the impetus of transforming Pakistan by wrangling in politics.

After rejecting Pakistani military's request to declare war on Kashmir as 'jihad', Maududi was imprisoned along with other leaders, who opposed Ayub's military rule. After his release from jail, Maududi decided that in order to keep the corrupt out of parliament, holding power was the only solution. Therefore, the JI decided to take part in the next 1970 national elections in Pakistan. However, it didn't do well in the elections, bagging only four out of 300 seats. Consequently, JI decided to return to its original mission of purifying the community. After Zia-ul-Haq, a sympathiser of JI's philosophy, came to power in a military coup in July 1977, the JI got a free hand in the state-controlled process of Islamisation in the country. Since then, it has always aligned itself with the military. The latter has exploited its street power to topple governments, and used governments as proxies in Afghanistan and Kashmir.

After partition, Jamaat was organised into two distinct units, JI Pakistan and JI Hind. Moreover, the JI Jammu and Kashmir too considers itself independent and distinct from the two JI units in India and Pakistan.[240] However, its counterpart in 'AJK', the JIAJK, is in essence a branch of JI Pakistan. Although it was launched in 'AJK' and Gilgit-Baltistan in July 1974 with an independent setup having no administrative control of JI Pakistan. The JIAJK in the beginning did not work as a political entity; it operated only as a revivalist movement. The JIAJK believes that complete Islamisation of the region will automatically lead to its unification with Pakistan.[241]

Electorally, like its mother organisation, it has not done too well in the region. There are various reasons why it has not emerged as a viable political party in 'AJK'. The JIAJK, unlike other political parties, lacked any systematic plan to develop economy, and deal with political crises and people's problems. It sees all the problems and their solutions through the prism of religion. Biradari system, feudalism and business tycoons play an important role in the overall political system in Pakistan. Votes are either bought or forced. On the other hand, the JIAJK's candidates are mostly from the middle-class background, give less importance to the biradari system and overemphasise Islam's message to attract votes.

The JIAJK and AJKPPP boycotted the 1985 elections. The JIAJK did not take part in the elections in protest against official favouritism of the 'AJK' Muslim Conference. It did not contest elections again in 1990. It "instead, demanded formation of a revolutionary government".²⁴² It participated in the 1996 elections, but performed poorly, getting only one seat. The AJKPPP won in 26 seats and the AJKMC eight. In the 2001 elections, which were held under army supervision, the total voter turnout was only 49 per cent, and the 'AJK' Muslim Conference got majority of the seats. However, the JIAJK fielded 33 candidates, but could not get even a single seat. It was accused by then AJKMC President, Sardar Abdul Qayyum Khan, of spending crores of rupees during elections.²⁴³

Again in the 2006 elections the JIAJK was part of the Muttahidda Majlis-e-Ammal (MMA), a coalition of various religious parties. The MMA was expecting a good result because of its prominent role in reconstruction and rehabilitation work after the 2005 earthquake. The MMA fielded 33 candidates, but drew a blank. Dejected with the election results, it organised a multi-party conference. Sardar Ijaz Khan, the MMA-AJK president not only denounced the results but also accused Islamabad's ruling class of rigging the elections.²⁴⁴ While commenting on the results, Islamabad-based analyst, Ershad Mahmud, with a distinct tilt towards JI stated, "These seats have become, simply, a tool of manipulation in the hands of the ruling government in Islamabad, and particularly Punjab, which has eight and half seats in its territorial jurisdiction. There is no doubt that successive federal governments have been gifting these seats to their allies. The ruling parties always use their leverage to ensure their allies' victory. Additionally ... a huge number of non-Kashmiris are registered as voters."²⁴⁵ The then JI leader, Qazi Hussain also termed the elections as a "trailer of upcoming engineered elections" to be held in Pakistan.²⁴⁶ In the 2011 elections, the JIAJK again failed to open its account. Same was the case in the elections in 2016.

Ideology and Objectives

The goals and objectives outlined by the party are similar to its parent organisation. The following are the three main goals outlined by the party:

(1) To invite all people, particularly those who are already Muslim, to be obedient to Allah.

(2) To free people from lives of hypocrisy, contradiction and the dichotomy of word and action – one should be true to one's claim and thus live like a true Muslim.

(3) To end the influence of the proponents of falsehood, the sinful and non-practising Muslims, from the prevalent system of life, and in place, transfer the leadership, from both theoretical and practical points of view, to those who are true believers and pious ones.²⁴⁷

Manifesto

The manifesto of JIAJK is analogous to that of JI Pakistan. It talks about ending slavery, overdependence on the US and reliance on the International Monetary Fund. The party claims to work for the restoration of Pakistan's independence and sovereignty. Other relevant issues included are ending load-shedding, curbing corruption, building five major dams within 10 years of coming into power, working towards an interest-free economy and dissolving all jagirs (feudal land grants).[248]

JIAJK's Take on Kashmir Issue

The JIAJK categorically believes that plebiscite as per the United Nations (UN) resolutions is the only solution of the Kashmir dispute. In this regard, the JIAJK's former Chief, Abdul Rashid Turabi has stated that an all-party coordination committee of Kashmiri leaders had conveyed its concerns to the Pakistani leaders and hoped for a clear-cut policy vis-à-vis Kashmir. He added that the coordination committee would also contact Islamabad-based foreign diplomats to apprise them of the prevailing political situation in the region.[249]

Following points highlight the JIAJK's Kashmir policy:[250]

(1) The whole nation and world should be made aware of the state of affairs of Kashmir's Azadi movement – the risks and dangers. All these issues should be brought into notice by Kashmiris and their concerned organisations.

(2) Kashmir Azadi Week should be celebrated from January 28 to February 5 annually.

(3) The UN Secretary General should be informed by letters and emails on February 5.

(4) A vigorous and full-fledged campaign should be started through print and electronic media for seeking cooperation from intelligentsia, particularly scholars and writers.

(5) The support of the general public must be sought for waging a continuous struggle in order to make the governments of both Azad Kashmir and Pakistan dutiful to the national interest.

(6) A district-wise meeting will be held in every six months for commemorating the martyrs.

Composition and Leadership of the JIAJK

The Jamaat is a well-organised cadre-based party led by an Emir (Leader), who is elected by the Majlis-e-Shura (Consultative Assembly) and the members of the party. A member should be a pious person. He should be able to read Quran. He must memorise the last 10 chapters of Quran along with its translation. He should know the 40 Hadiths (teachings of the Prophet), and read Islamic literature.[251]

The non-members are divided into different groups, depending on their degree of closeness with Jamaat's ideology. The highest in the hierarchy are called the Hamdard (sympathisers); the next as the Mutahtir (who recognise Jamaat's mission as a positive influence); the lowest ranking are termed the Mutaarif (who are just introduced to the objectives of the Jamaat, and have not been influenced or become sympathisers yet).[252] No one in the organisation can present himself or manoeuvre for the party's leadership. The party elects the 30 member Shura (Arakeen). It is the Shura which selects a panel before the General council and gets their opinion through a secret ballot. The members of the Shura are free to cast their individuals votes to anyone they liked, if they were not contesting the election themselves.

Siraj-ul-Haq is the current Emir of JI; Liyaqat Baloch is the Secretary; and Prof. Khurshid Ahmad, Hafiz Muhammad Idrees, Rashid Naseem, Assadullah Bhutto and Mian Mohmmad Aslam are the Deputy Presidents.[253]

Leadership of JIAJK

The JIAJK Emir is Dr Khalid Mahmood. He was elected in June 2017 as the fifth Emir of the JIAJK. Sheikh Aqeel Rehman, Dr Mushtaq Advocate, Noor ul Bhari, Mahmood ul Hassan Chowdhry, Dr. Khalid Mahmood Khan are Vice Presidents. Arshid Nadeem Advocate is a Secretary. Nisar Shaiq, Shamshir Khan, Ismael Shariah Yaar, Dr. Reyaz, Aftab Alam are Deputy Secretaries. Secretary for Information and Broadcasting is Raja Zakir Khan, and the Secretary for Finance is Abdul Waheed Abbasi. The previous Emir's included Maulana Abdul Bari, Col. (retd) Abdul Rashid Abbasi, Engr. Sardar Ejaz Afzal Khan and Abdul Rashid Turabi.

Relationship with Other Organisations

JIAJK's relationship with other organisations or parties is not necessarily out of its ideological consonance, rather out of its proximity in order to achieve short-term objectives. Its relationship with the Pakistan Army can be seen in the same vein. JI's support or opposition to incompetent governments depends on how much leeway is allowed for its activities. According to Frederic Grare, "Conversely, the Jamaat's criterion for support of opposition to the authorities depends on whether the government support to the causes that are most ideologically important to the Jamaat in matters of external policy is whole hearted or half-hearted."²⁵⁴ The Nawaz Sharif-led Pakistan PML-N was close to Jamaat, but on various occasions both have been at loggerheads, too. Nawaz Sharif's government had also financed Jamaat's activities in Kashmir.²⁵⁵

Jamaat's militant wing is the Hizbul Mujahideen (HM). HM replaced Jammu and Kashmir Liberation Front (JKLF) in Jammu and Kashmir, which was more or less an independent militant outfit fighting for independence. Formed in 1989, the HM considers jihad a duty and focuses on enemies and collaborators.²⁵⁶ Its main objectives are making Muslims aware about jihad and providing funds and training.²⁵⁷ Jamaat's student wing, the Islami Jamiat-e-Tulaba has provided the cannon fodder to the outfit. Thousands of Jamaat's cadres have received jihadi training. According to Muhammad Amir Rana, scores of Jamaat's student cadres have fought in Afghanistan and Kashmir and provide manpower to HM.²⁵⁸ Subtly, it endorses whatever HM does in Kashmir.

Funding

Most of the funding comes from charities, donations collected in mosques throughout Pakistan. Money and gold collected in the form of *Zakat*, *Usher* and remittances from overseas Pakistani and Kashmiri help the JI to fund HM's activities in Kashmir. JI allies with other political organisations and parties in the Muslim world, particularly the Islamist outfits, has helped the party to get financial support, for example, during the Afghan Jihad.

Current Status

Over the years, even when there has been a slight change in the perception of other political parties of Pakistan about India, the Jamaat's has maintained its rigid stance: no dialogue with India on any other issues unless the Kashmir dispute is settled. It is very critical of mending fences with India. For example, when Pakistan was toying with the idea of granting the Most Favoured Nation status (MFN) to India, the JIAJK's ex-Emir, Abdul Rashid Turabi, said that granting the MFN status to India was betrayal of the blood of Kashmiris martyrs and would put the solidarity of the country at stake.²⁵⁹ He further said that "Kashmir people are determined to continue their struggle till achievement of their right of self-determination adding they do not accept any solution with the constitutional administration of India".²⁶⁰ Therefore, any possibility of Jamaat changing or revamping itself along modern lines is bleak; in other words, there is no chance of Jamaat shunning its traditional ideology and accepting the new dynamics of the region.

KASHMIR VOICE INTERNATIONAL (KVI)

Introduction

A new international Kashmiri organisation named as Kashmir Voice International (KVI) was formed in London on 22 January 2017. The organisation was formed by a group of Academics, writers and professionals belonging to Kashmiri Diaspora in the U.K. with the aim to bring together prominent and liberal voices on Kashmir from both India and Pakistan in the U.K. to find a "dignified and honourable" solution to the issue.[261]

A meeting was held at Birkbeck University in this connection in London on 22 January 2017. An executive committee was formed under the chairmanship of Prof. Mohammad Abdullah Raina with Irshad Ahmad Malik as Vice Chairman and Javid Kakroo as the Secretary. The other six members in the committee are Gulam Nabi Falehi, Syed Abdullah Sherazi, Advocate Mohammad Saleem, Abdul Majed Bandey, Ulfat Hussain Zargar and Prof. Shahid Iqbal.[262]

Aims and Objectives

The main aim of the KVI is to reach out to the politicians in India and Pakistan, people of the valley, the real sufferers and political figures in both parts, and raise the voice of Kashmiris internationally. Elaborating about the objectives of the conference, a press conference was addressed by Prof. Raina and Javid Kakroo. The salient points of the conference were:[263]

(i) According to U.N. resolution adopted 70 years ago, Pakistan has to withdraw all its forces from Kashmir in order to get the U.N. resolutions implemented. But Pakistan has not given any indication of doing that.

(ii) There is a lack of trust between two countries because neither is willing to move from its stated position.

(iii) The Kashmiri diaspora is concerned that the real picture on the ground is not being projected. In this connection, KVI is intended to bring together prominent and liberal voices from Kashmir, from both India and Pakistan, in U.K. The members of this newly formed body will visit both the countries to interact with people from all walks of life including minorities and build opinion for an achievable and acceptable solution

(iv) The gun culture has promoted terrorism and defamed the freedom movement. As such, the KVI urges that guns from all sides should be silent and the movement be allowed to continue violence free.

(v) The KVI will raise the issues of human rights violations in 'AJK' and Gilgit-Baltistan with the Pakistan High Commission, London.

A political analyst on Kashmir affairs, R.C. Ganjoo says that the initiative to form KVI has come from eminent intellectuals who will work hard to find a lasting solution to the Kashmir issue.[264]

ENDNOTES

1. For the names of the registered political parties see http://ajkec.pk/wp-content/uploads/2016/03/List-of-Political-Parties-Aug2016.pdf, and for their symbols see http://ajkec.pk/wp-content/uploads/2016/03/LIST-OF-ELECTION-SYMBOLS.pdf. These lists are also provided as Appendices V, VI, VII at the end of the book.
2. For details see AJKEC website at http://ajkec.pk/wp-content/uploads/2016/07/Voters-Detail-Election-2016.pdf
3. See the detailed report "AJK elections: 427 in the run for 41 seats", *The Express Tribune*, June 13, 2016, at https://tribune.com.pk/story/187667/ajk-elections-427-in-the-run-for-41-seats/
4. The Maharaja accepted all the recommendations of the Glancy Commission.
5. Gull Mohd. Wani, *Kashmir Politics: Problems and Prospects*, Ashish Publishing House, New Delhi, 1993, p. 26.
6. Quoted in Sisir Gupta, *Kashmir: A Study in India-Pakistan Relations*, Asia Publishing House, New Delhi, 1967, p. 52.
7. Quoted in P.N. Bazaz, *The History of Struggle for Freedom*, Kashmir Publishing Co., New Delhi, 1954, p. 169.
8. See full text of All Jammu and Kashmir Muslim Conference, at http://archive.org/stream/AllJammuAndKashmirMuslimConference.
9. Ibid.
10. Sheikh Abdullah, *Aatish-e-Chinar*, Gulshan Books, Srinagar, 2008, pp. 163-172.
11. Sisir Gupta, *Kashmir: A Study in India-Pakistan Relations*, p. 57.
12. Christopher Snedden, *The Untold Story of the People of Azad Kashmir*, Hurst & Company, London, 2012, p. 20.
13. Quoted in P.N. Bazaz, *The History of Struggle for Freedom* p. 210.
14. Quoted in Gull Mohd. Wani, *Kashmir Politics: Problems and Prospects*, p. 32
15. Samuel Baid, "Politics in 'Azad Kashmir'", in Jasjit Singh, (ed.), *Pakistan Occupied Kashmir: Under the Jackboot*, Siddhi Books, New Delhi, 1995, p. 67.
16. Christopher Snedden, *The Untold Story of the People of Azad Kashmir*, p. 114
17. Ibid., p. 114
18. Ibid., p. 114
19. Ibid., p. 115.
20. Ibid., p. 116.
21. Samuel Baid, "Politics in 'Azad Kashmir'", p. 71.
22. Ibid.
23. Ibid., p. 72.
24. Parvez Dewan, "A History of PoK – 'Pakistan Occupied Kashmir'", in Virendra Gupta and Alok Bansal, (eds.), *Pakistan Occupied Kashmir: The Untold Story*, Manas Publications New Delhi, 2007, p. 107.
25. Samuel Baid, "Politics in 'Azad Kashmir'",, p. 99.
26. Christopher Snedden, *The Untold Story of the People of Azad Kashmir*, p. 118.

27. Ibid., p. 137.
28. Ibid., p. 190.
29. Samuel Baid, "Politics in 'Azad Kashmir'", p. 99.
30. Christopher Snedden, *The Untold Story of the People of Azad* Kashmir, p. 137.
31. Samuel Baid, "Politics in 'Azad Kashmir'", p. 102.
32. The United Front Alliance comprised the PPPAJK, Liberation League and Azad Muslim Conference – Ibrahim.
33. Quoted in Samuel Baid, "Politics in 'Azad Kashmir'", p. 112.
34. Christopher Snedden, *The Untold Story of the People of Azad* Kashmir.
35. Navnita Chadha Behera, *Demystifying Kashmir*, Brookings Institution Press, Washington, 2006, p. 196.
36. Quoted in Samuel Baid, "Politics in 'Azad Kashmir'", p. 119.
37. "Pakistan: Results of the 30 June 1996 elections in Azad Kashmir", Refworld, at www.refworld.org/docid/3ae6abc19c.html.
38. "All Jammu & Kashmir Muslim Conference (AJKMC)", at http://www.globalsecurity.org/military/world/pakistan/ajkmc.
39. http://ajkassembly.gok.pk/parliamentaryhistory.htm.
40. Ershad Mahmud, "Trouble Again: Azad Kashmir Experiences Instability – Once Again", *Greater Kashmir*, August 1, 2010, at http://www.greaterkashmir.com/news/2010/aug/1/trouble-again-2.asp.
41. "Sardar Attique Ahmed Khan", pakistantimes.com, at https://www.pakistantimes.com/topics/sardar-attique-ahmed-khan/
42. Ibid.
43. Farooq Tirmizi, "AJK Elections: An Unsurprising Result", *The Express Tribune*, June 27, 2011, at tribune.com.pk/story/197253/ajk-elections-an-unsurprising-result/
44. "PML-N grabs 31 seats in AJK elections", *Dawn*, July 23, 2016, at http://www.dawn.com/news/1272615
45. "Sardar Qayyum Calls for Making Jammu-Kashmir 'Danger-Free Area'", *Greater Kashmir*, April 27, 2007, at www.greaterkashmir.com/news/2007/Apr/28/sardar-qayyum-calls-for-making-jammu-kashmir-danger-free-71.asp.
46. Ibid.
47. Quoted in Shabir Choudhry, "Is There a Change of Heart in Kashmiri Politics", *The South Asia Tribune*, September 27, 2005 at http://satribune.wordpress.com/kashmir-peace-round-the-corner-but-jihad-also-escalating/is-there-a-change-of-heart-in-kashmiri-politics
48. Ibid.
49. Abdul Rasheed Azad, "AJK general elections: PTI, MC make seat adjustments," *The Business Recorder*, June 14, 2016, at http://www.brecorder.com/general-news/172/56441/t
50. A political group named as Plebiscite Front was first founded in August 1955 and formally launched in 1958 in the Indian state of Jammu and Kashmir. It was led by Mirza Muhammad Afzal Beg, a close confidante of Sheikh Muhammad Abdullah. It was formed following the removal of Sheikh Abdullah government in 1953. The party remained loyal to Sheikh Abdullah but toed the line that there should be a "popular plebiscite" to decide if the state would remain part of India, accede to Pakistan or become independent. Amanullah Khan established a party of the same name in AJK(PoK) in 1965. It was also known as Mahaz-i-Raisumari, as the name was translated in Urdu. It had an underground militant front named National Liberation Front, which was involved in the hijacking of Indian Airlines plane named Ganga on January 30, 1971. This Plebiscite Front had a chapter in Britain which later renamed itself as Jammu and Kashmir liberation Front in 1977.
51. Amanuallh Khan, *Jehad-e-Musalsal*, Rawalpindi, 1992, pp. 133-134.

52. Sumantra Bose, "JKLF and JKHM: Jammu and Kashmir Liberation Front and Jammu and Kashmir Hizbul-Mujahideen", in Marianne Heiberg, Brendan O'Leary and John Tirman (eds.), *Terror, Insurgency, and the State: Ending Protracted Conflicts*, University of Pennsylvania Press, USA, 2007.
53. See the Aims and Objectives of JKLF, at http://jklfworld.blogspot.in/p/jklf-aims-objectives.html
54. "Pakistan-administered Kashmir (Azad Kashmir and Gilgit-Baltistan)", COI Compilation, Report prepared by the Austrian Centre for Country of Origin & Asylum Research and Documentation (ACCORD), May 07, 2012.
55. Amir Mir, "JKLF Not for Pak Control in PoK", *DNA Analysis*, April 25, 2006, at www.dnaindia.com/world/reprt-jklf-not-for-pak-control-in-pok-1026112.
56. S.K. Sharma and A. Behera, *Militant Groups in South Asia*, Pentagon Press, New Delhi, 2014.
57. Immigration and Refugee Board of Canada, "Information on the Structure of the Jammu and Kashmir Liberation Front (JKLF) and the Means of Identification Used by Any Subgroups; on Any Humanitarian or Peaceful JKLF Factions and Their Leaders, and on the Names of Leaders of Militant JKLF Factions and Whether There Are Several Leaders within Different JKLF Factions", European Country of Origin Information Network, September 29, 1994, at https://www.ecoi.net/local_link/190564/308796_de.html.
58. See http://jklfajkgbzone.org/index.php/2012-11-23-13-21-14.
59. Shabir Choudhry, "Unity of JKLF groups and ISI", *Kashmir Watch*, August 23, 2011, at http://kashmirwatch.com/news/print.php/2011/08/23/unity-of-jklf-groups-and-isi.phtml.
60. See http://www.jklfajkgbzone.org/index.php/2012-11-23-13-24-14/2012-12-02-19-08-34/our-aims-and-objectives.
61. Ibid.
62. JKLF blog, at http://jklfworld.blogspot.in/p/jklf-aims-objectives.html.
63. Muralidhar Reddy, "JKLF Chief Assails Musharraf Move on LoC", *The Hindu*, January 19, 2003, at http://www.thehindu.com/thehindu/2003/01/19/stories/2003011902830900.htm.
64. "JKLF Protests against Gilgit, Baltistan Package", *The Dawn*, September 12, 2009, at http://www.dawn.com/news/490223/jklf-protests-aganist-gilgit-baltistan-package.
65. Alan Gray, "JKLF Marches up to 20,000 Protestors towards Islamabad", *News Blaze*, November 5, 2009.
66. "JKLF Launches Campaign for Return of Maqbool Butt's Mortal Remains", *The Greater Kashmir*, November 03, 2012, at https://www.greaterkashmir.com/=/jklf-launches-campign-for-return-of-maqbool-bhat-s-mortak-remains/132407=
67. JKLF blog, at http://jklfworld.blogspot.in/2009_08_31_archive.html.
68. Sumantra Bose, "JKLF and JKHM: Jammu and Kashmir Liberation Front and Jammu and Kashmir Hizbul-Mujahideen".
69. Mohd. Sadiq, "Elections in Pakistan occupied Kashmir: A Farce", *J & K Insights*, July 13, 2006, at www.jammu-kashmir.com/insight/20060713.ahtml
70. "Jammu and Kashmir Liberation Front", *Hindustan Times*, October 02, 2002.
71. Muralidhar Reddy, "JKLF Chief Assails Musharraf Move on LoC".
72. Immigration and Refugee Board of Canada, "Information on the Jammu and Kashmir People's National Party (JKPNP) and the Differences in Ideology with the Jammu and Kashmir Liberation Front (JKLF)", European Country of Origin Information Network, April 4, 1995, at https://www.ecoi.net/local_link/190507/294039_en.html.
73. Radha Vinod Raju, "Ghulam Nabi Fai and the ISI", Institute for Peace Studies and Conflict, #3523, December 18, 2011.
74. "Jammu and Kashmir Liberation Front", South Asian Terrorism Portal, at http://www.satp.org/

satporgtp/countries/india/states/jandk/terrorist_outfits/jammu_&_kashmir_liberation_front.htm.

75. Amir Mir, "JKLF Not for Pak Control in PoK".
76. Madhu Gurung and Ramtanu Maitra, "Pakistan, Northwest India insurgencies", *EIR*, 22 (41), October 13, 1995.
77. Immigration and Refugee Board of Canada, "The Kashmir Welfare Association of Lahore, Including When It Was Founded and by Whom, Its President in October/November 1998 and Its Position on Kashmir", European Country of Origin Information Network, March 30, 2000, at https://www.ecoi.net/local_link/190081/293602_en.html.
78. Immigration and Refugee Board of Canada, *Pakistan: The Jammu Kashmir Liberation League (JKLL), Including Its Structure, Mandate and Activities, Leaders, Current Status, and Treatment of Its Members by the Azad Kashmiri and Pakistani Authorities (1994 to September 1999)*, September 24, 1999, at http://www.refworld.org/docid/3ae6ad6e90.html.
79. Sushant Sareen, "Inside PoK: The Gilgit Grumble", Analyzing Pakistan (Blog), August 05, 2005, at http://sushantsareen.blogspot.in/2005/08/inside-pok-gilgit-grumble.html.
80. Information available at http://orkut.google.com/c6981110-tba305e1accb9d38d.html.
81. "Srinagar Boy Who Kept His Faith for Kashmir and Pakistan", *Pakistan Defence*, October 7, 2013, at http://defence.pk/threads/srinagar-boy-who-kept-his-faith-for-kashmir-and-pakistan.281914/.
82. Christopher Snedden, *The Untold Story of the People of Azad Kashmir*, p.190.
83. Samuel Baid, "Politics in 'Azad Kashmir'", p. 102.
84. Ibid., p 112.
85. Ibid., p. 113.
86. "Package for Affected Areas Promised: JK PML Manifesto Launched", *The Dawn*, June 30, 2006, at http://www.dawn.com/news/199323/package-for-affected-areas-promised-jk-pml-manifesto-launched.
87. "The Jammu Kashmir Liberation League", at http://www.jkonline.org/abour-us/.
88. Kashmir Information Centre, Islamabad, cited in *Refugee Review Tribunal*, Australia, Research Response Number: PAK 31088, January 29, 2007, at www.refworld.org/pdfid/4b6fe2d80.pdf.
89. Haruhiro Fukui, *Political Parties of Asia and the Pacific*, Greenwood Press, London, 1985, pp. 804-5.
90. "Our Constitution", at http://www.jkonline.org/our-constitution/
91. Ibid. Also see "Nationalist Parties Reject Ideology of the State's Accession to Pakistan, Demand Independent Constitution", *Pakistan Views*, May 16, 2016, at http://wp.pakistanviews.org/pakistan-news/kashmir-news/nationalist-parties-reject-ideology-of-the-states-s-accession-to-pakistan-demand-independent-constitution/
92. Op cit. note 90.
93. "Gilgit, Baltistan Is Part of State of J&K: Dr. Hassan", *The Asians*, December 21, 2014, at http://www.theasians.co.uk/print/20141221_misfar_kashmir.
94. "Pakistan: Follow-up to Pak32735.E of 24 September 1999 on the JKLL", at http://www.reworld.org/docid/3ae6ad7268.html; "K H Khurshid Paid Tribute on Death Anniversary", *The Nation*, March 12, 2013, at http://nation.com.pk/national/12-Mar-2013/kh-khurshid-paid-tribute-on-death-anniversary; "Gilgit, Baltistan Is Part of State of J&K: Dr. Hassan", No. 13.
95. *Refugee Review Tribunal*, Australia, Research Response Number: PAK 31088, January 29, 2007.
96. "Our Constitution", http://www.jkonline.org/our-constitution/.
97. Samuel Baid, "Politics in 'Azad Kashmir'", p 124.
98. "Politics – Pak-Police Denounced for Hampering Pro-Kashmiri Rally", *Pakistan Press*

International, October 28, 2003, cited in the Research Response Number, PAK31088, January 2007.
99. "Military Clampdown on PoK Parties Not Professing Allegiance to Pakistan", *Daily Excelsior*, July 4, 2001, cited in the Research Response Number, PAK31088, January 29, 2007.
100. "Police Seize Kashmir Leaders to Stop New March", Reuters, October 26, 1992, cited in Research Response Number, PAK31088, January 29, 2007.
101. "Demand for Plebiscite in Rallies across AJK", *Dawn*, January 27, 2005, at http://www.dawn.com/news/381250/demand-for-plebscite-in-rallies-across-AJK.
102. "Kashmir Solidarity Day Observed in Washington", *Kashmir Watch*, February 9, 2015, at http://kashmirwatch.com/news/print.php/2015/02/09/kashmir-solidarity-day-celebrated-in-washington.phtml.
103. United Nations Military Observers group in India and Pakistan (UNMOGIP) letter from Liberation League with civil societies on January 5, 2013, at http://www.jkllonline.org/unmogip-letter-from-liberation-league-with-civil-societies-on-5-january-2013/.
104. "An Appeal to the Members of the Non-Aligned Movement", at http://www.jkllonline.org//an-appeal-to-the-members-of-the-non-aligned-movement/.
105. Cited in "Pakistan Open to Idea of New Kashmir: Musharraf" CBS News, December 5, 2006, at http://www.cbc.ca/world/story/2006/12/05/pakistan-kashmir.html?ref=rss.
106. Mohinder Verma, "We Never Supported Terrorism, Violence against J&K: Former CJ Told PoK HC", *Daily Excelsior*, December 2014, at http://www.printfriendly.com/print?url=http://www.dailyexcelsior.com.
107. "Sultan Leaves PPP to Form People's ML", *The Dawn*, April 21, 2006, at http://www.dawn.com/news/188735/sultan-leaves-ppp-to-form-people.
108. "Package for Affected Areas Promised: JK PML Manifesto Launched", *The Dawn*, June 30, 2006, at http://www.dawn.com/news/199323/package-for-affected-areas-promised.
109. Christopher Snedden, *The Untold Story of the People of Azad Kashmir*, p. 211.
110. "Ruling MC Secures 20 Seats, AJKPP 7: Manipulation of Results Alleged", *The Dawn*, July 13, 2006, at http://www.dawn.com/news/201154/ruling-mc-secures-20-seats-ajkpp-7-manipulation-of-results-alleged.
111. For a detailed introduction, see: "United Kashmir Peoples National Party", at http://www.ukpnp.net
112. "United Kashmir Peoples National Party: A Brief History", at http://www.ukpnp.net/about-us/.
113. Ibid.
114. Ibid.
115. "Exiled leaders from PoK, Gilgit-Baltistan Blame Pak for Human Rights Violations", at http://www.aninews.in/newsdetail4/story207925/exiled-leaders-from-gilgit-baltistan-blame-pak.
116. Shaukat Ali Kashmiri, "Pakistan Administered Kashmir and Gilgit Baltistan: Solidarity with the Persecuted", *Asian Affairs*, June 2009, at http://asianaffairs.in/june2009/pakistan-administered.html.
117. Ibid.
118. Immigration and Refugee Board of Canada, February 3, 2003, at http://www.ecoi.net/local_link/189822/293320_en.html.
119. Ibid.
120. "Multi-Party Conference urges to make amendments in AJK Interim Act 1974 for independent, fair & transparent elections", *Sabah News*, May 15, 2016, at http://www.sabahnews.net/61656, and *The Express Tribune*, May 16, 2016, http://tribune.com.pk/story/1103962/kashmir-elections-nationalists-demand-right-to-contest-polls/
121. Jammu and Kashmir National Students Federation, at, http://jknsf.yolasite.com

122. http://kashooo.wordpress.com/2009/08/23/jammu-kashmir-national-awami-party-jknap-leaders-are-being-punished-opposing-jihadi-camps-in-pakistan-occupied-kashmirpok/
123. Naeem, 'AJK Interim Act 1974 and Human Rights', July 6, 2013, at http://kashooo.wordpress.com/category/news-and-politics/
124. Jammu Kashmir National Independence Alliance (JKNIA), at, http://kashooo.wordpress.com/tag/jammu-kashmir-national-independence
125. "New All-Party Alliance in PoK", *Hindustan Times*, June 22, 2003, at www.jammu-kashmir.com/archives/archives2003/kashmir20030622d.html.
126. Ibid.
127. "All Party National Alliance to Observe Oct. 22 as "Black Day" from Next Year", *ANI*, October 26, 2010, at http://in.news.yahoo.com/party-national-alliance-observe-oct-22-black-day.html.
128. Samuel Baid, "Pak Polity and Politicians", *Kashmir Images*, March 24, 2014, at http://www.dailykashmirimages.com/news-pak-polity-and-politicians-57197.aspx.
129. Senge H. Sering, "Political Dynamics of Culture and Identity in Baltistan", in K Warikoo (ed.), *The Other Kashmir: Society, Culture and Politics in the Karakoram Himalayas*, p. 84.
130. Noor, "APNA Brings Kashmiri Leaders and GB Nationalists Together in Islamabad", *Pamir Times*, January 11, 2010, at http://pamirtimes.net/2010/01/11/event-account-apna-brings-kashmiri-leaders-and-gb-nationalista-together-in-islamabad.
131. Zulfiqar Ali, "Kashmiris Protest at Killing of Sardar Arif Shahid", BBC News, May 16, 2013, at http://www.bbc.com/news/world-asia-22559730.
132. Ibid.
133. http://idp.world-citizenship.org-wp-archive-1069.
134. Azad Jammu and Kashmir Interim Constitution Act, 1974, at http://www.ajkassembly.gok.pk/ajkinterimconstitutionact1974.html.
135. "With Friends Like These: Human Rights Violations in Azad Kashmir", *Human Rights Watch Report 2006*, at http://www.hrw.org/reports/2006/pakistan0906/6.html.
136. Quoted in Shabir Choudhry, "Kashmiri leader Arif Shahid and his vision", WAAGA CUSUB Media, May 19, 2014, at http://waagacusub.net/articles/393/Kashmiri-leader-Arif-Shahid-and-his-vision
137. Ibid.
138. Ibid.
139. "Pakistan People's Party", at http://www.dailymotion.com/PPPOfficial
140. Official website of the PPP, at http://www.ppp.org.pk/history.html.
141. "Pakistan People's Party", *The Dawn*, January 17, 2012, at http//www.dawn.com/news/688790/Pakistan-peoples-party
142. Fakhar Zaman, "Pakistan People's Party – 1967–2000", at http://www.ppp.org.pk.history.html.
143. "People's Party of Pakistan", GlobalSecurity.org, at http://www.globalsecurity.org/military/world/pakistan/ppp.htm
144. Christopher Snedden, *The Untold Story of the People of Azad Kashmir*, p. 190.
145. Samuel Baid, "Politics in 'Azad Kashmir'", pp. 112-13.
146. Christopher Snedden, *The Untold Story of the People of Azad Kashmir*, p 191
147. Ibid., p. 192.
148. Samuel Baid, "Politics in 'Azad Kashmir'", p. 118.
149. Ibid., p. 124.
150. Ershad Mahmud, "AJK Polls: What Next ?", *Greater Kashmir*, July 3, 2011, at http://www.greaterkashmir.com/news/2011/ajk-polls-what-next.
151. Shamim-ur-Rahman, "Pakistan People's Party", in A.B.S. Jafri (ed.), *The Political Parties of Pakistan*, Royal Book Company, Karachi, 2002, pp. 103-10.

152. Akmal Hussain, "The Crisis of State Power in Pakistan", in Ponna Wignaraja and Akmal Hussain (eds.), *The Challenge in South Asia: Development, Democracy and Regional Cooperation*, Sage Publications, New Delhi, 1989, pp. 226-227.
153. Ibid.
154. "Party to Emerge Victorious in Polls", *The Nation*, May 24, 2011, at http://nation.com.pk/national/24-May-2011/Party-to-emerge-victorious-in-polls.
155. "Pak PM to Address Workers' Convention at Muzaffarabad on 23 May", *Kashmir Watch*, May 1, 2011, at http://kashmirwatch.com/news/print.php/2011/05/01/pak-pm-to-address.
156. Official Website of Pakistan People's Party.
157. Nadeem F. Paracha, "Political parties in Pakistan: Roots, fruit & Juice", *The Dawn*, May 2, 2013, at http://www.dawn.com/news/1026015/political-parties-in-pakistan-roots-fruit-juice.
158. "AJK Elections: PPP Sweeps AJK Polls Amid Rigging Charges", June 30, 2011, at http:www.elections.com.pk/newsemail.php?id=840.
159. Ershad Mahmud, "The Dynamics of AJK's Upcoming Assembly Elections", *Greater Kashmir*, June 20, 2011. at http://www.greaterkashmir.com/print/the-dynamics-of-ajk-s-upcoming/97132.html
160. Tom Hussain, " Pakistan People's Party Offers Coalition Deal after Easy Win in Kashmir Election", *The National*, June 28, 2011, at http://www.thenational.ae/news/world/south-asia/pakistan-peoples-party-offers-coalition-deal-after-easy-win.
161. Ibid.
162. For further detail see http://pppsb-kp.pk/history/
163. PPP (Shaheed Bhutto) prepping to make a comeback, *Daily Times*, March 7, 2016, at http://www.dailytimes.com.pk/national/07-Mar-2016/ppp-shaheed-bhutto-prepping-to-make-a-comeback
164. PPP (SB) announces contesting AJK polls, *The Nation*, March 16, 2016, at http://nation.com.pk/national/16-Mar-2016/ppp-sb-announces-contesting-polls
165. Pervaiz Iqbal Cheema, "The Muslim League: Decline of a National Party", in Subrata K. Mitra, Mike Enskat, Clemens Spieb (eds.), *Political Parties in South Asia*, Praeger Publishers, London, 2004, p. 132.
166. For further details, see official website of the Pakistan Muslim League-Nawaz (PML-N), at www.pmln.org.
167. Pervaiz Iqbal Cheema, "The Muslim League: Decline of a National Party", p. 136.
168. For details, see: Ibid., pp. 137-38.
169. www.http://Pml.org.pk
170. Ashraf Mumtaz, "Pakistan Muslim League", in A B S Jafri (ed.), *The Political Parties of Pakistan*, Royal Book Company, Karachi, 2002, p. 89.
171. www.revolvy.com/main/index.php?s=Pakistan%20Muslim%20League%20(J).
172. http://www.pmln.co.uk/consitution.html.
173. Samuel Baid, "Kashmir that Pakistan Occupies and Calls 'Azad'", Kashmir Information & Research Centre, New Delhi, 2001.
174. Quoted in Samuel Baid, "Politics in 'Azad Kashmir'", New Delhi, 1995, p. 124.
175. "PML-N Launched in AJK; Nawaz Comes Hard at Supporters of Dictators", *The Pakistan Times*, December 27, 2010, at http://www.pakistantimes.net/pt/detail.php?newsid=17594
176. "PML-N & JI to Contest Elections Jointly: Nawaz", *Sana News*, May 12, 2011, at http://www.sananews.net/english/2011/05/12/plm-n-ji-to-contest-ajk-elections-jointly-nawaz/
177. Assadullah Malik, "A Shift in AJK Politics", *Weekly Pulse*, July 01, 2011, at http://weeklypulse.org/details.aspx?contentID=900&storylist=1
178. "PPP Sweeps AJK Polls amid Rigging Charges", *The News*, June 27, 2011, at http://www.thenews.com.pk/TodaysPrintDetail.aspx?ID=7023&Cat=13&dt=6/27/2011

179. Tariq Naqash, "PTI's Sultan Mahmood Victorious in AJK by-Poll: Unofficial Result", *Dawn*, March 29, 2015, at www.dawn.com/news/1172637
180. "Nawaz Sharif Should Not Utilize Punjab Govt Resources during AJK Election: Watto", at http://www.onlinenews.com.pk/details.php?id=180725
181. Mateen Haider, "India Calls off Foreign Secretary Level Talks with Pakistan", *Dawn*, August 18, 2014, at www.dawn.com/news/1126123
182. "Nawaz Sharif Raises Kashmir Issue with US Senators", *The Times of India*, October 13, 2014, at timesofindia.indiatimes.com/world/Pakistan/Nawaz-Sharif-raises-Kashmir-issue-with-US-Senators/articleshow/44804562.cms
183. "Nawaz Sharif Asks Obama to Raise Kashmir during India Visit", *The Hindu*, November 22, 2014, at www.thehindu.com/news/international/south-asia/nawaz-sharif-asks-obama-to-raise-kashmir-during-india-visit/article6624359.ece
184. "MQM to Take Part in AJK Elections", *The World Affairs*, June 10, 2006, at http://www.worldaffairsboard.com/international-politics/12759-mqm-t.
185. "Ruling MC Secures 20 Seats, AJKPP 7: Manipulation of Results Alleged", *The Dawn*, July 13, 2006, at http://www.dawn.com/news/201154/ruling-mc-secures-20-seats-ajkpp-7-manipulation-of-results-alleged.
186. Mohd Sadiq, "Elections in Pakistan-Occupied Kashmir: A Farce" *Kashmir Insights*, July 13, 2006, at http://www.jammu-kashmir.com/insights/insight20060713a.html.
187. Christopher Snedden, *The Untold Story of the People of Azad Kashmir*, p. 210.
188. "Altaf Hussain Asks Kashmiris to Reject Oft-Tested Political Parties", June 19, 2011, at http://www.mqm.org/English-News/Jun-2011/ah-110619.htm
189. "The MQM Will Resolve the Kashmir Dispute", May 23, 2011, at http://www.mqm.org/English-News/May-2011/news110523.htm
190. Farhan Hanif Siddiqi, *The Politics of Ethnicity in Pakistan*, Routlege, London, 2012, p. 100.
191. Ibid., p. 106.
192. Syed Iftekhar Mir, "MQM and Altaf: Two Bodies but One Soul", April 22, 2014, at http://tastepakistan.pk/mqm-and-altaf-two-bodies-but-one-soul/
193. "Empowering People – MQM Manifesto 2013", at http://www.mqm.org/manifesto2013
194. "The MQM Will Resolve the Kashmir Dispute", May 23, 2011, at http://www.mqm.org/English-News/May-2011/news110523.htm
195. "About Muttahida Qaumi Movement (MQM)", at http:www.mqm.org/About MQM.
196. "Empowering People – MQM Manifesto 2013".
197. "Azad Kashmir Election 2011: MQM Announce Manifesto", May 20, 2011, at https://www.youtube.com/watch?v=zKoq1ptXuGM.
198. "Altaf Hussain Asks Kashmiris to Reject Oft-Tested Political Parties".
199. "Muttahida Qaumi Movement", http://mqminmyopinion.blogspot.in.
200. Nisar Mehdi, "MQM Names Newly Formed CEC", *The Nation*, November 21, 2011, at http://nation.com.pk/national/21-Nov-2011/MQM-names-newlyformed-CEC.
201. Ibid.
202. "About Muttahida Qaumi Movement (MQM)".
203. "MQM to Elect Office-Bearers through Democratic Way: Altaf Hussain", March 24, 2015, at http://www.mqm.org/englishnews/19677/mqm-to-elect-office-bearers-through-democratic-way-altaf-hussain.
204. Farhan Hanif Siddiqi, *The Politics of Ethnicity in Pakistan*, No. 7, pp. 104-5.
205. Farsahat Mohiuddin, "MQM Names 42 Members of Executive Council", *The News*, November 21, 2011, at http://www.thenews.com.pk/Todays-News-4-78581-MQM-names-42-members-of-executive-council

206. "Taliban Claim Responsibility for Attack on MQM Camp", *The Express Tribune*, November 22, 2014, at http://tribune.com.pk/story/795328/taliban-claim-karachi-attack-on-mqm-camp/
207. "Pakistan: Information on Mohajir/Muttahida Qaumi Movement-Altaf (MQM-A)", Resource Information Centre, USA Document No. PAK04002.OGC, February 9, 2004, at http://www.refworld.org/docid/414fe5aa4.html4
208. A. Khan, *Politics of Identity: Ethnic Nationalism and State in Pakistan*, Sage Publications, New Delhi, 2005, p. 152.
209. Assad Hashim, "Raid launched on Pakistan's MQM party offices", *Al Jazeera*, March 11, 2015, available at: http:www.aljazeera.com/news/asia/2015/03/police-raids-pakistan-mqm
210. "Pakistan: Information on Mohajir/Muttahida Qaumi Movement-Altaf (MQM-A)", No. 24.
211. Farhan Hanif Siddiqi, *The Politics of Ethnicity in Pakistan*, p. 104.
212. Yaroslav Trofimov, "Refugee Crisis Inflames Ethnic Strife in Pakistan ", *The Wall Street Journal*, May 30, 2009, at http://www.wsj.com/articles/SB124363974401367773t
213. The MIPT exclusively works on terrorism and is funded by the US Homeland Security Department. See: "US Think-Tank Lists MQM as Militant Outfit", June 11, 2007, at http://free-minds.org/forum/index.php?topic=14502.o
214. Vikhar Ahmad Sayeed, "The Muhajirs in the Promised Land", at Infichangeindia.org/agenda/migration-a-displacement/themuhajirs-in-the-promised-land-html
215. "Zardari Wins 100 Percent Votes from Sindh Assembly", Geo TV, September 8, 2008, at www.geo.tv/9-8-2008/24381.htm.
216. "Election Watch: Election Acid Test for MQM, Haqiqi, MMA", *Daily Times*, October 4, 2002, at Archives.dailytimes.com.pk/national/04-oct-2002/election-watch-election-acid-test-for-mqm.
217. Laurent Gayer, *Karachi: Ordered Disorder and Struggle for City*, Oxford University Press, New York, 2014.
218. Nafisa Hoodbhoy, *Abroad the Democracy Train: A Journey through Pakistan's Last Decade of Democracy*, Anthem Press, London and New York, 2011.
219. Jon Boone, "Imran Khan Blames MQM Leader Hussain for Killing of Activist", *The Guardian*, May 20, 2013, at http://www.theguardian.com/world/2013/may/19/imran-khan-pakistan-hussain-shahid-killing
220. *Constitution of Pakistan Tehreek-i-Insaf*, p. 2.
221. Hafeez Tunio, "ECP Results Show PTI Second Largest in Karachi", *The Express Tribune*, May 14, 2013, at http://tribune.com.pk/story/548862/ecp-results-show-pti-second-largest
222. Hassan Ali, "PTI, JI and QWP Agree to work on One Agenda in K-P", *The Express Tribune*, May 17, 2013, at http://www.tribune.com.pk/story/550372/pti-ji-and-qwp-agree-to-work-on-o.
223. Altaf Hamid Rao, "AJK to be Made 'Naya Azad Kashmir': Imran", *The Nation*, March 26, 2015, at http://nation.com.pk/national/26-Mar-2015/ajk-to-be-made-naya-azad-kashmir-imran.
224. Tariq Naqsh, "PTI's Sultan Mahmood Defeats N-backed PPP Candidate", *The Dawn*, March 30, 2015, at http://www.dawn.com/news/1172733/ptis-sultan-mahmood-defeats-n-backed-ppp-candidate.
225. *Constitution of Pakistan Tehreek-i-Insaf*, pp. 1-32.
226. Ibid.
227. "The Manifesto of Pakistan Tehreek-e-Insaf", at http://www.siasat.pk/forum/showthread.php?80340-The-Manifesto-of.
228. Ibid.
229. PTIAJK chapter announced its manifesto-Daily Messenger, May 25, 2016, at http://dailymessenger.com.pk/2016/05/25/pti-ajk-chapter-announced-its-manifesto/

230. *Constitution of Pakistan Tehreek-e-Insaf*, pp. 1-32.
231. Besides four Provincial Organisations – one each for Punjab, Sindh, Baluchistan and Khyber Pakhtunkhwa, a separate organisation each will be formed for the Federally Administered Tribal Areas, Gilgit Baltistan, Azad Jammu & Kashmir and for the overseas Pakistanis.
232. "PML-N Supporters Join PTI", *The Nation*, April 8, 2015, at http://nation.com.pk/national/08-april-2005/pml-n-supporters-join-pti-in-ajk
233. Asad Kharal, "PTI Members Who Are Eligible to Vote Number 350,000", *The Express Tribune*, October 31, 2012, at http://epaper.tribunr.com.pk/DisplayDetails.aspx?ENI_ID=112012103
234. "PML-N Supporters Join PTI in AJK", *The Nation*, April 8, 2015, at http://nation.com.pk/national/08-Apr-2015/pml-n-supporters-join-pti-in-ajk
235. *Constitution of Pakistan Tehreek-e-Insaf*, pp. 1-32.
236. Syed Irfan Raza, "ECP Seeks PTI Foreign Funding Details", *The Dawn*, April 2, 2015, at http://www.dawn.com/news/1173398.
237. "Azadi, Inqilab Sit-Ins: AJK's Political Leaders Oppose PTI, PAT Demands", *The Express Tribune*, August 20, 2014, at http://tribune.com.pk/story/750895/azadi-inqilab-sits-ins-ajks-political
238. "We Stand with People of Kashmir: Imran Khan", *The Nation*, February 04, 2015, at http://nation.com.pk/national/04-Feb-2016/we-stand-with-people-of-kashmir-imran-khan
239. Irfan Ahmad, "Genealogy of the Islamic state: Reflections on Maududi's Political thought and Islamism", *Journal of the Royal Anthropological Institute*, 15, N.S., 2009, p. 152.
240. Frederic Grare, *Political Islam in the Indian Subcontinent: The Jamaat-i-Islaami*, Monohar Publications, New Delhi, 2002, p. 75.
241. Ibid., p. 76.
242. Samuel Baid, *Kashmir That Pakistan Occupies and Calls "Azad"*, p. 38.
243. Ibid., p. 43.
244. Raja Asghar, "AJK Opposition Plans Protest Campaign", *Dawn*, July 20, 2006.
245. Quoted in Nirupama Subramanian, "What the Elections in PoK Mean", *The Hindu*, August 15, 2006, at http://www.thehindu.com/todays-paper/tp-opinion/what-the-elections-in-pok-mean/article3090448.ece
246. http://www.jamaat.org/news/2006S/jul/15/1001.html.
247. http://www.JIAJ&K.org/urdu/indux.php/2012-01-03-13-31-25/2012-01-03-14-48-30.
248. https://jamaat.org/ur/dastoorOrManshoor.php?cat_id=14.
249. Nisar Ahmed Thokar, "Kashmir Figures Prominently in Pak Elections", *Greater Kashmir*, April 16, 2013, at http://www.greaterkashmir.com/news/2013/Apr/16/kashmir-figure-prominantly.
250. www.JIAJ&K.org/urdu/index.php/2012-01-03-13-31-25/2012-04-25-12-28-48/2012-04-25-13-45-35.
251. Ibid.
252. Jackson Roy, *Mawlana Mawdudi & Political Islam*, Routledge, New York, 2011, p. 76.
253. https://jamaat.org/ur/central_leadership.php.
254. Frederic Grare, *Political Islam in the Indian Subcontinent: The Jamaat-i-Islaami*, p. 82.
255. Ibid.
256. Muhammad Amir Rana, *A to Z of Jehadi Organizations in Pakistan*, trans. Saba Ansari, Mashal Books, Lahore, 2004, p. 439.
257. Ibid., p. 440
258. Ibid., p. 448.
259. "Political Parties Should Put Kashmir on Top of Election Manifesto: JI", *Pakistan Observer*, December 31, 2012, at http://pakobserver.net/detailnews.asp?id=189528.
260. Ibid.
261. "Kashmir Voice International launched to give platform to Kashmiris in UK", *The New Nation*,

January 22, 2017 at http://www.newnation.in/world-news/kashmir-voice-international-launched-to-give-platform-to-kashmiris-in-uk/
262. R.C. Ganjoo, "Pakistan must withdraw from PoK", *Power Politics*, Vol.10, Issue 1, February 2017, p. 41
263. Ibid, "kashmiris in UK come together to find solution to Kashmir issue", *Hindustan Times*, January 23, 2017 at http://hindustantimes.com/india-news/kashmiris-in-uk-come-together-to-find-solution-to-kashmir-issue/ ; R.C. Ganju, "A New Voice from London"., *Northlines*, January 2017 at http://thenorthlines.com/new-voice-london/
264. Interview with R.C. Ganjoo on telephone, January 30, 2017.

3
Gilgit-Baltistan: A Historical Perspective

Introduction
Gilgit-Baltistan was officially referred to as the Northern Areas since its occupation by Pakistan in 1947, although the name was in popular use in the region before that. It was given its present name when the Pakistan People's Party (PPP) government in Islamabad promulgated the 'Gilgit-Baltistan Empowerment and Self-Governance Order (GBESGO)' in 2009.[1] In May 2018, just before demitting office, the outgoing Pakistan Muslim League-Nawaz (PML-N) government headed by Shahid Khaqan Abbasi repealed the order of 2009 and came out with a fresh "Government of Gilgit-Baltistan Order, 2018" which promised to offer more power to the elected legislature in matter concerning local governance, but in reality, the central government in Islamabad retained its absolute control over decision making in all spheres of governance.

Area and Population
The Gilgit-Baltistan region has a geographical area of 72,496 sq. km (as per Pakistani projections). Under an agreement reached between Pakistan and China on March 2, 1963, Pakistan handed over 5,180 square km of territory to China. Gilgit-Baltistan is administratively divided into three divisions[2] which in turn are divided into 10 districts, including Gilgit, Skardu, Diamer, Ghizer, Hunza, Nagar, Ghanche, Astore, Kharmang and Shigar.[3] The main centres of political activity are the towns of Gilgit, Ghizer and Skardu. Skardu is also the headquarters of Pakistan Army's Northern Light Infantry regiment.

Demography and Religion
According to 1998 census, the population of Gilgit-Baltistan was 870,347, while

estimated population in 2013 was 1.3 million with an annual growth rate of about 2.56 percent.[4] But several articles and books would put the population figure at 2 million in 2016-17. Approximately 81 percent population is rural and 19 percent urban.

In Gilgit-Baltistan, nearly 100 percent of population is Muslim. It is also the home of diverse languages, ethnicity, sectarian and tribal identities. There are eight major ethnic groups, namely Baltis, Shinas, Yashkuns, Moghals, Kashmiris, Pathans, Ladakhis and Turkis. They speak the dialects of Balti, Brushaski, Khawer, Wakhi, Turki, Tibeti, Pashto, Urdu and Persian.[5]

Four different sects of Islam are prevalent in Gilgit-Baltistan – Sunni, Shia, Ismail and Noorbakshi.[6] Although Shias constitute a clear majority in the region, except in Diamer and Astore districts, a study carried out by Prof. Omar Farooq Zain, shows a clear-cut variation on language, sect and ethnic lines.[7]

Ismailis comprise about 87 per cent of the Ghizer population. They belong to the Brusho tribe and speak Shina, Khowar and Brushashki languages. Gilgit and Hunza have a diverse population mix, the majority being Shias (about 54 per cent), and speak Shina, Brushashki and Wakhi languages. Gilgit also has a sizeable population of Ismailis (27 per cent) and Sunnis 19 (per cent). In Diamer and Astore, Sunnis constitute 90 per cent of the population, with only 10 per cent Shias. They mainly speak Shina. In Skardu, about 87 per cent of the population are Shias, 10 per cent Noorbakshis and 3 per cent Sunnis, with Balti as their major language. Noorbakshis constitute 96 per cent of the population in Ghangche and mainly speak Balti. There are also a small number of Kashmiris, Kohistanis, Gujars, Pakhtuns, Punjabis, Hazaras and Afghanis who are mostly migrants and labourers.

With the influx of Sunni businessmen and others from Punjab and Khyber Pakhtunkhwa since late 1980s, the demographic character of the terrain has been changing. Elaborating further, Samuel Baid says:

> The influx of outsiders has created two problems, depletion of employment opportunities for the locals and brutalisation of sectarian tension. Along with this there has come along a gun culture and gradual replacement of spiritual values by class materialism of the new middle class. The outsiders grab land and government jobs. It is not only the jobs that the outsiders grab, but also plunder their forest and natural resources. The funds allocated for the development of Gilgit and Baltistan are spent on the Army deployed there.[8]

The Pakistan Government has not done much to improve the economic condition of the people of Gilgit-Baltistan which is considered as the most backward in South Asia. Except tourism, no other industry has been set up in

Gilgit-Baltistan. It lacks basic amenities like education, roads, health care, and electricity. According to a report by the Pakistan Institute for Peace Studies, Islamabad, the region has a very low literacy, 14 per cent for men and 3.5 per cent for women.[9] However, data prepared by the Planning and Economic Development Department of Government of Gilgit-Baltistan in 2013 claimed that in 1998, literacy rate was 37.85 per cent (male 52.62 per cent, female 21.65 per cent) which was projected in 2013 as 60 per cent (male 70 per cent and female 50 per cent).

Further, according to this data, there were only 1,492 primary schools (both boys and girls) in the year 2011-12, where 105,869 students were enrolled. Total teaching staff in these primary schools was 36,554. Similarly, there were 418 middle schools for 63,897 students which had 2,787 teachers. For 60,713 students enrolled in 261 high schools, there were only 3,616 teachers. The condition of most of the public sector schools is pathetic, as almost 1,044 schools have no electricity, 954 schools lack drinking water and 913 schools are without any latrine facility.[10] In the whole of Gilgit-Baltistan, there were only 15 degree colleges in the year 2011-12, where only 182 teachers were employed to teach 6,438 students, both boys and girls.[11] The girls' schools have drawn the ire of Islamists in recent times. In 2018, for example, according to media reports in *Dawn* on August 3, Unidentified assailants burned down at least 12 schools in various places in Diamer district.

It may be noted that the Pakistan Government has not bothered to open medical or engineering colleges in the region, forcing many students to study in professional colleges in Karachi and other towns of Pakistan. However, the role of the Agha Khan Educational Services (AKES) is quite commendable in uplifting the educational standard of the people. The AKES operates 192 schools that educate over 36,000 students and employ over 1,600 teachers.[12] It provides education in the rural areas of Gilgit-Baltistan, and hence, supplements the efforts of the government.[13]

For such a vast region, there are just 33 hospitals with 986 beds. There is just one doctor for six thousand inhabitants although official data claim that there is one doctor for every 3,804 people and one hospital bed for 1,220 people.[14]

Economic Conditions

Gilgit-Baltistan is the most neglected, backward and poorest area in entire South Asia where 85 per cent of the people makes its living on subsistence farming,[15] but the state data shows only 23 per cent of the population living in poverty.[16] In this connection, a multi-party conference was organised in Gilgit on June 6,

2017 by Astore Supreme Council where the speakers held Islamabad responsible for keeping the people of Gilgit-Baltistan economically backward for the last seven decades. Moreover, heavy taxes have been imposed time and again through ordinances without providing basic fundamental rights, such as constitutional status to the region. Against the imposition of illegal taxation massive anti-government protests were held in Gilgit-Baltistan. That brought the socio-economic activities to a standstill as the traders observed strike for two months. The protest call was given jointly by G-B Markazi Anjuman-i-Tajran, lawyers and trade bodies, contractors, hotel and Petrol Pump Association and GB Chamber of Commerce and Industry who declared the imposition of new taxes as illegal and tantamount to "murder of traders".[17]

The Pakistan government was finally forced to withdraw the newly imposed taxation policy. But the Awami Action Committee maintained that it was less than convinced about the government's claim of withdrawing the tax as it wanted all taxes imposed over the years to be withdrawn.

The first direct taxation policy on Gilgit-Baltistan was introduced by the Pakistan Peoples' Party (PPP) in 2012. Before that, people of Gilgit-Baltistan were paying indirect taxes. This direct taxation policy by PPP was imposed through an act called the Gilgit-Baltistan Council Income Tax (Adaptation) Act, 2012. According to local analysts, after forming governments at the centre and in the region, the Pakistan Muslim League-Nawaz (PML-N) was "inclined to levy more taxes on the people in an attempt to derive maximum benefits out of the investments that are likely to make its way once the China-Pakistan Economic Corridor (CPEC) is functional."[18]

There has been increasing frequency of suicide incidents in the region. In Ghizer district alone over 300 youth both boys and girls committed suicides since 2000 (*The Nation* May 21, 2017). One major reason for committing the suicides is unemployment. Those who are educated either join the government services or Northern Light Infantry.[19] Moreover, there is discrimination in the pay structure as well. The natives who join the civil services are paid 25 per cent less than those in deputation from Punjab.[20]

Over 90 percent of the region's population is engaged in agriculture,[21] which is used for growing wheat, barley, maize, millet, potato, peas, vegetables and fruits such as pear, cherries, peach, apple, plum and mulberry. Gilgit-Baltistan had 640,000 hectares of forest area which has fallen to 295,000 hectares i.e. more than 50 percent in the last 20 years due to callous cutting of trees and illegal smuggling.[22]

The region earns most of its revenue from tourism and minerals. Major deposits include nickel, cobalt, copper, lead, tin, bismuth, mica, quartz, zircon, coal, actinolite, gold, silver, iron, zinc, marble, uranium, spinel tourmaline, sulphur, pyrite and feldspar.[23] Based on a survey report carried out by Australian Agency for International Development (AUAID) and Pakistan Mineral Development Corporation (PMDC) in 1995, it was estimated that there are 1,480 gold mines in this area out of which 123 contain superior quality to the gold mines in South Africa.[24] But the mining industry has not flourished. According to the Gilgit-Baltistan Metals Minerals and Gem Association (GBMMGA), this could be because the companies who were issued mining leases and exploration licenses have become powerful mafia intent on "keeping the sector backward for their ulterior motive".[25] These licenses were issued to 20 multinational mining companies during Musharraf's regime.[26] There are also reports that the Gem Association has protested the new mining rules announced by the then Prime Minister Nawaz Sharif. The Chairman of the Association, Shahbaz Khan has warned that it will deprive the locals of their natural wealth and "will fuel an uprising against the colonial policies" of Pakistan. The precious items covered under the new rules include mining, among other mineral resources, ruby, emerald, aquamarine, sapphire and tourmaline. Moreover, Pakistan has allowed China to exploit its mineral wealth. Apparently, 35 tonnes of certain mineral deposits from uranium-rich Karkalti village of Ghizer district in Yasin Valley were smuggled to China.[27] The locals have, however, resisted the entry of foreign companies. Senge Hasnan Sering writes in the *Economic Times*:

> In 2008, for instance, a local person was killed when the residents of uranium-rich Gindai valley (Yasin valley) in Ghizer district clashed with Chinese miners. A Pakistani company called Mohmand Minerals met the same fate in 2010 in Nasirabad valley of Hunza district where the Progressive Youth Front spearheads the resistance against the Pakistani and Chinese expansionism. Today, more than a 100 local right defenders are locked up in Pakistani jails and face sedition charges for denying space to the Chinese and Pakistani mining companies in their valleys.[28]

Karakoram Highway

The Karakoram Highway (KKH) links Pakistan with China and is beneficial for trade between the two countries, which runs into billions of dollars. The 857-km-long KKH constructed by Chinese engineers in 1978 was opened to the public in 1986. The importance of this road link was realised after Pakistan ceded 5180 square km of Shaksgam Valley to China in 1963 without consulting the local people.It is believed that the entire cost of the construction was met by China. Besides normal trade, the KKH is also used by Pakistan for bringing military equipment from China. To achieve further strategic military edge, KKH is being converted by China into a four-lane highway with three times more capacity to accommodate heavy-laden trucks in extreme weather conditions.[29] China and Pakistan are also planning to link the KKH to the southern Gwadar port of Balochistan through the Chinese aided the construction of Gwadar-Dalbandin railway, which extends up to Rawalpindi.[30]

Tourism Industry

One of the most beautiful places in the world, Gilgit-Baltistan is very popular among tourists both from Pakistan and abroad. Surrounded by the world's largest mountain ranges – Hindukush to the Karakoram in the northeast with western Himalayas in the south and Pamir in the extreme north – Gilgit-Baltistan borders the Chinese province of Xinjiang to the north, Jammu and Kashmir to the east, 'AJK' to the south, Afghanistan and Central Asia, through the Wakhan Corridor to the northwest and Pakistan's Khyber Pakhtunkhwa to the west. The region covers 32 snow-clad peaks and narrow valleys – 18,000 to 26,000 feet high – including the world's second-highest peak, K-2 or Chigori and the third-highest peak, Nanga Parbat.

Gilgit-Baltistan is home to snow-clad mountains, mighty glaciers, lush green valleys and freshwater lakes. The 80 per cent of foreign tourists coming to Pakistan visit Gilgit-Baltistan. However, the tourism industry, which was the only major source of employment, has suffered badly in recent years, particularly after Pakistan witnessed the rise in sectarian and militant violence that got exasperated after 9/11 terror attacks, earthquakes and floods that have ravaged the area and the brutal killing of nine foreign tourists (five Ukrainians, three Chinese, one Russian and a local guide) by militants at Nanga Parbat on June 23, 2013. In the immediate aftermath, the inflow of foreign tourists came down more than half, as only 4,524 foreign tourists visited Gilgit-Baltistan in 2013 as against 10,338 in 2007.[31] From the next year onwards, with improvement in security situation in Gilgit-Baltistan, the tourism industry witnessed an upward trend. According to Mubashir Ayub, Assistant Director, Gilgit-Baltistan Tourism Department, in 2017, around 1.72 million tourists visited G-B. The revival of tourism industry brought revenue worth PKR 300 million to the local economy and it had a potential to generate local business worth PKR one billion according to media reports.[32] As much of it would depend on the security situation in the region, the G-B government has decided to put curbs on public demonstrations and protests.[33] However, such highhandedness may backfire in future because it deprives people of the right to peaceful protests and holding rallies.

Political History

The region was originally known as Balwaristan or Boloristan. A number of small tribes, who were at odds with each other, ruled Gilgit-Baltistan until the beginning of the 19th century. According to some scholars, Gilgit was also known as Dardistan i.e. the land of Dards or Dardic people. However, F.M. Khan, the author of *The Story of Gilgit, Baltistan and Chitral*, refused to accept this description, saying, "There are no race such as *Dards* and no country as *Dardistan* in the entire region."[34] According to him, the Yashkuns were the predominant race before the first century and also in 1947. Baltistan was administered directly by the Kashmir Government as part of District Ladakh with headquarters at Leh. Not much is known about the political developments in Gilgit-Baltistan during the ancient period. It is believed that Gilgit was the home of Palola or Patola who practised Buddhism.

Between seventh century and early 19th century, parts of Gilgit-Baltistan were ruled by various dynasties including: Tarkhans of Gilgit, the Maghlots of Nagar, the Ayasho of Hunza, the Burshai of Punyal, the Maqpoons of Skardu, the Anchans of Shigar and the Yabgos of Khaplu. Sri Badat was the last ruler who patronised Buddhism and built many *Viharas* in Gilgit, Punial and Yasin. Sri Badat was killed by Shamsher around 1120 AD. It was during his rule that Islam was introduced in Gilgit. His first target was the poor sections of society, namely the Dooms, Kamins and Yashkuns.[35] In 1335 AD, forces of Taj Mughol, the King of Badakshan, invaded Chitral and captured the entire region from Gilgit to Hunza and introduced the Shia Imami Ismaili version of Islam. His followers now comprise the Noorbakshi sect.[36]

The later Mughal rulers also took interest in this region. After annexing Kashmir, Akbar captured some parts of Baltistan and Ladakh. However, the area remained largely independent. It was Mughal emperor Shahjahan who after capturing Ladakh, Baltistan and Kishtwar in 1634 AD merged these areas with Kashmir.[37] By 1842, the Sikh rule had been extended to Gilgit after Raja Karim Khan of Nagar went to meet the Sikh ruler of Punjab and invited him to occupy Gilgit. He even accompanied Dogra commander Colonel Nathe Shah with forces to capture Gilgit.[38] This was followed by Treaty of Amritsar of 1846. According to this treaty, the British transferred control of the territory to the Dogra rulers of Jammu and Kashmir. In 1848, the local tribal leaders led by Raja Gohar Aman rebelled and ousted the Maharaja's forces after defeating the Dogra forces led by General Bhup Singh. The region was, however, recaptured by Maharaja Ranbir Singh in 1860 who annexed it to the state of Jammu and Kashmir[39] and established a *Wazarat* in Gilgit in 1866.[40]

The control of the Kashmir State over the territories north of Gilgit and west of Skardu were always contested. The entire region was perpetually in turmoil both because of local intrigues among influential consanguine families eyeing local seats of power and ability of local adventurers to mobilise support from local chieftains against Dogra/British control. The state forces of Kashmir assisted by the British did attempt to hold on to the terrain in view of its strategic significance. However, they found it worrisome to quell episodic assaults from the tribal adventurers and deposed/defeated chieftains all the time. By the mid-1870s, the effects of the so-called 'great-game' on the thinking of the British colonial decision makers were evident. The British were suspicious of the Russian intent, despite its commitment vide the April 1875 treaty that it would not expand its footprints in Central Asia. The British decision makers at the top believed that the "very word Cashmerer (read Kashmir) exercise[d] a powerful charm over the Muscovite imagination" (Lord Lytton's communication with Salisbury at India Office before he became Viceroy of India) and by mid 1876, there was a dominant view in India office that "Gilgit [was] the best road from India to Central Asia" and that the British Indian government "should have an agent in that district".

In November 1876, Lord Lytton met Raja Ranbir Singh and urged him to exercise more effective control of the northern reaches of his kingdom and expressed his desire to station a British officer in Gilgit. Ranbir had no other option but to oblige the British. The Maharaja of the State of Jammu and Kashmir was authorised to extend his control over the states of Chitral and Yasin by a treaty in 1876-77. By the end of year 1877, a British political officer was posted as an 'officer on special duty' (OSD), as a defacto Political Agent, with the mandate to collect intelligence about events beyond the bounds of the Kashmir state and establish friendly relations with them, with the aim of bringing them gradually under the control of the Kashmir State. In Hunza, despite the stationing of an officer and a *wazir* (governor) appointed by the Maharaja of Kashmir, the local resistance continued to gather strength during this time and the Dogra-British controlled fortress of Chaprot situated at the tri-junction of Hunza, Nagar and Kashmir was a target of frequent attacks from the local rebels.

It was around this time that Russia sought to impose its mission on Afghanistan, and the Mirs of Hunza and Nagar were found to ingratiate themselves to the Chinese authorities in Sinkiang, so much so that the British ambassador to Peking had to emphasise the point that it was an act of impropriety by the chieftain of Hunza despite the fact that he was receiving an annual pension from as well as paying tribute to the Maharaja of Kashmir as a feudatory.

The second Anglo-Afghan war (1878-1880) led to change in the British approach, and by 1881, the British Agency was withdrawn from Gilgit. In the following days, however, fresh evidence of Russian interest in Afghanistan and the Russo-Afghan armed engagement during 1884-1885 led to a rethink of the British position on Gilgit, in view of its strategic import. Later in 1887, when the British Indian government sent a military contingent to the frontiers of Gilgit, it found evidence of Russian forays into Hunza through the gap between the Pamirs and Sinkiang. Hence, restoration of Gilgit Agency was considered necessary to strengthen British control over the strategic passes of the Hindu Kush and "to prevent at any cost, the establishment within this outlying country of the political preponderance of any other power" (as Lytton wrote in February 1879).

By 1889, four years into the rule by Pratap Singh, who was deemed weak compared to his predecessor Raja Ranbir Singh, the Gilgit Agency was restored. Two years later, the Kashmir forces stationed in the strategic forts of Chalt and Chaprot along the passes were threatened by a combined force of Hunza and Nagar. The rulers of these two states also insulted the emissary of the British agent leading to an armed engagement which resulted in a conclusive defeat for both the local chieftains. The subsequent instalment of loyal members of the local royal families, in the presence of two Chinese envoys, led to relative peace in the subsequent years. However, the British quietly encouraged the Mir of Hunza to cultivate tracts in the districts of Raksam and Taghdumbash, north of the Hindukush watershed jointly claimed by the rulers of Hunza and the Chinese administration in Kashgar. The British hold on these territories under the suzerainty of Maharaja of Kashmir continued. West of the terrain, following the uprising in Chitral in 1895, which the British put down with force, the control of the state was taken away from the Gilgit Agency which came under the suzerainty of the Maharaja of Kashmir and put under the control of the newly formed Malakand Agency by 1896.

After Pratap Singh died in 1925, his nephew, Hari Singh became the Maharaja of Kashmir. Political activities and political parties in Gilgit-Baltistan were controlled through a tough law called the Frontier Crime Regulation (FCR), which the British rulers had designed to keep the locals under complete control. Those found violating the orders were given harsh punishments. By 1935, thanks to the turns and twists in the geopolitics of Europe, the British concerns about Russian intent grew further. On March 26, that year, the British pressurised the Maharaja and obtained control of the sensitive terrain under a 60-year lease agreement which recognised suzerainty of the Maharaja and the

Art. II of the Agreement said that the "flag of His Highness will be flown at the official headquarters throughout the year". However, for all practical purposes the British took charge of the terrain until they decided through the doctrine of lapse of paramountcy to return it to the Maharaja restoring his suzerainty and control over it.

The British authorities took this step fearing threat to the northern frontier of India from Russian expansionist moves following the October 1917 revolution. Commenting on the strategic importance of Gilgit and Russian fears, eminent historian, E.F. Knight wrote: "It is necessary for the safeguarding of our Empire that we should at any rate hold our side of the mountain gates but unless we locked it in, Russia would soon have both sides under her control."[41] Similarly, the agreement gave the Viceroy the right to assume civil and military administration of the *Wazarat* while the territory continued to be part of Maharaja's dominion.[42] However, during this period the state flag remained hoisted over residency along with the Union Jack. The lease was, however, terminated with the announcement of the Partition of India in July 1947.

With the termination of the 1935 lease and lapse of the paramountcy in 1947, the British handed over the administrative control of all the areas included in the Gilgit agency to the Maharaja.[43] Maharaja Hari Singh sent Brigadier Ghansara Singh to take charge of Gilgit as its Governor. On October 31, 1947, Gilgit Scouts troops led by Major Brown surrounded the house of the Governor under a conspiracy and forced him to surrender. The rebels then headed towards Baltistan and after capturing it announced the formation of a provisional government. The provisional government was formed by Major Brown and other officers and was headed by one local Raja Shah Rais Khan.

The Provisional Government lasted only for a fortnight as it did not have the support of the common people. It appears that the provisional government did not sign a formal Instrument of Accession with Pakistan. Major Brown sent frantic wireless messages to Peshawar informing that Pakistan had taken over Gilgit[44] and asked them to send a civil administrator to rule over this region.[45] The Pakistan Government responded by sending Sardar Muhammad Alam, a tehsildar in the North-West Frontier Province (NWFP) government at that time, who assumed the post of Political Agent on November 16, 1947. Because of his strong leaning towards Pakistan, Major Brown played his cards by exploiting the "religious sentiments of the Muslims soldiers in Maharaja's army and Gilgit Scouts to incite them to revolt and detach Northern Areas from rest of Kashmir".[46] Presumably, for this act, he was appointed adviser to the provisional government.[47] Later he served in the Frontier Constabulary of the NWFP, now called Khyber Pakhtunkhwa. He and his family finally left Pakistan for their hometown in the UK in 1959.[48]

After appointing Sardar Mohammad Alam, a Sunni Pathan, as the agent of the region, Pakistan brought in the notorious Frontier Crimes Regulation (FCR) and retained all the anti-people laws included in the FCR. It used the FCR to ban political activities, rallies and processions. Under the FCR, people had no right to appeal, to legal representation or to present reasoned evidence. A group of judges and advocates started a movement for the people's rights and abolition of the FCR. They were sent to jail.

On April 28, 1949, Pakistan made this transfer formal by signing the Karachi Agreement with the President of "Azad Kashmir" and the Muslim Conference.[49] Under this agreement, the administrative control of Gilgit and Baltistan was temporarily transferred to the Government of Pakistan vide sub-clause 8 of Section-3 of the Agreement[50] and also gave the federal government responsibility for defence and foreign policy of PoK and negotiation with United Nations Commission for India and Pakistan.[51] It may be noted that the 1949 agreement was signed without the knowledge and consultation of the local people.

A former President of Northern Areas Bar Association Asadullah Khan, in an interview with Brussels based International Crisis Group called Karachi Agreement as "nothing more than a sale of human beings, in which Pakistan and Azad Kashmir were customers and we were the commodity on sale".[52] By virtue of this agreement the affairs of the Gilgit-Baltistan were brought under the control of a Political Agent appointed by the Government of Pakistan. Northern Areas have never figured in any of the Pakistan Constitution. Also, Pakistan describes Northern Areas as a disputed territory. In various Court cases Pakistan said that Northern Areas were not its part.

It was in 1970's that Pakistan undertook certain changes in the laws of governance of the region. In 1972, Chief Martial Law Administrator and President of truncated Pakistan, Zulfikar Ali Bhutto visited the area and promptly announced the abolition of all princely states and Gilgit-Baltistan was transformed into districts. In 1974, Bhutto abolished the Frontier Crime Regulation (FCR) and introduced a Northern Areas Council (NAC) which replaced the NAAC. The members of NAC were elected directly on the basis of universal adult franchise.[53] During the Martial Law Regime under General Zia-ul-Haq, Gilgit-Baltistan was governed as a separate Martial Law Zone.[54] In 1982, the Zia government granted observer status to the Gilgit-Baltistan members in the Majlis-i-Shura (the body he had established in the absence of a parliament). This was General Zia's attempt "to placate those who wanted

Gilgit-Baltistan to be made Pakistan's fifth province or merge it with NWFP".[55] The move was strongly opposed by 'AJK', nationalist Kashmiris and India. As a result General Zia dropped this idea. In fact, in 1972 the 'AJK' Legislative Assembly had passed a resolution demanding the return of Northern Areas, which had been taken over by Pakistan under the Karachi Agreement, according to a Pakistani analyst Khalid Hussain, a demand Pakistan has chosen to ignore.[56]

In 1993, 'AJK' High Court accepted a petition filed by Malik Mohammad Maskeen and Haji Amir Jan, both residents of Gilgit-Baltistan, and Sheikh Abdul Aziz, an advocate from Muzaffarabad, challenging Pakistan's authority to administer the Northern Areas. It ruled that Islamabad had "no legitimate cause to keep the Northern Areas and their residents (Jammu and Kashmir state subjects) detached from Azad Jammu and Kashmir". The High Court stressed that it was contradictory to claim that the Northern Areas were neither part of 'AJK' nor Pakistan. It accordingly directed the 'AJK' government to immediately assume the administrative control of the Northern Areas and annex it with the administration of 'AJK'. It also directed the government of Pakistan to provide adequate assistance and facility to the 'Azad Kashmir' government in attainment of the said objective.[57] Thereafter, the Pakistan Government filed an appeal in the 'AJK' Supreme Court which announced its decision on September 14, 1994. It said, "No doubt, that Northern Areas are part of the state of Jammu and Kashmir – but not of Azad Kashmir. Therefore, the government need not take administrative control of these areas."[58]

It was in 1994 that Prime Minister Benazir Bhutto in her second term approved a reform package. The package was known as the Northern Areas Legal Framework Order (LFO), 1994. It gave these areas a certain amount of representation by turning the Northern Area's Council into Northern Areas Legislative Council (NALC) comprising 24 members of whom six each shall be elected from Gilgit, Diamer and Baltistan districts, three each from Ghizir and Ghanche districts and five seats reserved for the women. Its other salient points were as follows:

(i) NALC shall be headed by the Chief Executive of the Northern Areas, who shall be the Federal Minister of Kashmir Affairs, Northern Areas, State and Frontier Region.

(ii) The Chief Executive shall appoint Deputy Chief from amongst the members of the council and Deputy Chief Executive, who shall be elected by the members of the council on the basis of majority votes. Person applied for the post will have a status of a minister.

(iii) Chief Executive will also appoint three advisors who will be given the status of Provincial Minister.

(iv) It was through this order that the certain Areas rules were enunciated. Under the new Judicial System, the areas will have courts mainly, courts of appeal, the Chief Court, Subordinate Judiciary and any other court, specially set up for any other purpose.

(v) NALC has been given power to legislate in 49 subjects listed in Schedule-II of the order.[59]

However, the NALC is empowered to legislate on 49 subjects and has been given a limited advisory functions but it still needs assent from the KANA minister's approval to pass a bill.[60]

Alarmed over the lack of political representation and denial of basic rights, the Supreme Court in its significant judgement in 1999 directed Islamabad to extend fundamental rights to the region's residents within six months:

> People of Northern Areas are citizens of Pakistan, for all intents and purposes and like other citizens have the right to invoke any of the fundamental rights and liable to pay taxes and other levies competently imposed. Said people are also entitled to participate in the governance of their area and to have an independent judiciary to enforce, inter alia, the fundamental rights. Supreme court directed the Federation of Pakistan to initiate appropriate administrative/legislative measures, with a period of six months from 28-5-1999 to make necessary enactments in the Constitution relevant statute /statutes/orders/rules/notifications, to ensure that the people of Northern Areas enjoy their fundamental rights, namely, to be governed through their chosen representatives and to have access to justice through an independent judiciary, inter alia, for the enforcement of their fundamental rights guaranteed under the Constitution. It is not understandable on what basis the people of Northern Areas can be denied the fundamental rights guaranteed under the Constitution.[61]

Accordingly, the Pakistan Government took the following decisions after delegating further administrative and financial powers to NALC:

(i) Separate divisions were created for Gilgit-Baltistan and 'AJK';
(ii) Some limited powers were given to the deputy chief executive regarding postings and transfers; and
(iii) Chief Secretary of Gilgit-Baltistan was to be treated at par with the chief secretaries of other provinces of Pakistan.[62]

Meanwhile, pressure was building up on the Pakistan Government both at home and abroad to take all necessary measures to grant fundamental rights to the people of Gilgit-Baltistan who had been living in a constitutional vacuum for over 68 years. Particularly because the international human rights organisations had reported extensively on the denial of human rights to the people of 'AJK' and Gilgit-Baltistan. One such report by the Human Rights Watch entitled, "With Friends Like These: Human Rights Violation in Azad Kashmir", elucidated:

> The controls on freedom of expression have been a hallmark of the Pakistani government's policy in Azad Kashmir and are also documented in this report. This control is highly selective. Pakistani-backed militant organizations promoting the incorporation of Jammu and Kashmir State into Pakistan have had free reign – particularly from 1989 when the insurgency began to 2001 – to propagate views and disseminate literature; by contrast, groups promoting an independent Kashmir find promoting their views sharply curtailed. But frequent official repression of freedom of expression and assembly is not limited to controls and censorship specific to Kashmiri nationalists, journalists and election cycles. This repression can also be violent and very publicly so.[63]

Another report which criticised the Pakistan Government over the absence of the basic rights to the people of Gilgit-Baltistan is the report by European Parliament that maintained:

> Deplores documented human rights violations by Pakistan including in Gilgit and Baltistan, where allegedly violent riots took place in 2004 and all too frequent incidents of terror and violence perpetrated by armed militant groups; urges Pakistan to revisit its concepts of the fundamental rights of freedom of expression, freedom association and freedom of religious practice in AJK and Gilgit and Baltistan, and notes with concern allegations by human rights associations such as Amnesty International of torture and detention without due process; strongly urges all parties involved to do all they can to address these violations.[64]

Further, the report by the International Crisis Group (ICG) blames the Pakistan military for not addressing the political problem in Gilgit-Baltistan. According to the ICG, the Force Command Northern Areas (FCNA) headed by a major general stationed in Gilgit exercises enormous influence in the internal affairs of the region. The FCNA controls both security and administrative affairs of the area. Even transfers and postings need the approval of the FCNA. While talking to the ICG, one analyst who did not want to be named, said that the army oversees the "recruitment and appointments and even approve government contracts and tenders".[65]

Despite the 1999 Supreme Court ruling, the people of Gilgit Baltistan were denied their basic rights and privileges. The Ministry of Kashmir Affairs and Northern Areas under the Federal Rules of Business of 1973 was still authorised to legislate for the Northern Areas.[66] Even the Pakistan Government did not trust the local bureaucracy, and instead senior officers were sent on deputation. In the 2007 reform package announced by General Musharraf upgraded the NALC into a Legislative Assembly and the deputy chief was made its chief executive.[67] In August 2009, the PPP government promulgated the Gilgit-Baltistan Empowerment and Self-Governance Order-2009 (GBESGO), brought some political reforms under which the region was not given the status of another province, but provided with legislative assembly with some powers and a nomenclature of a chief minister and governor. The new order which had 15 major parts replaced Northern Areas Governance Order 1994. Its salient features were:

(i) Name of the area changed from Northern Areas to Gilgit-Baltistan.
(ii) Offices of Governor, the Chief Minister are created.
(iii) On the pattern of 'AJK' Council, the Gilgit-Baltistan Council was formed. The Council was to be headed by the Prime Minister of Pakistan.
(iv) The Gilgit-Baltistan Assembly was given powers to approve budget. It also introduced concept of Consolidated Fund and increased the legislative powers of the Assembly from 49 to 61 subjects along with powers to legislate on all other subjects not in the domain of Gilgit-Baltistan Council.
(v) Gilgit-Baltistan Council was given the power to legislate on 55 subjects;
(vi) The Gilgit-Baltistan Assembly was empowered to formulate its own Rules of Procedures while legislation on various subjects pertinent to governance were to be done by the Council and Assembly in their respective jurisdiction.
(vii) Gilgit-Baltistan was entitled to have its own Public Service Commission, a Chief Election Commissioner and an Auditor General.
(viii) Auditor General was to be appointed by the Governor on the advice of the Council as the case in 'AJK'.
(ix) The Chief Judge and Judges of the Chief Court were to be appointed by the Chairman of the Council on the advice of the Governor on the same pattern as it was practised in 'AJK'. The number of judges increased from 3 to 5.[68]

Political Structure of GBESGO

Gilgit-Baltistan was still under the control of federal Ministry of Kashmir Affairs and Gilgit-Baltistan, and had a bicameral legislature:

Gilgit-Baltistan Legislative Assembly (GBLA): The GBLA consisted of 33 members (the number remains the same even after the G-B Order of May 2018) of which:
  (a) Twenty-four members are to be elected directly on the basis of adult franchise;
  (b) Six women members are to be elected in accordance with the system of reserved seats in Pakistan. One additional seat (total 7) was allotted to the newly created district of Hunza Nagar.
  (c) Three technocrats and professional members are to be elected on the lines of reserved seats in Pakistan.

Gilgit-Baltistan Council (GBC): The GBC consisted of the following members:
  (a) The Prime Minister of Pakistan;
  (b) The Governor of Gilgit-Baltistan, appointed by the President of Pakistan on the advice of Prime Minister;
  (c) Six members nominated by the Prime Minister of Pakistan from time to time from amongst Federal Ministers and members of Parliament, provided that the Federal Minister for Kashmir Affairs and Gilgit-Baltistan shall be an ex officio member and Minister in-charge of the Council;
  (d) The Chief Minister of Gilgit-Baltistan;
  (e) Six members to be elected by the Assembly in accordance with the system of proportional representation by means of a single transferable vote.
  (f) The Prime Minister of Pakistan was the Chairman of the GBC whereas the Governor was to be the Vice-Chairman of the GBC and the Minister of State for Kashmir Affairs and Gilgit-Baltistan was to be an ex-officio nonvoting member of GBC.

November 2009 Elections after the Promulgation of GBESGO

The first elections to the GBLA were held on November 14, 2009. The elections for the 24 assembly seats were contested by 256 candidates from 10 political parties. The total registered voters were over 714,000, the votes polled were 328,103, and the turnout was 46 per cent.[69] The PPP-GB won 14 seats of the 24 for which elections were held on November 12, 2009. In all, it got a total of 21 seats by winning four of the women seats and all the three reserved for technocrats. While the Jamiat Ulema-e-Islam-GB (JUI-GB) won 3 seats, Pakistan Muslim League-Quaid-e-Azam-GB (PMLQ-GB), Pakistan Muslim League-Nawaz-GB (PMLN-GB) and independents shared two seats each; the

Karachi-based Muttahida Quami Movement-GB (MQM-GB) won one seat.[70] Table 1 shows the political parties and seats they won in 2009 GBLA elections.

Table 1: Party Positions in 2009 Elections[71]

Party	General Seats	Women	Technocrats	Total
PPP-GB	14	4	3	21
PMLQ-GB	2	1		3
PMLN-GB	2			2
JUI-GB	3	1		4
MQM-GB	1			1
Independent	2			2
Total	24	6	3	33

The PPP-GB leader, Syed Mehdi Shah, became the first Chief Minister. Although the PPP had won absolute majority, the JUI-GB and PMLQ-GB were accommodated in the government.[72] The PMLN-GB which had won only two seats improved its tally to four when it won the by-elections held in Ghanche and Skardu constituencies in 2013.[73]

The party got a further boost just before the June 2015 elections when a senior leader of the PPP and some leaders of other political parties switched over their loyalties, including Haji Qurban, Agha Foker and Yahya Shah (all PPP-GB); Abdul Latif and Mahmoodal Hasan (both Pakistan Tehreek-e-Insaf [PTI-GB]); Aurangzeb Khan (Awami Party); and Raja Azam (MQM-GB).[74] Following completion of five years in office, the PPP government led by Syed Mehdi Shah stepped down. On December 13, 2014, a caretaker government was formed to conduct free and fair elections.

Legislative Assembly Elections June 2015

The second election under the GBESGO 2009 was held on June 8, 2015 under army supervision. Immediately after the announcement of elections, the then PML-(N) government in Islamabad appointed Chaudhry Birjees Tahir as Governor of Gilgit-Baltistan. Interestingly, Tahir was then holding the post of Minister of Kashmir Affairs and Gilgit-Baltistan. Thus, the appointment of Tahir as Governor of Gilgit-Baltistan was considered as an attempt to rig the elections.[75]

In all, 271 candidates from 17 political parties contested the elections. The breakdown of the political parties and the total number of constituencies (within brackets) where they fielded their candidates is as follows: PMLN-GB (24); PPP-GB (22); PTI-GB (21); Majlis-e-Wahadat-i-Muslimeen-GB (MWM-GB)

(15); All Pakistan Muslim League (APML-GB) (13); JUIF-GB (10); Pakistan Awami Tehreek-GB (PAT-GB) (7); Jamaat-e-Islami-GB (JI-GB) (6); and Tehreek-i-Islami (12). Besides, the MQM-GB, Sunni Ittehad Council-GB (SIC-GB) and independents were also part of the fray. While the Shia Ulema Council entered the scene under the banner of Islami-i-Tehreek Pakistan, the Quaid Muslim League boycotted the elections after all its three legislators in the last Assembly switched over to PMLN-GB. The revised NADRA voters' list reduced the number of registered voters from 750,000 in the 2009 Gilgit-Baltistan Assembly elections to 615,000 this time. The voter turnout was 60 percent.[76]

According to media reports, about 6,000 army personnel were deployed in 1143 polling booths to supervise the polling. While the women in the Diamer valley cast their ballots, the women in the Tangir valley followed the dictat of local Jirga declaring voting by women against cultural and religious norms. There were two women candidates from MQM-GB and PTI-GB parties but both of them lost. The PMLN-GB captured power by winning 15 seats out of 24 elected seats. Subsequently, an independent member, Fida Khan, elected from Ghizer joined the PMLN-GB, increasing its number to 16.

Out of GBLA's six seats reserved for women, and three for technocrats, the PMLN-GB grabbed four and two seats, respectively. By winning a technocrats' seat and a women's seat, Islami Tehreek Pakistan emerged as the main opposition party with four seats.[77] The MWM also got one women's seat.

With winning majority of seats, the PML-N formed Government and elected Hafeezur Rehman as new G-B Chief Minister. The then PML-N government at centre appointed Mir Ghazanfar Ali Khan as the new Governor. He was replaced by Raja Jalal Hussain Maqpoon. Mir Ghazanfar Ali Khan who resigned from the post after a controversy triggered by an alleged leaked video which was carried by the local daily news paper in which the former Governor was believed to making CPEC a controversial issue.

It may be mentioned that in August 2016, Mir Saleem, son of former G-B Governor, Mir Ghazanfar Ali Khan, was elected in a by-election from Hunza. The seat had fallen vacant after the appointment of his father as Governor of Gilgit-Baltistan. But on April 10, 2018, the Gilgit-Baltistan Supreme Appellate Court disqualified him on the grounds that he was a defaulter of the National Bank of Pakistan.

Table 2 shows the political parties and the seats they won in the 2015 elections:

Table 2: Results of 2015 Elections

Party	General seats	Women	Technocrats	Total
PMLN-GB	16	04	02	22
Majlis Wahadatul Muslimeen	02	01	—	03
Islami Tehreek Pakistan	02	01	01	04
PPP-GB	01			01
PTI-GB	01			01
JUIF-GB	01			01
Balwaristan National Front	01			01
Total	24	06	03	33

For further details see Appendixes XI, XII and XIII

The MQM, All Pakistan Muslim League and Jamaat-e-Islami could not win a single seat. However, the victory of Nawaz Khan Naji of the Balawaristan National Front was a boost to nationalists. About 10 candidates from pro-independence groups contested the elections. Naji won the seat from GBLA-19 (Ghizer-1) constituency. It may be noted that no pro-independence candidate won seats in the 2009 GBLA elections, although they had fielded 14 candidates. Out of 14, eight candidates pulled out of contest in protest against the abduction of the APNA chairman, Mirza Wajahat Hasan Khan and his younger brother by the law enforcement agencies on October 30. The following day, they were externed from Gilgit-Baltistan for 60 days.[78] Shabir Choudhry, the London-based Director of the Institute of Kashmir Affairs, alleged that local nationalist parties in Gilgit-Baltistan were marginalised and treated unfairly. According to him, this was because these nationalist parties did not have enough funds to compete with major Pakistan political parties. Moreover, they did not get the support from the "Pakistani imposed government and administration".[79]

Although the Chief Minister was an elected representative of the people, the 15-member Gilgit-Baltistan Council virtually wielded all authority and power over the affairs of the region. Not only this, the GBESGO gave extensive powers to the "Chairman of the Council" who was in fact the Prime Minister of Pakistan.[80] Ali Ashraf Khan of Karachi wrote in *Pakistan Today*:

> Until today Gilgit-Baltistan is neither represented in the National Assembly of Pakistan nor in the Senate and the GB Council that is the de facto government of GB have only one symbolic representation of the people of Gilgit-Baltistan. Refugees of Kargil and Ladakh living in Gilgit-Baltistan and other parts of Pakistan have no representation whereas refugees of Jammu and Kashmir have twelve seats reserved for them in AJK Assembly where till 1964 Kargil/Laddakh refugees also had one reserved seat: that is why it is considered as an instrument in the hands of the Ministry of Kashmir Affairs

and GB affairs. Thus the election to the 24 seat legislative assembly is a symbolic act at best and a fraud otherwise because elections will be rigged as they have been in KP [Khyber Pakhtunkhwa] and the rest of Pakistan and then the assembly will be a fig leaf of democracy.[81]

Reactions to GBESGO, 2009

The reactions to the GBESGO were mixed. While most of the political parties welcomed the order but the nationalist leaders and human rights bodies called it an "eye wash". They declared that they were not taken into confidence by the Pakistan Government, adding that by issuing this order India would get an upper hand "as it wants the existing line of control to be accepted as international border".[82] The Jammu and Kashmir Liberation Front termed the Gilgit-Baltistan reforms as a "conspiracy against the people of Kashmir".[83] Its President Syed Faisal Nazki said that, "the Kashmiris considered the Gilgit-Baltistan package as an attempt to divide the motherland".[84] Former JKLF supremo Amanullah Khan also rejected the package. He said that it appeared to be aimed at merging the disputed areas into Pakistan. The President of Jammu and Kashmir National Awami Party, Liaquat Hayat said that the GBESGO is "nothing but a little joke to the people of the region and the state of Jammu and Kashmir".[85] The APNA Chapter of Gilgit-Baltistan called it as "illegal and unconstitutional."[86] In a letter addressed to the former prime minister of Pakistan, Yousaf Gilani, the Gilgit-Baltistan National Alliance (GBNA) Chairperson Malika Baltistani described the package as a "provincial status, a political system without political empowerment, a constitutional package without constitutional rights, a constitutional draft for Gilgit-Baltistan without the input or suggestions by Gilgitis and Baltis, and last but not the least, your government "awards" us a presence in the main-stream economic strata without representation in National Finance Commission (NFC) awards." Strongly criticizing the package, Manzoor Parwana Chairman of Gilgit-Baltistan United Movement demanded 'AJK' like independent assembly till the resolution of Kashmir issue.[87] In the same vein, Christopher Snedden elucidates:

> While the 2009 political system was long overdue advancement for people in GB, the Gilgit-Baltistan (empowerment and self-governance) Order 2009 appeared to assume that this region is already a part of Pakistan. This becomes clear when comparing the political systems of GB and Azad Kashmir. While similar in the sense that both regions have a Council that links them to Pakistan, the two regions political systems vary in some significant ways. First and foremost Islamabad used the Ministry of Kashmir Affairs and Northern Areas to impose the 'order' on GB. Conversely the Azad Kashmir

Legislative Assembly formerly passed the Azad Kashmir Interim Constitution in 1974, albeit after Islamabad 'authorised' its introduction into the Azad Kashmir Legislative Assembly for consideration and passage. Second like Azad Kashmiris, G-Baltistanis are G-Bians, as they call themselves are not permitted to propagate against or take part in activities prejudicial or detrimental to the ideology of Pakistan. However, unlike Azad Kashmiris, legislators in GB do not have to swear allegiance to J&K joining Pakistan. Rather, they must swear that they 'will remain loyal to Pakistan', and oath that (incorrectly) seems to infer that their regions status (as part of Pakistan) has already been resolved.[88]

Writing in *The Nation*, Brigadier (Retired) Samson Simon Sharaf, an expert on 'AJK' and Gilgit-Baltistan affairs, said that successive governments have done little to address the separatist and sub nationalist sentiments which are on the rise and warned, "With time, alienation will breed forces of secession and then it will be too late."[89]

Despite these backlashes, the Ministry of Kashmir Affairs and Northern Areas continued to play its cards. Commenting on the new changes made in the GBESGO, Pakistan-based commentators on 'AJK' and Gilgit-Baltistan put it succinctly:

> For the people of GB, it was clear that the ministry of Kashmir Affairs and Northern Areas would not provide any advice that would compromise its hold over power in GB. The ministry has been used directly or indirectly to curtail people's rights in GB; the status quo did not change despite Gilani's new laws. GB still cannot claim a share in the National Finance Commission (NFC) award, for example.[90]

There are also flaws in the GBESGO 2009. Gilgit-Baltistan Council member Amjad Hussain of the PPP pointed out discrimination against the region saying that the regional elected assembly cannot make laws on the council subjects such as tourism, minerals, power generation, forest and trade with foreign countries. Moreover, Amjad Hussain said that the region has not been given a share in the National Finance Commission. This is inspite of the fact that the federal government earns Rs. 40 billion annually from Gilgit-Baltistan resources. However, in return, Gilgit-Baltistan gets only Rs. 26 billion.[91]

India's Response

India made it clear that the entire state of Jammu and Kashmir, which includes the regions of Gilgit and Baltistan, is an integral part of India. The Indian Government took serious note to the GBESGO. It summoned the Deputy

High Commissioner of Pakistan, Riffat Masood, and registered a strong protest against the order. An Indian Government spokesman described the GBESGO as yet another cosmetic exercise intended to camouflage Pakistan's illegal occupation of the region.India also raised strong objections to Pakistan's plan of holding elections in Gilgit-Baltistan in June 2015. In a strong statement on June 2, 2015, the External Affairs spokesperson, Vikas Swarup, said the proposed election in Gilgit and Baltistan under the so-called 'GBESGO' is an attempt by Pakistan to camouflage its forcible and illegal occupation of the regions.[92]

However, during the back-channel discussions on Kashmir, Pakistan accepted Gilgit-Baltistan as part of Jammu and Kashmir. In his book titled, *Neither a Hawk or a Dove*, former Pakistani Foreign Minister Khurshid Mahmud Kasuri writes:

> During the back channel negotiations also, the Indians made it abundantly clear that they could only accept an agreement regarding J&K, if the Northern Areas were also included in the entire scheme. We confronted a dilemma.... We therefore reached an agreement after many arguments and negotiations that there would be two units for the purpose of the agreement...comprising the areas respectively controlled by India and Pakistan.[93]

Political Developments

The efforts to establish a viable political system in Gilgit-Baltistan have been stunted by rich and influential Pakistan-based political parties. In the run up to the June 8, 2015 Assembly elections, it was clear that a section of the locals resented the presence of Pakistan-based political parties; however, a few others saw it as an opportunity for Gilgit-Baltistan because of these parties' links to the powers that be in Islamabad. Further, the ban on political activities under the FCR made sure that the indigenous political parties did not emerge in Gilgit-Baltistan. Locals' support to various protest movements, nonetheless, is a signal that locals can establish their own political identity, even though the colonised identity of Gilgit-Baltistan puts a damper on these signs.

The first attempt to form a political party in this region was made by Colonel Mirza Hasan Khan, a local man. He writes in his book, *Shamsher se Zanjir Tak* ("From Sword to Chains"), "I came to Gilgit and formed the political party (Gilgit League) in 1956. The objective was to bring this desolate region on a political map but God and the government did not like it. Two years later (1958), General Ayub Khan imposed Martial Law in Pakistan and outlawed politicians and their political activities. Although, there was no Martial Law in AJK, it enforced the same restrictions there, as did in Pakistan."[94]

The Muslim Conference, which had been installed into power in 'AJK' in 1947 opened its branch in Gilgit in 1951, but was at once told to wind it up. The Gilgit League was the first political party established in the region, but was not registered under the Pakistani rules. During the 1960s an organisation called "Gilgit and Baltistan Jamhoori Mahaz" (Democratic Front) emerged, but became defunct in 1972. It made efforts to educate the local people to fight for their constitutional and democratic rights. In this connection, the party staged rallies and demonstrations against the policies of the Pakistan government. This organisation was able to persuade the 'AJK' Assembly to adopt a resolution to demand that Northern Areas be joined with 'AJK'.[95] Leader of the Jammu and Kashmir Liberation Front (JKLF), Amanullah Khan in his autobiography, *Jehad-e-Musalsal* ("Continuous Struggle") had given a brief account of the political parties which were formed in Gilgit-Baltistan after 1951, when the Muslim Conference had to wind its Gilgit chapter up. Apart from the Gilgit and Baltistan Jamhoori Mahaz, he mentioned that in 1963, Gilgit and Baltistan Students' Central Organisation was started by the students of this region studying in Karachi. Later, similar bodies were formed in 'AJK' and some other cities in Pakistan. This led to the formation of a central body in the name of Gilgit-Baltistan Students Central Organisation in 1968. It was disbanded in 1976.[96]

In 1971, a local leader Johar Ali Khan formed the Tanzeem Milli Party in Gilgit. It demanded the abolition of the princely states and a provincial status to the Northern Areas.[97] But this party soon merged with the PPP. Formation of a political party, which enjoys locals' full support, has become difficult after 1988 when the region was split on sectarian lines in the wake of military action to quell locals' agitations for civil rights. Consequently, intelligence agencies and jihadis swarmed the region.

It was in 1994 that the then Prime Minister of Pakistan, Benazir Bhutto, introduced political reforms for Gilgit-Baltistan and allowed party-based elections. As mentioned earlier, her government approved the Northern Areas Council Legal Framework Order (LFO) 1994 through the Northern Areas Rules of Business. As per the LFO, the first party-based elections to a 24-member NALC were held in October 1994. But the NALC did not enjoy legislative authority. As per the reforms, it had only limited advisory functions and no control over the executive.[98] The real power remained with the Ministry of Kashmir Affairs and Northern Areas headed by Joint Secretary who operated from Islamabad and yielded unlimited powers.

Unlike in 'AJK', there are no established regional parties in Gilgit-Baltistan.

There are small electorally ineffective local parties. People do not vote for the nationalist parties and cast their lot with the Pakistan-based parties. Among them, the PPP was the first to open a branch here in 1972. As is evidenced in the discussion above, besides, the PML-N, PML-Q, Tehreek-e-Insaf, JUI (F) and MQM have also opened their chapters in Gilgit-Baltistan.

Local Government Act 2014

In its efforts to empower the citizens to have a say in the region's development, the GBLA on August 18, 2014 unanimously passed the Local Government Act 2014. The Act promises to maximise benefits of self-governance to citizens at lowest tier and introduce local participatory and democratic decision-making processes by holding local government elections on the party basis and under a single ward electoral system. Moreover, it aims to encourage women's participations in local governments and ensure the effective transfer of power from the regional to the local government.[99]

Before this legislation, Gilgit-Baltistan was operating under the Punjab Local Government Ordinance of 1979. Its local governance system was based on two tiers: District Councils and Union Councils/Municipal Committees below them. The middle tier of *Tehsil* council was not included.[100] Under this new Act, urban areas such as Gilgit and Skardu have been named city metropolitan corporations to be headed by a mayor and deputy mayor, while district councils will be formed in all districts headed by a chairman and vice-chairman. According to the new law, a Gilgit-Baltistan Finance Council will be formed to supervise financial matters of local bodies. The council's representatives will be nominated by the leader of the opposition in the assembly, finance minister and local government minister.[101]

On April 18, 2016, elections for the GBC were held after five years. The council was established in May 2009 under Article 33 of the Empowerment and Self-Governance 2009 Order. According to the 2009 Order, the GBC is represented by six members each from the Gilgit-Baltistan and the federal governments. Out of six candidates, PML-N got four seats. Islami Tehreek Pakistan got one and one seat was grabbed by an independent candidate. The PML-N members in the GBC are, Ashraf Sada, Wazir Ikhlaq, Sultan Ali Khan and Arman Shah. Agha Syed Abbas Rizvi from Islami Tehreek was also elected. Syed Afzal from Diamer made it as an independent candidate.[102]

Sectarianism in Gilgit-Baltistan

Sectarianism in Gilgit-Baltistan has deep roots in history with religious, political and geo-strategic connotations. Two developments played an important role in the emergence of sectarianism in Pakistan. One was the 1979 Iranian Revolution and the other was the Islamisation project of Zia-ul-Haq. In order to stem the Iranian influence in the region, Saudi Arabia funded the anti-Shia madrassas, outfits and regimes. Pakistan became the battle ground for the Sunni-Shia proxy war played by Iran and Saudi Arabia. The Shia revolution in Iran spurred the Shias in Pakistan, and Gilgit-Baltistan in particular. Shias in Gilgit-Baltistan started demanding the curriculum – primarily seeking exemptions on the basis of their sectarian identity. They demanded curriculum and textbooks similar to that of Iran; started going to Iran in large numbers for pilgrimage and also joined madrassas.

The sectarian feud started with religious leaders criticising and demonising the other sects in Friday sermons and other religious gatherings. Initially, the sectarian violence was limited only to the Gilgit district. The first clash erupted in 1983, over a dispute on the sighting of the moon. The Shia community ended fasting and started celebrating Eid on the declaration of moon sighting by their religious leaders. On the other hand, Sunnis did not end fasting. This was a major breach as Muslims are not allowed to fast on the day of Eid. Tensions quickly erupted and resulted in a bloody skirmish between the two groups.

Sectarianism again erupted in May 1988 when the Shias in Gilgit protested against the Sunni-dominated administration for being lenient towards Sunni extremists. In retaliation, a religious militia from outside, in connivance with the state, massacred the Shias. The offensive was apparently triggered by rumours of a Sunnis massacre in Gilgit by Shias, "deliberately spread to provide an excuse for Sunni militants to conduct the attacks".[103] An eyewitness in an interview to the International Crisis Group (ICG) revealed, "The laskhar consisted of thousands of people from Mansehra, Chilas, Kohistan and other areas in NWFP. They had travelled a long distance to reach Gilgit, but the government did not stop them. No government force intervened even as killings and rapes were going on. Instead, the government put the blame on RAW [Research and Analysis Wing, India's intelligence agency], Iran and CIA [Central Intelligence Agency]."[104] This carnage against the Shias marked a watershed moment in the history of Gilgit-Baltistan. After this mayhem, Shias in Gilgit-Baltistan realised how vulnerable they were against well-organized and well-equipped Sunni militant groups. They started looking for help and Iran was a natural ally that could provide financial and material help.[105]

Further, on August 17, 1993, 20 people were killed in riots in Gilgit on the occasion of Zia's death anniversary, as Shias, who are in a majority there, felt threatened by the large influx of Sunnis from other provinces, particularly from Punjab and Khyber Pakhtunkhwa. On June 3, 2004, another sectarian clash ensued on curriculum grounds. Shias objected to the Islamiyat (Islamic Studies) syllabus, as they felt that the texts and images were presented in a strictly Sunni way.[106] When the controversy was not resolved, sectarian clashes erupted in Skardu.

Whenever the situation in the region gets out of hand, army is called in to control the situation. But clearly military intervention is not a long-term solution, and sectarian killings have not come to an end. From 1988 to 2010, 117 sectarian-related murder cases were recorded; 44 were recorded in 2011 alone.[107] Further, in 2012, just to mention three incidents: 18 Shias were killed on February 28 on the KKH in Kohistan district while returning from Iran; 20 people were killed in Chilas on April 3; and 100 people were killed in August while commuting between Islamabad and Gilgit.[108] However, since 2013, the region has seen some respite in sectarian and terrorist violence.

Analysing the impact of sectarianism in Gilgit-Baltistan, Izhar Hunzai aptly states, "The development over the past three decades have left underlying sectarian tensions in Gilgit-Baltistan to simmer and grow. People increasingly think in sectarian terms and perceive the so-called other as problematic."[109]

The Diamer Bhasha Dam

The decision to build Bhasha Dam was taken after Pakistan government had to abandon the construction of Kalabagh Dam in Punjab following opposition from Sind, Baluchistan and Khyber Pakhtunkhwa provinces. The decision was taken as Pakistan has been facing acute water and power shortage.

The Project: Basic Features

- Maximum Height: 272 m
- Type: Roller compacted concrete (RCC)
- Diversion System: Tunnels: 02, Canals: 01
- Cofferdam: Upstream and Downstream
- Main Spillway: Gates: 09
- Size: 16.5×15.0 m
- Reservoir Level: 1160 m
- Min Operation Level Elevation: 1060 m
- Gross Capacity: 7,300,000 acre feet (9.0 km3)
- Live Capacity: 6,400,000 acre feet (7.9 km3)
- Outlets: Intermediate Level: 8

- Low Level: 4
- Powerhouses: No. of Powerhouses: 2
- Total Installed Capacity: 4,500 MW
- Location of Powerhouses: one each on right and left side
- No. of Generator Units: 8
- Capacity/Unit: 560 MW

Estimated Cost: US$ 14 Billion (2013 Estimate)

Dam Purpose: Water storage, irrigation and power generation

Environmental impact

1. Villages affected: 31
2. Houses affected: 4,100
3. Population affected: 35,000
4. Agricultural land submerged: 1,500 acres
5. Area under reservoir: 25,000 acres (100 km)

Pakistan has been talking about constructing the Diamer-Bhasha Dam, also known as the Bhasha Dam, on the Indus River for over five decades. The project has seen little progress despite two ceremonies for laying the foundation stone. Instead it has been mired in one controversy after another.

The concept of Bhasha Dam has much to do with an advisory of the World Bank (WB) on how Pakistan could overcome its recurring energy crunch. The Bank even identified a site in 1967 to build a run-of-water project, located at Bhasha, about 165 km from Gilgit, and hence the name.

Technically, Bhasha Dam is proposed to be built in Gilgit-Baltistan, but it falls within a 10 km stretch of land in Diamer Valley, which is claimed by both Gilgit-Baltistan and Kohistan region of the Khyber-Pakhtunkhwa province. The row remains unresolved till date, though the disputed stretch is demarcated for dam acquisition.

In the 1980s, the Pakistan Government decided to go beyond the WB brief and build the Bhasha Dam with an irrigation component. The decision was prompted by energy crunch and the inability to build the Kalabagh Dam, which was proposed as the lifeline of Punjab.

A Canadian firm, Monenco, completed the first feasibility study in 1984. An international consortium of hydropower consultants comprising a US firm, MWH, among others, took a relook at the technical, economic, financial and environmental aspects in 2004. Lahmeyer International of Germany, the world's top-ranked hydropower firm, carried out a review of earlier reports in 2008, and prepared a detailed engineering design and bidding documents.

Accordingly, the Bhasha Dam is to be built as a gravity dam.[110] It will be the highest RCC structure in the world. Built to a height of about 272 m (892 ft), the dam with 14 gates (each of 11.5 m × 16.24 m) will impound 15 per cent of the annual flow of the Indus. The reservoir will be spread over 25,000 acres. It could provide irrigation for 4 million acres. Two underground power houses will be built, one on either side of the main dam with six turbines on each side, and a total installed capacity of 4500 MW.

Furthermore, the dam will result in the submergence of 30 villages, affecting 35,000 people. Also to be submerged is 100 km stretch of the Karakoram Highway that connects Pakistan and China, and forms a key component of the China-Pakistan Energy Corridor (CPEC).

The foundation stone for the project has been laid twice – in 2006 by then President Pervez Musharraf, and in 2011 by then Prime Minister Yousaf Raza Gilani of the Pakistan People's Party (PPP). The Nawaz Sharif government, which came to power in 2013, too, energetically pursued the Bhasha Dam.

The initial cost of the project was estimated at around $ 6.5 bn. By 2016, the cost increased to $ 14 bn. The Asian Development Bank (ADB), WB and US had evinced interest, but went back on their promise of funding the venture.

The WB's reluctance to fund Bhasha Dam is primarily on account of Gilgit-Baltistan being a disputed area between Pakistan and India. The Bank insisted on a No Objection Certificate (NOC)[111] from India. India on its part has also been questioning the project's legality, saying that it is being built on a disputed territory. Moreover, India has raised objections on building such a massive dam with an irrigation component.

The WB's assistance to Pakistan for the period 2015-2019, approved in May 2014 makes no mention of the Bhasha Dam.[112] As mentioned earlier, the ADB and the US, too, after raising hopes have so far decided not to fund the project either directly or indirectly

Pakistan has also turned to China, its all-weather friend, to make Bhasha Dam a part of the US$ 60 billion CPEC project. The core focus of the CPEC is energy and laying of oil and gas pipelines from Gwadar on the Balochistan coast to Xinjiang in western China. Bringing Bhasha Dam under the CPEC ambit would be a natural and logical step. However, Beijing has not taken the call yet.

In August 2008, media reports in Pakistan suggested that China would not only pay for the construction costs,[113] but also send thousands of workers from its Three Gorges Dam site to Pakistan to construct, if not to replicate

'Three Gorges', then at least the largest hydropower project ever built on Pakistani soil. However, on a visit to Islamabad in 2015, the Chinese President Xi Jinping agreed to fund and build a $ 1.65 billion, 720-megawatt hydropower plant in Karot in 'AJK', "as the first project for his $40 billion Silk Road fund to build infrastructure in Asia". He made no mention of the Bhasha project.[114] It was a clear signal that China's push to finance infrastructure in Pakistan is not a blank cheque, as Bloomberg reported on April 23, 2015.[115]

The then PML-N government projected Bhasha Dam as a vital project, as vital as its Nuclear Plan, and has decided to build the dam at any cost, according to Minister for Planning and Development Ahsan Iqbal. Not building the dam will have negative consequences for entire South Asia and beyond as it will threaten Pakistan's food security, he told an audience of US scholars and researchers at the International Food Policy Research Institute (IFPRI) in Washington on November 5, 2016.[116]

The National Economic Council (ECNEC) of Pakistan, the apex body on economic policy, had fixed 2016 as the deadline for completion of Bhasha Dam. It also sanctioned Rs 60 billion for land acquisition. The deadline has not been met, and the land acquisition has ended up in a stinking scandal.[117]

Challenges

Not one but several factors have contributed to the stalling of the Bhasha Dam. Its height is certainly an issue. Moreover, several leading Pakistani geologists are worried that the project site is an earthquake-prone area. The Director General of the Geological Survey of Pakistan (GSP), Dr. Imran Ahmad Khan told the Senate Standing Committee on Petroleum and Natural Resources in March 2013 that the dam should not be built on the present site. According to him, as many as eight severe earthquakes have hit this area, therefore, major reservoirs should not be constructed there. He cautioned that construction of water reservoirs like Bhasha Dam may result in another severe incident like the Attabad Lake case.[118]

According to a noted architect, Sameeta Ahmed, who was part of team that studied the project details in 2008, the dam structure is not capable of controlling large floods. In Ahmed's assessment, the dam is located in the seismically riskiest zone. An earthquake and consequent flooding might forever damage the Indus River bed at this precious location. Ahmed cautioned, "When such an incident will occur, we will not be able to count in dollars the losses incurred by the devastation."[119]

A former Chief Technical Advisor to the United Nations (UN) and WB,

Engineer Bashir A. Malik has echoed Sameeta Ahmed's reservations. In an appeal to the Chief Justice of Pakistan (on January 17, 2012), he pointed out that there is no RCC dam anywhere higher than 620 feet. RCC is relatively soft and vulnerable to cracks and leakage compared to conventional concrete structures.[120] Moreover, the dam site falls in an earthquake-prone area:[121] An earthquake of 7.6 magnitude shook the area on October 8, 2005. More recently, a powerful 7.1 magnitude quake with its epicentre in the Hindukush Mountains jolted many parts of Pakistan including 'AJK' on April 11, 2016.[122]

Bhasha Dam area is also known for massive avalanches and landslides. But according to experts, the Bhasha project report does not address the risk of reservoir-induced seismicity, which is primarily due to immense weight of water stored in a dam. It can trigger tremors, and can prove to be very disastrous. China realised this the hard way in 2008 when it was hit by a 7.8 magnitude earthquake. Geologists attribute the quake to 320 million tons of water stored behind the 511-feet high Zipingpu Dam near the city of Dujiangyan, Sichuan Province in southwest China. The risk from Bhasha will be much more than Zipingpu, as it is located in a very active seismic zone.

Land Scam

The process of acquiring land for Bhasha Dam started in 2010 after the government signed an agreement with the landowners. It was to be completed by December 31, 2013, but it was stalled due to delay in payment of compensation within the agreed time frame, according to the Gilgit-Baltistan Chief Secretary, Tahir Hussain.[123] The PML-N government, then in power, claimed in March 2016 that it had acquired 70 to 80 per cent of land required for the project.

According to reports, massive irregularities of over Rs 500 million have been allegedly committed by the bureaucracy, in connivance with revenue officials, during the distribution of land compensation for the Diamer-Bhasha Dam project.[124] Barren land was shown as being cultivable in Gilgit-Baltistan. Instead of benefiting the dam-affected people, the category of land was altered to benefit bureaucrats and political elites– from local tehsildar to top office holders in the federal ministry in Islamabad. An officer of the rank of Assistant Commissioner unearthed the scandal, put the loss to the exchequer at Rs 572.66 million, and reported this to his seniors on October 8, 2015. Instead of taking action against those responsible, the Assistant Commissioner was removed from his office. The scam has heightened the demand for heftier payout for the lands already taken over.[125]

Threat to Buddhist Heritage

Bhasha dam site is a treasure trove of Buddhist relics.[126] It is spread over 135 km of the reservoir, according to archaeologists. At least 1,000-1,500 different kinds of rock carvings, sculptures and statues have been found during the technical work, and the archaeology department expects huge consignment when full-fledged reservoir building is started.[127]

The dam also has been a victim of a long-standing discord between Thore Valley of Diamer district in Gilgit-Baltistan and Kohistan region of Khyber-Pakhtunkhwa province. On March 13, 2014, the Gilgit-Baltistan Assembly unanimously passed a resolution against Khyber-Pakhtunkhwa for encroaching on its land (the disputed 10 km stretch). The House called for the immediate settlement of the boundary dispute with Khyber-Pakhtunkhwa through a boundary commission. This has not happened, and regular flare-ups are continually reported.[128]

The people in Thore Valley forcibly stopped the work on December 10, 2015, to protest encroachment by Kohistan on their land. The move was in retaliation to a similar protest by the people of Harban in Kohistan, who had stopped the realignment of the Karakoram Highway at Shatial, near Chilas, Gilgit-Baltistan. A similar flare-up in 2014 ended in the death of seven persons.

By 2014, it became clear that the then Nawaz Sharif government had begun looking for alternatives to Bhasha Dam to tide over power shortage in Pakistan. This new quest brought the Dasu hydropower project to the fore. Dasu is in the Khyber-Pakhtunkhwa Province, and the project will tap the Indus waters.

The former Prime Minister Nawaz Sharif laid the foundation stone for the 4,320 MW venture on June 25, 2016.[129] It is a run-of-river hydropower project with a small reservoir. The 242 m (794 ft) tall dam is being funded by the WB (US$ 700 million), the Industrial and Commercial Bank of China (US$ 1.5 billion), Deutsche Bank (US$ one billion) and Agha Khan Development Network (US$ 500 Million). The first stage will cost US$ 4.278 billion, and is expected to be ready by March 2019.

ENDNOTES

1. For further detail regarding GBESGO 2009 see Appendix IX.
2. "Gilgit-Baltistan Divided into Three Divisions", *The Express Tribune*, February 1, 2012, at http://tribune.com.pk/story/330126/gilgit-baltistan-divided-into-three-divisions.
3. The notification of the creation of three new districts was made by the Ministry of Kashmir Affairs and Gilgit-Baltistan on July 24, 2015. Hunza-Nagar was bifurcated into two separate districts – Hunza and Nagar – besides the two new districts, Kharmang and Shigar. Shabir Mir, "Dividing Governance: Three New Districts Notified in G-B", *The Express Tribune,* July

26, 2015, at http://tribune.com.pk/story/926380/dividing-governance-new-districts-notified-in.
4. Projected in the 1998 Census for 2013. See: "Gilgit-Baltistan at a Glance 2013", issued by the Statistical Cell, Planning and Development Department, Government of Gilgit-Baltistan, at www.gilgitbaltistan.gov.pk/DownloadFiles/GBFinancilCurve.pdf.
5. Muhammad Amir Rana and Mujtaba Rathore, *Northern Areas: Crisis and Prospects*, Pakistan Institute for Peace Studies, Lahore, 2007, p. 8.
6. Ismailism, is an offshoot of Shiism. The Ismailis are also known as Sevener Shias, as opposed to the orthodox Twelver Shias. While Twelver Shias believe that the line of Imams ended with the 12th, Ismailis have, from Ismail onwards, been led by an uninterrupted chain of hereditary Imams, with the current Agha Khan, Prince Karim, the spiritual leader of the world's Ismailis, the 49th in that chain. The Noorbakshi movement originated in the 15th century in Iran and Central Asia as a mystical, messianic order founded by Muhammad Noorbaksh, and Noorbakshis are presently found in parts of India and Pakistan. See: International Crisis Group (ICG), *Discord in Pakistan's Northern Areas*, Asia Report No. 131, Islamabad/Brussels, April 2, 2007.
7. Omar Farooq Zain, "A Socio-Political Study of Gilgit-Baltistan Province", *Pakistan Journal of Social Sciences*, 30 (1), September 2010, pp. 181-190, atwww.bzu.edu.pk/pjss/vol30no12010/final_pjss-3116.pdf.
8. Samuel Baid, "Suppression of Gilgit-Baltistan", in Virendra Gupta and AlokBansal (eds.), *Pakistan Occupied Kashmir: The Untold Story*, Manas Publications, New Delhi, 2007, p. 151.
9. Muhammad Amir Rana and Mujtaba Rathore, *Northern Areas: Crisis and Prospects*, p. 7.
10. Syed Waqas Ali and Taqi Akhunzada, "Unheard Voices: engaging youth of Gilgit-Baltistan", *Conciliating Resources*, London, January 2015, pp. 16-17, at www.c-r.org.download/cr%2020 Unheard/2020Voices%.20from%20Himalyas.pdf,
11. "Gilgit-Baltistan at a Glance 2013".
12. Syed Waqas Ali and Taqi Akhunzada, "Unheard Voices: engaging youth of Gilgit-Baltistan", p. 17.
13. Ibid.
14. "Gilgit-Baltistan at a Glance 2013".
15. Muhammad Amir Rana and Mujtaba Rathore, *Northern Areas: Crisis and Prospects*, Pakistan, p. 56.
16. "Gilgit-Baltistan at a Glance 2013".
17. Shabbir Mir, "Unfair Tax Imposition in G-B", *The Express Tribune*, January 2, 2018, at http://tribune.com.pk/story/1598123/6-unfair-tax-imposition-g-b/)
18. Ibid.
19. The Northern Light Infantry, which was picked up for the task of intrusion of heights of Kargil, comprises special troops, trained in anti-heliborne, commando operations and snow warfare. Some of these soldiers are sent on deputation to the Special Service Group (SSG). See: *Indian Defence Review*, 14 (3), July-September 1999.
20. Shafqat Inqalabi, "Economic exploitation of Gilgit-Baltistan", in Virendra Gupta and Alok Bansal (eds.), *Pakistan Occupied Kashmir : The Untold Story*, p. 192
21. "Pakistan: Economic Transformation Initiative-Gilgit-Baltistan", *IFAD*,EB 2015/114/r.14/rEV.1, April, 2015, at http://webapps.ifad.org/members/eb/114/docs/EB-2015-114-R-14-Rev-1pdf.
22. Shahzad Anwar, "Logging; G-B Stripped of More than 50% Forest Cover", *The Express Tribune*, January 25, 2015, at http://tribune.com.pk/story/827168/logging-g-b-stripped-of-more-than-50-forest-cover.
23. Omar Farooq Zain, "A Socio-Political Study of Gilgit-Baltistan Province" pp. 181-190,

24. Muhammad Amir Rana and Mujtaba Rathore, *Northern Areas: Crisis and Prospects*, p. 57
25. Raees Kamil, "Real Threat to Mineral Industry in Gilgit-Baltistan", *Gilgit-Baltistan Times*, July 10, 2011, at http://gbtimes.wordpress.com/2011/07/20/opinion-real-threat-to-mineral-industry-in-gilgit-baltistan/.
26. Ibid.
27. Ibid.
28. Senge Hasnan Sering, Chinese Mining Companies make Inroads into Gilgit's Mineral-rich Region, *The Economic Times*, June 30, 2011, at http://economictimes.indiatimes.com/industry/indl-goods/svs/metals-mining/chinese-mining-comapnies-make-inroads-into-gilgit-mineral-rich-region/
29. "Memo signed to initiate China-Pakistan Highway Renovation", CHINA.ORG.CN July 9, 2006 at http://www.china.org.en/english/2006/jul/174098.htm
30. "China, Pakistan to renovate Karakoram Highway", *The Hindu*, July 11.2006 at http://www.thehindu.com/todays-paper/tp/international/china-pakistan-to-ren
31. "Gilgit-Baltistan at a Glance 2013" at www.gilgitbaltistan.gov.pk
32. "Record 1.72 million tourists visit Gilgit-Baltistan in past 11 months", *Pamir Times*, November 29, 2017, at http://http://pamirtimes.net/2017/11/29/1-72-million-tourists-visit-gilgit-baltistan/)
33. "Gilgit-Baltistan government to boost tourism", *The Nation*, April 28, 2017, at http://nation.com.pk/28-apr-2017/gilgit-baltistan-government-to boost-tourism)
34. F.M. Khan, *The Story of Gilgit, Baltistan and Chitral: A Short History of Two Millenniums AD 7-1999*, Eejaz, Gilgit, 2002, p. 7. The word "Dard" was first used by Dr. G.W. Leitner in his book, *The Language and Races of Dardistan*, in 1887 citing evidence from Western classical sources. However, F. M Khan rejected his claim which he said was without the support of historical facts.
35. F.M. Khan, *The Story of Gilgit, Baltistan and Chitral: A Short History of Two Millenniums AD 7-1999*, p. 28.
36. P. Stobdan, "North-West under the Maharaja", in Jasjit Singh (ed.), Pakistan Occupied Kashmir: Under the Jackboot, Siddhi Books, New Delhi, 1995,p. 30.
37. Alok Bansal, "Gilgit-Baltistan: An Appraisal", Manekshaw Paper No. 37, 2013, cited in Mushtaquar Rahman, *Divided Kashmir: Old Problems, New Opportunities for India, Pakistan and the Kashmiri People*, Lynne Rienner Publishers Inc., London, 1996, p. 10.
38. F.M. Hassnain, *Gilgit: The Northern Gate of India*, Sterling Publishers, India, p.150
39. International Crisis Group, "Discord in Pakistan's Northern Areas", Asia Report No 31, April 2007, p. 3, at http://www.crisisgroup.org/home/index.
40. F.M. Khan, *The Story of Gilgit, Baltistan and Chitral: A Short History of Two Millenniums AD 7-1999*, pp. 41-43.
41. N.N. Raina, *Kashmir Politics and Imperialist Manoeuvres 1846-1980*, Patriot Publishers, New Delhi, 1988, p. 29.
42. Ahmad Hasan Dani, *History of the Northern Areas of Pakistan*, Sang-e-Meel Publication, Lahore, 2001,p.294). Accordingly the *Wazarat* of the Gilgit Province was also put under the charge of Viceroy and Governor General of India.
43. F.M. Hassnain, *Gilgit: The Northern Gate of India*, p.150
44. Ibid., p. 157.
45. Ahmad Hasan Dani, *History of Northern Areas of Pakistan*, Sang-e-Meel Publications, 2001, pp 348-349.
46. P. Stobdan, "Gilgit and Baltistan: The Historical Dimension", p. 44.
47. Ahmad Hasan Dani, *History of Northern Areas of Pakistan*, 2001, pp. 348-349.

48. "The Gilgit Rebellion 1947", *Hunza Development Forum*, February 7, 2011, at http://hisamullahbeg.blogspot.com/2010/12/gilgit-rebellion-1947-by-william-brown.html.
49. The signatories of the Karachi Agreement were Sardar Mohammad Ibrahim Khan, the PoK President, Mushtaq Ahmed Gurmani, Minister without Portfolio in the Pakistan Government who was former Prime Minister of the State of Bahawalpur; and Choudhry Ghulam Abbas, a representative from the Muslim Conference.
50. Text of the Karachi Agreement of April 1949 is given in Appendix II.
51. K Warikoo, *Himalayan Frontiers of India: Historical, Geo-Political and Strategic Perspectives*, Routledge, 2009, p. 73.
52. International Crisis Group, *Discord in Pakistan's Northern Areas*, p.5
53. Ibid., p.5
54. Ibid., p.6
55. Samuel Baid, "Suppression of Gilgit-Baltistan", p. 145.
56. Khalid Hussain, "Northern Areas Demystified", *The Friday Times*, April 25 -May 1, 2003
57. Excerpts of High Court Judgement, cited in Samuel Baid, "Northern Areas", in Jasjit Singh (ed.), *Pakistan Occupied Kashmir: Under the Jackboot*, pp. 147-67.
58. "History & Dispute", *Gilgit-Baltistan Tribune*, at http://gbtribune.blogspot.in/p/history-dispute.html.
59. The Northern Areas Council Framework Order-1994 at Appendix VIII.
60. International Crisis Group, *Discord in Pakistan's Northern Areas*, p. 12.
61. "Al-Jehad Trust vs Federation of Pakistan", *Supreme Court Monthly Review*, 1999, p. 1380, athttp://cmsdata.iucn.org.
62. Syed Waqas Ali and Taqi Akhunza, "Unheard Voices: Engaging Youth of Gilgit-Baltistan", p. 7.
63. "With Friends Like These: Human Rights Violations in Azad Kashmir", Human Rights Watch, 18(12)(C), September 2006, p. 7, at www.hrw.org/sites/default/files/reports/pakistan0906 webwcover_0.pdf
64. "On Kashmir Present Situation and Future Prospects", *European Parliament Report 2004-2009*, April 25, 2007, p. 11, at www.europarl.europa.eu/sides/getDoc.do?pubRef=-//EP//NONSGML+REPORT+A6-2007-0158+0+DOC+PDF+VO//EN.
65. International Crisis Group, *Discord in Pakistan's Northern Areas*, p. 11.
66. Ibid., p. 12.
67. Syed Waqas Ali and Taqi Akhunza, "Unheard Voices: Engaging Youth of Gilgit-Baltistan", pp. 1-24.
68. See text of the Gilgit-Baltistan Empowerment and Self–Governance Order 2009. See Appendix IX.
69. See Chief Election Commission of Secretariat - Gilgit-Baltistan, at http://ecgb.gov.pk/elec09.htm
70. Altaf Hussain, The Gilgit-Baltistan Reforms 2009, Forum of Federations Project, Pakistan, funded by the German Ministry of Foreign Affairs, December 2009 pp. 1-19, at http://gbpolicyinstitute.org/wp-content/uploads/Gilgit-Baltistan%20Reforms%20 AHussain%20 FinalDec09.pdf
71. Ibid.
72. Samuel Baid, "Debating Gilgit-Baltistan elections".
73. Ershad Mahmud, "The Battle for Gilgit-Baltistan", *Outpost,* June 7, 2015, at http://outpost.pk/gilgit-baltistan/452-the battle-for-gilgit-baltistan.html
74. S.K. Sharma, "Gilgit-Baltistan Goes to Polls on June 8 under Pak Army Care", *Business Standard,* June 7, 2015, at www.business-standard.com/article/printer-friendly-version?article_id=115060700705_1

75. Amir Wasim, "Minister made GB governor ahead of crucial polls", *The Dawn*, February 15, 2015, at http://www.dawn.com/news/1163731/minister-made-gb-governor-ahead-of-crucial-polls
76. Comments of Islamabad-based expert on 'AJK' and Gilgit-Baltistan, Ershad Mahmud to authors query on June 15, 2015. Some reports put as 618,364 registered voters in the region with 329,475 men and 288,889 women
77. Shabbir Mir, "33 Members of G-B Assembly Take Oath", *The Express Tribune*, June 25, 2015, at http://tribune.com.pk/story/909186/maiden-session-33-members-of-g-b-assembly-take-oath/
78. "Nationalists protest 'mock polls' in Gilgit-Baltistan, *Dawn*, November 13, 2009, at http://www.dawn.com/news/943158/nationalists-protest-mock-polls-in-Gilgit-Baltistan
79. Shabir Choudhry, "Sham Elections in Gilgit-Baltistan", *Kashmir Images*, June 8, 2015, at http://www.dailykashmirimages.com/news-sham- elections-in-gilgit-baltistan/
80. Section 33(2) of the 2009 Order
81. "The Case of Gilgit-Baltistan", *Pakistan Today*, June 8, 2015, at http://www.pakistantoday.com.pk/2015/06/08/comment/the-case-of-gilgit-baltistan
82. Altaf Hussain, The Gilgit-Baltistan Reforms 2009, pp. 1-19.
83. "JKLF protests against Gilgit Baltistan package", September 12, 2009 at http://www.dawn.com/news/490223/jklf-protests-against-gilgit-baltistan-package/
84. Ibid
85. "Pakistan's Ordinance Giving Internal Political Autonomy to Northern Jammu Kashmir Means Little", *Huffington Post*, at www.huffingtonpost.com/northern.region/pakistans-ordiance-given-to-279953.ht
86. "APNA rejects Gilgit-Baltistan reforms package", at, http://www.thefreelibrary.com/APNA+rejects+Gilgit+Baltistan+reforms+package
87. "Identity, Diversity and Kashmiriyat in South Asia", September 7, 2009 at http://www.greaterkashmir.com/news/gk-magazine/identity-diversity-andkashmiriyat-in-south-asia
88. Christopher Snedden, *Understanding Kashmir and Kashmiris*, Hurst & Company, London: 2015, pp. 221-22.
89. Samson Simon Sharaf, "Gilgit-Baltistan", *The Nation*, February 14, 2015, at http://nation.com.pk/columns/14-Feb-2015/gilgit-baltistan.
90. Zulfiqar Ali, Tariq Naqash and Jamil Nagri, "'Almost' Pakistan: Gilgit-Baltistan in a constitutional Limbo", *The Dawn*, August 9, 2015, at http://www.dawn.com/news/1198967/almost-pakistan-gilgit-baltistan-in-constituional-limbo.
91. Jamil Nagri, "The GB Council failed to play its due role", *The Dawn*, December 9, 2014, http://www.www.dawn.com/news/1149680/sound-bytes-the-gb-council-failed-to-play-due-role
92. "Official Spokesperson's response to a media question on elections which are to be held in Gilgit-Baltistan on June 8, 2015", Ministry of External Affairs, June 02, 2015, at http://www.mea.gov.in/media-briefings.htm?dtl/25307/Official_Spokespersons_ response_ to_ a_ media_question_on_election_on_elections_which-are-to_be_held_in-June.
93. Khurshid Mahmud Kasuri, *Neither a Hawk nor a Dove*, Penguin, India, 2015, pp. 339-41.
94. Colonel Mirza Hasan Khan, *Shamsher se Janjir Tak*, Romi Tral, Rawalpindi, 2002, p. 386.
95. "Northern Areas of Pakistan – Facts, Problems and Recommendations", *Policy Perspectives*, 1 (1), Institute of Policy Studies, Islamabad. at, www.ips.org.pk/northern-areas-of-pakistan-facts-problems-and-recommendations
96. Samuel Baid, "Northern Areas", Jasjit Singh (ed.), *Pakistan occupied Kashmir under the Jackboot*, Siddhi Books, New Delhi, 1995, pp. 135-137.

97. Quoted in "What Is Wrong in the Northern Areas", *Human Rights Commission of Pakistan – Newsletter*, Quarterly January, 1994.
98. International Crisis Group, *Discord in Pakistan's Northern Areas*, p. 9
99. For details, see: "Gilgit-Baltistan Legislative Assembly Passes Local Government Act 2014", United Nations Development Programme, August 18, 2014, at http://www.pk.undp.org/content/pakistan/en/home/presscentre/articles
100. Ibid.
101. Ibid.
102. "Gilgit-Baltistan Council: PML-N Bags Four Seats", *The Express Tribune,* April 19, 2016, at http://tribune.com.pk/story/1087330/gilgit-baltistan-council-pml-n-bags-four-seats.
103. Izhar Hunzai, *Conflict Dynamics in Gilgit-Baltistan*, United States Institute of Peace, Special Report 321, January 2013, p. 5.
104. International Crisis Group, *The State of Sectarianism in Pakistan*, Asia Report No. 95, April 18, 2005, p. 19. at, http://www.files.ethz.ch/isn/28410/095_the_state-of-sectarianism_in-pakistan.pdf
105. Ibid., p. 6.
106. Georg Stober, "Religious Identities Provoked: The Gilgit 'Textbook Controversy' and its Conflictual Context", *International Schulbuchforschung*, 29, 2007, p. 390.
107. "At Least 20 Shias pulled off Bus, Shot Dead in Northern Pakistan", *Dawn*, August 16, 2012, at www.dawn.com/2012/08/16/several-forced-off-buses-killed-in-northern-pakistan.
108. "Pakistan Shias Killed in Gilgit Sectarian Attack", BBC, August 2012, at www.bbc.com/news/world-asia-19280339.
109. Izhar Hunzai, *Conflict Dynamics in Gilgit-Baltistan*, p. 7.
110. Diamer-Bhasha Dam in Pakistan: Report from a Field Trip, Prepared by Sustainable Development Policy Institute for International Rivers, October 5, 2008, at https://www.internationalrivers.org/files/attached-files/bhasha_fact_finding_october_2008_final.pdf.
111. Zafar Bhutta, "Uncertainty Prevails: Lenders Seek Guarantees before Funding Bhasha Dam", *The Express Tribune,* Islamabad, July 5, 2013, at http://tribune.com.pk/story/572609/uncertainty-prevails-lenders-seek-guarantees-before-funding-bhasha-dam/; Imran Ali Kundi, "No World Bank Funds for Bhasha Dam Project", *The Nation,* Islamabad, May 3, 2014, at http://nation.com.pk/editors-picks/03-May-2014/no-world-bank-funds-for-bhasha-dam-project, Munawar Hasan, "Bhasha Dam Delayed till 2037", *The News,* Lahore, July 9, 2014, at http://www.thenews.com.pk/Todays-News-13-31478-Bhasha-Dam-delayed-till-2037.
112. Khaleeq Kiani, "World Bank Approves $12bn Loans", *The Dawn,* Islamabad, May 3, 2014, at http://www.dawn.com/news/1103851/world-bank-approves-12bn-loans.
113. Kamran Haider and Natalie Obiko Pearson, "Even China Won't Finance This Dam as Water Fight Looms", *Bloomberg,* April 23, 2015, at http://www.bloomberg.com/news/articles/2015-04-22/even-china-won-t-finance-this-pakistan-dam-as-water-fight-looms, "Diamer-Bhasha Dam", *International Rivers,* at http://www.internationalrivers.org/campaigns/diamer-bhasha-dam
114. Ibid.
115. Ibid.
116. Anwar Iqbal, "Bhasha Dam as Vital as N-plan: Minister", *The Dawn*, Washington, November 6, 2013, at http://www.dawn.com/news/1054454
117. Peer Muhammad, "Diamer-Bhasha Land Compensation: Irregularities Worth over Rs 500m Allegedly Committed", *The Express Tribune,* Islamabad, January 14, 2016, at http://tribune.com.pk/story/1027079/diamer-bhasha-land-compensation-irregularities-worth-over-rs500m-allegedly-committed/, Javed Mahmood, "Mega Dam & Mega Scam-Bhasha Dam",

Weekly Corporate Ambassador, Islamabad, September 13, 2015, at https://weeklycorporateambassador.wordpress.com/2015/09/13/mega-dam-mega-scam-_-bhasha-dam-2/

118. Alize Ahmed, "Geological Survey: Bhasha Dam Is in Dangerous Condition", *Aaj TV*, March 27, 2013, at http://aaj.tv/2013/03/geological-survey-bhasha-dam-is-in-dangerous-condition/
119. Sameeta Ahmed, "Diamer-Bhasha Dam: A Perspective", *The Dawn*, October 27, 2011, at http://www.dawn.com/news/669137/diamer-bhasha-dam-a-perspective
120. Diamer Dam Site Prone to Seismic Hazards': WB Chief Technical Advisor", *Pamir Times*, Islamabad, January 21, 2012, at http://pamirtimes.net/2012/01/21/diamer-dam-site-prone-to-seismic-hazards-wb-chief-technical-advisor/
121. Zafar Bhutta, "Diamer Bhasha Dam, Gwadar Port in Quake-Prone Zone", *The Express Tribune*, Islamabad, March 27, 2013, at http://tribune.com.pk/story/526826/diamer-bhasha-dam-gwadar-port-in-quake-prone-zone/.
122. "Earthquake in Pakistan: 6 Killed as Strong 7.1 Temblor Hits Islamabad, Khyber, Punjab; at least 28 Injured", *The Financial Express*, Islamabad, April 11, 2016, at http://www.financialexpress.com/article/world-news/earthquake-in-pakistan-6-killed-as-powerful-7-1-quake-rocks-islamabad-khyber-punjab-gilgit-baltistan/234869/
123. Shahzad Anwar, "Diamer-Bhasha Dam: 70-80% of Land Acquired, Remaining to be Bought Soon", at *The Express Tribune*, Islamabad, February 11, 2016, at http://tribune.com.pk/story/1044177/diamer-bhasha-dam-70-80-of-land-acquired-remaining-to-be-bought-soon/
124. Peer Muhammad, "Diamer-Bhasha Land Compensation: Irregularities Worth over Rs 500m Allegedly Committed".
125. Peer Muhammad, "Diamer-Bhasha Project: Heftier Payouts Offered to Residents Displaced by Dam", *The Express Tribune*, Islamabad, February 23, 2015, at http://tribune.com.pk/story/842669/diamer-bhasha-project-heftier-payouts-offered-to-residents-displaced-by-dam/
126. Murtaza Razvi, "Bhasha Dam and Heritage Sites", Dawn, November 1, 2011, at http://www.dawn.com/news/670721/bhasha-dam-and-heritage-sites, "Buddha Relics Found at Bhasha Dam Site", *Pak Tribune Islamabad*, April 4, 2008, at http://paktribune.com/news/Buddha-relics-found-at-Bhasha-dam-site-199138.html
127. Zafar Bhutta, "Diamer-Bhasha Project: Rock Carvings at Dam Site to be Preserved", *The Express Tribune*, Islamabad, August 23, 2013, at http://tribune.com.pk/story/594107/diamer-bhasha-project-rock-carvings-at-dam-site-to-be-preserved/.
128. Shabbir Mir, "Over 10 Feet of Land: Locals in Thore Valley Stop Construction on Bhasha Dam", *The Express Tribune*, Gilgit, December 11, 2015, http://tribune.com.pk/story/1007876/over-10-feet-of-land-locals-in-thore-valley-stop-construction-on-bhasha-dam/
129. "PM Lays Foundation Stone of Dasu Project", *Radio Pakistan*, at http://www.radio.gov.pk/25-Jun-2014/pm-lays-foundation-stone-of-dasu-power-project

4

Political Parties in Gilgit-Baltistan

There are 14 registered parties in Gilgit-Baltistan (see Appendix XI). In addition, there are many unregistered parties/groups which cannot take part in elections but they can put pressure on the government. Details of these parties/groups have also been given in this chapter.

PAKISTAN PEOPLE'S PARTY GILGIT-BALTISTAN (PPP-GB)

Introduction

The Pakistan People's Party Gilgit-Baltistan (PPP-GB) was formed in 1972. Its first President was Sheikh Ghulam Muhammad from Skardu. However, it was during Zulfiqar Ali Bhutto's time that the PPP was able to establish its stronghold in the region. In 1974, Bhutto introduced some welfare projects in the region by announcing an administrative and judicial reforms package, which included abolishing the Frontier Crime Regulation (FCR). A 14-member advisory council for Gilgit-Baltistan was set up for the governance of the area.[1] Later, Benazir Bhutto ensured the creation of the Northern Areas Legislative Council in 1994. Consequently, The PPP-GB participated in the first ever party-based elections in 1994, and later contested the 1999 and 2004 elections, too.

In 2009, when the PPP was again in power in Pakistan, the Gilgit-Baltistan Empowerment and Self-Governance Order (GBESGO 2009) was passed. Under this order, the people of Gilgit-Baltistan could elect their Legislative Assembly and Council. After winning the Legislative Assembly elections in November 2009, under the new Order, the PPP-GB elected Mehdi Shah as Chief Minister. (The party had fielded 23 candidates, of which it won 14 seats.) It formed a coalition government with the Pakistan Muslim League-Quaid-e-Azam

(PML-Q), Jamiat Ulema-e-Islam-Fazl (JUI-F), and the Muttahida Qaumi Movement (MQM). According to an International Crisis Group (ICG) report, "PPP has strong support partly because of Zulfiqar Ali Bhutto's reforms but also because the region's Shias and Ismailis view the centre-left party as more sympathetic to minority concerns than other mainstream Pakistani parties."[2]

Ideology/Objectives

The PPP has been a popular party in Gilgit-Baltistan, and has enjoyed a good representation in the Northern Areas Council. Its principal stand has two aspects: (i) the government can restore the rights of the people without damaging the cause of Kashmir, and (ii) it should act according to the spirit of the 1999 Supreme Court decision, which directed the Government of Pakistan to ensure the provision of equal rights to the people of Gilgit-Baltistan within six months.[3] The party promised to achieve the following objectives in its election manifesto for the June 8, 2015 elections:[4]

(1) To further enhance the autonomy and ensure the constitutional rights of the people of Gilgit-Baltistan.
(2) To further strengthen the local structure in order to enhance the people's participation in governance at the grass-roots level. In this connection, the Gilgit-Baltistan Government has already passed a Local Government Act in 2014 during the PPP regime.
(3) To facilitate fiscal and political devaluation allowing the people greater command over financial resources and ownership in local governance. In this connection, the party will set up a Gilgit Baltistan Tax Commission.
(4) To devise a medium-term development plan in the region: a planning and development department will be set up.
(5) To ensure fiscal autonomy by giving the people of Gilgit-Baltistan greater control over revenues generated within the area. The share of Gilgit-Baltistan from the federal revenue of Pakistan will be increased. The party will make Chief Minister of Gilgit-Baltistan to be the Vice Chairman of the Gilgit-Baltistan Council. Presently, the Gilgit-Baltistan Council is headed by the Prime Minister of Pakistan.
(6) To increase and strengthen the special police force.
(7) To provide employment opportunities for youth under a special development package for Gilgit-Baltistan.
(8) To set up a ministry of youth affairs on the lines of other provinces.
(9) To set up a medical college each in Gilgit and Skardu, besides setting up an information technology university.

(10) To set up special economic zones and export processing zones with substantial incentives for the people of Gilgit-Baltistan in the vicinity of the Pakistan-China Economic Corridor in order to boost local production and enhance the export of local products to China and Central Asia.

(11) To set up a special Gilgit-Baltistan-Xinjiang trade authority with bilateral participation and the representation of the private sector in order to promote border trade.

Organisation, Structure and Leadership

A committee headed by Amjad Hussain Advocate as the Provincial President looks after the party affairs. Other office bearers of the party are Engineer Mohammad Ismail (Provincial General Secretary), Jamil Ahmad (Provincial Senior Vice President), Imran Nadeem (Vice President) Zafar Iqbal (Vice President) Bashit Ahmad (Vice President) Attique Ahmad (Deputy General Secretary), Sania Danish (Secretary Information) and Sayed Jafar Shah as the Central Executive Member of the Central Executive Committee of the PPP.[5]

Cadre Strength and Funding

The post-1970s reforms allowed the party to establish strong bases in all districts. The party did not face a shortage of funds as it was in power both at the centre and the Gilgit-Baltistan region.

Network and Area of Influence

The party traditionally had a strong vote bank in Gilgit-Baltistan. However, because of its poor performance, it was convincingly voted out of power in the elections in June 2015.

Links and Alliances with other Political Parties

As mentioned earlier, the PPP-GB won a two-thirds majority in the 2009 elections, but still forged an alliance with the PML-Q, JUI-F and MQM. Even though part of the government, the PML-Q did not miss a chance to criticize the functioning of the government. During the 35th session of the GB Assembly, PML-Q lawmaker, Mirza Hussain termed the PPP-GB government and its ministers "corrupt", saying they "plundered national wealth during their years in power".[6] Upset by these remarks, the Chief Minister, Mehdi Shah, terminated PPP-GB's alliance with the PML-Q, calling the Muslim League's members "snakes in the grass".[7] However, the differences between the two alliances were sorted out.

Current Status

There is no doubt that most of the administrative reforms were made by the PPP in 1974, 1988, 1994 and 2009 when the party was in power. The PPP has deep roots in local politics as it is sole champion of problems of the locals. The local wing of PPP fielded 22 candidates in the June 2015 Assembly polls, but received a big jolt as it won only one seat. Even the former Chief Minister, Syed Mehdi Shah, his five ministers and former Deputy Speaker, Jamil Ahmed, were defeated. The defeat was ascribed to the anti-incumbency factor, internal party feuds and poor performance in the 2013 national elections. Ershad Mahmud, an Islamabad-based expert on region, puts the blame on the PPP local leadership that never cared for the party: "Mehdi Shah spent most of his time in the luxurious Gilgit-Baltistan House in Islamabad on the tax payers' money."[8] Moreover, he and his government cheated the people by selling government jobs.[9] Mehdi Shah washed his hands from of any responsibility by blaming the top leadership at the centre for not consulting them in making the decisions about the region. According to Ershad Mahmud, the PPP "introduced constitutional and administrative reforms but kept several major flaws in the Gilgit-Baltistan Empowerment and Self Governance Order 2009 which still haunt the people of this region".[10] Similar views were expressed by civil society and human right organisations who opined that some more concrete steps like changing and amendments in the constitution of Pakistan to include the area as its constitutional part was needed.[11]

PAKISTAN PEOPLE'S PARTY SHAHEED BHUTTO

Introduction

Pakistan People's Party Shaheed Bhutto, which was formed by Z.A. Bhutto's daughter-in-law, Ghinwa in 1997, one of PPP's breakaway factions, the PPP Shaheed Bhutto, led Murtaza Bhutto's widow, Ghinwa Bhutto, opened its chapter in Gilgit-Baltistan. It is however not popular among the local population. Its leaders are: Muhammad Abbas Safeer Advocate, President; Muhammad Faheem Wazir Advocate, General Secretary; Mustafa Abbas Akhondi, Information Secretary; and Azhar Ali Advocate, Financial Secretary.[12]

PAKISTAN MUSLIM LEAGUE-NAWAZ-GB (PMLN-GB)

Introduction

The PML-N opened its chapter in Gilgit Baltistan in 1994 with Saifur Rehman as its first President. It has played an active role in the electoral politics of Gilgit

Baltistan. The party contested the Northern Areas Legislative Council (NALC) elections in 1994, but was not able to secure any seat. It, however, won two seats in the NALC elections held in 2004. The PMLN-GB contested 15 seats in the Legislative Assembly elections held under the Gilgit Baltistan Empowerment and Self-Governance Order 2009 in November 2009 but won only two seats. It increased its tally to four after winning the two by-elections held in Ghanche and Skardu constituencies in 2013. In the elections held in June 2015, it emerged as largest party, winning 16 out of the 24 seats.

Ideology/Objectives

The PMLN-GB has welcomed the approval of self-governance for Gilgit-Baltistan saying the party would support every step which aims at bringing the people of this area into the mainstream. The party wants that the people of this area should be given resources to improve infrastructure and the social sector, and that a university should be set up for students to get higher education.[13]

Releasing the party Manifesto for the June 2015 elections, PMLN-GB regional head, Hafiz Hafeezur Rehman, said that the creation of employment opportunities, improving infrastructure and governance and putting an end to corruption were some of the key priorities of his party. In addition, the party will give greater attention to tourism which is the mainstay of the region's economy.[14] Anticipating a PMLN-GB victory, a dozen senior leaders of the PPP-GB, PTI-GB and other parties switched over their loyalties.

Organisation, Structure and Leadership

On the lines of setting up Provincial Councils (PCs) in all the provinces, the PMLN-GB has set up a council of 100 members for the Gilgit-Baltistan region as well.[15] The PC is headed by Hafiz Hafeezur Rehman, who was elected as Chief Minister of GB in 2015. He is the brother of Saifur Rehman, the first President, who was assassinated outside his home in Gilgit city in 2003. Hafiz Hafeezur Rehman has been closely associated with Nawaz Sharif to whom he remained loyal when majority of the party leaders deserted him and joined the PMLQ-GB which was formed with the blessing of the then military dictator, Gen. Musharraf, who had over thrown Sharif's government and forced him into exile in 2000. According to Ershad Mahmud, the PMLN-GB had never been a ruling party in Gilgit-Baltistan before the 2015 elections but made inroads due to dynamic leadership of its regional president Hafeezur Rehman who did not betray his party inspite of the pressure put by the former president

Gen. Musharraf. Another reason went in its favour was the support of G-B students by increasing their quota in institutions in Punjab.

Other office bearers include Haji Muhammad Akbar Taban (Provincial General Secretary), Ghulam Muhammad (Provincial Senior Vice President), Hayat Baig (Provincial Senior Vice President), Jafarullah Khan (Deputy General Secretary), Ibrahim Sanai (Provincial Senior Vice President), Col. (Retd.) Karim Shah (Provincial Vice President), Attiqa Gazanfer Ali Khan (Provincial Vice President), Haji Haider Khan (Provincial Vice President), Shafiq-ud-Din (Provincial Vice President), Shams Mir (Provincial Political Advisor), Dr. Muhammad Iqbal (Provincial Vice President), Tahir Ayub (Provincial Vice President) and Farooq Mir (Provincial Secretary Information).[16]

Network and Area of Influence

The party has been able to extend its influence in all the 10 districts of Gilgit-Baltistan. It has made a clean sweep by winning all the Assembly seats in the three districts of Gilgit, Astore and Ghanche. Earlier its influence was limited to Gilgit and Diamer.

PML-N's Election Manifesto for Gilgit-Baltistan

The PML-N's Gilgit-Baltistan manifesto guarantees magnificent development and prosperity of the region. The following are some of the highlighted points:[17]

(1) PMLN-GB has formulated an exemplary unique constitutional structure for Gilgit-Baltistan which would in an exemplary way reflect political, social and economic development in the region.
(2) Developing infrastructure in Gilgit-Baltistan has the top priority.
(3) PMLN-GB resolves to embrace reforms and plans to develop areas of administration in social and economic fields.
(4) PMLN-GB intends to complete the power projects in Gilgit-Baltistan under the China-Pakistan Economic Corridor project.
(5) Diamer Bhasha Dam would on completion provide thousands of jobs for the people, bringing prosperity to the people.
(6) PMLN-GB intended to complete the Karakoram Highway, Babusar Highway Gilgit-Skardu Road, Shonter Pass and Gilgit-Tashander Express, and also upgrade them as motorways.
(7) Under the Prime Minister Youth Loan Scheme, the PMLN-GB sought to provide better employment opportunities.
(8) PMLN-GB planned to have revolutionary projects to provide water and electricity to every person.

(9) PMLN-GB would accord the highest priority to enforcing the rule of law in Gilgit-Baltistan.
(10) Steps would be taken to safeguard and develop all local languages.
(11) PMLN-GB intended to bring a complete end to mal-administration and corruption.
(12) The party will strive hard to develop the tourist industry, mineral mining, herbal and other natural resources.
(13) PMLN-GB planned to establish a Bank of Gilgit-Baltistan for the residents.

The PML-N federal government in joint collaboration with its local chapter announced that some "unprecedented" measures for the development of the region had already been taken:

(1) First time in the history of Gilgit-Baltistan, a Federal Committee was constituted to accord constitutional status to the region.
(2) Approval for the construction of Gilgit-Skardu road.
(3) Approval for the formation of four new districts: Hunza, Nagar, Khar Mang, Shigar.
(4) Construction of Attabad tunnel.
(5) Approval of Hanzel, Skarkoi and Jilmish hydropower projects.
(6) Accumulating development projects and non-development projects.
(7) Rs 1400 crore to be utilised under the IFAD (International Fund for Agricultural Development) projects to irrigate barren land.
(8) Measures were taken to facilitate the business of precious stones and gems.
(9) Continuing wheat subsidies for Gilgit-Baltistan farmers. New price of Rs 11 to be fixed for cultivators.
(10) Approval of funds of Rs 10 crore for procurement of water in Jotiyal (Gilgit).
(11) Constitution of a boundary commission to settle disputes between Khyber Pakhtunkhawa and Gilgit-Baltistan, which played a crucial role in defusing tension between tribal sardars.
(12) Approval of National Action Plan to bring an end to terrorism, extremism in Gilgit-Baltistan.
(13) Approval for the construction of 14 MW hydel power projects Naltar (Gilgit)

Current Status

The then Prime Minister Nawaz Sharif during his election rally in Gilgit had announced a PKR 47 billion package for the construction of two dams, a specialised hospital, a university in Baltistan; setting up three new districts; and construction of road between Thakot and Raikot on the Karakoram Highway.[18] Earlier, under the pressure of the demands to declare Gilgit-Baltistan a province of Pakistan, Nawaz Sharif announced just before the June 2015 elections, the formation of a committee on the constitutional status of Gilgit-Baltistan. Local parties saw these promises as another ploy by the PMLN-GB "to win the upcoming (2015) elections".[19]

On July 8, 2015, a six-member cabinet of the ruling PMLN-GB took oath in Gilgit-Baltistan. The cabinet headed by Hafeezur Rehman included Farman Ali from Astore district, Mohammad Vakil Sobia Moqaddam and Janbaaz Khan from Diamer district, Ibrahim Sanai from Ghanche district and Dr. Mohammad Iqbal from Gilgit district. Haji Akbar Taban, General Secretary of PMLN-GB, who won the Skardu-1 constituency refused to take oath in protest against not being appointed as the region's governor.[20]

On June 1, 2018, just before the completion of five-year term, the PML-N government issued Gilgit Baltistan order 2018 replacing the GBSESGO 2009. Under the new order, all powers exercised by the GB Council including passing legislation regarding mineral, hydro-power and tourism have been transferred to GB Assembly. The order was opposed by the people who protested as they were not given any constitutional rights that they had expected.

PAKISTAN MUSLIM LEAGUE QUAID-I-AZAM-GB (PMLQ-GB)

Introduction

The Pakistan Muslim League Quaid-i-Azam (PML-Q) was formed by the leaders of the Pakistan Muslim League who had defected from the PML-N during Musharraf's regime just before the general elections in 2002. A few leaders of the now defunct Tehreek-e-Jafaria, a Shia outfit, also joined it after it was banned. The Gilgit-Baltistan chapter of the PMLQ-GB was set up soon after the formation of the PML-Q in 1999. Tracing its history, Muhammad Amir Rana and Mujtaba Rathore state:

> The PML-Q contested Elections-1999 but could not make any visible success. Before elections-2004, a couple of federal ministers stayed in Northern Areas for two months and reorganised the party. But, the PML-Q could win only five seats for Legislative Council out of 24. Later 10 independent winners joined the PML-Q after which it formed its government in the Legislative Council. The PML-Q also won 12 women and technocrat seats.[21]

According to another report, PMLQ-GB could win only four out of 24 seats and another 11 joined after they were promised adviser positions. The military government made it clear that there should be no political opposition. Thus Musharraf-backed PML-Q was able to manipulate the elections. Mir Ghazanfar Ali Khan was elected as DCE while Malik Muskeen became the Speaker.[22] it is worth mentioning that all the top leaders of PMLQ-GB including Mir Ghazanfar Ali Khan of Hunza and Malik Maskeen of Diamer quit the PMLN-GB. (*The Harald*, April 2006).

Current Status

In the November 2009 Assembly elections, the party fielded 14 candidates but could win only two seats – increasing its tally to three after bagging a reserved seat for women.[23] With three members it joined the coalition government of Chief Minister Mehdi Shah. Other coalition partners were the JUIF-GB and MQM-GB. The party boycotted the June 2015 Gilgit-Baltistan Assembly elections, primarily because many of its senior party leaders defected to the PTI-GB and PPP-GB. They included former minister Bashir Ahmad who defected to the PPP-GB and Amina Ansari and Mirza Hussain who joined the PTI-GB.[24]

ALL PAKISTAN MUSLIM LEAGUE-GB (APML-GB)

Introduction and Aims and Objectives

All Pakistan Muslim League (APML), which is headed by former President retired General Pervez Musharraf has a chapter in Gilgit-Baltistan. APML has sought a creation of separate province for Gilgit-Baltistan. In this connection the, chief coordinator of APML Ahmad Raza Kasuri has filed a petition in the Islamabad High Court seeking a constitutional amendment for turning Gilgit-Baltistan into the fifth province of the country. The petition was filed a few days before June, 2015 elections. In his petition Kasuri recalled that the Supreme Court had directed the Pakistan Government on May 28, 1999 to evolve a mechanism for protecting fundamental rights of the people of Gilgit-Baltistan. He said that the federal government under the direction was bound to give the people of Gilgit the right of self-governance. The petition claimed that in August, 2009, the PPP government instead of amending the Pakistan Constitution issued a Presidential Order titled 'The Gilgit-Baltistan Empowerment and Self Governance Order, 2009', which granted self-rule to the people of Gilgit-Baltistan. According to the petition, the order could not serve as a mechanism for creating the Gilgit-Baltistan Province.[25] The President of APML G-B, is Karim Khan popularly known KK. For June 2015 elections, it fielded candidates in 13 constituencies but failed to win any seat.

PAKISTAN TEHREEK-I-INSAF-GB (PTI-GB)

Introduction

The Pakistan Tehreek-i-Insaf (PTI) opened its Gilgit-Baltistan chapter in 2011. It appointed Abdul Latif and Mahmudal Ahsan as President and Vice President, respectively. However, both these leaders resigned and joined the PMLN-GB in May 2015. These leaders resented the central party leadership's decision to give party tickets for the June 2015 elections to rank newcomers.

Network

Although, the party has dedicated workers, it has not been able to spread its network in the region. The party contested the 2015 elections for 21 seats. The Party Chief, Imran Khan, extensively toured various parts of the region and addressed big election rallies. In these rallies, Imran Khan accused then PML-N federal government of pre-poll rigging by allocating huge funds for the development of the region. He also criticised the appointment of Federal Minister for Kashmir Affairs and Gilgit-Baltistan as a stopgap Gilgit-Baltistan governor.[26] The PTI's political agenda stands for an upgraded Gilgit-Baltistan Assembly with the right to vote in general elections and representation in the National Assembly and Senate. The PTI aims to abolish the Gilgit-Baltistan Council and transfer those powers to the concerned federal ministries, and seeks to apply the 1999 Supreme Court ruling to Gilgit-Baltistan.

Manifesto

The local leadership also released the party manifesto for the June 2015 elections. The salient features of the manifesto were as follows:[27]

(i) Ultimate integration of Gilgit-Baltistan with the Federation of Pakistan as a Constitutional Province, or a Constitutionally protected Autonomous Region, with full rights of a province, addressing the longstanding demand of the people of the region.

(ii) In the interim, this integration shall be considered as 'provisional' to accommodate Pakistan's internal and international stances on disputed territories; the precedence is Pak-China Border Agreement of 1962.

(iii) Empower and decentralise institutions of governance and economic management to local people, and restore political, economic, religious and cultural rights and freedoms of people.

(iv) Reform and establish a modern and equitable social sector, including the provision and promotion of high-quality services in health, education, sanitation, as well as well-being and social protection of the poorest and most vulnerable segments of the society.

(v) Develop and sustainably manage natural resources of the region, giving the highest priority to private sector-led development, promoting clean industries, creating jobs and ensuring local ownership of economic assets and participation in investment opportunities.

(vi) Encourage a merit-based system that provides equal opportunity for employment and upward social mobility for all, especially the working classes, youth and women.

(vii) Ensure an accountable and responsible system of governance, law and order, and promote regional peace and reconciliation.

(viii) Strive for cultural freedom, develop indigenous languages and promote traditional festivals and art.

(ix) Raise revenue from exploiting natural resources on our own and have 20 per cent share in the transit levies on the Economic Corridor, as well its due share in the national GST revenue.

In spite of Imran Khan's extensive election tour of Gilgit-Baltistan where he vowed to grant more regional autonomy and undertake more development work, the PTI-GB could win only one seat in the 2015 Assembly elections. The party alleged that then ruling PMLN-GB had resorted to massive rigging, and that it would challenge before the tribunals concerned the results of the various constituencies.[28] However, M Ismail Khan, a political analyst gives the following reason for the defeat of the PTI-GB:

(1) The PTI-GB failed to clarify its position on important matters;

(2) Imran Khan remained silent on major issues like Gilgit Baltistan's constitutional rights, its representation in Pakistan Parliament and other decision-making forums;

(3) He made no commitment to resolve Gilgit-Baltistan's boundary, power and water-related disputes with Khyber Pakhtunkhwa where PTI is in power;

(4) He didn't offer an increase in the number of seats in medical and engineering colleges for Gilgit-Baltistan's students in Khyber Pakhtunkhwa; and

(5) There was no impact of Imran's anti-Nawaz speeches on the common people of Gilgit-Baltistan.[29]

Current Status

The dismal performance of the party in 2015 Legislative Assembly elections forced central leadership for overhauling party leadership of the GB chapter. Its top leadership was changed and replaced by the new ones. Raja Jalal was chosen as the President, Shah Nasir as Vice-President and Fatehullah as General Secretary. Raja Jalal replaced Hashmatullah Khan who as a convener of the party, was the de-facto president and was also one of the founding leader of the party in GB. The decision has shocked the party workers as Hashmatullah Khan has not been given any role in the party leadership. The supporters of Hashmatullah Khan have slammed the central leadership for bypassing him and installing a newcomer as the regional chief. The cadres refused to cooperate with the new leadership. Therefore, the decision has given rise to discontent among the older cadre of the party in the region. It may be noted that Raja Jalal joined PTI-GB after the quitting the PPP on the eve of 2015 elections. However, Raja Jalal lost the election to PMLN-GB Akbar Taban. Fatehullah the new General Secretary of the party has joined the PTI after defecting from the PMLN around the same time.[30]

ISLAMI TEHREEK PAKISTAN (ITP)

Introduction, Aims and Objectives and Leadership

Shia Islami Council (SUC) contested the June 2015 Gilgit-Baltistan Assembly elections under the banner of ITP as the SUC has been registered with the Election Commission of Gilgit-Baltistan as ITP.[31] The main objective of the SUC is to protect the rights of Shia Muslims of Pakistan and give them voice in the Pakistan Parliament. The party has maintained cordial relations with Sunni organisations including Sunni Ittehad Council. The SUC had also formed an alliance with PPP to contest the National Assembly elections in 2013.[32] ITP won two seats in the June 2015 Gilgit Baltistan Legislative Assembly elections. And by winning one seat each in the women's and technocrat reserved seats, ITP emerged as the main opposition party with four seats. While Allama Sajid Naqvi is chief of SUC Pakistan, its Gilgit Baltistan Chapter is headed by Shaikh Shahadat Hashmi. Other prominent leaders of SUC are Shaikh Sultan Sabri, Ali Hussain, Shaikh Shabir Hakeemi and Shaikh Gulam Shakri.[33]

JAMIAT ULEMA-E-ISLAM-FAZLUR REHMAN-GB (JUIF-GB)

Introduction

The Jamiat Ulema-e-Islam-Fazlur Rehman (JUI-F) established its branch in

Gilgit-Baltistan in 1987 by four Islamic leaders: Qazi Inayatullah, Haji Muhammad Azeem, Qari Abul Hakeem and Maulana Haq Nawaz. Initially, the party concentrated on local issues like electricity and water. After consolidating its position, it focused on law and order problems and constitutional rights. The main demand of the party is to merge Gilgit-Baltistan with 'AJK'.[34] Most of its cadre strength comes from Sunni Muslims. It roped in Jamaat-i-Islami and Tehrik-e-Jafaria, to launch a movement against obscenity.[35]

The JUIF-GB had won three seats, including a seat reserved for women, in the 2009 elections to the Gilgit-Baltistan Assembly. It joined the coalition led by PPP-GB government headed by Mehdi Shah. For the June 2015 elections, it fielded 10 candidates, but secured only one seat. Its candidate, Haji Shah Baig won the sole seat from Diamer (GBLA-12) constituency. Baig was also elected as leader of the opposition in the Legislative Assembly. A major reason for its poor performance in the 2015 elections could be that its party chief, Fazlur Rehman, did not visit the region to campaign for the party's candidates.[36]

Manifesto
The JUIF-GB chapter follows the central manifesto of the party which demands the implementation of Islamic judicial system in Pakistan. The party is in favour of accession of Kashmir to Pakistan.[37]

Leadership
The organisational structure of the party is controlled by a committee whose office-bearers are Qari Inayatulla (President), Attaulla Shahab (General Secretary), and Maulana Luqman Hakeem. Other important leaders include Maulana Syed Mohammad, Maulana Haq Nawaz, Jamil Ahmad, Haji Gulberg, Qazi Imtiaz Ahmad Mir and Minahjuddin.[38]

JAMAAT-E-ISLAMI-GB (JI-GB)

Introduction
Jamaat-e-Islami (JI) had set up a chapter in Gilgit Baltistan in July 1974 but with a small following.[39] The JI favours merging of 'AJK' and Gilgit-Baltistan to form "one unit". It believes that Kashmir will soon be free, and if therefore, both the regions were to merge into one unit, it would strengthen the freedom movement, and also create more difficulties for India.[40] Commenting on the reforms package introduced through the Presidential Order on August 28, 2009,

JI pointed out that simple constitutional and administrative reforms would not suffice to solve the problems of the area. It suggested a need to bring a change at the leadership level in the country at large, in order to establish a government and society based on justice.[41] It did not field any candidates in the Assembly elections in November 2009. In the June 2015 Assembly elections, it gave tickets to six candidates but all of them lost.

Leadership

Office-bearers of the JI-GB are: Dr Khalid Mahmood (Emir), Maulana Abdus Sami (General Secretary), Mushtaq Ahmad (Vice President), who also happens to hold the post for the 'AJK' chapter, and advocate Noorul Bari.[42] Dr Mahmood replaced Abdul Rashid Turabi on June 30, 2017 who served party as an Emir for both the region of PoK for 22 years. The previous Emirs included Maulana Abdul Bari, Col. (retd.) Abdul Rashid Abbasi and Engr. Aziz Afzal Khan.

MUTTAHIDA QUAMI MOVEMENT-GB (MQM-GB)

Introduction

The Muttahida Quami Movement (MQM) strives for its own administration in Gilgit-Baltistan without interference by the Pakistan bureaucracy. It opened its Gilgit-Baltistan chapter during the first Legislative Assembly elections in November 2009. It fielded 20 candidates, but could win only one seat.[43] The party was supported by the people of Gilgit-Baltistan settled in Karachi, especially the youth who were sent by the party to Gilgit-Baltistan for campaigning. Also, for many voters, the MQM "is known for religious harmony in Karachi and it has given a voice to the middle class".[44] The party, however, could not secure any seat in June 2015 Assembly elections. In addition, the party's lone legislator, Raja Azam, quit the MQM-GB to join PML-N in April 2015. Raja Azam who was elected from Shigar area of Baltistan region in November 2009 became minister for planning in the PPP-led government. His loss completely demoralised the party cadre as Raja Azam was the sole member of the MQM Central Executive Committee in the region.[45]

MAJLIS-E-WAHADAT MUSLIMEEN GILGIT BALTISTAN (MWM-GB)

Introduction

Majlis-e-Wahadat Muslimeen (MWM) is a party formed by a group of Shias in Pakistan. It has branches in all the regions of Pakistan. Its Gilgit Baltistan chapter did not contest the November 2009 elections to the Legislative Assembly, although it has a strong following among the Shias in the region. In the June 2015 Assembly elections, 15 of its candidates contested, and two of them won. They include Rizwan Ali elected from GBLA-5 (Hunza-Nagar–II) and Imtiaz Haider Khan elected from GBLA-8 (Skardu-II) constituencies.

Leadership

Prominent leaders of the MWM Gilgit Baltistan are General Secretary Allama Sheikh Nayyar Abbas, Allam Raja Nasir Abbas Jafari, Head of MWM Baltistan Region; Allama Sheikh Nayyar Abbas, Provincial General Secretary; Allama Agha Ali Rizvi, General Secretary; Arif Qanbari, Provincial leader; Ghulam Abbas, Provincial Secretary Political Affairs Gilgit-Baltistan; and Mohammad Ali, Secretary Political Affairs Baltistan Division.

In April 2015, nine political activists of MWM were arrested for protesting against the Pakistan Government's decision to support Saudi Government's stance on its war in Yemen. The move was criticised by then Supreme Court Bar Association President, Late Asma Jahangir. She demanded release of the 40 political and human right activists who had been charged with sedition in the past six months simply for their peaceful protest against the denial of their political rights.[46]

In February 2016, the MWM Gilgit-Baltistan General Secretary, Allama Sheikh Nayyar Abbas, was sent to prison on judicial remand in a treason case by an anti-terrorist court. He had been at large for almost 10 months, and was declared a proclaimed offender by the court.

TANZEEM AHL-E-SUNNAT WAL JAMAAT (TASWJ)

Introduction

Tanzeem Ahl-e-Sunnat Wal Jamaat (TASWJ) is the main Sunni party of Gilgit-Baltistan. It was formed as a welfare organisation in the early 1980s to run mosques, madrassas, and orphanages. The organisation intensified its activities following the 1988 sectarian clashes. Being a staunch Sunni organisation, the TASWJ is closely associated with Anjuman Sipah-i-Sahaba Pakistan (ASSP), a radical sectarian outfit.[47]

NATIONALIST/PRESSURE GROUPS

BALAWARISTAN NATIONAL FRONT (BNF)

Introduction

The Balawaristan National Front (BNF) was formed by Nawaz Khan Naji in Gilgit on July 30, 1992. The main aim of the BNF was to fight for a sovereign and independent republic of Balawaristan. According to its official website, it considers Pakistan to be a 'usurper' whose control over the region is 'illegal' as per the international law.[48] The party has been voicing the grievances of the people by organising rallies, protests and conferences. One such conference was held on April 3, 1993 which was attended by different political, religious and national parties of Pakistan. This was followed by a protest meeting on March 24, 1994 and a huge public meeting at Shahi Polo ground in Gilgit in April 1994. The BNF observed "Black Jubilee" when Pakistan was celebrating its Golden Jubilee on August 14, 1997. The security forces arrested a number of its leaders and activists including Abdul Hamid Khan, who were charged with sedition and sent to jail and tortured.[49]

On the occasion of the 20th Anniversary of the Unrepresented Nations and Peoples Organisation (UNPO), Abdul Hamid Khan in a speech in The Hague on February 11, 2011 stated:

> In Balawaristan, arbitrary arrest, torture, detention and forcibly exile is the daily routine of the occupying regime of Pakistan, because of no higher and independent judicial system. Neither the people of this region have representation of their own nor have representation anywhere in the world. Human Rights organisations and independent media are out of question in this area. Hundreds and hundreds of local indigenous people were put behind bars for their religious and political differences and many political leaders including Mr. Wajahat Hassan, Ex Member of NAs Council and Col. (Retd) Nadir Hassan and others were arrested and were forcibly sent to exile to Pakistan from their home in Gilgit on 1st [November 1,] 2009, when they tried to hold peaceful public gathering during election campaign. Indigenous people are given death sentence without giving them right to justice in any High Court or Supreme Court.[50]

Earlier, in November 2004, in an open letter to the Prime Ministers of India and Pakistan, Abdul Hamid Khan appealed for early resolution of the mounting problems of the people of Gilgit-Baltistan. On April 28, 2017, BNF chairman said, "If referendum happens people will vote for India, they never committed atrocities on us." While praising India, he said, "Pakistan imposed war on us,

India never occupied our land. Pakistan's coward army gave Siachen to India." Commenting on the China-Pakistan Economic Corridor (CPEC), he said, "People are aware Gilgit-Baltistan is disputed, by arresting few, you (Pak) think CPEC will be built, 42 million (dollars) will be in your pocket, it's a dream."[51] In January 2017, Pakistan security agencies arrested a dozen activists of BNF accusing them of sabotage against CPEC at the behest of Indian intelligence agencies. The founder of the party, Nawaz Khan Naji contested against the religious and spiritual leader of the Ismail sect in 2004 Northern Areas Legislative Council elections but was defeated. The BNF was the only nationalist party which had fielded four candidates, but failed to win any seat in the November 2009 Assembly elections.

However, Nawaz Khan Naji surprised everyone by winning Ghizer constituency in the by-election held to the Gilgit Baltistan Legislative Assembly in 2011. According to Sohaib Bodla, the victory gave a big boost to the nationalist movement as earlier nationalist leaders in the area generally remained aloof from electoral politics.[52] Nawaz Khan Naji being the most influential nationalist leader has a large following among the youth. He won the Gilgit-Baltistan Legislative Assembly elections by a big margin twice, in 2011 and 2015. However, soon after the elections, differences emerged within the BNF regarding the future strategy of attaining the political objectives. Abdul Hamid Khan was expelled by Naji. This led the division of BNF into two groups: one led by Naji and the other by Abdul Hamid Khan. Khan's group (BNF-H) operates from Brussels where he is living in exile. However, Naji's adventure in mainstream politics has not gone well within the Nationalist circles. Although living in exile, Abdul Hamid Khan has established a good rapport with other nationalist groups. He is also in touch with international human right organisations, the UN and European Parliament, and on regular basis briefs them about the prevailing situation in Gilgit-Baltistan. In a letter addressed to the UN Secretary General Ban Ki Moon on March 14, 2016, Khan wrote:

> There is no legal, constitutional, judicial mechanism in place in Pakistan occupied Gilgit-Baltistan to protect people from human rights violations, except the UN and civilized world. Many political and religious people have been prosecuted in Gilgit-Baltistan jails without giving them access to legal, constitutional redress options or high court and Supreme Court. Local population working in administration, Police, Education and Security Forces are not promoted for the top jobs and are always put under the final control of Pakistani citizens. Indigenous people in government service have been insulted, degraded and never trusted.[53]

Ideology/Objectives

The BNF considers Gilgit-Baltistan a separate territory with a separate nation. According to the BNF, these areas were not a legitimate part of Jammu and Kashmir; rather, Kashmir was controlling them by military power in collaboration with the British Crown. The BNF has three slogans – independence, democracy and justice:

> The BNF calls for an independent state named Balawaristan, comprising the areas of GB plus districts of Kohistan and Chitral which are today part of Pakistan's Province Khyber Pakhtunkhwa: and it also includes Indian controlled Ladakh. The movement believes in a peaceful struggle for the ultimate cause of a separate homeland for the inhabitants of these areas.. Furthermore, the BNF has also struggled to highlight the demand that the people of GB should be given the right of determining their future in light of the long awaited plebiscite under the UN. Further the BNF wants to be a fourth party in the Kashmir dispute; India, Pakistan and Kashmir being the other parties. In the current set up, the people of GB do not have representation in the national legislature of Pakistan. Using electoral politics, the BNF is attempting to mobilise the local people to make sense of their own identity in a situation where they are surrounded by India, Kashmir and Pakistan's quest to take or to perpetuate control of the area.[54]

Besides the above-mentioned area which is under the control of India and Pakistan, the BNF also wants to include Gojal, which is under Chinese control, "in the proposed state on the basis of cultural affinity".[55] Explaining the nationalists' position, Nawaz Khan Naji said, "We are neither Pakistani nor part of Kashmir. After the Kashmir issue is resolved, we will decide whether our state, Balawaristan, will become an independent country or confederate with Pakistan." Till then, he said, he was ready to settle for autonomy within Pakistan, adding, "We should be allowed to have our president and prime minister."[56]

Pakistan earns an annual income Rs. 20 billion from Gilgit-Baltistan's natural and economic resources. However, the BNF alleged that it presents an annual budget of only Rs. 1.2 billion.[57] Even for the financial year 2017-18, the G-B Council has approved a budget with the total outlay of about PKR 2.4 billion. The party is against setting up mega projects as the area is still disputed. This issue came up for discussion in the Gilgit-Baltistan Legislative Assembly on January 11, 2014 after MLA Mirza Hussain presented an adjournment motion, asking the Assembly to deliberate on the construction of Railway Track and other mega projects in the region. Nawaz Khan Naji, too has opposed the construction of mega projects before determining the status of Gilgit-Baltistan.

Organisation, Structure, Leadership and Funding

The BNF is headed by a committee which has a Patron-in Chief, Chairman, President and General Secretary. Nawaz Khan Naji is the Patron-in-Chief of the party. Other office-bearers are Abdul Hamid Khan, Chairman; Muhammad Rafiq, President; Ali Madad Bai, General Secretary; Engineer Shafqat Inqilabi, Spokesman; and Shujat Ali and Engineer Akhtar Jan, both active members. The main hub of the political activity of the party is at Ghizer district where nationalists have been contesting elections for local bodies since 2004. The party's headquarters is, however, based at Majni Mahila, Gilgit.

BALAWARISTAN STUDENTS' NATIONAL ORGANISATION (BSNO)

Balawaristan Students' National Organisation (BSNO) is youth wing of BNF. Majority of its members come from the middle class. In addition, there are students who have returned from Karachi, Lahore and Peshawar after completing their studies and formed the Balawaristan Students' National Organisation (BSNO). Its main objective is to seek independence from Pakistan's colonial rule. The BSNO is headed by Faizullah Faruq. According to a senior leader of the BSNO, the main demands of the people of Gilgit-Baltistan are as follows:[58]

- (a) For the UN Security Council to ensure genuine political, judicial, economic and cultural autonomy in Gilgit-Baltistan as obligated under the UN resolution of January 5, 1949.
- (b) Given that Pakistan has failed to ensure security in Gilgit-Baltistan, the UN should station peace-keeping troops in the disputed region.
- (c) Pakistan must be asked to open traditional routes leading towards India and Tajikistan which can help sustain the local economy and provide safe alternate safe routes to travel, as, currently, travel on the Karakoram Highway is too dangerous.
- (d) The UN should ask Pakistan to respect UN resolutions and remove its citizens who have damaged the social fabric by spreading religious sectarianism in the region.
- (e) The UN should ask Pakistan to withdraw the fake sedition cases and release all political prisoners.
- (f) A UN commission must be sent to Gilgit-Baltistan to assess gross human rights violations, killings and torture of political workers.

The major funding of the party comes from its members and donors.

Network and Area of Influence

Major network of the Balawaristan movement is in Ghizer district, "which has now become synonymous with the Balawaristan struggle in entire Gilgit-Baltistan, according to Sohaib Bodla, leader of BSNO, who says: "The road from Gilgit to Ghizer is replete with slogans in favor of Balawaristan and its leadership."[59]

The BNF has voiced concern over the militant activities in 'AJK' and Gilgit-Baltistan in an article in the *Asia Times*. Salient points are as follows:

(i) In the past, the Ghizer valley had seen much militant activities. Post US military operation in Afghanistan, many al-Qaeda and Taliban leaders found safe haven in Pakistan's tribal areas. Most of the militants also took refuge in densely forests of Ghizer. Many anti-India militant organisations opened their camps in remote hilly areas of Hazara, Darel Yashote, Tangir, Astore, Skardu city and Gilgit.

(ii) There were also reports of the existence of a militant camp of Harkat ul Mujahedeen in Tangir in Diamar district. In addition, some camps were also located in Ghowadi village in Skardu, Juglote and Konodas near Gilgit.

(iii) About 1,000 al-Qaeda fighters crossed over to Pakistan after the US invasion of Afghanistan. Out of them, 600 escaped to Gilgit-Baltistan and another 200 pushed into the upper reaches of the Pir Panjal region in Kashmir.[60]

Current Status

The party is very active as more and more people are joining the BNF. The social media has become an important tool to spread the party's ideology, speeches of nationalist leaders and other happenings.

The BNF has opposed the so-called Gilgit-Baltistan Empowerment and Self-governance Order 2009 which it says is a ploy to occupy Gilgit Baltistan under the garb of an order. In a letter addressed to the President of the European Parliament, BNF Chairman, Abdul Hamid Khan, pointed out that the arrangement was an unconcerned attempt to (i) control the elected representatives of Gilgit-Baltistan and use the new political set up as a rubber stamp to get approval for the construction of six mega dams including Diamar/Bhasha Bonji; and (ii) to merge Gilgit-Baltistan with Pakistan by ignoring the will of the two million people as well as the United Nations Commission on

India and Pakistan (UNCIP) resolutions.⁶¹ Khan said that the resolution of the Kashmir dispute has been made even more difficult due to the intrusion of radical religious groups sponsored by the Pakistan State. In an interview with India-based security analyst, Yoginder Sikand, Khan said that "a viable solution to the Kashmir issue can emerge only after consulting all the many ethnic, religious, cultural and political groups which inhibit this land".⁶²

Similarly, the BNF believes that China-Pakistan Corridor project is a ploy to strengthen the hold of outsiders in Gilgit-Baltistan and keep the indigenous people in perpetual slavery. In a statement, the BNF Chairman said that his party not only rejects the project but also condemns Pakistan for envisaging it, adding the people of the region would never accept the mega project.⁶³

JAMMU AND KASHMIR LIBERATION FRONT (JKLF)

Introduction

The Jammu and Kashmir Liberation Front (JKLF) was founded in Birmingham (UK) in May 1977 by Amanullah Khan and Maqbool Bhat. It advocates independent Jammu and Kashmir comprising all Kashmir territory that is presently under the control of India, Pakistan and China. Moreover, according to the JKLF, Gilgit-Baltistan is a part of Jammu and Kashmir region, and should be completely independent.⁶⁴

It has termed the Gilgit-Baltistan Empowerment and Self Governance Order 2009 as a 'colonial-type' package which the Kashmiris consider "as an attempt to divide Kashmiris". Criticising the package, the JKLF Pakistan chapter President, Syed Faisal Nazki, said that power would not be vested in the people of the region but in the Gilgit Baltistan Council.⁶⁵ He rejected the package saying it that it appeared to be aimed at merging the disputed areas into Pakistan.⁶⁶ The JKLF has also stressed that making Gilgit-Baltistan a constitutional part of Pakistan "would be catastrophic for the country". In an interview with the Pakistan daily, *The Express Tribune*, Amanullah Khan said, "If GB does become part of Pakistan; it will be synonymous to committing suicide {....} I will not let this happen till I am alive, no one can separate G-B from Kashmir."⁶⁷

Before his death, Amanullah visited Gilgit to dissuade people from demanding a constitutional status for Gilgit-Baltistan. However, he has no reservations on the China-Pakistan Economic Corridor; rather, he supported Gilgit-Baltistan's demand for a larger share in the Corridor.⁶⁸ The party office was inaugurated by Amanullah Khan at Dar Plaza, Gilgit, in February 2016.

The function was also attended by JKLF's zonal president Dr Tawqeer Geelani, and its convener in Gilgit-Baltistan Saif ud Din Bhat.[69]

KARAKORUM NATIONAL MOVEMENT (KNM)

History

In 1986, a youth body in the name of Karakorum Students Organisation (KSO) was formed in Quetta, Balochistan, by Muhammad Qasim Sheraliyat and Dr Sharif. The movement was later extended to the other areas of Pakistan as well. In Gilgit-Baltistan, the KSO appointed Afsar Jan as its first Chairman. The youth body further decided to form a political party, called the Karakorum National Movement (KNM) with Qasim Sheraliyat as its chairman. As a part of its objective, the KNM has been struggling for the freedom of Karakorum (Gilgit-Baltistan). After shifting its office to Gilgit, it fanned out its leaders to Sindh and North-West Frontier Province (NWFP; now called Khyber Pakhtunkhwa) to meet college and university students in order to seek their support in struggle for the constitutional rights of the people of Gilgit-Baltistan.[70] The KNM along with other nationalist groups such as the Progressive Youth Front, Balor Forum and Gilgit Baltistan Democratic Alliance have been organising seminars and meetings on the issue of basic constitutional, social, economic and political rights. At a meeting in Hunza in August 2008, the speakers demanded that the Pakistan Government define the constitutional status of Gilgit-Baltistan and the region be given self-rule.[71]

Ideology

The KNM believes that Gilgit-Baltistan is not a territory of Pakistan as its future is yet to be decided in accordance with the United Nations resolutions. According to a KNM statement, quoted by the weekly, *Bang-e-Sahar*:

> When we don't want to join Pakistan, why are we being forced to do so? We have been saying that our constitutional status should be determined. We want an autonomous Gilgit-Baltistan but Pakistan's rulers have enslaved the people of Gilgit Baltistan for more than the last six decades without giving them their birth right of self-determination to decide about their future.[72]

To suppress the nationalist activists, Pakistani intelligence agencies have used state-sponsored terrorists to attack and weaken their cause. Over the years, a number of nationalist activists have been killed, namely Aflatoon, Gazi Anwer, Zakir Hussain, Ashiq Mir and Zubair Ali. KNM leaders like Muhammad Javed, Shah Zaman, Manzoor Parwana, Shabir Ali Shah, Syed Haider Shah Razvi, Iftikhar Husain and Amir Ali have faced rigorous torture and jail terms for demanding political rights for the people of Gilgit-Baltistan. Iftikhar Husain and Amir Ali were arrested when they were protesting against extra-judicial murders of two innocent citizens of Hunza Nagar. The demands of the KNM include end to terrorism, military and police-led torture, detentions and freedom of speech and expression.[73]

Leadership

The KNM which was until recently keeping low profile is one of the largest group among the nationalist groups. But of late it has been facing leadership crisis. It is believed that the KNM has now only about 500 members in the region.[74]

Some of the important leaders of KNM are Mohammad Iqbal Advocate (Chairman) and Amjad Changezi (Vice Chairman), and Mohammad Javed (President). Other leaders include Habib Yunuis, Comrade Naeemullah Baig, Mumtaz Nagri, Karim Hasan Sher Gazt and Faqir Hussain Chandio.

GILGIT BALTISTAN DEMOCRATIC ALLIANCE (GBDA)

Introduction

The Gilgit Baltistan Democratic Alliance (GBDA) is a leading conglomerate of eight nationalist parties of Gilgit-Baltistan. It demands complete freedom from occupation of Pakistan and an independent democratic government for the local indigenous people.[75] The coalition was initially formed in October 2009 by two major nationalist parties, the BNF and KNM.[76] The other alliance partners are the Gilgit Baltistan United Movement (GBUM), Balor Research Forum (BRF), Gilgit Baltistan Ladakh Democratic Movement (GBLDM), Progressive Youth Front (PYF), Boloristan[77] Labour Party (BLP) and Thinkers Forum (TF). The GBDA is closely associated with All Parties National Alliance (an amalgam of nationalist parties of both the regions of PoK). The GBDA jointly organises meetings, seminars rallies and conferences to create awareness about the fundamental rights of the people. Gilgit-Baltistan is represented at the UNPO by the GBDA.[78] The GBDA contested the November 2009 elections with 16 candidates on the issue of independence and autonomy. However, no candidate was able to win a seat.[79] Pakistani authorities were accused by the local nationalist leaders of not allowing their parties to hold election meetings, and of favouring pro-Pakistan political parties with funding and other kinds of support.[80] The GBDA has also criticised the Gilgit-Baltistan National Alliance (GBNA) for working against the nationalist cause and following the establishment's line.[81]

Leadership

The Chairman of the party is Ghulam Shehzad Agha and Senior Vice President is Advocate Ehsan Ali. Dr. Amjad Chengazi is Vice chairman, Burhanullah is General Secretary, Baba Jan Hunzai is Joint Secretary and Engineer Akbar Khan is Press Secretary. Other major leaders of the alliance include Convenor Muhammad Rafique, Engineer Amanullah Khan and Manzoor Hussain Parwana.

GILGIT BALTISTAN UNITED MOVEMENT (GBUM)

Introduction

Gilgit Baltistan United Movement (GBUM) is a prominent local political movement that is supported by local politicians. Based in Skardu, it demands a fully autonomous state comprising Gilgit and Baltistan.[82] GBUM believes that the people of Gilgit Baltistan didn't opt for Pakistan at the time of partition. The GBUM demanded that the 'Northern Areas' Legislative Council should be given the status of Legislative Assembly and given similar rights granted to the existing 'AJK' Legislative Assembly.[83]

The Chairman of the GBUM, Manzoor Hussain Parwana has strongly criticised Pakistan Government's proposal to make Gilgit-Baltistan a provisional province and its constitutional packages for the region as unlawful. In a press release, Parwana made it clear that Gilgit-Baltistan was not a part of Pakistan under the 1973 Constitution: "Pakistan had taken over the administrative control of the GB region in the wake of dubious 'Karachi pact' signed on April 28, 1949 in which GB was represented by no one."[84] Commenting further on the proposed provisional status, Parwana stated, "GB is the only area which neither has representation in the National Assembly and Senate of Pakistan nor does it have its own assembly to formulate the laws. So the proposed defacto Provisional Province will be cause of insecurity and scarcity for the people of Gilgit-Baltistan."[85]

On July 28, 2010 Manzoor Parwana was detained by the Pakistani security forces after his address to the BSNO in Gilgit. He was later shifted to an unknown place by the intelligence agencies for interrogation. He was arrested for expressing support to the Ladakhi refugees who were demanding the opening of Kargil-Skardu road. During his address Parwana raised the following issues:[86]

(i) The implementation of State Subject Rule, which Maharaja Hari Singh has promulgated in the region.
(ii) Withdrawal of Pakistani security forces from the region.
(iii) Denial of human rights to the people of Gilgit-Baltistan.

In an open letter addressed to then President of Pakistan, Asif Ali Zardari and Asian Human Rights Commission, the Chairman of the BNF, Abdul Hamid Khan appealed to them for immediate release of Manzoor Hussain Parwana and withdrawal of all charges against him.[87] Parwana was implicated in a false sedition case after his magazine *Kargil International* criticized Pakistan Army and General Musharraf for launching the Kargil misadventure. The magazine demanded the setting up of an independent commission to identify those officers responsible for launching Kargil war. The magazine alleged that hundreds of soldiers of Northern Light Infantry disguised as Mujahideen were killed. Consequently, *Kargil International* was banned by the Musharraf regime and all its copies were confiscated.[88] On November 4, 2004, the police arrested its publisher Ghulam Shehzad Agha. Agha who is also the Central President of GBUM, was however released after large scale protests by the party workers.

Further, in September 2013 Parwana also demanded that the Pakistan government should reveal the reasons behind the presence of Chinese in the region. Alarmed about the presence of foreign troops in the area, the GBUM Chairman stated, "Pakistan and China's unwarranted activities in Gilgit Baltistan are causing instability and may as well threaten the safety of natives in the long run. If terrorists attack passenger buses and foreign tourists near KKH, this is the conspiracy against the friendship between China and Pakistan and will be a constant threat to Gilgit Baltistan."[89]

GILGIT BALTISTAN UNITED ALLIANCE (GBUA)

Introduction, Aims and Objectives

The leftist parties established an alliance, Gilgit Baltistan United Alliance (GBUA), at a meeting attended by the representatives of the parties in January 2007 with the objective to:

(i) struggle against the bureaucratic colonial rule;
(ii) demand withdrawal of Pak troops from Gilgit-Baltistan and Indian troops from Ladakh and Kargil; and
(iii) demand establishment of two autonomous regions across the Line of Control (LoC).

The convenor of the Alliance is Ghulam Shehzad Agha. It comprises the Boloristan Labour Party, GBUM, KNM, BNF and Baltistan Students Federation.

The meeting was also attended by Manzoor Hussain Parwana, Chairman of the GBUM who stressed the need for greater understanding and unity among the nationalist and progressive parties.[90] This Alliance has been observing November 16 as day of repentance, marking it as the day when the freedom of Gilgit and Baltistan was seized in the name of Islam, Pakistan and Kashmir.[91] In one of the conferences held in Gilgit, the people openly raised slogans in support of independence from the colonial control of Pakistan.

GILGIT BALTISTAN NATIONAL ALLIANCE (GBNA)

Introduction

Formed in 2001, the Gilgit Baltistan National Alliance (GBNA) is an umbrella organisation of 14 political and religious parties of Gilgit-Baltistan. These parties include the PPP-GB, JI-GB, PMLN-GB, PMLQ-GB, JUI-GB, TeJ Pakistan, MQM-GB, BNF, KNM, JKLM, Awami Tehreek, National Rights Front, Thinkers' Forum and Gharib Qaumi Movement. The Alliance, which has practically split due to the differences within, aimed at a struggle for solution to the problems of Gilgit-Baltistan.[92] The Chairperson of the GBNA is Malika Baltistani. She became the founder President of Ladakh Baltistan United Front which was formed in 1963. She joined a protest march against the killings of Shias and minorities in front of Pakistan Embassy in Washington on April 14, 2012. The GBNA out rightly rejected the GBESGO 2009 and called it as deceptive.[93] But of late it has been noticed that GBNA has started cultivating its relationship with the Pakistan establishment.

AWAMI WORKERS PARTY (AWP)

Aims and Objectives

Awami Workers Party (AWP) was formed in 2012 with the merger of three leftist parties – Labour Party Pakistan, Workers' Party and Awami Party. According to its official website, the party was formed with the objective to:

   (i) take the primary responsibility of organising and planning the country's economy;
   (ii) nationalise major industries, including those run by the military and place them under the control of democratic state;
   (iii) resist imperialist aggression against the people in all manifestations, be they drone strikes, multinational capital or austerity measures imposed by the International Monetary Fund (IMF) and World Bank;
   (iv) stop privatisation policy – re-nationalise all private industries and re-instate the sacked employees;
   (v) permit workers to form trade unions;

(vi) implement radical land reforms and redistribute land among the peasantry in order to break the political and social power of big landlords; and

(vii) fundamentally change the state's hostile policy towards neighbouring countries.[94]

Leadership

AWP's leadership comprises Fanous Gujjar (Central Chairman); Farooq Tariq (General Secretary, earlier the spokesman of the Labour Party Pakistan); Baba Jan (Vice President, also the Chairperson of Progressive Youth Front of Gilgit Baltistan) and Farzana Bari (Secretary, women's wing).

It's vice president Baba Jan is currently serving 40 year jail term along with 11 other activists. He was arrested in 2011 and remained in jail for nearly two years. After a massive national and international campaign by various human rights organisations, he was released on bail on June 27, 2013. He was again arrested when an anti-terrorism court sentenced him to life imprisonment in September 2014 for raising his voice against police brutality and for demanding compensation to the affectees of Attabad Lake disaster. Baba Jan contested the June 2015 Gilgit Baltistan Legislative Assembly elections from jail from the GBLA-6 (Hunza) constituency on an appeal by the Committee for the Release of Political Prisoners. He was defeated. Meanwhile, an International Solidarity Campaign for Baba Jan and four of his party activists facing life sentence has been re-launched by Pierre Rousset, member of the leadership of the Fourth International and member of the New Anti-capitalist Party (NPA) in France. Pierre Rousset has also appealed to people for donation to help the families of Baba Jan and four others who are serving life sentence in jail.[95]

On November 20, 2014, the AWP held a country-wide protest to demand the release of its leaders including Baba Jan and to stop harassing people using the anti-terrorist laws. One such protest was held at Abpara Chowk (Islamabad). The protest meeting was also attended by the leaders of United Kashmir People's National Party (UKPNP) and National Students Federation Gilgit-Baltistan.[96] A delegation of the AWP met the visiting Fact Finding Mission of Human Rights Commission in Gilgit in August 2016 and shared their concern about the constitutional status of the region and the way it affected the legislative and judicial system of Gilgit-Baltistan.

GILGIT-BALTISTAN NATIONAL MOVEMENT (GBNM)

Introduction, Aim and Objectives

Gilgit-Baltistan National Movement (GBNM) is another nationalist group active in Gilgit-Baltistan. The party considers Gilgit-Baltistan a disputed area and maintains that until its status is decided in accordance with the UN resolutions, the area should be given an 'AJK'-like system of governance. Its chairman is Dr. Ghulam Abbas. Explaining the goal of his party, Abbas said, "We want a united state of Gilgit-Baltistan and Jammu and Kashmir and after achieving that goal if the people of GB wanted to separate themselves from the united country they should be given the option."[97] He criticised the 2009 Gilgit-Baltistan Empowerment and Self Governance Order, which according to him has no legal or constitutional status. In this connection, he filed a petition in the Gilgit-Baltistan Appellate Court. It was accepted by the court which directed the federal government and Ministry of Kashmir Affairs and Northern Areas to submit a report on the objections raised in the petition.[98] He also alleged that China considers Gilgit-Baltistan, Ladakh, Kargil and Aksai Chin as its integral part and is slowly and quietly occupying the whole region. He suspects that China is investing a considerable amount on the expansion of the Karakoram Highway and other projects as a part of its strategy.

GILGIT-BALTISTAN NATIONAL CONGRESS (GBNC)

Introduction

The Gilgit-Baltistan National Congress (GBNC) was formed in Washington to highlight the need of political, constitutional, economic, social and human rights for the people of both 'AJK' and Gilgit-Baltistan. It is headed by Imtiaz Hussain and Senge Hasnain Sering is its director. The group is supported by the GBDA and All Party National Alliance (APNA).

In one of its statements, GBNC stated:

> Pakistani forces have transformed this peaceful and picturesque region into a military garrison and commit rights violations with absolute impunity. In a memorandum submitted to UN observer in Islamabad on October 4, 2015, the organisation had demanded effective political and administrative system for PoK and GB which it alleged are being overtly and covertly dictated and governed by Pakistan through its bureaucracy military and its secret agencies in connivance with the so called peoples representative.[99]

Activities

The GBNC organised a conference titled, "Water Resource Exploitation,

Environment Pollution and Flashfloods in Pakistani Occupied Gilgit-Baltistan", at the United Nations Human Rights Council, Geneva, on September 24, 2010. The Member of European Parliament and the Chairperson of Friends of Gilgit-Baltistan Caucus in European Parliament, Jurgen Creutzmann, appealed to the Pakistan Government to improve its environment record which could help to reduce the damage caused by the flash floods in the future. In his support to the people of G-B, Creutzmann highlighted the following points:

- First, the extremist elements including the Taliban could benefit from the current situation in gaining sympathy from poverty-stricken flood victims.
- Second, Pakistan's policy of using Gilgit-Baltistan as a launching pad to advance militancy in Kashmir and Afghanistan exacerbates the security crisis of the region.
- Third, he expressed concern over Pakistan's tactics of exploiting river water dispute with India to advance militancy in Kashmir. Elaborating this point Creutzmann said, "Pakistan is largely interested in acquiring control over the rivers of Kashmir. Kashmir and water dispute with India have become tools to advance military and strategic interest, which destabilizes the region."
- Fourth, Creutzmann supported the demand of the people of Gilgit-Baltistan to regain control over their natural resources. He criticised Islamabad for exploiting these natural resources with impunity which has led to environmental degradation and glacier melting.[100]

In the same vein, Sange Hasnain Sering also highlighted the plight of the people who are constantly living under the shade of fear. According to Sering:

> Thousands of workers, soldiers and para-military with their equipment, explosives and vehicles are present on the soil of Gilgit-Baltistan. Further, several tunnels are being built adjacent to glacial moraines leading to their melting at alarming rate. In addition to environmental degradation, foreign workers compete with natives for jobs and services. In the name of development and infrastructural building, foreigners are encouraged to settle in the region and help change demography. Such policies will only damage the social fabric and add to ethnic violence.[101]

GILGIT-BALTISTAN THINKER'S FORUM (GBTF)

Introduction, Aims and Objectives

The Gilgit-Baltistan Thinker's Forum (GBTF) stands for the two-state formula in the region. The formation of these two independent states is based on ethnic and cultural lines. The first state would comprise two parts of Kashmir excluding Ladakh and the second state would include Gilgit, Baltistan and Ladakh areas.[102]

The Chairman of the GBTF is Col (retd.) Wajahat Hasan Mirza, who is living in exile, has been very active in highlighting the demand for complete independence from Pakistan at every forum. In a statement on September 10, 2000, Wajahat Mirza said, "Pakistan rule cannot be spread over Gilgit and Baltistan and these areas ought to be treated as a foreign country."[103] In March 2016, when the nationalist leaders protested at the UN Human Rights Council, Geneva, Mirza said, "In Gilgit-Baltistan all black laws are being enforced, the anti-terrorist courts and military courts are acting against the political activists and leaders."[104] Wajahat Hassan accused Islamabad of allowing foreign countries particularly China to exploit the resources of the region. Wajahat along with his brother Col. (retd.) Nadir Hasan suffered brutality at the hands of Pakistani security forces. Wajahat was kidnapped in Dubai in November 2010 and brought to Islamabad where he was handed over to the ISI. The entire operation was conducted under the supervision of Lt. Colonel Shoaib of the counter intelligence department of ISI in Islamabad.[105]

According to Nadir Hasan, depriving the people of Gilgit-Baltistan a right to self-rule by Pakistan is deliberate because it does not want a Shia state. The civilian and political administration according to Nadir is in the hands of Sunnis. Even the composition of Frontier Corps is Sunni-dominated, and they are being used to intimidate the Shias under the pretext of maintaining law and order.

The GBTF Convenor, Dr. G. Abbas has accused Pakistan of double talk. He said that on the one hand Pakistan claims that there is no dispute over the future status of Gilgit-Baltistan, but on the other hand, when a demand for self-rule is made, Pakistan declines it on the pretext that the area is part of the disputed state of Jammu and Kashmir.[106]

Nationalist leaders of 'AJK' and Gilgit-Baltistan to the great dismay of Pakistan do not recognise the Kashmiri separatists. Most of them are of the view that no one from the region has designated the Hurriyat or any other group in the region to represent them. In this context, Mirza Wajahat stated, "Neither we, nor the Hurriyat are elected by the common people. So, how can we claim to be their representative?"[107]

GILGIT-BALTISTAN BAR COUNCIL (GBBC)

Introduction

The lawyers of Gilgit-Baltistan have also joined the campaign to fight for basic rights for the people and to determine the constitutional status of Gilgit-

Baltistan. In this connection, lawyers belonging to different political parties have formed the Gilgit-Baltistan Bar Council. In one of its meetings, the Bar Council adopted an unanimous resolution raising three demands: i) Gilgit-Baltistan be declared the fifth province of the country; ii) there should be local government on the "pattern" of "Azad Kashmir"; and iii) if the two proposals are considered impractical, "Azad Kashmir" and Gilgit and Baltistan be declared one unit.[108] The Vice President of Gilgit-Baltistan Bar Council, Shehbaz Khan, said in Gilgit on January 8, 2015 that the federal government should either bring the region within the purview of Pakistan's Constitution or provide it with a separate constitution. He made it clear that the Gilgit-Baltistan Empowerment and Self-governance Order 2009 will not be accepted anymore, adding that "instead of introducing ceremonial changes in the order, the federal government should make arrangements to conduct elections for a constituent assembly".[109]

Network

The GBBC formed a committee of both the region of 'AJK' and Gilgit-Baltistan in January 2015. It issued a joint declaration in which the coordination committee demanded the abolition of Ministry of Kashmir Affairs and Gilgit-Baltistan as it poses a major stumbling block to constitutional rights.[110] The main aim to form the coordination committee was to launch a collective struggle for autonomy and eliminate misunderstandings between both regions. The declaration was signed by various lawyers of both the regions including Shehbaz Khan and the 'AJK' Bar Council advocate, Raja Khalid Mehmood.

In a letter addressed to the then Prime Minister of Pakistan Nawaz Sharif and the then Chairman Committee for Constitutional Status for GB Mr Sartaj Aziz, Shehbaz Khan wrote that refusal to allow fundamental rights to the two million people of Gilgit-Baltistan was a deliberate disobedience of the 1999 judgement of the Supreme Court of Pakistan as well wherein the federation of Pakistan has been directed to ensure fundamental rights to the people of Gilgit-Baltistan within six months to govern themselves through their chosen representatives and access to an independent judiciary guaranteed under the constitution. Further he invited the attention of these leaders that in both parts of the Kashmir, people are entitled to enjoy democratic, legal and constitutional rights but the people of GB are continued to be denied their constitutional rights since independence.[111]

GHARIB QAUMI MOVEMENT (GQM)

Introduction

The Gharib Qaumi Movement is basically a one-man party formed by Inayat-ullah Shumali, who is also its President. Shumali who hails from Chilas in Diamir district is also Chairman of the Gilgit Baltistan National Alliance. The party had earlier advocated the formation of a separate province on the lines of demands put forth by nationalists. However, it now demands that the Gilgit Baltistan Government be set up on the pattern of 'AJK'.[112] Meanwhile a reforms committee headed by the Advisor to the Prime Minister on Foreign Affairs, Sartaj Aziz has reportedly finalised recommendations to devolve more powers to the Gilgit-Baltistan Assembly. However, recommendations of the committee have not yet been revealed.[113]

CONCLUSION

The Pakistan Government leaves no stone unturned to silence the voice of the nationalsits in the region. There is discontent among the masses, as no concrete steps have been taken to ensure the people of Gilgit-Baltistan their basic democratic rights. Nationalist parties/groups complain of harassment of their workers including implicating hundreds in false sedition cases by the Pakistan security agencies. Number of their leaders and workers are living in exile abroad for fear of their life. They include Abdul Hamid Khan, Chairman of Balawaristan National Front (living in exile in Belgium since 1980s), Sardar Shaukat Ali Kashmiri, Chairman UKPNP (in exile in Switzerland since 1999), Col. Wajahat Hasan Mirza of Bolor Thinkers' Forum (in exile in Austria for the last 3 years) and Mumtaz Khan of UKPNP (in exile in Canada since 1998). The 1988 onslaught is still fresh in the memories of people and nationalists when thousands of Sunni tribesmen, predominantly from Khyber Pakhtunkhwa attacked Shiite villages of Gilgit. The entire operation was conducted under the supervision of General Musharraf who was then a Brigadier commanding the Special Services Group (SSG). According to Pakistani commentator, Sohaib Bodla, "Shiite villages were burnt down, Sunni tribesmen continued killings for days and went unhindered by the Pakistani Army that was deployed not far away from the villages under attack."[114] Moreover, with the abolition of state subject law, hundreds of the people from the adjoining states like Khyber Pakhtunkhwa (KP) have migrated to Gilgit-Baltistan where they have purchased properties and engaged in unlawful activities. The Kargil conflict in 1999 further aggravated the feelings of alienation as Pakistan government did not acknowledge the sacrifices of Northern Light Infantry (NLI) troops which suffered heavy casualties as Shia and Ismail soldiers were pushed into suicidal missions by Pakistani Sunni officers.[115] Not only this, Pakistan refused to receive the bodies of NLI soldiers. The worst was that their families were given only a meagre compensation. An editorial in *The Dawn* warned that a provocative sense of nationalism is getting stronger in Gilgit-Baltistan, "The same people who have unflinching loyalty towards the state of Pakistan and were considering themselves as Pakistanis are now talking about separation, freedom and a separate nation of Gilgit-Baltistan."[116]

ENDNOTES

1. Omar Farooq Zain, "A Socio-Political Study of Gilgit-Baltistan Province", *Pakistan Journal of Social Sciences*, 30 (1), September 2010, pp. 181-190, at www.bzu.edu.pk/pjss/vol30no12010/final_pjss-3116.pdf.
2. International Crisis Group (ICG), *Discord in Pakistan's Northern Areas*, Asia Report No. 131, April 2, 2007, p. 13. at http://www.crisisgroup.org/home/index
3. "History & Dispute", *Gilgit Baltistan Tribune*, at http://gbtribune.blogspot.in/p/history-dispute.html.
4. *Manifesto of PPP for Gilgit-Baltistan 2015*, at www.gbvotes.pk/english/WP-content/uploads/2015/03/PPP-final.pdf.
5. "PPP Announces Gilgit-Baltistan Office Bearers", Mountain TV Net, December 9, 2015, at http://www.mountaintv.net/ppp-announces-gilgit-baltistan-office-bearers.
6. Shabbir Mir, "Crisis Averted: PML-Q to stay in G-B Govt following Chief Minister's U-turn", *The Express Tribune*, May 8, 2014, at https://www.google.co.in/webhp?sourceid=chrome-instant&ion=1&espv=2&ie=UTF-8#q=Crosis+averted%3APML-Q+to+stay+in+G-B+govt+following+chief+minister's+u-turn.
7. "G-B Chief Minister Ends Alliance with PML-Q", *The Express Tribune*, May 6, 2014, at http://www.tribune.com.pk/story/704830/g-b-chief-minister-ends-alliance-with-pml-q/
8. Ershad Mahmud, "The Battle for Gilgit-Baltistan", *The News*, June, 7, 2015, at http://tns.thenews.com.pk/the-battle-for-gilgit-baltistan/#.VcL8h_OqpHw.
9. Ibid.
10. Ibid
11. Altaf Hussain, "Gilgit Baltistan Empowerment and Self-governance Order 2009", *The Gilgit-Baltistan Reforms*, December 2009, at, http://www.forumfd.org/en/pubs/pakistan/gilgit-baltistan%20AHussain%20FinalDec09.doc p. 8
12. http://pppSB-kp.pk/gilgitbaltistan-cabinet.
13. "PML-N Welcomes Approval of Self Governance Order: Ahsan", August 29, 2009, *Balochistan Times*, at http://www.thefreelibrary.com/PML-N+wecomes+approval+of+self+governance+for+NA+3A+AT.
14. Shabbir Mir, -"PML-N Announces Manifesto for G-B Polls", *The Express Tribune*, May 28, 2015, at http://tribune.com.pk/story/893330/full-speed-ahead-pml-n-announces-manifesto-for-g-b-polls.
15. http://pmln-constitution/theprovincial-organisation/.
16. "PMLN Leaders for Gilgit Baltistan Announced, Hafeez Gets the Top Slot", *Pamir Times*, at http://pamirtimesblog.tumblr.com/post/110256894016/pmln-leaders-for-gilgit-baltistan-announced.

17. *Election Manifesto of the Pakistan Muslim League (N) Gilgit-Baltistan.*
18. Ahmad Hassan, "Formation of GB Govt Likely by June-end", *The News*, June 15, 2013, at http://www.thenews.com.pk/Todays-News-2-323753-Formation-of-GB-govt-likely-by-june-end.
19. "Déjà vu: Committee on G-B Status Dubbed a Poll Ploy", *The Express Tribune*, May 4, 2015; http://tribune.com.pk/story/880453/deja-vu-committee-on-g-gb-status-dubbed-a-poll-ploy/
20. "Six-member GB Cabinet Takes Oath amid Controversy", *Dawn*, July 8, 2015, at http://www.dawn.com/news/1193113-six-member-gb-cabinet-takes-oath-amid-controversy.
21. Muhammad Amir Rana and Mujtaba Rathore, *Northern Areas: Crisis and Prospects*, Pakistan Institute for Peace Studies, Lahore, 2007, p 29.
22. International Crisis Group, "Discord in Pakistan's Northern Areas", pp.12-13
23. Altaf Hussain, "Gilgit Baltistan Empowerment and Self-governance Order 2009", p. 12.
24. Shabbir Mir, "PML-N Announces Manifesto for G-B Polls".
25. "APML seeks creation of GB province", *Dawn*, June 5, 2015, http://www.dawn,com/news/1186238/apml-seeks-creation-of-gb-province
26. Tariq Butt, "GB Polls: Major Parties Pin High Hopes", *The News*, June 8, 2015, at http://www.thenews.com.pk/Todays-News-2-322393-GB-polls-Major-parties-pin-high-hopes.
27. *The Manifesto of PTI for Gilgit-Baltistan*, March 2015, at www.gbvotes.pk/english/WP-content/uploads/2015/03/pti-final.pdf.
28. "PTI Cries Foul over GB Polls", *Dawn*, June 21, 2015, at http://www.dawn.com/news/1189443/pti-cries-foul-over-gb-polls.
29. M. Ismail Khan, "G B Elections: What Next?" *The News*, June 24, 2015, at http://www.thenews.com.pk/Todays-News-9-325253-GB-elections-what-next.
30. Shabbir Mir, "Loyalty unrewarded: PTI appoints Raja Jalal new G-B head", *The Express Tribune*, January 30 2017, at http://tribune.com.pk/story/1310903/loyalty-unrewarded-pti-appoints-raja-jalal-new-g-b-hed/
31. PPP and Shia Ulema Council forms Electoral Alliance, Shiite News, 18 April, 2013, http://www.shiitenews.org/index.php/component/k.2/item/2187-ppp-and-shia-ulema-council-forms-electoral-alliance/
32. Ibid.
33. "Allama Sajid Naqvi asks Shia Ulema Council's leaders to activate Party in Gilgit-Baltistan", *Shiite News*, May 13,2014, http://www.shiitenews.org/index.php/component/k2/item/8119-allama-
34. Samuel Baid, "Northern Areas", Jasjit Singh (ed.), *Pakistan occupied Kashmir under the Jackboot*, Siddhi Books, New Delhi, 1995, p. 137.
35. Muhammad Amir Rana and Mujtaba Rathore, *Northern Areas: Crisis and Prospects*, p. 3.
36. Ahmad Hassan, "PTI Rallies in GB Not to Effect PML-N's Position", *The News*, June 11, 2015, at http://www.thenews.com.pk/Todays-News-2-323079-PTI-rallies-in-G.
37. Muhammad Amir Rana and Mujtaba Rathore, *Northern Areas: Crisis and Prospects* pp. 31-33.
38. Ibid.
39. Ahmad Hassan "Formation of GB Govt Likely by June-end", *The News*, June 15, 2013.
40. "History & Dispute", *Gilgit Baltistan Tribune*.
41. Ibid.
42. Muhammad Amir Rana and Mujtaba Rathore, *Northern Areas: Crisis and Prospects*, pp. 33-34.
43. Altaf Hussain, "Gilgit Baltistan Empowerment and Self-governance Order 2009", p. 12.
44. Moosa Kaleem, "Tactical Shift", *The Herald*, December 2009, p. 37.
45. "Gilgit-Baltistan Elections: PML-N Ranks Swell as Raja Azam Quits MQM", *Out post*, April

23, 2015, at http://pk/national/364-gilgit-baltistan-elections-pml-n-ranks-swell-as-raja-azam-quits-mqm.htm.
46. "Asma against 'State Oppression' in GB", *Dawn*, April 5, 2015, at http://www.dawn.com/news/1174044/asma-aganist-state-oppression-in-gb.
47. Kamran Arif, "What Is Wrong in the Northern Areas", *Human Rights Commission of Pakistan – News Letter*, January 1994, pp. 21-24.
48. Official website of the Balawaristan National Front, at http://www.balawaristan.net/.
49. Official website of Balawaristan, at http://www.balawaristan.com/about-us/.
50. Speech of Abdul Hamid Khan, Chairman, Balawaristan National Front (BNF) in The Hague, Unrepresented Nations and Peoples Organization (UNPO), February 11, 2011, at www.unpo.org/downloads/156.pdf. See also Appendix X.
51. "Pakistan imposed war on us, India never occupied our land: Gilgit-Baltistan leader Abdul Hamid Khan," *Financial Express*, April 29, 2017 at http://www.financial express.com/india-news/if-referendum-happens-people-will-vote-for-india/
52. Sohaib Bodla, "Making a Nation in High Mountains: Balawars and Balwaristan Nationalism in Ghizer Districts of Gilgit Baltistan", *Ethno Scripts*, 1 (1), 2014, pp. 125-134.
53. "BNF Chief Asks UN to Save GB People from Vanishing", *Brooshaal Times*, n.d., at http://brooshaaltimes.com/bnf-chief-asks-save-gb-people-vanishing.
54. Ibid.
55. Muhammad Amir Rana and Mujtaba Rathore, *Northern Areas: Crisis and Prospects*, p. 50.
56. Moosa Kaleem, "Revolution out of Reach", *The Herald*, December 2009, pp. 36-37.
57. Muhammad Amir Rana and Mujtaba Rathore, *Northern Areas: Crisis and Prospects*, p. 50.
58. "Gilgit Baltistan: Activist Calls for End to Pakistani Occupation", UNPO, June 18, 2013, at http://www.unpo.org/article/16079.
59. Sohaib Bodla, "Making a Nation in High Mountains: Balawars and Balwaristan Nationalism in Ghizer Districts of Gilgit Baltistan", p 135
60. Abdul Hamid Khan, "Pakistan's Heart of Darkness", *Asia Times*, August 2, 2002, at http://www.a.times.com/a.times/South_asia/DH22Df03.html.
61. "'Package a Ploy to Occupy Gilgit Baltistan', Says BNF Chief", *Weekly Bang Karachi*, 2 (34), October 20-26, 2009, at http://weeklybaang.blogspot.in/2009/11/weekly-baang-karachi-volume-02-issue-34_27.html 34. (For details see Appendix X)
62. Yoginder Sikand, "'Treated by Pakistan as Virtual Slaves': An Interview with Abdul Hamid Khan", *Outlook*, June 28, 2002, at http://www.outlookindia.com/website/story/treated-by-pakistan-as-virtual-slaves/216236.
63. "'Corridor Project a Ploy to Enslave People of GB', Says BNF Chief", *Brooshal Times*, at http://brooshaltimes.com/corridor-corridor-project-ploy-enslave-people-gb-bnf/.
64. Muhammad Amir Rana and Mujtaba Rathore, *Northern Areas: Crisis and Prospects*, p. 44.
65. Pankaj Mathur, "'Pak's Gilgit-Baltistan reforms, Attempt to Divide Kashmiris': JKLF", TopNews.in, Lahore, November 4, 2009, at http://www.topnews.in/pak-s-gilgitbaltistan-reforms-attempt-divide-kashmiris-jklf-2232465.
66. "JKLF Rejects Gilgit-Baltistan Package", *Dawn*, September 7, 2009, at http://www.dawn.com/news/944451/jklf-rejects-gilgit-baltistan-package.
67. Shabbir Mir, "JKLF Leader Censures Giving GB Constitutional Status", *The Express Tribune*, February 29, 2016, at http://tribune.com.pk/story/1056106/jklf-leader-censures-giving-g-b-constituional-status/.
68. Ibid.
69. JKLF opens office in Gilgit-Baltistan, Greater Kashmir, February 3, 2016, at, http://www.greaterkashmir.com/news/pak-administered-kashmir/jklf-opnes-office-in-gilgit-baltistan

70. Mohammad Amir Rana and Mujtaba Rathore, *Northern Areas: Crisis and Prospects*, pp. 39-40.
71. "'Annul All Illegal Mining Leases Issued in Disputed Gilgit-Baltistan', Nationalists Demand in Hunza Valley", Hunza, July 21, 2008, cited in the Official website of Karakorum National Movement, August 21, 2008, at http://my/karakorum.blogspot.in/
72. Cited in Samuel Baid, "Gilgit-Baltistan's Elusive Self-Governance", The Democracy Forum, December 1, 2014, at http://thedemocracyforumltd.com/gilgit-baltistans-elusive-self-governance/
73. "Aims, Struggle and sacrifices of Karakuram National Movement (KNM)", *Pamir Times*, December 29, 2014, at http://pamirtimes.net/2014/12/29/aims-struggle-and-sacrifices-of-karakuram-nationa-movement
74. Shafaqat Inqalabi and Sange Sering, interview with the authors.
75. Paul Beersman, cited in K. Warikoo (ed.), *The Other Kashmir: Society, Culture and Politics in the Karakoram Himalayas*, Pentagon Press, New Delhi, 2014, p. 164.
76. Moosa Kaleem, "Revolution out of Reach".
77. Boloristan is an old name of Gilgit-Baltistanm.
78. See "Gilgit Baltistan", UNPO, at http://unpo.org/members/8727.
79. Moosa Kaleem, "Revolution out of Reach", Altaf Hussain, "Gilgit Baltistan Empowerment and Self-governance Order 2009", *Pakistan-administered Kashmir (Azad Kashmir and Gilgit – Baltistan): COI Compilation*, Austrian Centre for Country of Origin and Asylum Research and Documentation (ACCORD), Vienna, May 7, 2012, at http://www.refworld.org/docid/4fba0d042.html, "The Kashmir and Gilgit-Baltistan Dispute", Pakistan Defence, March 30, 2013, at http://defence.pk/threads/the-kashmir-and-gilgit-baltistan-dispute.242976/.
80. Freedom House, *Freedom in the World 2011: The Annual Survey of Political Rights and Civil Liberty*, Rowman and Littlefield Publishers, Washington, p. 783.
81. Mohammad Amir Rana and Mujtaba Rathore, *Northern Areas: Crisis and Prospects*, p. 46.
82. Official website of the Gilgit Baltistan United Movement, at http://skardu.blogspot.com
83. http://self.gutenberg.org/articles/gilgit_baltistan_united_movement/
84. "Dispute and Politic(k)s: 'Provisional Province is a Joke with GB'", *The Express Tribune*, July 12, 2015, at http://tribune.com.pk/story/919154/dispute-and-politicks-provisional-status-a-joke-with-gb.
85. "Provisional Province is a Joke with the People of Gilgit-Baltistan: Manzoor Parwana", Skardu Blogs, July 12, 2015, available at, http://skardu.blogspot.in/2015/07/provisional-province-is-joke-with-the-people-of-gilgit-baltistan
86. Senge Sering, "Gilgit Baltistan: Detainment of Manzoor Parwana is the Latest of Political Activists", UNPO, August 1, 2011, at http://www.unpo.org/article/12973.
87. http://www.humanrights.asia/news/forwarded-news/AHRC-FOL-009-2011.
88. "Book Musharraf as a Criminal", Press Release issued by Chairman Gilgit Baltistan United Movement (GBUM), Skardu, August 20, 2008.
89. "Gilgit-Baltistan: Chinese Presence Causes Concern", UNPO, September 23, 2013, at http://unpo.org/article/16406.
90. "Skardu: Call for Self-Rule in Gilgit, Baltistan", *The Dawn*, January 16, 2007, at http://www.dawn.com/news/228130/skardu-call-fi=or-self-rule-im-gilgit-baltistan.
91. "Day of Repentance Observed in Gilgit-Baltistan, Gilgit-Baltistan United Movement", December 13, 2007, at http://skardu.blogspot.in/2007/12/day-of-repentance-observed-in-gilgit-baltistan
92. Muhammad Amir Rana and Mujtaba Rathore, *Northern Areas: Crisis and Prospects*, p.44.
93. "Identity, Diversity and Kashmiriyat in South Asia,", *Greater Kashmir, September 7, 2009*, at http://www.greaterkashmir.com/news/gk-magazine/identity-diversity-and-kashmiriyat-in-south-asia

94. Website of Awami Workers Party (AWP), at http://gbelects.com.party/11/Awami+workers+party+(AWP).
95. "International Solidarity Campaign for Baba Jan Re-launched", *International Viewpoint*, May 27, 2015, at http://www.internationalviewpoint.org/spip.php?article4051.
96. "Stop the Abuse of Anti-Terror Laws against Political Activists – Release Jailed Workers", *International Viewpoint*, November 29, 2014, at http://www.internationalviewpoint.org/spip.php?page=imprimer_article.
97. "China Trying to Occupy Gilgit-Baltistan: GBNM Chief", *Brooshaal Times*, at http://brooshaaltimes.com/china-trying-to-occupy-gilgit-baltistan-gnbchief.
98. "SC Directs Government, KANA to File Replies, *Awaz TV*, February 23, 2012, at http://www.awaztoday.tv/News_SC-directs-govt-KANA-to-file-replies
99. R.C. Ganjoo, "European Parliament Supports Gilgit-Baltistan", Boloji.com, November 1, 2012, at http://www.boloji.com/index.cfm?md=Content&sd=Articles&ArticleID=13318.
100. "Pakistani Interventions in Gilgit-Baltistan Damage Fragile Ecosystem", PR Newswire, October 20, 2010, at http://www.prnewswire.com/news-releases/pakistani-interventions-in.gil.bal.
101. Ibid.
102. M Ilyas Khan, "Disagree and Be Damned", *The Herald*, Karachi, December 2000, p. 43-45.
103. "PoK Forum Demands Freedom for Gilgit, Baltistan", *The Hindu*, September 11, 2000, at, http://www.thehindu.com/2000/09/11/stories/0211000h.html.
104. "Pakistan Providing Safe Heavens to Terrorists, Claim PoK and Gilgit-Baltistan Leaders", *India TV*, March 12, 2016, at http://www.indiatvnews.com/print/news/india-pakistan-providing-safe-heavens-to-terrorisits.
105. "Pakistan Army and ISI is Kidnapping and Killing People of Gilgit-Baltistan", One India.Com, December 18, 2010, at http://www.oneindia.com/2010/12/18/pakistanarmy-and-isi-is-kidnapping-and-killing-people-of-gilgit-baltistan.
106. Sushant Sareen, "Inside PoK: The Gilgit Grumble", *Analyzing Pakistan*, August 5, 2005, at http://sushantsareen.blogspot.in/2005/08/inside-pok-gilgit-grumble.html.
107. Naveen Kapoor, "We Do Not Recognize Hurriyat, Say Gilgit Leaders", *The Tribune India*, May 21, 2006, at http://www.tribuneindia.com/2006/20060521/world.html.
108. Samuel Baid, "Northern Areas", p. 137, see also "History & Dispute", *Gilgit Baltistan Tribune*.
109. Shabbir Mir, "Lawyers Urge Government to End G-B's Constitutional Limbo", *The Express Tribune*, January 8, 2015, at http://tribune.com.pk/story/818361/now-or-never-lawyers-urge-government-to-end-g-bs-constituional-limbo.
110. Shabbir Mir, "Lawyers Demand Abolition of Ministry of Kashmir and G-B", *The Express Tribune*, February 2, 2015, at http://tribune.compk/story/831324/now-or-never-lawyers-demand-abolition-of-ministry-of-kashmir-and-g-b/.
111. Demands of Gilgit Baltistan Lawyers-Courting the Law, *Gilgit-Baltistan Bar Council*, November 26, 2015, at http://coutingthelaw.com/2015/11/26/updates/demands-of-gilgit-baltistan-lawyers/
112. Mohammad Amir Rana and Mujtaba Rathore, *Northern Areas: Crisis and Prospects*, p. 43.
113. Shabbir Mir, "Gilgit, Kashmir and the Identity Crisis", *The Express Tribune*, February 24, 2016, at www.tribune.com.pk/story/1052901/gilgit-kashmir-and-the-identityy-crisis/.
114. Sohaib Bodla, "Making a Nation in High Mountains: Balawars and Balwaristan Nationalism in Ghizer Districts of Gilgit Baltistan", pp. 125-134.
115. Paul Beersman, cited in K. Warikoo (ed.), *The Other Kashmir: Society, Culture and Politics in the Karakoram Himalayas*, Pentagon Press, New Delhi, 2014, pp. 166-167
116. "Political Unrest in Gilgit-Baltistan", *Dawn*, July 26, 2009, at http://www.dawn.com/news/881186/political-unrest-in-gilgit-baltistan

5

Demand for Provincial Status in Gilgit-Baltistan: Dilemmas of the Pakistan State

In September 2012, the legislative assembly of Gilgit-Baltistan (G-B) passed a resolution demanding provincial status for the region within Pakistan. All the mainstream political parties operating in the region supported this demand. After the elections of June 2015, in which PMLN-GB won a comfortable majority, there were regular demonstrations demanding inclusion of G-B as the fifth province of Pakistan. These demonstrations were well-attended and backed by the then ruling party at the ground level, leading the PML-N government in Islamabad to establish a committee headed by Sartaj Aziz, advisor to the prime minister on foreign affairs, to look into the demand carefully. There was a vigorous debate on this issue in Pakistan in general, and Pakistan occupied Kashmir (PoK) in particular, about the pros and cons of such a decision. Those opposing the demand seemed to influence government's decision with their argument that any decision to absorb G-B as a province of Pakistan would weaken Pakistan's stand on Kashmir vis-a-vis India. In this context, it is necessary to discuss the issue in detail.

Earlier debates on inclusion of 'AJK'

This is not the first time that such a debate has surfaced in Pakistan. In the early 1970s, when Zulfiqar Ali Bhutto, then President and first civilian Chief Martial Administrator of Pakistan, wanted to absorb "Azad Jammu and Kashmir" (AJK) as a province of Pakistan, he met lot of opposition from leaders of 'AJK' and Jamaat-e-Islami (JI) in Pakistan. Bhutto had said, "Pakistan's boundaries cannot be contracted anymore, they would be expanded". His statement came after reports appeared in the media that an alleged secret agreement had been reached at Simla to convert Line of Control (LoC) into international boundary. This was confirmed by former Indian Foreign Secretary J.N. Dixit who said, "At Simla, proposal to convert LoC to making it an international boundary was discussed where in Bhutto said, "I have no problem, I will do it, but please don't put it in the agreement formally."[1] Bhutto's statement on 'AJK' was taken as a suggestion that Pakistan would have five provinces again after the loss of East Pakistan. The debate over inclusion of 'AJK' into Pakistan died down after 1974, when Zulfiqar Ali Bhutto, who had become the prime minister of 'AJK' was gifted with an interim constitution, which remains truly "interim" to this day. With Bhutto's political fortunes plummeting by then, the issue was soon forgotten. It was never revisited afterwards by the succeeding leadership in Pakistan. During his visit to 'AJK' in the first week of November 1973, Bhutto said at a public meeting in Muzaffarabad, "How long will you hang between the two mountains?" He described the U.N. resolutions on Kashmir as mere scraps of paper if the people of Kashmir chose to ignore them. He said, he had invited the Kashmiri leaders to chalk out an agreed and workable proposal for an immediate solution to the Kashmir problem. At this meeting, he made three proposals; (i) 'AJK' can remain as it is; (ii) it could be a full-fledged province of Pakistan; or (iii) it would be accorded autonomous status. This led to immediate reactions from the student community of 'AJK'. They said, "We will die but not allow Kashmir to become a province of Pakistan", according to Lahore Weekly *Lail-o-Nihar*.[2] Later, commenting on the 1974 Act, the *Nawa-i-Waqt* wrote on February 2, 1975, that by virtue of the Kashmir Council which makes the Pakistan Prime Minister its Chairman, the 1974 Act has virtually rendered 'AJK' into a province of Pakistan.

The demand for representation in G-B

At that time, Gilgit-Baltistan which was then known as 'Northern Areas', did not feature in this discourse. However, in the same year (1974), Zulfiqar Ali Bhutto, who had become prime minister by then, abolished the notorious colonial era Frontier Crimes Regulation (FCR) under which it was ruled since 1947, and introduced the Northern Areas Council Legal Framework Order 1974–75. This order did introduce token administrative and judicial reforms, but did not fulfill the basic demands of the people of Gilgit-Baltistan for representative and responsible governance. Bhutto was soon displaced in a military coup, convicted in a case of murder and hanged. During General Zia-ul-Haq's dictatorship, some members of the Northern Areas Legislative Council (NALC) were selected to be members of *Majlis-e-Shura* (Zia's substitute for parliament); however, this was criticized by the political leadership of 'AJK' and nationalists in Northern Areas. The move was withdrawn following protests in both in 'AJK' and 'Northern Areas'.

This *ad hoc* system of a nominal council continued till 1994, when Benazir Bhutto's government, during her second stint as prime minister, introduced the Northern Areas Legal Framework Order (NA-LFO). The administrative system recommended by this order vested all executive powers with the Federal Minister for Kashmir Affairs and Northern Areas, who became the chief executive of NALC. He was accorded powers to amend the LFO at will without consulting the Council. He had the discretion to pick up his deputy from among the 24 members of the legislative council (six members each from Gilgit, Diamer and Baltistan and three each from Ghizar and Ghanche, plus five members, selected by the 24 elected members in the seats reserved for the women). The deputy chief executive served as a nominal administrative head and was assisted by all other members of NALC. In 1999, Pakistan's Supreme Court directed Islamabad to extend fundamental freedoms to the Northern Areas within six months. By this time, there was popular pressure from within Gilgit-Baltistan for change. The government of Pakistan was forced to delegate some of the administrative and financial powers to NALC. The chief secretary of Gilgit-Baltistan was treated at par with the chief secretaries of other provinces of Pakistan. In reform package, which followed in 2007, the NALC was replaced by a Legislative Assembly, and the position of deputy chief executive was renamed as chief executive. All powers continued to remain concentrated in the hands of the Minister for Kashmir Affairs who became the chairman of the new Legislative Assembly. However, at the local level, the demand for further delegation of powers to the local legislature continued.

Self-Governance Act of 2009

The debate on the future of Gilgit-Baltistan gathered further momentum after Yousuf Raza Gilani, the then Prime Minister of Pakistan, issued Gilgit Baltistan Empowerment and Self-governance Order in August 2009.

On 29 August 2009, the Gilgit-Baltistan Empowerment and Self-governance Order was passed by the Pakistan cabinet. The Order was an attempt to appease the local people as by creating among others things, an elected Gilgit Baltistan Legislative Assembly and its Council, a Governor and a Chief Minister with a six-member council of ministers. The council headed by the Prime Minister, exercises virtual power in important spheres of governance. Besides, it will also have supreme appellate court, headed by a chief judge, a public service commission, a chief election commissioner and an auditor-general.

Although the 2009 order conferred the region with a province like status, the Human Rights Commission of Pakistan while rejecting the order said that it fell short of people's expectations who had expected that "the region would either be made the fifth province of Pakistan or get an autonomous status or an interim constitutional set-up on the pattern of Azad Jammu and Kashmir". Pakistan commentator Ershad Mahmud writes:

> The people of Gilgit-Baltistan and their leadership are anxiously weighing the proposal to become a formal province of Pakistan. Gilgit-Baltistan Assembly has clearly demonstrated people's will through various resolutions. The people of Gilgit-Baltistan want representation in the National Assembly, Senate, and other policy making institutions, parallel and separate socio-political development has taken root in Gilgit-Baltistan and Azad Kashmir. Both the regions have not been able to develop shared interests and common democratic institutions which unite people and leadership. Gradually, Gilgit-Baltistan has developed more stakes in the Punjab and Khyber Pakhtunkhwa (KPK) instead of Azad Kashmir due to proximity and direct access through KKH. State Subject Law, which bars non-locals right to the acquisitions of lands ensuring demographic balance, was abolished in mid 1970s. It paved way to mass migration from across the country. Now over 50,000 Pashtuns and Punjabis own land properties and are running huge business in Gilgit-Baltistan. Their number is constantly growing.[3]

India' reaction was clear. The External Affairs Ministry summoned Pakistan Deputy High Commissioner Rifat Mahsud on 11 September 2009 and lodged its protest over its package for Northern Areas. India said that, "entire State of Jammu and Kashmir is an integral part of India by virtue of its accession in 1947. The so-called "Gilgit-Baltistan Empowerment and Self-governance Order 2009" is yet another cosmetic exercise intended to camouflage Pakistan's illegal occupation." India also said that Pakistan had for the last six decades denied basic democratic rights to the people in Pakistan occupied Kashmir (PoK).[4] Pakistan Foreign Office on the same day summoned an official from the Indian High Commission in Islamabad to tell him that New Delhi has no "locus standi" in the matter.[5] Again on March 16, 2017, India said that any 'unilateral step' by Pakistan to declare Gilgit-Baltistan as its fifth province and alter the boundary is completely unacceptable to it. Reacting to reports that a committee headed by Adviser to Pakistan Prime Minister on Foreign Affairs has proposed status of a province to Gilgit-Baltistan, Ministry of External Affairs spokesman, Gopal Baglay, said that any such step would not be able to hide the illegality of Pakistan's occupation of parts of Jammu and Kashmir, which it should vacate immediately.[6]

The Debate (2009-2017)

The debate on the future political status of G-B reflected three broad opinions at the popular level:

(i) Gilgit Baltistan should become another province of Pakistan;
(ii) Administration of Gilgit Baltistan should be returned to the government of 'AJK', and
(iii) Pakistan should vacate Gilgit Baltistan and allow it independence.

Of these three, first option is the most publicized one because it enjoys the support of Pakistan-based political parties in Gilgit-Baltistan. The second one is not so well-publicized because holders of this view are not powerful in the region and they do not have strong links with the leaders of 'AJK', even though the 'AJK' High Court in 1993 had upheld a petition to this effect. The third option is held by the nationalists whose views and activities are hardly covered by the Pakistani media. As Human Rights Commission of Pakistan (HRCP) disclosed in its fact-finding report on Gilgit-Baltistan on March 3, 2017, local journalists and nationalist politicians face crackdown by security forces.[7] It is well-known that the nationalists are strongly opposed to provincial or quasi-provincial status to Gilgit-Baltistan as this would undermine the local people's right to independence. Because of media insensitivity to their opinion, this view is not so well known as those who are demanding provincial status. Without proper empirical assessment of the strength of this constituency, it would not be correct to say what the people of this region actually want. Whatever is being said is based on Pakistani newspapers reports and the local people influenced by Pakistan-based politicians.

Kashmiri leaders on both sides of Line of Control (LoC) have slammed the empowerment package as also move to declare Gilgit-Baltistan as the fifth province of Pakistan. Several Kashmiri separatist leaders including Tehriq-i-Hurriyat leader Syed Ali Shah Gilani, Hurriyat leader Mirwaiz Umar Farooq and JKLF chief Yasin Malik opposed the merger of Gilgit-Baltistan into Pakistan and maintained that such move will provide a justification to India to revoke the special status of Jammu and Kashmir and further consolidate the process of integration of the state into the Indian Union.[8] Yasin Malik, on a visit to Pakistan at the time the empowerment order was proclaimed, had criticized the package and termed it "as an arrow that has been shot into the hearts of Kashmiris."[9] An old veteran of JKLF, Late Amanullah Khan, also denounced the move as a ploy to absorb the territory into Pakistan. He said that "it was on account of Pakistan's "wavering stand" on the Kashmir issue that it had lost the support of the Security Council, and now it was squandering any goodwill left for it by "merging" Gilgit-Baltistan with Pakistan."[10]

As stated above, after the legislative election of June 2015, there was a fresh round of popular protest in favour of inclusion as fifth province of Pakistan. The demonstrations to this effect were orchestrated by the local branch of PML-N and supported by other Pakistan-based political parties, civil society organisations and trade unions. Complete shutter down and wheel jam strikes were observed across G-B, protest rallies were held in Gilgit, Diamer, Hunza, Skardu, Ghizer, Astore, and Nagar since August 2015 and continued till the first half of 2016. The Gilgit-Baltistan Assembly has already adopted a unanimous resolution on August 11, 2015 demanding inclusion of Gilgit-Baltistan as a constitutional province within Pakistan. The resolution also demanded that the Gilgit-Baltistan be given representation in the National Assembly and Senate till the solution of the Kashmir issue in the light of UN resolutions. On January 24, 2016, youths from all over Gilgit-Baltistan organised a demonstration at Gilgit Press Club demanding constitutional rights for the region, declaring Gilgit-Baltistan the fifth province of Pakistan and raising their voice for due and equal share in the CPEC. Similar protests were held by people from the region at the press clubs in Islamabad, Karachi and other cities. According to the *Express Tribune* (January 25, 2016), it was the first time in the history of the region that youth from all walks of life gathered for a common cause. Although Gilgit Baltistan has adopted a resolution to declare Gilgit-Baltistan as a constitutional province, there are different opinions among the political parties as to what type of status be given to Gilgit-Baltistan.

The reactions from 'AJK' leaders to such demands have been on expected lines. The 'AJK' government warned the Pakistan government against any move to convert Gilgit-Baltistan into a province of Pakistan. Addressing a press conference in Muzaffarabad, the then 'AJK' Prime Minister Chaudhry Abdul Majeed made it clear that, "Gilgit-Baltistan is a part and parcel of the State of Jammu and Kashmir. Any attempt to merge it into Pakistan will deal a fatal blow to our stand in the light of UN resolutions envisaging right to self-determination for the Kashmiris." A former Prime Minister of 'AJK' Sardar Attique Khan also warned Pakistan for taking any such decision. He maintained that such a move would be tantamount to the division of Jammu and Kashmir and unacceptable. He further said, "Kashmiris living on either side of the Line of Control (LoC) as well as in Ladakh, Aksai Chin and Gilgit-Baltistan are party to the Kashmir issue along with Pakistan and India".[11] Sardar Ibrahim also jumped into the fray and said that annexing Gilgit-Baltistan without plebiscite was not possible. According to Ibrahim by this "the PML-N regime is strengthening India's case on Kashmir. This is tantamount to division of Kashmir which we would never allow. We strongly oppose any such move".[12] Ershad Mahmud writes in *The News*, January 24, 2016:

It is a hard reality that government of Pakistan has discouraged social and political linkages between the two regions gradually [allowing the gap between the communities to], turn into trust deficit and finally generated deep seated mutual suspicion and hatred leading to wrangling at public forums. The ongoing debate about the future of Gilgit-Baltistan has further deepened the gulf between the two regions.

Since there is no clarity to what should be the future status of Gilgit-Baltistan, it is useful to study a survey, which was conducted by Centre for Peace, Development and Reforms (CPDR), Islamabad under the aegis of Conciliation Resources, London in 2012-13. The survey was based on the interviews, discussions with the youth of the region. Its findings are:

(I) Majority of the youth want Gilgit-Baltistan fully integrated as a fifth province of Pakistan.

(II) Some young people belonging to nationalist parties are strongly against giving provincial or quasi-provincial status to Gilgit-Baltistan.

(III) 'AJK' is an obstacle in bringing reforms in this region. Most of the young people were of the opinion that there is a lack of trust between the people of both sides due to lack of communication channels. Some of the youth suggested that people of both regions should launch a joint struggle for their common socio economic political rights. To establish regular contact, many feel there is need to reopen the old road link between the two regions.

(IV) There was a common view that from the Pakistani side, there was a sustained denial of constitutional and political rights under the pretext of the Kashmir conflict and its treatment of the people of the region was unacceptable.

(V) Although majority of the participants called Gilgit-Baltistan Empowerment and Self Governance Order 2009 'a positive step" which has given them their 'identity" and "might" usher a new era of empowerment and self-rule, many of them criticised it as it has failed to give the region a political status and representation at the national level within Pakistan.

Another survey was conducted by Colonel Imtiaz ul Haque for his Master's thesis titled "Determining the Political Status of Gilgit-Baltistan: Future Perspective", submitted in the National University of Modern Languages, Islamabad in 2012. The responses in Imtiaz ul Haque's survey were very thought-provoking. When respondents were asked whether they suffered from any identity crisis, more than 85 percent answered in the affirmative. On Gilgit-Baltistan's historical link with erstwhile Jammu and Kashmir State, members of the GB legislative Assembly and students dismissed any such notion. Interestingly, when respondents were asked whether Gilgit-Baltistan was a part of Pakistan 'liberated' in 1947, more than 80 percent said 'yes', and only 12 percent answered in the negative. On future status of the region as an independent and an autonomous entity, 45 per cent said 'yes' while 32 per cent said 'no', and 22 per cent remained neutral. To a question whether Empowerment and Self-Governance Order 2009, addressed political and administrative and governance issues of the region, 40 percent of the respondents said 'yes', while a number of the respondents said 'no'. Not surprisingly, 76 per cent of the respondents demanded representation in the National Assembly of Pakistan and more than 68 per cent opposed the idea of merger with 'AJK', while only 28 per cent shared that opinion.[13]

GB Reforms Order 2018

In view of the persisting demands for absorption of the region as the fifth province of Pakistan, the then Prime Minister Nawaz Sharif announced his decision to form a committee on the constitutional status of Gilgit-Baltistan, just before June 2015 legislative elections. The committee headed by Sartaj Aziz was formed on October 29, 2015.

Pakistan raised the hopes to the people of Gilgit-Baltistan by indirectly assuring them to change the political status of the region by turning it into a province of Pakistan. However, the leadership knew that it could not possibly do that, especially when Pakistan continually emphasised on the disputed nature of the Kashmir issue and demanded its early resolution according to the UN resolutions. In this context, if provincial status were to be given to Gilgit-Baltistan, it would be violating these very resolutions that it wanted India to honour and this will weaken its stance on Kashmir.

Secondly, it is going to deepen the sense of alienation among the people of PoK (both 'AJK' and G-B), and lose credibility and trust among the people of Jammu and Kashmir. To avoid this dilemma, a well-known analyst from 'AJK', Ershad Mahmud, has suggested a setup on the lines of AJK, which may address aspirations of people of Gilgit-Baltistan for empowerment. In comparison, Colonel Imtiaz-ul-Haque, whose research work on the subject has been cited above, has suggested "interim provisional status to Gilgit-Baltistan, with right to vote and representation in Parliament of Pakistan" as the best possible alternative. But this can only be done by necessary legislation and amendment in the Pakistani Constitution of 1973.

It was proposed that each district of Gilgit-Baltistan would have representation by sending one member to the National Assembly and representation in the Senate as in the case of other states. Colonel Haque admitted there would be protests from India and the Kashmiri leadership, "but the action can be justified and legalized adding only one word "interim" or "provisional", which is covered under Karachi Agreement 1949". In this connection, he also referred to the Supreme Court of Pakistan's directive to Government of Pakistan in 1999, to initiate and legalise steps, through necessary amendments in the Constitution and statutes, to ensure that the people of Gilgit-Baltistan enjoy fundamental rights. He added that with the enforcement of the 2009 Order, a portion of the Supreme Court judgment had been fulfilled. But to ensure better integration of Gilgit-Baltistan, there was a need to establish a forum where the elected representatives from Gilgit-Baltistan could participate and give their suggestions. This is not possible in the Gilgit-Baltistan Council where only regional subjects could be discussed.

Gilgit-Baltistan remained focus of so much attention that a committee headed by Adviser to Pakistan Prime Minister Sartaj Aziz looked into the popular demand for granting provincial status to the region. According to political observers, the government in Islamabad took the issue seriously which might have been necessitated by the US$ 46 billion (now raised to US$ 60 billion) China Pakistan Economic Corridor (CPEC) being implemented jointly by China and Pakistan. Reports from Pakistan held that the decision to incorporate Gilgit-Baltistan as a new province was taken following pressure from China to bring clarity to the legal status of Gilgit-Baltistan, especially because India called it a disputed territory and objected to any investment in this region.

With PML-N, then the ruling party, dragging its feet over the demand for grant of separate province status to GB, Pakistan Tehreek-i-Insaf (PTI) committed internal autonomy to the region if voted to power. The All Pakistan Muslim League (APML) headed by former President General (retd.) Pervez Musharraf filed a petition in the Islamabad High Court, seeking constitutional amendment for turning Gilgit-Baltistan into the fifth province of Pakistan.

Jamaat-i-Islami and Jamiat Ulema-i-Islam-Fazlur Rahman (JUI-F) favoured merging of Gilgit with 'AJK'. The Majlis Wahadat Muslimeen (MWM) also fully supported complete merger of Gilgit-Baltistan with Pakistan. According to Spokesman of the MWM Ilyas Siddiqui, there were forces who deliberately created hurdles in the way of basic rights of people of Gilgit-Baltistan by making this region controversial,[14] and he would even say that people of the region fought against Dogra ruler for independence and after that ceded to Pakistan "under the love of Islam and Pakistan. Pakistan should have declared this region as its part to respond the selfless love and dedication."[15]

The nationalist groups, including Balawaristan National Front, Karakoram National Movement, Gilgit Baltistan Democratic Alliance, Gilgit Baltistan United Movement, G-B Thinkers' Forum etc have been fighting with the government either for autonomy or independence and thus were lukewarm to the demands for inclusion of GB as the fifth province of Pakistan. Amid such divergent views, the people of the region noticed Pakistan's ambivalence over the issue of incorporating Gilgit-Baltistan into the constitution as the fifth province of Pakistan.

On January 3, 2018, the nine-member parliamentary committee headed by Sartaj Aziz submitted its report to the federal government as per a report in *Dawn* on February 8, 2018. The recommendations of the Ministry of Kashmir Affairs based on the report were submitted to the prime minister on January 3, and to the federal cabinet on February 7, 2018. As per the *Dawn* report:

> The committee recommended de-facto integration of GB with Pakistan but not a de-jure change since that will affect Pakistan's principle position on Kashmir. It recommended delegating further legislative, administrative and financial powers to GB to enhance the people's sense of participation and to improve service delivery. The committee [also] recommended that to bring GB Legislative Assembly on a par with other the provincial assemblies, all legislative subjects, other than those enumerated in article 142 of constitution of Pakistan and its fourth schedule may be devolved from the GB Council to GBLA.

Another report in the same newspaper on February 17, 2018, suggested that the government had decided to remove GB Council and the Powers exercised by the council were to be shifted to the elected GB Legislative Assembly.

However, pending government's announcement of the reforms, there were protests by opposition parties rejecting the draft package. There was a fear that even after abolishing the unrepresentative GB Council, the new framework would weaken GB government even further by taking away whatever autonomy was given to its assembly in the previous arrangement. They objected to the approach of the government in Islamabad to frame policies towards GB without consulting the local representatives. On May 18, the opposition members in GB Legislative Assembly boycotted an in-camera session convened especially to take lawmakers into confidence about the draft political and administrative reforms in GB.

The Government of Gilgit Baltistan Reforms Order 2018 was promulgated by local Legislative Assembly dominated by PMLN-GB on May 22, 2018, after the formal approval by the federal cabinet and endorsement by the National Security Council. This "Order" was notified following the approval by the president on June 1, 2018. (For details see Appendix XV)

According to the Order, the prime minister of Pakistan had been given the authority to legislate over 68 subjects. As the chief executive of the region, he had also been invested with the power to overrule any law passed by the GB Assembly. Despite the claims from the ruling party that the Order was more comprehensive, wide-ranging and all-inclusive compared to 2009 empowerment act, because it would permit GB Assembly to legislate over mineral, hydropower and tourism, the local opposition was overly critical of the move arguing that it did not even grant GB the powers that were made available to the 'AJK' vide the Interim Constitution of 1974.

On May 25, 2018, the Human Rights Commission of Pakistan (HRCP) criticised the reforms package and said:

> In claiming to grant the people of GB their fundamental freedoms, the GB Order has clipped their right to freedom of association and expression. It has denied any Gilgit-Baltistani the right to become a chief judge of the Supreme Appellate Court or to have any say in internal security. Above all, it has disregarded people's needs despite continual public pressure in GB to address their problems fairly and in accordance with local aspirations. The continuing imprisonment of Baba Jan and his comrades for having stood up for their fundamental rights is a sore case in point. There is nothing in the GB Order to protect others like Baba Jan in the future.[16]

The issue took an interesting turn when the GB Supreme Appellate Court, which had stayed the order pending its hearing of a petition on the legality of such an order, came out with a verdict to suspend the GB Reforms order on June 20, 2018. The Supreme Court of Pakistan responding to a petition from the government restored the order on August 7, 2018. The issue of devolution of more powers to GB and according greater autonomy to the region at par with other provinces of Pakistan continues to agitate the minds of the local populace. With the new PTI government in power in Islamabad with its promise to bring province-like status to GB, the popular demand for greater autonomy continued in the following days. The prevailing uncertainty gave rise to nationalist feelings which alarmed the government in Islamabad prompting it to adopt restrictive measures on the local media. As per the fact-finding report brought out by HRCP in August 2018[17], Pakistan government put restrictions on the local press in GB and specifically warned them not to give coverage to nationalists and report negatively about state institutions and government departments. Even advertisers were instructed by the ministry of information not to place advertisements in the newspapers publishing nationalist materials. Many journalists were rounded up and their newspapers were banned leading to widespread disaffection. Such harsh actions by the Pakistan government indicated its extreme sensitivity to growing nationalist feelings among the people in the region, which is likely to intensify if the government fails to meet local aspirations on the one hand and resorts to coercive measures on the other.

ENDNOTES

1. "The Errors of Simla", Interview with Jyotindra Nath 'Mani' Dixit by Sheela Bhat, Rediff.com. July 15, 2001, at https://www.rediff.com/news/2001/jul/15spec.htm
2. Cited in Samuel Baid, "Politics in Azad Kashmir", in Jasjit Singh (ed.) *Pakistan Occupied Kashmir under the Jackboot*, Siddhi Books, New Delhi, 1995, pp. 105-106.
3. Ershad Mahmud, "Gilgit-Baltistan: A Province or not", *The News*, January 24, 2016, http://tns.thenews.com.pk/gilgit-baltistan-province/#comments
4. India Objects to Pakistan Package for PoK, *The Hindu*, September 12, 2009, http//www.thehindu.com/news/national/India-objects-to-Pakistan-package-for-PoK
5. Nirupama Subramanian, "Pakistan Rejects India's Protests", *The Hindu*, September 12, 2009, http://www.thehindu.com/news/national/Pakistan-rejects-Indias-protess
6. Vineeta Pandey, India Flays Pak's Move to Declare Gilgit-Baltistan as 5th Province, *The Pioneer*, March 17, 2017, http://www.dailypioneer.com/print.php?printFOR=storydetail&story_u
7. *BBC* Urdu Service 20:30 hrs March 3, 2017. The detailed report titled, "Gilgit-Baltistan: Aspirations for identity, integration & autonomy", can be accessed at http://hrcp-web.org/publication/wp-content/uploads/2017/04/Gilgit-Baltistan-report-Aspirations-for-identity-integration-autonomy.pdf (accessed on January 18, 2019)
8. Both Yasin Malik and Nawaz Sharif exchanged letters, see details at Appendix XIV.
9. Nirupama Subramanian, "Measures for Gilgit-Baltistan generate suspicion", *The Hindu*, September 1, 2009, http://www.thehindu.com/todays-paper/tp-international/Measures-for-Gilgit-Baltistan-generate-suspicion/article16506357.ece
10. Ibid.
11. Ghulam Abbas, "Constitutional' reforms finalized: GB likely to have place in Senate, NA shortly, *Pakistan Today*, February 13, 2017, www.pakistantoday.com.pk/2017/02/12/police-arrest-two-over-anti-state-activities-in-gb/
12. Ibid.
13. Colonel Imtiaz-ul-Haque, "Determining the Political Status of Gilgit-Baltistan: Future Perspective" Unpublished Master's Thesis, submitted in the National University of Modern Languages, Islamabad 2012.
14. Majlis Wahdat Muslimeen fully support the peaceful struggle of youth of Gilgit-Baltistan in the region:Ilyas Siddiqui, at, http://english.mwmpak.org/index.php/explore/gilgit-baltistan-news/ite
15. Ibid.
16. As reported by daily *Dawn*, May 25, 2018, available at https://www.dawn.com/news/1409777
17. See the report titled "Curbs on freedom of expression in Pakistan", fact-finding report, HRCP, August 2018, available at http://hrcp-web.org/hrcpweb/wp-content/uploads/2018/09/HRCP_Report-on-curbs-on-freedom-of-expression_2018-EN.pdf (accessed January 19, 2019)

6

China-Pakistan Economic Corridor and Gilgit-Baltistan

The China-Pakistan Economic Corridor (CPEC), if it fully materialises, is believed to be a game changer for Pakistan's economy. The CPEC is part of the ambitious Chinese Silk Road initiative, more widely known as 'One Belt One Road (OBOR)' or 'Belt and Road Initiative (BRI)', connecting Kashgar in Xinjiang with Gwadar Port in Pakistan. The relationship between Communist China and the Islamic Republic of Pakistan is a fine example of intricate interplay of geo-strategic and geo-economic aspirations of two countries in the region. It is against this backdrop that the implications and importance of CPEC and handing over of Gwadar port to China on lease for 40 years must be understood.[1] Apart from its economic and trade benefits, Gwadar will enable China to monitor the sea lines of communication through which, according to the US Department of Defence, 82 per cent of all Chinese crude oil and 30 per cent of natural gas imports transit.[2] Gwadar will help China to bypass the Strait of Malacca and will lessen the leverage the US enjoys in the South China Sea.

The bilateral relations between China and Pakistan go back to 1963 when both signed the trade and border agreement. The trade relationships between the two were strengthened under the Free Trade Agreements (FTAs) signed on November 24, 2006 and February 21, 2009. According to the *Pakistan Economic Survey 2014-15*, Pakistan's trade with China has increased 10 per cent in 2013-14 and 9 per cent in 2014-15. In 2012-13, Pakistan's total exports to China were worth Rs. 252.5 billion. In 2013-14, there was a slight decrease in Pakistan's exports to China, the total share was 10 per cent. But in Fiscal Year 2014-15, the trade volume in terms of Pakistan's exports to China has seen further reduction; it stands for Rs. 169.9 billion that constitutes a share of 9 per cent of Pakistan's overall exports to other countries.[3] China's non-financial investment in Pakistan reached one billion dollar in 2014, a dramatic increase from the previous year.[4] China's major investment fields in Pakistan include telecommunications, chemical industry, electricity, oil and gas, among others.

The relationship between Pakistan and China has much to do with the leverage that the two sides gain in their rivalries with India. The animosity vis-à-vis India has underpinned the Pak-China security cooperation, too. Both countries have also benefited from each other by sharing military and nuclear technology; over the years, China has invested heavily in Pakistan's energy sector as well. Moreover, China has shown great interest in Pakistan-occupied Kashmir particularly in Gilgit-Baltistan. The range of infrastructure projects it has undertaken in these areas in the recent past highlights their importance to China. The area provides China a strategic edge both in economic and security realms. China has invested a massive amount of money and manpower in improving and expanding the Karakoram Highway (KKH) – the highest motorway in the world.

On September 14, 2015, Pakistan's then Prime Minister Nawaz Sharif inaugurated the seven-km-long five tunnels, which are the part of the 24-km-long portion of the KKH. These tunnels are known as the Pakistan-China Friendship Tunnels, constructed by China over Attabad Lake in Gilgit-Baltistan's Hunza valley.[5] The KKH's almost 1,300 km stretch runs from China's Kashgar area to Islamabad. China is also involved in the construction of a 750 km railway – from Havelian to the 4,730 m high Khunjerab Pass in Gilgit-Baltistan.[6] Other Chinese investments include a range of projects, particularly in the energy sector, the construction of a hydro-power station in Bunji, the construction of a dry port at Sost, water diversion channels and telecommunication facilities.

The $ 46 billion (now gone up to around $60 billion), CPEC provides the opportunity to kick off major projects in Pakistan. It also envisages establishing various Special Economic Zones (SEZs) along the corridor.[7] The Planning Commission of Pakistan has stated that $ 11 billion will be allocated for infrastructure development and the remaining money will be set aside for energy projects.[8] China is very committed to the CPEC, and wants to pursue the project despite all odds – the topography of the region, unrest in Baluchistan and security of its engineers and workers. Underscoring the importance of the CPEC, Shannon Tiezzi states, "For China, meanwhile, the project is a must if the broader Silk Road Economic Belt, with its attendant benefits for China's domestic economy, geopolitical clout, and regional stability, is to get off the ground ... China also sees the CPEC in particular as a way to diversify its energy supply, lessening reliance on easily disrupted maritime trade routes."[9]

The launch of a major investment drive under the CPEC has helped Gilgit-Baltistan to acquire the status of a gateway to Central Asia. Although it would be premature to predict how much the CPEC benefits Gilgit-Baltistan; nonetheless, the region might gain some infrastructure in terms of roads and rail services. However, not much is being expected by the people of the region partly because the federal government hasn't announced any SEZs in the region. All other provinces through which the Corridor is passing are getting SEZs, except Gilgit-Baltistan.[10] An editorial in a leading daily of Gilgit-Baltistan concludes thus, "Any confrontation by Gilgit-Baltistan would snap the trade ties between the two countries. The tragedy is that Pakistan has always been keen on signing agreements with China but it has deliberately kept Gilgit-Baltistan ignorant of all these developments! In accomplishing mega economic projects, Pak-China highway, and other projects, road goes through Gilgit-Baltistan."[11]

The leadership of Gilgit-Baltistan has never been consulted on CPEC. That is not the case even with the restive provinces of Pakistan that are part of the Corridor, who have at least some say in its policy development. For example, when the federal government wanted to change the route of the Corridor, the leaders from Khyber-Pakhtunkhwa (KP) and Balochistan protested and forced the government to initiate work on the western route. The route from Gwadar to Kashghar was initially planned to pass through Bisima, Khuzdar, Kalat and Quetta, Zhob, Dera Ismail Khan, Hassan Abdal and onwards to Kashghar. However, the route was reportedly changed from Bisima, through Ratodero towards Punjab bypassing the risk-prone Baloch and Pakhtun areas. This high-handed approach of the Punjab-dominated federal government could simmer the already existing alienation against the Punjab province and affect the CPEC.[12] Nonetheless, after months of wrangling, the then PML-N government called an All Parties Conference (APC) in order to address the grievances of KP and Balochistan regarding the corridor. A consensus was reached, and the political leaders from KP and Balochistan were successful in persuading the Nawaz Sharif government to show flexibility and give in to the demands of other parties.[13]

However, such a case is not possible for the leadership of Gilgit-Baltistan: first, they do not have representation in the National Assembly; second, Islamabad does not take them seriously. As an editorial in a Gilgit-Baltistan daily puts it:

> At the end of the APC, all the political leaders went home happily as their reservations had been met by the federal government. But unfortunately no one even bothered to ask the people of Gilgit-Baltistan if they had any

reservations about the CPEC as it would pass through over 400 kilometres land in their area. The government did not bother to take the people of the region on board about the project. It also showed that the people having no representation in power corridors and deprived of their basic rights have no avenue to go to when they are discriminated against. Same has been done with the people of Gilgit-Baltistan for seven decades.[14]

It is also believed that with the extension of the KKH, the Pakistani Government has decided to shift the dry port which was to be built up in Sost in Gilgit-Baltistan to Havelian in Hazara division of KP, which would have rendered thousands of people from Gilgit-Baltistan jobless.[15] Reacting on the relocating of the dry port, former president of the Chamber of Commerce and Industry, Javed Hussaini, said, "Livelihood of thousands of families of Gilgit-Baltistan is linked with the Sost dry port and it would be an economic disaster for them if existing activities are shifted to the newly proposed dry port at Havelian."[16] In the same vein, the former speaker of Gilgit-Baltistan Legislative Assembly, Wazir Baig said, "We are not clear about the benefits of the CPEC we will get, but we are much certain about the adverse effects due to relocation of the dry port."[17]

The Federal government has verbally assured Gilgit-Baltistan of establishing two SEZs to compensate the people of the region, but nothing concrete has emerged in writing. The mainstream political parties of Gilgit-Baltistan have ostensibly supported the Corridor, but at the same time, expressed their reservations about the progress and benefits for the region. Jhanzaib Yaseen, a leader of the Gilgit-Baltistan chapter of the Pakistan Tehreek-i-Insaf (PTI), said that if economic zones are not established in the region, the CPEC is meaningless for the people of the Gilgit-Baltistan, adding that the CPEC will only benefit Punjab, and Gilgit-Baltistan will only get cheap labour and dust.[18] The nationalist parties, particularly the Balawaristan National Front (BNF), are very vocal in their criticism of the CPEC project. The Brussels-based Chairman of BNF asserts, "Under the CPEC project, Islamabad has virtually handed over the disputed territory to China clandestinely ... China has not only been taking away gold and copper from Gilgit-Baltistan but was also looting the wildlife of the region."[19] Nationalists although are not against the Corridor per se, but they have the reservations over its ownership. While commenting on the CPEC, the Gilgit Baltistan United Movement (GBUM) Chief, Manzoor Hussain Parwana, revealed his stance on the CPEC. He said that Gilgit-Baltistan should be one of the three major parties to the project, and therefore, should be given an equal share: "As the area has its own distinct cultural and historical identity, without including it in the CPEC project as a partner, none of the two countries – China and Pakistan – can construct and operate the CPEC route through Gilgit-Baltistan."[20] He also demanded that economic zones should be set up in Gilgit, Skardu and Chilas under the CPEC.

While commenting on the growing presence of China in Gilgit-Baltistan, Senge Hasnan Sering, who heads the Institute of Gilgit-Baltistan Studies in Washington and is a vocal advocate of Gilgit-Baltistan's independence, claimed, "All the mining sites in the region were given to Chinese companies who are strengthening their bases there."[21] He further argued that constitutionally Gilgit-Baltistan is not a part of Pakistan, however, "it (Pakistan) just exploits our resources and wants to continue with its political hegemony. Even the latest empowerment package is a farce as the power centre continues to be in Pakistan".[22]

On the other hand, Chinese Ambassador to Pakistan, Yao Jing underscored the importance of Gilgit-Baltistan for the CPEC and assured the people of the region that they would get maximum benefit from the project. While meeting a delegation of the Gilgit-Baltistan Chamber of Commerce and Industry (GBCCI) in Islamabad on March 31, 2018, he would assure that the project would contribute to the "development of the residents through trade activities between GB and neighbouring Xinjiang province".[23]

In a pre-emptive strategy to thwart any discontent emerging from the region, China granted five billion Pakistani rupees to develop infrastructure in G-B,[24] prioritising education, health and road connectivity. However, these funds were to be released to G-B through the federal government. Moreover, China is also reportedly planning to create a regional forum, consisting of G-B, Tajikistan and Afghanistan for border development. The purpose of this forum is to link these bordering regions to CPEC.[25]

However, the resentment is growing among the people regarding land acquisition. The provincial government of Gilgit-Baltistan's land acquisition drive for the SEZ at Maqpun Das in Gilgit, created controversy. The Gilgit-Baltistan government took forcefully the land without due compensation for the community.[26] According to Amjad Hussain, the president of the Pakistan People's Party-Gilgit-Baltistan (PPP-GB), "A compensation of Rs two billion is yet to be provided by the government for land used for extension in KKH 2007. So, that being the case, public concerns are rising and [the people remain] sceptical of government promises of compensation for the land taken for CPEC".[27] Amjad further emphasised that, "The government must acquire the land for CPEC through the Land Acquisition Act of Gilgit-Baltistan and it shall introduce a Shamilat-e-Deh Act like other provinces. If the government fails to provide compensation, CPEC will become an international controversy and it will be huge failure on Pakistan's account".[28]

The PPP-GB along with other political activists and oppositions leaders held many protests on the land grabbing by the Gilgit-Baltistan government. One thing that stands clear is that if economic development, that too without consent of the local people, proceeds over political development of the region, the CPEC will get in to controversy and the already existing resentment among the people regarding constitutional crisis will flare up.

CPEC and Kashmir Issue

The positive and negative impact of the CPEC is a broad subject with different and partly interrelated dimensions. As mentioned earlier, the Corridor passes through the disputed area of Gilgit-Baltistan, which is a part of the erstwhile state of Jammu and Kashmir. The region does not enjoy any constitutional status and was, until 2018, governed by the controversial Self Governance Order of 2009. The people from Gilgit-Baltistan find themselves in a constitutional limbo: on the one hand, being considered a part of the larger issue of Kashmir, and on the other, fully 'controlled' by Pakistan sans any constitutional identity. According to a recent survey conducted by the Conciliation Resources, the majority of the people from Gilgit-Baltistan want to associate themselves with the larger political and constitutional structure of Pakistan. Around 82 per cent, according to the survey, prefer to call themselves Pakistanis and disassociate themselves from the larger Kashmiri identity.[29] However, at the same time, the Nationalist parties strongly oppose any integration or quasi-provincial status for Gilgit-Baltistan. They believe that any such attempt will undermine the "organic unity of the former state of Jammu and Kashmir".[30]

Before and during the last held elections, the ruling party of Gilgit-Baltistan, PML-N promised that if voted in power, they would give constitutional status to the region. In this regard, Nawaz Sharif constituted a committee headed by Sartaj Aziz that would invite suggestions and proposals from legal and constitutional experts to determine the constitutional status for Gilgit-Baltistan.[31] But ever since the announcement of the committee, a deliberate ambiguity has been created regarding its members, mandate and the time period. Nothing specific has been deliberated. At the same time, there have been protests from 'AJK' leadership and other power corridors from Pakistan regarding the same.

Interestingly, it is China that was pushing the then government of Nawaz Sharif to grant a constitutional status to Gilgit-Baltistan. According to media sources, China's dream project, the Silk Road passes through the disputed land, where the Chinese are investing billions of dollars; therefore, naturally, it wants Pakistan to legally solve this issue so that the Corridor does not face any hindrances. China has apparently made clear to Pakistan that the work on CPEC will not start until Gilgit-Baltistan is made a province of Pakistan.[32] The CPEC project is a bilateral treaty between Pakistan and China, but the latter does not consider Gilgit-Baltistan as a part of Pakistan. Moreover, China knows that India has reservations on Chinese investment in the region.

Further, the completion of the US$ 60 billion Corridor will further strengthen the Chinese control of the territory. The huge investment and presence in the region will provide China a leverage to become a de facto member of the dispute. Thus, the Corridor has all the "ingredients to exacerbate the complexities of the Kashmir issue threaten peace and cement China's stake in Jammu & Kashmir".[33] Moreover, as in the past, the people of Gilgit-Baltistan will not have any say on the decision-making when it comes to the handing over of natural resources to the Chinese companies. Apart from the political ramifications, the corridor will also have a deleterious impact on the ecology of the region. According to M Ismail Khan, Gilgit-Baltistan, which is home to 5,000 big and small glaciers, is facing a "myriad of sustainability challenges including climate change which now threatens faster melting of glaciers".[34]

There is also a fear that if SEZs are established in the region, the outsiders from Punjab and Khyber Pakhtunkhwa would get maximum jobs due to lack of human resource in Gilgit-Baltistan, which in turn would further imbalance the ethnic demography in favour of Sunni sect.[35] Expressing opinions on CPEC and its impact on region does not go well with the security agencies. According to the International Crisis Group report, "Instead of addressing such concerns, authorities have regularly invoked the 1997 Anti-Terrorism Act and the 2016 cybercrimes law against political party and human rights activists. Intelligence officials have warned local journalists in Gilgit-Baltistan against criticising CPEC".[36]

ENDNOTES

1. "Gwadar port leased to Chinese company for 40 years, Senate told", *The Nation*, April 20, 2017, at https://nation.com.pk/20-Apr-2017/gwadar-port-leased-to-chinese-company-for-40-years-senate-told
2. Ibid.
3. For details, see: Ministry of Finance, "Chapter 8", *Pakistan Economic Survey 2014-15*, Government of Pakistan, at www.finance.gov.pk/survey_1415.html.
4. Ambassador Sun Weidong's Remarks at The Round Table Conference on "Pakistan-Paradise Investment", September 14, 2015, at http://pk.chineseembassy.org/eng/zbgx/t1296377.htm.

5. "PM Nawaz Inaugurates Pak-China Friendship Tunnels over Attabad Lake", *Dawn*, September 14, 2015, at www.dawn.com/news/1206911.
6. Hasnain Kazim, "The Karakoram Highway: China's Asphalt Powerplay in Pakistan", *Der Spiegel*, July 17, 2012, at www.spiegel.de/international/world/china-expands-karakoram-highway-to-pakistan-a-844282.html.
7. For details, see: Ministry of Planning, Development & Reform, CPEC, at www.pc.gov.pk/?page_id=2731.
8. Ibid.
9. Shannon Tiezzi, "The China-Pakistan Economic Corridor Gets Even More Ambitious", *The Diplomat*, August 12, 2015, at http://thediplomat.com/2015/08/the-china-pakistan-economic-corridor-gets-even-more-ambitious/.
10. For details on SEZ, see: Ministry of Planning Commission of Pakistan's report, *China-Pakistan Economic Corridor: Investment & Business Prospects*, August 2015, at http://202.83.172.247:8080/Complaints/China%20Pakistan%20Economic%Corridor%20%28English %20Booklet%29.pdf.
11. "Nawaz Sharif's Visit to China and Gilgit-Baltistan", *Daily Bang-e-Sehar*, March 11, 2014, at http://www.bangsehar.net//popoup.php?date=11-03-2014.
12. "Economic Corridor: ANP Denounces Change in Route, Calls APC", *Dawn*, May 1, 2015, at www.dawn.com/news/1179361.
13. "APC Consensus: Parties Settle on Corridor Route", *The Express Tribune*, May 29, 2015, at http://www.tribune.com.pk/story/894068/apc-consensus-parties-settle-on-corridor-route/.
14. "CPEC, Where Does Gilgit-Baltistan Stand?", *Daily Bang-e-Sahar*, June 3, 2015, at http://www.bangesahar.net/popup.php?lang=en&r_date=06-03-2015&story=06-03-2015page-1-5.
15. "CPEC to Cause Unemployment in Gilgit-Baltistan", *The Express Tribune*, November 16, 2015, at http://tribune.com.pk/story/992728/anticipating-effects-cpec-to-cause-enemplyment-in-gilgit-baltistan/.
16. Ibid.
17. Ibid.
18. "CPEC Will Benefit Punjab and Gilgit-Baltistan Will Only Get Labour and Dust, Jhanzaib", *Bang-e-Sahar*, November 30, 2015, at www.bangesahar.net/popup.php?r_date=11-30-2015&img=11-30-2015page-1-2.
19. "CPEC Equal to Handing over GB to China, Says BNF Chief", *Bang-e-Sahar*, November 18, 2015, at http:// www.bangesahar.net/popup.php?r_date=11-18-2015&story=11-18-2015page-1-1.
20. "Gilgit-Baltistan: The Problem of CPEC Strikes Again", Unrepresented Nations and Peoples Organisation (UNPO), February 26, 2016, at http://unpo.org/article/18956.
21. Hakeem Irfan, "Kashmiri Activists Seek India's Support to 'Save' PoK' from China's Increasing Strength", *Mail Online India*, February 23, 2012, at http://www.dailymail.co.uk/indiahome/indianews/article-2105531.
22. Ibid.
23. Jamil Nagri, CPEC to benefit Gilgit-Baltistan the most: Chinese envoy, *Dawn*, April 1, 2018, at, http://www.dawn.com/news/1398814/cpec-to-benefit-gilgit-baltistan-the-most-chinese-envoy
24. China has granted 5 billion for Gilgit-Baltistan, *Daily K2*, February 25, 2018, at http://epaper.dailyK2.com/index.php?eid=1&nid=1&date=1519516800
25. Ibid.
26. Afzal Ali Shigri, Land Ownership Rights, *Dawn*, April 15, 2017, at http://www.dawn.com/news/1327031

27. Khadija Zahid, Fate of Gilgit-Baltistan under CPEC, *Pakistan Today*, April 2, 2017, at, http://www.pakistantoday.com/pk/2017/04/02/fate-of-gilgit-baltistan-under-cpec/
28. Ibid.
29. Syed Waqas Ali and Taqi Akhunzada, "Unheard Voices: Engaging Youth of Gilgit-Baltistan", *Conciliation Resources: Working together for Peace*, January 2015.
30. Ibid., p. 3.
31. "PM Announces Several Dev. Projects for Gilgit-Baltistan", *Pakistan Observer*, April 15, 2015, at http://www.pakobserver.net/detailnews.asp?id=262015.
32. Shabir Hussain, "Rahdari Mansoobay Gilgit-Baltistan ko Sooba Banany say Mashroot Karnay ka Inkishaaf", *Daily Express News*, December 14, 2015, at http://www.express.pk/story/415338.
33. Junaid Qureshi, "China Pakistan Economic Corridor and Jammu and Kashmir", *Kashmir Images*, November 15, 2015, at http://dailykashmirimages.com/Details/96364/china-pakistan-economic-corridor-and-jammu-kashmir. For further details on the implications of the CPEC on Kashmir, see: Fahad Shah, "A Costly Corridor: How China and Pakistan Could Remake Asia", *Foreign Affairs*, December 3, 2015, at http://www.foreignaffairs.com/articles/asia/2015-12-03/cotsly-corridor.
34. For further details, see: M Ismail Khan, "Gilgit-Baltistan: Melting Water Towers of the Indus", Institute of Peace and Conflict Studies (IPCS), IPCS Discussion papers on Indus Water, 2014, at www.ipcs.org/pdf_file/1412-indusPapers-Ismailkhan.pdf.
35. 'China-Pakistan Economic Corridor: Opportunities and Risks', *International Crisis Group*, Asia Report No. 297, June 29, 2018, p. 15.
36. Ibid., p. 15

7

Profiles of Prominent Leaders of 'AJK' and Gilgit-Baltistan

(A) PROMINENT LEADERS OF 'AJK'

Amanullah Khan (1934-2016)

One of the founders of pro-independence party, Jammu and Kashmir Liberation Front (JKLF), Amanullah Khan was born in Astore district of the Gilgit region on August 24, 1934. He had his early education in the Kashmir valley. He migrated to Pakistan in 1952, where he studied law from Karachi University and became a co-founder of the Kashmir Independent Committee in 1963. Two years later, in 1965, he was elected as the Secretary General of the Jammu and Kashmir Plebiscite Front (JKPF). He co-founded the Jammu and Kashmir National Liberation Front (JKNLF) with Maqbool Bhat. Khan was charged with being an Indian agent, and consequently, spent 15 months in Gilgit prison in 1970-72. Moreover, he was also tried in absentia in Srinagar, allegedly for being an agent of Pakistan. In 1976, he went to England where he formed the JKLF by renaming the England branch of the JKNLF. He was arrested in England in September 1985, and was acquitted only after being deported to Pakistan in December 1986. Once in Pakistan, he became the chief architect of the armed struggle in 1988 in Jammu and Kashmir. Amanullah Khan's only daughter, Asma, married Sajjad Ghani Lone, the son of Late Abdul Ghani Lone, Chairman of the Jammu and Kashmir People's Conference (JKPC) in November 2000. She is based in Srinagar and writes about different aspects of Kashmir and the regional geo-political issues. Amanullah Khan died in Rawalpindi on 26 April, 2016.

Sardar Attique Ahmed Khan

Sardar Attique Ahmed Khan is the son of Sardar Mohammad Abdul Qayyum Khan (April 4, 1924-July 10, 2015), a renowned political figure and founder-member of the All Jammu and Kashmir Muslim Conference. He was born in Ghaziabad in 'AJK' on January 21, 1955. A post-graduate in international relations, he studied Arabic at the Islamic University of Medina, Saudi Arabia. He became the Prime Minister of 'AJK' twice on July 24, 2006 to 6 January 2009 and between 29 July 2010 till 26 July 2011. He is the President of the 'AJK' Muslim Conference (AJKMC). He has led many political and diplomatic missions to several international organisations and countries alike, namely the United Nations (UN), Organisation of Islamic Cooperation (OIC) and the US.

Raja Zulqarnain Khan

Elected as President of 'AJK' in July 2006 by an Electoral College, comprising of the members of 'AJK' Legislative Assembly and the Kashmir Council, Raja Zulqarnain Khan had a distinguished career. He was born on March 15, 1936 in Gujrat. His father, Khan Bahadur Raja Muhammad Afzal Khan, who was also a member of the Indian Civil Service (ICS), served as the Home, Education and Revenue Minister in the princely state of Jammu and Kashmir during 1930-1941, and he was a close confidant of Maharaja Hari Singh. After falling out with the Maharaja he went back to the ICS cadre and after the establishment of Pakistan served as Commissioner of Lahore.[1] Raja Zulqarnain Khan studied in Srinagar, New Delhi and Lahore, and graduated in French language. He started his formal political career in 1960 by associating himself with K H Khurshid and founding the Jammu Kashmir Liberation League in 1962 and serving as its first General Secretary. He served in the Local government System in 'AJK' during the phase of Basic Democracy (BD) by Ayub Khan government, and was inducted as a minister in 1969 by then 'AJK' President Major General (Retd) Abdul Rehman. In 1975, Raja Zulqarnain Khan was elected to the AJK Legislative Assembly from Samani constituency (then in Mirpur, now in Bhimber district). He was in line for the Prime Minister's post but made way for Khan Abdul Hameed Khan. In Sardar Abdul Qayyum Khan's government he served as a Minister for Finance. In 1985, he was elected as lawmaker and became Minister for Finance, Planning & Development, Health and Revenue in the government of Prime Minister Sikander Hayat. He also won as a member of legislative assembly in the 1991 elections. In 1996, he was elected as member of the Jammu and Kashmir Council and held the office for five years. During this period, he also acted as Advisor to the Chairman of 'AJK' Council.

Sardar Sikandar Hayat Khan

Sardar Sikandar Hayat Khan is the son of Sardar Fateh Muhammad Khan Karelvi, who is remembered to this day in Gilgit-Baltistan for raising the banner of revolt against the Dogra rule in the 1930s. He was born on June 1, 1934, and received his early schooling in his native village of Karela in tehsil Fatehpur Thakiala (now in District Kotli) and in Poonch city. He graduated from the famous Gordon College (Rawalpindi) in 1956 and took a law degree from the University Law College in Lahore in 1958. His political baptism took place in the elections to the Kotli municipality. In 1970, he was elected to the 'AJK' Legislative Assembly and became Revenue Minister two years later. He served as the acting President of the Jammu and Kashmir Muslim Conference (AJKMC) in the 1976-78, and was elected President in 1978, a position he held for a decade. He served as the Prime Minister and President of 'AJK' twice, and was also the longest serving Prime Minister. In 1985, he was elected Prime Minister of AJK(PoK) and retained the office for the next five years. He remained leader of the opposition in the Assembly during the next two years, before he was elected President of 'AJK' for a five-year term in 1991. On July 25, 2001, he was sworn in as Prime Minister of 'AJK' for the second time; he retired from active politics in July 2006 after completing his second term. Later he played a major role in introducing Pakistan Muslim League-Nawaz (PML-N) in 'AJK', for which he was given the position of Senior Vice President of PML-N in 2011. His son, Farooq Sikandar, was elected in the July 2016 local elections as a member of the legislative assembly.

Sardar Shaukat Ali Kashmiri

Sardar Shaukat Ali Kashmiri heads the United Kashmir Peoples' National Party (UKPNP). He was born on May 25, 1958 in Papanar, near Trarkhal, in 'AJK'. He had his education in his native Tarkhan and in Karachi. During his Karachi days, he struggled for the educational and democratic rights of the students and organised many demonstrations and strikes. He has spent considerable time in jail, in both Pakistan and 'AJK'. He was also abducted by the Inter-Services intelligence (ISI) in 1994 and 1998. He was released only after UKPNP and other like-minded parties and groups demonstrated against his illegal confinement and detention throughout AJK(PoK) and Pakistan.

In 1980, he founded the Kashmir Nationalist Students' Federation in Karachi, and became its Chairman. From 1985 to 1997, he practiced law in different courts of 'AJK'. In 1994, he became the founding Chairman of the UKPNP. Between 1980 and 1997 he organised seminars in different cities of 'AJK' on human rights violations and right to self-determination of the people of Kashmir, Gilgit-Baltistan and demanded the withdrawal of Pakistan Army from 'AJK'. He organised many demonstrations against theo-fascism and Pakistan's proxy war with India. In 1993, he represented the UKPNP in the European Parliament Round Table Conference held in Brussels, Belgium. From 1999 to 2004, he addressed the United Nations Human Rights Commission (UNHRC) and Sub Commission on Human Rights in Geneva, on the subject of human rights violations and the Kashmiris' right to self-determination for the establishment of an independent Kashmir. Since 2002, he is Secretary General, International Kashmir Alliance (IKA), which consists of secular political parties struggling for the independence of Kashmir and Gilgit-Baltistan. The Amnesty International declared him as a prisoner of conscience. He is living in exile in Switzerland since April 25, 1999.

Sardar Muhammad Abdul Qayyum Khan

Sardar Muhammad Abdul Qayyum, who passed away at the old age of 91 in July 2015, was a doctor by profession. He is considered as one of the founders of the Kashmir Liberation Movement and the supreme leader of the Muslim Conference, which is the oldest political party in the 'AJK' region. Abdul Qayyum became President of 'AJK' for the first time in September 1956 and ended his last presidency in July 1991, and was then Prime Minister until 1996. In 1971, the day Zulfiqar Ali Bhutto took over as Pakistan's President, Sardar Qayyum, too, was elected President of 'AJK'. He held ideological difference with Bhutto, but always secured the support of the Pakistani generals. He was also known as Mujahid-e-Awal ("the first holy warrior"), believed to have fired the first bullet in the 1947 War of Liberation to establish 'AJK'. He was a supporter of the campaign aimed at bringing an Islamic system in 'AJK'.

Sultan Mahmood Chaudhry

A former Prime Minister of 'AJK', Barrister Sultan Mahmood Chaudhry as a member of AJKMC, joined AJKPPP in 2011, and later Imran Khan's Pakistan Tehreek-e-Insaf (PTI) in February 2015. He belongs to a highly influential and distinguished political family from Mirpur in 'AJK'. His father Chaudhry Noor Hussain was a prominent Kashmiri Leader. This Mirpur-born barrister had created history in 1996 by becoming the first Mirpuri Prime Minister of 'AJK'. The Chaudhry family has 'a long history of playing an active role in trying to bring the Kashmir issue in to the limelight by continuously raising the issue on an international level'.[2] Barrister Chaudhry lost his assembly seat (to a AJKPML-N candidate) for the first time in his political career in July 2016 elections as a member of the AJKPTI.

Sardar Arif Shahid

Sardar Arif Shahid was a prominent nationalist leader of 'AJK'. He was the Chairman of All Party National Alliance (APNA). He was assassinated near his residence in Rawalpindi on May, 2013. He wanted to have a united and independent Jammu and Kashmir with liberal, democratic and secular ideas. Arif Shahid was a man of vision and wanted to promote democratic values and fundamental human rights for all citizens of the state of Jammu and Kashmir. He believed that religion was a personal matter of individuals sand religion must be kept out of politics. He was the Chairman of the APNA whose main objective is to liberate Kashmir from both India and Pakistan. APNA was developed in parallel with the All Parties Hurriyat Conference of J&K which was patronized by Pakistan government. He was a vocal critic of Pakistan's alleged role in sending militants to fight proxy war in J&K. He also criticized Pakistan policy of treating Kashmir and opposed Pakistan's occupation of 'AJK' and Gilgit Baltistan.

Arif Shahid was also an author of a number of books pertaining to freedom struggle in Kashmir. He was an outspoken person who held sentiments of freedom for 'AJK' and Gilgit Baltistan. He was jailed when he stood for the restoration of K-2 Newspaper which was banned by Pakistan authorities. He was also taken into custody and deported from Gilgit before holding a public meeting to condemn Karachi Agreement. Three months before his killing, police in Rawalpindi registered a case against him. Pakistan Government banned him for travelling abroad in 2009 and later confiscated his passport and other identification documents. It was later returned after a court battle. He was warned by the Pakistan intelligence agencies to stop anti-Pakistan activities. He refused to surrender and was silenced. It was widely believed that he was killed by the secret agencies of Pakistan because he exposed their nefarious designs on Kashmir.

Chaudhry Abdul Majid

A politician from Mirpur, Chaudhry Abdul Majid was elected Prime Minister of 'AJK' on 26th July, 2011. He first became a member of the 'AJK' Assembly in 1985. He is B.A. LL.B. He is a member of the AJKPPP and remained its president for a long period till he resigned following his party's loss in July 2016 elections. He was elected sixth time as member of the 'AJK' legislative Assembly. Prior to this position, he had served as Minister for Revenue and Agriculture of 'AJK' government and Speaker of 'AJK' Legislative Assembly from 1998 to 2001.

Sardar Muhammad Yaqoob Khan

Sardar Muhammad Yaqoob Khan was President of 'AJK' during 2011-2016. He was also Prime Minister during 2009-2011. He was born in 1953 in Ali Sojal, Rawalakot. He started his political career as a Central Office bearer of Punjabi Pakhtoon Ittehad in Karachi. Later, he became a Senior Vice President of the Tehreek-e-Amal Party's 'AJK' chapter. He stood first for the Sindh Legislative Assembly and later on for 'AJK' Legislative Assembly. He was a minister in the 'AJK' Government from 2001-2006 and in 2009, and held different portfolios. He became the 'AJK' Prime Minister on January 6, 2009. Two years later, in 2011, he was elected as the President of 'AJK'. He is also a noted businessman.

Dr. Shabir Choudhry

Dr Shabir Choudhry is the London-based founder member of the JKLF. He became its Secretary General in 1985, and President of the JKLF's Europe unit in 1999. Born in Nakker Shamali (near Panjeri) in Bhimber district of 'AJK', he went to the UK in 1966, and holds a dual nationality. A regular contributor to various newspapers and author of more than 25 books, he has done extensive research on the Kashmir issue, as also on India-Pakistan relations. He regularly takes part in the proceedings of UN Human Rights Council and has attended various International conferences on Kashmir. His blog[3], has a good following for the alternative view it provides on the Kashmir dispute and politics of South Asia. He is now the spokesman of International Kashmir Alliance and Kashmir National Party and Director Institute of Kashmir Affairs, London. He is also president of the foreign affairs committee of the United Kashmir Peoples National Party (UKPNP).

Raja Farooq Haider Khan

Currently Prime Minister of 'AJK' after leading his party AJKPML-N to a spectacular victory in July 2016 elections, Raja Farooq Haider Khan was prime minister earlier too during October 2009-July 2010. A senior leader of AJKPML-N, Raja Farooq Haider Khan belongs to a well-known political family. He was born on February 14, 1955 at Muzaffarabad, and studied at the Abbottabad Public School, one of the historic educational institutions in north-west Pakistan. He graduated from Government College, Lahore. His father, Raja Muhammad Haider Khan, was President of the AJKMC in 1960 and 1963. His mother, Mohterma Saeeda Khan, was the first female Member of the 'AJK' Legislative Assembly. His uncle, Raja Muhammad Latif Khan, was elected to the 'AJK' Legislative Assembly in 1970, and his sister, Naureen Haider, was an 'AJK' lawmaker from 1991 to 1996.

Raja Haider Khan headed the Muslim Conference's Muzaffarabad chapter from 1986 to 1990, and in 1989 was elected Chairman of the party's 'AJK' Central Parliamentary Board for two years. He held several organisational posts in the 'AJK' party chapter. In 1985, and 1991, he was elected to AJK Assembly and served as Minister. From 2003 to 2006, he remained Special Assistant to Prime Minister of 'AJK'. In 2006, he was again elected as a lawmaker and was made Chairman of the Public Accounts Committee (PAC) of the Assembly, which ensures accountability for public spending. After joining PML-N in 2010, he worked sincerely towards strengthening its reach in 'AJK'. The success of AJKPML-N in July 2016 elections, was largely credited to him by analysts in Pakistan.

Syed Ghulam Raza Naqvi

Founder-Chairman of the Jammu and Kashmir Islamic Democratic Party (JKIDP), Syed Ghulam Raza Naqvi is one of the few 'AJK' politicians who are recognised internationally. He was born in Sehnsa in 'AJK' and had his education in 'AJK' and Karachi. He belongs to the Naqvi Albukhari family. He was baptised into politics by becoming the mayor of Sehnsa. A great orator and passionate believer in peaceful coexistence, he advocates basic human rights, and has been threatened many times by state and non-state organisations during his student life and early political career. He has been a member of Jammu and Kashmir Council and Chairman of the PAC.

Chaudhry Ghulam Abbas (1904-1967)

Lawyer-politician Chaudhry Ghulam Abbas was born in a middle-class Rajput family of Chaudhry Nawab Khan on February 4, 1904 at Jammu. After he started his career as a lawyer in Jammu, he was offered the post of a sub-judge; however, he declined to serve the then Dogra ruler. He became an associate of Kashmir's prominent leader, Sheikh Abdullah, when the All Jammu and Kashmir National Conference was established, and became its secretary general. However, Ghulam Abbas parted company with Sheikh Abdullah when the latter moved closer to the Congress and Jawaharlal Nehru. As the idea of Pakistan gained ground, he revived the Muslim Conference, and headed it in the princely state of Jammu and Kashmir. As he hailed from Jammu, he did not know the Kashmiri language and had distinct problem of communicating with the people of the valley. His friend turned political foe, Sheikh Abdullah, who hailed from the valley had larger political appeal. After his migration to 'AJK', he became the Supreme Head of the 'AJK' Government, was known as Quaid-e-Kashmir. In 1951, he resigned from the headship of the 'AJK' government and quit active politics. He died of cancer in Rawalpindi on December 18, 1967.

Khawaja Abdul Ghaffar (1926-2014)[4]

Acknowledged as one of the most influential personalities in 'AJK', Khawaja Abdul Ghaffar migrated from Wazapora, Mahraj Gunj (old Srinagar), where he was born in 1926, to 'AJK' in 1948, when he was still in the college. On migration to 'AJK', in September 1948, he was offered the position of Information Officer in Pakistan Government, and later, the post of a lecturer. But after three years, he quit government service, and started his own business. He had a personal rapport with leading Pakistani figures, namely Faiz Ahmed Faiz and Zulfiqar Ali Bhutto. An old ideologue of the Muslim Conference, an ardent admirer of Mohammad Ali Jinnah and a veteran Kashmiri leader, Khawaja Abdul Ghaffar was a kingmaker in 'AJK' politics, though he distanced himself from the power politics. He passed away at the age of 88 in June 2014.

Sardar Muhammad Ibrahim Khan (1915-2003)

Ibrahim Khan was born on April 19, 1915 in Kot Mattay Khan, a village near Rawalakot. He received his BA degree from Islamia College Lahore, and later the Bar-at-Law from Lincoln's Inn. He practised law in Srinagar for a while and joined the State Legal Service, serving as state prosecutor in Mirpur in 1943, and later, at the State Advocate General office in Srinagar. In 1946, he resigned from government service, and successfully contested for the J&K State Assembly (Rajya Sabha) in the same year. The Azad Muslim Conference platform and his demand for accession of the Jammu and Kashmir State to Pakistan pitted him against the Dogra rulers. In 1947, he led Kashmiri rebels against the Maharaja of Kashmir. In October 1947, he became the first President of 'AJK'. He was used by Pakistan to spread propaganda regarding Kashmir at the international level in the United Nations in subsequent years. It was due to his untiring efforts that the Pakistan Government finally allowed the creation of the 'AJK' Legislative Assembly during the Yahya Khan regime. He was elected to the Assembly thrice, the last being in 1975. A close lieutenant of Zulfiqar Ali Bhutto, Ibrahim Khan refused to betray his leader in 1977 despite mounting pressure from the then military dictator, Gen. Zia-ul-Haq. He paid the price for it and was dismissed as President of 'AJK'. He was re-elected again as the President of 'AJK' in August 1996 and remained in that position until August 2001. He died in 2003 at his son's home in Islamabad.

Khurshid Hasan Khurshid (1924-1988)[5]

Born in a modest middle-class family of Srinagar in 1924. Khurshid was active in politics from his student days. He started the Kashmir Muslim Student's Federation to 'educate' people on mass uprising against the British colonial masters. In 1942, as General Secretary of the Federation, he met Muhammad Ali Jinnah for the first time in Jallandhar. That interaction brought him close to Jinnah, and he worked for him over the next several years. When Jinnah died, he decided to quit politics and launched a weekly magazine. His magazine venture did not do well, and he went to Karachi where he started working with Jinnah's sister, Fatima. On her advice, he enrolled in Lincoln's Inn and became a barrister in 1954. His contemporaries were Zulfiqar Ali Bhutto and Margaret Thatcher. In 1956 he was appointed the Foreign Publicity Advisor by the 'AJK' Government. Three years later, in May 1959, Khurshid was appointed by Ayub Khan as the President of 'AJK' and simultaneously, established his own party, the Jammu Kashmir Liberation League. Under his leadership the first ever 'Basic Democracy' elections were held in 'AJK' in 1962, and he was re-elected as the President. Later, he developed serious differences with the military-led government and resigned in August 1964. Subsequently, his party did not perform well in the elections though he remained politically active until his death. He died on March 11, 1988 in a road accident while travelling from Gujarat to Lahore.

Sardar Ghulam Sadiq Khan

Born to Subedar Bagga Khan, Sardar Ghulam Sadiq Khan was elected Speaker of the Legislative Assembly of 'AJK' on July 25, 2011. He is a member of the AJKPPP, and has been elected as a 'AJK' Legislative Assembly three times. He also served in the past as Advisor to prime minister of Pakistan, Syed Yousaf Raza Gillani, and was a member of the Public Accounts Committee 'AJK'. He was disqualified from contesting the July 2016 elections, by the 'AJK' High Court for misusing power and embezzling government funds, drawing salary on two accounts, both as 'adviser' to the 'AJK' Council chairman (prime minister of Pakistan) and assembly member for more than 31 months. He was even made to deposit PKR 2.09 million in the government treasury.[6]

Raja Mumtaz Hussain Rathore

During his student days, Raja Mumtaz Hussain Rathore founded the Jammu and Kashmir National Student Federation. In 1970, on AJKMC ticket, he contested the Legislative Assembly elections and won. Later, he joined the AJKPPP and also served as a senior minister, holding finance, forest and revenue ministry portfolios. He was elected as the Prime Minister of 'AJK' and served in that position from June 1990 to July 1991. Rathore was ousted from office and then arrested after refusing to accept defeat in the assembly elections. He was heading a coalition government. After his arrest, he was flown by helicopter from Muzaffarabad to Rawalpindi. The then Prime Minister Benazir Bhutto made a statement in London saying that the government had made "a historic error" in arresting Rathore. He also served as Acting President, Speaker, Senior Minister of 'AJK'. He died of heart attack on June 16, 1999 in Hevali.

Maj. Gen. Sardar Muhammad Anwar Khan

Major General (Retd) Sardar Muhammad Anwar Khan was born on May 9, 1945 in Tain, Poonch District, 'AJK' and served as the President of 'AJK' from 2001 to 2006. Sardar Anwar Khan received his early education in the Tain village. In 1966, he joined the Pakistan Army and was commissioned in the Azad Kashmir Regiment. He is a graduate of the Command and Staff College, Quetta; Pakistan Navy Staff College, Karachi; and National Defence College, Rawalpindi. He also attended the US Army War College in Pennsylvania and received a master's degree in War Studies. During his distinguished Army career span of 35 years, he held various important commands of staff and instructional appointments. As a young officer he also actively participated in 1971 War in the Kashmir Sector. He made significant contribution to the leadership development within the Pakistan Army as an Instructor at the Pakistan Military Academy, School of Infantry and Tactics, Command and Staff College, Quetta and as the Chief Instructor at National Defence College, Islamabad from December 1996 to December 1998. He retired from the army as Vice Chief of General Staff (VCGS) in July 2001. He also served as the colonel commandant of the Azad Kashmir Regiment till April 2003.

Chaudhry Latif Akbar

Chaudhry Latif Akbar was appointed President of the AJKPPP in early 2017. He has a distinguished career in the party following his lifelong affiliation with party and Bhutto's since the emergence of the PPP. He has replaced Chaudhry Abdul Majeed, the ex-prime minister of 'AJK' in the last PPP led coalition government in 'AJK'. Chaudhry Latif hails from Muzaffarabad district. He has also been holding office of the Secretary General of the party. He was a minister in the various PPP led government including in the Chaudhry Majeed led government as finance minister besides holding many other portfolios in the Raja Mumtaz Hussain Rathore and Barrister Sultan Mehmood governments.

Faisal Mumtaz Rathore

Faisal Mumtaz Rathore is the Secretary General of the AJKPPP. He is son of former 'AJK' prime minister late Raja Mumtaz Hussain Rathore. Rathore is from Haveili district of Poonch division. He is considered to be a seasoned and sincere worker of the party. He has also been minister in the cabinet of Chaudhry Abdul Majeed's PPP government which lost the 2016 elections.

Dr. Khalid Mahmood

Dr. Khalid Mahmood is the current Emir of Jamaat-i-Islami 'Azad Jammu & Kashmir' (AJK) and Gilgit-Baltistan (GB). He was elected for a three-year term on June 30, 2017. He replaced Abdul Rashid Turabi, who remained the chief for 22 years after the party that was launched in these two regions in July 1974 with an independent set-up having no administrative control by JI Pakistan. Turabi is, however, member of the 'AJK' Legislative Assembly, against a special seat reserved for the technocrats. Dr. Mahmood, who has been practicing medicine in Rawalakot, was chosen for the slot by the party's General Council, comprising around 1,500 members from 'AJK', GB and Pakistan-based Kashmiris refugees, from among the panel of three candidates who included the incumbent emir.

Dr. Mahmood was born in Rihara village of district Poonch in 1956. He completed his MBBS degree from Larkana in Sindh where he became member of Islami Jamiat Tulaba (IJT) and later its Nazim for the Chandika Medical College as well as member of provincial shoora of Sindh. After serving for five years in government health department, he shifted to Rawalakot where besides practice, he also carried on his organizational activities, holding the office of JI city and later district president in Poonch. He also contested 'AJK' Assembly elections from Rawalakot but was defeated.

Raja Muhammad Mushtaq Minhas

The journalist turned politician, Raja Muhammad Mushtaq Minhas was born on 12 June 1965 in Bagh, 'AJK' where he had early education. He had higher studies in Lahore where he did his B.A. in Political Science and Journalism and later Masters in Mass Communication from Punjab University in 1992. Pakistan government had awarded him 'Best Reporter Award' for his outstanding and quality reporting during earthquake in 'AJK' in 2005. He is founder of National Press Club, Islamabad and is associated with number of journalist unions of Pakistan and socially very active.

Mushtaq Minhas who belongs to Malalayal clan joined PML-N in March 2016. He contested from Bagh-II constituency and won the seat by defeating Khurshid Ahmad of PTI in July 2016 elections. According to media reports, he was also one of the prominent faces during Nawaz Sharif visit to AJK' before the July 2016 elections and the latter always gave importance to Minhas's suggestions on the political developments in 'AJK'. There were also reports of Mushtaq Minhas would also be in the race of 'AJK' Premiership as he maintained strong relations with PML-N top leadership and had played active role in formation of PML-N chapter in 'AJK'. Mushtaq Minhas was appointed Minister for Information, Tourism and Information Technology in the Farooq Haider's cabinet. At a function in Muzaffarabad on April 21, 2017, he said that it was bureaucracy that was ruling the roost in 'AJK'.

(B) Prominent Leaders of Gilgit-Baltistan

Hafiz Hafeezur Rehman

A dynamic politician, Hafiz ur Rehman is known as a moderate. He has been a pillar of strength to the Pakistan Muslim League – Nawaz in Gilgit-Baltistan (G-B). He bravely faced the wrath of the military ruler General Parvez Musharraf but did not betray his party, which rewarded him with the stewardship of the PML–N, G-B chapter. Earlier, he was made the party's chief organiser for G-B. He inherited the mantle from his brother, Saif ur Rehman, who was assassinated outside his home in their native Kashrote (Gilgit city) in 2003. He was elected to the G-B Legislative Assembly (GBLA) from GBLA-2 constituency in the June 2015 elections; and became the unanimous choice for the post of Chief Minister. A moderate and champion of sectarian harmony and peace, he had a brief but loose association with the Jamiat Ulema-i-Islam-Fazl (JuI-F). Hafiz ur Rehman favours strong ties between G-B and the Punjab province but does not advocate close relations with Khyber Pakhtunkhwa (KP), which, he alleges, has flooded Gilgit Baltistan with weapons. Strained relationship between G-B and KP dates back to 1988, the year when then Army ruler General Zia ul Haq had sent Sunnis from Khyber Pakhtunkhwa to loot and butcher Shias.

Mir Ghazanfar Ali Khan, Gilgit-Baltistan

Mir Ghazanfar is the son of last Mir of Hunza, Muhammad Jamal Khan who died in 1976. A close friend of Nawaz Sharif, he was appointed Governor of Gilgit-Baltistan in November, 2015. His wife Rani Atiqa is also a lawmaker in the Gilgit Baltistan Legislative Assembly. Ghazanfar had represented Hunza, his home constituency, in various representative bodies of Gilgit-Baltistan. He also served as the Deputy Chief Executive and Chief Executive of the then Northern Areas Legislative Council from 2004 to 2009 during the regime of president Gen. Musharraf. He resigned from his post on September 15, 2018.

Manzoor Hussain Parwana

A rights activist, poet, environmentalist, and freelance journalist, Manzoor Parwana is a chemical engineer by profession. His political career started in 1990 when he was a secondary level student. Fifteen years later in 2005, he entered national political scene, when he floated the Gilgit Baltistan United Movement (GBUM), a pro-independence organisation in Gilgit-Baltistan. It was an off-shoot of Balwaristan Students Federation, (BSF) of which he was Information Secretary. Manzoor Parwana belongs to a middle class farmer family. He was born on April 2, 1975 in Thowar village of Skardu district. He faced persecution for his political views and his writings, and went to jail several times. Monthly magazine, *Kargil International* of which he is the chief editor has been banned. He was arrested for an article published in the magazine. The trial lasted five-years. His first book, titled *Sach Likhna Jurm Hai* (Writing Truth is a crime) was published in 2005. Musharraf's government banned the book. He was arrested on sedition charges in July 2011 as he spoke about the illegal activities of Pakistan forces and their intelligence agencies in G-B at a convention of Balawaristan National Students Organisation (BNSO). He was sent to prison several times for championing the cause of basic rights and freedom of the people of Gilgit Baltistan.

Shafqat Inqalabi

Shafqat Inqalabi shot into fame when he challenged "the Gilgit-Baltistan Empowerment and Self-Governance Order 2009" in the 'AJK' Supreme Court on March 4, 2010. This legal recourse earned for him the wrath of the government which had been subjecting him to harassment. He was also forced to stop his construction business putting him to grave financial loss. The Interior Ministry has put his name on the Exit Control List, impounded his passport and Identity Card thus putting a blanket ban on his foreign travels. Inqalabi hails from Bubur in Puniyal tehsil of Ghizer district in Gilgit-Baltistan. He is a qualified Civil Engineer. He had established a district level political party, 'Ghizar National Movement' in 1997. After its merger with Karakoram National Movement" in 2000, Inqalabi headed the Karakoram Students Organisation (KSO) and from 2000 to 2003 served as its President and from 2003 to 2005, as its Central Chairman. He joined Balwaristan National Front (BNF) in 2005 and has been its spokesperson since then. He regularly writes for local newspapers and magazines.

Syed Jaffar Shah

Syed Jaffar Shah hails from Jalalabad, Gilgit. He entered politics in 1983 after a seven-year stint as a lawyer in Karachi. He has won Legislative Council elections thrice in 1983, 1987 and 1999. He was, however defeated in the 1994 elections. Shah also served as President of the Gilgit High Court Bar Association and Chairman of the legal committee of the Council. He is the president of G-B chapter of PPP.

Bashir Ahmed

Bashir Ahmed had his political baptism with the PML-N. He had a stint in the PML-Q, which was floated during the Musharraf era as the King's party. He defected to PPP before the 2015 Assembly election.

Qazi Inayatullah

A founding member of the Jamiat Ulema-e-Islam (Fazlur) he runs his own seminary. He is also President of the Gilgit Baltistan chapter of JUI (F)–. An affiliate of Tableeghi Jammat, he is widely travelled across the world. Inayatullah who hails from Goharabad, Diamer, entered politics after a stint as a teacher at a Madrassa.

Sobia Moqaddam

A lone female minister in the G-B government, the 33-year-old Sobia Moqaddam hails from the Diamer Valley where the literacy rate for women remains abysmally low and cultural barriers prevent women from voting. She moved to Diamer from her native Jhelum after her marriage in 2007. Overcoming local prejudices and various other obstacles, she successfully contested in the 2015 elections and became one of the six women members in the Gilgit-Baltistan Legislative Assembly.

Haji Fida Muhammad Nashad

A politician and a writer, Haji Fida Muhammad Nashad belongs to the illustrious Maqpon family (royal family of Gilgit-Baltistan). His father, Kacho Amir Baig, a renowned poet (of Balti language) was amongst the few of Baltistan's elite who rose against the Dogras to "liberate" the area. Born on February 27, 1945, he graduated from the Punjab University. In 1983, he was elected to the Baltistan District Council. Soon afterwards he became Chairman of the Council. In 1994, he was elected to the then Northern Areas Council from NA-9 Skardu constituency. Five years later, in 1999, he won his second term, unopposed, and became the Deputy Chief Executive. During his third term, from 2004, the Northern Areas Legislative Council was upgraded as the Northern Areas Legislative Assembly. After the Gilgit-Baltistan Legislative

Assembly was created, he won the by-election held in October 2013. After the PML-N won the 2015 elections, he was elected as the Speaker of the Gilgit-Baltistan Legislative Assembly. Before entering politics, Nashad served in the Northern Areas Administration in various capacities, including as Public Relations Officer (1963-1978). He also worked for Pakistan's news agency, APP for two years. He balances his political activism and his profession as a journalist, writing for both the local newspapers as well as the leading Pakistani dailies like *Daily Jang*, *Nawa-e-Waqt*, *Muslim* and *Pakistan Times*.

Haji Jaffar Ullah Khan

A senior PML-N leader, Haji Jaffar Ullah Khan was born on April 12, 1966 in Gilgit. In 2015, he was elected from the GBLA-1 constituency in a multi-corner contest by a comfortable margin, and later elected the Deputy Speaker of the Gilgit-Baltistan Legislative Assembly.

Haji Shah Baig

Haji Shah Baig is the lone member of the JUI-F in the current Gilgit-Baltistan Legislative Assembly. Baig was elected from Diamer Valley in the 2015 elections, and became the Leader of the Opposition in the Assembly when PPP, PTI, and Majlis Wahdat-e-Muslimeen (MWM), besides the JUI-F, agreed to try their luck for the post through a draw.

Haji Akbar Taban

Known as a strong pillar of PML-N in Skardu, Haji Akbar Taban has become a dissident after the 2015 Gilgit-Baltistan Legislative Assembly elections. As general secretary of the party, he expected to become either Speaker or Deputy Speaker after his election from Skardu-1 constituency. Instead he was asked to join the cabinet, that too, without a key portfolio. In protest, he did not turn up at the swearing in ceremony. Taban then angled for the post of Governor saying that since the Chief Minister is from the Gilgit region, the Governor should be from the Baltistan region. However, the PML-N leadership rejected his demand.

Baba Jan

Baba Jan, the Vice President of Awami Workers Party (AWP) created history by contesting the 2015 elections to the Gilgit-Baltistan Legislative Assembly from behind bars. He stood for the GBLA-6 seat in Gilgit, but lost in a four-corner contest, facing PML-N's Mir Ghazanfar, PPP's Zafar Iqbal and PTI's Izhar Hunzai.

Jan was sentenced to life term by an anti-terrorism court in 2014 on charges of ransacking police stations and torching government property in Hunza during a protest in August 2011 by families affected by the formation of Attabad Lake. Soon afterwards Baba Jan became a local hero.

A Labour Party of Pakistan Press Release carried by media stated that Baba Jan was treated brutally in jail and tortured badly. "Baba Jan was subjected to torture for three to four hours at a stretch, beaten with sticks and his feet crushed under heavy boots for three days in a row. He was denied treatment for his many injuries despite the orders of the Court."

According to International View Point, Baba Jan and his comrades are not activists who took up arms against state. They simply raised their voices for the fate of thousands of people of the Hunza Valley who were displaced as a result of a climate disaster in January 2010 and protested against corruption and against the violent repression that had been unleashed against the victims demonstrating in August 2011.

Syed Mehdi Shah

Syed Mehdi Shah, a PPP veteran, is the first Chief Minister of Gilgit-Baltistan. He lost the 2015 elections to a PTI candidate. His defeat was one of the biggest surprises of the elections. He is native of Baltistan educated in local school and completed Secondary School Certificate course. He joined college studies but did not complete his Intermediate course. Before joining PPP, he was teaching in one of the schools in Baltistan.

Agha Rahat Hussain Al-Hussaini

Agha Rahat Hussain Al-Hussaini is a Shia cleric from Gilgit. He is an Imam at Gilgit's Central Imamia Mosque. In the run-up to the 2015 elections, he managed to broker a deal between Islami Tehreek Pakistan and Majlis-e-Wahdatul Muslimeen.

Nawaz Khan Naji

53-year old, Nawaz Khan Naji is the founder chairman of the Balawaristan National Front (BNF). He is a graduate and has been a political activist since his student days. The BNF calls for an independent state named Balawaristan, comprising the areas of G-B plus districts of Kohistan and Chitral. Naji contested the first Gilgit Baltistan Legislative Assembly (GBLA) elections held in November 2009 but was defeated. But he surprised everyone by winning by-election held in April 2011. In the June 2015 elections, he was again elected to the second GBLA. He is the only legislator representing nationalist parties in the GBLA. BNF does not accept the Karachi Agreement of 28 April 1949 and believes that the agreement deprived the people of Balawaristan of their basic fundamental rights.

Abdul Hamid Khan

Abdul Hamid Khan is a Chairman of the Balawaristan National Front. He is living in exile in Belgium. He was born in a small village of Yasin in Ghizer district on July 10, 1953. Abdul Hamid Khan is in regular touch with international human rights organisations, UN and European Parliament and briefing them about prevailing situation in Gilgit-Baltistan.

Dr. Ghulam Abbas

Dr. Ghulam Abbas is a Convenor of Astore Supreme Council. It organized a multi-party conference in Gilgit on June 11, 2017 where speakers from all walks of life held Pakistan government responsible of Gilgit-Baltistan economically backward and sufferings of the people who have been struggling for their fundamental rights for the last seven decades.

Raja Jalal Hussain Maqpoon

Raja Jalal Hussain Maqpoon was appointed as the new Governor of Gilgit-Baltistan by the PTI on September 30, 2018. He took over after Mir Ghazanfar Ali Khan resigned from the post. Raja Jalal hails from Skardu, from Maqpoon family which ruled the area before the Sikh and Dogra rule. He was defeated by PMLN candidate Akbar Khan Taban in the G-B Assembly election from Skardu constituency in 2015.

(C) SOME OTHER LEADERS AND CURRENT CABINET OF GILGIT-BALTISTAN

Following are some other prominent leaders of Gilgit-Baltistan:

1. Syed Raziuddin Rizvi (PPP)
2. Fida Muhammad Nashad (PML-N)
3. Syed Pir Karam Ali Shah (PPP)
4. Engineer Muhammad Ismail (PPP)
5. Hashmatullah (President – PTI)
6. Amjad Hussain Advocate (PPP)

7. Sultan Madad (PML-N)
8. Ghulam Muhammad (PML-N)
9. Izhar Hunzai (PTI)
10. Muhammad Zaman (PTI)
11. Muhammad Jafar (PPP)
12. Agha Muhammad Ali (PML-N)
13. Malik Miskeen (PML-N)
14. Haji Janbaz Khan (PML-N)
15. Zafar Iqbal (PPP)
16. Muhammad Ali Akhtar (PPP)
17. Mirza Hussain (PTI)
18. Amina Ansari (PTI)
19. Sadia Danish (PPP)
20. Muhammad Ayub Shah (PPP)
21. Muhammad Naseer (PPP)
22. Karim Khan (aka) KK (President – APML)
23. Mehboob Ali Advocate (BNF)
24. Ali Ghulam (BNF)
25. Afaq Blor (BNF)
26. Maulana Abdul Sami (Jamaat-e-Islami)
27. Sayeda Danish (Information Secretary – PPP)
28. Raja Jehnzaib (PTI)

Following are the Cabinet Members of the Present Gilgit Baltistan Government

- Chief Minister: Hafeez-ur-Rehman
- Minister for Education and Information: Muhammad Ebrahim Sanaei (Ghanche)
- Minister for Food, Agriculture, Livestock & Fisheries: Haji Janbaz Khan (Diamer)
- Minister for Works: Dr Muhammad Iqbal (Gilgit)
- Minister for Excise & Taxation & Local Bodies: Farman Ali (Astore)
- Minister for Forests & Environment: Muhammad Wakil (Diamer)
- Minister for Women's development & Youth Affairs: Sobia Jabeen Muqaddam (Diamer)

The Cabinet has no representation from Skardu, Hunza-Nagar and Ghizer districts.

Members of the Gilgit-Baltistan Council Nominated and Elected

Nominated Members

(1) Capt. (retd.) Muhammad Safdar
(2) Mr. Khalid Hussain Magsi
(3) Dr. Darshan
(4) Syed Ittikhar ul Hassan
(5) Mr. Isphanyar M. Bhandara
(6) Dr Tariq Fazal Chaudhary

Elected Members

(1) Arman Shah (PMLN)
(2) Sultan Ali Khan (PMLN)
(3) Muhammad Ashraf (PMLN)
(4) Wazir Ikahlaq Hussain (PMLN)
(5) Syed Muhammad Abbas Rizvi (ITP)
(6) Syed Afzal (Independent)

ENDNOTES

1. See his profile at http://rajazulqarnain.blogspot.in/2006/08/ajk-president-raja-zulqarnain-khan.html (Last accessed March 10, 2017)
2. See his profile on https://www.pakistantimes.com/topics/barrister-sultan-mahmood-chaudhry/ (Last accessed on March 10, 2017).
3. See http://drshabirchoudhry.blogspot.in/ (Last accessed on March 10, 2017)
4. See for details his short obituary at http://www.kashmirlife.net/khawaja-abdul-ghaffar-issue17-vol06-61305/ & http://www.greaterkashmir.com/news/news/kashmiri-leader-khawaja-abdul-ghaffar-passes-away/172901.html
5. See Nisar Thokar, "Kh Khursheed – the Kashmiri who fought along jinnah", *Greater Kashmir*, March 12, 2008, at http://www.greaterkashmir.com/news/news/kh-khursheed-the-kashmiri-who-fought-along-jinnah/30418.html, also see "K. H. Khurshid's death anniversary today", Dawn, March 11, 2011, at https://www.dawn.com/news/612297/k-h-khurshids-death-anniversary-today
6. See M.A. Mir, "AJK Court disqualifies assembly speaker from contesting upcoming polls", *Express Tribune*, July 18, 2016, at https://tribune.com.pk/story/1144220/ajk-court-disqualifies-assembly-speaker-contesting-upcoming-polls/

Conclusion

Local politics in both the regions of Pakistan occupied Kashmir (PoK) – consisting of both 'AJK' and Gilgit-Baltistan (GB) – is firmly under the control of the central government in Pakistan. Local political parties have been progressively overtaken by mainstream political parties in Pakistan, who have set up their local branches and engineered defection from local parties to strengthen their political hold in these areas. The problem with the growth of local political parties in PoK is associated with the freedom granted to Pakistan-based parties by the establishment. Over the years, the government in Islamabad has suppressed freedom of opinion in PoK and political parties and groups questioning Pakistan's control over the terrain have been dealt with force and absolute scorn. Some of them have not been allowed to participate in the elections while many others have been placed under tight control by the army units operating at the local level.

Pakistan's move to grant Gilgit-Baltistan a constitutional status generated a debate within the region about the future course of the relationship between Islamabad and the region and also between Gilgit-Baltistan and 'AJK' since the middle of 2015. A committee headed by Sartaj Aziz was established in October 2015, to look into various proposals related to Gilgit-Baltistan's future political and constitutional status. These proposals included granting Gilgit-Baltistan a "provisional" provincial status, introduction of an 'AJK' type administrative structure, and complete integration of Gilgit-Baltistan into Pakistan, by bringing about necessary amendment in the constitution and making it Pakistan's fifth province. Yet another proposal was to bifurcate Gilgit-Baltistan into two parts, separating Gilgit from Baltistan. The last proposal was handed over to the committee spearheading the constitutional crisis of Gilgit-Baltistan by the local Jamaat-e-Islami leader, Maulana Abdul Sami. According to this, proposal only those areas which were directly under the control of Maharaja Hari Singh would be treated as 'disputed', while the remaining areas would be merged with Pakistan.

Going by this argument, six districts from Gilgit and four from Baltistan, including Astore district remain disputed, whereas four districts that of Ghizer, Hunza, Nagar and Diamer were proposed to be merged with Pakistan.[1] However, this peculiar formula drew flak from various circles in Gilgit-Baltistan including both mainstream and nationalist political parties. Therefore, it might not be plausible for Pakistan to divide the region on these grounds. Moreover, these districts were very much under the suzerainty of the Maharaja of Jammu and Kashmir at the time of partition. It is being argued that this would mean dividing the region on sectarian grounds which would have a deleterious impact not only on the society, but also hinder economic development of the region, further jeopardising the CPEC project. Nevertheless, it is not the first time a committee had been established in this regard. In the past, three such committees were formed, and they all failed to deliver. The first such committee was formed in 1975 by Zulfiqar Ali Bhutto, the second by Gen. Zia-ul-Haq and the third by Asif Ali Zardari.

The present leadership of Gilgit-Baltistan is facing two challenges: one is about the CPEC and the other concerns Gilgit-Baltistan's constitutional status, as outlined above. On CPEC, almost all the stakeholders, whether they are mainstream political parties or nationalist groups, excepting a few, share the common perception: They all want more shares in the CPEC. Mainstream parties want written documents from Islamabad assuring them establishment of Special Economic Zones (SEZs) in the region. And the nationalist groups are demanding that Gilgit-Baltistan be made the third partner in the project along with China and Pakistan and given more space in the decision-making concerning CPEC.[2] It is obvious that these stakeholders are not opposing the CPEC, but want to use it as a tool for scoring political points over each other. Even cutting across sectarian divide, there is a tentative consensus that CPEC will bring tremendous fortune to the region and its people if it were implemented well.

Regarding the region's constitutional status, the nationalist leaders of Gilgit-Baltistan as well as the leaders of 'AJK' have condemned Pakistan's move to fully integrate Gilgit-Baltistan as a province. The Pakistani leadership is caught between the devil and the deep sea: on the one hand is the over US $60 billion. Corridor that Islamabad cannot afford to jeopardise by ignoring the demand and adding to internal security challenges by provoking yet another wave of popular demonstrations in favour of full political representation in Pakistan legislative bodies; and on the other hand, it would not like to annoy the leadership in 'AJK' and the Kashmiri separatists by integrating Gilgit-Baltistan pending resolution of the Kashmir dispute.

There is a strong view in Pakistan that the proposed move to grant Gilgit-Baltistan full provincial status will erode the credibility of Pakistan's stand on Kashmir, and with that it may lose whatever political constituency it has in whole of PoK and Indian State of Jammu and Kashmir. Nonetheless, some commentators apprehend that the military establishment acting under pressure, possibly from China, may prevail upon the civilian leadership to change the demographic and political status of the region. In the Gilgit Baltistan Order 2018, which was based on the final report by the Sartaj Aziz Committee and promulgated on May 21, 2018, the existing structure of relationship between Pakistan and Gilgit-Baltistan was largely maintained with minor modifications to assuage the feelings of the people of the region. Following this, several petition (more than 30 in number) were filed in the Supreme Court challenging this order and inquiring into various dimensions of the constitutional status of the relationship between GB and Pakistan, since August 2018.

It may be noted that the then Chief Justice of Pakistani Supreme Court, Mian Saqib Nisar, after his visit to GB in July 2018, took keen interest in the issue and assured the people of GB to "deal with their issues on an urgent basis".[3] In October 2018, a three-judge bench headed by then Chief Justice Saqib Nisar appointed senior lawyers Barrister Aitzaz Ahsan and Khawaja Haris as amicus curiae (friend of the court) in the case of appointment of judges in the courts of the Gilgit-Baltistan. The petitioner had argued that the GB Council had been given extraordinary powers to appoint all the judges including the chief judge of the GB Supreme Appellate Court, which violated the principle of independence of the judiciary.

It needs to be mentioned here that after winning the elections on July 27, 2018, and assuming office in August, the new government in Pakistan with Imran Khan as Prime Minister, took up the case and informed the Supreme Court on November 16, 2018 that his government had appointed yet another high-level committee to examine the constitutional, administrative and governance reforms for Gilgit-Baltistan. The Committee consisted of the federal minister for Kashmir Affairs and Gilgit-Baltistan as its convener and the federal law minister, the Attorney General, GB governor, the GB law minister, the secretaries for defence, foreign affairs and Kashmir and GB Affairs, the GB chief secretary, and the joint secretary (finance) of GB Council, as members. The committee was tasked with the review of reforms in the light of the GB Order of May 2018, the judgment of the Supreme Court in Al Jihad Trust case in 1999, recommendations of the attorney general, the status of GB in the light of UN resolutions on Kashmir and the stand taken by the government at the international level. The committee came out with a recommendation to grant interim/provisional provincial status to GB pending the final resolution of the Kashmir issue, which reportedly enjoyed the approval of Imran Khan himself.[4]

Soon afterwards, amid reports[5] that Imran Khan's cabinet refused to accept the recommendations of the high-level committee to accord special provisional status to GB, the Supreme Court heard the case on December 7, 2018. As per the court's orders, a fresh committee was constituted to look into the case, with Barrister Aitzaz Ahsan, the *amicus curiae* in another case pertaining to GB, as a member. The other members were GB Bar Council vice chairman Javed Ahmed, petitioner's counsel Salman Akram Raja, Secretary of the Ministry of Kashmir Affairs and Gilgit-Baltistan Chaudhry Afrasiab and GB Law Minister Aurengzeb Khan.[6]

On January 7, 2019, a seven-judge bench headed by the chief justice was informed by Attorney General of Pakistan that the government had drawn up a draft constitutional amendment bill, which intended to hand over the authority over law enforcement and administrative matters to the GB government in line with the Pakistani Constitution. It also reportedly recommended granting of all the fundamental rights guaranteed under the Pakistani constitution from Article 6 to 25 to the GB citizens. The other provisions in the bill reportedly included grant of policy-making powers to the GB government over all subjects which had been devolved to the provinces under the 18th Amendment. Aitzaz Ahsan, however, argued that the recommendations of the Sartaj Aziz committee should also be incorporated into the draft bill. Three days before his retirement, Justice Saqib Nisar, known for his 'populist grandstanding' as "an unelected individual wading into the political realm",[7] heading the same seven-judge bench came out with the order that was deferred earlier, on January 14, 2019.

Quite expectedly, India summoned the deputy high commissioner of Pakistan in New Delhi on January 18, and lodged a strong protest saying that this order was an interference in its internal affairs. It held that Pakistan Government or judiciary had "no locus standi on territories illegally and forcibly occupied by it" and "any action to alter the status of these occupied territories by Pakistan" had no legal basis whatsoever. It rejected such attempts by Pakistan "to bring material change in the occupied territories" and "to immediately vacate all areas under its illegal occupation".[8]

The order issued by the Supreme Court ruled that it had jurisdiction over GB and it looked into the "historical and constitutional issues involving the status, authority and powers" of GB including that of its judiciary and the rights available to its people. After dwelling at length on the history of the problem, it looked into a series of administrative structures and laws that were applied to GB since 1947. It concurred with the conclusions of the Sartaj Aziz Committee that "further reforms were required to enhance the sense of participation of the people of GB and to upgrade the standard of governance and public service delivery", however, "the reforms proposed should not prejudice Pakistan's principled position in the context of UN resolutions on Kashmir". It opined that "there should be no discrepancy in the fundamental rights available to those in GB relative to Pakistani citizens anywhere in the country", and "the right to self-government through an empowered GB Assembly as well as a robust system of local bodies is entirely uncontroversial and must be enforced as early as possible".

Notably, it held that the jurisdiction of the supreme appellate court or the chief court of GB was "territorially bound" and would not extend to any matter beyond GB. It could, therefore, interpret and implement the 2018 order of the government; and while it can strike down any law made by the GB legislature, it cannot judge the validity of the 2018 Order, from which it derived its authority.

Turning to the apex court's ruling in 1999 in the Al Jehad Trust case, the order said that even if the court had articulated "the basic position as regards the status and rights of the people of GB in the case...two decades ago, the actual realization by the Executive of that expression has remained fitful at best", which was "not acceptable". It recognised the proposed modifications of the government order of 2018, by the committee under the PTI government and instructed the President to promulgate the order with the aid of the federal government within a fortnight.

Not just "to provide judicial imprimatur to the order" but "to give it permanence", the court said that the proposed order would neither be amended after due promulgation "except in terms of the procedure provided in Article 124" of the order, "nor shall it be repealed or substituted", without placing it "before [the Supreme Court] by the Federation through an application that will be treated as a petition under Article 184(3)" of the Pakistani Constitution. The proposed order annexed to the judgment in its preambular section clearly acknowledged the limitations of the government even if it "intends to give Gilgit-Baltistan the status of a provisional Province, subject to the decision of the Plebiscite to be conducted under the UN Resolutions". It recognized that "a proper Constitutional Amendment needs to be made in the Constitution of the Islamic Republic of Pakistan" which would need two thirds majority in the Parliament and would take time".

Therefore, the order was only to be treated as "an interim measure", to give people of GB such fundamental rights as given to the people in other provinces and to "provide for greater empowerment" to GB to bring it "at par with other provinces".[9] The proposed order has 128 (instead of 122 articles in the previous order of 2018) and it is a modified version of it. In an appendix, the court order amended few articles of the proposed order and asked the government to comply with it.

It is believed that the incumbent government will abide by the judgment of the court and soon promulgate an order, which is intended to fulfill the local aspirations. However, the uncertainty over evolution of a policy acceptable to the people of GB continued to prevail at the time of publication of this book. In fact, in the immediate aftermath of the apex court's verdict, members of various political parties, students' organisations and civil society bodies organised a strong protest in Gilgit, Skardu, Islamabad and even Karachi against the verdict and launched a movement for permanent settlement of the status of GB.[10] Shabir Choudhry, President of the Foreign Affairs Committee of UKPNP, London termed the judgment 'controversial' and said it indicated the 'imperial designs of Pakistani rulers', "obsessed with occupying the territory of Jammu and Kashmir, which does not belong to Pakistan".[11]

Clearly, Islamabad has never taken either Gilgit-Baltistan or 'AJK' leadership on board before deciding on such critical issues concerning the region. The leaders of Gilgit-Baltistan like their cousins in 'AJK' have traditionally been kept out of the consultative processes on issues of critical importance – whether it is on the CPEC or while deciding the future political status of Gilgit-Baltistan. The Gilgit-Baltistan Assembly has passed many resolutions – from seeking representation in the National Assembly and other decision-making institutions to weighing the proposal for becoming the fifth province of Pakistan. In contrast, the 'AJK' Assembly passed a resolution against the proposed provincial status for Gilgit-Baltistan, as it believed that such status would affect Pakistan's position on Kashmir. Thus, this stance taken by 'AJK' Assembly had earlier irked the Gilgit-Baltistan leadership.

The mistrust between 'AJK' and Gilgit-Baltistan is not new. It has a long history which goes back to the period when the Karachi Agreement was signed by leaders from 'AJK' without consulting the people of Gilgit-Baltistan. In fact, throughout most of its history, the people of Gilgit-Baltistan were never consulted by the 'AJK' leadership on the Kashmir issue, even if G-B was very much a party to the dispute. It is a hard reality that the government of Pakistan has also actively discouraged social and political linkages between the two regions.[12] Thus, the two regions have developed separate geo-cultural identities even if they form part of the Jammu and Kashmir state. With very little interaction among the political leadership of the two regions as well as local political parties, the two regions have developed separate political dynamics, unrelated to each other. This situation is likely to continue in future.

ENDNOTES

1. Abdul Jabar Nasir, "The Formula of Division, Is it True?", *Daily Bang-e-Sahar*, January 14, 2016, at http://www.bangesahar.net/popup.php?r_date=01-14-2016&img=01-14-2016page-2-5 (accessed on January 19, 2019).
2. For details, see: "Pakistan and China Should Accept Gilgit-Baltistan as Third Partner, BNF and BSO", *Daily Bang-e-Sahar*, March 14, 2016, at http://www.bangesahar.net/popup.php?r_date=03-14-2016&img=03-14-2016page-1-2 (accessed on January 19, 2019).
3. "CJP Justice Nisar sways to traditional music during Gilgit-Baltistan tour", *The News*, July 28, 2018, at https://www.thenews.com.pk/latest/342867-cjp-justice-nisar-sways-to-traditionalmusic-during-gilgit-baltistan-tour (accessed on January 19, 2019)
4. Ghulam Abbas, "Cabinet refuses to give provisional province status to GB", *Pakistan Today*, December 6, 2018, at https://www.pakistantoday.com.pk/2018/12/06/cabinet-refuses-to-giveprovisional-province-status-to-gb/ (accessed on January 18, 2019).
5. "PM approves interim province status for G-B", *The Tribune*, November 28, 2018, at https://tribune.com.pk/story/1855919/1-pm-imran-approves-interim-province-status-g-b/ (accessed on January 19, 2019)
6. Mentioned in "SC reserves ruling on cases about rights of GB people", *Dawn*, January 8, 2019, at https://www.dawn.com/news/1456187 (accessed on January 18, 2019).
7. "CJP Nisar's legacy", Editorial, *Dawn*, January 18, 2019, at https://www.dawn.com/news/1458280 (accessed on January 18, 2019).
8. "India protests to Pakistan against recent order by Supreme Court of Pakistan on so-called "Gilgit-Baltistan"", January 18, 2019, at https://mea.gov.in/press-releases.htm?dtl/30919/India_protests_to_Pakistan_against_recent_order_by_Supreme_Court_of_Pakistan_on_socalled_GilgitBaltistan (accessed on January 19, 2019).
9. The whole order can be downloaded from http://www.supremecourt.gov.pk/web/user_files/File/Const.P._50_2018.pdf (accessed on January 19, 2019.
10. Jamil Nagri, "Protesters vow to start movement over GB's political status", The Dawn, January 21, 2019 https://www.dawn.com/news/1458793 (accessed February 7, 2019)
11. Shabir Choudhry, "Gilgit Baltistan and Pakistani game plan", *Daily Excelsior*, February 2, 2019, at http://www.dailyexcelsior.com/gilgit-baltistan-and-pakistani-game-plan/ (accessed February 7, 2019)
12. Ershad Mahmud, "Gilgit-Baltistan: A Province or Not", *The News*, January 24, 2016, at http://tns.thenews.com.pk/gilgit-baltistan-province/#.VqYEBpp97Gg (accessed on January 19, 2019).

Chronology of Developments in PoK with special focus on Gilgit Baltistan

July 1947: British Indian Government terminates the lease for Gilgit-Baltistan granted to it by the Maharaja.

Late July, Maharaja appoints Brig Ghansara Singh as Governor of Gilgit, who flies in on July 30, 1947. Takes over power from Lt. Col. Bacon, the then British Political Agent, on 01 August 1947.

Early August 1947: The Mirs of Hunza and Nagar remain defiant; so does the Gilgit Scouts formed by the British, dominated by recruits from Hunza and Nagar. Subedar Major Babar Khan, the uncle of the Mir of Nagar and married to the sister of the Mir of Hunza leads the rebellious section within the Scouts. The civil bureaucracy is also non-cooperative and demands special pay and perks. These elements are provoked by two British officers of the Gilgit Scouts, whose services had been retained by the State, namely Major W.A. Brown and Captain Matheson.

October 22, 1947: As tribal lashkar marches towards Srinagar, the Muslim component of Maharaja's soldiery starts showing its disaffection. Major Brown orchestrates a revolt in the ranks of the Scouts. A local commander of the Scouts, Col. Mirza Hassan Khan, leads a successful rebellion against Ghansara Singh's forces and easily deposes his government.

November 1, 1947: A government is formed in Gilgit and the Independent state of Gilgit is announced. Shah Raees Khan becomes the president of this republic and goes on to become the chief of the Gilgit Scouts later.

November 16, 1947: On the basis of an orchestrated request from the new government in Gilgit to join Pakistan, Jinnah decides to take over administration of Gilgit. A political agent named Sardar Alam Khan is sent in, while the Frontier Crimes Regulation (FCR) is imposed as the law of the land. Even though the princely states stay intact, Pakistan takes over administrative control of Gilgit. However, Pakistan does not officially annex it, in view of the overall controversy over Kashmir since the case was referred to the United Nations (UN). The UN Commission on India and Pakistan (UNCIP) Resolution adopted on 13 August 1948. (Document No. 1100, Para. 75, dated the 9th November, 1948), which looks for a plebiscite-oriented solution states clearly that Pakistani troops would have to evacuate the territory occupied by them first and states later:

PART II, TRUCE AGREEMENT

(3) Pending a final solution, the territory evacuated by the Pakistan troops will be administered by the *local authorities* under the surveillance of the Commission.

December 22, 1949: Proposal in respect of Jammu and Kashmir made by **General A.G.L. McNaughton, President of the United Nations Security Council (UNSC)**, pursuant to the decision of the Council taken at its 457th meeting, on 22 December, 1949, also makes a case for withdrawal of Pakistani forces.

DEMILITARISATION PREPARATORY TO THE PLEBISCITE

The programme of demilitarisation should include the withdrawal from the State of Jammu and Kashmir of the regular forces of Pakistan; and the withdrawal of the regular forces of India not required for purposes of security or for the maintenance of local law and order on the Indian side of the Cease-Fire Line;

The "Northern Area" should also be included in the above programme of demilitarisation, and its administration should, subject to United Nations supervision, be continued by the existing local authorities.

April 28, 1949: Karachi Agreement is signed between the Government of Pakistan and leaders of 'A.K.' ('Azad Kashmir' as it was known then) – more precisely, the signatories were Nawab Mushtaq Gurmani, a Pakistani Minister without Portfolio, and President of 'Azad Kaashmir' Sardar Ibrahim Khan and Chaudhry Ghulam Abbas, who were leaders of Muslim Conference, widely seen as mouth piece of Pakistan. The signing parties agree to allow Pakistan to administer the area known then as 'Gilgit-Ladakh'. No leader from the region is invited to the discussions. Pakistan sets up a Ministry of Kashmir Affairs, which is entrusted with the responsibility to govern the area through its agents. It is later (in 1970) termed 'Northern Areas (NA)' by Pakistan and the Ministry is called Ministry of Kashmir and Northern Areas (KANA).

1949-1970: The NA is under exclusive control of Pakistan. The princely states in NA continue to operate under the overall control of the agent. Restrictions on outsiders settling down in the area are gradually removed. Sunni Wahabi migration into the region, otherwise Shia-dominated, starts, which later peaks during the 1980s.

March 2, 1963: Pakistan and China sign a Boundary Agreement whereby Pakistan concedes large tracts of land (around 5,180 square kilometres) to China along the Shaksgam Valley.

> Article 6 of the agreement states:
> *The two Parties have agreed that after the settlement of the Kashmir dispute between Pakistan and India, the sovereign authority concerned will reopen negotiations with the Government of the People's Republic of China, on the boundary as described in Article Two of the present Agreement*, so as to sign a formal Boundary Treaty to replace the present agreement:
> Provided that in the event of that sovereign authority being Pakistan, the provisions of this agreement and the aforesaid Protocol shall be maintained in the formal Boundary Treaty to be signed between the Peoples Republic of China and Pakistan.
> Responding to Indian protest in the UN on March 16, 1963, Zulfikar Ali Bhutto, then foreign minister of Pakistan notes:
> "My Government is bound by its duty to declare in the Security Council that, pending determination of the future of Kashmir, through the will of the people impartially ascertained, no position taken or adjustments made by either of the parties to the present controversy between India and China or any similar controversy in the future shall be valid or affect the status of the territory of Jammu and Kashmir or the imperatives or demilitarization and self-determination of the state of Jammu and Kashmir laid down in the resolution of 21 April 1948, 30 March 1951, 24 January 1957, and in resolutions of the United Nations Commissions for India and Pakistan, dated 13 August 1948, and 5 January 1949, which have been jointly accepted by both India and Pakistan.."

1970: A single administrative unit comprising Gilgit Agency, the Baltistan region, and the former princely states of Hunza and Nagar is formed. It is officially called 'Northern Areas'.

July-August 1972: Bhutto visits Northern Areas and announces abolition of princely states. The first ever representative body in NA is formed, – named Northern Areas Advisory Council (18 members are directly elected, functions under a commissioner).

1973: The Constitution of Pakistan and PoK states that Pakistan's territories include "such States and territories as are or may be included in Pakistan, whether by accession or otherwise". Article 257 of the constitution further elaborates that "when the people of the State of Jammu and Kashmir decide to accede to Pakistan, the relationship between Pakistan and that State shall be determined in accordance with the wishes of the people of that State."

The Constitutions for 'AJK':

1970: The first formal Constitution for 'AJK' is drafted, referred to as Act of 1970. Presidential and Legislative Assembly elections are held for the first time on the basis of adult franchise. Executive and legislative powers are vested, respectively, in the President and the Legislative Assembly except in respect of defence and security, currency and the external affairs. The Assembly is also empowered to amend the Act.

1971: The 'AJK' Assembly amends the Act, without having to seek prior permission of the Pakistan government, and gives fundamental rights to the people, writ-jurisdiction to the High Court and establishes an Apex (appellate) Court. The President of 'AJK' is given powers to appoint judges to the superior courts. The subjects of foreign trade and foreign aid were also in the domain of the 'AJK' government, raising the profile of its internal autonomy.

1974: Interim Constitution Act is introduced. It allows a parliamentary form of government, but drastically curtails the powers of the vested in the 'AJK' government reversing the trend towards autonomy for the region. A new institution is established – the 'AJK' Council – with Prime Minister of Pakistan as chairman, and the Minister KANA as members. The Council is given wide ranging power including power to appoint 'AJK' high and supreme courts judges and the chief election commissioner.

1977: Zia-ul-Haq extends martial law to the region (Zone E), promises representation in Majlis-e-Shoora. He regards Northern Areas as an integral part of Pakistan even if it had been part of the Kashmir State once upon a time.

April 1982: Three members are nominated by Zia as observers in the 'AJK' Council.

July 1982: Zia says publicly that Northern regions of Gilgit, Hunza and Skardu were integral parts of Pakistan. Under pressure from 'AJK' leadership, Zia later revises his position and becomes less vocal about the status of Northern Areas thereafter.

1984: The importance of NA shoots up at the domestic level with the opening of the Karakoram Highway.

May 1988: Anti-Shia violence takes place in NA. The collusion of Pakistan military is suspected. There is a demand for separate provincial status in certain quarters.

December 1988-1990: Benazir Bhutto government forms a new body to suggest political reforms.

1994: Benazir Bhutto introduces the Legal Framework Order (LFO)-1994, which turned the *Northern Areas Council into the Northern Areas Legislative Council*. The leader of the house of this body is the deputy chief executive, while the minister of KANA serves as the chief executive. Northern Areas Rules of Business are framed, Chief Secretary and Civil Secretariats are established and judicial reforms are introduced.

1993: AJK High Court ruling on the legal status of Northern Areas

March 18, 1993: Responding to a petition filed by Mohammad Miskeen and Haji Bashir Khan of Gilgit, and Shaikh Abdul Aziz Advocate of Muzaffarabad, *to establish the constitutional future of the Northern Areas, the full bench of the 'AJK' High Court held that*

> "Northern Areas (Gilgit and Baltistan) are part of Azad Kashmir, historically and constitutionally; the Azad Kashmir government should establish administrative and legal institutions in these areas; Under the Provisional Constitutional Act, 1974, the (A.K.) High Court has the right to hear all petitions concerning Azad Kashmir; and (the Court) also has right to hear cases in all matters pertaining to Northern Areas.
> 'AJK' Supreme Court's ruling on Northern Areas-1994
> "AJK" Govt appeals against the 1993 verdict of the AJK High Court in 'AJK' Supreme Court

September 14, 1994: The 'AJK' SC in its verdict states: "No doubt, that Northern Areas are part of the state of Jammu and Kashmir – but not of Azad Kashmir. Therefore, the government need not take administrative control of these areas."

Pakistan Supreme Court ruling on Northern Areas

May 28 1999: In 1994, A petition on AJK HC's decision is brought before the Supreme Court of Pakistan by Habib Wahab al-Khairi (founder of Al-Jihad Trust, Rawalpindi), making Secretary, Ministry of Kashmir Affairs and N.A. defendant to the lawsuit. The Supreme Court of Pakistan came out with a 42-page verdict on May 28, 1999[1] that:

> ..."that Northern Areas were constitutional part of the state of Jammu and Kashmir... that the people of the Northern Areas are citizens of Pakistan for all intent and purposes".
> The government of Pakistan should ensure that basic human rights and other political and administrative institutions are provided in

the areas within six months. However, the action should not adversely affect Pakistan's stand concerning the Kashmir dispute.

"...the geographical location of the Northern Areas is very sensitive because it is bordering India, China, Tibet and USSR, and as the above areas in the past have also been treated differently, this Court cannot decide what type of Government should be provided to ensure the compliance with the above mandate of the Constitution. Nor we can direct that the people of Northern Areas should be given representation in the Parliament as, at this stage it may not be in the larger interest of the country because of the fact that a plebiscite under the auspices of the United Nations is to be held. The above questions are to be decided by the Parliament and the Executive. This Court at the most can direct that the proper administrative and legislative steps should be taken to ensure that the people of Northern Areas enjoy their above rights under the Constitution."

1999: The LFO of 1994 is amended delegating more powers to the Northern Areas Legislative Council (NALC). NALC is empowered to legislate on 49 subjects as envisaged in schedule –II of the LFO.

July 7, 2000: Musharraf reconstitutes NALC. It has 29 members with 5 seats reserved for women. His government authorizes NALC to legislate on 40 items. He granted NA Legislative Assembly the right to amend the LFO.

2007: The Northern Areas Legal Framework Order 1994 renamed as Northern Areas Governance Order 1994 and amended, similarly NALC is renamed as Northern Areas Legislative Assembly.

September 8, 2009: "Gilgit-Baltistan Empowerment and Self-Government Order (GBESGO)-2009" is introduced by PPP government.

The term "Northern Areas" is replaced with "Gilgit-Baltistan."

The GB Council comprised 15 members, six of whom were elected from the GB Legislative Assembly while the rest were elected members from Pakistani assemblies.

The Council has greater powers than the GB Legislative Assembly and most important decisions are to be taken by them.

Art 92. Order not to prejudice stance – The provision of this Order shall not derogate form, or in any manner prejudice, the declared stand of the Government of Pakistan regarding the right of self-determination for the people of Jammu and Kashmir in accordance with the United Nations Resolutions.

Developments in GB since 2009

Demand for Provincial Status in GB

September 2012: GB Legislative Assembly passes a resolution demanding provincial status within Pakistan. Sets off a debate on the issue. Apart from the nationalists, most of the mainstream political parties support the demand.

> Some political groups opposed the resolution, calling it an effort to divide the "undivided state of Jammu and Kashmir". They said that giving GB a provincial status will provide precedence for India to annex the parts of Kashmir under its control.
>
> **In 2012,** a retired Colonel named Imtiaz ul Haque, whose father had served in the Gilgit Scouts, which rebelled against the Maharaja in October-November 1947, came out with a dissertation titled: "Determining Political Status of Gilgit Baltistan – Future Prospects".
> **Col Imtiaz was one of the members of a committee formed by GB Government to make recommendations for the constitutional status of Gilgit-Baltistan.**
> His main recommendations were:
> [I]t may not be possible for Government of Pakistan, to take a U turn on its principle[d] stance on the subject and integrate Gilgit Baltistan in its constitutionally defined territories, due to its commitments with people of Jammu and Kashmir, United Nations, India and international community.....
>
> However, provision of interim provincial status, right of vote and due representation in the Constituent Assemblies of Pakistan, is the best viable option to address the issue of identity of crisis and sense of political deprivation, thereby ensuring better future integration of Gilgit Baltistan with Pakistan.

April 2014: Standing Committee of Senate on Human Rights took notice of Human Rights violation in GB with special reference to constitutional deprivation of the people of Gilgit Baltistan for the past several decades.

July 2014: The sub-committee of the Senate Functional committee on human rights led by Senator Raja Rabbani told by G-B government "(then Chief Minister Mehdi Shah) that neither the UN resolution on Kashmir nor the Establishment is [an obstacle] in providing constitutional rights to the people of G-B. But there is a need for [political will by the leaders], in this regard". G-B must be given its due share in the National Finance Commission (NFC) awards, and allowed to collect GST and custom duty.

September 2014: Extra-ordinary Meeting of **Gilgit Baltistan Bar Council** was held at Gilgit presided by Vice Chairman Advocate Shehbaz Khan. The meeting thoroughly discussed various issues and unanimously resolved on each point separately including the issue of "Constitutional Status of Gilgit Baltistan".

Gilgit Baltistan is no doubt a Jugular Vein for Pakistan because of its geographical, strategic & economic importance, but the rulers of Pakistan have not bothered to realize this fact and they have not been treating the people and the region accordingly by bringing G-B at par with other provinces, 'AJK' or even 'Indian Occupied J&K' in terms of constitutional & political rights.

The G-B Council, in which GB is only symbolically represented, is based in Islamabad and it is a meaningless institution, working under the Ministry of Kashmir and Gilgit-Baltistan Affairs, safeguarding and catering to the interests of the Ministry, not the people of GB". G-B has been made a sacrificial goat in the name of the so-called Kashmir Dispute with a malafide intention of keeping the area and the people under the clutches of (the Pakistani) bureaucratic system, depriving the people of their basic fundamental rights.

"AJK", which was liberated by the Pak Army with the help of Tribal Lashkar, is comparatively in a better position compared to GB, having an "Act" based governing system at least since 1969 & 1974 although not having a constitutional status.

The people of 'Indian occupied Jammu & Kashmir', have also got special constitutional status and full representation in the Central Government under Article 370 of Indian Constitution since 1948, in addition to having their own Jammu & Kashmir Constitution 1957 passed by the Constituent Assembly in 1957.

The people of Gilgit Baltistan are very much concerned and aware of the historical existence of the Pakistan China Agreement made in 1963 wherein 2000 Sq Km of their land has been given to China in exchange of just 700 km. They have a right to question legitimacy of this pact concerning the territories of GB, if it is a disputed territory. They are justified to ask whether giving away such a huge tract of land affected Pakistan stance on the Kashmir Dispute??? If not, how will it then affect their stance on Kashmir if the people of Gilgit Baltistan were to be given their fundamental rights to govern themselves through their chosen representatives guaranteed under a "constitution" under the domain of Local Authority as committed by GOP with UNCIP??

Denial of political rights to the people of Gilgit Baltistan will not be in the larger interest of Pakistan having crucial strategic & economic interests in this sensitive region. The dream of making Pakistan an Economical Tiger of Asia through Economic Corridor crossing 600 Km of GB will not become a reality until and unless the two million people of GB are given their due constitutional, political, social and economic rights.

The [pattern] of political governing system in 'Indian Occupied Jammu Kashmir' prevailing since 1948 & 1957 is the most suitable and viable in this regard as the same will not only cater to the [strategic] interest of Pakistan in this region but also redress the prolong[ed] sense of deprivation of people of GB as well without harming the princip[led] stan[ce] of Pakistan on Kashmir Issue if the following steps are taken:

Declare the next general elections in GB for holding "Constituent Assembly" and thereafter to draft, table and pass Constitution of GB accordingly.

Making amendments in the Constitution of Pakistan by the Pakistani Parliament giving the GB a "Special Status" & representation in the constitutional institutions of the Federation "provisionally".

Conversion of GB Governance Order 2009 into an "ACT" after amendments

October 29, 2015: A nine-member parliamentary committee headed by Sartaj Aziz is established to recommend steps to bring about reforms in GB to cater to the growing demands from the people of GB for absorption into Pakistan as its fifth province. The mandate of the committee includes: (a) review of the current constitutional and administrative arrangements in Gilgit Baltistan and analyse any shortcomings in relation to aspirations of the people;(b) after studying the historic record and relevant treaties, examine whether the existing eternal boundaries of the territories that constitute Gilgit-Baltistan overlap with territories that formed part of the state Jammu and Kashmir and if so, make recommendations for corrective measures; and (c) recommend constitutional and administrative reforms for GB, keeping in view the implications of these recommendations vis-a-vis the UN resolutions on Kashmir.

December 2015: The committee formed by Gilgit-Baltistan's Chief Secretary to prepare a document on the history of GB, boundaries and treaties signed so far, and future constitutional status **submitted its final report**. The committee comprised of Brig (r) Hissamullah Baig, Professor Usman Ali, Sherbaz Barcha, AIG (r) Dilpazir, Col (r) Imtiaz SI(M), Qasim Naseem and Israruddin Israr.

The committee [sic] recommended:

"Interim or provisional status to Gilgit-Baltistan with right of vote and representation in Parliament of Pakistan" as best possible option. For this purpose, necessary legislation and amendment in 1973 Constitution can be made, as permissible vide para 1 (2) (d) of the Constitution of Pakistan 1973.

Since representation in the National Assembly is based on population ratio, conveniently three elected representatives, one each for three divisions, i.e. Gilgit, Baltistan and Diamer respectively. While one woman seat can be kept for Gilgit Baltistan.

For representation in the Senate of Pakistan, Gilgit-Baltistan may be considered as an interim federating unit with due recognition and representation as in case of other federating units. Pakistan can justify its stance, as India has already extended its constitutional jurisdiction to the part of Jammu and Kashmir under its administrative control, including Laddakh region. Moreover, Kashmir issue also remains unhurt due to interim nature of the provision.

Other recommendations are:

1) Extension of bench of Supreme Court of Pakistan, bringing GB under wider judicial umbrella.

2) Establishment of institutions like office of Provincial Public Service Commission, Provincial Ombudsman, office of Provincial Consolidated Fund, etc, as permissible under the Constitution of Pakistan 1973.

3) Due representation of GB in NFC award and other national level forums, having representation of federating units.

4) Determination of due share / royalty of projects of national magnitude, like Diamer Basha Dam, Bunji hydel project and mineral, tourism and water resources.

5) Safeguarding economic interests of GB in Pak-China Economic Corridor project.

January 7, 2016: Sajjadul Haq, spokesperson for the chief minister of G-B, Hafiz Hafeez ur Rehman, told AFP: "A high level committee formed by the prime minister is working on the issue, you will hear good news soon." The committee under the leadership of Sartaj Aziz met thrice till February 3, 2016.

January 12, 2016: On 12 January, Jammu Kashmir Liberation Front (JKLF) leader *Yasin Malik wrote a letter to Nawaz Sharif* urging him not to change the status of the occupied J&K territory as it would adversely affect the nature of Kashmir dispute. "If your government incorporates Gilgit-Baltistan into Pakistan, and if as a consequence, India consolidates its hold in Kashmir, this would amount to bartering of people's aspirations…Kashmir is not about territory. It is about rights of people. Bartering these rights for land means killing the aspirations of the people".

Hurriyat(G) chairman Syed Ali Shah Geelani said Islamabad had no "constitutional or moral justification" to merge Gilgit Baltistan and that such a move would be betrayal of Kashmiris... "It is also clear violation of the UN resolutions on Kashmir".

January 13, 2016: *AJK' Legislative Assembly unanimously passed two resolutions* against the proposed move. "Making Gilgit-Baltistan a fifth province will weaken Pakistan's national stand on J&K at the international level," one of the resolutions said.

"Gilgit-Baltistan was part of the state of J&K and whenever a plebiscite is conducted the people of Gilgit-Baltistan will also have the right to decide their future with the people of other parts of the state of J&K".... The move to give G-B a provincial status will not only serve the interests of India but also negate the stand of Pakistan Prime Minister Nawaz Sharif and Army chief General Raheel Sharif on Kashmir dispute....."It is time to work for internal autonomy, political and constitutional rights than taking an initiative that would lead us towards the division of the state of Jammu and Kashmir".

The resolutions were presented by Finance Minister Latif Akber and All J&K Muslim Conference ('AJK'MC) member Sayab Khalid. Besides the treasury members, *the opposition Pakistan Muslim League Nawaz PML (N), "AJK" chapter unexpectedly supported the resolution.* Muttahida Quami Movement (MQM) and All J&K Muslim Conference ('AJK'MC) also supported the resolutions while Pakistan Tehreek-e-Insaaf (PTI) member Barrister Sultan Mahmood did not attend the session.

"AJK'" rehabilitation minister, Abdul Majid Khan said that it was *"our collective responsibility to stand against every move that paves the way for the division of the state of J&K".*

Sardar Abid Hussain Abid, 'AJK' Minister for Information while talking to the press.

"Any prudent and visionary person cannot take this step which I believe in all fairness and honesty is bound to harm the Kashmir issue beyond retrieve." *The alleged Chinese insistence was a 'lame excuse'.* *"China is making investment worth billions in our territory which too is not part of the federation of Pakistan.* Therefore, this logic does not hold ground," he said. He pointed out that the GB and 'AJK' practically enjoyed the status of de facto provinces of Pakistan, but if the same status was given official approval, it could cause more damage than the perceived benefits.... Even if there are some momentary benefits, for Pakistan, the losses in the long run are far greater."...

"Nevertheless, if some people want to do it, they should firstly issue a declaration that the Kashmir issue stands closed from today and Pakistan doesn't have any interest in its resolution...

We have a better status than GB but even then we are not satisfied with it and have unanimously passed recommendations for constitutional reforms. And in the same spirit, we support more constitutional powers for our brethren in Gilgit-Baltistan Even more than us.... But the federal government should avoid annexing the territory as a province, lest India may use it a justification to annex the territories of Jammu and Kashmir under its control".

On January 24, 2016: Hundreds of people from different political and religious parties attended the gathering in Islamabad in front of National Press Club, organised by the Youth of Gilgit-Baltistan, a non-political platform representing the youth of the area.

They protested what they called "Pakistan's sidelining of Gilgit-Baltistan" while launching the CPEC project and imposing taxes in the area. *"CPEC will pass through 600 kilometres area of GB but it is unfortunate that we are not getting even a single industrial zone or any project for the development of the area,"* Chairman of the GB Youth's coordination committee, Hasnain Kazmi.

January 2016: A resolution passed in the G-B legislative assembly demanded that there should be three hubs of CPEC in GB but only one station is being given to us for loading and unloading of goods. Moreover, no industrial zone is being set up in GB.

People of the GB could not get their basic rights even after over 68 years. Against any division of G-B. Rumours of Gilgit being merged into K-P. Demand for internet facility. A fibre optic cable is being laid from China to Pakistan but GB to get internet cable from Rawalpindi instead of the main line passing through the area from China. Demand for subsidy on wheat supply. During the previous PPP government, two million bags of wheat was allocated for GB on 50 per cent subsidised rates, but the new PML-N government initially decreased the rate of subsidy and later due to public protest, reduced the number to 1.1 million bags.

February 2, 2016: President Mammon Hussain meets members of GBLA and said that the government could not afford any compromise on its long-standing policy on the issue of Kashmir. However, the government, he added, was sincerely working on different proposals to give the people of Gilgit-Baltistan more powers in accordance with their expectations. Governor Gilgit-Baltistan Mir Ghazanfar Ali Khan, Chief Minister Hafiz Hafizur Rehman, federal minister for Kashmir affairs Birjees Tahir and others were also present during the meeting.

March 10, 2017: The Sartaj Aziz committee submits its first Report to the government. It recommends: (a) de-facto integration of GB with Pakistan but not a de-jure change since that will affect Pakistan's principle position on Kashmir. It recommended delegating further legislative, administrative and financial powers to GB to enhance the people's sense of participation and to improve service delivery. (b) The GB Legislative Assembly be brought on a par with other the provincial assemblies, with all legislative subjects, other than those enumerated in article 142 of constitution of Pakistan and its fourth schedule be devolved from the GB Council to the GB Legislative assembly; (c) The GB government may be given representation in constitutional bodies like National Economic Council (NEC), Executive Committee of the National Economic Council (ECNEC), the National Financial Commission (NFC), and Indus River System Authority (IRSA) as an observer; (d) One or more SEZs be set up in GB under CPEC to provide larger employment opportunities for GB people; and (e) People of Gilgit Baltistan be given special representation in the parliament.

July 3, 2017: The Sartaj Aziz committee is reconstituted to include the Ministers of Finance, Lawand Kashmir Affairs.

September 26, 2017: The Committee submits a Supplementary Report making additional recommendations which include:(a) Provision of funds through an agreed formula to cover the revenue deficit in GB budget; (b) Transfer of development funds directly to Gilgit-Baltistan Government rather than through the ministry of Kashmir Affairs; (c) Shifting of budget of Gilgit Baltistan Supreme Appellate Court and Chief Court to Gilgit Baltistan Council; (d) The Ministry of Kashmir Affairs to consult the Government of Gilgit Baltistan. before extending any federal government notification to Gilgit Baltistan; (e) Gilgit Baltistan to be accorded 'Observer' status in the Executive Committee of the National Economic Council (ECNEC), the National Economic Council (NEC), the Indus River System Authority (IRSA)and the Council of Common Interests (CCI) which was formed under the 1973 Constitution and presently consists of the Prime Minister of Pakistan and all four provincial Chief Ministers. The CCI is mandated under the Constitution to meet at least once in 90 days.

January 3, 2018: The committee headed by Sartaj Aziz submits its report to then Prime Minister Shahid Khaqan Abbasi.

February 17, 2018: The federal government decides to remove GB Council and the powers exercised by the Council are to be shifted to the elected GB Legislative Assembly.

May 18, 2018: An in-camera session is convened especially to take lawmakers into confidence about the draft political and administrative reforms in GB. The opposition members in GB Legislative Assembly boycott the session.

May 26, 2018: The Government of Gilgit Baltistan Reforms Order 2018 is promulgated by the local Legislative Assembly dominated by PML-N, 2018, after the formal approval by the federal cabinet and endorsement by the National Security Council.

June 1, 2018: The Government of Gilgit Baltistan Reforms Order 2018 is notified following the approval by the president.

June 20, 2018: Hearing a petition on the legality of the GB Order 2018, the GB Supreme Appellate Court comes out with a verdict to suspend the GB Reforms order.

August 7, 2018: The Supreme Court of Pakistan responding to a petition from the government restores the GB Order on August 7, 2018.

August 2018-October 2018: Several petitions filed in the Supreme Court of Pakistan challenging various aspects of GB Order of May 2018.

October 17, 2018: A three-judge bench headed by then Chief Justice Saqib Nisar appointed senior lawyers Barrister Aitzaz Ahsan and Khawaja Haris as *amicus curiae* (friend of the court) in the case of appointment of judges in the courts of the Gilgit-Baltistan. The petitioner argues that the GB Council had been given extraordinary powers to appoint all the judges including the chief judge of the GB Supreme Appellate Court, which violated the principle of independence of the judiciary.

November 16, 2018: The federal government informs the seven-judge Supreme Court bench, headed by then Chief Justice Mian Saqib Nisar that it has appointed a high-level committee to examine the constitutional, administrative and governance reforms for Gilgit-Baltistan. The Committee consists of the federal minister for Kashmir Affairs and Gilgit-Baltistan as its convener and the federal law minister, the Attorney General, GB governor, the GB law minister, the secretaries for defence, foreign affairs and Kashmir and GB Affairs, the GB chief secretary, and the joint secretary (finance) of GB Council, as its members.

December 7, 2018: After hearing the case, the Supreme Court orders formation of a fresh committee to look into the case, with Barrister Aitzaz Ahsan, as a member. The other members were GB Bar Council vice chairman Javed Ahmed, petitioner's counsel Salman Akram Raja, Secretary of the Ministry of Kashmir Affairs and Gilgit-Baltistan Chaudhry Afrasiab and GB Law Minister Aurengzeb Khan.

January 7, 2019: A seven-judge bench headed by the chief justice is informed by Attorney General of Pakistan that the government had drawn up a draft constitutional amendment bill, which intended to hand over the authority over law enforcement and administrative matters to the GB government in line with the Pakistani Constitution. It also reportedly recommended granting of all the fundamental rights guaranteed under the Pakistani constitution from Article 6 to 25 to the GB citizens.

January 14, 2019: The same seven-judge bench came out with the order which concurred with the conclusions of the Sartaj Aziz Committee that "further reforms were required to enhance the sense of participation of the people of GB and to upgrade the standard of governance and public service delivery", however, "the reforms proposed should not prejudice Pakistan's principled position in the context of UN resolutions on Kashmir". It opined that "there should be no discrepancy in the fundamental rights available to those in GB relative to Pakistani citizens anywhere in the country", and "the right to self-government through an empowered GB Assembly as well as a robust system of local bodies is entirely uncontroversial and must be enforced as early as possible".

ENDNOTES

1. The whole judgment is available at http://www.supremecourt.gov.pk/web/user_files/File/Const.P._72_2015.pdf

APPENDICES

APPENDIX I

The Boundary Agreement Between China and Pakistan, 1963

The Government of the People's Republic of China and the Government of Pakistan;

Having agreed, with a view to ensuring to prevailing peace and tranquility on the border, to formally delimit and demarcate the boundary between China's Sinkiang and the contiguous areas the defence of which is under the actual control of Pakistan, in a spirit of fairness, reasonableness, mutual understanding and mutual accommodation, and on the basis of the ten principles as enunciated in the Bandung conference;

Being convinced that this would not only give full expression to the desire of the peoples of China and Pakistan for the development of good neighbourly and friendly relations, but also help safeguard Asian and world peace.

Have resolved for this purpose to conclude the present agreement and have appointed as their respective plenipotentiaries the following:

For the Government of the People's Republic of China; Chen Yi, Minister of Foreign Affairs;

For the Government of Pakistan; Mr. Zulfikar Ali Bhutto, Minister of External Affairs;

Who, having mutually examined their full powers and found them to be in good and due form, have agreed upon the following:

Article 1

In view of the fact that the boundary between China's Sinkiang and contiguous areas the defence of which is under the actual control of Pakistan has never been formally delimited, two parties agree to delimit it on the basis of the traditional customary boundary line including natural features and in a spirit of equality, mutual benefit and friendly co-operation.

Article 2

(One) In accordance with the principle expounded in Article 1 of the present agreement, the two parties have fixed, as follows the alignment of the entire boundary line between China's Sinkiang and the contiguous areas the defence of which is under the actual control of Pakistan:

(1) Commencing from its north-western extremity at height 5630 metres (a peak, the reference co-ordinates of which are approximately longitude 74 degrees 34 minutes east and latitude 37 degrees 03 minutes north), the boundary line runs generally eastward and then southeastward strictly along the main watershed between the tributaries of the Tashkurgan river of the Tarim river system on the one hand and tributaries of the Hunza river of the Indus river system on the other hand, passing through the Kalik Daban (Dawan), the Mintake Daban (pass), the Kharchanai Daban (named on the Chinese map only), the Mutsjilga Daban (named on the Chinese map only), and the Parpik Pass (named on the Pakistan map only), and reaches the Khunjerab (Yutr) Daban (Pass).

(2) After passing through the Khunjerab (Yutr) Daban (pass), the boundary line runs generally southward along the above mentioned main watershed up to a mountain-top south of this Daban (pass), where it leaves the main watershed to follow the crest of a spur lying generally in a southeasterly direction, which is the watershed between the Akijilga river (a nameless corresponding river on the Pakistan map) on the one hand, and the Taghumbash (Oprang) river and the Koliman Su (Oprang Jilga) on the other hand.

According to the map of the Chinese side, the boundary line, after leaving the southeastern extremity of this spur, runs along a small section of the middle line of the bed of the Keliman Su to reach its confluence with the Kelechin river. According to the map of the Pakistan side, the boundary line, after leaving the southeastern extremity of the spur, reaches the sharp bend of the Shaksgam or Muztagh River.

(3) From the aforesaid point, the boundary line runs up the Kelechin river (Shaksgam or Mistagh river) along the middle line of its bed to its confluence (reference co-ordinates approximately longitude 76 degrees 02 minutes east and latitude 36 degrees 26 minutes north) with the Snorbulak Daria (shimshal river or Braldu river).

(4) From the confluence of the aforesaid two rivers, the boundary line, according to the map of the Chinese side, ascends the crest of a spur and runs along it to join the Karokoram range main watershed at a mountain-top (reference co-ordinates approximately longitude 75 degrees 54 minutes east and latitude 36 degrees 15 minutes north) which on this map is shown as belonging to the Shorgulak mountain. According to the map of the Pakistan side, the boundary line from the confluence of the above-mentioned two rivers ascends the crest of a

corresponding spur and runs along it, passing through height 6520 metres (21,390 feet) till it joins the Karakoram range main watershed at a peak (reference co-ordinates approximately longitude 75 degrees 57 minutes east and latitude 36 degrees 03 minutes north).

(5) Thence, the boundary line, running generally southward and then eastward, strictly follows the Karakoram range main watershed which separates the Tarim river drainage system from the Indus river drainage system, passing through the east Mustagh pass (Mustagh pass), the top of the Chogri peak (K-2), the top of the broad peak, the top of the Gasherbrum mountain 8068, the Indirakoli pass (names on the Chinese maps only) and the top of the Teram Kankri peak, and reaches its southeastern extremity at the Karakoram pass.

(Two) The alignment of the entire boundary line as described in section one of this article, has been drawn on the one million scale map of the Chinese side in Chinese and the one million scale map of the Pakistan side in English which are signed and attached to the present agreement. (Not attached in this book)

(Three) In view of the fact that the maps of the two sides are not fully identical in their representation of the topographical features the two parties have agreed that the actual features on the ground shall prevail, so far as the location and alignment of the boundary described in Section one is concerned, and that they will be determined as far as possible by joint survey on the ground.

Article 3
The two parties have agreed that:

Wherever the boundary follows a river, the middle line of the river, the middle line of the river bed shall be the boundary line; and that

Wherever the boundary passes through Daban (pass), the water-parting line thereof shall be the boundary line.

Article 4
I. The two parties have agreed to set up, as soon as possible, a joint boundary demarcation commission. Each side will appoint a chairman, one or more members and a certain number of advisers and technical staff. The joint boundary demarcation commission is charged with the responsibility, in accordance with the provisions of the present agreement, to hold concrete discussions on and carry out the following tasks jointly:

(1) To conduct necessary surveys of the boundary area on the ground, as stated in Article 2 of the present agreement, so as to set up boundary markers at places considered to the appropriate by the two parties and to delineate the boundary line of the jointly prepared accurate maps.

(2) To draft a protocol setting forth in detail the alignment of the entire boundary line and the location of all the boundary markers and prepare and get printed detailed maps, to be attached to the protocol, with the boundary line and the location of the boundary markers shown on them.

II. The aforesaid protocol, upon being signed by the representatives of the Government of the two countries, shall become an annex to the present agreement, and the detailed maps shall replace the maps attached to the present agreement.

III. Upon the conclusion of the above-mentioned protocol, the tasks of the joint boundary demarcation commission shall be terminated.

Article 5

The two Parties have agreed that any dispute concerning the boundary, which may arise after the delimitation of the boundary line actually existing between the two countries shall be settled peacefully by the two parties through friendly consultations.

Article 6

The two Parties have agreed that after the settlement of the Kashmir dispute between Pakistan and India, the sovereign authority concerned will reopen negotiations with the Government of the People's Republic of China, on the boundary as described in Article Two of the present Agreement, so as to sign a formal Boundary Treaty to replace the present agreement:

Provided that in the event of that sovereign authority being Pakistan, the provisions of this agreement and the aforesaid Protocol shall be maintained in the formal Boundary Treaty to be signed between the Peoples Republic of China and Pakistan.

##Ariticle 7

The present agreement shall come into force on the date of its signature.

Done in duplicate in Peking on the second day of March, 1963, in the Chinese and English language, both texts being eqully authentic.

Marshal Chen Yi,
Plenipotentiary of the
Government of the
People's Republic of China

Zulfikar Ali Bhutoo,
Plenipotentiary of the
Government of Pakistan

APPENDIX II

Karachi Agreement

Heads of agreement between Hon'ble Minister without Portfolio. The President of All Jammu and Kashmir Muslim Conference and the President of the Azad Kashmir Government.

Civil Administration and Azad Kashmir Areas

(i) The Azad Kashmir Cabinet shall formulate policy and generally supervise administration in Azad Kashmir area. Day to day administration hall however, be entrusted to executive officers viz. the Heads of Departments who shall also be secretaries to government for their respective Departments.

(ii) Besides the Heads of Departments the Azad Kashmir Government will have only the following two secretaries:
1. Secretary, Finance Department, and
2. Cabinet Secretary.

The Cabinet Secretary besides maintaining records of Cabinet proceedings will be directly responsible to keep the Cabinet well-posted with all matters connected with the plebiscite and for all correspondence with the Plebiscite Administrator.

(iii) The details of the set up will be as follows:

	Subjects	Head of Deptt.-cum-Secretary	Minister Incharge
1.	Law and Order Including Jails and Police	Commissioner-cum-Chief Secretary	Hon'ble president
2.	Food and Civil Supplies	Director of Food and Civil Supplies and Secretary to Government Civil Supplies Deptt.	Minister for Civil Supplies

3.	Revenues (including Forests, Customs) and Public Works.	Commissioner-cum-Chief Chief Secretary.	Revenue & Finance Minister
4.	Finance Minister	Finance Secretary	Revenue & Finance
5.	Rehabilitation & Secretary Rehabilitation Deptt.	Director of Rehabilitation	Minister for Rehabilitation
6.	Medical & Health Secretary	Director of Health Services & Health Services	Minister for Health and Education
7.	Education Secretary	Director of Education & Education	Ministry of Health and Education
8.	Cabinet & Plebiscite Works	Cabinet Secretary	Hon'ble President

(iv) No one below the rank of Head of Department/Secretary shall have access to the Ministers and orders to lower staff shall always be communicated through the head of Department/Secretary

(v) Heads of Department/Secretaries shall submit all important cases to their Ministers and shall generally keep them fully informed of developments in their respective Departments.

(vi) Heads of Department/Secretaries who are at present located outside Azad Kashmir area may continue to be so located. But they would meet their Ministers once or twice a week and put up cases on which orders of Ministers have to be obtained.

(vii) Whenever a Head of Department feels that an order passed by an Hon'ble Minister needs revision, he would bring the case to the notice of the Commissioner who in capacity as Chief Secretary to the Azad Kashmir Government, will endeavour to have the matter satisfactory settled, if necessary, in consultation with the Chief Plebiscite Adviser to the Pakistan Government, who will also be notified by the Azad Kashmir Government as their Chief Advisor.

(viii) Officers loaned to Azad Kashmir Government will formally appointed as Officers-on-Specific Duty with the Chief Plebiscite Adviser and their services will informally be placed at the disposal of Azad Kashmir Government who would formally appoint them to office by notification in their own Gazette. All correspondence of the Azad Kashmir Government with the Secretariat of the Minister without Portfolio, Government of Pakistan, will be through the Chief Plebiscite Advisor.

(ix) Pending the appointment of a Public Service Commission for Azad Kashmir an ad hoc Committee consisting of the following may be

appointed to recommend future recruitment and promotions in services in Azad Kashmir Government.
1. Commissioner (Chairman).
2. Judge of Azad Kashmir High Court.
3. The Head of the Department concerned.
4. Cabinet Secretary as Member-Secretary.

II. Financial Arrangements

(i) Monies advanced to the A.K. Government for specific purposes shall be spent for those purposes and no other. The Pakistan Government shall satisfy themselves that they have been properly spent.

(ii) Moneys advanced to the A.K. Government as general grants-in-aid shall be given only after the A.K. Government has produced a budget statement for the Government as a whole. In the case of these funds, the Government of Pakistan shall satisfy themselves that A.K. Government spend according to the budget proposals. For this purpose, they may ask for periodical statement of account from that Government.

(iii) The Pakistan Government shall loan the services of an Accounts Officer for employment as Accountant General of the Azad Kashmir Government.

III. Division of functions between the Government of Pakistan, The Azad Kashmir Government and the Muslim Conference.

A. *Matters within the Purview of Pakistan Government*

(i) Defence, (Complete Control over A.K. Government).
(ii) Negotiations with U.N.C.I.P.
(iii) Foreign Policy of A.K. Government.
(iv) Publicity in Pakistan and Foreign Countries.
(v) Coordination of arrangements for relief and rehabilitation of refugees.
(vi) All activities within Pakistan itself with regard to Kashmir such as procurement of food and civil supplies transport, running of refugee camps, medical arrangements etc.
(vii) All affairs of the Gilgit and Ladakh areas under the control of Political Agent at Gilgit.

B. *Matters within the Purview of A.K. Government*

(i) Policy with regard to administration in Azad Kashmir.
(ii) General Supervision of administration in Azad Kashmir.
(iii) Publicity with regard to activities of the A.K. Government and its administration.

(iv) Advise to H.M. without portfolio with regard to negotiations with U.N.C.I.P.
(v) Development of economic resources of A.K. area.

C. *Matters within the Purview of Muslim Conference*
  (i) Publicity with regard to plebiscite in A.K. Government.
  (ii) Field work and publicity in the Indian occupied area of the State.
  (iii) Organisation of political activities in the A.K. and the Indian occupied areas of the State.
  (iv) Preliminary arrangements in connection with plebiscite.
  (v) Organisation for contesting the plebiscite.
  (vi) Political work and publicity among Kashmir refugees in Pakistan.
  (vii) General guidance of the A.K. Government.
  (viii) Advice to H.M. without portfolio with regard to negotiations with U.N.C.I.P.

Sd/-	Sd/-	Sd/-
(Mohammad Ibrahim)	(Ghulam Abbas)	(M.A. Gurmani)
President Azad Kashmir Govt.	President All Jammu and Muslim Conference	Minister without Portfolio, Govt. of Pakistan.
28/4/49	28/4	

APPENDIX III

Simla Agreement, July 2, 1972

The Simla Agreement signed by Prime Minister Indira Gandhi and President Zulfikar Ali Bhutto of Pakistan on 2nd July 1972 was much more than a peace treaty seeking to reverse the consequences of the 1971 war (i.e. to bring about withdrawals of troops and an exchange of PoWs). It was a comprehensive blue print for good neighbourly relations between India and Pakistan. Under the Simla Agreement both countries undertook to abjure conflict and confrontation which had marred relations in the past, and to work towards the establishment of durable peace, friendship and cooperation.

The Simla Agreement contains a set of guiding principles, mutually agreed to by India and Pakistan, which both sides would adhere to while managing relations with each other. These emphasize: respect for each other's territorial integrity and sovereignty; non-interference in each other's internal affairs; respect for each others unity, political independence; sovereign equality; and abjuring hostile propaganda. The following principles of the Agreement are, however, particularly noteworthy:

- A mutual commitment to the peaceful resolution of all issues through direct bilateral approaches.
- To build the foundations of a cooperative relationship with special focus on people to people contacts.
- To uphold the inviolability of the Line of Control in Jammu and Kashmir, which is a most important CBM between India and Pakistan, and a key to durable peace.

India has faithfully observed the Simla Agreement in the conduct of its relations with Pakistan.

SIMLA AGREEMENT
Agreement on Bilateral Relations Between The Government of India and The Government of Pakistan:

1. The Government of India and the Government of Pakistan are resolved that

the two countries put an end to the conflict and confrontation that have hitherto marred their relations and work for the promotion of a friendly and harmonious relationship and the establishment of durable peace in the sub-continent, so that both countries may henceforth devote their resources and energies to the pressing talk of advancing the welfare of their peoples.

2. In order to achieve this objective, the Government of India and the Government of Pakistan have agreed as follows:
    o That the principles and purposes of the Charter of the United Nations shall govern the relations between the two countries;
    o That the two countries are resolved to settle their differences by peaceful means through bilateral negotiations or by any other peaceful means mutually agreed upon between them. Pending the final settlement of any of the problems between the two countries, neither side shall unilaterally alter the situation and both shall prevent the organization, assistance or encouragement of any acts detrimental to the maintenance of peaceful and harmonious relations;
    o That the pre-requisite for reconciliation, good neighbourliness and durable peace between them is a commitment by both the countries to peaceful co-existence, respect for each other's territorial integrity and sovereignty and non-interference in each other's internal affairs, on the basis of equality and mutual benefit;
    o That the basic issues and causes of conflict which have bedevilled the relations between the two countries for the last 25 years shall be resolved by peaceful means;
    o That they shall always respect each other's national unity, territorial integrity, political independence and sovereign equality;
    o That in accordance with the Charter of the United Nations they will refrain from the threat or use of force against the territorial integrity or political independence of each other.
3. Both Governments will take all steps within their power to prevent hostile propaganda directed against each other. Both countries will encourage the dissemination of such information as would promote the development of friendly relations between them.
4. In order progressively to restore and normalize relations between the two countries step by step, it was agreed that;
    o Steps shall be taken to resume communications, postal, telegraphic, sea, land including border posts, and air links including overflights.
    o Appropriate steps shall be taken to promote travel facilities for the nationals of the other country.

- Trade and co-operation in economic and other agreed fields will be resumed as far as possible.
- Exchange in the fields of science and culture will be promoted.

In this connection delegations from the two countires will meet from time to time to work out the necessary details.

5. In order to initiate the process of the establishment of durable peace, both the Governments agree that:
   - Indian and Pakistani forces shall be withdrawn to their side of the international border.
   - In Jammu and Kashmir, the line of control resulting from the cease-fire of December 17, 1971 shall be respected by both sides without prejudice to the recognized position of either side. Neither side shall seek to alter it unilaterally, irrespective of mutual differences and legal interpretations. Both sides further undertake to refrain from the threat or the use of force in violation of this Line.
   - The withdrawals shall commence upon entry into force of this Agreement and shall be completed within a period of 30 days thereof.
6. This Agreement will be subject to ratification by both countries in accordance with their respective constitutional procedures, and will come into force with effect from the date on which the Instruments of Ratification are exchanged.
7. Both Governments agree that their respective Heads will meet again at a mutually convenient time in the future and that, in the meanwhile, the representatives of the two sides will meet to discuss further the modalities and arrangements for the establishment of durable peace and normalization of relations, including the questions of repatriation of prisoners of war and civilian internees, a final settlement of Jammu and Kashmir and the resumption of diplomatic relations.

Sd/-
(Indira Gandhi)
Prime Minister
Republic of India

Sd/-
(Zulfikar Ali Bhutto)
President
Islamic Republic of Pakistan

APPENDIX IV

'AJK' Interim Constitution (Thirteenth Amendment) Act, 2018

"Muzaffarabad"
Dated: The 2nd day of June, 2018

No.LD/Legis-Act/37-52/2018. The following Act of the Azad Jammu and Kashmir, passed by the Joint Sitting and assented by the President on the 1st day of June, 2018, is hereby published for general information:

[Act III of 2018]

An Act

further to amend the Azad Jammu and Kashmir Interim Constitution Act, 1974 **WHEREAS** it is expedient further to amend the Azad Jammu and Kashmir Interim Constitution Act, 1974 (VIII of 1974), for the purposes hereinafter appearing; It is hereby enacted as follows:-

1. Short title and commencement. - (1) This Act may be called the Azad Jammu and Kashmir Interim Constitution (Thirteenth Amendment) Act, 2018.

(2) It shall come into force at once.

2. Amendment in the Preamble of the Azad Jammu and Kashmir Interim Constitution Act, 1974. - In the Azad Jammu and Kashmir Interim Constitution Act, 1974 (VIII of 1974), hereinafter referred to as the Constitution, in the Preamble, between third and fourth paragraphs, the following new paragraphs shall be inserted:-

"**AND WHEREAS** the Muslims shall be enabled to order their lives in the individual and collective spheres in accordance with the teachings and requirements of Islam as set out in the Holy Quran and Sunnah;

AND WHEREAS, it is necessary to cause further empowerment of the Legislative Assembly of Azad Jammu and Kashmir and Azad Government of the State of Jammu and Kashmir as being chosen representative of the people of Azad Jammu and Kashmir to exhaustively exercise their legislative powers and executive authority, as the case may be, for the better governance, socio-economic development and in particular for general welfare of people of Azad Jammu and Kashmir in the sustained manner and other matters ancillary thereto beside pursuing and fostering our cause of securing self-determination under the UN Charter and according to the UNCIP Resolutions through the democratic method of free and fair plebiscite under the auspices of the United Nations;"

3. General amendment in the Constitution. - In the Constitution, -
  (i) for the words "**this Act**" wherever occurring, the words "**the Constitution**" shall be substituted and referred as such;
  (ii) for the words "**Section**" and "**sub-section**", wherever occurring, the words "**Article**" and "**sub-Article**" shall be substituted and referred as such respectively.

4. Amendment of Article 1 of the Constitution. - In the Constitution, sub-Article (1) of Article 1 shall be substituted as under, -
  "(1) This Constitution shall henceforth be known as the Azad Jammu and Kashmir Interim Constitution, 1974."

5. Amendment of Article 2 of the Constitution. - In the Constitution, in Article 2, in sub-Article (1),-
  (i) the definition of term '**Joint Sitting**' shall be omitted;
  (ii) in the definition of term '**Judge**', between the words "an" and "additional", the words "ad-hoc Judge of the Supreme Court and" shall be inserted.
  (iii) in the definition of term 'Service of Azad Jammu and Kashmir' the words "or Advisor appointed under Article 21" shall be omitted.
  (iv) for sub-Article (2), the following shall be substituted:-
  "(2) In the Constitution, Act of the Assembly, shall include an Ordinance promulgated under sub-Article (1) of Article 41."

6. Addition of new Article 3-A to 3-J of the Constitution. - In the Constitution, after Article 3, the following new Article 3-A, 3-B, 3-C, 3-D, 3-E, 3-F, 3-G, 3-H, 3-I, and 3-J shall be added, namely. -

  "**3-A. Principles of Policy.** - (1) The Principles set out in Article 3-A, 3-B, 3-C, 3-D, 3-E, 3-F, 3-G, 3-H, 3-I and 3-J shall be known as the Principles of Policy, and it is the responsibility of each organ and authority of the State, and of each person performing functions on behalf of an organ or authority of the State, to act in accordance with these Principles in so far as they relate to the functions of the organ or authority.
  (2) In so far as the observance of any particular Principle of Policy may be dependent upon resources being available for the purpose, the Principle shall be regarded as being subject to the availability of resources.
  (3) In respect of each year, the President shall cause to be prepared and laid before the Assembly, a report on the observance and implementation of the Principles of Policy and provision shall be made in the rules of procedure of the Assembly for discussion on such report.

3-B. Responsibility with respect to Principles of Policy. - (1) The responsibility of deciding whether any action of an organ or authority of the State, or of a person performing functions on behalf of an organ or authority of the State, is in accordance with the Principles of Policy is that of the organ or authority of the State, or of the person, concerned.
(2) The validity of an action or of a law shall not be called in question on the ground that it is not in accordance with the Principles of Policy, and no action shall lie against the State or any organ or authority of the State or any person on such ground.

3-C. Islamic way of life. - (1) Steps shall be taken to enable the Muslim State Subjects, individually and collectively, to order their lives in accordance with the fundamental principles and basic concepts of Islam and to provide facilities whereby they may be enabled to understand the meaning of life according to the Holy Quran and Sunnah.
(2) The state shall endeavor, as respects the Muslims of State:-
(a) to make the teaching of the Holy Quran and Islamiat compulsory, to encourage and facilitate the learning of Arabic language and to secure correct and exact printing and publishing of the Holy Quran;
(b) to promote unity and the observance of the Islamic moral standards; and
(c) to secure the proper organization of zakat, usher, auqaf and mosques.

3-D. Promotion of local Government institutions. - The State shall encourage local Government institutions composed of elected representatives of the areas concerned and in such institutions special representation will be given to peasants, workers and women.

3-E. Parochial and other similar prejudices to be discouraged. - The State shall discourage parochial, racial, tribal and sectarian prejudices among the State Subjects.

3-F. Full participation of women in life. - Steps shall be taken to ensure full participation of women in all spheres of life.

3-G. Protection of family, etc. - The State shall protect the marriage, the family, the mother and the child.

3-H. Protection of minorities. - The State shall safeguard the legitimate rights and interests of minorities including their due representation in the Service of Azad Jammu and Kashmir.

3-I. Promotion of social justice and eradication of social evils. - The State shall,-
(a) promote, with special care, the educational and economic interests of backward classes or areas;
(b) remove illiteracy and provide free and compulsory secondary education within minimum possible period;

(c) make technical and professional education generally available and higher education equally accessible to all on the basis of merit;
(d) ensure inexpensive and expeditious justice;
(e) make provision for securing just and humane conditions of work, ensuring that children and women are not employed in vocations unsuited to their age or sex, and for maternity benefits for women in employment;
(f) enable the people of different areas, through education, training, agricultural and industrial development and other methods, to participate fully in all forms of national activities, including employment in the service of Azad Jammu and Kashmir;
(g) prevent prostitution, gambling and taking of injurious drugs, printing, publication, circulation and display of obscene literature and advertisements;
(h) prevent the consumption of alcoholic liquor otherwise than for medicinal and, in the case of non-Muslims, religious purposes; and
(i) decentralise the Government administration so as to facilitate expeditious disposal of its business to meet the convenience and requirements of the public.

3-J. Promotion of social and economic well-being of the people. - The State shall, -
(a) secure the well-being of the people, irrespective of sex, caste, creed or race, by raising their standard of living, by preventing the concentration of wealth and means of production and distribution in the hands of a few to the detriment of general interest and by ensuring equitable adjustment of rights between employers and employees, and landlords and tenants;
(b) provide for all citizens, within the available resources of the State, facilities for work and adequate livelihood with reasonable rest and leisure;
(c) provide for all persons employed in the service or otherwise, social security by compulsory social insurance or other means;
(d) reduce disparity in the income and earnings of individuals, including persons in the various classes of the service; and
(e) eliminate *riba* as early as possible.

7. Amendment of Article 4 of the Constitution. - In the Constitution, in sub-Article (4) of Article 4, in paragraphs relating to fundamental rights,-
(i) in paragraph 1, between the words "**of**" and "**liberty**" the words "**life or**" shall be inserted;
(ii) in paragraph 2, for the sub- paragraph (4) and (5), the following shall be substituted, namely:-

"(4) No law providing for preventive detention shall be made except to deal with persons acting in a manner prejudicial to the integrity, security or defense of Azad Jammu and Kashmir or Pakistan or any part thereof, or public order, or the maintenance of supplies or services, and no such law shall authorize the detention of a person for a period exceeding three months unless the Review Board has, after affording him an opportunity of being heard in person, reviewed his case and reported, before the expiration of the said period, that there is, in its opinion, sufficient cause for such detention, and, if the detention is continued after the said period of three months, unless the Review Board has reviewed his case and reported, before the expiration of each period of three months, that there is, in its opinion, sufficient cause for such detention.

Explanation-I: In this clause, "the Review Board" means a Board appointed by the Chief Justice of Azad Jammu and Kashmir consisting of a Chairman and two other persons, each of whom is or has been a Judge of the Supreme Court or a High Court.

Explanation-II: The opinion of the Review Board shall be expressed in terms of the views of the majority of its members.

(5) When any person is detained in pursuance of an order made under any law providing for preventive detention, the authority making the order shall, within fifteen days from such detention, communicate to such person the grounds on which the order has been made, and shall afford him the earliest opportunity of making a representation against the order:

Provided that the authority making any such order may refuse to disclose facts which such authority considers it to be against the public interest to disclose.

(6) The authority making the order shall furnish to the Review Board all documents relevant to the case unless a certificate, signed by a Secretary to the Government concerned, to the effect that it is not in the public interest to furnish any documents, is produced.

(7) Within a period of twenty four months commencing on the day of his first detention in pursuance of an order made under a law providing for preventive detention, no person shall be detained in pursuance of any such order for more than a total period of eight months in the case of a person detained for acting in a manner prejudicial to public order and twelve months in any other case:

Provided that this clause shall not apply to any person who is employed by, or works for, or acts on instructions received from, the enemy, or who is acting or attempting to act in a manner prejudicial to the integrity, security or defense of Azad Jammu and Kashmir or Pakistan or any part thereof or who commits or attempts to commit any act which amounts to an anti-national activity as defined in a law or is a member of any association which has for its objects, or which indulges in, any such anti-national activity.

(8) The Review Board shall determine the place of detention of the person detained and for a reasonable subsistence allowance for his family.

(9) Nothing in this clause shall apply to any person who for the time being is an enemy alien.

(iii) In paragraph 3,-
    (a) in sub-paragraph (2), between the words "**labour**" and "**are**" the words "**and traffic in human beings**" shall be inserted and thereafter the following new sub-paragraph (2-a) shall be added;
    "(2-a) No child below the age of fourteen years shall be engaged in any factory or mine or any other hazardous employment."
    (b) the full stop at the end of clause (b) of sub-paragraph (3) shall be substituted by a colon and thereafter the following proviso shall be added:
    "Provided that no compulsory service shall be of a cruel nature or incompatible with human dignity."

(iv) for paragraph 7, the following shall be substituted, namely:-

"**7. Freedom of association.** - (1) Every State Subject shall have the right to form association or unions, subject to any reasonable restrictions imposed by law in the interest of sovereignty or integrity of Pakistan and Azad Jammu and Kashmir, morality or public order.

(2) Every State Subject, not being in the Service of Azad Jammu and Kashmir, shall have the right to form or be a member of a political party, subject to any reasonable restrictions imposed by law in the interest of the sovereignty or integrity of the State and such law shall provide that where the Government declares that any political party has been formed or is operating in a manner prejudicial to the sovereignty or integrity of the State, the Government shall, within fifteen days of such declaration, refer the matter to the Supreme Court whose decision on such reference shall be final.

(3) No person or political party in Azad Jammu and Kashmir shall be permitted to propagate against, or take part in activities prejudicial or detrimental to, the ideology of the State's accession to Pakistan.

(4) Every political party shall account for the source of its funds in accordance with law."

(v) in paragraph 8, in clause (c),-
    (a) the words "**or Council**" appearing between the words

"**Government**" and "**or**" shall be omitted; and

    (b) the words and comma "**or the Council,**" appearing between the words "**Government**" and "**of**" shall be omitted.

(vi) In the paragraph 14,-

    (a) in sub-paragraph (3), in clause (b), after the words "**under any law**" , at the end, the words and brackets, "**(not being property which has ceased to be evacuee property under any law)**" shall be added; and

    (b) after sub-paragraph (3), the following new sub-paragraph (4) shall be added,-

"(4) The adequacy or otherwise of any compensation provided for by any such law as is referred to in this Article, or determined in pursuance thereof, shall not be called in question in any court."

  (vii) For paragraph 15, the following shall be substituted, namely. -

"15. **Equality of State Subjects**. - (1) All State Subjects are equal before law and are entitled to equal protection of law.

(2) There shall be no discrimination against any State Subject on the basis of sex.

(3) Nothing in this Article shall prevent the state from making any special provision for the protection of women and children.

    (viii) The paragraph 16 shall be renumbered into sub-paragraph (1) and thereafter the following new sub-paragraph (2) shall be added, namely,-

"(2) Nothing in sub-Article (1) shall prevent the state from making any special provision for women and children."

  (ix) For paragraph 17, the following shall be substituted namely:-

"17. **Safeguard against discrimination in services**. - No State Subject otherwise qualified for appointment in the service of Azad Jammu and Kashmir shall be discriminated against in respect of any such appointment on the ground only of race, religion, caste, residence, sex or place of birth: Provided that in the interest of the said service, specified posts or services may be reserved for members of either sex if such posts or services entail the performance of duties and functions which cannot be adequately performed by members of the other sex:

Provided further that under-representation of any class or area in the service of State may be redressed in such manner as may be determined by an Act of Assembly.

    (x) After paragraph 18, the following new paragraphs 19, 20, 21, 22, 23 and 24 shall be added, namely:-

"19. **Right to fair trial**. - For the determination of his civil rights and obligations or in any criminal charge against him, a person shall be entitled to a fair trial and due process.

20. Protection against double punishment and self- incrimination. - No person shall,-
- (i) be prosecuted or punished for the same offence more than once; or
- (ii) when accused of an offence, be compelled to be a witness against himself.

21. Inviolability of dignity of man, etc. -
- (i) The dignity of man and, subject to law, the privacy of home, shall be inviolable.
- (ii) No person shall be subjected to torture for the purpose of extracting evidence.

22. Right to information. - Every State Subject shall have the right to have access to information in all matters of public importance subject to regulation and reasonable restrictions imposed by law.

23. Right to education. - The State shall provide free and compulsory education to all children of the age of five to sixteen years in such manner as may be determined by law.

24. Preservation of language, script and culture. - Without prejudice to the national language of Azad Jammu and Kashmir as may be declared by the Government, any section of society having a distinct language, script or culture shall have the right to preserve and promote the same and subject to law, establish institutions for that purpose."

8. Amendment of Article 5 of the Constitution. - In the Constitution, in Article 5, in sub-Article (1), for the words "**Joint Sitting**", appearing twice, the word "**Assembly**" shall be substituted.

9. Amendment of Article 6 of the Constitution. - In the Constitution, in Article 6, for the words "**Joint Sitting**", wherever appearing, the word "**Assembly**" shall be substituted.

10. Amendment of Article 12 of the Constitution. - In the Constitution, in Article 12, the words and comma "Subject to this Act," shall be omitted.

11. Amendment of Article 14 of the Constitution. - In the Constitution, in Article 14, in sub-Article (1), the proviso, shall be substituted as under:-

"Provided that from next term of Assembly, total strength of Ministers in the cabinet shall not exceed thirty percent of the total membership of the Assembly."

12. Substitution of Article 14-A of the Constitution. - In the Constitution, for Article 14-A the following shall be substituted, namely:-

"**14-A. Appointment of Advisors, Special Assistants and Parliamentary**

Secretaries. - (1) The Prime Minister may appoint Advisors and Special Assistants to Government, of whom total strength in each case shall not exceed two, for the performance of such duties and functions as may be prescribed by law.

(2) The Prime Minister may also appoint Parliamentary Secretaries, not exceeding five from amongst the members of the Assembly to perform such functions as may be prescribed by law.

(3) The Advisor, Special Assistant or Parliamentary Secretary, as the case may be, by writing under his hand addressed to the Prime Minister, may resign from his office or may be removed from his office by the Prime Minister."

13. Amendment of Article 17 of the Constitution. - In the Constitution, in sub-Article (3) of Article 17, for the comma and words "**, for any reason, the Prime Minister is unable to perform his functions**" the words "**the Prime Minister is unable to perform his functions due to physical incapacitation or sickness**" shall be substituted.

14. Amendment of Article 18 of the Constitution. - In the Constitution, for sub-Article (1) of Article 18, the following shall be substituted, namely,-

"(1) A resolution for a vote of no-confidence (hereinafter in this Article referred to as the resolution) moved by not less than twenty five per centum of the total membership of the Assembly may be passed against the Prime Minister by the Assembly."

15. Substitution of Article 19 of the Constitution. - In the Constitution, for Article 19, the following shall be substituted, namely:-

"**19. Extent of executive authority of Government.** - (1) The executive authority of the Government shall extend to the matters with respect to which the Assembly has power to make laws including Part-B of Third Schedule and shall be so exercised as,-

(a) not to impede or prejudice the responsibilities of Government of Pakistan in relation to the matters specified in sub-Article (3) of Article 31; and

(b) to secure compliance with the laws made in relation to matters specified in Third Schedule as set out under sub-Article (3) of Article 31.

(2) The Government, if deems necessary or expedient in the public interest and to secure paramount purpose of social and economic wellbeing of the people of the State, may with the consent of the Government of Pakistan, entrust, either conditionally or unconditionally, to the Government of Pakistan or to any of its subordinate authority including a ministry, division, organization or statutory body or entity of Pakistan, to perform any of such functions within territory of the State as may be prescribed by law.

(3) The Government of Pakistan may also entrust, either conditionally or unconditionally, any of its functions to the Government in relation to any matter specified in Part-B of the 'Third Schedule' as set out under sub-Article (3).

(4) The relationship between Government of Pakistan with the Government shall be such as manifested in sub-Article (3) of Article 31 and the Cabinet Division D.O. No. 8/9/70-Cord-1 dated the 11th May, 1971 of the Government of Pakistan with respect to peculiar political status of Azad Jammu and Kashmir and shall be the guiding principles to maintain direct working relationship of Government with the Government of Pakistan.".

16. Amendment of Article 21 of the Constitution. - In the Constitution, in Article 21,-

    (i) sub-Articles (7), (8), (9), (10), (11), (12) and (13) shall be omitted; and

    (ii) sub-Article (14) shall be renumbered as sub-Article (7) thereof and thereafter the following new sub-Article (8) shall be added, namely:-
"(8) The Council shall have an advisory role in respect of matters and subjects, referred to in sub-Article (3) of Article 31 and in respect of the responsibilities of Government of Pakistan under the UNCIP Resolutions.".

17. Amendment of Article 22 of the Constitution. - In the Constitution, in Article 22,-

    (i) in sub-Article (1), for the words "**forty nine**" the words "**fifty three**" shall be substituted;

    (ii) for clause (a) of sub-Article (1), the following shall be substituted, namely;-
"(a) forty five shall be elected directly on the basis of adult franchise, out of whom,-

      (i) thirty three members to be elected by the State Subjects residing in the Azad Government of the State of Jammu and Kashmir as defined in Article 2:
Provided that this amendment shall take effect from the next term of the Assembly;

      (ii) six members to be elected from amongst themselves by the refugees from the occupied areas of districts of Muzaffarabad, Anantnag (Islamabad) and Baramula as these existed on the 14th day of August, 1947, who are now residing in any of the province of Pakistan;

      (iii) six members to be elected from amongst themselves by such of the State Subjects from occupied areas of districts of Jammu, Kathua, Reasi, Udhampur, Poonch State and Mirpur as existed on the 14th day of August, 1947 and Mangla Dam affectees who are now residing in any of the province of Pakistan:

Provided that the members represented under sub-clauses (ii) and (iii), hereinabove, shall be deemed to have been elected and shall always to have been validly represented and elected under this Article.

18. Amendment of Article 27 of the Constitution. - In the Constitution, for sub-Article (3) of Article 27, the following shall be substituted, namely:-

"(3) The Assembly shall meet for not less than sixty working days in each year.".

19. Amendment of Article 30-A of the Constitution. - In the Constitution, in Article 30-A, the words "**or the Council or the joint sitting**" shall be omitted.

20. Substitution of Article 31 of the Constitution. - In the Constitution, for Article 31, the following shall be substituted, namely:-

"**31. Legislative Power.** - (1) Subject to sub-Article (3) the Assembly shall have the power to make laws,-

(a) for the territories of Azad Jammu and Kashmir;

(b) for all state subjects, wherever they may be; and

(c) for all persons in the Service of Azad Jammu and Kashmir, wherever they may be.

(2) The Assembly shall have exclusive power to make laws on any matter not enumerated in Part-A of the Third Schedule.

(3) The Government of Pakistan shall have exclusive power to make laws with respect to any matter enumerated in 'Part-A' of the Third Schedule.

(4) The Assembly shall, with the consent of Government of Pakistan, make laws with respect to any matters enumerated in 'Part-B' of the Third Schedule.

(5) All taxes including the income tax shall be levied for the purposes of the territories of Azad Jammu and Kashmir by or under the authority of an Act of the Assembly.

(6) No law shall be repugnant to the teachings and requirements of Islam as set out in the Holy Quran and Sunnah and all existing laws shall be brought in conformity with the Holy Quran and Sunnah.

Explanation.—In the application of this sub-Article to the personal law of any Muslim sect, the expression "Quran and Sunnah" shall mean the Quran and Sunnah as interpreted by that sect.".

21. Substitution of Article 32 of the Constitution. - In the Constitution, Article 32 shall be substituted as under,-

"**32. Council of Islamic Ideology**. - (1) There shall be a Council of Islamic Ideology, hereinafter referred to as the Islamic Council.

(2) The Islamic Council shall consist of such members, being not less than

five nor more than ten, as the President may appoint, on the advice of the Prime Minister, from amongst persons having knowledge of principles and philosophy of Islam as enunciated in the Holy Quran and Sunnah, or understanding of the economic, political, legal or administrative problems of Azad Jammu and Kashmir.

(3) While appointing members of Islamic Council, the President shall ensure that,-

    (a) so far as practicable, various school of thought are represented in the Islamic Council

    (b) not less than one of the members are persons each of whom is or has been a judge of the Supreme Court or of a High Court; and

    (c) not less than one third of the members are persons each of whom has been engaged for a period of not less than fifteen years, in Islamic research or instruction.

(4) The President shall appoint one of the members of Islamic Council to be Chairman of Islamic Council.

(5) If one-third members of the total strength of the Assembly so requires, the Assembly may refer to Islamic Council or Islamic Ideology Council of Pakistan constituted under Article 228 of the Constitution of Pakistan, for solicitation of advice as to whether a proposed law is or is not repugnant to the injunctions of Islam:

Provided that the Government may also make such reference for advice of Islamic Council or Islamic Ideology Council of Pakistan, if deems expedient in the public interest.

(6) When a proposed law or a question is referred under sub-Article (6), the Islamic Council, or the Islamic Ideology Council of Pakistan, as the case may be, shall, within fifteen days, inform the Assembly or the Government of the period within which the council expects to be able to furnish that advice:

Provided that the Islamic Council may refer the question so received, with or without its opinion, to the Council of Islamic Ideology of Pakistan for advice.

(7) Where the Assembly considers that in the public interest, the making of the proposed law in relation to which the question arose should not be postponed until the advice of the Islamic Council or Islamic Ideology Council of Pakistan is furnished, the law may be made before the advice is furnished;

Provided that, where a law is referred for advice under sub-Article (7) and it is advised that the law is repugnant to the injunctions of Islam, the Assembly shall reconsider the law so made.

(8) A member of Islamic Council shall hold office for a period of three years.

(9) A Member may, by writing under his hand addressed to the President, resign his office or maybe removed by the President upon the passing of a resolution for his removal by a majority of the total membership of the Islamic Council.

(10) The proceedings of the Islamic Council shall be regulated by rules of

procedure to be made by the Council with the approval of the Government.

22. Substitution of Article 33 of the Constitution. - In the Constitution, for Article 33 the following shall be substituted, namely,-

> "**33. Amendment of the Act.** - (1) The provisions of the Constitution may be amended in accordance with the following provisions.

(2) No amendment shall be made in Articles 31, 33 and 56, without the prior approval of the Government of Pakistan.

(3) A bill to amend the Constitution, shall be originated in the Assembly and when the bill has been passed with or without amendment by the votes of not less than two-third of total membership of the Assembly, the bill shall be presented to the President for assent.".

23. Omission of Article 33-A of the Constitution. - In the Constitution, Article 33-A shall be omitted.

24. Substitution of Article 34 of the Constitution. - In the Constitution, for Article 34, the following shall be substituted, namely:-

> "**34. Validity of Proceedings of the Assembly.** - (1) The validity of any proceedings in the Assembly shall not be questioned in any court.

(2) An officer or member or an authority to whom powers are vested for the regulation of proceedings, conduct of business, maintenance of order in the Assembly shall not, in relation to the exercise of any of those powers, be subject to the jurisdiction of any court.

(3) A member of, or a person entitled to speak in the Assembly shall not be liable to any proceedings in any court in respect of anything said by him or any vote given by him in the Assembly or in any committee thereof.

(4) A person shall not be liable to any proceedings in any court in respect of publication by or under the authority of the Assembly, of any report, paper, vote or proceedings.

(5) No process issued by a court or other authority shall, except with the leave of the Speaker be served or executed within the precincts of the place where a meeting of the Assembly is being held.

(6) Subject to this Article, the privileges of the Assembly, the committees and members of the Assembly and of the persons entitled to speak in the Assembly may be determined by law."

25. Omission of Article 35 of the Constitution. - In the Constitution, Article 35 shall be omitted.

26. Amendment of Article 36 of the Constitution. - In the Constitution, in Article 36, in sub-Article (1), the words '**or a Joint Sitting**' shall be omitted.

27. Omission of Article 37 of the Constitution. - In the Constitution, Article 37 shall be omitted.

28. Amendment of Article 37-A of the Constitution. - In the Constitution, in Article 37-A,-
> (i) in sub-Article (1), between the words **"revenue"** and **"received"** the words "**taxes including income tax**" shall be inserted; and
> (ii) in sub-Article (2), in clause (b), between the words "**the**" and "**High Court**" the words "**Supreme Court and the**" shall be inserted.

29. Amendment of Article 41 of the Constitution. - In the Constitution, in Article 41,-
> (i) in sub-Article (2), in the clause (a), the semi-colon at the end shall be substituted by a colon and the word "and" at the end shall be omitted and thereafter following proviso shall be added:
> "Provided that the Assembly may by a resolution extend the Ordinance for a further period of four months and it shall stand repealed at the expiration of the extended period." and
> (ii) sub-Article (4) shall be omitted.

30. Amendment of Article 42-A of the Constitution. - In the Constitution, in Article 42-A, in sub-Article (4), for the words "**Council**" the words "**Government**" shall be substituted.

31. Amendment of Article 42-D of the Constitution. - In the Constitution, in Article 42-D, the words "**or the Council**" shall be omitted.

32. Amendment of Article 43 of the Constitution. - In the Constitution, in Article 43, after sub-Article (1-A), the following new sub-Article (1-B), (1-C) and (1-D) shall be added, namely,-
> "(1-B) There shall be a Shariat Appellate Bench of the High Court as constituted by an Act of the Assembly consisting of Chief Justice of High Court, all the Muslim Judges of the High Court and an Aalim Judge, to perform such functions and exercise such jurisdiction as may be conferred upon it by an Act of the Assembly.
> (1-C) The Aalim Judge shall be appointed by the President on the advice of the Prime Minister and after consultation with the Chief Justice of the Supreme Court and the Chief Justice of High Court, from amongst the persons having such qualification and experience and on such terms and conditions, as may be, prescribed by an Act of the Assembly.
> (1-D) The Shari'at Appellate Bench of the High Court, existing at the time of enforcement of this Amendment Act, 2018 shall be deemed to have been constituted under this Article.

33. Amendment of Article 47 of the Constitution. - In the Constitution, in Article 47, -
> (i) In sub-Article (1), the words "**Council in respect of matters to which its executive authority extends and**" shall be omitted.

(ii) in clause (b) of sub-Article (1), the words "**the Council or**" shall be omitted.

34. Substitution of Article 48 of the Constitution. - In the Constitution, for Article 48, the following shall be substituted:-

"**48. Public Service Commission.** - (1) There shall be a Public Service Commission consisting of a Chairman and such number of members who shall be having such qualification as may be prescribed by an Act of the Assembly.

(2) The appointment of the Chairman Public Service Commission and members shall be made by the President on advice of the Prime Minister on such terms and conditions as may be prescribed by an Act of the Assembly:

Provided that in respect of appointment of Chairman, the Prime Minister, may solicit the opinion of Leader of Opposition in the Assembly before making advice to the President for such appointment.

(3) The Chairman and members of Public Service Commission appointed immediately before the commencement of this amending Act, 2018 shall be deemed to have been appointed under this Article subject to terms and conditions already determined and notified at the time of their appointment."

35. Substitution of Article 50 of the Constitution. - In the Constitution, for Article 50 the following shall be substituted, namely:-

"**50. Election Commission.** - (1) There shall be an Election Commission for Azad Jammu and Kashmir, hereinafter referred to as "the Commission".

(2) The Commission shall consist of the Chief Election Commissioner, who shall act as the Chairman and two Members.

(3) The Chief Election Commissioner, hereinafter referred to as the Commissioner, shall be appointed by the President on the advice of the Chairman of the Council.

(4) The Prime Minister after consultation with the Leader of Opposition in the Assembly shall finalize the nominees for the appointment as Commissioner.

(5) No person shall be appointed as the Commissioner unless he has been a Judge of the Supreme Court or High Court or has been a civil servant of BPS-21 and above, in the service of Azad Jammu and Kashmir.

(6) The members of the Commission possessing the qualification as mentioned for Commissioner in sub-Article (5) above, shall be appointed by the President on the advice of the Prime Minister.

(7) It shall be duty of the Commission to organize and conduct the election for the office of the President, the Assembly, the Council and local government bodies and to make such arrangements as are necessary to ensure that the election is conducted honestly, justly, fairly and in accordance with the law.

(8) The Commission shall have such powers and perform such functions as are conferred on it under the Constitution and Act of the Assembly.

(9) At any time when the office of Commissioner is vacant or the Commissioner is absent or unable to perform the functions of his office due to any cause, the senior member of Commission duly designated at the time of appointment shall act as Commissioner for a period not exceeding six months.

(10) Before entering upon office, the Commissioner shall make oath before the Chief Justice of Azad Jammu and Kashmir and the members before the Commissioner in the form set out in the First Schedule.

(11) Subject to this Article, the Commissioner and each member, as the case may be, shall hold office for a term of five years from the day he enters upon his office:

Provided that the Chief Election Commissioner appointed before the commencement of the Azad Jammu and Kashmir Interim Constitution (Thirteenth Amendment) Act, 2018 shall be deemed to have been appointed under this Article for remaining period of his term.

(12) The Commissioner and members shall not be removed from their office except in the manner prescribed in Article 42-E.

(13) The Commissioner or the member may, by writing under his hand addressed to the President, resign from his office.

(14) The terms and conditions, other than mentioned hereinabove, for the office of the Commissioner and member shall be such as may be prescribed by an Act of Assembly.

(15) The Commissioner or a member shall not,-
   (a) hold any other office of profit in the Service of Azad Jammu and Kashmir or Pakistan; or
   (b) occupy any other position carrying the right to remuneration for the rendering of such services.

(16) A person who has held office as Commissioner or the member shall not hold any office of profit in the Service of Azad Jammu and Kashmir or Pakistan before the expiration of two years after he has ceased to hold that office.

(17) The Commission shall perform such functions as may be determined by Act of Assembly.

(18) It shall be the duty of all executive authorities in the state to assist the Commission in the discharge of its functions.

(19) Until Assembly by law otherwise provides, the Commission may, on the advice of the Prime Minister and with the approval of the President, make rules providing for the appointment of officers and servants to be employed in connection with the functions of the Commission and for their terms and conditions of employment.".

36. Amendment of Article 50-A of the Constitution. - In the Constitution, in

Article 50-A, in sub-Article (1), for the word 'Council', the words "**Chairman of the Council**" shall be substituted.

37. Amendment of Article 51 of the Constitution. - In the Constitution, in Article 51, the existing provision shall be renumbered to as sub-Article (1) and thereafter the following new sub-Article (2) shall be added, namely: -

"(2) Subject to the Constitution, all laws of Azad Jammu and Kashmir which, from time to time, made by the Azad Jammu and Kashmir Council and in force immediately before the commencement of the Azad Jammu and Kashmir Interim Constitution (Thirteenth Amendment) Act, 2018, shall continue to be in force until amended or altered or repealed by the Act of the Assembly or by the order, notification etc., of the Government of Pakistan or, as the case may be, by the Azad Government of the State of Jammu and Kashmir:

Provided that the reference of Azad Jammu and Kashmir Council made in the existing laws, on the commencement of the Azad Jammu and Kashmir Interim Constitution (Thirteenth Amendment) Act, 2018, shall, as far as practicable, be construed and referred to as the Assembly, or as the case may be, Government of Pakistan or the Azad Government of the State of Jammu and Kashmir.".

38. Insertion of new Article 51-A of the Constitution. - In the Constitution, after Article 51, the following new Article 51-A shall be inserted, namely:-

"**51-A. Transfer of Employees, Assets and Liabilities.** - (1) On the commencement of the Azad Jammu and Kashmir Interim Constitution (Thirteenth Amendment) Act, 2018, all moveable and immovable properties and assets, moneys or funds received by and deposited in the Azad Jammu and Kashmir Council Consolidated Fund or made part of Public Finance, all savings or fixed deposits of the Council in all bank accounts and also such liabilities which were incurred under any law, shall immediately be transferred or invested with Azad Jammu and Kashmir Consolidated Fund or, as the case may be, to the Government.

(2) All existing employees in the service of Azad Jammu and Kashmir Council who immediately before the commencement of the Azad Jammu and Kashmir Interim Constitution (Thirteenth Amendment) Act, 2018 were serving on regular basis under superintendence and control of Azad Jammu and Kashmir Council for any department, secretariat or any statutory body or institution or organizations duly constituted or setup under any law or through its executive authority shall stand transferred or shifted to the Government forthwith on commencement of this amending Act, 2018.

(3) The rights of the persons under existing laws of Azad Jammu and Kashmir who were, immediately before the commencement of the Azad Jammu and Kashmir Interim Constitution (Thirteenth Amendment) Act, 2018, serving under the Azad Jammu and Kashmir Council shall be protected and officers and servants on

deputation from the Federal Government or any province shall be entitled for repatriation to their parent organizations.

(4) The persons serving on contractual or temporary basis shall not be entitled to claim any right to continue their employment and they shall be dealt in accordance with prevailing service rules of Azad Jammu and Kashmir and terms of their appointments.

(5) Subject to Article 51, the perks, privileges and allowances to the elected members of the Council and also salary, allowances and pensionary benefits of the employees of the Council in the Service of Azad Jammu and Kashmir, as admissible to them under the law, shall be borne by the Government, for which budgetary requirements shall be made out of the Azad Jammu and Kashmir Consolidated Fund."

39. Substitution of Article 52-A of the Constitution. - In the Constitution, for Article 52-A, the following shall be substituted, namely:-

"**52-A. Power to acquire property and to make contracts, etc.** - (1) The executive authority of the Government shall extend, subject to an Act of the Assembly, to the grant, sale, disposition or mortgage of any property vested in, and to the purchase or acquisition of property on behalf of the Government and to the making of contracts.

(2) All property acquired for the purpose of the Government shall vest in the President.

(3) All contracts made in the exercise of the executive authority of the Government shall be expressed to be made in the name of the President and all such contracts and all assurances of property made in the exercise of that authority shall be executed on behalf of the President by such persons and in such manner as the President may direct or authorize.

(4) The President shall not be personally liable in respect of any contract or assurance made or executed in the exercise of the executive authority of the Government and no person making or executing any such contract or assurance on his behalf shall be personally liable in respect thereof.

(5) Transfer of land or property by the Government shall be regulated by law."

40. Addition of Articles 52-B and 52-C in the Constitution. - In the Constitution, after Article 52-A, following Articles 52-B and 52-C shall be added:-

"**52-B. Ownerless property.** - Any property which has no rightful owner, if located within Azad Jammu and Kashmir, shall vest in the Government.

52-C. Natural Resource endowment. - (1) The natural resource of Azad Jammu and Kashmir which having a potential of economic value and providing for the sustenance of life for future generations shall be preserved and regulated by an Act of the Assembly.

(2) Without prejudice to sub-Article (1), the natural resource of Azad Jammu

and Kashmir may be utilized under the law, in the economic and efficient manner, by the Government and also may be authorized under an Act of Assembly to utilize any resource of the State by any person, entity or authority of Pakistan in consideration of valuable economic benefits for the public interest such as net-hydel profit or royalty or any other acceptable form or benefit but without affecting the pristine environmental value of the inherent endowment of the State."

41. Amendment of Article 53 of the Constitution. - In the Constitution, in Article 53,-

    (i) in sub-Article (2), for the words "**a joint sitting**" the words "**the Assembly**" shall be substituted.

    (ii) in sub-Article (2-A), the words "**unless it has earlier been approved by a resolution of the Council**" shall be omitted.

42. Amendment of Article 54 of the Constitution. - In the Constitution, in Article 54, in sub-Article (1), full stop at the end shall be substituted by a colon and thereafter the following proviso shall be added:

"Provided that the Assembly shall, in no case be dissolved on account of issuance or pendency of the proclamation under the Constitution."

43. Amendment of Article 58 of the Constitution. - In Article 58, between the words "may" and "make", the commas and words "**on the advice of Prime Minister,**" shall be substituted.

44. Amendment of the First Schedule of the Constitution. - In the Constitution, in First Schedule,-

    (i) form of "Oath of Advisor" shall be omitted; and

    (ii) form of oath for office of Chief Election Commissioner and Member of the Election Commission shall be added as under,-

"CHIEF ELECTION COMMISSIONER OR A MEMBER OF THE ELECTION COMMISSION

[See Article 50]

I, _____, do solemnly swear that as Chief Election Commissioner or member of the Election Commission, I shall discharge my duties, and perform my functions honestly, to the best of my ability, faithfully in accordance with the Azad Jammu and Kashmir Interim Constitution, 1974 and the law, and without fear or favor, affection or ill will, and that I shall not allow my personal interest to influence my official conduct or my official decisions.

May Allah Almighty help and guide me (A'meen)."

45. Substitution of Third Schedule of the Constitution. - In the Constitution, for the Third Schedule the following shall be substituted, namely,-

"THIRD SCHEDULE
[See Article 31 (3) and (4)]

'Part-A'

1. The responsibilities of the Government of Pakistan under the UNCIP Resolutions.
2. Defense and security of Azad Jammu and Kashmir.
3. The current coin or the issue of bills, notes or other paper currency.
4. The External affairs of Azad Jammu and Kashmir including foreign trade and foreign aid.
5. Post and Telegraphs, including Telephones, Wireless, Broad- Casting and other like forms of communications; post office saving Bank.
6. Nuclear energy, including:
   (a) mineral resources necessary for the generation of nuclear energy;
   (b) the production of nuclear fuels and the generation and use of nuclear energy; and
   (c) ionizing radiations.
7. Aircraft and air navigation; the provision of aerodromes; regulation and organization of air traffic and of aerodromes.
8. Beacons and other provisions for safety of aircraft.
9. Carriage of passengers and goods by air.
10. Copyright, inventions, designs, trademarks and merchandise marks.
11. Opium so far as regards sale for export.
12. State Bank of Pakistan; banking, that is to say, the conduct of banking business by corporations other than corporations owned or controlled by Azad Jammu and Kashmir and carrying on business only within the Azad Jammu and Kashmir.
13. The law of insurance, except as respects insurance undertaken by Azad Jammu and Kashmir and the regulation of the conduct of insurance business, except as respects business undertaken by Azad Jammu and Kashmir.
14. Stock exchanges and future markets with objects and business not confined to Azad Jammu and Kashmir.
15. Corporations, that is to say, the incorporation, regulation and winding-up of trading corporations, including banking, insurance and financial corporations, but not including corporations owned or controlled by Azad Jammu and Kashmir or cooperative societies, and of corporations, whether trading or not, with objects not confined to Azad Jammu and Kashmir, but not including universities.
16. Planning for economic coordination including planning and coordination of scientific and technological research.
17. Highways, continuing beyond the territory of Azad Jammu and Kashmir

and also roads declared by the Government of Pakistan to be of strategic importance.
18. External affairs; the implementing of treaties and agreements, including educational and cultural pacts and agreements, with other countries; extradition, including the surrender of criminals and accused persons to Governments outside Pakistan.
19. Foreign exchange; cheques, bills of exchange, promissory notes and other like instruments.
20. Administrative Courts and Tribunals for subjects under this Part.
21. Libraries, museums, and similar institutions controlled or financed by the Government of Pakistan.
22. Government of Pakistan agencies and institutes for the following purposes, that is to say, for research, for professional or technical training, or for the promotion of special studies.
23. Education as respects Azad Jammu and Kashmir students in foreign countries and foreign students in Azad Jammu and Kashmir.
24. Import and export across customs frontiers as defined by the Government of Pakistan.
25. International treaties, conventions, agreements and International arbitration.
26. Surveys including geological surveys and meteorological organizations.
27. Establishment of standards of weights and measures.
28. Duties of customs, including export duties.
29. Taxes on corporations.
30. Offences against laws with respect to any of the matters in this Part.
31. Inquiries and statistics for the purposes of any of the matters in this Part.
32. Matters incidental or ancillary to any matter enumerated in this Part.

'Part-B'

1. Railways.
2. Mineral oil and natural gas; liquids and substances declared by Government of Pakistan to be dangerously inflammable.
3. National planning and national economic coordination, including planning and coordination of scientific and technological research.
4. Supervision and management of public debt.
5. Boilers
6. Census.
7. State Property until transfer to the Government of AJK.
8. Electricity except the power generation planned and made by Government of AJK.

9. Terminal taxes on goods or passengers carried by railway or air, taxes on their fares and freights.
10. Extension of the powers and jurisdiction of members of a police force belonging to Azad Jammu and Kashmir, or any Province of Pakistan to any area in such province or the Azad Jammu and Kashmir but not so as to enable the police of Azad Jammu and Kashmir or such province to exercise power and jurisdiction in such province or Azad Jammu and Kashmir and without the consent of the Government of that province or the Azad Jammu and Kashmir.
11. Measures to combat certain offences committed in connection with matters concerning the subjects included in this list.
12. Removal of prisoners and accused persons from Azad Jammu and Kashmir to Pakistan or from Pakistan to Azad Jammu and Kashmir.
13. Prevention of the extension from Azad Jammu and Kashmir to Pakistan or from Pakistan to Azad Jammu and Kashmir of infections of contagious diseases or pests affecting men; animals or plants.
14. Curriculum, syllabus, planning, policy, centers of excellence and standards of education.
15. Medical and other professions excluding legal profession.
16. Standards in institutions for higher education and research, scientific and technical institutions.
17. Matters concerning coordination between Azad Jammu and Kashmir and other Provinces of Pakistan.
18. The salaries, allowance and privileges of the members and including salaries and pension payable to employees of the council.
19. Jurisdiction and powers of all courts with respect to any of the matters enumerated in this list.
20. Offences against laws with respect to any of the matters in this Part.
21. Inquiries and statistics for the purposes of any of the matters in this Part.
22. Matters incidental or ancillary to any matter enumerated in this Part."

sd/-
(**Irshad Ahmed Qureshi**)
Secretary Law

APPENDIX V
List of Political Parties in 'AJK' Alongwith Names of the Party Heads & General Secretaries

S.No.	Name of Party	Party Head	Contact Number	General Secretary Name & No.
1	All Jammu & Kashmir Muslim Conference	Sardar Attique Ahmed Khan, (President) Mujahid Munzil 83-A/1, Satellite Town, Rawalpindi.	111-456789 0345-5091948, 0300-9896578 (Wajid) 0321-5025678 (Personal Attique Sb) 0322-9403776 (Rizwan), 0300-5050854 (Khalid), 051-4852136 (Fax Mujahid Manzil)	Ms. Mahr-un-Nisa 0344-5473-489
2	Pakistan People's Party Azad Kashmir	Choudary Abdul Majeed, (President), House No. 167, Sector F-2, Mirpur.	0300-5191384	Ch. Latif Akbar 0300-9856966
3	Pakistan Muslim League (N), Azad Kashmir	Raja Farooq Haider Khan, (Chief Organizer) Shoukat Line Muzaffarabad.		Shah Ghulam Qadir 0333-5138112, 0355-760-6842
4	Pakistan Muslim League Jammu & Kashmir	Sardar Mansha Jamal Advocate, (President), Kotli Bar Azad Kashmir.	0302-4802516	Malik Aftab
5	Jammu & Kashmir Liberation League	Justice (R.) Abdul Majeed Malik, (President), House No. 38, Sector B-2, Allama Iqbal Road, Mirpur, AJK.	05827-443711 (Office) 05827-446434 (Res) 0333-5889228	Ghulam Akbar Advocate Kh. Manzoor Qadir 0301-5713-129920092

List of Political Parties in 'AJK'

S.No.	Name of Party	Party Head	Contact Number	General Secretary Name & No.
6	Jammu & Kashmir People's Party.	**Sardar Khalid Ibrahim Khan,** (President) 35 Park Road F8/1, Islamabad.	0301-5555360	Zahid Akram Advocate 0300-5188709
7	Jamiat-ul-Ullema AJ&K.	**Sahibzada Attique-ur-Rehman Faizpuri,** (President) 122-A-F/2, Sector Faiz Pur Shareef House, Mirpur, AJ&K.	0344-8802829	Moulana Muhammad Imtiaz Ahmed Siddique 0333-9415637
8	Jamat-e-Islami AJ&K	**Abdul Rasheed Trabi,** (Ameer) 415 Poonch House Complex Sadar Rawalpindi.	0300-850-5298 051-5511417 051-5565531 051-5510197 (Fax)	Mahmood-ul-Hassan Chaudhry 0344-5558050
9	All Jammu & Kashmir Justice Party.	**Professor Maqsood Jaffri,** (Chairman) NW-706/A, Saidpur Road Rawalpindi.		
10	Swad-i-Azam Ahlay Sunnat Wa Al Jamat AK.	**Mollana Mufti Mahmood-ul-Hassan Shah Masoodi,** (Ameer) Jamaia Abu Hurrara Muhallah Sadiq Abad Ranjata Muzaffarabad.	05822-446080 0321-9555921 0300-2187329 (Gen Secretary)	
11	Jammu & Kashmir Awami Tehreek.	**Sardar Mansoor Khan,** (President) Silver Line School System Opp. Ayub Park GT Road Rawalpindi.		
12	Kashmir Freedom Movement,	**Choudary Khaliq Hussain Advocate,** (President) Muslim Bazar Bhimber, AK.	0355-6502003 05828-444033	
13	Jammu Kashmir Liberation Front,	**Sardar Sagheer,** (Chairman) District Courts, Rawalakot.	0333-5713450	Sardar Shamas Kashmiri

S.No.	Name of Party	Party Head	Contact Number	General Secretary Name & No.
14	Jammu Kashmir National Liberation Front	Shoukat Maqbool Butt, (President) C/O Minhas General Store, Ghari Pan Chowk, Muzaffarabad AJ&K.		
15	Jammu Kashmir Islamic Democratic Party, AJ&K.	Syed Ghulam Raza Naqvi, (President) Tehsil Sehnsa, District Kotli.	0300-5139840	
16	Kashmir Freedom Front.	Mufti Sana-ul-Haq Bukhari, (President) Mufti Kashmir House, Muree.	0345-5532450 0355-8133150 0301-5382272	Farooq Wani
17	Pakistan People's Party (Shaheed Bhutto) AJ&K.	Munir Hussain Choudary, (President) House No. 14 Sanwala Sector F/2, Mirpur.	05827-444137 0300-4838882	Professor Muhammad Hanif Khawaja
18	Nazaam-e-Mustafa Conference	Sahibzada Syed Muhammad Nadeem Ahmed Gillani, (President) Jamia Gosia Rizivia Sethi Bagh, Muzaffarabad.	0321-9884575 0300-9738347 0312-9001014	Yasir Mughal
19	Pakistan Jamiat Ullema-e-Islam J&K.	Mufti Muhammad Younas Choudary, (Markazi Ameer) Akbar Road B-5, Mirpur, Azad Kashmir		
20	Suni Tehreek AJ&K	Sardar Abdul Shakoor Ladhalvi, (Convener) Devisional Office Sunni Tehreek, Tehsil Nakyal, District Kotli.	05827-479552	
21	MQM Azad Jammu & Kashmir.	Muhammad Tahir Khokhar, (Parlimani Leader) 5-C Sunset Line-3, Phase ii DHA, EXT, Karachi.	0345-8553390	

List of Political Parties in 'AJK'

S.No.	Name of Party	Party Head	Contact Number	General Secretary Name & No.
22	Jamiat Ullema-e-Islam J&K.	Moulana Saeed Yousaf, (Ameer) Darul Aloom Taleem-ul-Quran, Palandri, J&K	0300-5556863 Naib Ameer Abdul Haye 0300-5250635	Maulana Imtiaz Abbasi 0346-5161105 0314-516-1105
23	Jammu & Kashmir Milli Tehreek	Syed Muhammad Ali Raza Bukhari, (Chairman) 137 Faisal Colony Near Airport Rawalpindi.		
24	Markazi Jamiat-e-Ahllay Hadees AJ&K.	Mollana Muhammad Anwar Ruknudin, (Ameer) Allama Iqbal Colony, Bagh City.		
25	UN Parh Party AJ&K.	Muhammad Ismail Chohan, (Chairman) Ward #9 Tariq Abad Near Water Supply Pump Muzaffarabad AJ&K.	0322-9403389	
26	All Jammu & Kashmir Muslim League	Muhammad Sajjad Advocate, (Markazi President) Old Secretariat Muzaffarabad A.K.	0300-9709404	
27	Jamaat-e-Falah-e-Insaniat AJ&K	Muhammad Mudassar Afzil Choudary, (Chairman) Tehsil Dodyal, Mirpur, Azad Jammu & Kashmir	0342-6110000 05827-466000	
28	Peopls National Party, United Kashmir (PNP,UK)	Syed Waqar Hussain Kazmi, (Chairman) Bar Council Muzaffarabad, A.K.	0322-9422434 0301-5374678	
29	Jammu & Kashmir Public Rights Party	Shehzad khursheed rathore, (Chairman) House # 36-A, Sector F-8/3, Islamabad	051-2266277, 0332-5131559	

S.No.	Name of Party	Party Head	Contact Number	General Secretary Name & No.
30	Jaffaria Supreme Council AJ&K	**Syed Shabir Hussain Bukhari,** (Chairman), Imam Bargah Takiya Bari Imam Shoukat Line Muzaffarabad	05822-442134 0300-9855724	Raja Anwar-ul-Saqlain Advocate Murpur 0301-5823181 0344-5133769
31	Pak Kashmir National League	**Nisar Ahmed,** (Chairman) Office No. 7, Usman Ghani First Flour District Kachehri, Rawalpindi	0300-5158856	
32	Pakistan Tehreek-e-Insaf Kashmir	**Barister Sultan Mahmood Chaudry** (President), 22, Main Margala Road, F-3/6, Islamabad.	051-2277-226	0300-855-7892 0300-855-3466
33	Majilis Wahdat-e-Muslimeen Pakistan	**Syed Tasawar Hussain Jafri,** Secretary General (Head), Near Boys High School Narul, Domail Syedan Muzaffarabad.	05822-202848 0315-5121471 0345-6452318	Syed Abdul Rehman Shah Kazmi Deputy Secretary General
34	Al Jammu & Kashmir Jamiat Ulma Islama	**Mahmood-ul-Hassan Ashraf,** (Markazi General Secretary) Jamaia Daraul Aloom-ul-Islamia Muzaffarabad.	05822-432502 0300-2187-329 0344-1914-810 0321-5631-389	Markazi Nazam Prof. Abdul Malik Advocate 0345-5082-806
35	Rah-e-Haq Party AJK	**Hafiz Aftab Ahmed Kashir** (President) Bangoin Khas Post Office Paniola, Tehsil Rawlakot, District Poonch.	0302-8988-929	Muhammad Afraz Khan General Secretary 0321-2330-409
36	Al-Jammu & Kashmir Sunni Irihad Council	**Abdul Khaliq Naqshbandi** (President) Near Jammia Taleem-ul-Quran, Naqshbandia, Pallak Post Office Tehsil & District Mirpur	0300-5043-088 0315-5043-088	Fiaz Hussain Mustafai General Secretary 0345-4476-502 0302-5196-825

List of Political Parties in 'AJK'

S.No.	Name of Party	Party Head	Contact Number	General Secretary Name & No.
37	Qoumi Itihad Party (QIP)	Shahzad Hussain Khan (Chairman) Khora Mangiryout Neriyan Post Office Khas Tehsil Trarkhal District Sudhnoti	0316-5061-267	Israr Farooq General Secretary 0341-4733-131
38	Meri Apni Party (MAP)	Mirza Abdul Qadeer Farooqi (Founder & President) PO & Tehsil Samahni, Village Sohlnan District Bhimber	0347-655-4037	Muhammad Usman General Secretary 0346-5130-192
39	All Pakistan Aam Admi Party	Muhammad Bashir Raja (President) H# 309-B, Valley Road opposite Maryam Memorial Hospital Peshawar Road Rawalpindi	0333-511-4535 0315-511-4535	Nazma Shafiq
40	Jammu & Kashmir Qoumi Movement	Raja Khursheed Khan Nick Name Kala Bawa (President) R/O Chella Bandi near Nisar Camp District Tehsil & Muzaffarabad	0302-5634-686	Raja Muhammad Arif Kiani 0343-8511-881
41	Front National Azad Jammu & Kashmir	Amir Sohail (President) 305/9, Street 19, Westridge, Peshawar Road, Rawalpindi	Hina Manzoor 0303-566-1822	
42	Muslim League Functional Azad Kashmir	Saeed Mahboob Hussain Shah Bukhari (Founder and Chief Organizer) R/O Moil Post Office Kot Jamel Tehsil Barnala District Bhimber	0346-500-9215	Syed Makhdoom Hussain Shah 0342-8136-196

S.No.	Name of Party	Party Head	Contact Number	General Secretary Name & No.
43	All Pakistan Muslim League State of Azad Jammu & Kashmir	Javed Ahmed Mughal (Chief Organizer) R/O Mohalla Tagara Eid Gah Road Muzaffarabad	0347-5637-950	Syed Naseer Hussain Kazmi 0344-8892-355 0355760-1606
44	Aam Admi Party Azad Jammu & Kashmir	Muhammad Khurram Mushtaq (President) Secretariat Near Jan Milk Shop, Police Lines, Naluchi, Muzaffarabad	0345-5127-301 0335-7123-457	Nawaz Saijad

APPENDIX VI

Presidents/Prime Ministers of 'AJK'

A. Presidents of 'AJK'

S.No.	Name	From	To
1	Sardar Muhammad Ibrahim Khan	24 Oct, 1947	12 May 1950
2	Col. (R) Syed Alhi Ahmed Shah	13 May, 1950	04 Dec, 1951
3	Mir Waiz Molana Muhammad Yousf Shah	05 Dec, 1951	20 Jun, 1952
4	Colonel (R) Sher Ahmed Khan	21 Jun, 1952	30 May, 1956
5	Mir Waiz Molana Muhammad Yousf Shah	31 May, 1956	07 Sep, 1956
6	Sardar Muhammad Abdul-Qayyum Khan	08 Sep, 1956	12 Apr, 1957
7	Sardar Muhammad Ibrahim Khan	13 Apr, 1957	30 Apr, 1959
8	Mr. K.H. Khursheed	01 May, 1959	06 Aug, 1964
9	Khan Abdul Hameed Khan	07 Aug, 1964	07 Oct, 1968
10	Brig. (later Maj. Gen) Abdur-Rehman	08 Oct, 1968	11 Nov, 1970
11	Sardar Muhammad Abdul-Qayyum Khan	12 Nov, 1970	15 Apr, 1975
12	Sheikh Manzar Masaud (Acting President)	16 Apr, 1975	04 June, 1975
13	Sardar Muhammad Ibrahim Khan	05 Jun, 1975	30 Oct, 1978
14	Brig. (R) Muhammad Hayat Khan	01 Nov, 1978	31 Jan, 1983
15	Major General (R) Abdur Rehman	01 Feb, 1983	29 Sep, 1985
16	Sardar Muhammad Abdul-Qayyum Khan	30 Sep, 1985	19 Jul, 1991
17	Sahibzada Muhammad Ishaq Zafar (Acting President)	20 Jul, 1991	28 July, 1991
18	Mr. Abdul Rashid Abbasi (Acting President)	29 Jul 1991	11 August 1991
19	Sardar Sikandar Hayat Khan	12 Aug, 1991	11 May, 1996
20	Mr. Abdul Rashid Abbasi (Acting President)	12 May, 1996	22 May, 1996

S.No.	Name	From	To
21	Sardar Sikandar Hayat Khan	23 May, 1996	11 Aug, 1996
22	Raja Mumtaz Hussain Rathore	12 Aug, 1996	24 Aug, 2001
23	Sardar Muhammad Ibrahim Khan	25 Aug 1996	24 Aug, 2001
24	Major General (R) Sardar Muhammad Anwar Khan	25 Aug, 2001	24 Aug, 2006
25	Raja Zulqurnain Khan	25 Aug 2006	24 Aug, 2011
26	Sardar Muhammad Yaqoob Khan	25 Aug, 2011	24 Aug, 2016
27	Sardar Masood Khan	25 Aug 2016	Continued

B. Prime Ministers of 'AJK'

S.No.	Name	From	To
1	Khan Abdul Hameed Khan	05 Jun, 1975	11 Aug, 1977
2	Sardar Siksndar Hayat Khan	17 Jun, 1985	28 Jun, 1990
3	Mumtaz Hussain Rathore	29 Jun, 1990	05 Jul, 1991
4	Sardar Muhammad Abdul-Qayyum Khan	29 Jul, 1991	29 Jul, 1996
5	Barrister Sultan Mehmood Chaudry	30 Jul, 1996	24 Jul, 2001
6	Sardar Siksndar Hayat Khan	25 Jul, 2001	23 Jul, 2006
7	Sardar Attique Ahmed Khan	24 Jul, 2006	06 Jan, 2009
8	Sardar Muhmmad Yaqoob Khan	07 Jan, 2009	21 Oct, 2009
9	Raja Farooq Haider Khan	22 Oct, 2009	28 Jul, 2010
10	Sardar Attique Ahmed Khan	29 Jul, 2010	25 Jul, 2011
11	Chaudry Abdul Majid	26 Jul, 2011	30 Jul, 2016
12	Raja Farooq Haider Khan	31 Jul, 2016	Continued

APPENDIX VII

Members 'AJK' Legislative Assembly 2016

S.No.	Name	Position
1	Ch. Masood Khalid	MLA
2	Chaudhry Abdul Majeed	MLA
3	Ch. Muhammad Saeed	Minister
4	Rukhsar Ahmed	MLA
5	Waqar Ahmed Noor	MLA
6	Ali Shan Chaudhry	MLA
7	Ch. Tariq Farooq	Senior Minister for, Physical Planning & housing, Agriculture & Live Stock
8	Malik Muhammad Nawaz Khan	MLA
9	Farooq Sikandar Khan	Minister Revenue and Rehabilitation
10	Raja Naseer Ahmad Khan	MLA
11	Choudhary Muhammad Yasin	Opposition Leader
12	Raja Nisar Ahmed Khan	Minister Law, Parliamentarian affairs, Justice and Human Rights, Electricity
13	Sardar Attique Ahmed Khan	MLA
14	Mushtaq Ahmed Minhas	Minister Information, Tourism and Information Technology
15	Sardar Mir Akbar Khan	Minister Forests, Wild Life and Fisheries
16	Ch. Muhammad Aziz	Minister Public Works and Communications
17	Ch. Muhammad Yasin Gulshan	MLA
18	Sardar Khan Bahadur Khan	MLA
19	Khalid Ibrahim Khan	MLA
20	Muhammad Saghir Khan	MLA
21	Dr. Muhammad Najeeb Naqvi Khan	Minister Treasury, Planning & Development and Public Health
22	Sardar Farooq Ahmed Tahir	Deputy Speaker Legislative Assembly Azad Jammu and Kashmir

S.No.	Name	Position
23	Shah Ghulam Qadir	Speaker Legislative Assembly Azad Jammu and Kashmir
24	Noreen Arif	Minister Industries, Labor, Mineral Resources, Social Welfare and Women Development
25	Chaudhry Shazad Mehmood	MLA
26	Syed Iftekhar Ali Gillani	Minister Higher Education, Elementary & Secondary Education, Muzaffarabad City Development Project
27	Raja Abdul Qayyum Khan	MLA
28	Raja Muhammad Farooq Haider Khan	Prime Minister, Azad Jammu & Kashmir
29	Mustafa Bashir Abbasi	MLA
30	Nasir Hussain Dar	Minister
31	Chaudhry Muhammad Ismail	MLA
32	Muhammad Ishaq	MLA
33	Mian Muhammad Yasir Rasheed	MLA
34	Chaudhry Javed Akhtar	MLA
35	Raja Muhammad Siddique	MLA
36	Amir Abdul Ghaffar	MLA
37	Ghulam Mohi ud Din Dewan	MLA
38	Syed Shoukat Ali Shah	Minister
39	Asad Aleem Shah	MLA
40	Muhammad Ahmed Raza Qadri	MLA
41	Abdul Majid Khan	MLA
42	Mrs. Riffat Aziz	MLA
43	Mrs. Sehrish Qamar	MLA
44	Mrs. Shazia Akbar Ch.	MLA
45	Mrs. Faiza Imtiaz	MLA
46	Mrs. Naseema Khatoon	MLA
47	Syed Muhammad Ali Raza Bukhari	MLA
48	Javed Iqbal	MLA
49	Abdul Rashid Turabi	MLA

Source: Azad Jammu and Kashmir Legislative Assembly.

APPENDIX VIII

The Northern Areas Council Legal Frame Work Order, 1994
(With Amendments)

No. 12(34)/93-NA-I
GOVERNMENT OF PAKISTAN
KASHMIR AFFAIRS & NORTHERN AFFAIRS
DIVISION ISLAMABAD

Islamabad, the 12th June, 1994.

WHEREAS the Northern Areas Electoral Rolls Act, 1975 provides for the preparation of electoral rolls for the purpose of election of representatives to the Council for Northern Areas on the basis of adult franchise;

AND WHEREAS it is expedient to provide for the Constitution of the Council for Northern Areas and to introduce the people of this area to democratic institution and to give them a sense of participation in their affairs;

NOW, THEREFORE, the Government of Pakistan is pleased to make the following order:

1. Short title, extent and commencement. – (1) This Order may be called the Northern Areas Council, Legal Frame Work Order, 1994.

(2) It extends to the whole of the Northern Areas.

(3) It shall come into force at once.

2. Definition. – In this order, unless there is any thing repugnant in the subject or context:

Compiled by Hafiz-Ur-Rahman, B.A., LL.B., Secretary, Northern Areas Legislative Council Gilgit, 1st November, 2001.

(a) "Adviser" means a person appointed under section-5;
¹[(b) " **********];
(c) "Chief Executive" means the Federal Minister for Kashmir Affairs, Northern Areas, state & Frontier Regions Division.
(d) "Commissioner" means the Election Commissioner appointed under the Northern Areas Electoral Rolls Act, 1975;
(e) "Council" means the ²[Northern Areas Legislative Council] constituted under section-6;
(f) "Deputy Chief Executive" means a person elected as such by the Council under section-4;
(ff) "Deputy Speaker" means the Deputy Speaker of the Council NACLF (Amendment) Order 2002, No. 1 (11)/93-NA. II, dated 19 Nov. 2002.
(g) "Electoral Rolls" means the electoral rolls prepared under the Northern Areas Electoral Rolls Act, 1975;
(h) "Member" means member of the Council;
(i) "Northern Areas" has the same meaning as in Northern Areas Electoral Rolls Act, 1975;
(j) "Provincial Government" means the Chief Executive, the Deputy Chief Executive and the Chief Secretary, Northern Areas;
(k) "Rules of Business" means the Northern Areas Rules of Business, 1994;
(l) "Rules of Procedure" means rules framed by the Northern Areas Council for the conduct of its business;
(m) "Secretary of the Council" means the officer so designated by the ³[Chief Executive]; and
(n) ⁴["Speaker" means the Speaker of the Council]

3. Chief Executive. – (1) There shall be. a Chief Executive of Northern Areas who shall be the Federal Minister for Kashmir Affairs, Northern Areas, Stale and Frontier Regions.

(2) The Chief Executive shall exercise powers specified in sub-rule (1) of rule 5 of the Rules of Business.

⁵[(3) The Chief Executive shall address the opening and closing sessions of the Northern Areas Legislative Council (NALC) in every financial year wherein he shall detail his policy for the Northern Areas and review the working of Northern

---

1. Omitted by Amendment Order dated 1st July 2000.
2. Substituted by Amendment Order dated 28th October 1999.
3. Substituted by Amendment Order, dated 1st July, 2000.
4. Substituted by Amendment Order ibid.
5. Added by Amendment Order ibid.

Areas Government in that year respectively. He may also address the Council at his discretion and for that purpose may require the attendance of the members].

(4) The Chief Executive shall work towards continued empowerment of the elected representatives and power of the Northern Areas.

4. Deputy Chief Executive. – The Chief Executive shall appoint, from amongst the members of the Council, a Deputy Chief Executive who shall:

    (a) be elected by the members of the Council on the basis of majority votes;
[1][(b) *****************************];
    (c) be a person with the status of a Minister of State;
    (d) exercise such powers as may be delegated to him by the Chief Executive under clause (I) of rule-6 of Rules of Business; and
    (e) perform such functions as are assigned to him under clauses (II) and (iii) of rule-6 of the Rules of Business.

[2][**4-A. Speaker.** – The Council shall elect from amongst its members a Speaker who shall conduct the business of the Council in accordance with Rules of Procedure of the Council. The Speaker shall be entitled to the status of Provincial Minister.

4AA. The Council shall elect from amongst its members a Deputy Speaker who shall conduct the business of the Council in accordance with the Rule of Procedure of the Council in the absence of Speaker. The Deputy Speaker shall be entitled to the status of Provincial Minister.

4-B. Panel of Presiding Officers. – At the commencement of each Session, the Speaker shall nominate, In order of precedence, from amongst the members, a panel of not more than three presiding officers and, in the absence of the Speaker the member having precedence amongst those present shall preside over the meeting.]

5. Advisers. – (1) The Chief Executive shall, in consultation with the Deputy Chief Executive, appoint, from amongst the members of the Council, not less than [3][three] find not more then [4][five] advisors [5][****] The advisers appointed under sub-section (1) shall be entitled to the status of a Provincial Minster.

---

1. Omitted by Amendment Order ibid.
2. Section 4-A and 4-B inserted by Amendment Order dated 1st July, 2000.
3. Substituted by Amendment Order ibid.
4. Substituted by Amendment Order ibid.
5. Columns words omitted by Substituted by Amendment Order dated 28th Oct 1999.

¹[(2) An Advisor shrill hold office during the pleasure of the Chief Executive].

²[(3) Thee Advisers shall **monitor** the functioning of the departments assigned to them.]

6. Composition of the Council for Northern Areas. – (1) The Council shall consist of:

    (a) ³[****] The Chief Executive for Northern Areas appointed under section-3;

⁴[(b) ******]

    (c) twenty four members, ⁵[*****], of whom six each shall be elected from Gilgit, Diamer and Baltistan Districts and three each from Ghizer and Ghanche Districts; and

    (d) ⁶[Five] women ⁷[*****] members to be elected in the manner as provided in sub-section 1 A);].

⁸|(1A) Of the members referred to in clause (d) of sub-section (1), one woman ⁹[******] shall be elected from each District by the members referred to in clause (C) of sub-section (1)] ¹⁰[******]

(2) The ¹¹[Chief Executive Northern Areas] may associate any person, whether official or non-official, for the proceedings of the Council;

7. Delimitation of constituencies. – (1) For the purpose of election to the Council, the Commissioner shall divide each district into as many separate territorial constituencies as the number of seats allocated to that district under sectioh-6.

(2) All constituencies for the seats in the Council shall be so delimited, having regard to administrative convenience, so that each constituency is a compact area and in doing so due regard shall be had, as far as practicable to the distribution of population.

---

1. Sub-section 2 added by Amendment Order ibid.
2. Sub-section 3 added by Amendment Order dated 1ˢᵗ July, 2000.
3. Omitted by Amendment Order dated 1ˢᵗ July, 2000.
4. Omitted by Amendment Order ibid.
5. Omitted by Amendment Order ibid.
6. Word two substituted by Amendment Order dated 28th October, 1999.
7. Omitted by Amendment Order dated 1st July, 2000.
8. Sub-Section I-A inserted by Amendment Order deled 28st October, 1999.
9. Omitted by Amendment Order dated 1st July, 2000.
10. Omitted by Amendment Order dated 1st July, 2000.
11. Substituted by Amendment Order dated 1st July, 2000.

(3) The Commissioner shall, after making such inquiries and examining such, records as it may deem necessary and considering such representations as may be received by him, publish a preliminary list of territorial constituencies specifying the areas proposed to be included in each such constituency together with a notice inviting objections and suggestions within a period specified in such *a* notice.

(4) The Commissioner shall, after bearing and considering the objections and suggestions, if any, received by him, make such amendments, alterations or modifications in the preliminary list published under sub-section (3), as he may deem fit or necessary and shall publish the final list of territorial constituencies showing the areas including in each such constituency.

8. Validity of Act of Commissioner not questionable. – The validity of the delimitation or formation of any constituency, or of any proceedings taken or anything done by, or under the authority of, the commissioner under this Order shall not be called in question in any Court.

9. Term of office. – (1) The term of Office of the Council shall be five years commencing on the day of its first session;

Provided that it may be dissolved earlier if a resolution to that effect is passed by the Council by a majority of two-third of its members;

Provide further that if the government of Pakistan is of the opinion that the Council has failed to perform its functions in accordance with this Order, it may dissolve the Council earlier than the five years.

(2) The members shall assume office on such date and place as may be appointed by the government of Pakistan.

Provided that the period intervening between the declaration of the official result of the election to the Council and the date for assumption of office of member shall not exceed thirty days.

(3) On the expiry of the term of office of the Council, or on its dissolution earlier under the first or second proviso to sub-section (1), if there be any delay in the assumption of office by the next Council the powers and functions of (fie Council shall be exercised and performed by such person as the Chief Executive may appoint in this behalf in accordance with such directions as the Chief Executive may issue from time to time.

10. Notice for the first session. – (1) The first Session of the council shall be held on the date and place appointed by the Chief Executive for the assumption of office of its members;

¹[(2) After first Session of the Council it shall meet at such times and places as provided by the Rules of Procedure of the Council];

Provided that the interval between two sessions shall not exceed ninety days;

Provided further that the session of the council next following its first session shall be held before the day of expiration of seven days following the first session.]

²[(3) *******]

³[(4) The session of the Council shall be presided over by the Speaker, and, in his absence, by a member nominated by the Speaker in the manner specified in section 4-8.]

11. Assumption of office and taking of oath. – (1) At the first session of the Council, the ⁴[Chief Executive] shall take oath before the Chairman, Chief Court, in Form "A" and thereafter ⁵[Speaker administer oath to the members present in Form "B" as provided in Schedule-I].

(2) If any member of the Council is for any reason not present at the first session of the Council, the ⁶[Chief Executive] shall, at the next following session of the Council, administer oath of office to such member and on his taking the oath of office he shall be deemed to have assumed his office.

⁷[(3) The Deputy Chief Executive, the Speaker and Advisers shall make oath before the Chief Executive of Northern Areas as specified in Forms 'C', 'D' and 'E' respectively.

12. Qualification and disqualification of member. – (1) A person shall, subject to the provisions of sub-section (2), be qualified to be elected as a member if:

    (a) he is bona fide resident of the Northern Areas;
    (b) he has attained the age of twenty five year; and
    (c) his name appears on the electoral roll for any constituency in the district from which he seeks election.

(2) A person shall be disqualified from being elected as, and from being a member if:

---

1. Sub-Section 2 is substituted by Amendment Order dated 1 July, 2000.
2. Sub-Section 3 omitted by Amendment Order ibid.
3. Sub-Section A is substituted by Amendment Order ibid.
4. Substituted by Amendment Order dated 1st July, 2000.
5. Substituted by Amendment Order ibid.
6. Substituted by Amendment Order ibid.
7. Sub-Section 3 is added by Amendment Order ibid.

(a) he is of unsound mind and stands so declared by a competent court, or
(b) he is an un-discharged insolvent, unless a period of ten years has elapsed since his being adjudged and insolvent; or
(c) he has been, on conviction of any offence, sentenced to imprisonment for a term of not less than two years, Unless a period of five years, or such less period as the Government of Pakistan may allow in any particular case, has elapsed since his release;
(d) he holds any office in the service of the Northern Areas or service of Pakistan other than an office which is not a whole time office remunerated either by salary or by fee; or
(e) he has been dismissed for misconduct from the service of the Northern Areas or of Pakistan, unless a period of five years, or such less period as the Government of Pakistan may allow in any particular case, has elapsed since his dismissal; or
(f) he, whether by himself or by any person or body of persons in trust for him or for his benefit or on his account, has any share or interest in a contract, not being a contract between a cooperative society and the Government of Pakistan, for the supply of goods to or for the execution of any contract or the performance of any services undertaken by, the Provincial Government or Government of Pakistan.

Provided that the disqualification under clause (f) shall not apply to a person:
 (i) where the share of interest in the contract devolves oh him by inheritance or succession or as i a legatee, executor or administrator, until the expiration of six months after it has so devolved on him or such longer period as the Government of Pakistan, may in any particular case, allow, or
 (ii) where the contract has been entered into by a public company as defined in the Companies Ordinance, 1904 (XLVII of 1984), of which he is a share holder but is neither a director of the said company or a person holding an office of profit under the company nor a Managing Agent.

(3) If any question arises whether a member has, after his election, become subject to any disqualification, the Commissioner shall place the question before the Chief Execute, and if the opinion of the Chief Executive be that the member has been so subjected to disqualification his seal shall become vacant:

Provided that no member shall be disqualified unless he is afforded an opportunity of being heard:

13. Resignation and removal. – (1) A member may resign his member-ship of the Council by notice in writing addressed to the Chairman.

(2) If a member is absent without leave of the Chairman, from three consecutive sessions of the Council, his seat shall become vacant.

(3) If a member fails to lake and subscribe an oath in accordance with section-11, his seat shall become vacant.

(4) A member shall render himself liable to removal from membership if he incurs any of the following disqualification, namely:

- (a) it he becomes a whole-time or part-time salaried official in the service of the Government of Pakistan or service of Northern Areas, or of a public statutory corporation, a local body or other local authority;
- (b) if he is under contract for work to be done or goods to be supplied to the Council or has otherwise any peculiar interest in its affairs;
- (c) if he has been convicted of any offence for corrupt or illegal practice relating to election or has been found guilty of any such offence or practices in any proceedings questioning the validity or regularity of an election, unless, four years or such less period as the Government of Pakistan may by notification determine specially in his behalf, has elapsed from the date of the order, or from the date of expiry of the sentence, if any;
- (d) if he is guilty of an abuse of power or of, any misconduct in the discharge of his duties as a member or has been responsible for any loss or misappropriation of any money or property of the Government of Pakistan or Northern Areas or of any local body or local authority.
- (e) If a vote of no-confidence is passed against him by not less than two third of the members in a session held on a written requisition signed by at least one-half of them calling upon the Chairman to convene a special meeting of the council lo consider the no-confidence motion; or
- (f) If he is engaged or is reasonably suspected of being engaged in subversive activities, or is reasonably suspected of being associated with others engaged in subversive activities.

Explanation. – In this sub-section the term "misconduct" includes bribery, corruption, nepotism or any attempt at, or abutment of, such misconduct or failure to perform the functions of office.

(5) A person who renders himself liable to removal from membership under sub-section (4) may be removed from membership by an order of the Chairman

and shall not be eligible for election to the Council for such a period not exceeding five years as the Chairman may determine.

14. Bar against double membership. – No person shall, at the same time, be member in respect of more than one constituency or member of a Local Council as defined in the explanation to section 19-A of the Northern Areas Local government Order, 1979.

15. Casual vacancy. – If the seal of a member becomes vacant during the term of the office of the Council, it shall be filled by election and such member shall hold office for the residue of the term of his predecessor.

16. Allowances and privileges of members. – The members shall be entitled to such honorarium, allowance and privileges as may be prescribed by rules.

[1][**17. Power to make laws.** – (1) Subject to such limitations as the Government of Pakistan may, from time to time, impose, the Council may make laws with respect to any matter enumerated in schedule-II to this order.

(2) The Council shall not make any law, which is repugnant to the injunctions of Islam as laid down in Holy Quran and Sunnah or adversely affecting personal law rights of any Muslim sect].

[2][**17A. Chief Executive assent to bills.** – (1) Subject to this Order, when a Bill has been passed by the Council, it shall be presented to the Chief Executive for assent.

(2) When a Bill is presented to the Chief Executive for assent, the Chief Executive shall within fifteen days:

(a) assent to the Bill or
(b) return the Bill to the Council with a message requesting that the Bill or any specified provision thereof, be reconsidered and that any amendment specified in the message may be reconsidered.

(3) When the Chief Executive has assented to a Bill, it shall become law and be called an Act of Council].

[3][**17B. Legislative powers of the Government of Pakistan.** – The Government of Pakistan may, by an Order make laws with respect to matters not enumerated in schedule-II to this Order].

---

1. Substituted by Amendment Order dated 28th October, 1999.
2. Inserted by Amendment Order ibid.
3. Inserted by Amendment Order ibid.

¹[**17C. Inconsistency between Law made by Government of Pakistan and Council.** – If any provision of a law made by the Council is repugnant to the law made by the Government of Pakistan the law made by the Government of Pakistan, whether made before or after the law made by the Council, shall prevail].

²[**17D. Budget.** – Annual budget allocated shall be presented before the Council in the form of a statement].

18. Rules of procedure and quorum. – (1) The procedure of the Council shall be regulated by rules of procedure to be framed by the Council at its first session.

(2) If, at any time during a session of the Council, the attention is drawn to the fact that the number of members present is less than one-third of the total number of members, the person presiding shall either suspend the session until number of members present is not less than one-third or adjourn the session.

(3) The proceedings of the Council shall be conducted in Urdu and the minutes of the session of the Council shall be drawn up and recorded by the Secretary of the Council.

³[**19. Development Forums.** – The Chief Executive shall, by Order in writing, constitute recommending, approving and monitoring fora for development schemes in accordance with guidelines issued by the Planning Commission of Pakistan].

⁴[**19A. Fundamental Rights.** – (1) The people of the Northern Areas shall have the Fundamental Rights specified in Chapter-I of Part-II of the Constitution of the Islamic Republic of Pakistan.

(2) The Chief Court may, if it is satisfied that no adequate remedy is provided by law, on the application of any aggrieved person, make an order giving such direction to any person or authority exercising any power or performing any functions in, or in relation to, any territory within the jurisdiction of that Court as may be appropriate for the enforcement of any of the Fundamental Rights].

⁵[**19B. Liability to Pay Tax.** – The people of Northern Areas shall be liable to pay taxes arid other levies competently imposed under an Act of the Council or under any law made by the Government of Pakistan].

---

1. Inserted by Amendment Order dated 20th October, 1999.
2. Inserted by Amendment Order ibid.
3. Substituted by Amendment Order ibid.
4. Inserted by Amendment Order ibid.
5. Inserted by Amendment Order of 1999.

[19C. Judicial System. – (1) Judicial system in the Northern Areas shall consist of the following Courts, namely:

    (i) the Court of Appeals;
    (ii) the Chief Court;
    (iii) Subordinate Judiciary; and
    (iv) Any other court specially set-up for any other purpose.

(2) The composition of, and the jurisdiction exercisable by, each court shall be such as has been, or may be, determined by law.

(3) The Courts existing immediately before the commencement of the Northern Areas Council Legal Frame Work (Amendment) Order, 1999, shall continue and the Court of appeals shall be established as soon as possible].

20. Bar of Jurisdiction. – No Court shall have jurisdiction to enquire into or question the validity of any act done, or any order or resolution passed, Under this Order.

21. Power of Government to make rules. – The Government of Pakistan may make Rules for carrying out the purposes of this Order.

22. Repeal. – The Northern Areas Council Legal Frame Work Order, 1975 is hereby repealed.

---

1. Inserted by Amendment Order of 1999.

SCHEDULE-1

FORM "A"

OATH OF OFFICE OF THE CHIEF EXECUTIVE NORTHERN AREAS

(See Section 11)

I,... being the Chief Executive of the Northern Areas, do solemnly swear that I will bear true faith and allegiance to Pakistan and uphold the sovereignty and integrity of Pakistan.

That, as Chief Executive of the Northern Areas, I will be faithful to the declaration of the Founder of Pakistan, Quaid-i-Azam Muhammad All Jinnah, that Pakistan would be a democratic State based on Islamic principles of Social Justice;

That I will perform my functions honestly and faithfully;

That I shall strive to preserve the Islamic ideology which is the basis for the emotion of Pakistan;

That I shall strive to preserve and to maintain religious/sectarian harmony in the Northern Areas and shall not indulge in any activity prejudicial to the cause, and

That I will not directly or indirectly communicate or reveal to any person any official secret which may come to my knowledge as Chief Executive of the Northern Areas Council.

Signature of Chief Executive

Place ....
Date ....

Signature of Chairman Chief Court

FORM "B"
OATH OF OFFICE OF THE MEMBER NORTHERN AREAS LEGISLATIVE COUNCIL

(See Section 11)

I,..., have been elected as a Member of the Northern Areas Legislative Council, do solemnly swear that I will bear true faith and allegiance to Pakistan and uphold the sovereignty and integrity of Pakistan.

That, as Member of the Northern Areas Legislative Council, I will be faithful to the declaration of the Founder of Pakistan, Quaid-i-Azam Muhammad All Jinnah, that Pakistan would be a democratic State based on Islamic principles of social justice.

That I will perform my functions honestly and faithfully.

That I shall strive to preserve the Islamic ideology which is the basis for the creation of Pakistan;

That I shall strive to preserve and to maintain religious/sectarian harmony in the Northern Areas and shall not indulge in any activity prejudicial to this cause, and

That I will not directly or indirectly communicate or reveal to any person any official secret which may come to my knowledge as Member of the Northern Areas Legislative Council.

Signature of Member

Place ....
Date ....

Signature of Speaker Northern Areas Council

[FORM "C"][1]
OATH OF OFFICE OF THE DEPUTY CHIEF EXECUTIVE NORTHERN AREAS LEGISLATIVE COUNCIL

[Section 11(3)]

I, ...being the Deputy Chief Executive of the Northern Areas Legislative Council, do solemnly swear that I will bear faith and allegiance lo Pakistan and uphold the sovereignty and integrity of Pakistan.

That as Deputy Chief Executive of the Northern Areas Legislative Council, I will be faithful to the declaration of the Founder of Pakistan, Quaid-e-Azam Muhammad Ali Jinnah, that Pakistan would be democratic State based on Islamic principles of social justice;

That I will perform my functions honestly and faithfully;

That I shall strive to preserve the Islamic ideology which is the basis for the creation of Pakistan

That I shall strive to preserve and lo maintain religious/sectarian harmony in the Northern Areas and shall not indulge in any activity prejudicial to this cause; and

That I will not directly or indirectly communicate or reveal to any person any official secret which may come to my knowledge as Deputy Chief Executive of the Northern Areas Legislative Council.

Signature of Deputy Executive, Northern Areas

Place ....
Date ....

Signature of Chief Executive]

---

1. Form "C" added by Amendment Order dated 1 July, 2000.

[FORM "D"
OATH OF OFFICE OF THE SPEAKER
NORTHERN AREAS LEGISLATIVE COUNCIL
(Section 11(3)]

I..being the Speaker of the Northern Areas Legislative Council, do solemnly swear that I will bear faith and allegiance to Pakistan and uphold the sovereignty and integrity of Pakistan.

That as Speaker of the Northern Areas Legislative Council, i will be faithful to the declaration of the Founder of Pakistan, Quaid-I-Azam Muhammad All Jinnah, that Pakistan would be democratic State based on Islamic principles of social Justice;

That I will perform my functions honestly and faithfully;

That I shall strive to preserve the Islamic ideology which is the basis for the creation of Pakistan;

That I shall strive to preserve and to maintain religious/sectarian harmony in the Northern Areas and shall not indulge in any activity prejudicial to this cause; and

That I will not directly or indirectly communicate or reveal to any person any official secret which may come to my knowledge as Speaker of the Northern Areas Legislative Council.

Signature of Speaker Northern Areas

Place ....
Date ....

Signature of Chief Executive Northern Areas]

---

1. Form "D" added by Amendment Order dated 1st July, 2000.

[FORM "E"][1]

OATH OF OFFICE OF THE ADVISOR
NORTHERN AREAS LEGISLATIVE COUNCIL

[Section 11(3)]

I, ...being the Advisor of the Northern

Areas Legislative Council, do solemnly swear that I will bear faith and allegiance to Pakistan and uphold the sovereignty and integrity of Pakistan.

That as Advisor of the Northern Areas Legislative Council, I will be faithful to the declaration of the Founder of Pakistan, Quaid-i-Azam Muhammad Ali Jinnah, that Pakistan would be democratic State based on Islamic principles of social Justice;

That I will perform my functions honestly and faithfully;

That I shall strive to preserve the Islamic ideology which is the basis for the creation of Pakistan

That I shall strive to preserve and to maintain religious/sectarian harmony in the Northern Areas and shall not indulge in any activity prejudicial to this cause; and

That I will not directly or indirectly communicate or reveal to any person any official secret which may come to my knowledge as Advisor of the Northern Areas Legislative Council.

Signature of Advisor, Northern Areas

Place ....
Date ....

Signature of Chief Executive Northern Areas]

---

1. Form "E" added by Amendment Order dated 1st July, 2000.

SCHEDULE-II
(See Section-17)

1. Public order (but not including the use of Naval, Military, Air Force, or any other aimed forces of the Federation in aid of the civil power).
2. Preventive detention for reasons in connection with the maintenance of public order; persons subjected to such detention.
3. Prisons, reformatories, borstal institution and other institutions of a like nature and persons detained therein, arrangements with other provinces for the use of prisons and other institutions.
4. I and, that is to say, rights in or over land; land tenures, including the relation of landlord and tenant, and the collection of rents: transfer, alienation and devolution of agricultural land; land improvement and agricultural loans; colonization.
5. Land revenue; including the assessment and collection of revenue, the maintenance of land records, survey for revenue purpose and records of lights and alienation of revenues.
6. Works, lands and buildings vested in or in the possession of the Northern Areas Administration.
7. Compulsory acquisition or requisitioning of property.
8. Agriculture, including agricultural education and research protection against posts and prevention of plant diseases.
9. Local Government, that is to say, the constitution and powers of municipal corporations, improvement trusts, district councils settlement authorities and other local authorities for the purpose of local self-government or village administration.
10. Preservation, protection and improvement of stock, and prevention of animal diseases; veterinary training and practice.
11. Pounds and the prevention of cattle trespass.
12. Water, including water supplies, irrigation and canals, drainage and embankments, water storage and water power; flood control.
13. Libraries, museums and ancient and historical monuments.
14. Bolanical, zoological and anthropological surveys.
15. Theaters: cinemas; sports; entertainments and amusement.
16. Public health and sanitation; hospitals and dispensaries.
17. Registration of births and deaths.
18. Burials and burial grounds; cremations and cremation grounds.
19. Relief of the disabled and un-employed.
20. Intoxicating liquors, that is to say, the production, manufacture, possession, transport, purchase and sale of intoxicating liquors and other narcotic drugs.

21. Boilers.
22. Markets and fairs.
23. Money lending and moneylenders; relief of indebtedness.
24. Protection of wild animals and birds.
25. Prevention of cruelty to animals.
26. Adulteration of foodstuff and other goods.
27. Retting and gambling.
28. Fisheries.
29. Professions.
30. Inns and in-keepers.
31. Orphanages and poor houses.
32. Taxes on agricultural income and on the value of agricultural land.
33. Lunacy and mental deficiency including places for reception of treatment of lunatics and mental deficient.
34. Duties in respect of succession to agricultural land.
35. Estate Duly in respect of agricultural land.
36. Taxes on lands and buildings.
37. Taxes on advertisement.
30. Taxes on goods and passengers carried by road or on inland waterways.
39. I fixes on vehicles, whether mechanically propelled or not, suitable for use on a road; on boats, launches and streamers on inland water; on tram cars.
40. I axes on animals and boats.
41. Tolls.
42. Capitation taxes
43. I fixes on luxuries, including taxes on entertainment and amusements.
44. Taxes on profession, trades, callings and employment.
45. Relief of poor; un-employment.
46. Offences against laws with respect of any of the matters in this list.
47. Inquiries and statistics for the purpose of any of the matters in this list.
40. Cases on the entry of goods into a local area for consumption, use or sale therein.
49. Duns on passengers and goods carried on roads or inland waterways.

CHAPTER-I
FUNDAMENTAL RIGHTS

[See Section 19-A]

Note: Fundamental Rights specified in Chapter 1 of part II of the Constitution of the Islamic Republic of Pakistan (See Section 19A)

ARTICLE

8. Laws inconsistent with or in derogation of fundamental rights to be void. – (1) Any law, or any custom or usage having the force of laws in so far as it is inconsistent with the rights conferred by this Chapter, shall, to the extent of such inconsistency, be void.

(2) The State shall not make any law, which takes away or abridges the rights so conferred and any law made in contravention of this clause shall, to the extent of such contravention, be void.

(3) The provisions of this Article shall not apply to,-

(a) any law relating to members of the Armed Forces, or of the police or of such other forces as are changed with the maintenance of public order, for the purpose of ensuring the proper discharge of their duties of the maintenance of discipline among them; or

1[(b) any of the
  (i) laws specified in the First Schedule as in force immediately before the commencing day or as amended by any of the law specified in that Schedule;
  (ii) other laws specified in Part I of the First Schedule:] and no such law nor any provision thereof shall be void on the ground that such law or provision is inconsistent with, or repugnant to, any provision of this Chapter.

(4) Notwithstanding anything contained in paragraph (b) of clause (3), within a period of two years from the commencing day, the appropriate Legislature shall bring the laws specified in 2[part II of the first Schedule] into conformity with the rights conferred by this Chapter.

Provided that the appropriate legislature may by resolution extend the said period of two years by a period not exceeding six months.

---

1. By Constitution (First Amendment) Act, 1974 (33 of 1974), in "day" the words or as amended by any of the laws specified in that schedule were added. This amended paragraph (b) was then substituted by the present one through the Constitution (Fourth Amendment) Act, 1975 (71 of 1975).
2. Substituted by the Constitution (Fourth Amendment) Act, 1975 (71 of 1975), tor the words "the First Schedule, not being a law which relates to, or is connected with, economic reforms".

Explanation. If in respect of any law [Majlish-E-Shoora (Parliament)] is the appropriate legislature, such resolution shall be a resolution of the national Assembly.

(5) The rights conferred by this Chapter shall not be suspended except as expressly provided by the Constitution.

9. Security of person. – No person shall be deprived of life or liberty save in accordance with law.

10. Safeguards as to arrest and detention. – (1) No person who is arrested shall be detained in custody without being informed, as soon as may be, of the grounds for such arrest, not shall he be denied the right to consult and be defended by a legal practitioner of his choice.

(2) Every person who is arrested arid detained in custody shall be produced before a magistrate within a period of twenty four. hours of such arrest, excluding the time necessary for the journey from the place of arrest to the court of the nearest magistrate, and no such person shall be detained in custody beyond the said period without the authority of a magistrate.

(3) Nothing in clause (1) and (2) shall apply to any person who is arrested or detained under any law providing for preventive detention.

(4) No law providing for preventive detention shall be made except to deal with persons acting in a manner prejudicial to the integrity, security or defence of Pakistan or any part thereof, or external affairs of Pakistan, or public order, or the maintenance of supplies or services, and ho such law shall authorize the detention of a person for a period exceeding [1][three months] Unless the appropriate Review Board has, after affording him an opportunity of being heard in person, reviewed his case and reported, before the expiration of the said period, that there is, in its opinion, sufficient cause for such detention, and, if the detention is continued after the said period of [2][three months], unless the appropriate Review Board has reviewed his case and reported, before the expiration of each period of three months, that there is, in its opinion, sufficient cause for such detention.

Explanation-I. In this Article, "the appropriate Review Board" means:
    (i) in the case of a person detained under a Federal Law, a Board appointed by the Chief Justice of Pakistan arid consisting of a Chairman arid two other persons, each of whom is or has been a Judge of the Supreme Court or a High Court; and
    (ii) in the case of a person detained under a Provincial Law, a board appointed by the Chief Justice of the High Court concerned and consisting of

---

1. Substituted by the Constitution (third Amendment) Act, 1975 for the words one month.
2. Substituted by the Constitution (third Amendment) Act, 1975 for the words one month.

Chairman and two other persons, each of whom is or has been a Judge of a High court.

Explanation-II. The opinion of a Review Board shall be expressed in terms of the views of the majority of its members.

(5) When any person is detained in pursuance of an order made under any law providing for preventive detention, the authority making the order shall, [1][within fifteen days] from such detention, communicate to such person the grounds on which the order has been made, and shall afford him the earliest opportunity of making a representation against the order;

Provided that the authority making any such order may refuse to disclose facts which such authority considers it to be against the public interest to disclose.

(6) The authority making the order shall furnish to the appropriate Review Board all documents relevant to the case unless a certificate, signed by a Secretary to the Government concerned, to the effect that it is not in the public interest to furnish any documents, is produced.

(7) Within a period of twenty-four months commencing on the day of his first detention in pursuance of an order made under a law providing for preventive detention, ho person shall be detained in pursuance of any such order for more than a total period of eight months in the case of. a person detained for acting in manner prejudicial to public order and twelve months in any other case;

Provided that this clause shall not apply to any person who is employed by, or works for, or acts on instruction received from the enemy [2][or who is acting or attempting to act in a manner prejudicial to the integrity, security or defence of Pakistan or any part thereof or who commits or attempts to commit any act which amounts to an anti-national activity as defined in a Federal law or is a member of any association which has for its objects, or which indulges, in, any such anti-national activity].

(8) The appropriate Review Board shall determine the place of detention of the person detained and fix a reasonable subsistence allowance for his family.

(9) Nothing in this Article shall apply to any person who for the time being is an enemy alien.

11. Slavery, forced labour, etc. prohibited. – (1) Slavery is non-existent and forbidden and no law shall permit or facilitate its introduction into Pakistan in any form.

(2) All firms of forced labour and traffic in human beings are prohibited.

---

1. Substituted by the Constitution (Third Amendment) Act, 1975.
2. Added by Constitution (Third Amendment) Act, 1975.

(3) No child below the age of fourteen years shall be engaged in any factory or mine or any other hazardous employment.

(4) Nothing in this Article shall be deemed to affect compulsory service:

    (a) by any person undergoing punishment for an offence against any law; or

    (b) required by any law for public purpose:

        Provided that no compulsory service shall be of a cruel nature or incompatible with human dignity.

12. Protection against retrospective punishment. – (1) No law shall authorize the punishment of a person:

    (a) for an act or omission that was not punishable by law at the time of the act or omission; or

    (b) for an offence by a penalty greater then, or of a kind different from, the penalty, prescribed by law for that offence at the time the offence was committed.

(2) Nothing in clause (I) or in Article 270 shall apply to any law making acts of abrogation or subversion of a Constitution in force in Pakistan at any time since the twenty third day of March, one thousand nine hundred and fifty six, an offence.

13. Protection against double punishment and self-incrimination. – No person:

    (a) shall be prosecuted or punished for the same offence more than once; or

    (b) shall, when accused of an offence, be compelled to be a witness against himself.

14. Inviolability of dignity of man, etc. – (1) The dignity of man and, subject to law, the privacy of home, shall be inviolable.

(2) No person shall be subjected to torture for the purpose of extracting evidence.

15. Freedom of movement, etc. – Every Citizen shall have the right to remain, in and, subject to any reasonable restriction imposed by law in the public interest, enter and move freely throughout Pakistan and to reside and settle in any part thereof.

16. Freedom of assembly. – Every citizen shall have the right to assemble peacefully and without arms, subject to any reasonable restrictions imposed by law in the interest of public order.

17. Freedom of association. – (1) Every citizen shall have the right to form associations or unions, subject to any reasonable restrictions imposed by law in the interest of [1][sovereignty or integrity of Pakistan, public order or morality].

---

1. Substituted by the Constitution (fourth Amendment) Act, 1975.

[1][(2) Every citizen, not being in the service of Pakistan, shall have the right to form or be a member of a political party subject to any reasonable restrictions imposed by law in the interest of the Sovereignty or integrity of Pakistan and such law shall provide that where the Federal Government declares that any political party has been formed or is operating in a manner prejudicial to the Sovereignty or integrity of Pakistan, the Federal Government shall, within fifteen days of such declaration, refer the matter to the Supreme Court whose decision on such reference shall be final.

(3) Every political party shall account for the source of its funds in accordance with law.]

18. Freedom of trade, business or profession. – Subject to such qualifications, if any, as may be prescribed by law, every citizen shall have the right to enter upon any lawful profession or occupation, and to conduct any lawful trade or business:

Provided that nothing in this Article shall prevent:
   (a) the regulation of any trade or profession by licensing system; or
   (b) the regulation of trade, commerce or industry in the interest of free competition therein; or
   (c) the carrying on, by the Federal Government or a Provincial Government, or by a corporation controlled by any such Government, of any trade, business, industry or service, to the exclusion, complete or partial, of other persons.

19. Freedom of speech, etc. – Every citizen shall have the right to freedom of speech and expression, and there shall be freedom of the press, subject to any reasonable restrictions imposed by law in the interest of the glory of Islam or the integrity, security or defence of Pakistan or any part thereof, friendly relations with foreign States, public order, decency or morality, or in relation to contempt of court, [2][commission of] or incitement to an offence.

20. Freedom to profess religion and to manage religious institutions. – Subject to law, public order and morality:
   (a) every citizen shall have the right to profess, practice and propagate his religion; and
   (b) every religious denomination and every sect thereof shall have the right to establish, maintain and manage its religious institutions.

---

1. Clause (20 and (3) substituted by the Constitution (first Amendment) Act, 1974 for clause (2) which read as under:
   "(2) Every citizen not being in the service of Pakistan shall have the right to form or be a member of a political party. Every political party shall account for the source of its funds in accordance with law".
2. Substituted by the Constitution (Fourth Amendment) Act, 1975 for the word "definition".

21. Safeguard against taxation for purposes of any particular religion. – No person shall be compelled to pay any special tax the proceeds of which are to be spent on the propagation, or maintenance of any religion other than his own.

22. Safeguards as to educational institutions in respect of religion, etc. – (1) No person attending any educational institution shall be required to receive religious instruction, or take part in any religious ceremony, or attend religious worship, if such instruction, ceremony or worship relates to a religion other than his own.

(2) In respect of any religious institution, there shall be no discrimination against any community in the granting of exemption or concession in relation to taxation.

(3) Subject to law,
  (a) no religious community or denomination shall be prevented from providing religious instruction for pupils of that community or denomination in any educational institution maintained wholly by that community or denomination; and
  (b) no citizen shall be denied admission to any educational institution receiving aid from public revenues on the ground only of race, religion, caste or place of birth.

(4) Nothing in this Article shall prevent any public authority from making provisions for the advancement of any socially or educationally backward class of citizens.

23. Provision as to property. – Every citizen shall have the right to acquire, hold and dispose of property in any part of Pakistan, subject to the Constitution and any reasonable restrictions imposed by law in the public interest.

24. Protection of property rights. – (1) No person shall be compulsorily deprived of his property save in accordance with law.

(2) No property shall be compulsorily acquired or taken possession of save for a public purpose, and save by the authority of law which provides for compensation therefore and either fixes the amount of compensation or specifies the principles on and the manner in which compensation is to be determined and given.

(3) Nothing in this Article shall affect the validity of:
  (a) any law permitting the compulsory acquisition or taking possession of any property for preventing danger to life, property or public health; or
  (b) any law permitting the taking over of any property which has been acquired by, or come into the possession of, any person by any unfair means, or in any manner, contrary to law; or
  (c) any law relating to the acquisition, administration or disposal of any

property which is or is deemed to be enemy property or evacuee property under any law (not being property which has ceased to be evacuee property under any law); or

(d) any law providing for taking over of the management of any property by the State for a limited period, either in the public interest or in order to secure the proper management of the property, or for the benefit of its owner, or

(e) any law providing for the acquisition of any class of property for the purpose of:
   (i) providing education and medical aid to all or any specified class of citizens; or
   (ii) providing housing and public facilities and services such as roads, water supply, sewerage, gas and electric power to all or any specified class of citizens; or
   (iii) providing maintenance to those who on account of unemployment, sickness, infirmity or old age are unable to maintain themselves or

(f) any existing law or any law made in pursuance of Article 253.

(4) The adequacy or otherwise of any compensation provided for by any such law as is referred to in this Article, or determined in pursuance thereof, shall not be called in question in any court.

25. Equality of citizens. – (1) All citizens are equal before law and are entitled to equal protection of law.

(2) There shall be no discrimination on the basis of sex alone.

(3) Nothing in this Article shall prevent the State from making any special provision for the protection of women and children.

26. Non-discrimination in respect of access to public places. – (1) In respect of access to places of public entertainment or resort, hot intended for religious purpose only there shall be no discrimination against any citizen on the ground only of race religion, caste sex residence or place of birth.

(2) Nothing in clause (I) shall prevent the State from making any special provision for women and children

27. Safeguard against discrimination in services. – (1) No citizen otherwise qualified for appointment in the service of Pakistan shall be discriminated against in respect of any such appointment on the ground only of race, religion, caste sex residence or place of birth,

Provided that, for a period not exceeding ¹[twenty] years from the commencing

---

1. Substituted by P.O. No. 14 of 1985 for word "ten".

day, posts may be reserved for persons belonging to any class or area to secure their adequate, representation in the service of **Pakistan;**

Provided further that, in the interest of the said service, specified posts or services may be reserved for members of either sex if such posts of services entail the performance of duties and functions which cannot be adequately performed by members of the other sex.

(2) Nothing in clause (I) shall prevent any Provincial Government, or any local or other authority in a Province, from prescribing, in relation to any post or class of service under that Government or authority, conditions as to residence in the Province, for a period not exceeding three years, prior to appointment under that Government or authority.

28. Preservation of language, script and culture. – Subject to Article 251, any section of citizens having a distinct language, script or culture shall have the right lo preserve and promote the same and subject to law, establish institutions for that purpose.

APPENDIX IX

Gilgit-Baltistan (Empowerment and Self-Governance) Order, 2009

GOVERNMENT OF PAKISTAN
MINISTRY OF KASHMIR AFFAIRS AND
NORTHERN AREAS

****

Islamabad, the 9th September, 2009

AN

ORDER

to provide greater political empowerment and better governance to the people of Gilgit-Baltistan;

WHEREAS it is expedient to undertake necessary legislative, executive and judicial reforms for granting self-governance to the people of Gilgit-Baltistan and for matters connected therewith or incidental thereto;

NOW, THEREFORE, the Government of Pakistan is pleased to make the following Order:-

1. Short title, extent and commencement. – (1) This Order may be called the Gilgit-Baltistan (Empowerment and Self-Governance) Order, 2009.

    (2) It extends to the whole of areas Gilgit-Baltistan.

    (3) It shall come into force on at once.

PART I - PRELIMINARY

2. Definitions. – (1) In this Order, unless there is anything repugnant in the subject or context:

    (a) **"Assembly"** means the Gilgit-Baltistan Legislative Assembly;

    (b) **"Citizen"** unless otherwise expressed in this Order "citizen" means a person who has a domicile of Gilgit-Baltistan;

(c) **"Council"** means the Gilgit-Baltistan Council constituted under this Order;
(d) **"Chairman"** means the Chairman of the Council who shall be the Prime Minister of Pakistan;
(e) **"Financial year"** means the year commencing on the first day of July and ending on the thirtieth day of June;
(f) **"Gilgit-Baltistan"** means the areas comprising districts of Astore, Diamer, Ghanche, Ghizer, Gilgit, Hunza-Nagar, Skardu and such other districts as may be created from time to time;
(g) **"Governor"** means the Governor of Gilgit-Baltistan and includes a person for the time being acting as, or performing the functions of the Governor;
(h) **"Government"** means the Government of Gilgit-Baltistan;
(i) **"Joint Sitting"** means a joint sitting of the Assembly, the Federal Minister in-charge of the Council Secretariat and the members of the Council;
(j) **"Judge"** in relation to the Gilgit-Baltistan Supreme Appellate Court or the Gilgit-Baltistan Chief Court, includes the Chief Judge of the Gilgit-Baltistan Supreme Appellate Court and the Chief Court;
(k) **"Person"** includes any body politic or corporate;
(l) **"Prescribed"** means prescribed by law or rules made thereunder;
(m) **"Property"** includes any right, title or interest in property, movable or immovable, and any means and instruments of production;
(n) **"remuneration"** includes salary and pension;
(o) **"Service of Gilgit-Baltistan"** means any service, post or office in connection with the affairs of Gilgit-Baltistan including the Council, but does not include service as Chairman of the Council, Governor, Speaker, Deputy Speaker, Chief Minister, Minister, Federal Minister in-charge of the Council Secretariat or Advisor, Parliamentary Secretary, Advisor to the Minister or a member of the Assembly or member of the Council; and
(p) **"Speaker"** means Speaker of the Assembly and includes any person acting as the Speaker of the Assembly.
(q) **"Vice Chairman of the Council"** means the Governor of Gilgit-Baltistan.

PART II - FUNDAMENTAL RIGHTS

3. Security of person. – No person shall be deprived of liberty save in accordance with law.

4. Safeguard as to arrest and detention. – (1) No person who is arrested shall be detained in custody without being informed, as soon as may be, of the grounds for such arrest, nor shall he be denied the right to consult and be defended by a legal practitioner of his choice.

(2) Every person who is arrested and detained in custody shall be produced

before the nearest Magistrate within a period of twenty-four hours of such arrest excluding the time necessary for the journey from the place of arrest to the Court of the Magistrate, and no such person shall be detained in custody beyond the said period without the authority of a Magistrate.

(3) Nothing in Clauses (1) and (2) shall apply to any person-
   (a) who for the time being is an enemy alien, or
   (b) who is arrested or detained under any law providing for preventive detention.

(4) No law providing for preventive detention shall authorize the detention of a person for a period exceeding three months unless the review board set up by the Government has reported before the expiration of the said period of three months that there is, in its opinion, sufficient cause for such detention.

(5) When any person is detained in pursuance of an order made under any law providing for preventive detention, the authority making the order shall as soon as may be, communicate to such person the grounds on which the order has been made, and shall afford him the earliest opportunity of making a representation against the order:

Provided that the authority making any such order may refuse to disclose facts which such authority considers it to be against the public interest to disclose.

5. Slavery and forced labour prohibited. – (1) No person shall be held in slavery, and no law shall permit or in any way facilitate the introduction into Gilgit-Baltistan of slavery in any form.

(2) All forms of forced labour are prohibited.

(3) Nothing in this clause shall be deemed to affect compulsory service-
   (a) by persons undergoing punishment for offences under any law; or
   (b) required by any law for a public purpose.

6. Protection against retrospective punishment. – No law shall authorize the punishment of a person –
   (a) for an act or omission that was not punishable by law at the time of the act or omission; or
   (b) for an offence by a penalty greater than, or of a kind different form, the penalty prescribed by law for that offence at the time the offence was committed.

7. Freedom of movement. – Subject to any reasonable restrictions imposed by law in the public interest, every citizen shall have the right to move freely throughout the Gilgit-Baltistan and to reside and settle in any part thereof.

8. Freedom of assembly. – Every citizen shall have the right to assemble peacefully and without arms, subject to any reasonable restrictions imposed by law in the interest of morality or public order.

9. Freedom of association. – (1) Subject to this Order, every citizen shall have the right to form association or unions, subject to any reasonable restrictions imposed by law in the interest of morality or public order.

(2) No person or political party in the area comprising Gilgit-Baltistan shall propagate against, or take part in activities prejudicial or detrimental to the ideology of Pakistan.

10. Freedom of trade, business or profession. – Every citizen possessing such qualifications, if any, as may be prescribed by law in relation to his profession or occupation shall have the right to enter upon any lawful profession or occupation, and to conduct any lawful trade or business:

Provided that nothing in this Article shall prevent –
  (a) the regulation of any trade or profession by a licensing system; or
  (b) the regulation of trade, commerce or industry in the interest of free competition therein; or
  (c) the carrying on, by Government or the Council, or by a corporation controlled by Government or the Council, of any trade, business, industry or service, to the exclusion, complete or partial, or other persons.

11. Freedom of speech. – Every citizen shall have the right to freedom of speech and expression, subject to any reasonable restrictions imposed by law in the interest of the security of area Gilgit-Baltistan, public order, decency or morality, or in relation to contempt of Court, commission of, or incitement to an offence.

12. Freedom of religion. – Subject to law, public order and morality-
  (a) every citizen has the right to profess and practice his religion; and
  (b) every religious denomination and every sect thereof has the right to establish, maintain and manage its places of worship.

13. Safeguard against taxation for purposes of any particular religion. – No person shall be compelled to pay any special tax the proceeds of which are to be spent on the propagation or maintenance of any religion other than his own.

14. Safeguard as to educational institutions in respect of religion etc. – (1) No person attending any educational institution shall be required to receive religious instructions or take part in any religious ceremony, or attend religious worship, if such instruction, ceremony or worship relates to a religion other than his own.

(2) No religious community or denomination shall be prevented from providing religious instruction for pupils of that community or denomination in any educational institution maintained wholly by that community or denomination.

(3) No citizen shall be denied admission to any educational institution receiving aid from public revenues on the ground only of race, religion, caste or place of birth.

(4) In respect of any religious institution, there shall be no discrimination against any community in the granting of exemption or concession in relation to taxation.

(5) Nothing in this paragraph shall prevent any public authority from making provision for the advancement of any society or educationally backward class.

15. Provisions as to property. – Subject to any reasonable restrictions imposed by law in the public interest, every citizen shall have the right to acquire, hold and dispose of property.

16. Protection of property. – (1) No person shall be deprived of his property save in accordance with law.

(2) No property shall be compulsorily acquired or taken possession of save for a public purpose, and save by the authority of law which provides for compensation therefor and either fixes the amount of compensation or specifies the principles on which and the manner in which compensation is to be determined and given.

(3) Nothing in this clause shall, affect the validity of –
  (a) any law permitting the compulsory acquisition or taking possession of any property for preventing danger to life, property or public health; or
  (b) any law relating to the acquisition, administration or disposal of any property which is or is deemed to be evacuee property under any law; or
  (c) any law permitting the taking over of any property which has been acquired by, or come into the possession of, any person by any unfair means, or in any manner, contrary to law ; or
  (d) any law providing for the taking over of the management of any property by the Government for a limited period, either in the public interest or in order to secure the proper management of the property, or for the benefit of its owner; or
  (e) any law providing for the acquisition of any class of property for the purpose of –
    (i) providing education and medical aid to all or any specified class of citizen; or
    (ii) providing housing and public facilities and services such as roads, water supply, sewerage, gas and electric power to all or any specified class of citizen; or
    (iii) providing maintenance to those who, on account of unemployment, sickness, infirmity or old age, are unable to maintain themselves; or

(f) any law in force immediately before the coming into force of this Order.

Explanation. – In clauses (2) and (3), the expression 'property' means immovable property, or any commercial or industrial undertaking, or any interest in any undertaking.

17. Equality of citizens. – All citizens are equal before law and are entitled to equal protection of law.

18. Non-discrimination in respect of access to public places. – In respect of access to places of public entertainment or resort, not intended for religious purposes only, there shall be no discrimination against any citizen on the ground only of race, religion, caste, sex or place of birth, but nothing herein shall be deemed to prevent the making of any special provision for women.

19. Safeguard against discrimination in services. – No citizen otherwise qualified for appointment in the services of areas comprising Gilgit-Baltistan shall be discriminated against in respect of any such appointment on the ground only of race, religion, caste or sex:

Provided that, in the interest of the said service, specified posts or services may be reserved for members of either sex.

PART III - GOVERNOR

20. The Governor. – (1) There shall be a Governor of the Gilgit-Baltistan who shall be appointed by the President of Pakistan on the advice of the Prime Minister of Pakistan:

    (a) Notwithstanding any thing contained in this Order, the Federal Minister for Kashmir Affairs and Gilgit-Baltistan shall act as the Governor of Gilgit-Baltistan till the appointment of the first Governor.

    (b) provided that after the first election under this Order, in the absence of Governor, the Speaker of Legislative Assembly shall act as acting Governor.

(3) A person shall not be appointed as Governor unless he is qualified to be elected as a member of the Assembly or the National Assembly of Pakistan and is not less than thirty five years of age.

(4) The Governor shall hold office during the pleasure of the President and shall be entitled to such salary, allowances and privileges as the President may determine.

(5) The Governor may, by writing under his hand addressed to the President, resign his office.

(6) The President may make such provision as he thinks fit for the discharge of the functions of the Governor in any contingency not provided for in this Order.

(7) Before entering upon office, the Governor shall make before the Chief Judge of the Gilgit-Baltistan Supreme Appellate Court an oath in the form set out in the First Schedule.

(8) The Governor shall not hold any office of profit in the service of Gilgit-Baltistan or of Pakistan nor occupy any other position carrying the right to remuneration for the rendering of services.

(9) The Governor shall not be a candidate for election as a member of the Assembly, and, if a member of the Assembly is appointed as Governor, his seat in the Assembly shall become vacant on the day he enters upon his office.

21. Governor to act on advice, etc. – (1) Subject to this Order in the performance of his functions, the Governor shall act in accordance with the advice of the Cabinet or the Chief Minister:

Provided that the Governor may require the Cabinet or, as the case may be, the Chief Minister to reconsider such advice, whether generally or otherwise, and the Governor shall act in accordance with the advice tendered after such reconsideration.

(2) The question whether any, and if so what, advice was tendered to the Governor by the Chief Minister or the Cabinet shall not be inquired into in, or by, any court, tribunal or other authority.

PART IV - THE GOVERNMENT

22. The Government. – (1) Subject to this Order, the executive authority of Gilgit-Baltistan shall be exercised in the name of the Governor by the Government through Cabinet consisting of the Chief Minister and the Ministers, which shall act through the Chief Minister who shall be the Chief Executive.

(2) In the performance of his functions under this Order, the Chief Minister may act either directly or through the Ministers.

(3) The Chief Minister and the Ministers shall be collectively responsible to the Assembly.

(4) Orders and other instructions made and executed in the name of the Governor shall be authenticated in such manner as may be specified in rules to be made by the Government, and the validity of an order or instruction which is so authenticated shall not be questioned in any court on the ground that it is not an order or instruction made or executed by the Governor.

(5) The Governor, in consultation with Chairman of the Council, may regulate the allocation and transaction of its business and may for the convenient transaction of that business delegate any of its functions to officers or authorities subordinate to it.

23. The Chief Minister. – (1) The Assembly shall meet on the thirtieth day following the day on which a general election to the Assembly is held, unless sooner summoned by the Governor.

(2) After the election of the Speaker, and the Deputy Speaker, the Assembly shall, to the exclusion of any other business, proceed to elect, without debate, one of its members to be the Chief Minister.

(3) The Chief Minister shall be elected by the votes of the majority of the total membership of the Assembly;

Provided that, if no member secures such majority in the first poll, a second poll shall be held between the members who secure the two highest numbers of votes in the first poll and the member who secures a majority of votes of the members present and voting shall be declared to have been elected as Chief Minister:

Provided further that, if the number of votes secured by two members securing the highest number of votes is equal, further poll shall be held between them until one of them secures a majority of the members present and voting.

(4) The member elected under clause (3) shall be invited by the Governor to assume the office of Chief Minister and he shall, before entering upon the office make before the Governor oath in the form set out in the First Schedule.

24. Ministers. – (1) The Governor shall appoint Ministers from amongst the members of the Assembly on the advice of Chief Minister.

(2) Before entering upon office, a Minister shall make before the Governor oath in the form set out in the First Schedule.

(3) A Minister may, by writing under his hand addressed to the Chief Minister, resign his office or may be removed from office by the Chief Minister.

25. Advisors to Chief Minister. – The Governor may, on the advice of Chief Minister, appoint not more then two Advisors on such term and conditions, as he may determine.

26. Parliamentary Secretaries. – (1) The Chief Minister may appoint Parliamentary Secretaries from amongst the members of the Assembly to perform such functions as may be prescribed.

(2) A Parliamentary Secretary may, by writing under his hand addressed to the Chief Minister, resign his office or may be removed from office by the Chief Minister.

27. Resignation of Chief Minister. – (1) Subject to clause (2) the Chief Minister may, by writing under his hand addressed to the Governor, resign his office and, when the Chief Minister resigns, the Ministers shall cease to hold office.

(2) If the Assembly is in session at the time when the Chief Minister resigns his office, the Assembly shall forthwith proceed to elect a Chief Minister, and if the Assembly is not in session the Governor shall for that purpose summon it to meet within fourteen days of the resignation.

28. Vote of no-Confidence against Chief Minister. – (1) A resolution for a vote of no-confidence moved by not less than twenty percent of the total membership of the Assembly may be passed against the Chief Minister by the Assembly.

(2) A resolution shall not be moved in the Assembly unless by the same resolution the name of another member of the Assembly is put forward as the successor.

(3) A resolution shall not be moved in the Assembly while the Assembly is considering demands for grants submitted to it in the Annual Budget.

(4) A resolution shall not be voted upon before the expiration of three days, or later than seven days, form the date on which it is moved in the Assembly.

(5) If the resolution is passed by majority of the total membership of the Assembly, the Chief Minister and the Ministers appointed by him shall cease to hold office.

(6) If a resolution is not passed another such resolution shall not be moved until a period of six months has elapsed.

29. Chief Minister Continuing in Office. – The Governor may ask the Chief Minister to continue to hold office until his successor enters upon the office of the Chief Minister.

30. Minister performing functions of Chief Minister. – (1) In the event of the death of the Chief Minister or the office of the Chief Minister becoming vacant by reason of his ceasing to be member of the Assembly or he resigns his office, the most senior Minister for the time being shall be called upon by the Governor to perform the functions of that office and the Minister shall continue in office until a new Chief Minister has been elected and has entered upon his office.

(2) If the Assembly is in session at the time when the Chief Minister dies or the office of the Chief Minster becomes vacant, the Assembly shall forthwith proceed to elect a Chief Minister, and if the Assembly is not in session the Governor shall for that purpose summon it to meet within fourteen days of the death of the Chief Minister or, as the case may be, of the office becoming vacant.

(3) When, for any reason, the Chief Minister is unable to perform his functions, the most senior Minister for the time being shall perform functions of Chief Minister until the Chief Minister resumes his functions.

(4) In this Article 'most senior Minister' means the Minister for the time being designated as such by the Chief Minister by notification in the official Gazette.

31. Extent of Executive Authority of Government. – (1) Subject to this Order, the executive authority of the Government shall extend to the matters with respect to which the Assembly has power to make laws.

(2) The executive authority of the Government shall be so exercised as to secure compliance with the laws made by the Council and Pakistan laws.

(3) Notwithstanding anything contained in this Order, the Government may with the consent of the Council, entrust, either conditionally or unconditionally,

to the Council, or to its officers functions in relation to any matter which the executive authority of the Government extends.

32. Advocate General. – (1) The Governor shall appoint a citizen, being a person qualified to be appointed as Judge of the Gilgit-Baltistan Chief Court, to be the Advocate General for Gilgit-Baltistan.

(2) It shall be the duty of the Advocate General to give advice to Government upon such legal matter, and to perform such other duties of a legal character, as may be referred or assigned to him by the Government.

(3) The Advocate General shall hold office during the pleasure of the Governor.

(4) The Advocate General may, by writing under his hand addressed to the Governor resign his office.

(5) The person holding the office as Advocate General immediately before the commencement of this Order shall be deemed to be the Advocate General, appointed under this Order.

PART V - GILGIT-BALTISTAN COUNCIL

33. Gilgit-Baltistan Council. – (1) There shall be a Gilgit-Baltistan Council consisting of –
- (a) the Prime Minister of Pakistan;
- (b) the Governor;
- (c) six members nominated by the Prime Minister of Pakistan from time to time from amongst Federal Ministers and members of Parliament:Provided that the Federal Minister for Kashmir Affairs and Gilgit-Baltistan shall be an *ex officio* member and Minister Incharge of the Council:
- (d) the Chief Minister of Gilgit-Baltistan;
- (e) six members to be elected by the Assembly in accordance with the system of proportional representation by means of a single transferable vote.

(2) The Prime Minister of Pakistan shall be the Chairman of the Council.

(3) The Governor shall be the Vice-Chairman of the Council.

(4) The Minister of State for Kashmir Affairs and Gilgit-Baltistan shall be an *ex officio* non voting member of the Council.

(5) The qualifications and disqualifications for being elected, as, and for being, a member of the Council shall, in the case of a member referred to in sub-clause (e) of clause (1), be the same as those for being elected as, and for being a member of the Assembly.

(6) The seat of a member of the Council elected by the Assembly, hereinafter referred to as an elected member, shall become vacant,-
- (a) if he resigns his seat by notice in writing under his hand addressed to

the Chairman or, in his absence, to the Secretary of the Council;
(b) if he is absent, without the leave of the Chairman, from ten consecutive sittings of the Council;
(c) if he fails to make the oath referred to in clause (11) within a period of ninety days after the date of his election, unless the Chairman, for good cause shown, extends the period; or
(d) if he ceases to be qualified for being a member under any provision of this Order or any other law for the time being in force.

(7) If any question arises whether a member has, after his election, become disqualified from being a member of the Council, the Chairman shall refer the question to the Chief Election Commissioner and, if the Chief Election Commissioner is of the opinion that the member has become disqualified, the member shall cease to be member and his seat shall become vacant.

(8) An election to fill a vacancy in the office of an elected member shall be held not later than thirty days from the occurrence of the vacancy or, if the election cannot be held within that period because the Assembly is dissolved, within thirty days of the general election to the Assembly.

(9) The manner of election of elected members and filling of a casual vacancy in the office of an elected member shall be such as may be prescribed.

(10) An elected member shall hold office during term of the Council.

(11) An elected member shall, before entering upon office, make before the Chairman or the Vice Chairman oath in the form set out in the First Schedule.

(12) The executive authority of the Council shall extend to all matters with respect to which the Council has power to make laws and shall be exercised, in the name of the Council, by the Chairman who may act either directly or through the Secretariat of the Council of which Federal Minister for Kashmir Affairs and Gilgit-Baltistan shall be incharge.

Provided that the Council may direct that, in respect of such matters it may specify, its authority shall be exercisable by the Vice-Chairman of the Council, subject to such conditions, if any, as the Council may specify.

(13) The Chairman may from among the elected members of the Council appoint not more than three Advisors on such terms and conditions as he may determine.

(14) An advisor shall, before entering upon office, make before the Chairman oath in form set out in the First Schedule.

(15) An Advisor who is a member of the Assembly shall have the right to speak in, and otherwise take part in the proceedings of the Council, but shall not by virtue of this clause be entitled to vote.

(16) The Council may make rules for regulating its procedure and the conduct of its business, and shall have power to act notwithstanding any vacancy in the membership thereof, and any proceedings of the Council shall not be invalid on

the ground that a person who was not entitled to do so sat, voted or otherwise took part in the proceedings.

(17) Orders and other instruments made and executed in the name of the Council shall be authenticated in such manner as may be specified in rules to be made by the Council and the validity of an order or instrument which is so authenticated shall not be called in question on the ground that it is not an order or instrument made or executed by the Council.

(18) The Chairman may regulate the allocation and transaction of the business of the Council and may, for the convenient transaction of that business, delegate any of its functions to officers and authorities subordinate to it.

Explanation: In this Article the expression 'Chairman' means Chairman of the Council.

34. Chairman of Council power to pardon and reprieve. – The Chairman shall have power to grant pardons, reprieves and respites and to remit, suspend or commute any sentence passed by any court, tribunal or other authority.

PART VI - THE LEGISLATURE

35. Legislative Assembly. – (1) The Legislative Assembly shall consist of **thirty three** members of whom-
- (a) **twenty four** members shall be elected directly on the basis of adult franchise;
- (b) **six** women members shall be elected on the pattern as in case of reserved seat in Pakistan.
- (c) **three** technocrats and other professional members shall be elected on the pattern as in case of reserved seat in Pakistan.

Explanation. – In sub-clause (c), the expression "technocrat or other professional" includes a person who is in possession of such qualification or experience as may be prescribed.

(2) The manner of election of the members of the Assembly and the manner of filling casual vacancies shall be such as may be prescribed.

(3) The Assembly, unless sooner dissolved, shall continue for five years from the date appointed for their first meeting.

(4) A general election to the Assembly shall be held within a period of sixty days immediately proceeding the day on which the term of the Assembly is due to expire, unless the Assembly has been sooner dissolved, and result of the election shall be declared not later than fourteen days before that day.

36. Oath of members of the Assembly. – (1) A person elected as a member of the Assembly shall not take his seat in the Assembly until he makes before such person as is prescribed by rules of the Assembly an oath in the form set out in the First Schedule.

(2) The oath may be made when the Assembly is in session.

(3) If any person sits or votes in the Assembly knowing that he is not qualified to be, or is disqualified from being a member of the Assembly he shall be liable in respect of every day on which he so sits or votes; shall be guilty of an offence punishable for a term which shall not be less than seven years and a fine which shall not be less than two hundred thousand rupees.

37. Qualifications of members of the Assembly. – (1) A person shall be qualified to be elected as, and to be, a member of the Assembly if –
    (a) he is a citizen;
    (b) he is not less than twenty-five years of age; and
    (c) his name appears on the electoral roll of any constituency in Gilgit-Baltistan.

(2) A person shall be disqualified from being so elected if –
    (a) he is of unsound mind and stands so declared by a competent court; or
    (b) he is an undischarged insolvent unless a period of ten years has elapsed since his being adjudged as insolvent; or
    (c) he has been on conviction for any offence sentenced to transportation for any term or imprisonment for a term of not less than two years unless a period of five years has elapsed since his release; or
    (d) he holds any office of profit in the service of Gilgit-Baltistan or in the service of Pakistan other than a office which is not a whole time office remunerated either by salary or by fee other than an office specified in the Second Schedule; or
    (e) he has been in the service of Gilgit-Baltistan, Pakistan and AJ&K or of any statutory body or any body which is owned or controlled by the Government of Pakistan, AJ&K and Gilgit-Baltistan or in which the Government has a controlling share or interest, unless a period of two years has elapsed since he ceased to be in such service; or
    (f) he has been dismissed for misconduct from the service of Gilgit-Baltistan or the service of Pakistan unless a period of five years has elapsed since his dismissal; or
    (g) he is otherwise disqualified from being a member of the Assembly by this Order or by any other law.

38. Seat in Assembly becomes vacant under certain circumstances. – (1) The seat of a member of the Assembly shall become vacant if –
    (a) he resigns his seat by notice in writing under his hand addressed to the Speaker, in his absence, to the Secretary of the Assembly; or
    (b) he is absent from the Assembly without the leave of the Assembly for thirty consecutive sitting days of the Assembly; or
    (c) he fails to make the oath referred to in Article 36 within a period of

ninety days after the date of his election unless the Speaker for good cause shown extends the period; or

(d) he is elected as member of the Council; or

(e) he ceases to be qualified for being a member under any provision of this Order or any other law.

(2) If the member of the Assembly is elected to more than one seat, he shall within a period of thirty days after the declaration of result for the last such seat, resign all but one of his seats, and if he does not so resign, all the seats to which he has been elected shall become vacant at the expiration of the said period of thirty days except the seat to which he has been last elected or, if he has been elected to more than one seat on the same day, the seat for election to which his nomination was filed last.

(3) If any question arises whether a member of the Assembly has, after his election become disqualified from being a member of the Assembly, the Speaker shall refer the question to the Chief Election Commissioner and, if the Chief Election Commissioner is of the opinion that the member has become disqualified the member shall cease to be a member and his seat shall become vacant.

(4) When except by dissolution of the Assembly, a seat in the Assembly has become vacant not later than one hundred and twenty days before the term of the Assembly is due to expire, an election to fill the seat shall be held within sixty days from the occurrence of the vacancy.

39. Right of Governor to address the Assembly. – (1) The Governor may address the Assembly and may for that purpose require the attendance of the members.

(2) The Advocate General shall have the right to speak and otherwise take part in the proceedings of the Assembly or any Committee thereof of which he may be named a member, but shall not by virtue of this Article be entitled to vote.

40. Meetings of the Assembly. – (1) The Assembly shall assemble at such times and at such places as the Governor may appoint, and the Governor may prorogue a session of the Assembly except when the Assembly has been summoned by the Speaker.

(2) Any meeting of the Assembly may be adjourned by the Speaker or other person presiding thereat.

(3) There shall be at least three sessions of the Assembly every year, and not more than one hundred and twenty days shall intervene between the last sitting of the Assembly in one session and the date appointed for its first sitting in the next session.

Provided that the Assembly shall meet for not less than one hundred and thirty working days in each parliamentary year.

(4) On a requisition signed by not less than one-third of the total membership of the Assembly, the Speaker shall summon the Assembly to meet, at such time

and place as he thinks fit, within fourteen days of the receipt of the requisition, and when the Speaker has summoned the Assembly, only he may prorogue it.

41. Dissolution of the Assembly. – (1) The Governor shall dissolve the Assembly if so advised by the Chief Minister, and the Assembly shall, unless sooner dissolved, stands dissolved at the expiration of the forty-eight hours after the Chief Minister has so advised.

Explanation. – Reference in this Article to Chief Minister shall not be construed to include reference to a Chief Minister against whom a resolution for a vote of no-confidence has been moved in the Assembly but has not been voted upon or against whom such a resolution has been passed or who is continuing in office after his resignation or after the dissolution of the Assembly or a Minister performing the functions of Chief Minister under clause (I) or clause (3) of Article 30.

(2) When the Assembly is dissolved a general election to the Assembly shall be held within a period of ninety days after the dissolution, and the result of the election shall be declared not later than fourteen days after the conclusion of the polls.

42. Speaker of the Assembly. – (1) After a general election, the Assembly shall, at its first meeting and to the exclusion of any other business, elect from amongst its members a Speaker and a Deputy Speaker of the Assembly.

Provided that the period intervening between the declaration of the official result of the election to the Assembly and the date for assumption of office of members shall not exceed thirty days.

(2) Before entering upon office, a member of the Assembly elected as Speaker or Deputy Speaker shall make before the Assembly an oath in the form set out in the First Schedule.

(3) All the proceedings of the Assembly shall be conducted in accordance with rules of procedures made by the Assembly and approved by the Governor.

(4) The Speaker shall preside the meetings of the Assembly except when a resolution for his removal from the office is being considered and, when the office of the Speaker is vacant, or the Speaker is absent, or is unable to perform his functions due to any cause, the Deputy Speaker shall act as Speaker and if at that time, the Deputy Speaker is also absent or is unable to act as Speaker due to any cause, such member of the Assembly present as may be determined by the Rules of Procedure of the Assembly shall preside at the meeting of the Assembly.

(5) Soon after as the office of Speaker or Deputy Speaker becomes vacant, the Assembly shall elect one of its members to fill the office.

(6) The Speaker may resign from his office by writing under his hand addressed to the Governor.

(7) The Deputy Speaker may resign his office by writing under his hand addressed to the Speaker.

(8) The office of the Speaker or Deputy Speaker shall become vacant if-
  (a) except as provided in clause (9) he ceases to be a member of the Assembly; or
  (b) he is removed from office by a resolution of the Assembly, of which not less than seven days' notice by not less than one-fourth of the total membership of the Assembly has been given and which is passed by a majority of total membership of the Assembly.

(9) When the Assembly is dissolved, the Speaker shall continue in his office till the person elected to fill the office by the next Assembly enters upon his office.

43. Voting in Assembly and quorum. – (1) Subject to this Order, -
  (a) a decision in the Assembly shall be taken by a majority of the votes of the members present and voting but the Speaker or the person presiding in his absence shall not vote except when there is an equality of votes in which case he shall exercise his casting vote;
  (b) the Assembly may act notwithstanding any vacancy in its membership; and
  (c) any proceedings in the Assembly shall not be invalid on the ground that some person who was not entitled to do so sit, voted or otherwise took part in the proceedings.

(2) If at any time during the meeting of the Assembly the attention of the person presiding at the meeting is drawn to the fact that number of the members is less than one-third of the total membership of the Assembly, it shall be the duty of the person presiding either to adjourn the meeting or to suspend the meeting till such number of members are present.

44. Restriction on discussion in Assembly, etc. – No discussion shall take place in the Assembly or the Council or the joint sitting with respect to matters relating to Foreign Affairs, Defence, Internal Security and Fiscal Plans of Government of Pakistan and the conduct of the any Judge of the Gilgit-Baltistan Supreme Appellate Court or the Gilgit-Baltistan Chief Court in the discharge of his duties.

45. Finance Committee. – (1) The expenditure of the Assembly within authorized appropriation shall be controlled by the Assembly acting on the advice of the Finance Committee.

(2) The Finance Committee shall consist of the Speaker, the Finance Minister and such other members as may be elected thereto by the Assembly.

46. Secretariat of the Assembly. – (1) The Assembly shall have a separate Secretariat.

(2) The Assembly may by law regulate the recruitment and conditions of service of persons appointed to the Secretariat Staff of the Assembly.

(3) Until provision is made by the Assembly under clause (2) the persons appointed to the Secretariat Staff of the Assembly shall continue to be governed by conditions of service for the time being applicable to them.

PART VII - DISTRIBUTION OF LEGISLATIVE POWERS

47. Legislative Powers. – (1) Subject to the succeeding provisions of this Article, both the Council and the Assembly shall have the power to make laws,-
- (a) for the territories of Gilgit-Baltistan;
- (b) for all citizens of Gilgit-Baltistan; and
- (c) for the officers of the Council or as the case may be, the Government, wherever they may be.

(2) Subject to clause (3):
- (a) the Council shall have exclusive power to make laws with respect to any matter in the Council Legislative List set out in the Third Schedule, hereinafter referred to as the Council Legislative List; and
- (b) the Assembly shall, and the Council shall not, have power to make laws with respect to any matter enumerated in the Fourth Schedule referred to as the Assembly Legislative List.
- (c) The Council shall have the powers to adopt any amendment in the existing Laws or any new Law in force in Pakistan.

(3) The Government of Pakistan shall have exclusive power to make laws in respect of any matter not enumerated in the Council Legislative List or the Assembly Legislative List by Order notified in the official Gazette.

48. Tax to be levied by laws only. – No tax shall be levied for the purposes of the territories of Gilgit-Baltistan except by or under the authority of an Act of the Council or the Assembly and all taxes and levies competently imposed under an Act of the Assembly or the Council or under any law made by the Government of Pakistan shall remain in force..

PART VIII - ISLAMIC PROVISIONS

49. No laws against Islamic Injunctions, etc. – No law shall be repugnant to the teachings and requirements of Islam as set out in the Holy Quran and Sunnah and all existing laws shall be brought in conformity with the Holy Quran and Sunnah.

50. Reference to Council of Islamic Ideology. – (1) If one-third of the total number of the members of the Assembly or, as the case may, the Council so requires, the Assembly or the Council shall refer to the Council of Islamic Ideology constituted under the Constitution of Islamic Republic of Pakistan (hereinafter referred to as the Islamic Council) for advice on any question as to whether a proposed law is or is not repugnant to the injunctions of Islam.

(2) When a question is referred by the Assembly or the Council, as the case may be, the Council of Islamic Ideology shall, within fifteen days thereof, inform the Assembly or the Council, as the case may be, of the period within which the Council of Islamic Ideology expects to be able to furnish that advice.

(3) Where the Assembly or, as the case may be, the Council considers that in the public interest, the making of the proposed law in relation to which the question arose should not be postponed until the advice of the Council of Islamic Ideology is furnished, the law may be made before the advice is furnished.

Provided that, where a law is referred for advice to the Council of Islamic Ideology and the Council advises that the law is repugnant to the injunctions of Islam, the Assembly or, as the case may be, the Council shall reconsider the law so made.

51. General provisions regarding Council, etc. – (1) The validity of any proceedings in the Council or the Assembly shall not be questioned in any Court.

(2) An officer or member or an authority in whom powers are vested for regulation of proceedings, conduct of business, maintain order in the Council or the Assembly shall not, in relation to exercise by him of any of those powers, be subject to the jurisdiction of any Court.

(3) A member of, or a person entitled to speak in, the Council or the Assembly, shall not be liable to any proceedings in any Court in respect of anything said by him or any vote given by him in the Council or the Assembly or in any Committee thereof.

(4) A person shall not be liable to any proceedings in any Court in respect of publication by or under the authority of the Council or the Assembly, of any report, paper, vote or proceedings.

(5) No process issued by a Court or other authority shall except with the leave of the Chairman of the Council or the Speaker be served or executed within the precincts of the place where a meeting of the Council or, as the case may be, the Assembly is being held.

(6) Subject to this Article, the privileges of the Council, the Assembly, the Committees and members of the Council, or the Assembly and of the persons entitled to speak in the Council, or the Assembly, may be determined by law.

52. Authentication of Bills Passed by the Council. – A Bill passed by the Council shall not require the assent of the Governor and shall, upon its authentication by the Chairman of the Council, become law and be called an Act of the Council.

53. Governor's assent to Bills. – (1) Subject to this Order, when a Bill has been passed by the Assembly it shall be presented to the Governor for assent.

(2) When a Bill is presented to the Governor for assent, the Governor shall, within thirty days,-
    (a) assent to the Bill; or
    (b) in the case of a Bill other then a Money Bill, return the Bill to the Assembly with a massage requesting that the Bill, or any specified provision thereof, be reconsidered and that any amendment specified in the message be considered.

(3) When the Governor has returned a Bill to the Assembly, it shall be reconsidered by the Assembly and, if it is again passed, with or without amendment, by the Assembly, by the votes of the majority of the members of the Assembly present and voting, and in accordance with the provision of this Order and in not in any manner prejudicial to the security, integrity, solidarity and strategic interest of Pakistan, it shall be again presented to the Governor and Governor shall not withhold assent therefrom.

(4) When the Governor has assented to a Bill, it shall become law and be called an Act of Assembly.

PART IX - FINANCIAL PROCEDURE

54. Council Consolidated Fund. – (1) All revenues received by the Council, all loans raised by the Council and all moneys received by it in payment of any loan shall form a part of Consolidated Fund, to be known as the Council Consolidated Fund.

(2) All other moneys –
   (a) received by or on behalf of the Council; or
   (b) received by or deposited with the Gilgit-Baltistan Supreme Appellate Court or any other Court established under the authority of this Order shall be credited to the Public Account of the Council.

(3) The Custody of the Council Consolidated Fund, the payment of money into that Fund, the withdrawal of money there from, the custody of other moneys received by or on behalf of the Council, their payment into, and withdrawal from the Public Account of the Council, and all matters connected with or ancillary to the matters aforesaid, shall be regulated by the Act of the Council or, until provision in that behalf is so made, by rules made by the Chairman of the Council.

(4) The Council shall, in respect of every financial year, cause to be prepared, and approve, a statement of estimated receipts and expenditure of the Council for that year.

(5) The Chairman of the Council shall authenticate by his signature the statement approved by the Council under clause (4), and no expenditure from the Council Consolidated Fund shall be deemed to be duly authorized unless it is specified in the statement so authenticated.

(6) If in respect of any financial year it is found:
   (a) that the amount authorized to be expended for a particular service for the current financial year is insufficient, or that a need has arisen for expenditure upon some new service not included in the statement referred to in clause (4) for that year; or
   (b) that any money has been spend on any service during a financial year in excess of the amount granted for that year, the Chairman of the Council shall have the power to authorize expenditure from the Council

Consolidated Fund and shall cause to be laid before the Council a supplementary statement or, as the case may be, an excess statement, setting out the amount of that expenditure, and the provision of clause (3) and (4) shall apply to theses statements as they apply to the statement referred to in clause (3).

(7) Notwithstanding anything contained in the foregoing provisions of this Article, the Council shall have power to make any grant in advance in respect of the estimated expenditure for a part of any financial year, not exceeding four months, pending completion of the procedure prescribed in clause (3) and (4).

55. Gilgit-Baltistan Consolidated Fund. – (1) All revenues received by the Government, all loans raised by the Government with the approval of Government of Pakistan and all moneys received by it in payment of any loan shall form a part of Consolidated Fund, to be known as the Gilgit-Baltistan Consolidated Fund.

(2) All other moneys –
 (a) received by or on behalf of the Government; or
 (b) received by or deposited with any other Court established under the authority of the Government, shall be credited to the Public Account of the Government.

(3) The custody of the Gilgit-Baltistan Consolidated Fund, the payment of money into that Fund, the withdrawal of money therefrom, the custody of other moneys received by or on behalf of the Government, their payment into, and withdrawal from the Public Account of the Government, and all matters connected with or ancillary to the matters aforesaid, shall be regulated by the Act of the Assembly or, until provision in that behalf is so made, by rules made by the Governor.

56. Budget. – (1) The Government shall, in respect of every financial year, cause to be laid before the Assembly a statement of estimated receipts and expenditure for that year, to be called the Annual Budget.

(2) The Annual Budget shall be submitted to the Assembly in the form of demands for grant and the Assembly shall have power to assent to, or to refuse to assent to any demand, or to assent to any demand subject to a reduction of the amount specified therein.

(3) No demand for a grant shall be made except on the recommendation of the Government.

(4) The Annual Budget as passed by the Assembly shall be placed before the Governor who shall authenticate it by his signature.

(5) If in respect of any financial year it is found:
 (a) that the amount authorized to be expended for a particular service for the current financial year is insufficient, or that a need has arisen for expenditure upon some new service not included in the Annual Budget

for that year; or
  (b) that any money has been spend on any service during a financial year in excess of the amount granted for that year, the Government shall have the power to authorize expenditure from the Gilgit-Baltistan Consolidated Fund and shall cause to be laid before the Assembly a Budget or, as the case may be, an excess Budget, setting out the amount of that expenditure, and the provisions of this Article shall apply to those Budgets as they apply to the Annual Budget.

(6) Notwithstanding anything contained in the foregoing provisions of this section, the Assembly shall have power to make any grant in advance in respect of the estimated expenditure for a part of any financial year, not exceeding four months, pending completion of the procedure prescribed in clause (2) for the voting of such grant and the authentication of the Budget as passed by the Assembly in accordance with the provisions of clause (4) in relation to the expenditure.

57. Special provisions regarding Budget, etc. – (1) Where the Annual Budget for any financial year cannot be passed by the Assembly by reason of its having been dissolved, the Chief Minister shall cause to be prepared an Annual Budget for that year and, by his signature, authenticate the Budget.

(2) The Annual Budget for any financial year authenticated by the Chief Minister under clause (1) shall, for the purpose of this Act, be deemed to have been passed by the Assembly.

58. Restriction on expenditure. – No expenditure shall be incurred by the Government except authorized by the Annual or Supplementary Budget as passed or deemed to have been passed by the Assembly.

PART X - ORDINANCE

59. Power to make Ordinance. – (1) The Governor may, except when the Assembly is in session, if satisfied that circumstances exist which render it necessary to take immediate action, make and promulgate an Ordinance as the circumstances may require.

(2) An Ordinance promulgated under this Article shall have the same force and effect as an Act of the Assembly and shall be subject to like restrictions as the power of the Assembly to make law, but every such Ordinance;
  (a) shall be laid before the Assembly and shall stand repealed at the expiration of four months from its promulgation or, if before the expiration of that period a resolution disapproving it is passed by the Assembly, upon the passing of that resolution; and
  (b) may be withdrawn at any time by the Governor.

(3) Without prejudice to the provisions of clause (2) an Ordinance laid before the Assembly or the Council shall be deemed to be a Bill introduced in the Assembly or the Council, as the case may be.

(4) The Governor shall likewise, except when the Council is in session, if so advised by the Chairman of the Council, make, promulgate and withdraw an Ordinance as the circumstances may require, and the provisions of clause (2) and clause (3) shall apply to an Ordinance so made as if references therein to 'Act of the Assembly and, Assembly were references respectively to' Act of the Council and Council.

PART XI - THE JUDICATURE

60. Gilgit-Baltistan Supreme Appellate Court. – (1) There shall be constituted a Gilgit-Baltistan Supreme Appellate Court, referred to as the Supreme Appellate Court to be the highest Court of Appeal.

(2) Subject to the provisions of this Order, the Supreme Appellate Court shall have such jurisdiction as is or may be conferred on it by this Order or by under any law.

(3) The Supreme Appellate Court shall consist of a Chief Judge to be known as Chief Judge of Gilgit-Baltistan and **two other Judges**:

Provided that the Government of Pakistan may from time to time increase the number of judges.

(4) The person holding office as Chief Judge or other Judge of the Supreme Appellate Court immediately before the commencement of this Order shall be deemed to be the Chief Judge or other Judge as the case may be appointed under this Order.

(5) The Chief Judge of Supreme Appellate Court shall be appointed by the Chairman of the Council on the advice of the Governor and other Judges shall be appointed by the Chairman on the advice of Governor after seeking views of the Chief Judge.

(6) A person shall not be appointed as the Chief Judge or Judge of the Supreme Appellate Court of Gilgit-Baltistan unless he:
- (a) has been a judge of Supreme Court of Pakistan or is qualified to be a judge of the Supreme Court of Pakistan; or
- (b) has for a period of, or for periods aggregating, not less than five years been a Judge of a Chief Court; or
- (c) for a period of or for periods aggregating, not less than fifteen years has been an advocate of a High Court.

Explanation. – In this sub-clause, the expression 'High Court' includes,-
- (a) the Chief Court of Gilgit-Baltistan, or an equivalent Court that existed in Gilgit-Baltistan before the 1st day of August, 2009; and
- (b) a High Court in Pakistan including a High Court that existed in Pakistan at any time before the 1st day of July, 2009.

(7) Before entering upon office, the Chief Judge of Gilgit-Baltistan shall make before the Governor and any other Judge of the Supreme Appellate Court of Gilgit-

Baltistan shall make before the Chief Judge, oath in the form set out in the First Schedule.

(8) The Chief Judge and judges of the Supreme Appellate Court of Gilgit-Baltistan shall be appointed for a term not exceeding three years and may be appointed for such further term as the Government of Pakistan may determine, unless they sooner resign or are removed from office in accordance with law.

(9) At any time when the office of Chief Judge of Gilgit-Baltistan is vacant, or the Chief Judge, is absent or unable to perform the functions of his office due to any other cause, the next senior Judge of the Supreme Appellate Court to act as Chief Judge of Gilgit-Baltistan.

(10) The remuneration and other terms and conditions of service of the Chief Judge and of a Judge of the Gilgit-Baltistan Supreme Appellate Court shall be such as are admissible to the Chief Justice of Pakistan and Judges of the Supreme Court of Pakistan.

(11) Subject to the succeeding provision of this Article, the Supreme Court of Gilgit-Baltistan shall have jurisdiction to hear and determine appeals from judgments, decrees, final orders or sentences of the Chief Court of Gilgit-Baltistan.

(12) An appeal shall lie to the Supreme Appellate Court of the Gilgit-Baltistan from any judgment, decree, final order or sentence of the Chief Court of Gilgit-Baltistan, –

    (a) if the Chief Court has on appeal reversed an order of acquittal of an accused person and sentenced to death or to imprisonment for life; or, on revision, has enhanced a sentence to a sentence as aforesaid; or.

    (b) if the Chief Court has withdrawn for trial before itself any case from any court subordinate to it and has in such trial convicted the accused person and sentenced him as aforesaid; or

    (c) if the Chief Court has imposed any punishment on any person for contempt of the Chief Court; or

    (d) if the amount or value of the subject matter of the dispute in the court of first instance was, and also in dispute in appeal is, not less than fifty thousand rupees or such other sum as may be specified in that behalf by Act of the Council and judgment, decree or final order appealed from has varied or set aside the judgment, decree or final order of the court immediately below; or

    (e) if the judgment, decree or final order involved directly or indirectly some claim or question respecting property or the like amount or value and the judgment, decree or final order appealed from has varied or set aside the judgment, decree or final order of the court immediately below; or

    (f) if the Chief Court certifies that the case involves a substantial question of law as to the interpretation of this Order.

(13) An appeal to the Gilgit-Baltistan Supreme Appellate Court of from a judgment, decree, order or sentence of the Chief Court in a case to which clause (11) does not apply shall lie only if the Supreme Appellate Court of grants leave to appeal.

(14)   (a)   an appeal to Gilgit-Baltistan the Supreme Appellate Court shall be heard by a Bench consisting of not less than two judges to be constituted or reconstituted by the Chief Judge;

       (b)   if the Judges hearing a petition or an appeal are divided in opinion, the opinion of majority shall prevail;

       (c)   if there is no such majority as aforesaid the petition or appeal, as the case may be, shall be placed for hearing and disposal before another Judge to be nominated by the Chief Judge:

Provided that in case of difference of opinion as aforesaid, the decision of the Supreme Appellate Court shall be expressed in term of opinion of the senior of the two Judges.

(15) The person holding office as Chief Judge of the Gilgit-Baltistan Supreme Appellate Court of Gilgit-Baltistan immediately before the commencement of this Order shall as from such commencement hold office as Chief Judge of Supreme Appellate Court under this Order on terms and conditions prescribed in this Order provided these are not inferior to the terms an conditions applicable to him immediately before such commencement.

(16) All legal proceedings pending in the Gilgit-Baltistan Supreme Appellate Court, immediately before the commencement of this Order, shall on such commencement, stand transferred to, and be deemed to be pending before the Supreme Appellate Court for determination and any judgment or order of the Supreme Appellate Court delivered or made before such commencement shall have the same force and effect as if it had been delivered or made by the Supreme Appellate Court.

61. Original Jurisdiction. – (1) Without prejudice to the provisions of Article-71, the Supreme Appellate Court, on an application of any aggrieved party, shall if it considers that a question of general public importance with reference to the enforcement of any of the fundamental right conferred by Part II of this Order is involved, have the power to make declaratory order of the nature mentioned in the said Article.

(2) An application made under clause (1) shall be heard by a Bench comprising not less than two Judges to be constituted by the Chief Judge.

62. Issue and execution of processes of Supreme Appellate Court. – (1) The Supreme Appellate Court shall have powers to issue such directions, orders or decrees as may be necessary for doing complete justice in any case or matter pending before it including an order for the purpose of securing the attendance of any person or the discovery or production of any document.

(2) Any such direction, order or decree shall be enforceable throughout Gilgit-Baltistan as if it has been issued by the Gilgit-Baltistan Chief Court.

(3) All executive and judicial authorities throughout Gilgit-Baltistan shall act in aid of the Supreme Appellate Court.

(4) Subject to this Order and Law, the Supreme Appellate Court may, in consultation with the Council, make rules regulating the practice and procedure of the Court:

Provided that till the new rules are framed, the rules framed by the Supreme Appellate Court shall, so far as they are not inconsistent with this Order and any other law, deemed to have been made by the Supreme Appellate Court until altered or amended and references to the Supreme Appellate Court in these rules shall be construed to be referred to the Supreme Appellate Court.

63. Decisions of Supreme Appellate Court binding on other Courts. – Any decision of the Supreme Appellate Court shall, to the extent that it decides a question of law or is based upon or enunciates a principle of law, be binding on all other Courts in the Gilgit-Baltistan.

64. Seat of the Supreme Appellate Court. – (1) The Seat of the Supreme Appellate Court shall be at Gilgit.

(2) The Supreme Appellate Court may sit at such other place or places as the Chief Judge of Gilgit-Baltistan, with the approval of the Governor, may appoint.

65. Review of judgment or order by the Supreme Appellate Court. – The Supreme Appellate Court shall have powers, subject to the provisions of an Act of the Assembly or the Council and of any rules made by the Supreme Appellate Court, to review any judgment pronounced or any order made by it.

66. Supreme Judicial Council. – (1) There shall be a Supreme Judicial Council of Gilgit-Baltistan.

(2) The Supreme Judicial Council shall consist of,_
   (a) the Chief Judge of Gilgit-Baltistan who shall be its Chairman.
   (b) the Senior Judge of the Supreme Appellate Court; and
   (c) the Chief Judge of the Chief Court .

(3) A Judge of the Supreme Appellate Court or of the Chief Court shall not be removed from office except as provided by this Article.

Explanation: The expression "Judge" includes the Chief Judge of Gilgit-Baltistan and the Chief Judge of Chief Court of Gilgit-Baltistan.

(4) If on information received from the Supreme Judicial Council or from any other source, the Chairman of the Gilgit-Baltistan Council or the Governor is of the opinion that a Judge of the Supreme Appellate Court or of the Chief Court,
   (a) may be incapable of properly performing the duties of his office by

reason of physical or mental incapacity; or

(b) may have been guilty of misconduct, the Chairman or the Governor, as the case may be, shall direct the Supreme Judicial Council to inquire into the matter.

(5) If, upon any matter inquired into by the Supreme Judicial Council, there is a difference of opinion amongst its members, the opinion of the majority shall prevail, and the report of the Supreme Judicial Council shall be expressed in terms of the view of the majority.

(6) If, after inquiring into the matter, the Supreme Judicial Council reports to the Chairman of the Gilgit-Baltistan Council that it is of the opinion.

(a) that the Judge is incapable of performing the duties of his office or has been guilty of misconduct; and

(b) that he should be removed from office, the Chairman shall advise the Governor to remove the Judge from his office and the Governor shall pass orders accordingly.

(7) The Supreme Judicial Council shall issue a Code of conduct to be observed by Judges of the Gilgit-Baltistan Supreme Appellate Court, and of the Gilgit-Baltistan Chief Court.

(8) If at any time the Supreme Judicial Council is inquiring the conduct of a Judge who is a member of the Supreme Judicial Council, or a member of the Supreme Judicial Council is absent or is unable to act due to illness or any other cause, than;

(a) If such member is the Chief Judge or the Judge of the Supreme Appellate Court the Judge of the Supreme Appellate Court who is next in seniority;

(b) If such member is the Chief Judge of Gilgit-Baltistan Court, the most senior most of the other Judges of the Chief Court, shall, act as a member of the Supreme Judicial Council in his place.

(9) If, upon any matter inquired into by the Supreme Judicial Council, there is a difference of opinion amongst its member, the opinion of the Supreme Judicial Council shall be expressed in terms of the view of the majority.

67. Power of Supreme Judicial Council to enforce attendance of persons, etc. –

(1) for the purpose of inquiring into any matter, the Supreme Judicial Council shall have the same powers as has the Supreme Appellate Court, to issue directions or order for securing the attendance of any person or the discovery or the production of any document and any such direction or order shall be enforceable as if it has been issued by the Supreme Appellate Court.

(2) The provisions of Article 60, shall, mutatis mutandis apply to the Supreme Judicial Council as they apply to the Gilgit-Baltistan Supreme Appellate Court and the Gilgit-Baltistan Chief Court.

68. Bar of Jurisdiction. – The proceedings before the Supreme Judicial Council, and the removal of a Judge under Article 66, shall not be called in question in any Court.

69. Gilgit-Baltistan Chief Court. – (1) There shall be a Gilgit-Baltistan Chief Court, hereinafter called the Chief Court, which shall consist of a Chief Judge and four other judges of whom 60% will be appointed from lawyers community and 40% from subordinate judiciary:

Provided that the Government of Pakistan may from time to time increase the number of judges.

(2) The function of the Chief Court may be performed by a Single Bench, a Division Bench or a Full Bench:, but the Chief Judge may recall a case pending before a Bench and make it over to another Bench or constitute a larger Bench for the purpose.

(3) In case of difference of opinion in a Full Bench, the opinion of the majority shall prevail;

(4) In case of difference of opinion in a Division Bench, the matter shall be referred to a third judge and the decision of the Chief Court shall be expressed in terms of judgment of the majority.

(5) The person holding office as Chief Judge or other Judge of the Chief Court Immediately before the commencement of this Order shall be deemed to be the Chief Judge or other Judge as the case may be appointed under this Order.

(6) The Chief Judge and Judges of the Chief Court shall be appointed by the Chairman of the Council on the advice of the Governor.

(7) A person shall not be appointed as a Judge of the Chief Court unless–
   (a) he has for a period, or for periods aggregating, not less than ten years, been an Advocate of the Chief Court or a High Court in Pakistan. Provided that the expression "High Court" herein shall include a High Court or an equivalent Court that existed at any time before the 1st day of August, 2009; or
   (b) he has for a period of not less than ten years held a judicial office out of which not less than three years shall have been as District and Sessions Judge.

(8) Before he enters upon his office, the Chief Judge of the Chief Court shall make before the Governor, and judge of the Chief Court shall make before the Chief Judge, an oath in the form set out in the First Schedule.

(9) The Chief Judge or a Judge of the Chief Court shall hold office until he attains the age of sixty two years, unless he sooner resigns or is removed from office in accordance with law:

Provided that the Chairman of the Gilgit-Baltistan Council may appoint a retired Judge of any High Court of Pakistan to be the Chief Judge or a Judge of the Chief Court for a period not exceeding three years and such person shall hold office till he attains the age of sixty-five years.

(10) If at any time any Judge of the Chief Court is absent or is unable to perform his functions due to illness or some other cause, the Chairman of the Gilgit- Baltistan Council may appoint a person qualified for appointment as a Judge of the Chief Court to be an Additional Judge for the period for which the Judge is absent or unable to perform his functions.

(11) A Judge of the Chief Court shall not, –
- (a) hold any other office of profit in the service of the Gilgit-Baltistan if his remuneration is thereby increased; or
- (b) occupy any other position carrying the right to remuneration for the rendering of services, but this clause shall not be construed as preventing a Judge from holding or managing private property.

(12) A person who has held office as Judge of the Chief Court shall not hold any office of profit in the service of Gilgit-Baltistan not being a Judicial or quasi-Judicial office or the office of Chief Election Commissioner or of Chairman or member of the Public Service Commission, before the expiration of two years after he ceased to hold that office.

(13) The remuneration and other terms and conditions of service of the Chief Judge and Judges of Chief Court shall be such as admissible the Chief Justice and the Judges of the High Courts of Pakistan.

70. Acting Chief Judge. – At any time when –
- (a) the Office of Chief Judge of Chief Court is vacant;
- (b) the Chief Judge of Chief Court is absent or is unable to perform the functions of his office due to any other cause, the Governor shall appoint the most senior Judge of the Chief Court to act as Chief Judge.

71. Jurisdiction of Chief Court. – (1) The Chief Court shall have such jurisdiction as is conferred on it by this Order or by any other law.

(2) Subject to this Order, the Chief Court may if it is satisfied that no other adequate remedy is provided by law, –
- (a) the Government, exercising any power or performing any function in, or in relation to, Gilgit-Baltistan as may be appropriate for the enforcement of any of the fundamental rights conferred by this Order. on the application of any aggrieved party, make an order, –
    - (i) directing a person performing functions in connection with the affairs of Gilgit-Baltistan or local authority to refrain from doing that which he is not permitted by law to do, or to do that which he is required by law to do; or
    - (ii) declaring that any act done or proceeding taken by a person performing functions in connection with the affairs of the Gilgit-Baltistan or a local authority has been done or taken without lawful authority, and is of no legal effect; or

    (b) on the application of any person, make an order, –
        (i) directing that a person in custody in Gilgit-Baltistan be brought before the Chief Court so that the Court may satisfy itself that he is not being held in custody without lawful authority or in an unlawful manner; or
        (ii) requiring a person holding or purporting to hold a public office in connection with the affairs of Gilgit-Baltistan to show under what authority of law he claims to hold that office; or
    (c) on the application of any aggrieved person, make an order giving such directions to the person or authority, including the Council.

(3) An order shall not be made under clause (2) on application made by or in relation to a person in the Armed Forces of Pakistan in respect of his terms and conditions of service, in respect of any matter arising out of his service or in respect of any action in relation to him as a member of the Armed Forces of Pakistan.

(4) Where, –
    (a) an application is made to the Chief Court for an order under sub-clause (a) or sub-clause (c) of clause (2); and
    (b) the Court has reason to believe that the making of an interim order would have the effect of prejudicing or interfering with the carrying out of a public work or otherwise being harmful to the public interest, the Court shall not make an interim order unless the Advocate-General has been given notice of the application and the Court, after the Advocate-General or any officer authorized by him in this behalf has been given an opportunity of being heard, is satisfied that the making of the interim order would not have the effect referred to in sub-clause (b) of this clause.

(5) In this Article unless the context otherwise requires, the expression "person" includes any body politic or corporate, any authority of or under control of the Council or the Government and any court or tribunal other than the Gilgit-Baltistan Supreme Appellate Court, the Chief court or a Court or tribunal establish under a law relating to the Armed Forces of Pakistan.

72. Rules of procedure. – Subject to this Order and law the Chief Court may in consultation with the Government, make rules regulating practice and procedure of the Court or of any Court subordinate to it.

73. Decision of Chief Court binding on subordinate Courts. – Subject to Article 47, any decision of Chief Court shall, to the extent that it decides a question of law or is based upon or enunciates a principle of law, be binding on all Courts subordinate to it.

74. Seat of the Chief Court. – (1) The permanent seat of the Chief Court shall be at Gilgit.

(2) The Chief Court may, from time to time, sit at such other place as the Chief Judge of the Chief Court, with the approval of the Governor, may appoint.

75. Contempt of Court. – (1) In this Article the expression "Court" means the Gilgit-Baltistan Supreme Appellate Court or the Chief Court.

(2) A Court shall have power to punish any person who –
   (a) abuses, interferes with or obstructs the process of the Court in any way or disobeys any order of the Court;
   (b) scandalizes the Court or otherwise does anything which tends to bring the Court or a judge of the Court into hatred, ridicule or contempt;
   (c) does anything which tends to prejudice the determination of a matter pending before the Court; or
   (d) does any other thing which, by law, constitutes contempt of the Court.

(3) The exercise of the power conferred on a Court by this Article may be regulated by law and, subject to law, by rules made by the Court.

76. The Chief Court to superintend and control all courts subordinate to it, etc. – (1) The Chief Court shall superintend and control all other courts that are subordinate to it.

(2) A Court so established shall have such jurisdiction as conferred on it by law.

(3) No Court shall have any jurisdiction which is not conferred on it by this Order or by or under any other law.

77. Advisory jurisdiction. – (1) If, at any time, the Chairman of the Council or the Governor desires to obtain the opinion of the Gilgit-Baltistan Supreme Appellate Court on any question of law which he considers of public importance, he may refer the question to the Supreme Appellate Court of Gilgit-Baltistan for consideration.

(2) The Gilgit-Baltistan Supreme Appellate Court shall consider a question so referred and report its opinion on the question to the Chairman of the Council or as the case may be, the Governor.

78. Administrative Courts and Tribunals. – (1) Notwithstanding any thing herein before contained, the Council in respect of matters to which its executive authority extends, and the Assembly in respect of matters to which the executive authority of the Government extends may by Act provide for the establishment of one or more Administrative Courts or Tribunals to exercise exclusive jurisdiction in respect of, –
   (a) matters relating to the terms and conditions of persons who are or have been in the service of Gilgit-Baltistan including disciplinary matters;
   (b) matters relating to claims arising from tortuous acts of the Council or the Government or any person in the service of Gilgit-Baltistan or of

any local or other authority empowered by law to levy any tax or cess and any servant or such authority acting in the discharge of his duties as such servant; or

(c) matters relating to acquisition, administration and disposal of any property which is deemed to be enemy property under any law.

(2) Notwithstanding anything herein before contained, where any Administrative Court of Tribunal is established under clause (1), no other Court shall grant an injunction, maker any order or entertain any proceedings in respect of any matter to which the jurisdiction of such Administrative Court or Tribunal extends and all proceedings in respect of any such matter which may be pending before such other court immediately before the establishment of the Administrative Court or Tribunal shall abate on such establishment.

(3) An appeal to the Gilgit-Baltistan Supreme Appellate Court from a judgment, decree, order or sentence of an Administrative Court or Tribunal shall lie only if the Supreme Appellate Court of Gilgit-Baltistan being satisfied, that the case involves a substantial question of law of public importance, grants leave to appeal.

79. Employees of Court. – The Gilgit-Baltistan Supreme Appellate Court and the Gilgit-Baltistan Chief Court, with the approval of the Governor, may make rules providing for the appointment of employees of the Court and for their terms and conditions of employment.

PART XII - SERVICES

80. Public Service Commission. – There shall be a Public Service Commission for Gilgit-Baltistan which shall consist of such number of members, including a Chairman to be appointed by the Chairman of the Council on the advice of Governor, and perform such functions as may be prescribed on such terms and conditions as may be determined by the Governor.

81. Services. – (1) Subject to this Order, the appointment of persons to, and the terms and conditions of service of persons in the service of Gilgit-Baltistan may be regulated by law.

(2) Until an Act of the Council in respect of persons in the service of Gilgit-Baltistan employed in connection with the affairs of the Council, or an Act of the Assembly in respect of such persons employed in connection with the affairs of the Government, makes provision for the matters referred to in clause (1), all rules and orders in force immediately before the commencement of this Order, shall continue to be in force and may be amended from time to time by the Council or, as the case may be, the Government.

(3) Notwithstanding anything contained in clause (1) or (2) the position or vacancy sharing formula between the Government of Gilgit-Baltistan and the Government of Pakistan, i.e. Gilgit-Baltistan Civil Service and All Pakistan Unified

Grades or District Management Group, shall be as specified in the Fifth Schedule.

82. Chief Election Commissioner. – There shall be a Chief Election Commissioner to be appointed by the Chairman of the Council on the advice of Governor on such terms and conditions as may be prescribed.

83. Auditor-General. – (1) There shall be an Auditor General of Gilgit-Baltistan who shall be appointed by the Governor on the advice of the Council.

(2) Before entering upon office, the Auditor General shall make before the Chief Judge of Gilgit-Baltistan oath in the form set out in the Schedule

(3) The terms and conditions of service, including the terms of office, of the Auditor-General shall be determined by Act of the Council and, until so determined, by rules made by the Council.

(4) The Auditor-General shall, in relation to –
- (a) the accounts of the Council and any authority or body established by the Council; and
- (b) the accounts of the Government and any authority or body established by the Government, perform such functions and exercise such powers as may be determined, by or under Act of the Council and, until so determined, by rules made by the Council.

(5) The accounts of the Council and of the Government shall be kept in such form and in accordance with such principles and methods as may be determined by the Auditor-General with the approval of the Council.

(6) The reports of the Auditor-General relating to the accounts of the Council shall be submitted to the Chairman of the Council; who shall cause them to be laid before the Council; and the reports of the Auditor-General relating to the accounts of the Government shall be submitted to the Governor who shall cause them to be laid before the Assembly.

PART XIII - GENERAL

84. Continuance of existing laws. – Subject to the provisions of this Order, all laws which immediately before the commencement of this Order, were in force in Gilgit-Baltistan shall continue to be in force until altered, repealed or amended by an Act, of the appropriate authority.

Explanation. – In this Article, –
- (a) The expression 'laws includes Ordinance, Orders, rules, bye-laws, regulations and any notification and other legal instruments having the force of law, and
- (b) The expression 'in force' in relation to any law, means having effect as law whether or not the law has been brought into operation.

85. General provision regarding Governor and Ministers. – (1) The Governor, the Chief Minister, a Minister or an Advisor shall not, –

(a) hold any other office of profit in the service of Gilgit-Baltistan or any other country; or

(b) occupy any other position carrying the right to remuneration for the rendering of services; but this action shall not be construed as preventing the Governor, the Chief Minister, a Minister or an Advisor from holding or managing his private property.

(2) No criminal proceedings whatsoever shall be instituted or continued against the Governor or the Chairman of the Council while he is in office.

(3) No civil proceedings in which relief is claimed against the Governor or the Chairman of the Council shall be instituted while he is in office in respect of anything done or not done, or purporting to have been done or not done, by him in his personal capacity, whether before or after he enters upon his office unless at least sixty days before the proceedings are instituted, notice in writing has been delivered to him, or sent to him, stating the nature of the proceedings, the cause of the action, the name, description and place of residence of the party by whom the proceedings are to be instituted and the relief which he claims.

(4) Except in relation to proceedings referred to in clause (3) no process whatsoever shall be issued from any court or tribunal against the Governor or the Chairman of the Council, whether in a personal capacity or otherwise, while he is in office.

(5) Subject to this Order, the Governor, the Chief Minister, the Chairman of the Council, the Federal Minister who is a member of the Council, a Minister or an Advisor shall not except in respect of anything done or not done by him in contravention of law, be answerable to any court or Tribunal in the exercise of the powers, or the performance of the duties, of his office or for any act done or purporting to be done by him in the exercise of those powers or in the performance of those duties:

Provided that nothing in this clause shall be construed as restricting the right of any person to bring appropriate proceedings against the Council or as the case may be, the Government.

86. Power to acquire property and to make contracts, etc. – (1) The executive authority of the Government and of the Council shall extend, subject to any Act of the appropriate authority to the grant, sale, disposition or mortgage of any property vested in, and to the purchase or acquisition of property on behalf of, the Government or as the case may be, the Council, and to the making of contracts.

(2) All property acquired for the purpose of the Government or of the Council shall vest in the Government or, as the case may be, in the Council.

(3) All contracts made in the exercise of the executive authority of the Government or of the Council shall be expressed to be made in the name of the Governor, or as the case may be, the Council and all such contracts and all assurances of property made in the exercise of that authority shall be executed on

behalf of the Governor or the Council by such persons and in such manner as the Governor, or as the case may be, the Council may direct or authorize.

(4) Neither the Governor, nor the Chairman of the Council, shall be personally liable in respect of any contract or assurance made or executed in the exercise of the executive authority of the Government or, as the case may be the Council, nor shall any person making or executing any such contract or assurance on behalf of any of them be personally liable in respect thereof.

(5) Transfer of land by the Government or the Council shall be regulated by law.

PART XIV - EMERGENCY PROVISIONS

87. Power to issue proclamation. – (1) If the Chairman of the Gilgit-Baltistan Council, on receipt of a report from Governor of Gilgit-Baltistan or otherwise, is satisfied that a grave emergency exists in which the security of Gilgit-Baltistan is threatened by war or external aggression or by internal disturbances, in which the Government of the Gilgit-Baltistan cannot be carried on in accordance with the provisions of this Order, Chairman of the Council shall issue Proclamation of Emergency, hereinafter referred to as the Proclamation.

(2) Assume to himself, or direct the Governor of the Gilgit-Baltistan to assume on behalf of the Chairman of the Council, all or any of the functions of the Government of the Gilgit-Baltistan, and all or any of the powers vested in, or exercisable by, any body or authority in the Gilgit-Baltistan, other than the Assembly;

(3) A Proclamation shall be laid before a Joint Sitting of the Council and the Assembly which shall be summoned by the Chairman of the Council on the advice of Governor to meet within thirty days of the Proclamation being issued and –

    (a) shall, cease to be in force at the expiration of two months unless before the expiration of that period it has been approved by a resolution of the Joint Sitting; and

    (b) shall, subject to the provisions of sub-clause (a), cease to be in force upon a resolution disapproving the resolution being passed by the votes of the majority of the total membership of the Joint Sitting.

(4) Notwithstanding anything contained in clause (2), if the Assembly stands dissolved at the time when the Proclamation is issued, the Proclamation shall continue in force for a period of four months but, if a general election to the Assembly is not held before the expiration of that period, it shall cease to be in force at the expiration of that period unless it has earlier been approved by a resolution of the Council.

(5) A Proclamation may be made before the actual occurrence of war or external aggression if the Governor is satisfied that there is imminent danger thereof.

88. Power to suspend fundamental rights. – (1) While a Proclamation is in operation, the Governor may, by order, declare that right to move any Court for the enforcement of such of the rights conferred by Chapter as may be specified in the order, and all proceedings pending in any Court for the enforcement of the rights so specified, shall remain suspended for the period during which the Proclamation is in force.

(2) Every order made under clause (1), shall, as soon as may be, laid before the Assembly.

89. Power to vary or rescind proclamation. – (1) A Proclamation issued under Article 87 may be varied or revoked by a subsequent Proclamation.

(2) The validity of any Proclamation issued or order made under Article 87 or Article 88 shall not be questioned in any Court.

90. Failure to comply with requirement as to time does not render an act invalid. – When any act or thing is required by this Order to be done within a particular period and it is not done within that period, the doing of the act or thing shall not be invalid or otherwise ineffective by reason only that it was not done within that period.

PART XV - MISCELLANEOUS

91. Oath of office. – (1) An oath required to be made by person under this Order shall be made in a language that is understood by that person.

(2) Where, under this Order, an oath is required to be made before a specified person and for any reason, it is impracticable for the oath to be made before that person, it may be made before such other person as may be nominated by that person.

(3) Where, under this Order, a person is required to make an oath before he enters upon an office, he shall be deemed to have entered upon the office on the day on which he makes the oath.

92. Order not to prejudice stance. – The provision of this Order shall not derogate form, or in any manner prejudice, the declared stand of the Government of Pakistan regarding the right of self-determination for the people of Jammu and Kashmir in accordance with the United Nations Resolutions.

93. Power to amend. – The Government of Pakistan may, by notified Order, amend the provisions of this Order.

94. Power to make rules. – The Governor or as the case may be, the Chairman of the Council, may make rules for carrying out the purposes of this Order.

95. Order to override other laws, etc. – (1) The provision of this Order shall have effect notwithstanding anything contained in the provisions of any law for the time being in force except that in case of conflict between the laws of Pakistan and the laws framed under this Order, the laws of Pakistan shall prevail.

(2) No Court, including the Gilgit-Baltistan Supreme Appellate Court and

the Gilgit-Baltistan Chief Court, shall call into question or permit to be called into question, the validity of this Order or an Act to amend it.

96. Repeal and saving. – (1) The Northern Areas Governance Order, 1994 hereinafter referred to as the said Order, together with the Orders amending it, and the rules made there-under are hereby repealed.

(2) On the commencement of this Order –
- (a) the Legislative Assembly in existence shall stand dissolved and General Election shall be held within one hundred and twenty days of such commencement; and
- (b) in all documents, proceedings and references, a reference to the expression "Northern Areas" shall mean and be construed as reference to "Gilgit-Baltistan."

97. Effect of repeal. – Where a law is repealed, or is deemed to have been repealed, by, under, or by virtue of this Order, the repeal shall not, except as otherwise provided in this Order:
- (a) revive anything not in force or existing at the time at which the repeal takes effect;
- (b) affect the previous operation of the law or anything duly done or suffered under the law;
- (c) affect any right, privilege, obligation or liability acquired, accrued or incurred under the law;
- (d) affect any penalty, forfeiture, or punishment incurred in respect of any offence committed against the law; or
- (e) affect any investigation, legal proceeding or remedy in respect of any such right, privilege, obligation, liability, penalty, forfeiture or punishment; and any such investigation, legal proceedings or remedy may be instituted, continued or enforced, and any such penalty, forfeiture or punishment may be imposed, as if the law had not been repealed.

FIRST SCHEDULE
OATH OF OFFICE GOVERNOR
[*See* Article 20(7)]

I,................................do hereby solemnly swear in the name of Allah;

That, as Governor of Gilgit-Baltistan, I will remain loyal to Pakistan;

That I will perform my functions as Governor honestly and faithfully; and

That I will not directly or indirectly communicate or reveal to any person any official secret which, may, come to my knowledge as Governor.

So help me Allah.

Signature of Governor

Place: ....
Date: ....

Signature of Chief Judge
Supreme Appellate Court, Gilgit-Baltistan

CHIEF MINISTER
[*See* Article 23(4)]

I,................................do hereby solemnly swear in the name of Allah;

That, as Chief Minister of Gilgit-Baltistan, I will remain loyal to Pakistan;

That I will perform my functions as Chief Minister honestly and faithfully; and

That I will not directly or indirectly communicate or reveal to any person any official secret which, may, come to my knowledge as Chief Minister;

So help me Allah.

Signature of Chief Minister

Place: ....
Date: ....

Signature of Governor
Gilgit-Baltistan

MINISTER

[*See* **Article** 24(2)]

I,…………………………..do hereby solemnly swear in the name of Allah;

That, as Minister of Gilgit-Baltistan, I will remain loyal to Pakistan;

That I will perform my functions as Minister honestly and faithfully; and

That I will not directly or indirectly communicate or reveal to any person any official secret which, may, come to my knowledge as Minister;

So help me Allah.

Signature of Minister

Place: ……………..

Date: ……………..

Signature of Governor
Gilgit-Baltistan

SPEAKER OR DEPUTY SPEAKER OF LEGISLATIVE ASSEMBLY

[*See* **Article** 42(2)]

I,…………………………..having been elected as Speaker or Deputy Speaker of Gilgit-Baltistan Legislative Assembly do hereby solemnly swear in the name of Allah;

That I will remain loyal to Pakistan;

That I will perform my functions as Speaker or Deputy Speaker of the Legislative Assembly honestly and faithfully; and

That I will not directly or indirectly communicate or reveal to any person any official secret which, may, come to my knowledge as Speaker or Deputy Speaker of the Assembly;

So help me Allah.

Signature of Speaker/Deputy Speaker

Place: ……………..

Date: ……………..

Signature of Outgoing Squeaker /Sitting Speaker
Gilgit-Baltistan Legislative Assembly

MEMBER OF LEGISLATIVE ASSEMBLY

[*See* **Article 36**]

I,................................having been elected as Member of Gilgit- Baltistan Legislative Assembly do hereby solemnly swear in the name of Allah;

That I will remain loyal to Pakistan;

That I will perform my functions as Member of the Legislative Assembly honestly and faithfully; and

That I will not directly or indirectly communicate or reveal to any person any official secret which, may, come to my knowledge as Member of the Legislative Assembly;

So help me Allah.

Signature of Member

Place: ....
Date: ....

Signature of Speaker
Gilgit-Baltistan Legislative Assembly

MEMBER OF GILGIT-BALTISTAN COUNCIL

[*See* **Article 33(11)**]

I,................................having been elected as Member of Gilgit- Baltistan Council do hereby solemnly swear in the name of Allah;

That I will remain loyal to Pakistan;

That I will perform my functions as Member of the Gilgit-Baltistan Council honestly and faithfully; and

That I will not directly or indirectly communicate or reveal to any person any official secret which, may, come to my knowledge as Member of the Council;

So help me Allah.

Signature of Member

Place: ....
Date: ....

Signature of Chairman/Vice Chairman
Gilgit-Baltistan Council

CHIEF JUDGE/JUDGE OF GILGIT – BALTISTAN SUPREME APPELLATE COURT

[*See* **Article 60(6)**]

I,................................having been appointed Chief Judge of Gilgit - Baltistan Supreme Appellate Court do solemnly swear and I will bear true faith and allegiance to Pakistan and that I will faithfully perform the duties of my office to the best of my ability, knowledge and judgment and will administer justice according to the law in force Gilgit- Baltistan, without fear or favour, affection or ill-will.

Signature of Chief Judge/Judge

Place: ....
Date: ....

Signature of Governor/Chief Judge
Gilgit-Baltistan

OATH OF CHIEF JUDGE/JUDGE OF GILGIT-BALTISTAN CHIEF COURT

[*See* **Article 69(8)**]

I,................................having been appointed Chief Judge of Gilgit-Baltistan Chief Court do solemnly swear that I owe allegiance to Allah and that I will faithfully perform the duties of my office to the best of my ability, knowledge and judgment and will administer justice according to the law in force in the Areas comprising Gilgit-Baltistan, without fear or favour, affection or ill-will.

Signature of Chief Judge/Judge

Place: ....
Date: ....

Signature of Governor/Chief Judge
Gilgit-Baltistan

OATH OF ADVISOR

[*See* **Article 33 (14)**]

I,.............................. do hereby solemnly swear in the name of Allah;

That I will remain loyal to Pakistan;

That I will perform my functions as Advisor honestly and faithfully; and

That I will not directly or indirectly communicate or reveal to any person any official secret which, may, come to my knowledge as Advisor;

So help me Allah.

Signature of Advisor

Place: ....

Date: ....

Signature of Chairman of Council
Gilgit-Baltistan

AUDITOR-GENERAL
[*See* Article 83]

I,.......................do hereby solemnly swear and bear true faith and allegiance to Pakistan.

That, as Auditor-General of the Areas comprising Gilgit- Baltistan, I will perform my functions honestly, faithfully, in accordance with the Gilgit-Baltistan (Empowerment and Self-Government) Order, 2009, and the law and to the best of my knowledge, ability and judgment, without fear or favour, affection or ill-will.

Signature of Auditor General

Place: ....

Date: ....

Signature of Chief Judge of Supreme Appellate Court
Gilgit-Baltistan

CHIEF ELECTION COMMISSIONER
[*See* Article 82]

I,.......................do hereby solemnly swear and bear true faith and allegiance to Pakistan.

That, as Chief Election Commissioner of the Areas comprising Gilgit-Baltistan, I will perform my functions honestly, faithfully, in accordance with the

Gilgit-Baltistan (Empowerment and Self-Government) Order, 2009, and the law and to the best of my knowledge, ability and judgment, without fear or favour, affection or ill-will.

Signature of Auditor General

Place: ....
Date: ....

Signature of Chief Judge of Supreme Appellate Court
Gilgit-Baltistan

SECOND SCHEDULE

[*See* Article 37(2)(d)]

1. An office, which is not a whole time office remunerated either by salary or by fee.
2. The office of Lamberdar, Inamdar, Sufedposh and Zaildar, whether called by this or any other title.
3. The office of the Chairman of any elective body constituted under any law relating to the Local Government.
4. Reserve of the Armed Forces.
5. Any other office which is declared by an Act of the Assembly not to disqualify its holder from being elected as, or from being a member of the Assembly.

THIRD SCHEDULE

COUNCIL LEGISLATIVE LIST

[*See* Article 47(2)(a)]

1. Post and telegraphs, including telephones, wireless, broad-casting and other like forms of communications; Post Office Saving Bank.
2. Public debt of the Council, including the borrowing of money on the security of the Council Consolidated Fund.
4. Council public services and Council Public Service Commission.

5. Council pensions, that is to say, pensions payable by the Council or out of the Council Consolidated Fund.
6. Administrative courts for Council subjects.
7. Council agencies and institutions for the following purpose, that is to say, for research, for professional or technical training, or for the promotion of special studies.
8. Nuclear energy, including:
   (a) mineral resources necessary for the generation of nuclear energy;
   (b) the production of nuclear fuels and the generation and use of nuclear energy; and
   (c) ionizing radiations.
9. Aircraft and air navigation; the provision of aerodromes; regulations and organization of air traffic and of aerodrome.
10. Beacons and other provisions for safety of aircraft.
11. Carriage of passengers and goods by air.
12. Copyright, inventions, designs, trade marks and merchandise marks.
13. Opium so far as regards sale for export.
14. Banking, that is to say, the co-ordination with the Government of Pakistan of the conduct of banking business.
15. The law for insurance and the regulation of the conduct of insurance business.
16. Stock-exchange and future markets with object and business not confined to the areas comprising Gilgit-Baltistan. .
17. Corporations, that is to say, the incorporation regulation and winding up of trading corporations including banking, insurance and financial corporations, but not including corporations owned or controlled by the Provincial Government of Gilgit-Baltistan and carrying on business, co-operative societies, and of corporations, whether trading or not, with object not confined to the Gilgit-Baltistan, but not including universities.
18. Planning for economic coordination, including planning and coordination of scientific and technological research.
19. Highways, continuing beyond the territory of the Gilgit-Baltistan excluding roads declared by the Government of Pakistan to be strategic importance.
20. Council surveys including geological surveys and Council meteorological organizations.
21. Works, lands and buildings vested in, or in the possession of the Council, for the purpose of the Council (not being Military, Naval or Air Force works), but as regards property situated in the Gilgit-Baltistan, subject always to law made by the Legislative Assembly, save in so far as law made by the Council otherwise provides.
22. Census.

23. Establishment of standards of weights and measures.
24. Extension of the powers and jurisdiction of members of a police force belonging to the Gilgit-Baltistan or any Province of Pakistan to any area in such Province or the Gilgit-Baltistan, but not so as to enable the police of the Gilgit-Baltistan or such province to exercise powers and jurisdiction in such Province or the Gilgit-Baltistan without the consent of the Government of that Province or the Gilgit-Baltistan; extension of the powers and jurisdiction of members of a police force belonging the Gilgit-Baltistan or a Province of Pakistan to railway areas outside the Gilgit-Baltistan or that Province.
25. Election to the Council.
26. The salaries, allowances and privileges of the members of the Council and Advisors.
27. Railways.
28. Mineral oil natural gas; liquids substances declared by law made by the Council to be dangerously inflammable.
29. Development of industries, where development under Council control is declared by law made by Council to be expedient in the public interest.
30. Removal of prisoners and accused persons from the Gilgit-Baltistan to Pakistan or from Pakistan to the Gilgit-Baltistan.
31. Measures to combat certain offences committed in connection with matters concerning the Council and the Government and the establishment of police force for that purpose or the extension to the Gilgit-Baltistan of the jurisdiction of police force established in Pakistan for the investigation of offences committed in connection, with matters concerning the Government of Pakistan.
32. Prevention of the extension from the Gilgit-Baltistan to Pakistan or from Pakistan to the Gilgit-Baltistan of infections or contagious diseases or pests affecting men, animals or plants.
33. Boilers.
34. Electricity and bulk water storage.
35. Newspapers, books and printing presses.
36. Works, lands and buildings vested, or in the possession of Government for the purpose of Gilgit-Baltistan Council (not being air force, military or navel works) save in so far as the Council Act otherwise provides.
37. Curriculum, syllabus, planning, policy, centers of excellence and standards of education.
38. Sanctioning of cinematography films for exhibition.
39. Tourism.
40 Forest.

41. Minerals and Mineral Wealth.
42. Duties of customs, including export duties.
43. Duties of excise, including duties on salt but not including duties on alcoholic liquors, opium and other narcotics.
44. Taxes on income other than agricultural income.
45. Taxes on corporations.
46. Taxes on the sale and purchases of goods and services imported, exported, produced, manufactured or consumed.
47. Taxes on the capital value of the assets, not including taxes on capital gains on immovable property.
48. Taxes and duties on the production capacity of any plant, machinery, under taking, establishment or installation in lieu of the taxes and duties specified in entries 42 and 43 or in lieu of either or both of them.
49. Terminal taxes on goods or passengers carried by railway or air, taxes on their fares and freights.
50. Fees in respect of any of the matters enumerated in this list, but not including fees taken in any court.
51. Jurisdiction and powers of all courts with respect to any of the matters enumerated in this list.
52. Offences against laws with respect to any of the matters enumerated in this list.
53. Inquires and statistics for the purpose of any of the matters enumerated in this list.
54. Matters which under the Act are within the legislative competence of the Council or relates to the Council.
55. Matter incidental or ancillary to any of the matters enumerated in this list.

FOURTH SCHEDULE
ASSEMBLY LEGISLATIVE LIST
[*See* **Article 47 (2) (b)**]

1. Public order (but not including the use of Naval, Military, Air Force, or any other armed forces of the Federation in aid of the civil power).
2. Preventive detention for reasons in connection with the maintenance of public order; persons subjected to such detention.
3. Prisons, reformatories, borstal institution and other institutions of a like nature and persons detained therein, arrangements with other provinces for the use of prisons and other institutions.
4. Land, that is to say, rights in or over land; land tenures, including the relation of landlord and tenant, and the collection of rents; transfer, alienation and devolution of agricultural land; land improvement and agricultural loans; colonization.
5. Land revenue, including the assessment and collection of revenue, the maintenance of land records, survey for revenue purpose and records of rights and alienation of revenues.
6. Works, lands and buildings vested in or in the possession of the Gilgit-Baltistan Administration.
7. Compulsory acquisition or requisitioning of property.
8. Agriculture, including agricultural education and research protection against pests and prevention of plant diseases.
9. Local Government, that is to say, the constitution and powers of municipal corporations, improvement trusts, district councils settlement authorities and other local authorities for the purpose of local self-government or village administration.
10. Preservation, protection and improvement of stock, and prevention of animal diseases; veterinary training and practice.
11. Pounds and the prevention of cattle trespass.
12. Drinking water supplies, irrigation and canals, drainage and embankments; flood control.
13. Libraries, museums and ancient and historical monuments.
14. Botanical, zoological and anthropological surveys.
15. Theaters; cinemas; sports; entertainments and amusements.
16. Public health and sanitation; hospitals and dispensaries.
17. Registration of births and deaths.
18. Burials and burial grounds; cremations and cremation grounds.
19. Relief of the disabled and un-employed.

20. Intoxicating liquors, that is to say, the production, manufacture, possession, transport, purchase and sale of intoxicating liquors and other narcotic drugs.
21. Markets and fairs.
22. Money lending and moneylenders; relief of indebtedness.
23. Protection of wild animals and birds.
24. Prevention of cruelty to animals.
25. Adulteration of food-stuff and other goods.
26. Betting and gambling.
27. Fisheries.
28. Professions.
29. Inns and in-keepers.
30. Orphanages and poor houses.
31. Taxes on agricultural income and on the value of agricultural land.
32. Lunacy and mental deficiency including places for reception of treatment of lunatics and mental deficient.
33. Duties in respect of succession to agricultural land.
34. Estate Duty in respect of agricultural land.
35. Taxes on lands and buildings.
36. Taxes on advertisement.
37. Taxes on goods and passengers carried by road or on inland waterways.
38. Taxes on vehicles, whether mechanically propelled or not, suitable for use on a road; on boats, launches and steamers on inland water; on tram cars.
39. Taxes on animals and boats.
40. Tolls.
41. Capitation taxes.
42. Taxes on luxuries, including entertainments and amusements. Taxes.
43. Taxes on profession, trades, callings and employment.
44. Relief of poor; un-employment.
45. Offences against laws with respect of any of the matters in this list.
46. Inquiries and statistics for the purpose of any of the matters in this list.
47. Cesses on the entry of goods into a local area for consumption, use or sale therein.
48. The salaries, allowances and privileges of the Speaker, Deputy Speaker, Chief Minister, Ministers and Members of the Assembly.
49. Dues on passengers and goods carried on roads or inland water-ways.
50. Management of Gilgit – Baltistan Consolidated Fund.
51. Environmental pollution and ecology.
52. Population planning and social welfare.
53. The setting up and carrying on of labour exchanges, employment information bureaus and training establishments.

54. Regulation of labour and safety in mines and factories.
55. Trade unions; industrial and labour disputes.
56. Gilgit–Baltistan public services and Public Service Commission.
57. Gilgit–Baltistan pensions, that is to say, pension payable out of Gilgit–Baltistan Consolidated Fund.
58. Administrative Courts for subjects within purview of Gilgit – Baltistan Legislative Assembly.
59. Gilgit–Baltistan agencies and institutions for the following purpose, that is to say, for research, for professional or technical training, or for the promotion of special studies.
60. Fees in respect of any of the matters enumerated in this list, but not including fees taken in any court.
61. Jurisdiction and powers of all Courts with respect to any of the matters enumerated in this list.

FIFTH SCHEDULE
SERVICES
[*See* Article 81]

Position or Vacancy Sharing Formula Between the Government of Pakistan and the Government of Gilgit-Baltistan

Government of Gilgit-Baltistan	APUG/DMG/APS	BS-17	BS-18	BS-19	BS-20	BS-21
		25%	40%	50%	60%	65%

N.B.: Percentage showing the share earmarked for APUG/DMG/APS, out of total number of vacancies in Gilgit-Baltistan (on the pattern of Federal Government and Provinces of Pakistan).
No. F. 3 (i)/2009 NA-I

(Muhammad Ikram)
Deputy Secretary (NA)

APPENDIX X

BALAWARISTAN NATIONAL FRONT

HEAD OFFICE: MAJINI MOHALLA, GILGIT, BALAWARISTAN
(Pakistan Occupied Gilgit Baltistan)

Date 22nd Dec. 2009
Ref......................

Mr. Jerzy BUZEK
President
European Parliament
Rue Wiertz PHS 11B011
B-1047 Brussels

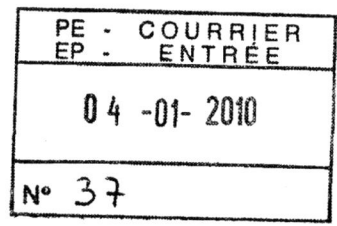

Sub: Xmas Greetings

I represent Balawaristan National Front (BNF) being exile here in Brussels because of the ISI threat to my life and I am also representative of a lonely nationalist alliance of Balawaristan (China and Pakistan Occupied Gilgit Baltistan) namely GBDA (Gilgit Baltistan Democratic Alliance) of an alliance consists of 6 indigenous parties, which demand for freedom and independence from the occupation of both Pakistan and China. I wish you all the best on the auspicious occasion of Holy Christmas on behalf of 2 million slave people of this world.

It's my pleasure as well as an honour for the 2 million people of Balawaristan (Pakistan and China Occupied Gilgit Baltistan), because European Union and its Parliament has shown its interest in this most deprived and neglected part of the world, who even have no right of representation and no access to Justice and Pakistani regime both Military and Civilians have been violating all kind of human political, economical, educational and fundamental rights since 16th Nov 1947 by violating UNCIP resolutions. This is the only part of the world where people have no place to go against human rights violation. The 2 million people of Gilgit Baltistan are very thankful of European Parliament resolution of 24th May 2007 by taking the issue of this part of the world seriously. EU resolution states that:

"19. Very much regrets the continuing ambivalence of the current Government of Pakistan with regard to the ethnic identity of Gilgit and Baltistan, whereby statements made by the President are contradicted by official government communications; strongly recommends that the Government of Pakistan endorse and Implement the judgment of the Supreme Court of Pakistan of 28 May 1999 which validates the Kashmiri heritage of the people of Court of Pakistan of 28 May 1999 which validates the Kashmiri heritage of the people of Gilgit and Baitistan and states that the Government should implement their fundamental human rights, democratic freedoms and access to justice;

20: the people of digit and Baitistan are under the direct rule of the military and enjoy no democracy."

The people of this disputed region are offering their gratitude to all the members of EP for the declaration passed Strasburg session before this Holy Christmas in Strasburg Session in which it raised serious concerns over Pakistan's proxy rule in Gilgit Baitistan.

We pray for prosperity and good health for you and your family.

Yours Sincerely,

Abdul Hamid Khan
Chairman
Balawaristan National Front (BNF)
Head Office: Majini Mania, Gilgit, Balawaristan (Pakistan Occupied Gilgit Baitistan)
Website: www.balawaristan.net
Email: Balawaristan@gmail.com, Balawaristan(£),hotmail.com
Present Add:
Avenue d'Auderghem 57/18
1040 Brussels
Tele/Fax: 022311750
Cell: 0488409035

Website: www.balawaristan.net
Email: balawaristan@usa.com balawaristan@gmail.com
Contact: Tel/Fax. 0032 22 311 750

FREEDOM   DEMOCRACY   JUSTICE

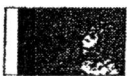

Abdul Hamid Khan
Chairman

BALAWARISTAN NATIONAL FRONT (BNF)
Head Office : Majini Mahla ,Gilgit , Balawaristan
(Pakistan Occupied Gilgit Baltistan)
www.balawaristan.net
balawaristan@gmail.com, balawaristan@hotmail.com

ADDRESS: Avenue Auderghem 57
Bt -18, Etterbeek 1040
Brussels Belgium
Tel/Fax : 0032 2 231 17 50
0032 488 40 90 35

Avenue d'Auderghem 57/18
1040 Etterbeek, Brussels,
Belgium

Mr. Jerzy BUZEK
President
European Parliament
Rue Wiertz PHS 11B011
B-1047 Brussels

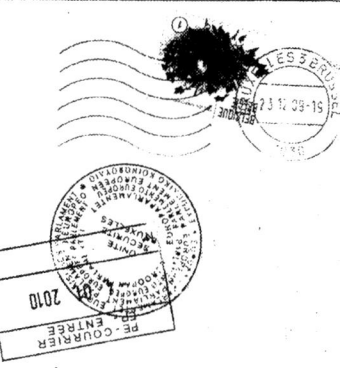

APPENDIX XI

Registered Political Parties of Gilgit-Baltistan with Election Symbols

S.No.	Name of Registered Political Party	Symbol Allotted	Symbol Name
01	All Pakistan Aam Admi Party		Star
02	All Pakistan Muslim League		Eagle
03	Gilgit-Baltistan Qoumi Movement Gilgit	...	Not mentioned by EC
04	Islami Tehreek Pakistan		Key with Lock
05	Jammat Islami Pakistan		Scale
06	Jamiat Ulmae Islam Pakistan		Book
07	Majlis Wahdat-e-Muslimeen Pakistan		Tent
08	Muttahida Qoumi Movement		Kite

Registered Political Parties of Gilgit-Baltistan with Election Symbols

S.No.	Name of Registered Political Party	Symbol Allotted	Symbol Name
09	Pakistan Awami Tehreek		Crescent
10	Pakistan Muslim League (N)		Tiger
11	Pakistan People's Party		Arrow
12	Pakistan Tehreek-e-Insaf		Bat
13	Qaumi Watan Party Pakistan		Chiragh/Lamp
14	Sunni Ittehad Council Pakistan		Horse

Source: http://ecgb.gov.pk/symbolalloted.htm

APPENDIX XII

Electoral Rolls of Gilgit-Baltistan Election 2015

Final Electoral Rolls Voter State

Districts	Male Voters		Male Voters	Female Voters
Gilgit	GBLA-1		16,849	13,548
Gilgit	GBLA-2		18,734	15,491
Gilgit	GBLA-3		18,226	16,187
		Total	53,809	45,226
Hunza Nagar	GBLA-4		10,024	8,794
Hunza Nagar	GBLA-5		6,353	5,639
Hunza Nagar	GBLA-6		18,931	17,486
		Total	35,308	31,919
Skardu	GBLA-7		8,871	7,613
Skardu	GBLA-8		18,461	15,820
Skardu	GBLA-9		11,070	9,510
Skardu	GBLA-10		11,316	10,490
Skardu	GBLA-11		11,766	10,192
Skardu	GBLA-12		15,806	14,607
		Total	77,290	68,232
Astore	GBLA-13		15,016	12,683
Astore	GBLA-14		12,916	11,536
		Total	27,932	24,219
Diamer	GBLA-15		13,238	13,842
Diamer	GBLA-16		15,439	12,498
Diamer	GBLA-17		13,063	12,559
Diamer	GBLA-18		8,936	6,764
		Total	50,676	45,663
Ghizer	GBLA-19		16,547	14,709
Ghizer	GBLA-20		18,695	15,705
Ghizer	GBLA-21		14,986	12,591
		Total	50228	43005
Ghanche	GBLA-22		13,079	11,642
Ghanche	GBLA-23		12,416	10,870
Ghanche	GBLA-24		8,737	8,113
		Total	34,232	30,625
	Grand	Total	329,475	288,889

©2015 Chief Election Commissioner Secretariate Gilgit-Baltistan.
http://ecgb.gov.pk/elecroll.htm.

APPENDIX XIII

Members of Gilgit-Baltistan Assembly

Members of Gilgit-Baltistan Legislative Assembly. Names of all elected members and their party affiliation of GilgitBaltistan Assembly 2015.

GBLA-01	Jaffarullah Khan	PMl-N
GBLA-02	Hafiz HafeezurRahman	PML-N
GBLA-03	Doctor Muhammad Iqbal	PML-N
GBLA-04	Doctor Muhammad Ali Haidar	ITP
GBLA-05	Rizwan Ali	MWM
GBLA-06	Shah Saleem Khan	PML-N
GBLA-07	Haji Akbar Khan Taban	PML-N
GBLA-08	KachoImtiazHaidar Khan	MWM
GBLA-09	Haji Fida Muhammad Nashad	PML-N
GBLA-10	Caption (R) Muhammad Sikandar	ITP
GBLA-11	Iqbal Hassan	PML-N
GBLA-12	Imran Nadeem	PPP
GBLA-13	Farman Ali	PML-N
GBLA-14	Barkat Jamil Siffat	PML-N
GBLA-15	Haji Shah Baig	JUl-F
GBLA-16	Janbaz Khan	PML-N
GBLA-17	Haidar Khan	PML-N
GBLA-18	Muhammad Wakeel	PML-N
GBLA-19	Nawaz Khan Naji	BNF
GBLA-20	Fida Khan	Independent
GBLA-21	Raja Jahanzaib	PTI
GBLA-22	Muhammad Ibrahim Sanai	PML-N
GBLA-23	GhulamHussain Advocate	PML-N
GBLA-24	MuhamamdShafiq	PML-N

Women Seats

1	Sherian Akhtar	PML-N
2	Nasreen Bano	PML-N
3	Rani Atiqa	PML-N
4	Sobia Jabein	PML-N
5	Rehana Abbadi	ITP
6	Bibi Saleema	MWM

Technocrat Seats

1	Aurungzaib Khan Advocate	PML-N
2	Major (R) Muhammad Amin	PML-N
3	Caption (R) Muhammad Shafi	ITP

Source: 2010-2016 www.pakinformation.com

APPENDIX XIV

Letters Exchanged Between Yasin Malik and Nawaz Sharif

Date: January 12, 2016

His Excellency
Muhammad Nawaz Sharif
Prime minister of Islamic republic of Pakistan

Assalam u Alaikum Warahmatullah

I take this opportunity to offer my good will and good faith to you. I am writing because media reports say that you are holding a meeting to discuss the future constitutional status of Gilgit Baltistan. I will pour my heart out with the hope you will see and appreciate the sentiment behind it.

Respected Prime Minister: reports say that on the 14th of January, your government is holding a meeting where the future of Gilgit Baltistan is going to be deliberated upon. Apprehensions have been raised in various quarters that your government may reach a consensus to merge Gilgit Baltistan with Pakistan. This will have implications on the dispute over Jammu and Kashmir. If Pakistan imposes its sovereign writ over Gilgit Baltistan, India will then have a political and moral right to integrate Kashmir with it. With one stroke, Pakistan will be helping India to consolidate its writ on Kashmir.

Respected Prime Minster: I, as someone who represents the aspirations and sentiments of the people of Jammu and Kashmir urge and appeal to you to stay away from such a course of action. It is not only political wisdom that makes me make this appeal but also respect for the sentiments, sacrifices and aspirations of Kashmiri people. From 1947 people of Jammu Kashmir have been striving for their birth right and lakhs of people have given their lives for this struggle in Kashmir, people have lost their near and dear ones, homes and yet people of Kashmir hold the struggle dear to their heart. If your government incorporates Gilgit Baltistan into Pakistan, and if as a consequence, India consolidates its hold in Kashmir, this would amount to a bartering of people's aspirations. Kashmir is not about territory. It is about rights of people. Bartering these rights for land means killing the aspirations of people.

Respected prime Minister: Media has reported that China Pakistan corridor is making you change the constitutional status of Gilgit Baltistan. Economic development is good but you have no moral right to make policy that will adversely affect the future of millions of Kashmiris. I know that Pakistan is in a phase of history that is delicate. But this does not mean trading people's rights. I know you in personal capacity. When you met me in Lahore, in 2009, you made some promises to me. I want to remind you of these promises. You clearly vindicated Kashmiri position on Gilgit Baltistan and opposed any proposal that will change its legal or constitutional status. I will also add that history is not made by small bargaining and territorial exchanges but by respecting the will of the people. The will of people in Kashmir is what everyone including your good self knows. History, morality and ethics dictate that will of people prevail. History also judges people in light of greatness and great achievements they make. So I urge you to take a long view of history and not short term interest.

I appeal you to think of the legacy you will leave if you become party to depriving people of their historical, political and moral rights for which they have given their lives. Bartering away territory for economic growth does not make you statesman. It is opportunity for you to become a statesman by not bowing to economic pressures. Become a statesman and resist short term temptations.

Thank you

Yours brotherly,
Muhammad Yasin Malik
Chairman
Jammu Kashmir Liberation Front (JKLF)

Copy of Yasin Malik's Letter in Urdu
12 January 2016

بسم اللہ الرحمن الرحیم

عزت مآب محترم المقام جناب محمد نواز شریف صاحب (حفظ اللہ تعالیٰ)

السلام علیکم و رحمۃ اللہ و برکاتہ

میں آپ کے لئے اپنی نیک خواہشات اور خیر خوابی کے جذبات پیش کرتا ہوں۔ میں آج یہ خط اسلئے رقم کر رہا ہوں کیونکہ کچھ اطلاعات ہیں کہ آپ کی حکومت عنقریب گلگت بلتستان کی آئینی حیثیت کے بارے میں ایک میٹنگ منعقد کر رہی ہے۔ میں اپنا دل آپ کے سامنے رکھ رہا ہوں اور امید رکھتا ہوں کہ آپ میرے جذبات کی قدر کریں گے

محترم وزیر اعظم پاکستان : اطلاعات ہیں کہ 14 جنوری 2016ء کو آپ کی حکومت گلگت بلتستان کے مستقبل کے حوالے سے ایک اجلاس منعقد کر رہی ہے ۔اس حوالے سے بہت سے حلقوں کے اندر خدشات ظاہر کئے جا رہے ہیں کہ آپ کی حکومت گلگت بلتستان کو پاکستان میں ضم کرنے کے لئے کسی قسم کی اتفاق رائے پیدا کرنا چاہتی ہے۔ اس فیصلے سے مسئلہ جموں کشمیر پر دوررس منفی نتائج مرتب ہوں گے ۔اگر پاکستان نے اپنی خودمختار عملداری کا اطلاق گلگت بلتستان کے خطے پر کر دیا تو بھارت کے پاس ایک سیاسی اور اخلاقی جواز ہو گا کہ وہ بھی اپنے زیر قبضہ کشمیر کے علاقوں کو بھارت کے اندر ضم کر دے۔ اس کا صاف مطلب ہو گا کہ پاکستان بیک جنبش قلم کشمیر پر بھارت کے قبضے کو مضبوط تر کرنے میں مدد کرے گا۔

جناب وزیر اعظم : میں ' بحیثیت جموں کشمیر کے عوام کے جذبات و احساسات کے ایک حقیقی ترجمان آپ پر زور دیتا ہوں اور آپ سے اپیل کرتا ہوں کہ آپ اس قسم کی کاوش سے دور رہیں۔ یہ میری سیاسی فراست ہی نہیں بلکہ کشمیریوں کے جذبات و احساسات اور قربانیوں کا عزت و وقار ہے جو مجھے یہ اپیل کرنے پر آبھار رہے ہیں۔ 1947 سے ہی جموں کشمیر کے لوگ اپنے بنیادی پیدائشی حق کے لئے جہد کر رہے ہیں اور اس دوران لاکھوں کشمیریوں نے اپنے جان کی قربانی بھی دی ہے۔ یہاں لوگوں نے اپنے عزیز و اقارب کو کھویا ہے ، اپنے گھر بار کو لٹایا ہے اور ابھی بھی کشمیر کے باسی اپنی جہد اور تحریک کو سینے سے لگائے ہوئے ہیں۔ اگر آپ کی حکومت گلگت بلتستان کو پاکستان کے اندر ضم کر دیتی ہے تو اس کے نتیجے میں اگر بھارت مقبوضہ کشمیر پر اپنے تسلط اور قبضے کو مستحکم بنانے میں کامیاب ہو جائے ' تو اس کا صاف مطلب یہ ہو گا کہ لوگوں کے جذبات و احساسات کا سودا کیا جا رہا ہے ۔ کشمیر کوئی سرحدی یا زمین کا تنازعہ نہیں ہے، یہ لوگوں کے حقوق کا مسئلہ ہے اور زمین کے لئے حقوق کا سودا کرنا لوگوں کے جذبات و احساسات کو قتل کر دینا ہے۔

محترم وزیر اعظم : میڈیا نئی اطلاعات میں کہا جا رہا ہے کہ چائنا پاکستان اکانامک کاریڈور کی وجہ سے آپ گلگت بلتستان کے آئینی حیثیت کو تبدیل کرنا چاہئے ہیں۔ معاشی ترقی بہت اچھی ہے لیکن آپ اس ضمن میں کوئی اخلاقی جواز نہیں رکھتے کہ آپ کوئی ایسی پالیسی اختیار کریں جو لاکھوں کروڑوں کشمیریوں کے مستقبل پر منفی اثرات مرتب کرے گا۔ میں جانتا ہوں اور ہمیں احساس ہے کہ پاکستان اس وقت تاریخ کے نازک دور سے گزر رہا ہے لیکن اس کا قطعاً یہ مطلب نہیں کہ آپ لوگوں کے جذبات کا سودا کریں۔ میں آپ کو ذاتی طور پر بھی جانتا ہوں۔ جب آپ 2009 میں مجھ سے لاہور میں ملاقی ہوئے تھے اور آپ نے میرے ساتھ کئی وعدے کیے تھے۔ میں آپ کو وہ سارے وعدے بھی یاد دلانا چاہتا ہوں۔ آپ نے صاف طور پر اس وقت گلگت بلتستان پر کشمیریوں کے موقف کو تسلیم کیا تھا اور گلگت بلتستان کی آئینی حیثیت کو تبدیل کرنے کی مخالفت کی تھی۔ میں یہاں پر ایک اور چیز شامل کرنا چاہتا ہوں کہ تاریخ معمولی قسم کی سوداباری اور علاقوں کی ادلا بدلی سے نہیں بنائی جاتی ہے بلکہ تاریخ میں نیک نامی لوگوں کے جذبات و احساسات کی قدر کر کے حاصل کی جا سکتی ہے۔ اور کشمیریوں کے جذبات و احساسات اور خواہشات سے سبھی بشمول آپ بخوبی واقف ہیں۔ تاریخ اور اخلاقیات ہمیں بتاتے ہیں کہ لوگوں کی خواہشات ہی بالآخر آجاتی ہیں۔ تاریخ کو انکی عظمت اور بڑے اہداف کی بناء پر یاد رکھتی ہے اسلئے میں آپ سے اپیل کرتا ہوں کہ آپ تاریخ کی لمبی سوچ رکھیں اور مختصر وقتی مفادات کو ترک کر دیں۔

میں آپ سے اپیل کرتا ہوں کہ آپ اس میراث کو سمجھیں جو آپ لوگوں کو انکے تاریخی، سیاسی، اور اخلاقی حقوق سے محروم نہیں بن سکتا ۔ یہ آپ statesman کر کے اپنے پیچھے چھوڑیں گے ۔ معاشی ترقی کے لئے زمین کا سودا کرنے سے کوئی statesman نہیں بنتا۔ یہ موقع ہے کہ آپ معاشی دباؤ کے سامنے سر تسلیم خم نہ کریں اور آپ ایک statesman کے لئے ایک اور مختصر وقتی ترغیبات کو ترک کر دیں۔ شکریہ

آپ کا بھائی

محمد یاسین ملک ، چیرمین جموں کشمیر لبریشن فرنٹ

(Available at https://www.facebook.com/YasinMalikJKLF/photos/yasin-malik-writes-letter-to-nawaz-shareef-on-gilgit-baltistanhis-excellency-muh/1169014663126717/)

بِسْمِ اللهِ الرَّحْمٰنِ الرَّحِيْمِ

Islamabad
18th March 2016

PRIME MINISTER

Dear Yasin Malik Sahib,

I have received your letter with great pleasure and read it with deep interest.

I appreciate your views on the impact of any possible change in the constitutional status of Gilgit-Baltistan on the Kashmir cause. Your concerns and suggestions are valuable and are being examined with meticulous care.

I would like to make it unambiguously clear that Pakistan is fully aware of the sensitivities attached to Gilgit-Baltistan with regard to the Jammu & Kashmir dispute. Media speculations are a result of either misperceptions, or misinterpretations. The reforms intended in Gilgit-Baltistan are aimed at empowering the people of this region and giving them a greater say in their governance.

I would like to assure you that Pakistan will never compromise on its principled stance on the Jammu and Kashmir dispute, which is based on the UN Security Council resolutions. Nor will Pakistan take any measure that may cause harm to the valiant struggle of the people of Indian Occupied Jammu and Kashmir, for their inalienable right to self-determination, promised to them by the UN Security Council resolutions.

You may rest assured of Pakistan's continued moral, diplomatic and political support for the just resolution of the Kashmir issue, in accordance with the UN Security Council resolutions and the aspirations of its people.

With warmest wishes,

Hoping to see you soon.

Yours sincerely,

(Muhammad Nawaz Sharif)

Mr. Muhammad Yasin Malik,
Chairman,
Jammu Kashmir Liberation Front
Srinagar, Jammu Kashmir

APPENDIX XV

Pakistan Supreme Court Order on Gilgit Baltistan on 17 January 2019

(Available at http://www.supremecourt.gov.pk/web/user_files/File/Const.P._50_2018.pdf)

IN THE SUPREME COURT OF PAKISTAN
(ORIGINAL JURISDICTION)

PRESENT: MR. JUSTICE MIAN SAQIB NISAR, HCJ MR. JUSTICE SH. AZMAT SAEED

MR. JUSTICE UMAR ATA BANDIAL MR. JUSTICE FAISAL ARAB

MR. JUSTICE IJAZ UL AHSAN MR. JUSTICE SAJJAD ALI SHAH MR. JUSTICE MUNIB AKHTAR

CONST. PETITIONS NO.50/2018, 51/2018 & 63/2011, CIVIL MISC. APPLICATIONS NO.4922, 5382/2011, 695/2012 & 724/2017 IN CONST. PETITION NO.63/2011, CONST. PETITIONS NO.6/2012, 16/2015 & 20/2015, CIVIL MISC. APPLICATION NO.6966/2017 IN CONST. PETITION NO. 20/2015, CONST. PETITION NO.3/2016, CIVIL MISC. APPLICATION NO.6800/2017 IN CONST. PETITION NO.3/2016, CONST. PETITION NO.13/2016, 32/2016, 34/2016, CIVIL MISC. APPEAL NO.184/2016 IN CONST. PETITION NO.NIL/2016, CIVIL MISC. APPLICATION 7367/2016 IN CONST. PETITION NO.2/2017, 30/2017, 41/2018, CIVIL MISC. APPEAL NO.202/2016 IN CONST. PETITION NO.NIL/2016, CONST. PETITION NO.49/2018, 55/2018, 30/2015, 31/2015 32/2015, 36/2015, 64/2015, 6/2017 IN CIVIL MISC. APPEAL NO.31/2017, CONST. PETITION NO.61/2017 IN CIVIL MISC. APPEAL NO.243/2017, CONST. PETITION NO.18/2018 AND CIVIL MISC. APPLICATION NO.10872/2018 IN CONST. PETITION NO.16/2015

Const.P.50/2018:	Civil Aviation Authority Vs. Supreme Appellate Court Gilgit Baltistan etc.
Const.P.51/2018:	Prince Saleem Khan Vs. Registrar Supreme Appellate Court Gilgit Baltistan etc.
Const.P.63/2011:	Dr. Ghulam Abbas Vs. Federation of Pakistan etc.

C.M.A.4922/2011: in Const.P.63/2011	Application for impleadment by Supreme Appellate Court Bar Association Gilgit-Baltistan
C.M.A.5382/2011: in Const.P.63/2011	Application for Impleadment Dolat Jan
C.M.A.695/2012: in Const.P.63/2011	Application for Impleadment by Wazir Farman Ali
C.M.A.724/2017: in Const.P.63/2011	Application for Impleadment by Taqdir Ali Khan Vs. Federation of Pakistan and others
Const.P.6/2012:	Gilgit Baltistan Chief Court Bar Association through its Vice President Vs. Federation of Pakistan etc.
Const.P.16/2015:	Gilgit Baltistan, Bar Council through its Vice Chairman Vs. Federation of Pakistan etc.
Const.P.20/2015:	Gilgit Baltistan, Supreme Appellate Court Bar Association Vs. Federation of Pakistan etc.
C.M.A.6966/2017: in Const.P.20/2015	Gilgit Baltistan, Supreme Appellate Court Bar
Const.P.3/2016:	Association Vs. Federation of Pakistan & others
C.M.A.6800/2017: in Const.P.3/2016	Shaheen Air International Ltd., Karachi Vs. The Registrar, Supreme Appellate Court, Gilgit-Baltistan etc. Shaheen Air International Ltd. Karachi Vs. The Registrar, Supreme Appellate Court, Gilgit-Baltistan & others
Const.P.13/2016:	Zafar Ali Khan Maqpoon Vs. Government of Pakistan etc.
Const.P.32/2016:	Muhammad Ibrahim Vs. Fed. of Pakistan etc.
Const.P.34/2016:	Pak Agricultural Research Council Vs. Govt. of GB through Chief Secretary, Gilgit Baltistan etc.
C.M.Appeal.184/2016: in Const.P.Nil/2016	Pak Agricultural Research Council Vs. Govt. of GB through Chief Secretary, Gilgit Baltistan & others
C.M.A.7367/2016: in Const.P.34/2016	Pak Agricultural Research Council Vs. Govt. of GB through Chief Secretary, Gilgit Baltistan & others
Const.P.2/2017:	Federal Board of Intermediate & Secondary Educations through its Chairman & another Vs. Federations of Pakistan through M/o Kashmir Affair & Northern Areas etc.
Const.P.30/2017:	Chairman F.B.R., Islamabad Vs. Registrar Supreme Appellate Court, Gilgit Baltistan
Const.P.41/2018:	Federation of Pakistan through Secretary Ministry of Kashmir Affairs and Gilgit Baltistan, Islamabad Vs. Registrar Supreme Appellate Court, Gilgit-Baltistan & another
C.M.Appeal.202/2016: in Const.P.Nil/2016	Air Blue Company Ltd. Vs. The Registrar S.C. Appellate Court Gilgit-Baltistan

Const.P.49/2018:	Federation of Pakistan through Secretary Ministry of Kashmir Affairs and Gilgit Baltistan, Islamabad & another Vs. The Registrar Supreme Appellate Court, Gilgit-Baltistan etc.
Const.P.55/2018:	Gilgit Baltistan Bar Council & another Vs. Federation of Pakistan etc.
Const.P.30/2015:	Amna Ansari & another Vs. Chairman Gilgit-Baltistan Council etc.
Const.P.31/2015:	Amna Ansari & another Vs. Chairman Gilgit-Baltistan Council etc.
Const.P.32/2015:	Amna Ansari & another Vs. Chairman Gilgit-Baltistan Council etc.
Const.P.36/2015:	Ameer Khan Vs. Federation of Pakistan etc.
Const.P.64/2015:	Prof. Abdul Rasheed Mian etc. Vs. Federation of Pakistan through Secretary M/o Health Services Regulations and Coordination, Islamabad etc.
Const.P.6/2017:	Pakistan Tourism Development Corporation Vs. Registrar Supreme Appellate Court & another
Const.P.61/2017:	Hotels and Restaurants Association of Gilgit-Baltistan & another Vs. Federation of Pakistan through Secy. Cabinet Division, Islamabad etc.
Const.P.18/2018:	Abdul Qayyum Khan Vs. Ministry of Kashmir Affairs & Gilgit-Baltistan through its Secretary, Islamabad etc.
C.M.Appeal.10872/ 2018 in Const.P.16/2015:	Impleadment application by Lt. Co. (R) Syed Iqbal Hashmi
For the petitioner(s):	Mr. Salam Akram Raja, ASC Syed Rifaqat Hussain Shah, AOR **(In Const.P.6/2012, 20/2015 & 55 of 2018 & 64/2015)**
	Mian Shafaqat Jan, ASC Syed Rafaqat Hussain Shah, AOR **(In Const.P.50/2016 & Const.P.18 of 2018)**
	Barrister Masroor Shah, ASC **(In Const.P.51/2011)**
	Mr. Ikram Chaudhry, ASC **(In Const.P.63/2011)**
	Rai M. Nawaz Kharal, ASC Syed Rifaqat Hussain Shah, AOR **(In Const.Ps.16/2015 & 61/2017 & C.M.A.6966/2017)**

	Mr. Bhajandas Tejwani, ASC Ch. Akhtar Ali, AOR **(In Const.P.3/2016)**
	Syed Qalb-i-Hassan, ASC **(In Const.P.13/2016)**
	Mian Shafaqat Jan, ASC **(In Const.P.32/2016)**
	Nemo **(In Const.P.34/2016)**
	Mr. Mir Afzal Malik, ASC Mr. Tariq Aziz, AOR **(In Const.P.2/2017)**
	Mr. Ghulam Shoaib Jally, ASC **(In Const.P.30/2017)**
	Mr. Sajid Ilyas Bhatti, Addl. A.G.P. **(In Const.Ps.41 & 49/2018)**
	Mr. Asif Fasih ud Din Vardag, ASC Ch. Akhtar Ali, AOR **(In Const.Ps.30 & 32/2015)**
	Mr. M. Munir Peracha, ASC Mr. Mehmood A. Sheikh, AOR **(In Const.P.6/2017)**
	Nemo **(In Const.P.36/2015)**
	Mr. M. Ikhlaque Awan, ASC **(In C.M.A.5382/2011 & C.M.Appeal 202/2018)**
On Court's notice:	Mr. Anwar Mansoor Khan, A.G.P. Amicus Curiae: Ch. Aitzaz Ahsan, Sr. ASC
For the respondent(s):	Mr. Saeed Iqbal, Dy. A.G. Gilgit-Baltistan Mr. Aurangzeb Khan, Minister of Law & Parliamentary Affairs, Gilgit Baltistan
	Mr. Dil Muhammad Khan Alizai, ASC Ch. Afrasiab Khan, ASC **(For respondent No.2 in Const.P.49/2018)**
	Mr. M. Iqbal Hashmi, Advocate in person **(in C.M.A.10872/2018)**
	Mr. Waseem Sajjad, Sr. ASC **(For respondent in Const.P.63/11)**
	Raja Abdul Ghafoor, AOR **(For the Federation)**
	Mr. Abdullah Baig **(Respondent in person)**
Date of hearing:	7.01.2019

ORDER

MIAN SAQIB NISAR, CJ. – Succinctly, the instant matters pertain to a very important historical and constitutional issue involving the status, authority and powers of Gilgit-Baltistan (GB) including the judiciary and the rights available to its people. Although similar issues emanate from the various constitution petitions filed before this Court, it would be pertinent to briefly discuss the factual background of each case before proceeding further, –

  i. In Constitution Petition No.63/2011, the petitioner who is a political and social activist, seeks the enforcement of the independence of the judiciary in GB and thus challenges the *vires* of the Gilgit-Baltistan Empowerment and Self-Governance Order 2009 *(2009 Order) (and the Gilgit Baltistan Order, 2018 (2018 Order) by amendment of the petition through a C.M.A.)* in light of Article 175 and 203 of the Constitution of the Islamic Republic of Pakistan, 1973 *(Constitution)*;

  ii. In Constitution Petition No.6/2012, the GB Chief Court Bar Association claims that the 2009 Order did not make sufficient provisions for the appointment of judges to the GB Supreme Appellate Court and this oversight threatens the establishment of an independent judiciary in GB and thus the *vires* of the relevant provisions *[Articles 60(5), (6) and (8) of the 2009 Order]* have been challenged.

  iii. In Constitution Petition No.16 and 20/2015, the petitioner, GB Bar Council *(in both the petitions)* seeks appropriate directions to the respondents to arrange for issuance of an order contemplated by Article 258 of the Constitution read with Article 1(2)(d) thereof, to provide for good governance for GB in compliance with the direction already issued by this Court in paragraph No.28 of the judgment reported as **Al-Jehad Trust through Habibul Wahab Al-Khairi, Advocate and 9 others Vs. Federation of Pakistan through Secretary, Ministry of Kashmir Affairs, Islamabad and 3 others (1999 SCMR 1379)** to enforce fundamental rights;

  iv. In Constitution Petitions No.30, 31, 32 and 36/2015 the petitioner challenged the appointments of the Chief Election Commissioner GB, Governor of GB and the Chief Minister of GB made under the 2009 Order and sought a declaration to the effect that the said Order was *ultra vires* and the fundamental rights extended to the people of GB be enforced;

  v. Petitioners No.1 and 2 in Constitutional Petition No.64/2015 are faculty members of various medical colleges and petitioners No.1, 3 and 4 are also members of the Pakistan Medical and Dental Council *(PMDC)*. Through the instant petition they claim that Section 2 of the PMDC

(Amendment) Ordinance, 2015 on account of being discriminatory to the people of Azad Jammu and Kashmir and GB be declared *ultra vires* of Article 25 of the Constitution, fresh elections be announced for members of council of PMDC and Regulation No.9(2) of the PMDC Regulations 2015 be declared unreasonable, arbitrary and of no legal effect;

vi. In Constitutional Petition No.2/2016 the judgments against the Federal Board of Intermediate & Secondary Education by the lower fora were upheld by the GB Supreme Appellate Court. Through the instant petition, the impugned judgment was sought to be declared as beyond the jurisdiction of the said Court and the declaration that no civil proceedings may be initiated against it in the territory of GB and any such proceedings should have no legal effect;

vii. In Constitutional Petition No.3/2016, the petitioner Shaheen Airline Limited was issued directions in Suo Moto Case No.2/2009 by the Supreme Appellate Court to operate flights to Gilgit Baltistan despite it not being commercially feasible for the petitioner. Through this petition, the petitioner seeks that the said *suo moto* proceedings and all the orders issued therein be declared unconstitutional, *ultra vires* of the Constitution and void ab initio;

viii. In Constitutional Petition No.13/2016, the petitioner, *inter alia*, seeks the implementation of the judgment passed in **Al-Jehad Trust**'s case *(supra)* as well as the declaration that the 2009 Order is *ultra vires* of the Constitution and has no legal value unless the Constitution is amended;

ix. In Constitutional Petition No.34/2016, the Pakistan Agriculture Research Council seeks reversal of the transfer of 24 *kanals* and 3 *marlas* to Pakistan State Oil under the mistaken belief that the said land was owned by the Government of GB whereas according to the petitioner the said land was owned by the Government of Pakistan and could not be unilaterally so transferred. The said matter was *sub judice* when it was taken up in suo moto proceedings by the GB Supreme Appellate Court in S.M.C. No.8 of 2016 and directions have been issued to facilitate said transfer. The petitioner seeks, *inter alia*, that the jurisdiction of the said Court be outlined in light of the Constitution of Pakistan and the said transfer of land be declared void and without lawful authority.

x. In Constitutional Petition No.3/2016, the petitioner, *inter alia*, seeks implementation of the **Al-Jehad Trust**'s case *(supra)* as well as the declaration that Order 2009 is ultra vires of the Constitution and has no legal value unless the Constitution is amended and therefore should be declared ultra vires;

xi. In Constitutional Petition No.6/2017, there was a dispute regarding *shamlat* land measuring 30 *kanals* in Satpara Lake which the Pakistan Tourism and Development Corporation *(PTDC)* wanted to acquire. *Vide* impugned order dated 19.11.2015 in S.M.C. No.3/2009, this Court issued directions to PTDC to bring its work at the Satpara Lake in conformity with the environmental standards it laid out which directions the PTDC states that it has complied with. Subsequently, through suo moto case No. 2/2016, the GB Supreme Appellate Court passed a series of adverse orders against PTDC. The petitioner seeks, *inter alia*, that the proceedings be declared illegal, unconstitutional and coram non judice and be quashed.

xii. In Constitutional Petition No.30/2017, the Federal Board of Revenue, Islamabad, Pakistan *(petitioner)* seeks a declaration by this Court that the GB Supreme Appellate Court exceeded its jurisdiction when in suo moto case No.11/2010 it passed orders issuing notices and orders to and against the petitioner, declaring the same to be unconstitutional, coram non judice and consequently quash the same;

xiii. In Constitutional Petition No.61/2017, the petitioner is a representative body of Hotels and Restaurants in GB which seeks the implementation of the **Al-Jehad Trust** case *(supra)* which, *inter alia*, provides for the right of access to justice and independence of judiciary to the people of GB. Thus directions are sought from this Court to implement the same in letter and spirit;

xiv. In Constitutional Petition No.49/2018, the Supreme Appellate Court of GB after taking cognizance of the matter *vide* judgment dated 13.7.2018 set aside the 2018 Order. The Federation of Pakistan through the instant petition seeks that the said judgment be set aside and such action of the said Court be declared unconstitutional and beyond its jurisdiction;

xv. In Constitutional Petition No.51/2018, the petitioner seeks the quashment of the impugned judgment wherein the GB Supreme Appellate Court declared the by-election held in petitioner's constituency to be void, illegal and without any legal authority, thus it was set aside seeking *inter alia* that: (1) the GB Supreme Appellate Court exceeded its jurisdiction by taking *suo motu* notice under Article 61 read with Article 95 of the 2009 Order; (2) *suo motu* notice was taken of a fact not pleaded in the *lis*; (3) the impugned judgement is per incuriam for having been rendered in derogation of the express words used in Article 61 of the 2009 Order;

xvi. In Constitutional Petition No.55/2018, the petitioner, GB Bar Council, *inter alia*, seek that the 2018 Order be declared illegal, void ab initio and without legal authority;

xvii. In Constitutional Petition No.50/2018, the Petitioners, Civil Aviation Authority seek that the declaration that the jurisdiction of the Chief Court in terms of article 71 of the 2009 Order is only to the extent of the Government of GB therefore the latter does not have the jurisdiction to issue writs/directions to the former;

xviii. In Constitutional Petition No.18/2018 the petitioner is a citizen of Pakistan after remaining in the permanent and pensionable service of the Armed Forces Medical College Rawalpindi. This is mainly a service dispute and the petitioner seeks implementation of the judgment of the Federal Service Tribunal against the Principal Public School & College, Jutial, Gilgit. The petitioner seeks quashment of the judgment passed in Writ Petition No.108/2017 filed by the respondents to be declared without lawful authority, coram non judice and not maintainable; and

xix. In Constitutional Petition No.41/2018, the Federation of Pakistan through Secretary Ministry of Kashmir Affairs and Gilgit Baltistan Islamabad seeks quashment of the impugned judgment wherein the GB Supreme Appellate Court *vide* order dated 20.06.2018 stayed the operation of the 2018 Order and its implementation process was suspended till the decision of the suo moto taken by the said Court.

2. The following common but key questions stem from the foregoing factual background:
   i. Would granting fundamental rights and a status, role and recognition to the people of GB within the constitutional scheme of Pakistan prejudice Pakistan's cause for the resolution of the Kashmir dispute by such appropriate means as may be acceptable to Pakistan (which could, for example, be a United Nations sanctioned and supervised plebiscite)?
   ii. What rights can be granted to the people of GB?
   iii. Is the GB Supreme Appellate Court a constitutional court?

To answer the foregoing questions, it is pertinent to examine some of the commitments made to the people of Jammu and Kashmir. Their importance is enhanced by some special provisions in the constitutions of both Pakistan and India. These constitutional provisions are not only a continuing reminder of those commitments but especially from Pakistan's side most definitely and certainly reiterate its commitment to a peaceful resolution of the Kashmir dispute in accordance with International Law and the aspirations of the people of Kashmir.

3. The Kashmir issue, starting as it did in the dying days of the British Raj and erupting and escalating into a dispute *(and indeed armed conflict)* shortly

thereafter, became one of Partition's defining moments. A process that could have produced two empowered, independent countries — countries with a shared history and hopes of a productive and cooperative future—instead embroiled Pakistan in strife that it did not want and was not of its making. The origins of the dispute lay in the contrived *(some might even say coerced)* accession of Kashmir to India by the Hindu ruler of a Muslim majority state, which was contrary to the expectations of the population and to the basis professed to be preferred by the British for accession by Princely States. The resultant heroic uprising and resistance by the majority was but inevitable. Subsequent United Nations *(UN)* intervention recommended, and Pakistan and India accepted, a de-escalatory approach leading up to calls for a plebiscite to determine the wishes of the people of the region. Successive Security Council Resolutions asked the UN to facilitate a *"free and impartial plebiscite to decide whether the State of Jammu and Kashmir is to accede to India or Pakistan."*

4. What does require clarification is that the commitment to a plebiscite was, at least ostensibly, echoed also from Indian side, perhaps in an attempt to calm the uproar around the obvious injustice of Maharaja Hari Singh's alleged declaration of accession to India. Thus, the then Prime Minister of India, Pandit Jawaharlal Nehru unambiguously committed himself to the plebiscite arrangement. His telegrams to the Prime Ministers of Pakistan and the United Kingdom *(UK)* sought to create the impression that any Indian recognition of the Maharaja's accession to India was only provisional and that the question of the future of Jammu and Kashmir *(i.e., whether as part of Pakistan or India)* would be determined by its own people after the restoration of law and order. What, after all, could *(at least facially)* be more unambiguous than Mr. Nehru's telegram to the British Prime Minister, Clement Attlee where, in paragraph No.3, he committed that *"I would like to make it clear that the question of aiding Kashmir in this emergency is not designed in any way to influence the State to accede to India. Our view which we have repeatedly made public is that **the question of accession in any disputed territory or State must be decided in accordance with the wishes of people and we adhere to this view.**"*[1]

[Emphasis supplied] This commitment of the Prime Minister of India was repeated and forwarded by the Prime Minister of Britain to the Prime Minister of Pakistan on 27th October, 1947 by stating that *"He adds that he would like to make it clear that the question of aiding Kashmir in this emergency is not designed in any way to influence the State to accede to India."*[2]

---

1 Reproduced in Modern History of Jammu and Kashmir: Ancient times to Shimla Agreement by J. C. Aggarwal, S. P. Agrawal (originally published in 1995, page 35, paragraph 3).
2 Kashmir: The Case for Freedom By Tariq Ali, Arundhati Roy, Pankaj Mishra, Hilal Bhatt, Angana P. Chatterji (originally published in 2011, page 125).

5. Mr. Nehru continued his protestations of supporting the right of the Kashmiri people to so decide their future in direct communications with Pakistan's leaders. Thus in his telegram of 28th October, 1947 to Mr. Liaquat Ali Khan, Mr. Nehru reiterated that:

"In regard to accession also it has been made clear that this is subject to reference to people of State and their decision. The Government of India have no desire to impose any decision and will abide by people's wishes."[3]

Similarly, in his telegram of 31st October, 1947 to the Prime Minister of Pakistan, the Prime Minister of India reasserted as follows:

"Our assurance that we shall withdraw our troops from Kashmir as soon as peace and order are restored and leave the decision regarding the future of this State to people of the State is not merely a pledge to your Government but also to the people of Kashmir and to the world."[4]

Mr. Nehru's claims of sincerity in empowering the people of Kashmir to so decide their future continued unabated. In his telegram of 4th November, 1947 to the Prime Minister of Pakistan, Mr. Nehru declared, yet again that:

"I wish to draw your attention to broadcast on Kashmir which I made last evening. I have stated our Government's policy and made it clear that we have no desire to impose our will on Kashmir but to leave final decision to people of Kashmir. I further stated that we have agreed on impartial international agency like United Nations supervising any referendum. This principle we are prepared to apply to any state where there is a dispute about accession."[5]

Mr. Nehru's claims of fealty to the rights to the Kashmiris were echoed by his government's representatives. The Indian representative to the UN, Mr. Gopalaswami Ayyangar, made a policy statement in the UN Security Council on 15th January, 1948 where he claimed that India desired *"only to see peace restored in Kashmir and to ensure that the people of Kashmir are left free to decide in an orderly and peaceful manner the future of their State. We have no further interest, and we have agreed that a plebiscite in Kashmir might take place under international auspices after peace and order have been established."*

6. It was on the basis of such assurances that the UN Security Council passed resolutions on 17th and 20th January, 1948 establishing the UN Commission for India and Pakistan *(UNCIP)*. The UNCIP was directed to investigate the facts and to report its advice. On 6th February, 1948, the Security Council

---

3 Modern History of Jammu and Kashmir: Ancient times to Shimla Agreement By J. C. Aggarwal, S. P. Agrawal (originally published in 1995, page 41).

4 Regional and Ethnic Conflicts: Perspectives from the Front Lines By Judy Carter, George Irani, Vamik D Volkan (originally published in 2009, page 44).

5 Quoted in "Unravelling the Kashmir Knot" by Aman M. Hingorani (originally published in May 2016).

made an appeal to both parties to agree on a just settlement of the Kashmir problem, to put an end to violence and hostilities and to withdraw all regular and irregular forces who had entered the State from outside. These resolutions were supplemented by a comprehensive resolution passed on 21st April, 1948 and the UNCIP's resolutions of 13th August, 1948 and 5th January, 1949. Truce was declared on 1st January, 1949. However, rather than adopting the process of demilitarization as envisaged in the aforesaid resolutions India has made the area that it holds in Kashmir as one of the most militarized areas in the world.

7. We have taken the liberty of citing at length from the statements of the Indian leadership because it is important to understand that the concept of the international nature of the Kashmir dispute was not a demand put forth merely by Pakistan. To the contrary, the repeated statements of Mr. Nehru make clear that the right of self-determination of the Kashmiri people was a right acknowledged, promoted and committed to by the Government of India as well as the Government of Pakistan and embraced and sanctified by the international community through the UN.

8. Commitments of this nature ought to be inviolable. Pakistan has certainly not resiled from its commitments—whether to the people of Kashmir or the international community. However, and this is a sad but hard reality, despite the passage of seven decades the promised plebiscite has yet to be held and the territory of Kashmir continues to remain divided—Jammu and Kashmir under the Indian Constitution, increasingly subsumed into India *(hereinafter referred to as "Indian Occupied Kashmir" or "IOK")* on the one hand, and the State of Azad Jammu and Kashmir *(hereinafter referred to as "AJK")* and the territory of GB on the other.

9. Over the decades the trajectories of the divided region have diverged. The part under Pakistan's administrative control *(i.e., GB)*—subject to the writ of the Constitution of the Islamic Republic of Pakistan, 1973 *(the Constitution)*— and that aligned with Pakistan *(i.e., AJK)* have progressed *(though perhaps not as swiftly or as much as Pakistanis would have desired)* and remained largely at peace, while the portion of Kashmir under Indian control has been convulsed with resistance and rebellion—expressions of popular sentiment that have been met with ever worsening repression and suppression.

10. The situation at present in IOK is dire. To reach such conclusion we need not turn to any official document or statement from Pakistan. Reliance can be placed upon the most recent report of the Office of the UN High Commissioner for Human Rights *(OHCHR)* issued in the summer of 2018 which pulls no punches and is damning. It notes widespread allegations of *"human rights violations [that] include torture and custodial deaths, rape, enforced disappearances and extrajudicial killings."* With some 500,000 to 700,000 troops in the territory,

the OHCHR report noted that *"Indian Kashmir"* is *"one of the most militarized zones in the world." "Impunity for human rights violations and a lack of access to justice"* are just a few of the human rights challenges in IOK. This impunity is sanctioned and promoted by such draconian laws as the Armed Forces (Jammu and Kashmir) Special Powers Act, 1990 *(AFSPA)* that grants broad powers to the security forces and effectively bestows immunity from prosecution in civilian courts for their conduct by requiring the central government to sanction all prospective prosecutions prior to being launched. As per the OHCHR, the law *"gives virtual immunity against prosecution for any human rights violation. In the nearly 28 years that the law has been in force in Jammu and Kashmir, there has not been a single prosecution of armed forces personnel granted by the central government."* The provisions of AFSPA fly in the face of the most basic international norms and conventions. For example, section 4 thereof allows any personnel operating under the law to use lethal force not only in cases of self-defence but also against any person contravening laws or orders *"prohibiting the assembly of five or more persons."* The use of pellet guns is regarded as directly responsible for the blinding, and thus incapacitation, of hundreds of Kashmiri youth. Others have been bound, in some of the most bizarre sights of the modern era, in front of military vehicles, self-evidently as so-called "human shields" against stones lobbed by unarmed youth facing the terrible might of one of the world's largest and most well-equipped armies.
11. In contrast, circumstances on the Pakistan side of the Line of Control *(LOC)* are markedly better. Tellingly, the OHCHR Report devotes most of itself to the situation in Indian-held Kashmir. There is of course an obvious and understandable reason for this. In all of the seven decades since Independence even when Pakistan itself was caught in, and convulsed by, turmoil of the most tragic nature, there was always an obvious and popular acceptance of, and for, Pakistan by the people, both in AJK and GB. On the Indian side however state sanctioned violence seems to go on and on.
12. As acknowledged by the OHCHR Report, AJK is neither a police state, nor are military laws or rules in place. Basic rights are available to the population and most elements of due process exist. Relative to IOK, the region is empowered, peaceful and prosperous. But a relative improvement as compared with the dire situation across the border is not the standard that Pakistan should ever be satisfied with. Nor is this Court prepared to tolerate or condone any violation of human rights on this side of the prevailing divide even though those breaches involve no violence as reported from the other side. We should seek to hold ourselves to the highest standards of conduct in relation to the territories for which Pakistan bears responsibility. In this context, there is always more work to be done.
13. As noted, Pakistan has responsibilities in relation to two regions: AJK and GB.

In 1948, UNCIP recognized the existence of local authorities *(as distinct from the Government of Pakistan)* for the territories. We are of course here concerned with GB alone. The region has not been incorporated into Pakistan as it is considered to be a part of the disputed State of Jammu and Kashmir. However, it has always remained completely under Pakistan's administrative control.

14. For the governance of the region, a series of administrative structures and laws have been applied to GB since 1947. These have included the following *(up to 1999)*:

Year	Legal instrument	Description
1947	Frontier Crimes Regulations (FCR) implemented	First law to be enforced was a continuation of the colonial law of FCR. Under this British law for the tribal areas and GB, a civil bureaucracy exercised all judicial and administrative power.
1949	Karachi Agreement	On 28th April, 1949, officials of the Pakistan Government met with those of the AJK Government to ink the Karachi Agreement. Under this accord, it was agreed that the affairs of Gilgit would be run by the Pakistan Government. It appears that no leader from Gilgit was included in this agreement.[6]
1950	Ministry of Kashmir Affairs and Northern Areas created	Affairs of Northern Areas handed over to the Ministry of Kashmir Affairs and Northern Areas *(KANA)*. Joint Secretary of the Ministry of Kashmir Affairs has been performing duties of Resident in the Northern Areas with all administrative and judicial authority since 1952.[7]
1952	Political Resident Appointed	Joint Secretary of the Ministry of Kashmir Affairs who headed the local administration and judiciary; was responsible for enforcement of the FCR and was also the financial and revenue commissioner. The Resident also exercised legislative powers in the Northern Areas in consultation with the Federal Government.[8]
1967	Political Agents appointed	KANA transferred powers of the High Court and Revenue Commissioner to the Resident and appointed two Political Agents, one each for Gilgit and Baltistan.[9]

---

6   Information retrieved from http://gbla.gov.pk/page/history#advocuncil.
7   AJK and Gilgit-Baltistan, Journal of Contemporary Studies, Vol. V, No. 1, Summer 2016, at page 80, paragraph 2, available at: https://ndu.edu.pk/fcs/Publications/fcsjournal/JCS_2016_summer/5.AJK-and-Gilgit- Baltistan.pdf.
8   Ibid at paragraph 2.
9   *Supra*.

1970	Advisory Council for Northern Areas Council Constitutional Order	Between Pakistan and the Azad Kashmir Government. 21 elected and non-elected members headed by the then Resident for GB as Chairman under KANA Division O.M. No.NA-1(6)/70 dated 18th November, 1970. 16 members of Northern Areas Advisory Council *(NAAC)* were elected in 1970.[10]
1975	Northern Areas Council Legal Framework Order 1975FCR Abolished	Major administrative, judicial and political reforms were introduced. The *jagirdari nizam* was abolished. GB was transformed into districts like those in Pakistan. The FCR was abolished, and the civil and criminal law was extended to the Northern Areas. The Advisory Council for Northern Areas was replaced by Northern Areas Council (NAC).[11]
1994	Northern Areas Council Legal Framework Order *(LFO)* of 1994	Administrative instrument devised by KANA, supplemented by the Northern Areas Rules of Business *(NARoB)* (also of 1994) serving as a sort of basic law but with only limited advisory functions devolved on the council.[12]
1999	Al Jehad Trust judgment (1999 SCMR 1379)	This Court declared it could not prescribe a form of government for the region, nor could it direct that the region be represented in the Parliament since that could undermine Pakistan's stand on Kashmir. It left such issues to the Federal Government and the Parliament. However, it directed the Government to take "proper administrative and legislative steps" to ensure that the people of the Northern Areas enjoyed their rights under Pakistan'sConstitution.[13]
1999	Northern Areas Council Legal Framework (Amendment) Order, 1999	The Northern Areas Council was renamed as the Northern Areas Legislative Council (NALC) which was given the powers to legislate on 49 subjects. The post of Speaker and three women seats were also created.[14]

15. As of today, the situation ultimately to emerge both for AJK and GB, as also of course for the rest of the erstwhile State, is enshrined in the aspiration expressed

---

10 Information retrieved from http://gbla.gov.pk/page/history#advcouncil.
11 Information retrieved from http://gbla.gov.pk/page/history#advcouncil.
12 Volume 7, page 108, paragraph 35.
13 Volume 7, Pg 108, Paragraph 36.
14 Information retrieved from http://gbla.gov.pk/page/history.

in Article 257 of the Constitution, which provides that *"When the people of the State of Jammu and Kashmir decide to accede to Pakistan, the relationship between Pakistan and that State shall be determined in accordance with the wishes of the people of that State."*

16. Be that as it may, in 1999, this Court in the seminal judgment reported as **Al-Jehad Trust through Habibul Wahab Al-Khairi, Advocate and 9 others Vs. Federation of Pakistan through Secretary, Ministry of Kashmir Affairs, Islamabad and 3 others 1999 SCMR 1379** directed the Pakistan Government to extend fundamental freedoms to the Northern Areas *(now of course referred to as GB)* within six months. The judgment declared that Pakistan exercised both *de facto* and *de jure* administrative control over the Northern Areas. This Court ruled that the people of the region were *"citizens of Pakistan for all intents and purposes...and could invoke constitutionally guaranteed fundamental rights."* *(at page 1393)* The ruling emphasized that the people of the Northern Areas were *"entitled to participate in the governance of their area and to have an independent judiciary to enforce...Fundamental Rights."* *(at page 1396).*

17. This Court has thus been sensitive for a long time to the fundamental rights of the people of GB. At the same time it was recognized that in the prevailing circumstances the Northern Areas' Legislative Council could not simply be equated with a Provincial Government. The problem clearly required a resolution. However, there was no immediate follow-up to the judgment passed in the **Al-Jehad Trust** case *(supra)* as the executive procrastinated. But after the lapse of a decade, the Federal Government promulgated the 2009 Order which, it argued, would establish a system of full internal governance in GB. The 2009 Order was a step towards the empowerment of the people of GB, but was not a complete solution. Thus, the Human Rights Commission of Pakistan (HRCP) emphasized, in a 2016 report based on a fact-finding mission, that the 2009 Order *"falls short of providing a democratic system in which the people of Gilgit-Baltistan could enjoy the rights available to other Pakistan citizens."* Other deficiencies noted in the report included, in part, that it *(the 2009 Order)* did not guarantee the right to protection against double punishment nor a right to information and the right to education. According to the report, discrimination on the basis of sex was not prohibited nor was the State obliged to take affirmative action in favour of women and children. This situation appears to be most unsatisfactory to this Court. Even though some rights are indeed available in GB, albeit under laws such as the Pakistan Penal Code and the Code of Criminal Procedure, 1898 *(CrPC)*, and are given effect by the respective courts, these are not protected under any overarching framework of a constitutional nature. This therefore remains unsatisfactory. Perhaps unsurprisingly, the 2009 Order failed to fully address the aspirations of the people of GB for full empowerment and representation. Reflecting this discontent, the GB Legislative Assembly

passed a unanimous resolution in August 2015 demanding that the region be included in Pakistan as a constitutional Province with representation in Parliament. The desire of the people of GB to participate fully in the national life of Pakistan is palpable. The HRCP mission had noted that *"a large number of people living in Gilgit-Baltistan aspire to have **full rights** as citizens of Pakistan. They argue that whenever it suits the federal government they are viewed as Pakistanis but **when they ask for equal rights they are reminded of their controversial constitutional status.**"* [Emphasis supplied]

18. The division of Kashmir has dragged on for more than seven decades. Given continued Indian policy to deny a plebiscite, it is possible that it may persist for a considerable further period. Under these circumstances, it is surely a denial of fundamental rights to have the people of GB linger on in legal limbo—deprived of rights simply because they await a future event that may not practically occur within their individual lifetimes. Quite obviously, the question of fundamental rights cannot be addressed in isolation. Such rights do not hang in the air. In order to have meaningful life and force, they must be embedded in *(thereby drawing support and sustenance from, and in turn, fertilizing and enhancing)* a properly articulated system of governance of a constitutional nature. These two—fundamental rights and a system of governance—of necessity go hand in hand. The former without the latter is not possible and only desirable, and the latter without the former, though possible, is not desirable. To attempt to put in place one but not the other would be a lopsided exercise, lacking the proper balance that must exist. Fortunately, a path forward is already available in the recommendations of the Committee on Constitutional and Administrative Reforms in GB *(Committee)* constituted by the Prime Minster in 2015. The Committee, which submitted its report in March 2017, was tasked with reviewing the constitutional and administrative arrangements in GB and recommending reforms, as well as reviewing the existing internal arrangements of the region. The Committee was led by the veteran civil servant and former Foreign Minister Mr. Sartaj Aziz. The report of the Committee concluded that further reforms were required to enhance the sense of participation of the people of GB and to upgrade the standard of governance and public service delivery. At the same time, the Committee noted that **the reforms proposed should not prejudice Pakistan's principled position in the context of UN resolutions on Kashmir.**

19. We are in agreement with the conclusions of the Committee on both the above noted counts: (i) that there is a need for further substantive reforms to enhance the participation of GB's citizenry in governance; and (ii) that in no way and at no point should the proposed reforms prejudice Pakistan's principled position regarding the status of Kashmir. Indeed, the latter point is of crucial importance and must guide and inform any and all recommendations regarding reforms in

GB. It is within the context of the above framework that we must examine the recommendations of the Committee. The Committee recommended, in part, that, –
    i. GB be accorded a "provisional" and special status of a Province pending final settlement of the Jammu and Kashmir dispute;
    ii. The region be given representation in the National Assembly and the Senate of Pakistan through amendments to Articles 51 and 57 of the Constitution, rather than an amendment to Article 1 thereof;
    iii. All legislative subjects other than those enumerated in Article 142 of the Constitution and its Fourth Schedule be assigned to the GB Assembly;
    iv. GB be given representation in all constitutional bodies; and
    v. A robust local bodies system be introduced.

The Committee also suggested broad reforms in other key areas including infrastructure development, socio-economic uplift and the civil service.

20. We are cognizant of the fact that nothing this Court recommends or orders should affect the nature and status of the Kashmir issue. It is within this light that we have reflected upon the recommendations of the Committee with great care. We also recognize that some of the recommendations may require Acts of Parliament and even amendments to the Constitution. At the same time, we have also been comforted by the fact that the Committee itself was acutely aware of the sensitivities of the issue before it, and provided its recommendations only after considering their implications, if any, on the status of the Kashmir dispute. It must be emphasized that **all** the above measures must be predicated by the caveat that these are subject to the result of the plebiscite, which is duly recognized in Article 257 already alluded to above. The Committee's recommendations have been considered in the backdrop of Pakistan's international commitments and their constitutional endorsement. As a responsible member of the comity of nations Pakistan remains aware of its obligations in such terms. As and when the promised plebiscite is organized by the parties to the dispute, it will be up to the people of all of Jammu and Kashmir, and of GB, to make their choice. Till then, it is surely incumbent upon both India as well as Pakistan to ensure that the people of this region enjoy maximum rights for areas within each country's control. Therefore, till such time that the plebiscite is held, a proper arrangement must be provided for by Pakistan for the people of GB for purposes of governance within a framework of a constitutional nature, including most importantly the enjoyment of fundamental rights.

21. This Court has already held in the case of **Al-Jehad Trust** *(supra)* that the people of GB are *"citizens of Pakistan for all intents and purposes…and could invoke constitutionally guaranteed fundamental rights"* and emphasized that they were *"entitled to participate in the governance of their area and to have an*

independent judiciary to enforce...Fundamental Rights." (at page 1393) This Court's observations in the noted case find expression in the Committee's report which distinguishes between the *(yet to be finally resolved)* status of GB, and the legitimate aspirations of the people of the region to participate in national life. It is clear that granting full rights to them does not in any way prejudice the eventual determination of the status of Jammu and Kashmir. A state of vacuum cannot be created for the people of GB. They, after all, are as entitled to all the fundamental rights as are enjoyed by others. Therefore there can be no prejudice to Pakistan's position on the plebiscite issue if the men, women and children living in GB are guaranteed basic human rights and a role in their own governance within a framework of a constitutional nature. Indeed, full rights for the people of GB can only bolster Pakistan's case for the right of self-determination for all the people of Kashmir. Pakistan has the principled position that the people of Kashmir deserve to exercise all fundamental rights **including the right of self-determination in terms of the plebiscite, the promise of which remains yet to be actuated.**

22. Regrettably, this latter right is not solely within Pakistan's own prerogative to proffer. It is a right that can only be exercised with the participation of India and the international community through the UN. However, Pakistan does have the ability to itself empower the people of GB with all those fundamental rights that Pakistanis enjoy, without the involvement of India or the international community, and without prejudice to the right of self-determination through a plebiscite of *all* the people of Jammu and Kashmir. **These rights for GB residents would include the right to representation as well as all other rights enjoyed by the citizens of Pakistan.** In conferring these rights Pakistan is not only discharging its obligations to the people in the territory that it controls and administers, it is also making a loud and clear statement in favour of providing all rights to all the people of Kashmir. As such, its actions can only strengthen the case for self-determination of Kashmir in accordance with the commitment to ensure exercise of all fundamental rights. It may be mentioned clearly, and without any ambiguity, that the most fundamental and basic right, the right of self-determination is for all the people of Jammu and Kashmir, and it remains a matter of satisfaction that their right to choose through a plebiscite remains a solemn commitment. That is why we hold that the Committee's recommendations relating to the provision and enforcement of fundamental rights provided by the Constitution must be implemented immediately and with full force and effect. As a matter of law as well as morality, there should be no discrepancy in the fundamental rights available to those in GB relative to Pakistani citizens anywhere in the country. As for a framework for governance, of a constitutional and political nature, for GB we are of the view that the right to self-government through an empowered GB Assembly as well as a robust

system of local bodies is entirely uncontroversial and must be enforced as early as possible.

23. We hold the above while yet again emphasizing our considered view that these changes do not in any way prejudice or affect Pakistan's principled stance on Kashmir. As such, these reforms are by definition provisional until the time when the people of Kashmir exercise their right of self-determination under the plebiscite. They have been deprived of this choice for far too long and at far too great a cost. Our judgment today merely states and upholds the obvious—that the parties to the Kashmir issue have an obligation to hasten the final resolution of this dispute and until that takes place, we must do everything in our power to minimize the suffering that this region has had to bear on account of its prolonged division.

24. Another question before this Court is whether the GB Supreme Appellate Court lacks the judicial power and jurisdiction to suspend, set aside or vary an Order promulgated by the President of Pakistan for the governance of GB, i.e., the 2018 Order or any Order amending, substituting or replacing the same. Now, given the present status of GB, i.e., as a region that is fully within the administrative control of Pakistan, and where Pakistan functionally exercises all aspects of sovereignty, it is clear that the Federation *(i.e., Parliament and the Federal Government)* is fully empowered to make arrangements for the governance of the region. This power extends to enacting and putting into place, whether on the executive side by means of an Order promulgated by the President or on the legislative side by an Act of Parliament, a framework and system of governance that is of a constitutional nature. The 2018 Order was issued in exercise of these powers, and the courts in GB were created under the same. The question now being considered can be put in more general terms: what would be the position *(i.e., status, powers and jurisdiction)* of the judicial, legislative and executive organs established by an instrument of the nature of the 2018 Order? In accordance with well-established principles of law, the GB legislature would only have such powers as are conferred upon it by the Federation through the Proposed Order. The courts created by such Order shall have the power to judicially review the laws enacted by such legislature. Of course, the organs created by the 2018 Order, and especially any legislative body, would be bound not merely by the Order, but also by the Constitution *(under which the Order itself came into existence)*. For the present purposes, the more immediate point is that a court created by the 2018 Order, such as the GB Supreme Appellate Court or the Chief Court, can examine whether the GB Assembly has exceeded the remit of its competence as conferred by the Order *(when, e.g., enacting a law)*, and can declare it to be *ultra vires* the same. However, this jurisdiction is of necessity territorially bound. It can only apply and operate in relation to GB, and to things done or purported to be done

under the 2018 Order. It cannot extend to any matter beyond or outside GB, or the *vires* or validity of the 2018 Order itself. The jurisdiction of a GB court of the sort being considered in the present context is confined to the territory of GB. Therefore, it may be concluded that the intention was to give the GB Supreme Appellate Court and the Chief Court the status of a "constitutional" court within the ambit of GB and the 2018 Order, but confining the scope to interpreting and implementing the said Order and conducting judicial review within the territory of GB in this regard. It is thus a "constitutional" court inasmuch as it has the jurisdiction to strike down any law made by a GB legislature on the recognized concept of *ultra vires*. But it would not be in a position to question, in any manner and on any ground whatsoever, the very law that created it. This view is bolstered by the fact that an ouster clause has been inserted as Article 118 of the 2018 Order, whereby the GB courts have been restrained from calling into question the validity of the 2018 Order. The said Article reads as under:

"118. Order to override other laws, etc.– (1) The provision of this Order shall have effect notwithstanding anything contained in the provisions of any law for the time being in force except that in case of conflict between the laws of Pakistan and the law framed under this Order, the laws of Pakistan shall prevail.
(2) No Court, including the Gilgit-Baltistan Supreme Appellate Court and the Gilgit-Baltistan High Court, shall call into question or permit to be called into question, the validity of this Order."

25. Therefore it may be concluded that the GB Court does not sit as a court having the power of judicial review in respect of the territory of Pakistan, nor can it declare Orders made or legislation passed by the President or the Parliament as *ultra vires*, nor can it initiate judicial review of departments working outside of GB. Instead, the 2018 Order can be challenged by, inter alia, the people of GB, but only before this Court, either under Article 184 of the Constitution or in the manner herein after provided.

26. We now turn to a question of importance, which is crucial for the success of the project of creating a framework of governance for GB of a constitutional nature. Any framework of such a nature necessarily implies, and indeed it could be said demands, a degree of continuity in the manner provided in the Proposed Order *(hereinafter referred to)*. Otherwise, what good is it? Of what value are the fundamental rights enshrined in such a framework, and how independent can a judiciary created thereby be, if the structure is impermanent, and even ephemeral? This is all the more so where the framework is put in place in exercise of executive authority, by means of an Order promulgated by the President. Such an Order can be put in place, as it were, with a stroke of the pen, but likewise instantly cast into oblivion. Indeed, the manner in which the

2009 Order was replaced by the 2018 Order is a telling illustration of the point now under consideration. During the course of the hearing of these petitions, and in light of the submissions by various learned counsel and the observations of the Court, the Federal Government constituted a committee shepherded by the learned Attorney General, to review the entire matter, and place before the Court a draft of a fresh Order for the governance of GB. This was duly done, and the draft so placed was examined by the Court in light of the submissions made before it. In our view, that draft, as modified in the manner hereinafter stated, does provide a suitable framework in the hue of constitutional nature for the governance of GB. The Federal Government stands committed to promulgating the same *(hereinafter referred to as the "Proposed Order")*, in substitution of the 2018 Order. However, the question of permanence remains. It is this point that must now be considered.

27. As noted above, the matters before us have been instituted under Article 184(3) of the Constitution. The jurisdiction thereby conferred upon this Court has been considered in a number of decisions, which have settled a well-known jurisprudence that requires no elaborate rehearsal. There is also Article 187 of the Constitution, which confers a special jurisdiction on this Court. As the text of Article 184(3) *supra* indicates, this Court can give *"such directions to any person or authority including any Government… as may be appropriate for the enforcement of any of the Fundamental Rights conferred by Chapter 1 of Part II"* of the Constitution. It is now well settled that this constitutional power, within the scope of the grant, is not just plenary; it is also dynamic and flexible. Indeed, if we may adapt *(in a somewhat modified manner)* for present purposes a famous metaphor used by the Privy Council in relation to the Canadian constitution, in granting fundamental rights the Constitution has planted a *"living tree capable of growth and expansion"*. Understandings of both the nature of fundamental rights, and what must be done to ensure their meaningful enjoyment in full, have developed and evolved over the decades and will undoubtedly continue to do so in times to come. Thus, to take but one example, the meaning of the right to life conferred by Article 9 of the Constitution has developed in a manner that would, perhaps, be breathtaking for previous generations. The categories and varieties of cases involving or raising issues of fundamental rights of public importance can never be closed. They are shaped by the human condition and the vagaries of the human experience, which by its very nature is limitless. This is not to say that the scope of the constitutional power is, as a matter of law, boundless, but only to stress that any artificial straitjacketing, based on preconceived notions or whatever passes for orthodoxy or received wisdom in a particular age, is to be avoided. Now, precedent is too often perceived as a limitation. Certainly, at least in the common law tradition, it is a defining characteristic of judicial power. It should however, perhaps also be given greater

recognition as a useful tool in the judicial arsenal. It must never be forgotten that while we are certainly tied to the past we are not shackled by it. And this is perhaps all the more so when the jurisdiction is of the nature as conferred by Article 184(3) *supra*. To this must be added the power conferred on this Court under Article 187 *supra*, to *"issue such directions, orders or decrees as may be necessary to do complete justice"* in any pending case or matter. Keeping these provisions in mind, and the special nature of the issue before us—the settling of a framework, of a constitutional nature, for the governance of GB—we are of the view that our jurisdiction extends to the giving of suitable directions to the Federation, both to promulgate the Proposed Order and also for ensuring its continuity. It is only in this way that fundamental rights can be granted to the people of GB in the meaningful and realistic manner envisaged by this Court in the case of **Al-Jehad Trust** *(supra)*. At the same time, as indeed was accepted on behalf of the federation, the directions that we can give extend to making certain modifications in the Proposed Order, again in order to properly effectuate the objective sought to be achieved. It is in the foregoing terms that we have, indeed, made certain modifications to the Proposed Order, which have been incorporated therein, and have also for convenience been gathered in the appendix to this judgment.

28. Before concluding, we would like to make one last point. It is a matter of some concern that although this Court had articulated the basic position as regards the status and rights of the people of GB in the case of **Al-Jehad Trust** *(supra)* two decades ago, the actual realization by the Executive of that expression has remained fitful at best. This is not acceptable. This Court has not hesitated in the past to give legal recognition to the aspirations of people who have unhesitatingly, enthusiastically (and if we may out it like that, joyously) cast their lot with Pakistan right from the beginning. We do not hesitate now to take the matter further. Therefore, we do not just provide judicial imprimatur to the proposed framework: we also give it permanence, so that the people of GB have unassailable confidence that their rights, and the enjoyment thereof, is not subject to the whims and caprice of every passing majority, but are firmly grounded in the Constitution itself. And let it be clearly understood: we will not hesitate in future, should the need and occasion arise, to take, within our constitutional mandate, all such steps as may be required. The human rights jurisprudence of this Court has served, and will continue to serve, as the sheet-anchor of the liberties and rights of all the people. Those of Gilgit-Baltistan are no exception.

29. Accordingly, we hereby direct and order as follows:
    i. The Proposed Order, which *(modified as noted above)* is annexed to this judgment, shall be forthwith promulgated by the President on the advice of the Federal Government, and in any case within a fortnight hereof;

ii. No amendment shall be made to the Order as so promulgated except in terms of the procedure provided in Article 124 of the same, nor shall it be repealed or substituted, without the instrument amending, repealing or substituting *(as the case may be)* the same being placed before this Court by the Federation through an application that will be treated as a petition under Article 184(3) of the Constitution. Nothing in this judgment shall be construed to limit the jurisdiction conferred on this Court by the Proposed Order itself; and

iii. If the Order so promulgated is repealed or substituted by an Act of Parliament the validity thereof, if challenged, shall be examined on the touchstone of the Constitution.

30. In light of the foregoing, the instant matters are disposed of accordingly, save those petitions in which a specific order or judgment, of either the GB Supreme Appellate Court or the Chief Court, has been challenged. Such petitions *(being only Constitution Petitions No.2/2016, 3/2016, 34/2016, 6/2017, 30/2017, 18/2018, 50/2018 and 51/2018)* shall be deemed pending and be treated and disposed of as the leave petitions envisaged under Article 103 of the Proposed Order, when promulgated. Such petitions shall be listed in the normal course before an appropriate Bench.

CHIEF JUSTICE

JUDGE

JUDGE

JUDGE

JUDGE

JUDGE

Announced in open Court
on **17.01.2019** at **Islamabad**
Approved for Reporting
M. Azhar Malik

JUDGE

No. F.13 (2)/2018-Admn(GBC)
GOVERNMENT OF PAKISTAN MINISTRY OF KASHMIR AFFAIRS AND GILGIT-BALTISTAN

****

Islamabad, the January, 2019

AN ORDER

to provide for further political empowerment and good governance in Gilgit-Baltistan

WHEREAS the Federal Government intends to give Gilgit-Baltistan the status of a provisional Province, subject to the decision of the Plebiscite to be conducted under the UN Resolutions, with all privileges provided by the Constitution, however, a proper Constitutional Amendment needs to be made in the Constitution of the Islamic Republic of Pakistan. This needs two thirds majority in the Parliament and would take time. However, as an interim measure the Federal Government intends to give such Fundamental Right as given to the other Province.

WHEREAS it is expedient to provide for greater empowerment so as to bring Gilgit-Baltistan at par with other provinces and to initiate necessary legislative, executive and judicial reforms for the aforesaid purposes;

NOW, THEREFORE, the President of Islamic Republic of Pakistan is pleased to make the following Order:

1. Short title, extent and commencement. – (1) This Order may be called the Gilgit-Baltistan Governance Reforms, 2019.

(2) It extends to whole of the Gilgit-Baltistan.

(3) It shall come into force on at once.

PART I: PRELIMINARY

2. Definitions. – (1) In this Order, unless there is anything repugnant in the subject or context. –

(a) "**Assembly**" means the Gilgit-Baltistan Legislative Assembly;

(b) "**Citizen**" means a person who has a domicile or resident of Gilgit-Baltistan;

(c) "**Council**" means the Gilgit-Baltistan Council constituted under this Order;

(d) "**Chairman**" means the Chairman of the Council who shall be the Prime Minister of Pakistan;

(e) "**Federation**" means the Federal Government of Islamic Republic of Pakistan;

(f) "**Financial year**" means the year commencing on the first day of July and ending on the thirtieth day of June;

(g) **"Gilgit-Baltistan"** means the areas comprising districts of Astore, Diamer, Ghanche, Ghizer, Gilgit, Hunza, Nagar, Skardu, Shigar, Kharmang and such other districts as may be created from time to time;

(h) **"Governor"** means the Governor of Gilgit-Baltistan and includes a person for the time being acting as Governor;

(i) **"Government"** means the Government of Gilgit-Baltistan;

(j) **"Joint Sitting"** means a joint sitting of the Assembly, the Federal Minister in-charge of the Council Secretariat and the members of the Council;

(k) **"Judge"** in relation to the Gilgit-Baltistan Supreme Appellate Court or the Gilgit-Baltistan Chief Court, includes the Chief Judge of the Gilgit-Baltistan Supreme Appellate Court and the Chief Court;

(l) **"person"** includes any body politic or corporate;

(m) **"prescribed"** means prescribed by law or rules made there under;

(n) **"President"** means the President of Islamic Republic of Pakistan;

(o) **"Property"** includes any right, title or interest in property, movable or immovable, and any means and instruments of production;

(p) **"remuneration"** includes salary and pension;

(q) **"Service"** means the Service of Pakistan, Service of Gilgit-Baltistan and Service of Azad Jammu and Kashmir;

(r) **"Service of Gilgit-Baltistan"** means any service, post or office in connection with the affairs of Gilgit-Baltistan, but does not include service of Council, service as Governor, Speaker, Deputy Speaker, Chief Minister, Minister or Advisor, Parliamentary Secretary, Advisor to the Minister or a member of the Assembly;

(s) **"Service of Council"** means any service, post or office in connection with the affairs of Gilgit-Baltistan Council which shall be the service of Pakistan, but does not include service as the Chairman of the Council, Advisor to Chairman, Member of the Council, Chairman of the Council's Committees;

(t) **"Speaker"** means Speaker of the Assembly and includes any person acting as the Speaker of the Assembly;

(u) **"Supreme Court of Pakistan"** means the Supreme Court as defined by the Constitution of the Islamic Republic of Pakistan, 1973; and

(v) **"Vice Chairman of the Council"** means the Governor of Gilgit-Baltistan.

3. **Elimination of exploitation.** – The Government shall ensure the elimination of all forms of exploitation and the gradual fulfillment of the fundamental principle, from each according to his ability to each according to his work.

4. **Right of individuals to be dealt with in accordance with law, etc.** – (1) To enjoy equal protection of law and to be treated in accordance with law is the inalienable right of every citizen, wherever he may be, and of every other person for the time being in Gilgit-Baltistan.

(2) In particular—
- (a) no action detrimental to the life, liberty, body, reputation or property of any person shall be taken except in accordance with law;
- (b) no person shall be prevented from or be hindered in doing that which is not prohibited by law; and
- (c) no person shall be compelled to do that which the law does not require him to do.

5. Obedience to this Order. – Obedience to this Order and law is the inviolable obligation of every citizen, wherever he may be, and of every other person for the time being within Gilgit-Baltistan.

PART II: FUNDAMENTAL RIGHTS

6. Laws inconsistent with or in derogation of Fundamental Rights to be void. – (1) Any law, or any custom or usage having the force of law, in so far as it is inconsistent with the rights conferred by this part, shall, to the extent of such inconsistency, be void.

(2) The Government shall not make any law which takes away or abridges the rights so conferred by this Order and any law made in contravention of this clause shall, to the extent of such contravention, be void.

(3) The Provisions of this Article shall not apply to any law relating to members of the Armed Forces, or of the Police or of such other forces as are charged with the maintenance of public order, for the purpose of ensuring the proper discharge of their duties or the maintenance of discipline among them and no such law nor any provision thereof shall be void on the ground that such law or provision is inconsistent with, or repugnant to, any provision of this Part.

(4) The rights conferred by this Part shall not be suspended except as expressly provided by this Order.

7. Security of person. – No person shall be deprived of life or liberty save in accordance with law.

8. Safeguard as to arrest and detention. – (1) No person who is arrested shall be detained in custody without being informed, as soon as may be, of the grounds for such arrest, nor shall he be denied the right to consult and be defended by a legal practitioner of his choice.

(2) Every person who is arrested and detained in custody shall be produced before the nearest Magistrate within a period of twenty-four hours of such arrest excluding the time necessary for the journey from the place of arrest to the Court of the Magistrate, and no such person shall be detained in custody beyond the said period without the authority of a Magistrate.

(3) Nothing in clause (1) and (2) shall apply to any person who is arrested or detained under any law providing for preventive detention.

(4) No law providing for preventive detention shall be made except to deal with persons acting in a manner prejudicial to the integrity, security or defence of Pakistan or any part thereof, or external affairs of Pakistan, or public order, or the maintenance of supplies or services, and no such law shall authorize the detention of a person for a period exceeding three months unless the Review Board has, after affording him an opportunity of being heard in person, reviewed his case and reported, before the expiration of the said period, that there is, in its opinion, sufficient cause for such detention, and, if the detention is continued after the said period of three months, unless the Review Board has reviewed his case and reported, before the expiration of each period of three months, that there is, in its opinion, sufficient cause for such detention.

Explanation I.— In this article, "the Review Board" means, a Board appointed by the Chief Judge of the Supreme Appellate Court of Gilgit-Baltistan consisting of a Chairman, the Secretary of the Department concerned with Home Affairs and a person, who is or has been a Judge of the Supreme Appellate Court or the Chief Court.

Explanation II.—The opinion of the Review Board shall be expressed in terms of the views of the majority of its members.

(5) When any person is detained in pursuance of an order made under any law providing for preventive detention, the authority making the order shall, within fifteen days from such detention, communicate to such person the grounds on which the order has been made, and shall afford him the earliest opportunity of making a representation against the order:

Provided that the authority making any such order may refuse to disclose facts which such authority considers it to be against the public interest to disclose.

(6) The authority making the order shall furnish to the Review Board all documents relevant to the case unless a certificate, signed by a Secretary to the Government, to the effect that it is not in the public interest to furnish any documents, is produced.

(7) Within a period of twenty-four months commencing on the day of his first detention in pursuance of an order made under a law providing for preventive detention, no person shall be detained in pursuance of any such order for more than a total period of eight months in the case of a person detained for acting in a manner prejudicial to public order and twelve months in any other case:

Provided that this clause shall not apply to any person who is employed by, or works for, or acts on instructions received from, the enemy, or who is acting or attempting to act in a manner prejudicial to the integrity, security or defence of Pakistan or any part thereof or who commits or attempts to commit any act which amounts to an anti-national activity as defined in any law or is a member of any association which has for its objects, or which indulges in, any such anti-national activity.

(8) The Review Board shall determine the place of detention of the person detained and fix a reasonable subsistence allowance for his family.

(9) Nothing in this article shall apply to any person who for the time being is an enemy alien.

9. Right to fair trial. – For the determination of his civil rights and obligations or in any criminal charge against him a person shall be entitled to a fair trial and due process.

10. Slavery and forced labour prohibited. – (1) No person shall be held in slavery, and no law shall permit or in any way facilitate the introduction into Gilgit-Baltistan of slavery in any form.

(2) All forms of forced labour and traffic in human beings is prohibited.

(3) No child below the age of fourteen years shall be engaged in any factory or mine or any other hazardous employment.

(4) Nothing in this clause shall be deemed to affect compulsory service-
 (a) by persons undergoing punishment for offences under any law; or
 (b) required by any law for a public purpose.

11. Protection against retrospective punishment. – No law shall authorize the punishment of a person –
 (a) for an act or omission that was not punishable by law at the time of the act or omission; or
 (b) for an offence by a penalty greater than, or of a kind different from, the penalty prescribed by law for that offence at the time the offence was committed.

12. Protection against double punishment and self-incrimination. – No person—
 (a) shall be prosecuted or punished for the same offence more than once; or
 (b) shall, when accused of an offence, be compelled to be a witness against himself.

13. Inviolability of dignity of man, etc. (1) The dignity of man and, subject to law, the privacy of home, shall be inviolable.

(2) No person shall be subjected to torture for the purpose of extracting evidence.

14. Freedom of movement. – Every citizen shall have the right to remain in, and, subject to any reasonable restrictions imposed by law in the public interest, enter and move freely throughout Gilgit-Baltistan and to reside and settle in any part thereof.

15. Freedom of assembly. – Every citizen shall have the right to assemble peacefully and without arms, subject to any reasonable restrictions imposed by law in the interest of morality or public order.

16. Freedom of association. – (1) Subject to this Order, every citizen shall have the right to form association or unions, subject to any reasonable restrictions imposed by law in the interest of morality or public order.

(2) No person or political party in the area comprising Gilgit-Baltistan shall propagate against, or take part in activities prejudicial or detrimental to the ideology of Pakistan.

(3) Every citizen, not being in the Service, shall have the right to form or be a member of a political party, subject to any reasonable restrictions imposed by law in the interest of the sovereignty or integrity of Pakistan or any part thereof and such law shall provide that where the Government declares that any political party has been formed or is operating in a manner prejudicial to the sovereignty or integrity of Pakistan or any part thereof, the Government of Gilgit-Baltistan shall, within fifteen days of such declaration, refer the matter to the Supreme Appellate Court whose decision on such reference shall be final.

(4) Every political party shall account for the source of its funds in accordance with law.

17. Freedom of trade, business or profession. – Every citizen possessing such qualifications, if any, as may be prescribed by law in relation to his profession or occupation shall have the right to enter upon any lawful profession or occupation, and to conduct any lawful trade or business:

Provided that nothing in this article shall prevent –
   (a) the regulation of any trade or profession by a licensing system; or
   (b) the regulation of trade, commerce or industry in the interest of free competition therein; or
   (c) the carrying on, by Government or by a corporation controlled by Government, of any trade, business, industry or service, to the exclusion, complete or partial, or other persons.

18. Freedom of speech. – Every citizen shall have the right to freedom of speech and expression, subject to any reasonable restrictions imposed by law in the interest of the security, public order, decency or morality, or in relation to contempt of Court, commission of, or incitement to an offence.

19. Right to information. –Every citizen shall have the right to have access to information in all matters of public importance subject to regulation and reasonable restrictions imposed by law.

20. Freedom to profess religion and manage religious institutions. – Subject to law, public order and morality, –
   (a) every citizen has the right to profess and practice his religion; and
   (b) every religious denomination and every sect thereof has the right to establish, maintain and manage its places of worship.

21. Safeguard against taxation for purposes of any particular religion. – No person shall be compelled to pay any special tax the proceeds of which are to be spent on the propagation or maintenance of any religion other than his own.

22. Safeguard as to educational institutions in respect of religion etc. – (1) No person attending any educational institution shall be required to receive religious instructions or take part in any religious ceremony, or attend religious worship, if such instruction, ceremony or worship relates to a religion other than his own.

(2) No religious community or denomination shall be prevented from providing religious instruction for pupils of that community or denomination in any educational institution maintained wholly by that community or denomination.

(3) No citizen shall be denied admission to any educational institution receiving aid from public revenues on the ground only of race, religion, caste or place of birth.

(4) In respect of any religious institution, there shall be no discrimination against any community in the granting of exemption or concession in relation to taxation.

(5) Nothing in this paragraph shall prevent any public authority from making provision for the advancement of any society or educationally backward class.

23. Provisions as to property. – Subject to any reasonable restrictions imposed by law in the public interest, every citizen shall have the right to acquire, hold and dispose of property.

24. Protection of property. – (1) No person shall be deprived of his property save in accordance with law.

(2) No property shall be compulsorily acquired or taken possession of save for a public purpose, and save by the authority of law which provides for compensation thereof and either fixes the amount of compensation or specifies the principles on which and the manner in which compensation is to be determined and given.

(3) Nothing in this clause shall, affect the validity of –
   (a) any law permitting the compulsory acquisition or taking possession of any property for preventing danger to life, property or public health; or
   (b) any law relating to the acquisition, administration or disposal of any property which is or is deemed to be evacuee property under any law; or
   (c) any law permitting the taking over of any property which has been acquired by, or come into the possession of, any person by any unfair means, or in any manner, contrary to law ; or
   (d) any law providing for the taking over of the management of any property by the Government for a limited period, either in the public interest or in order to secure the proper management of the property, or for the benefit of its owner; or

(e) any law providing for the acquisition of any class of property for the purpose of –
  (i) providing education and medical aid to all or any specified class of citizen; or
  (ii) providing housing and public facilities and services such as roads, water supply, sewerage, gas and electric power to all or any specified class of citizen; or
  (iii) providing maintenance to those who, on account of unemployment, sickness, infirmity or old age, are unable to maintain themselves; or
(f) any law in force immediately before the coming into force of this Order:

Explanation. – In clause (2) and (3), the expression 'property' means immovable property, or any commercial or industrial undertaking, or any interest in any undertaking.

(4) The adequacy or otherwise of any compensation provided for by any such law as is referred to in this Article, or determined in pursuance thereof, shall not be called in question in any court.

25. Equality of citizens. – (1) All citizens are equal before law and are entitled to equal protection of law.

(2) There shall be no discrimination on the basis of gender.

(3) Nothing in this Article shall prevent the Government from making any special provision for the protection of women and children.

26. Right to education. – The Government shall provide free and compulsory education to all children of the age of five to sixteen years in such manner as may be determined by law.

27. Non-discrimination in respect of access to public places. – In respect of access to places of public entertainment or resort, not intended for religious purposes only, there shall be no discrimination against any citizen on the ground only of race, religion, caste, gender or place of birth, but nothing herein shall be deemed to prevent the making of any special provision for women.

28. Safeguard against discrimination in services. – No citizen otherwise qualified for appointment in the service of Gilgit-Baltistan, shall be discriminated against in respect of any such appointment on the ground only of race, religion, caste or gender:

Provided that, in the interest of the said service, specified posts or services may be reserved for members of either sex.

29. Preservation of language, script and culture. – Subject to Article 117 any section of citizens having a distinct language, script or culture shall have the right to preserve and promote the same and subject to law, establish institutions for that purpose.

PART III: PRINCIPLES OF POLICY

30. Principles of Policy. – (1) The Principles set out in this Part shall be known as the Principles of Policy, and it is the responsibility of each organ and authority of the Government, and of each person performing functions on behalf of an organ or authority of the Government, to act in accordance with those Principles in so far as they relate to the functions of the organ or authority.

(2) In so far as the observance of any particular Principle of Policy may be dependent upon resources being available for the purpose, the Principle shall be regarded as being subject to the availability of resources In respect of each year, the Governor shall cause to be prepared and laid before the Assembly, a report on the observance and implementation of the Principles of Policy, and provision shall be made in the rules of procedure of the Assembly, for discussion on such report.

31. Responsibility with respect to Principles of Policy. – (1) The responsibility of deciding whether any action of an organ or authority of the Government, or of a person performing functions on behalf of an organ or authority of the Government, is in accordance with the Principles of Policy is that of the organ or authority of the Government, or of the person, concerned.

(2) The validity of an action or of a law shall not be called in question on the ground that it is not in accordance with the Principles of Policy, and no action shall lie against the Government or any organ or authority of the Government or any person on such ground.

32. Islamic way of life. (1) Steps shall be taken to enable the Muslims of Gilgit-Baltistan, individually and collectively, to order their lives in accordance with the fundamental principles and basic concepts of Islam and to provide facilities whereby they may be enabled to understand the meaning of life according to the Holy Quran and Sunnah.

(2) The Government shall endeavor:
  (a) to make the teaching of the Holy Quran and Islamiat compulsory, to encourage and facilitate the learning of Arabic language and to secure correct and exact printing and publishing of the Holy Quran;
  (b) to promote unity and the observance of the Islamic moral standards; and
  (c) to secure the proper organization of zakat, ushr, auqaf and mosques.

33. Promotion of local Government institutions. – The Government shall encourage local Government institutions composed of elected representatives of the areas concerned and in such institutions special representation will be given to peasants, workers and women.

34. Parochial and other similar prejudices to be discouraged. – The Government shall discourage parochial, racial, tribal and sectarian prejudices among the citizens.

35. Full participation of women in national life. – Steps shall be taken to ensure full participation of women in all spheres of national life.

36. Protection of family, etc. – The Government shall protect the marriage, the family, the mother and the child.

37. Protection of minorities. – The Government shall safeguard the legitimate rights and interests of minorities, including their due representation in the service of Gilgit-Baltistan.

38. Promotion of social justice and eradication of social evils. – The Government shall:

(a) promote, with special care, the educational and economic interests of backward classes or areas;

(b) remove illiteracy and provide free and compulsory secondary education within minimum possible period;

(c) make technical and professional education generally available and higher education equally accessible to all on the basis of merit;

(d) ensure inexpensive and expeditious justice

(e) make provision for securing just and humane conditions of work, ensuring that children and women are not employed in vocations unsuited to their age or sex, and for maternity benefits for women in employment;

(f) enable the people of different areas, through education, training, agricultural and industrial development and other methods, to participate fully in all forms of national activities, including employment in the service of Gilgit-Baltistan;

(g) prevent prostitution, gambling and taking of injurious drugs,printing, publication, circulation and display o obscene literature and advertisements;

(h) prevent the consumption of alcoholic liquor otherwise than for medicinal and, in the case of non-Muslims, religious purposes; and

(i) decentralize the Government administration so as to facilitate expeditious disposal of its business to meet the convenience and requirements of the public.

39. Promotion of social and economic well-being of the people. – The Government shall:

(a) secure the well-being of the people, irrespective of sex, caste, creed or race, by raising their standard of living, by preventing the concentration of wealth and means of production and distribution in the hands of a few to the detriment of general interest and by ensuring equitable adjustment of rights between employers and employees, and landlords and tenants;

(b) provide for all citizens, within the available resources of the Gilgit-Baltistan, facilities for work and adequate livelihood with reasonable rest and leisure;

(c) provide for all persons employed in the service of Gilgit-Baltistan or otherwise, social security by compulsory social insurance or other means;

(d) provide basic necessities of life, such as food, clothing. housing, education and medical relief, for all such citizens, irrespective of sex, caste, creed or race, as are permanently or temporarily unable to earn their livelihood on account of infirmity, sickness or unemployment;

(e) reduce disparity in the income and earnings of individuals, including persons in the various classes of the service of Gilgit-Baltistan; and

(f) eliminate riba as early as possible.

40. Participation of people in Armed Forces. – The Government shall enable people from all parts of Gilgit-Baltistan to participate in the Armed Forces of Pakistan.

PART IV: GOVERNOR

41. The Governor. – (1) There shall be a Governor of the Gilgit-Baltistan who shall be appointed by the President on the advice of the Prime Minister.

(2) When the Governor, by reason of absence from Gilgit-Baltistan or for any other cause, is unable to perform his functions, the Speaker of the Assembly and in his absence any other person as the President may nominate shall perform the functions of Governor until the Governor returns to Gilgit-Baltistan or, as the case may be, resumes his functions.

(3) A person shall not be appointed a Governor unless he is qualified to be elected as a member of the Assembly and is not less than thirty-five years of age and is a registered voter and resident of Gilgit-Baltistan.

(4) The Governor shall hold office during the pleasure of the President and shall be entitled to such salary, allowances and privileges as the President may determine.

(5) The Governor may, by writing under his hand addressed to the President, resign his office.

(6) The President may make such provision as he thinks fit for the discharge of the functions of the Governor in any contingency not provided for in this Order.

(7) Before entering upon office, the Governor shall make before the Chief Judge of the Gilgit-Baltistan Supreme Appellate Court an oath in the form set out in the First Schedule.

(8) The Governor shall not hold any office of profit in the Service nor occupy any other position carrying the right to remuneration for the rendering of services.

(9) The Governor shall not be a candidate for election as a member of the

Assembly, and, if a member of the Assembly is appointed as Governor, his seat in the Assembly shall become vacant on the day he enters upon his office.

42. Governor to act on advice, etc. – (1) Subject to this Order in the performance of his functions, the Governor shall act in accordance with the advice of the Cabinet or the Chief Minister:

Provided that the Governor may require the Cabinet or, as the case may be, the Chief Minister to reconsider such advice, whether generally or otherwise, and the Governor shall act in accordance with the advice tendered after such reconsideration.

(2) The question whether any, and if so what, advice was tendered to the Governor by the Chief Minister or the Cabinet shall not be inquired into or by, any court, tribunal or other authority.

PART V: THE GOVERNMENT

43. The Government. – (1) Subject to this Order, the executive authority of Gilgit-Baltistan shall be exercised in the name of the Governor by the Government, consisting of the Chief Minister and the relevant Minister(s), which shall act through the Chief Minister, who shall be the Chief Executive.

(2) In the performance of his functions under this Order, the Chief Minister may act either directly, through the Ministers or through their subordinate Officers.

44. The Cabinet. – (1) There shall be a Cabinet of Ministers, with the Chief Minister at its head, to aid and advise the Governor in the exercise of his functions.

(2) The Assembly shall meet on the twenty-first day following the day on which a general election to the Assembly is held, unless sooner summoned by the Governor.

(3) After the election of the Speaker and the Deputy Speaker, the Assembly shall, to the exclusion of any other business, proceed to elect without debate one of its members to be the Chief Minister.

(4) The Chief Minister shall be elected by the votes of the majority of the total membership of the Assembly:

Provided that, if no member secures such majority in the first poll, a second poll shall be held between the members who secures the two highest numbers of votes in the first poll and the member who secures a majority of votes of the members present and voting shall be declared to have been elected as Chief Minister:

Provided further that, if the number of votes secured by two or more members securing the highest number of votes is equal, further polls shall be held between them until one of them secures a majority of votes of the members present and voting.

(5) The member elected under clause (4) shall be called upon by the Governor to assume the office of Chief Minister and he shall, before entering upon the office, make before the Governor oath in the form set out in the First Schedule:

(6) The Cabinet shall be collectively responsible to the Assembly and the total strength of the Cabinet shall not exceed twelve members or eleven percent of the total membership of the Assembly, whichever is higher:

Provided that the aforesaid limit shall be effective after the next general elections.

(7) The Chief Minister shall hold office during the pleasure of the Governor, but the Governor shall not exercise his powers under this clause unless he is satisfied that the Chief Minister does not command the confidence of the majority of the members of the Assembly, in which case he shall summon the Assembly and require the Chief Minister to obtain a vote of confidence from the Assembly.

(8) The Chief Minister may, by writing under his hand addressed to the Governor, resign his office.

(9) A Minister who for any period of six consecutive months is not a member of the Assembly shall, at the expiration of that period, cease to be a Minister and shall not before the dissolution of that Assembly be again appointed a Minister unless he is elected a member of that Assembly.

(10) Nothing contained in this Article shall be construed as disqualifying the Chief Minister or any other Minister for continuing in office during any period during which the Assembly stands dissolved, or as preventing the appointment of any person as Chief Minister or other Minister during any such period.

(11) The Chief Minister shall not appoint more than two Advisers.

45. Governor to be kept informed. – The Chief Minister shall keep the Governor informed on matters relating to administration and on all legislative proposals the Government intends to bring before the Assembly.

46. Ministers. – (1) Subject to clause (9) and (10) of Article 44, the Governor shall appoint Ministers from amongst members of the Assembly on the advice of the Chief Minister.

(2) Before entering upon office, a Minister shall make before the Governor oath in the form set out in the First Schedule.

(3) A Minister may, by writing under his hand addressed to the Governor, resign his office or may be removed from office by the Governor on the advice of the Chief Minister.

47. Vote of no-confidence against Chief Minister. – (1) A resolution for a vote of no-confidence moved by not less than twenty per centum of the total membership of the Assembly may be passed against the Chief Minister by the Assembly.

(2) A resolution referred to in clause (1) shall not be voted upon before the expiration of three days, or later than seven days, from the day on which such resolution is moved in the Assembly.

(3) If the resolution referred to in clause (1) is passed by a majority of the total membership of the Assembly, the Chief Minister shall cease to hold office.

48. Chief Minister continuing in office. – The Governor may ask the Chief Minister to continue to hold office until his successor enters upon the office of Chief Minister, in case of a vote of no confidence.

49. Extent of executive authority of Government. – Subject to this Order, the executive authority of the Government shall extend to the matters with respect to which the Assembly has power to make laws:

Provided that, in any matter with respect to which both Council and the Assembly has power to make laws, the executive authority of the Government shall be subject to, and limited by law made by the Council

50. Conferring of functions on subordinate authorities. – On the recommendation of the Government, the Assembly may by law confer functions upon officers or authorities subordinate to the Government.

51. Conduct of business of Government. – (1) All executive actions of the Government shall be expressed to be taken in the name of the Governor.

(2) The Government shall by rules specify the manner in which orders and other instruments made and executed in the name of Governor shall be authenticated, and the validity of any order or instrument so authenticated shall not be questioned in any court on the ground that it was not made or executed by the Governor.

(3) The Government shall also make rules for regulation, allocation and transaction of its business and may for the convenient transaction of that business delegate any of its functions to the officers or authority subordinate to it.

52. Parliamentary Secretaries. – (1) The Chief Minister may appoint Parliamentary Secretaries from amongst the members of the Assembly to perform such functions as may be prescribed.

(2) A Parliamentary Secretary may, by writing under his hand addressed to the Chief Minister, resign his office or may be removed from office by the Chief Minister.

53. Advocate-General. – (1) The Governor, shall appoint a citizen, being a person qualified to be appointed as Judge of the Gilgit-Baltistan Chief Court, to be the Advocate-General for Gilgit-Baltistan.

(2) It shall be the duty of the Advocate-General to give advice to Government upon such legal matters, and to perform such other duties of a legal character, as may be referred or assigned to him by the Government.

(3) The Advocate-General shall hold office during the pleasure of the Governor and shall not engage in private practice so long as he holds the office of the Advocate General.

(4) The Advocate-General may, by writing under his hand addressed to the Governor resign his office.

(5) The person holding the office as Advocate-General immediately before

the commencement of this Order shall be deemed to be the Advocate-General, appointed under this Order.

PART VI: GILGIT-BALTISTAN COUNCIL

54. Gilgit-Baltistan Council. – (1) There shall be a Gilgit-Baltistan Council consisting of, –
- (a) the Prime Minister of Pakistan;
- (b) the Governor;
- (c) six members nominated by the Prime Minister of Pakistan from time to time from amongst Federal Ministers and members of Parliament: Provided that the Federal Minister for Kashmir Affairs and Gilgit-Baltistan shall be an *ex officio* member and Minister-in-Charge of the Council:
- (d) the Chief Minister of Gilgit-Baltistan;
- (e) six members to be elected by the Assembly in accordance with single non-transferable majority vote.

(2) The Prime Minister of Pakistan shall be the Chairman of the Council.

(3) The Governor shall be the Vice-Chairman of the Council.

(4) The Minister of State for Kashmir Affairs and Gilgit-Baltistan shall be an *ex officio* non-voting member of the Council.

(5) The qualifications and disqualifications for being elected, as, and for being, a member of the Council shall, in the case of a member referred to in sub-clause (e) of clause (1), be the same as those for being elected as, and for being a member of the Assembly.

(6) The seat of a member of the Council elected by the Assembly, hereinafter referred to as an elected member, shall become vacant, –
- (a) if he resigns his seat by notice in writing under his hand addressed to the Chairman or, in his absence, to the Secretary of the Council;
- (b) if he is absent, without the leave of the Chairman, from ten consecutive sittings of the Council;
- (c) if he fails to make the oath referred to in clause (11) within a period of ninety days after the date of his election, unless the Chairman, for good cause shown, extends the period; or
- (d) if he ceases to be qualified for being a member under any provision of this Order or any other law for the time being in force.

(7) If any question arises whether a member has, after his election, become disqualified from being a member of the Council, the Chairman shall refer the question to the Chief Election Commissioner and, if the Chief Election Commissioner is of the opinion that the member has become disqualified, the member shall cease to be member and his seat shall become vacant.

(8) An election to fill a vacancy in the office of an elected member shall be

held not later than thirty days from the occurrence of the vacancy or, if the election cannot be held within that period because the Assembly is dissolved, within thirty days of the general election to the Assembly.

(9) The manner of election of elected members and filling of a casual vacancy in the office of an elected member shall be such as may be prescribed.

(10) An elected member shall hold office for a term of five years from the day he enters upon his office.

(11) An elected member shall, before entering upon office, make before the Chairman or the Vice Chairman oath in the form set out in the First Schedule.

(12) The executive authority of the Council shall extend to all matters with respect to which the Council has power to make laws and shall be exercised, in the name of the Council, by the Chairman who may act either directly or through the Secretariat of the Council of which Federal Minister for Kashmir Affairs and Gilgit-Baltistan shall be incharge.

Provided that the Council may direct that, in respect of such matters it may specify, its authority shall be exercisable by the Vice-Chairman of the Council, subject to such conditions, if any, as the Council may specify.

(13) The Chairman may from among the elected members of the Council appoint not more than three Advisors on such terms and conditions as he may determine.

(14) An advisor shall, before entering upon office, make before the Chairman oath in form set out in the First Schedule.

(15) An Advisor who is a member of the Assembly shall have the right to speak in, and otherwise take part in the proceedings of the Council, but shall not by virtue of this clause be entitled to vote.

(16) The Council may make rules for regulating its procedure and the conduct of its business, and shall have power to act notwithstanding any vacancy in the membership thereof, and any proceedings of the Council shall not be invalid on the ground that a person who was not entitled to do so sat, voted or otherwise took part in the proceedings.

(17) Orders and other instruments made and executed in the name of the Council shall be authenticated in such manner as may be specified in rules to be made by the Council and the validity of an order or instrument which is so authenticated shall not be called in question on the ground that it is not an order or instrument made or executed by the Council.

(18) The Chairman may regulate the allocation and transaction of the business of the Council and may, for the convenient transaction of that business, delegate any of its functions to officers and authorities subordinate to it.

55. Chairman of Council power to pardon and reprieve. – The Chairman shall have power to grant pardons, reprieves and respites and to remit, suspend or commute any sentence passed by any court, tribunal or other authority.

PART VII: THE LEGISLATURE

56. Legislative Assembly. – (1) The Legislative Assembly shall consist of **thirty three** members of whom –
- (a) **twenty four** members shall be elected directly on the basis of adult franchise;
- (b) **six** women members shall be elected on the pattern as in case of reserved seat in Pakistan.
- (c) **three** technocrats and other professional members shall be elected on the pattern as in case of reserved seat in Pakistan.

Explanation. – In sub-clause (c), the expression "technocrat or other professional" includes a person who is in possession of such qualification or experience as may be prescribed.

(2) The manner of election of the members of the Assembly and the manner of filling casual vacancies shall be such as may be prescribed.

(3) The Assembly, unless sooner dissolved, shall continue for five years from the date appointed for their first meeting.

(4) A general election to the Assembly shall be held within a period of sixty days immediately preceding the day on which the term of the Assembly is due to expire, unless the Assembly has been sooner dissolved, and result of the election shall be declared not later than fourteen days before that day.

(5) On dissolution of Assembly on completion of its term, or in case it is dissolved under Article 62, the Chairman of the Council shall appoint a care- taker Cabinet:

Provided that the care-taker Chief Minister shall be selected by the Chairman of the Council in consultation with the Chief Minister, the leader of the Opposition in the outgoing Assembly and the Minister for Kashmir Affairs and Gilgit-Baltistan:

Provided further that the members of the care-taker Cabinet shall be appointed on the advice of the care-taker Chief Minister:

Provided also that if the Chief Minister, the Leader of the Opposition in the outgoing Assembly and the Minister for Kashmir Affairs and Gilgit-Baltistan do not agree on any person to be appointed as care-taker Chief Minister, the Chairman of the Council may appoint, in his discretion, a care-taker Chief Minister.

57. Oath of members of the Assembly. – (1) A person elected as a member of the Assembly shall not take his seat in the Assembly until he makes before such person as is prescribed by rules of the Assembly an oath in the form set out in the First Schedule.

(2) The oath may be made when the Assembly is in session.

(3) If any person sits or votes in the Assembly knowing that he is not qualified to be, or is disqualified from being a member of the Assembly he shall be liable in respect of every day on which he so sits or votes; shall be guilty of an offence

punishable for a term which shall not be less than seven years and a fine which shall not be less than two hundred thousand rupees.

58. Qualifications of members of the Assembly. – (1) A person shall be qualified to be elected as, and to be, a member of the Assembly if –
    (a) he is a citizen;
    (b) he is not less than twenty-five years of age;
    (c) his name appears on the electoral roll of any constituency in Gilgit-Baltistan; and
    (d) he is not a dual national.
(2) A person shall be disqualified from being so elected if-
    (a) he is of unsound mind and stands so declared by a competent court; or
    (b) he is an un-discharged insolvent unless a period of ten years has elapsed since his being adjudged as insolvent; or
    (c) he has been on conviction for any offence sentenced to transportation for any term or imprisonment for a term of not less than two years unless a period of five years has elapsed since his release; or
    (d) he holds any office of profit in the Service of Gilgit-Baltistan or Azad Jammu and Kashmir or Pakistan other than an office which is not a whole time office remunerated either by salary or by fee other than an office specified in the Second Schedule; or
    (e) he has been in the Service or of any statutory body or anybody which is owned or controlled by the Government of Pakistan or Gilgit-Baltistan or Azad Jammu and Kashmir or in which such Government has a controlling share or interest, unless a period of two years has elapsed since he ceased to be in such service; or
    (f) he has been dismissed for misconduct from the Service unless a period of five years has elapsed since his dismissal; or
    (g) he is otherwise disqualified from being a member of the Assembly by this Order or by any other law.

59. Seat in Assembly becomes vacant under certain circumstances. – (1) The seat of a member of the Assembly shall become vacant if –
    (a) he/she resigns his seat by notice in writing under his hand addressed to the Speaker, in his absence, to the Secretary of the Assembly; or
    (b) he/she is absent from the Assembly without the leave of the Assembly for thirty consecutive sitting days of the Assembly; or
    (c) he/she fails to make the oath referred to in Article 57 within a period of ninety days after the date of his election unless the Speaker for good cause shown extends the period; or
    (d) he/she is elected as member of the Council; or
    (e) he/she ceases to be qualified for being a member under any provision of

this Order or any other law.

(2) If the member of the Assembly is elected to more than one seat, he shall within a period of thirty days after the declaration of result for the last such seat, resign all but one of his seats, and if he does not so resign, all the seats to which he has been elected shall become vacant at the expiration of the said period of thirty days except the seat to which he has been last elected or, if he has been elected to more than one seat on the same day, the seat for election to which his nomination was filed last.

(3) If any question arises whether a member of the Assembly has, after his election become disqualified from being a member of the Assembly, the Speaker shall refer the question to the Chief Election Commissioner and, if the Chief Election Commissioner is of the opinion that the member has become disqualified the member shall cease to be a member and his seat shall become vacant.

(4) When except by dissolution of the Assembly, a seat in the Assembly has become vacant not later than one hundred and twenty days before the term of the Assembly is due to expire, an election to fill the seat shall be held within sixty days from the occurrence of the vacancy.

60. Right of Governor to address the Assembly. – (1) The Governor may address the Assembly and may for that purpose require the attendance of the members.

(2) The Advocate General shall have the right to speak and otherwise take part in the proceedings of the Assembly or any Committee thereof of which he may be named a member, but shall not by virtue of this Article be entitled to vote.

61. Meetings of the Assembly. – (1) The Assembly shall assemble at such times and at such places as the Governor may appoint, and the Governor may prorogue a session of the Assembly except when the Assembly has been summoned by the Speaker.

(2) Any meeting of the Assembly may be adjourned by the Speaker or other person presiding thereat.

(3) There shall be at least three sessions of the Assembly every year, and not more than one hundred and twenty days shall intervene between the last sitting of the Assembly in one session and the date appointed for its first sitting in the next session.

Provided that the Assembly shall meet for not less than one hundred and thirty working days in each parliamentary year.

(4) On a requisition signed by not less than one-third of the total membership of the Assembly, the Speaker shall summon the Assembly to meet, at such time and place as he thinks fit, within fourteen days of the receipt of the requisition, and when the Speaker has summoned the Assembly, only he may prorogue it.

62. Dissolution of the Assembly. – (1) The Governor shall dissolve the Assembly if so advised by the Chief Minister, and the Assembly shall, unless sooner dissolved, stands dissolved at the expiration of the forty-eight hours after the Chief Minister has so advised.

Explanation. – Reference in this Article to Chief Minister shall not be construed to include reference to a Chief Minister against whom a resolution for a vote of no-confidence has been moved in the Assembly but has not been voted upon or against whom such a resolution has been passed or who is continuing in office after his resignation or after the dissolution of the Assembly.

(2) When the Assembly is dissolved a general election to the Assembly shall be held within a period of ninety days after the dissolution, and the result of the election shall be declared not later than fourteen days after the conclusion of the polls.

(3) Notwithstanding anything in the Order, if at any time it is not possible for any reason to hold general election to the Assembly, the Chairman of the Council may postpone the election for a period not exceeding ninety days at a time.

63. Speaker of the Assembly. – (1) After a general election, the Assembly shall, at its first meeting and to the exclusion of any other business, elect from amongst its members a Speaker and a Deputy Speaker of the Assembly.

Provided that the period intervening between the declaration of the official result of the election to the Assembly and the date for assumption of office of members shall not exceed thirty days.

(2) Before entering upon office, a member of the Assembly elected as Speaker or Deputy Speaker shall make before the Assembly an oath in the form set out in the First Schedule.

(3) All the proceedings of the Assembly shall be conducted in accordance with rules of procedure made by the Assembly and approved by the Governor.

(4) The Speaker shall preside the meetings of the Assembly except when a resolution for his removal from the office is being considered and, when the office of the Speaker is vacant, or the Speaker is absent, or is unable to perform his functions due to any cause, the Deputy Speaker shall act as Speaker and if at that time, the Deputy Speaker is also absent or is unable to act as Speaker due to any cause, such member of the Assembly present as may be determined by the Rules of Procedure of the Assembly shall preside at the meeting of the Assembly.

(5) Soon after as the office of Speaker or Deputy Speaker becomes vacant, the Assembly shall elect one of its members to fill the office.

(6) The Speaker may resign from his office by writing under his hand addressed to the Governor.

(7) The Deputy Speaker may resign his office by writing under his hand addressed to the Speaker.

(8) The office of the Speaker or Deputy Speaker shall become vacant if-
    (a) except as provided in clause (9) he ceases to be a member of the Assembly; or

(b) he is removed from office by a resolution of the Assembly, of which not less than seven days' notice by not less than one-fourth of the total membership of the Assembly has been given and which is passed by a majority of total membership of the Assembly.

(9) When the Assembly is dissolved, the Speaker shall continue in his office till the person elected to fill the office by the next Assembly enters upon his office.

64. Voting in Assembly and quorum. – (1) Subject to this Order, –
   (a) a decision in the Assembly shall be taken by a majority of the votes of the members present and voting but the Speaker or the person presiding in his absence shall not vote except when there is an equality of votes in which case he shall exercise his casting vote;
   (b) the Assembly may act notwithstanding any vacancy in its membership; and
   (c) any proceedings in the Assembly shall not be invalid on the ground that some person who was not entitled to do so sit, voted or otherwise took part in the proceedings.

(2) If at any time during the meeting of the Assembly the attention of the person presiding at the meeting is drawn to the fact that number of the members is less than one-third of the total membership of the Assembly, it shall be the duty of the person presiding either to adjourn the meeting or to suspend the meeting till such number of members are present.

65. Restriction on discussion in Assembly, etc. – No discussion shall take place in the Assembly or the Council or the joint sitting with respect to matters relating to Foreign Affairs, Defence, Internal Security and Fiscal Plans of Government of Pakistan and the conduct of the any Judge of the Gilgit-Baltistan Supreme Appellate Court or the Gilgit-Baltistan Chief Court in the discharge of his duties.

66. Finance Committee. – (1) The expenditure of the Assembly within authorized appropriation shall be controlled by the Assembly acting on the advice of the Finance Committee.

(2) The Finance Committee shall consist of the Speaker, the Finance Minister and such other members as may be elected thereto by the Assembly.

67. Secretariat of the Assembly. – (1) The Assembly shall have a separate Secretariat.

(2) The Assembly may by law regulate the recruitment and conditions of service of persons appointed to the Secretariat Staff of the Assembly.

(3) Until provision is made by the Assembly under clause (2) the persons appointed to the Secretariat Staff of the Assembly shall continue to be governed by conditions of service for the time being applicable to them.

PART VIII: DISTRIBUTION OF LEGISLATIVE POWERS

68. Legislative Powers. – (1) Subject to the succeeding provisions of this Article,

both the Council and the Assembly shall have the power to make laws, –
  (a) for the territories of Gilgit-Baltistan;
  (b) for all citizens of Gilgit-Baltistan; and
  (c) for the officers of the Council or as the case may be, the Government, wherever they may be.
 (2) Subject to clause (3) –
  (a) the Council shall have exclusive power to make laws with respect to any matter in the Legislative List set out in the Third Schedule, hereinafter referred to as the Legislative List; and
  (b) subject to clause 2 (a), the assembly shall and the Council shall not, have power to make laws with respect to any matter not enumerated in the Legislative List.
  (c) The Council shall have the powers to adopt any amendment in the existing Laws or any new Law in force in Pakistan.
(3) Notwithstanding anything contained in this Order, the Government of Pakistan shall have exclusive powers and the Council and the Assembly shall not have powers to make any law in respect of the following matters. –
  (a) the defence and external security of Gilgit-Baltistan;
  (b) the current coin of the issue of any bills, notes or other paper currency; or
  (c) the external affairs of Gilgit-Baltistan including foreign trade and foreign aid; or
  (d) such other matters as the President may specify by Order.

69. Tax to be levied by laws only. – No tax shall be levied for the purposes of the territories of Gilgit-Baltistan except by or under the authority of an Act of the Council or the Assembly and all taxes and levies competently imposed under an Act of the Assembly or the Council or under any law made by the Government of Pakistan shall remain in force.

PART IX: ISLAMIC PROVISIONS

70. No laws against Islamic Injunctions, etc. – No law shall be repugnant to the teachings and requirements of Islam as set out in the Holy Quran and Sunnah and all existing laws shall be brought in conformity with the Holy Quran and Sunnah.

71. Reference to Council of Islamic Ideology. – (1) If one-third of the total number of the members of the Assembly or, as the case may, the Council so requires, the Assembly or the Council shall refer to the Council of Islamic Ideology constituted under the Constitution of Islamic Republic of Pakistan (hereinafter referred to as the Islamic Council) for advice on any question as to whether a proposed law is or is not repugnant to the injunctions of Islam.
  (2) When a question is referred by the Assembly or the Council, as the case

may be, the Council of Islamic Ideology shall, within fifteen days thereof, inform the Assembly or the Council, as the case may be, of the period within which the Council of Islamic Ideology expects to be able to furnish that advice.

(3) Where the Assembly or, as the case may be, the Council considers that in the public interest, the making of the proposed law in relation to which the question arose should not be postponed until the advice of the Council of Islamic Ideology is furnished, the law may be made before the advice is furnished.

Provided that, where a law is referred for advice to the Council of Islamic Ideology and the Council advises that the law is repugnant to the injunctions of Islam, the Assembly or, as the case may be, the Council shall reconsider the law so made.

72. General provisions regarding Council, etc. – (1) The validity of any proceedings in the Council or the Assembly shall not be questioned in any Court.

(2) An officer or member or an authority in whom powers are vested for regulation of proceedings, conduct of business, maintain order in the Council or the Assembly shall not, in relation to exercise by him of any of those powers, be subject to the jurisdiction of any Court.

(3) A member of, or a person entitled to speak in, the Council or the Assembly, shall not be liable to any proceedings in any Court in respect of anything said by him or any vote given by him in the Council or the Assembly or in any Committee thereof.

(4) A person shall not be liable to any proceedings in any Court in respect of publication by or under the authority of the Council or the Assembly, of any report, paper, vote or proceedings.

(5) No process issued by a Court or other authority shall except with the leave of the Chairman of the Council or the Speaker be served or executed within the precincts of the place where a meeting of the Council or, as the case may be, the Assembly is being held.

(6) Subject to this Article, the privileges of the Council, the Assembly, the Committees and members of the Council, or the Assembly and of the persons entitled to speak in the Council, or the Assembly, may be determined by law.

73. Authentication of Bills Passed by the Council. – A Bill passed by the Council shall not require the assent of the Governor and shall, upon its authentication by the Chairman of the Council, become law and be called an Act of the Council.

74. Governor's assent to Bills. – (1) Subject to this Order, when a Bill has been passed by the Assembly it shall be presented to the Governor for assent.

(2) When a Bill is presented to the Governor for assent, the Governor shall, within thirty days, –

    (a) assent to the Bill; or

    (b) in the case of a Bill other than a Money Bill, return the Bill to the

Assembly with a message requesting that the Bill, or any specified provision thereof, be reconsidered and that any amendment specified in the message be considered.

(3) When the Governor has returned a Bill to the Assembly, it shall be reconsidered by the Assembly and, if it is again passed, with or without amendment, by the Assembly, by the votes of the majority of the members of the Assembly present and voting, and in accordance with the provision of this Order and in not in any manner prejudicial to the security, integrity, solidarity and strategic interest of Pakistan, it shall be again presented to the Governor and Governor shall not withhold assent thereform.

(4) When the Governor has assented to a Bill, it shall become law and be called an Act of Assembly.

PART X: FINANCIAL PROCEDURE

75. Council Consolidated Fund. – (1) All revenues received by the Council, all loans raised by the Council and all moneys received by it in payment of any loan shall form a part of Consolidated Fund, to be known as the Council Consolidated Fund.

(2) All other moneys –
   (a) received by or on behalf of the Council; or
   (b) received by or deposited with the Gilgit-Baltistan Supreme Appellate Court or any other Court established under the authority of this Order shall be credited to the Public Account of the Council.

(3) The Custody of the Council Consolidated Fund, the payment of money into that Fund, the withdrawal of money there from, the custody of other moneys received by or on behalf of the Council, their payment into, and withdrawal from the Public Account of the Council, and all matters connected with or ancillary to the matters aforesaid, shall be regulated by the Act of the Council or, until provision in that behalf is so made, by rules made by the Chairman of the Council.

(4) The Council shall, in respect of every financial year, cause to be prepared, and approve, a statement of estimated receipts and expenditure of the Council for that year.

Provided that the Government of Pakistan shall provide grant in aid to the Council to meet its revenue deficit.

(5) The Chairman of the Council shall authenticate by his signature the statement approved by the Council under clause (4), and no expenditure from the Council Consolidated Fund shall be deemed to be duly authorized unless it is specified in the statement so authenticated.

(6) If in respect of any financial year it is found:
   (a) that the amount authorized to be expended for a particular service for the current financial year is insufficient, or that a need has arisen for

expenditure upon some new service not included in the statement referred to in clause (4) for that year; or

(b) that any money has been spend on any service during a financial year in excess of the amount granted for that year, the Chairman of the Council shall have the power to authorize expenditure from the Council Consolidated Fund and shall cause to be laid before the Council a supplementary statement or, as the case may be, an excess statement, setting out the amount of that expenditure, and the provision of clause (3) and (4) shall apply to these statements as they apply to the statement referred to in clause (3).

(7) Notwithstanding anything contained in the foregoing provisions of this Article, the Council shall have power to make any grant in advance in respect of the estimated expenditure for a part of any financial year, not exceeding four months, pending completion of the procedure prescribed in clause (3) and (4).

76. Gilgit-Baltistan Consolidated Fund. – (1) All revenues received by the Government, all loans raised by the Government with the approval of Government of Pakistan and all moneys received by it in payment of any loan shall form a part of Consolidated Fund, to be known as the Gilgit-Baltistan Consolidated Fund.

(2) All other moneys –
  (a) received by or on behalf of the Government; or
  (b) received by or deposited with any other Court established under the authority of the Government, shall be credited to the Public Account of the Government.

(3) The custody of the Gilgit-Baltistan Consolidated Fund, the payment of money into that Fund, the withdrawal of money therefrom, the custody of other moneys received by or on behalf of the Government, their payment into, and withdrawal from the Public Account of the Government, and all matters connected with or ancillary to the matters aforesaid, shall be regulated by the Act of the Assembly or, until provision in that behalf is so made, by rules made by the Governor.

77. Budget. – (1) The Government shall, in respect of every financial year, cause to be laid before the Assembly a statement of estimated receipts and expenditure for that year, to be called the Annual Budget.

(2) The Annual Budget shall be submitted to the Assembly in the form of demands for grant and the Assembly shall have power to assent to, or to refuse to assent to any demand, or to assent to any demand subject to a reduction of the amount specified therein.

(3) No demand for a grant shall be made except on the recommendation of the Government.

(4) The Annual Budget as passed by the Assembly shall be placed before the Governor who shall authenticate it by his signature.

(5) If in respect of any financial year it is found_
   (a) that the amount authorized to be expended for a particular service for the current financial year is insufficient, or that a need has arisen for expenditure upon some new service not included in the Annual Budget for that year; or
   (b) that any money has been spend on any service during a financial year in excess of the amount granted for that year, the Government shall have the power to authorize expenditure from the Gilgit-Baltistan Consolidated Fund and shall cause to be laid before the Assembly a Budget or, as the case may be, an excess Budget, setting out the amount of that expenditure, and the provisions of this Article shall apply to those Budgets as they apply to the Annual Budget.

(6) Notwithstanding anything contained in the foregoing provisions of this Article, the Assembly shall have power to make any grant in advance in respect of the estimated expenditure for a part of any financial year, not exceeding four months, pending completion of the procedure prescribed in clause (2) for the voting of such grant and the authentication of the Budget as passed by the Assembly in accordance with the provisions of clause (4) in relation to the expenditure.

78. Special provisions regarding Budget, etc. – (1) Where the Annual Budget for any financial year cannot be passed by the Assembly by reason of its having been dissolved, the Chief Minister shall cause to be prepared an Annual Budget for that year and, by his signature, authenticate the Budget.

(2) The Annual Budget for any financial year authenticated by the Chief Minister under clause (1) shall, for the purpose of this Order, be deemed to have been passed by the Assembly.

79. Restriction on expenditure. – No expenditure shall be incurred by the Government except authorized by the Annual or Supplementary Budget as passed or deemed to have been passed by the Assembly.

PART XI: ORDINANCE

80. Power to make Ordinance. – (1) The Governor may, except when the Assembly is in session, if satisfied that circumstances exist which render it necessary to take immediate action, make and promulgate an Ordinance as the circumstances may require.

(2) An Ordinance promulgated under this Article shall have the same force and effect as an Act of the Assembly and shall be subject to like restrictions as the power of the Assembly to make law, but every such Ordinance;
   (a) shall be laid before the Assembly and shall stand repealed at the expiration of four months from its promulgation or, if before the expiration of that period a resolution disapproving it is passed by the

Assembly, upon the passing of that resolution; and
(b) may be withdrawn at any time by the Governor.

(3) Without prejudice to the provisions of clause (2) an Ordinance laid before the Assembly or the Council shall be deemed to be a Bill introduced in the Assembly or the Council, as the case may be.

(4) The Governor shall likewise, except when the Council is in session, if so advised by the Chairman of the Council, make, promulgate and withdraw an Ordinance as the circumstances may require, and the provisions of clause (2) and clause (3) shall apply to an Ordinance so made as if references therein to 'Act of the Assembly and, Assembly were references respectively to' Act of the Council and Council.

PART XII: THE JUDICATURE

81. Appointment of Judges to the Supreme Appellate Court and Chief Court, Gilgit-Baltistan. – (1) There shall be a Judicial Commission of Gilgit-Baltistan, hereinafter in this Article referred to as the Commission, for appointment of Judges of the Supreme Appellate Court and Chief Court as hereinafter provided.

(2) For appointment of Judges of the Supreme Appellate Court, the Commission shall consist of –

i.	Chief Judge, Supreme Appellate Court;	Chairman
ii.	Secretary Kashmir Affairs & Gilgit-Baltistan	Member
iii.	One most senior Judge of the Supreme Appellate Court;	Member
iv.	One former Judge of the Supreme Court of Pakistan to be nominated by the Chief Justice of Pakistan for a terms of two years	Member
v.	Minister for Law, Govt. of Gilgit-Baltistan;	Member
vi.	Chief Secretary, Gilgit-Baltistan; and	Member
vii.	A Senior Advocate of the Supreme Appellate Court of Gilgit-Baltistan nominated by the Bar Council for a term of two years.	Member
viii.	Joint Secretary, Gilgit-Baltistan Council	Secretary

(3) On recommendation of the Commission, the Gilgit-Baltistan Council shall move a summary to the Chairman Gilgit-Baltistan Council for approval of the appointment of Judge, Supreme Appellate Court;

(4) Notwithstanding anything contained in clause (1), clause (2) or clause (3), the Chief Judge of the Supreme Appellate Court shall be appointed by the above Commission. However, the Secretary, Kashmir Affairs and Gilgit-Baltistan shall replace the Chairmanship of Commission.

(5) The Commission may make rules regulating its procedure.

(6) For appointment of Judges of the Chief Court, Gilgit-Baltistan the Commission shall in clause (2) shall also include the following, namely:

i.	Chief Judge, Chief Court;	Member
ii.	One most senior Judge of the Chief Court;	Member
iii.	iii. A Senior Advocate of the Chief Court of Gilgit-Baltistan nominated by the concerned Bar Council for a term of two years	Member

Provided that for appointment of the Chief Judge of the Chief Court, the most Senior Judge mentioned in paragraph (ii) shall not be member of the commission.

82. Gilgit-Baltistan Supreme Appellate Court. – (1) There shall be a Gilgit-Baltistan Supreme Appellate Court, referred to as the Supreme Appellate Court to be the highest Court of Appeal.

(2) Subject to the provisions of this Order, the Supreme Appellate Court shall have such jurisdiction as is or may be conferred on it by this Order or by under any law.

(3) The Supreme Appellate Court shall consist of a Chief Judge to be known as Chief Judge of Gilgit-Baltistan and two other Judges:

Provided that the Government of Pakistan may from time to time increase the number of judges.

(4) The person holding office as Chief Judge or other Judge of the Supreme Appellate Court immediately before the commencement of this Order shall be deemed to be the Chief Judge or other Judge as the case may be appointed under this Order.

(5) A person shall not be appointed as the Chief Judge or Judge of the Supreme Appellate Court of Gilgit-Baltistan unless he –

- (a) has been, or is qualified to be, a judge of the Supreme Court of Pakistan; or
- (b) has for a period of, or for periods aggregating, not less than five years been a Judge of a Chief Court; or
- (c) for a period of or for periods aggregating, not less than fifteen years has been an advocate of a High Court.

Explanation. – In this sub-clause, the expression 'High Court' includes, –

- (a) the Chief Court of Gilgit-Baltistan, or an equivalent Court that existed in Gilgit-Baltistan before this order; and
- (b) a High Court in Pakistan including a High Court that existed in Pakistan at any time before this order.

(6) Before entering upon office, the Chief Judge of Gilgit-Baltistan shall make before the Governor and any other Judge of the Supreme Appellate Court of Gilgit-Baltistan shall make before the Chief Judge of Supreme Appellate Court, oath in the form set out in the First Schedule.

(7) The Chief Judge and judges of the Supreme Appellate Court of Gilgit-Baltistan shall be appointed by the Chairman on recommendation of the

Commission and shall hold office until he/she attains the age of 65 years, or unless he/she sooner resigns or is removed from office in accordance with law:

Provided that if the Chief Judge or a Judge is a person who has been a Judge of the Supreme Court of Pakistan, he/she shall hold office until he/she attains the age of 70 years, or unless he/she sooner resigns or is removed from office in accordance with law.

(8) At any time when the office of Chief Judge of Gilgit-Baltistan is vacant, or the Chief Judge, is absent or unable to perform the functions of his office due to any other cause, the Chairman shall appoint the senior most Judge of the Supreme Appellate Court to act as Chief Judge of Gilgit-Baltistan.

(9) The remuneration and other terms and conditions of service of the Chief Judge and of a Judge of the Gilgit-Baltistan Supreme Appellate Court shall be such as are admissible to the Chief Justice of Pakistan and Judges of the Supreme Court of Pakistan.

Provided that Council will provide funds to Supreme Appellate Court Gilgit-Baltistan.

83. Original Jurisdiction. – (1) Without prejudice to the provisions of Article-94, the Supreme Appellate Court, on an application of any aggrieved party, shall if it considers that a question of general public importance with reference to the enforcement of any of the fundamental right conferred by Part II of this Order is involved, have the power to make declaratory order of the nature mentioned in the said Article.

(2) An application made under clause (1) shall be heard by a Bench comprising not less than two Judges to be constituted by the Chief Judge.

84. Appellate Jurisdiction. – (1) Subject to the succeeding provision of this Article, the Supreme Appellate Court of Gilgit-Baltistan shall have jurisdiction to hear and determine appeals from judgments, decrees, final orders or sentences of the Chief Court of Gilgit-Baltistan.

(2) An appeal shall lie to the Supreme Appellate Court of the Gilgit-Baltistan from any judgment, decree, final order or sentence of the Chief Court of Gilgit-Baltistan, –

 (a) if the Chief Court has on appeal reversed an order of acquittal of an accused person and sentenced to death or to imprisonment for life; or, on revision, has enhanced a sentence to a sentence as aforesaid; or.

 (b) if the Chief Court has withdrawn for trial before itself any case from any court subordinate to it and has in such trial convicted the accused person and sentenced him as aforesaid; or

 (c) if the Chief Court has imposed any punishment on any person for contempt of the Chief Court; or

 (d) if the amount or value of the subject matter of the dispute in the court of first instance was, and also in dispute in appeal is, not less than fifty thousand rupees or such other sum as may be specified in that behalf by Act of the Council and judgment, decree or final order appealed from has varied or set aside the judgment, decree or final order of the court immediately below; or

(e) if the judgment, decree or final order involved directly or indirectly some claim or question respecting property or the like amount or value and the judgment, decree or final order appealed from has varied or set aside the judgment, decree or final order of the court immediately below; or

(f) if the Chief Court certifies that the case involves a substantial question of law as to the interpretation of this Order.

(3) An appeal to the Gilgit-Baltistan Supreme Appellate Court of from a judgment, decree, order or sentence of the Chief Court in a case to which clause (11) does not apply shall lie only if the Supreme Appellate Court grants leave to appeal.

(4) (a) an appeal to Gilgit-Baltistan the Supreme Appellate Court shall be heard by a Bench consisting of not less than two judges to be constituted or reconstituted by the Chief Judge; (b) if the Judges hearing a petition or an appeal are divided in opinion, the opinion of majority shall prevail; (c) if there is no such majority as aforesaid the petition or appeal, as the case may be, shall be placed for hearing and disposal before another Judge to be nominated by the ChiefJudge:

Provided that in case of difference of opinion as aforesaid, the decision of the Supreme Appellate Court shall be expressed in term of opinion of the senior of the two Judges.

(5) The person holding office as Chief Judge of the Gilgit-Baltistan Supreme Appellate Court of Gilgit-Baltistan immediately before the commencement of this Order shall as from such commencement hold office as Chief Judge of Supreme Appellate Court under this Order on terms and conditions prescribed in this Order provided these are not inferior to the terms and conditions applicable to him immediately before such commencement.

(6) All legal proceedings pending in the Gilgit-Baltistan Supreme Appellate Court, immediately before the commencement of this Order, shall on such commencement, stand transferred to, and be deemed to be pending before the Supreme Appellate Court for determination and any judgment or order of the Supreme Appellate Court delivered or made before such commencement shall have the same force and effect as if it had been delivered or made by the Supreme Appellate Court.

85. Issue and execution of processes of Supreme Appellate Court. – (1) The Supreme Appellate Court shall have powers to issue such directions, orders or decrees as may be necessary for doing complete justice in any case or matter pending before it including an order for the purpose of securing the attendance of any person or the discovery or production of any document.

(2) Any such direction, order or decree shall be enforceable throughout Gilgit-Baltistan as if it has been issued by the Gilgit-Baltistan Chief Court.

(3) All executive and judicial authorities throughout Gilgit-Baltistan shall act in aid of the Supreme Appellate Court.

(4) Subject to this Order and Law, the Supreme Appellate Court may, in consultation with the Council, make rules regulating the practice and procedure of the Court:

Provided that till the new rules are framed, the rules framed by the Supreme Appellate Court shall, so far as they are not inconsistent with this Order and any other law, deemed to have been made by the Supreme Appellate Court until altered or amended and references to the Supreme Appellate Court in these rules shall be construed to be referred to the Supreme Appellate Court.

86. Decisions of Supreme Appellate Court binding on other Courts. – Any decision of the Supreme Appellate Court shall, to the extent that it decides a question of law or is based upon or enunciates a principle of law, be binding on all other Courts in the Gilgit-Baltistan.

87. Seat of the Supreme Appellate Court. – (1) The Seat of the Supreme Appellate Court shall be at Gilgit.

(2) The Supreme Appellate Court may sit at such other place or places as the Chief Judge of Gilgit-Baltistan, with the approval of the Governor, may appoint.

88. Review of judgment or order by the Supreme Appellate Court. – The Supreme Appellate Court shall have powers, subject to the provisions of an Act of the Assembly or the Council and of any rules made by the Supreme Appellate Court, to review any judgment pronounced or any order made by it.

89. Supreme Judicial Council. – (1) There shall be a Supreme Judicial Council of Gilgit-Baltistan.

(2) The Supreme Judicial Council shall consist of, –
    (a) the Chief Judge of Gilgit-Baltistan who shall be its Chairman.
    (b) the Senior Judge of the Supreme Appellate Court; and
    (c) the Chief Judge of the Chief Court .

(3) A Judge of the Supreme Appellate Court or of the Chief Court shall not be removed from office except as provided by this Article.

Explanation: The expression "Judge" includes the Chief Judge of Gilgit-Baltistan and the Chief Judge of Chief Court of Gilgit-Baltistan.

(4) If on information received from the Supreme Judicial Council or from any other source, the Chairman of the Gilgit-Baltistan Council or the Governor is of the opinion that a Judge of the Supreme Appellate Court or of the Chief Court,_

(a) may be incapable of properly performing the duties of his office by reason of physical or mental incapacity; or
  (b) may have been guilty of misconduct, the Chairman or the Governor, as the case may be, shall direct the Supreme Judicial Council to inquire into the matter.

(5) If, upon any matter inquired into by the Supreme Judicial Council, there is a difference of opinion amongst its members, the opinion of the majority shall prevail, and the report of the Supreme Judicial Council shall be expressed in terms of the view of the majority.

(6) If, after inquiring into the matter, the Supreme Judicial Council reports to the Chairman of the Gilgit-Baltistan Council that it is of the opinion.
  (a) that the Judge is incapable of performing the duties of his office or has been guilty of misconduct; and
  (b) that he should be removed from office, the Chairman shall advise the Governor to remove the Judge from his office and the Governor shall pass orders accordingly.

(7) The Supreme Judicial Council shall issue a Code of conduct to be observed by Judges of the Gilgit-Baltistan Supreme Appellate Court, and of the Gilgit-Baltistan Chief Court.

(8) If at any time the Supreme Judicial Council is inquiring the conduct of a Judge who is a member of the Supreme Judicial Council, or a member of the Supreme Judicial Council is absent or is unable to act due to illness or any other cause, than:
  (a) If such member is the Chief Judge or the Judge of the Supreme Appellate Court the Judge of the Supreme Appellate Court who is next in seniority;
  (b) If such member is the Chief Judge of Gilgit-Baltistan Court, the most senior most of the other Judges of the Chief Court, shall, act as a member of the Supreme Judicial Council in his place.

(9) If, upon any matter inquired into by the Supreme Judicial Council, there is a difference of opinion amongst its member, the opinion of the Supreme Judicial Council shall be expressed in terms of the view of the majority.

90. Power of Supreme Judicial Council to enforce attendance of persons, etc. – (1) for the purpose of inquiring into any matter, the Supreme Judicial Council shall have the same powers as has the Supreme Appellate Court, to issue directions or order for securing the attendance of any person or the discovery or the production of any document and any such direction or order shall be enforceable as if it has been issued by the Supreme Appellate Court.

(2) The provisions of Article 81, shall, mutatis mutandis apply to the Supreme Judicial Council as they apply to the Gilgit-Baltistan Supreme Appellate Court and the Gilgit-Baltistan Chief Court.

91. Bar of Jurisdiction. – The proceedings before the Supreme Judicial Council, and the removal of a Judge under Article 87, shall not be called in question in any Court.

92. Gilgit-Baltistan Chief Court. – (1) There shall be a Gilgit-Baltistan Chief Court, hereinafter called the Chief Court, which shall consist of a Chief Judge and six other judges, of whom 60% will be appointed from lawyers community and 40% from subordinate judiciary:

Provided that the Government of Pakistan may from time to time increase the number of judges.

(2) The function of the Chief Court may be performed by a Single Bench, a Division Bench or a Full Bench:, but the Chief Judge may recall a case pending before a Bench and make it over to another Bench or constitute a larger Bench for the purpose.

(3) In case of difference of opinion in a Full Bench, the opinion of the majority shall prevail;

(4) In case of difference of opinion in a Division Bench, the matter shall be referred to a third judge and the decision of the Chief Court shall be expressed in terms of judgment of the majority.

(5) The person holding office as Chief Judge or other Judge of the Chief Court Immediately before the commencement of this Order shall be deemed to be the Chief Judge or other Judge as the case may be appointed under this Order.

(6) A person shall not be appointed as a Judge of the Chief Court unless he is 45 years of age and:

> (a) he has for a period, or for periods aggregating, not less than ten years, been an Advocate of the Chief Court or a High Court in Pakistan. Provided that the expression "High Court" herein shall include a High Court or an equivalent Court; or
>
> (b) he has for a period of not less than ten years held a judicial office out of which not less than three years shall have been as District and Sessions Judge.

(7) Before he enters upon his office, the Chief Judge of the Chief Court shall make before the Governor, and judge of the Chief Court shall make before the Chief Judge, an oath in the form set out in the First Schedule.

(8) The Chief Judge or a Judge of the Chief Court shall hold office until he attains the age of sixty two years, unless he sooner resigns or is removed from office in accordance with law.

(9) If at any time any Judge of the Chief Court is absent or is unable to perform his functions due to illness or some other cause, the Chairman of the Gilgit-Baltistan Council may appoint a person qualified for appointment as a Judge of the Chief Court to be an Additional Judge for the period for which the Judge is absent or unable to perform his functions.

(10) A Judge of the Chief Court shall not, –
  (a) hold any other office of profit in the service of the Gilgit-Baltistan if his remuneration is thereby increased; or
  (b) occupy any other position carrying the right to remuneration for the rendering of services, but this clause shall not be construed as preventing a Judge from holding or managing private property.

(11) A person who has held office as Judge of the Chief Court shall not hold any office of profit in the service of Gilgit-Baltistan not being a Judicial or quasi-Judicial office or the office of Chief Election Commissioner or of Chairman or member of the Public Service Commission, before the expiration of two years after he ceased to hold that office.

(12) The remuneration and other terms and conditions of service of the Chief Judge and Judges of Chief Court shall be such as admissible the Chief Justice and the Judges of the High Courts of Pakistan.

93. Acting Chief Judge. – At any time when –
  (a) the Office of Chief Judge of Chief Court is vacant;
  (b) the Chief Judge of Chief Court is absent or is unable to perform the functions of his office due to any other cause, the Chairman shall appoint the most senior Judge of the Chief Court to act as Chief Judge.

94. Jurisdiction of Chief Court. – (1) The Chief Court shall have such jurisdiction as is conferred on it by this Order or by any other law.

(2) Subject to this Order, the Chief Court may if it is satisfied that no other adequate remedy is provided by law, –
  (a) the Government, exercising any power or performing any function in, or in relation to, Gilgit-Baltistan as may be appropriate for the enforcement of any of the fundamental rights conferred by this Order. on the application of any aggrieved party, make an order,—
    (i) directing a person performing functions in connection with the affairs of Gilgit-Baltistan or local authority to refrain from doing that which he is not permitted by law to do, or to do that which he is required by law to do; or
    (ii) declaring that any act done or proceeding taken by a person performing functions in connection with the affairs of the Gilgit-Baltistan or a local authority has been done or taken without lawful authority, and is of no legal effect; or
  (b) on the application of any person, make an order, –
    (i) directing that a person in custody in Gilgit-Baltistan be brought before the Chief Court so that the Court may satisfy itself that he is not being held in custody without lawful authority or in an unlawful manner; or

(ii) requiring a person holding or purporting to hold a public office in connection with the affairs of Gilgit-Baltistan to show under what authority of law he claims to hold that office; or

(c) on the application of any aggrieved person, make an order giving such directions to the person or authority, including the Council.

(3) An order shall not be made under clause (2) on application made by or in relation to a person in the Armed Forces of Pakistan in respect of his terms and conditions of service, in respect of any matter arising out of his service or in respect of any action in relation to him as a member of the Armed Forces of Pakistan.

(4) Where, –

(a) an application is made to the Chief Court for an order under sub-clause (a) or sub-clause (c) of clause (2); and

(b) the Court has reason to believe that the making of an interim order would have the effect of prejudicing or interfering with the carrying out of a public work or otherwise being harmful to the public interest, the Court shall not make an interim order unless the Advocate-General has been given notice of the application and the Court, after the Advocate-General or any officer authorized by him in this behalf has been given an opportunity of being heard, is satisfied that the making of the interim order would not have the effect referred to in sub-clause (b) of this clause.

(5) In this Article unless the context otherwise requires, the expression "person" includes any body politic or corporate, any authority of or under control of the Council or the Government and any court or tribunal other than the Gilgit-Baltistan Supreme Appellate Court, the Chief court or a Court or tribunal establish under a law relating to the Armed Forces of Pakistan.

95. Rules of procedure. – Subject to this Order and law the Chief Court may in consultation with the Government, make rules regulating practice and procedure of the Court or of any Court subordinate to it.

96. Decision of Chief Court binding on subordinate Courts. – Subject to Article 86, any decision of Chief Court shall, to the extent that it decides a question of law or is based upon or enunciates a principle of law, be binding on all Courts subordinate to it.

97. Seat of the Chief Court. – (1) The permanent seat of the Chief Court shall be at Gilgit.

(2) The Chief Court may, from time to time, sit at such other place as the Chief Judge of the Chief Court, with the approval of the Governor, may appoint.

98. Contempt of Court. – (1) In this Article the expression "Court" means the Gilgit-Baltistan Supreme Appellate Court or the Chief Court.

(2) A Court shall have power to punish any person who –
  (a) abuses, interferes with or obstructs the process of the Court in any way or disobeys any order of the Court;
  (b) scandalizes the Court or otherwise does anything which tends to bring the Court or a judge of the Court into hatred, ridicule or contempt;
  (c) does anything which tends to prejudice the determination of a matter pending before the Court; or
  (d) does any other thing which, by law, constitutes contempt of the Court.

(3) The exercise of the power conferred on a Court by this Article may be regulated by law and, subject to law, by rules made by the Court.

99. The Chief Court to superintend and control all courts subordinate to it, etc. – (1) The Chief Court shall superintend and control all other courts that are subordinate to it.

(2) A Court so established shall have such jurisdiction as conferred on it by law.

(3) No Court shall have any jurisdiction which is not conferred on it by this Order or by or under any other law.

100. Advisory jurisdiction. – (1) If, at any time, the Chairman of the Council or the Governor desires to obtain the opinion of the Gilgit-Baltistan Supreme Appellate Court on any question of law which he considers of public importance, he may refer the question to the Supreme Appellate Court of Gilgit-Baltistan for consideration.

(2) The Gilgit-Baltistan Supreme Appellate Court shall consider a question so referred and report its opinion on the question to the Chairman of the Council or as the case may be, the Governor.

101. Administrative Courts and Tribunals. – (1) Notwithstanding anything herein before contained, the Council in respect of matters to which its executive authority extends, and the Assembly in respect of matters to which the executive authority of the Government extends may by Act provide for the establishment of one or more Administrative Courts or Tribunals to exercise exclusive jurisdiction in respect of, -
  (a) matters relating to the terms and conditions of persons who are or have been in the service of Gilgit-Baltistan including disciplinary matters;
  (b) matters relating to claims arising from tortuous acts of the Council or the Government or any person in the service of Gilgit-Baltistan or of any local or other authority empowered by law to levy any tax or cess and any servant or such authority acting in the discharge of his duties as such servant; or
  (c) matters relating to acquisition, administration and disposal of any property which is deemed to be enemy property under any law.

(2) Notwithstanding anything herein before contained, where any

Administrative Court or Tribunal is established under clause (1), no other Court shall grant an injunction, make any order or entertain any proceedings in respect of any matter to which the jurisdiction of such Administrative Court or Tribunal extends and all proceedings in respect of any such matter which may be pending before such other court immediately before the establishment of the Administrative Court or Tribunal shall abate on such establishment.

(3) An appeal to the Gilgit-Baltistan Supreme Appellate Court from a judgment, decree, order or sentence of an Administrative Court or Tribunal shall lie only if the Supreme Appellate Court of Gilgit-Baltistan being satisfied, that the case involves a substantial question of law of public importance, grants leave to appeal.

Provided that Council will provide funds to Administrative Courts and Tribunals of Gilgit-Baltistan fall under Council legislative list.

102. Employees of Court. – The Gilgit-Baltistan Supreme Appellate Court and the Gilgit-Baltistan Chief Court, with the approval of the Chairman and Governor respectively, may make rules providing for the appointment of employees of the Court and for their terms and conditions of employment.

103. Supreme Court of Pakistan. – (1) The Supreme Court shall, to the exclusion of every other court including the Supreme Appellate Court and the Chief Court, have original jurisdiction in respect of:

    (i) any dispute between the Government, the Federation or the Government of a Province of Pakistan;

    (ii) any challenge to, or dispute raising any issue regarding, the *vires* or validity of this Order or any amendment hereto or modification herein, including an Order repealing, replacing or substituting this Order, and clause (2) of Article 126 hereof shall apply accordingly.

(2) Any aggrieved person may, subject to clause (3), appeal to the Supreme Court against any judgment, order or decree of the Supreme Appellate Court or the Chief Court made in any proceedings where the subject matter of the dispute or the matter in issue is not exclusively in relation to or under this Order or any law made hereunder or Gilgit-Baltistan.

(3) An appeal under clause (2) shall lie only if the Supreme Court grants leave to appeal.

(4) A decision of the Supreme Court, whether made under any of the foregoing clauses or otherwise, shall be as binding on all courts established by or under this Order as it is in terms of Article 189 of the Constitution on all courts in Pakistan, and Article 86 and Article 96 hereof shall apply accordingly.

PART XIII: SERVICES

104. Public Service Commission. – There shall be a Public Service Commission for Gilgit-Baltistan which shall consist of such number of members, including a

Chairman to be appointed by the Chairman of the Council on the advice of Governor, and perform such functions as may be prescribed on such terms and conditions as may be determined by the Governor.

Provided that till the establishment of the Gilgit-Baltistan Public Service Commission, the Federal Public Service Commission shall continue recruitment functions on behalf of Gilgit-Baltistan Government.

105. Services. – (1) Subject to this Order, the appointment of persons to, and the terms and conditions of service of persons in the service of Gilgit-Baltistan and Council shall be regulated by law.

(2) Until an Act of the Council in respect of persons employed in connection with the affairs of the Council, or an Act of the Assembly in respect of such persons employed in connection with the affairs of the Government, makes provision for the matters referred to in clause (1), all rules and orders in force immediately before the commencement of this Order, shall continue to be in force and may be amended from time to time by the Council or, as the case may be, the Government.

(3) Notwithstanding anything contained in clause (1) or (2) the position or vacancy sharing formula between the Government of Gilgit-Baltistan and the Government of Pakistan, i.e. Gilgit-Baltistan Civil Service and Pakistan Administrative Service (PAS), Police Service of Pakistan (PSP), or all Pakistan Service (APS) shall be as specified in the Fourth Schedule.

(4) Gilgit-Baltistan shall be given representation in Federal Services in accordance with provisions made for the purpose thereof for the provinces. Necessary, civil service reforms, including up gradation of posts, commensurate with the increased delegation of powers and in line with other provinces shall be carried out in Gilgit-Baltistan.

PART XIV: ELECTIONS

106. Chief Election Commissioner. – (1) There shall be a Chief Election Commissioner to be appointed by the Chairman of the Council on the advice of Governor on such terms and conditions as may be prescribed.

(2) Before entering upon office, the Chief Election Commissioner shall make before the Chief Judge of Gilgit-Baltistan oath in the form set out in the First Schedule.

PART XV: AUDITOR GENERAL

107. Auditor-General. – (1) There shall be an Auditor General of Gilgit-Baltistan who shall be appointed by the Governor on the advice of the Council.

Provided that till the appointment of Auditor-General of Gilgit-Baltistan, the Chairman of the Gilgit-Baltistan Council may ask Auditor- General of Pakistan to work as Auditor-General of Gilgit-Baltistan also.

(2) Before entering upon office, the Auditor General shall make before the

Chief Judge of Gilgit-Baltistan oath in the form set out in the first Schedule

(3) The terms and conditions of service, including the terms of office, of the Auditor-General shall be determined by Act of the Council and, until so determined, by rules made by the Council.

(4) The Auditor-General shall, in relation to –
- (a) the accounts of the Council and any authority or body established by the Council; and
- (b) the accounts of the Government and any authority or body established by the Government, perform such functions and exercise such powers as may be determined, by or under Act of the Council and, until so determined, by rules made by the Council.

(5) The accounts of the Council and of the Government shall be kept in such form and in accordance with such principles and methods as may be determined by the Auditor-General with the approval of the Council.

(6) The reports of the Auditor-General relating to the accounts of the Council shall be submitted to the Chairman of the Council; who shall cause them to be laid before the Council; and the reports of the Auditor-General relating to the accounts of the Government shall be submitted to the Governor who shall cause them to be laid before the Assembly.

PART XVI: GENERAL

108. Continuance of existing laws. – Subject to the provisions of this Order, all laws which immediately before the commencement of this Order, were in force in Gilgit-Baltistan shall continue to be in force until altered, repealed or amended by an Act, of the appropriate authority.

Explanation. – In this Article. –
- (a) The expression 'laws includes Ordinance, Orders, rules, bye- laws, regulations and any notification and other legal instruments having the force of law, and
- (b) The expression 'in force' in relation to any law, means having effect as law whether or not the law has been brought into operation.

109. General provision regarding Governor and Ministers. – (1) The Governor, the Chief Minister, a Minister or an Advisor shall not, –
- (a) hold any other office of profit in the service of Gilgit-Baltistan or any other country; or
- (b) occupy any other position carrying the right to remuneration for the rendering of services; but this action shall not be construed as preventing the Governor, the Chief Minister, a Minister or an Advisor from holding or managing his private property.

(2) No criminal proceedings whatsoever shall be instituted or continued against the Governor or the Chairman of the Council while he is in office.

(3) No civil proceedings in which relief is claimed against the Governor or the Chairman of the Council shall be instituted while he is in office in respect of anything done or not done, or purporting to have been done or not done, by him in his personal capacity, whether before or after he enters upon his office unless at least sixty days before the proceedings are instituted, notice in writing has been delivered to him, or sent to him, stating the nature of the proceedings, the cause of the action, the name, description and place of residence of the party by whom the proceedings are to be instituted and the relief which he claims.

(4) Except in relation to proceedings referred to in clause (3) no process whatsoever shall be issued from any court or tribunal against the Governor or the Chairman of the Council, whether in a personal capacity or otherwise, while he is in office.

(5) Subject to this Order, the Governor, the Chief Minister, the Chairman of the Council, the Federal Minister who is a member of the Council, a Minister or an Advisor shall not except in respect of anything done or not done by him in contravention of law , be answerable to any court or Tribunal in the exercise of the powers, or the performance of the duties, of his office or for any act done or purporting to be done by him in the exercise of those powers or in the performance of those duties:

Provided that nothing in this clause shall be construed as restricting the right of any person to bring appropriate proceedings against the Council or as the case may be, the Government.

110. Power to acquire property and to make contracts, etc. – (1) The executive authority of the Government and of the Council shall extend, subject to any Act of the appropriate authority to the grant, sale, disposition or mortgage of any property vested in, and to the purchase or acquisition of property on behalf of, the Government or as the case may be, the Council, and to the making of contracts.

(2) All property acquired for the purpose of the Government or of the Council shall vest in the Government or, as the case may be, in the Council.

(3) All contracts made in the exercise of the executive authority of the Government or of the Council shall be expressed to be made in the name of the Governor, or as the case may be, the Council and all such contracts and all assurances of property made in the exercise of that authority shall be executed on behalf of the Governor or the Council by such persons and in such manner as the Governor, or as the case may be, the Council may direct or authorize.

(4) Neither the Governor, nor the Chairman of the Council, shall be personally liable in respect of any contract or assurance made or executed in the exercise of the executive authority of the Government or, as the case may be the Council, nor shall any person making or executing any such contract or assurance on behalf of any of them be personally liable in respect thereof.

(5) Transfer of land by the Government or the Council shall be regulated by law.

PART XVII: EMERGENCY PROVISIONS

111. Power to issue proclamation. – (1) If the Chairman of the Gilgit-Baltistan Council, on receipt of a report from Governor of Gilgit-Baltistan or otherwise, is satisfied that a grave emergency exists in which the security of Gilgit-Baltistan is threatened by war or external aggression or by internal disturbances, in which the Government of the Gilgit-Baltistan cannot be carried on in accordance with the provisions of this Order, Chairman of the Council shall issue Proclamation of Emergency, hereinafter referred to as the Proclamation.

(2) Assume to himself, or direct the Governor of the Gilgit-Baltistan to assume on behalf of the Chairman of the Council, all or any of the functions of the Government of the Gilgit-Baltistan, and all or any of the powers vested in, or exercisable by, anybody or authority in the Gilgit-Baltistan, other than the Assembly;

(3) A Proclamation shall be laid before a Joint Sitting of the Council and the Assembly which shall be summoned by the Chairman of the Council on the advice of Governor to meet within thirty days of the Proclamation being issued and-

    (a) shall, cease to be in force at the expiration of two months unless before the expiration of that period it has been approved by a resolution of the Joint Sitting; and

    (b) shall, subject to the provisions of sub-clause (a), cease to be in force upon a resolution disapproving the resolution being passed by the votes of the majority of the total membership of the Joint Sitting.

(4) Notwithstanding anything contained in clause (2), if the Assembly stands dissolved at the time when the Proclamation is issued, the Proclamation shall continue in force for a period of four months but, if a general election to the Assembly is not held before the expiration of that period, it shall cease to be in force at the expiration of that period unless it has earlier been approved by a resolution of the Council.

(5) A Proclamation may be made before the actual occurrence of war or external aggression if the Governor is satisfied that there is imminent danger thereof.

112. Power to suspend fundamental rights. – (1) While a Proclamation is in operation, the Governor may, by order, declare that right to move any Court for the enforcement of such of the rights conferred by Part as may be specified in the order, and all proceedings pending in any Court for the enforcement of the rights so specified, shall remain suspended for the period during which the Proclamation is in force.

(2) Every order made under clause (1), shall, as soon as may be, laid before the Assembly.

113. Power to vary or rescind proclamation. – (1) A Proclamation issued under Article 108 may be varied or revoked by a subsequent Proclamation.

(2) The validity of any Proclamation issued or order made under Article 108 or Article 109 shall not be questioned in any Court.

114. Failure to comply with requirement as to time does not render an act invalid. – When any act or thing is required by this Order to be done within a particular period and it is not done within that period, the doing of the act or thing shall not be invalid or otherwise ineffective by reason only that it was not done within that period.

PART XVIII: MISCELLANEOUS

115. Oath of office. – (1) An oath required to be made by person under this Order shall be made in a language that is understood by that person.

(2) Where, under this Order, an oath is required to be made before a specified person and for any reason, it is impracticable for the oath to be made before that person, it may be made before such other person as may be nominated by that person.

(3) Where, under this Order, a person is required to make an oath before he enters upon an office, he shall be deemed to have entered upon the office on the day on which he makes the oath.

116. Chairman may make laws of indemnity, etc. – Nothing in the Order shall prevent the Chairman from making any law indemnifying any person in the service of Gilgit-Baltistan, or any other person, in respect of any act done in connection with the maintenance or restoration of order in any area in Gilgit-Baltistan.

117. Protection to Chairman, Governor, Minister, etc. – (1) The Chairman, the Governor, the Chief Minister, and Ministers shall not be answerable to any court for the exercise of powers and performance of functions of their respective offices or for any act done or purported to be done in the exercise of those powers and performance of those functions:

Provided that nothing in this clause shall be construed as restricting the right of any person to bring appropriate proceedings against the Government.

(2) No criminal proceedings whatsoever shall be instituted or continued against the President, Chairman or Governor in any court during his term of office.

(3) No process for the arrest or imprisonment of the President, Chairman or a Governor shall issue from any court during his term of office.

(4) No civil proceedings in which relief is claimed against the Chairman or Governor shall be instituted during his term of office in respect of anything done or not done by him in his personal capacity whether before or after he enters upon his office unless, at least sixty days before the proceedings are instituted, notice in writing has been delivered to him, or sent to him in the manner prescribed by law,

stating the nature of the proceedings, the cause of action, the name, description and place of residence of the party by whom the proceedings are to be instituted and the relief which the party claims.

118. Legal proceedings. – Any legal proceedings which, but for this Order, could have been brought by or against the Government in respect of a matter which, immediately before the commencing day, was the responsibility of the Council and has, under the Order, become the responsibility of the Assembly, shall be brought by or against the Government and if any such legal proceedings were pending in any court immediately before the commencing day then, in those proceedings, for the aforesaid Council the Government shall, as from that day, be deemed to have been substituted.

119. Failure to comply with requirement as to time does not render an act invalid. – When any act or thing is required by this Order to be done within a particular period and it is not done within that period, the doing of the act or thing shall not be invalid or otherwise ineffective by reason only that it was not done within that period.

120. Official language. – (1) The official language of Gilgit-Baltistan is Urdu.

(2) Subject to clause (1), the English language may be used for official purposes until arrangements are made for its replacement by Urdu.

(3) Without prejudice to the status of the National language, the Assembly may by law prescribe measures for the teaching, promotion and use of any other language in addition to the National language.

121. Private armies forbidden. – (1) No private organization capable of functioning as a military organization shall be formed, and any such organization shall be illegal.

(2) The Chairman shall, by law, provide for the punishment of persons found guilty of the offence under this Article and such law may also provide for establishment of special courts for trial of such offence.

122. Local Government. – (1) The Government shall, by law, establish a local government system and devolve political, administrative and financial responsibility and authority to the elected representatives of the local governments.

(2) Elections to the local governments shall be held by the Election Commission.

123. Order not to prejudice stance. – The provision of this Order shall not derogate form, or in any manner prejudice, the declared stand of the Government of Pakistan regarding the right of self-determination for the people of Jammu and Kashmir in accordance with the United Nations Resolutions.

124. Power to amend. – (1) The President on advice of the Federal Government may, by notified Order, amend the provisions of this Order:

Provided that no amendment shall be made or take effect unless it has been placed before the Supreme Court under application moved by the Federal

Government, which shall be treated as a petition under clause (3) of Article 184 of the Constitution, and the Supreme Court has not disapproved of the amendment.

(2) For the purposes of this Article, any Order proposing or seeking to repeal or replace this Order shall be deemed to be a measure to amend it.

125. Power to make rules. – The Governor or as the case may be, the Chairman of the Council, may make rules for carrying out the purposes of this Order.

126. Order to override other laws, etc. – (1) The provision of this Order shall have effect notwithstanding anything contained in the provisions of any law for the time being in force except that in case of conflict between the laws of Pakistan and the laws framed under this Order, the laws of Pakistan shall prevail.

(2) No Court, including the Gilgit-Baltistan Supreme Appellate Court and the Gilgit-Baltistan Chief Court, shall call into question or permit to be called into question, the validity of this Order or an Act to amend it.

127. Repeal and saving. – (1) The Government of Gilgit-Baltistan Order, 2018, hereinafter in this Article referred to as "the Repealed Order" together with the Orders amending it, is hereby repealed.

(2) Any rules made under the Repealed Order is so far as they are not inconsistent with the provisions of this Order shall continue to be in force unless altered amended or repealed by the competent authority.

128. Effect of repeal. – Where a law is repealed, or is deemed to have been repealed, by, under, or by virtue of this Order, the repeal shall not, except as otherwise provided in this Order: –

    (a) revive anything not in force or existing at the time at which the repeal takes effect;

    (b) affect the previous operation of the law or anything duly done or suffered under the law;

    (c) affect any right, privilege, obligation or liability acquired, accrued or incurred under the law;

    (d) affect any penalty, forfeiture, or punishment incurred in respect of any offence committed against the law; or

    (e) affect any investigation, legal proceeding or remedy in respect of any such right, privilege, obligation, liability, penalty, forfeiture or punishment; and any such investigation, legal proceedings or remedy may be instituted, continued or enforced, and any such penalty, forfeiture or punishment may be imposed, as if the law had not been repealed.

****

FIRST SCHEDULE
OATH OF OFFICE OF- GOVERNOR
[*See* Article 41(7)]

I, ... do hereby solemnly swear in the name of Allah;

That, as Governor of Gilgit-Baltistan, I will remain loyal to Pakistan;

That I will perform my functions as Governor honestly and faithfully; and

That I will not directly or indirectly communicate or reveal to any person any official secret which, may, come to my knowledge as Governor.

So help me Allah.

Place   Signature of Governor

Date

Signature of Chief Judge
Supreme Appellate Court, Gilgit-Baltistan

CHIEF MINISTER
[*See* Article 44(5)]

I, ... do hereby solemnly swear in the name of Allah;

That, as Chief Minister of Gilgit-Baltistan, I will remain loyal to Pakistan;

That I will perform my functions as Chief Minister honestly and faithfully; and
That I will not directly or indirectly communicate or reveal to any person any official secret which, may, come to my knowledge as Chief Minister;

So help me Allah.

Place   Signature of Chief Minister

Date

Signature of Governor
Gilgit-Baltistan

MINISTER
[*See* Article 46(2)]

I, ... do hereby solemnly swear in the name of Allah;

That, as Minister of Gilgit-Baltistan, I will remain loyal to Pakistan;

That I will perform my functions as Minister honestly and faithfully; and

That I will not directly or indirectly communicate or reveal to any person any official secret which, may, come to my knowledge as Minister;

So help me Allah.

Place
Date

Signature of Minister

Signature of Governor
Gilgit-Baltistan

SPEAKER OR DEPUTY SPEAKER OF LEGISLATIVE ASSEMBLY
[*See* Article 63(2)]

I, …………………………….. having been elected as Speaker or Deputy Speaker of Gilgit-Baltistan Legislative Assembly do hereby solemnly swear in the name of Allah;

That I will remain loyal to Pakistan;

That I will perform my functions as Speaker or Deputy Speaker of the Legislative Assembly honestly and faithfully; and

That I will not directly or indirectly communicate or reveal to any person any official secret which, may, come to my knowledge as Speaker or Deputy Speaker of the Assembly;

So help me Allah.

Place
Date

Signature of Speaker/Deputy Speaker

Signature of Outgoing Squeaker /Sitting Speaker
Gilgit-Baltistan Legislative Assembly

MEMBER OF LEGISLATIVE ASSEMBLY
[*See* Article 57(1)]

I, …………………………….. having been elected as Member of Gilgit-Baltistan Legislative Assembly do hereby solemnly swear in the name of Allah;

That I will remain loyal to Pakistan;

That I will perform my functions as Member of the Legislative Assembly honestly and faithfully; and

That I will not directly or indirectly communicate or reveal to any person any official secret which, may, come to my knowledge as Member of the Legislative Assembly;

So help me Allah.

Place
Date
                                                        Signature of Member

Signature of Speaker
Gilgit-Baltistan Legislative Assembly

MEMBER OF GILGIT-BALTISTAN COUNCIL
[*See* **Article 54(11)**]

I, ………………………….. having been elected as Member of Gilgit-Baltistan Council do hereby solemnly swear in the name of Allah;

That I will remain loyal to Pakistan;

That I will perform my functions as Member of the Gilgit-Baltistan Council honestly and faithfully; and

That I will not directly or indirectly communicate or reveal to any person any official secret which, may, come to my knowledge as Member of the Council;

So help me Allah.

Place
Date
                                                        Signature of Member

Signature of Chairman/Vice Chairman
Gilgit-Baltistan Council

CHIEF JUDGE/JUDGE OF GILGIT-BALTISTAN SUPREME APPELLATE COURT
[*See* **Article 82(6)**]

I, …………………. having been appointed Chief Judge/Judge of Gilgit-Baltistan Supreme Appellate Court do solemnly swear and I will bear true faith and allegiance to Pakistan and that I will faithfully perform the duties of my office to the best of my ability, knowledge and judgment and will administer justice according to the law in force Gilgit-Baltistan, without fear or favour, affection or ill-will.

Place
Date
                                          Signature of Chief Judge/Judge

Signature of Governor/Chief Judge
Gilgit-Baltistan

OATH OF CHIEF JUDGE/JUDGE OF GILGIT-BALTISTAN CHIEF COURT
[*See* Article 92(7)]

I, ………………………. having been appointed Chief Judge/Judge of Gilgit-Baltistan Chief Court do solemnly swear that I owe allegiance to Allah and that I will faithfully perform the duties of my office to the best of my ability, knowledge and judgment and will administer justice according to the law in force in the Areas comprising Gilgit-Baltistan, without fear or favour, affection or ill-will.

Place
Date

Signature of Chief Judge/Judge

Signature of Governor/Chief Judge
Gilgit-Baltistan

OATH OF ADVISOR
[*See* Article 54(14)]

I, ……………………………. do hereby solemnly swear in the name of Allah; That I will remain loyal to Pakistan.

That I will perform my functions as Advisor honestly and faithfully; and That I will not directly or indirectly communicate or reveal to any person any official secret which, may, come to my knowledge as Advisor; So help me Allah.

Place
Date

Signature of Advisor

Signature of Chairman of Council
Gilgit-Baltistan

AUDITOR-GENERAL
[*See* Article 107(2)]

I, ……………………. do hereby solemnly swear and bear true faith and allegiance to Pakistan.

That, as Auditor-General of the Areas comprising Gilgit-Baltistan, I will perform my functions honestly, faithfully, in accordance with the Gilgit-Baltistan (Empowerment and Self-Government) Order, 2009, and the law and to the best of my knowledge, ability and judgment, without fear or favour, affection or ill-will.

Place
Date

Signature of Auditor-General

Signature of Chief Judge of Supreme Appellate Court
Gilgit-Baltistan

CHIEF ELECTION COMMISSIONER
[*See* Article 106(2)]

I, ... do hereby solemnly swear and bear true faith and allegiance to Pakistan.

That, as Chief Election Commissioner of the Areas comprising Gilgit-Baltistan, I will perform my functions honestly, faithfully, in accordance with the Gilgit-Baltistan (Empowerment and Self-Government) Order, 2009, and the law and to the best of my knowledge, ability and judgment, without fear or favour, affection or ill-will.

Place
Date

Signature of Chief Election Commissioner

Signature of Chief Judge of Supreme Appellate Court
Gilgit-Baltistan

****

SECOND SCHEDULE
[*See* Article 58(2)(d)]

1. An office, which is not a whole time office remunerated either by salary or by fee.
2. The office of Lamberdar, Inamdar, Sufedposh and Zaildar, whether called by this or any other title.
3. The office of the Chairman of any elective body constituted under any law relating to the Local Government.
4. Reserve of the Armed Forces.
5. Any other office which is declared by an Act of the Assembly not to disqualify its holder from being elected as, or from being a member of the Assembly.

****

THIRD SCHEDULE
COUNCIL LEGISLATIVE LIST
[See Article 68 (2) (a)]

1. Nationality, citizenship and naturalization.
2. Migration from or into, or settlement in Gilgit-Baltistan.
3. Admission into, and emigration and expulsion from Gilgit-Baltistan, including in relation thereto the regulation of the movements in Gilgit-Baltistan of persons not domiciled in Gilgit-Baltistan; pilgrimages to places beyond Pakistan.
4. Post and telegraphs, including telephones, wireless, broadcasting and other like forms of communications; Post Office Saving Bank.
5. Foreign Exchange; cheques, bills of exchange, promissory notes and foreign aid.

6. Public debt, including the borrowing of money on the security of the Gilgit-Baltistan Council Consolidated Fund.
7. Public debt of the Federation, including the borrowings of money on the security of the Federal Consolidated Fund; foreign loan and foreign aid.
8. Council [of] public services.
9. Pensions, that is to say, pensions payable by the Council out of the Council Consolidated Fund.
10. Ombudsman.
11. Administrative courts for the subjects in legislative list.
12. Libraries, museums, and similar institutions controlled by the Council.
13. Federal agencies and institutions for the following purpose, that is to say, for research, for professional or technical training, or for the promotion of special studies.
14. Education as respects students of Gilgit-Baltistan in foreign countries and foreign students in Gilgit-Baltistan.
15. Nuclear energy, including. –
    (a) mineral resources necessary for the generation of nuclear energy;
    (b) the production of nuclear fuels and the generation and use of nuclear energy; and
    (c) ionizing radiations.
    (d) boilers
16. Ports quarantine, seamens and marine hospitals and hospitals concerned with port quarantine.
17. Maritime shipping and navigation, including shipping and navigation on tidal waters, Admiralty jurisdiction.
18. Aircraft and air navigation; the provision of aerodromes; regulations and organization of air traffic and of aerodrome.
19. Light Houses, including lightships, beacons and other provisions for safety of aircraft.
20. Carriage of passengers and goods by sea or by air.
21. Copyright, inventions, designs, trademarks and merchandise marks.
22. Opium so far as regards sale for export.
23. Import and exports across customs frontiers as defined by the Federal Government, inter-provincial trade and commerce with foreign countries; standards of goods to be exported out of Pakistan.
24. State Bank of Pakistan; banking, that is to say, the co-ordination with the Government of Pakistan of the conduct of banking business by corporations other than corporations owned or controlled by Gilgit-Baltistan and carrying out business only within Gilgit-Baltistan.
25. The law for insurance, except as respects insurance undertaken by Government of Gilgit-Baltistan, and the regulation of the conduct of insurance business,

except as respect to business under taken by Government of Gilgit-Baltistan, Government insurance, except so far as undertaken by the Government of Gilgit-Baltistan by virtue of any matter within the legislative competence of the Assembly.
26. Stock-exchange and future markets with object and business not confined to the areas comprising Gilgit-Baltistan.
27. Corporations, that is to say, the incorporation regulation and winding up of trading corporations including banking, insurance and financial corporations, but not including corporations owned or controlled by the Provincial Government of Gilgit-Baltistan and carrying on business, cooperative societies, and of corporations, whether trading or not, with object not confined to the Gilgit-Baltistan, but not including universities.
28. International treaties conventions and agreements and international arbitration
29. National Highways, strategic roads, and highways continuing beyond the territory of the Gilgit-Baltistan.
30. Federal surveys including geological surveys and Federal meteorological organizations.
31. Fishing and fisheries beyond territorial waters
32. Works, lands and buildings vested in, or in the possession of the Government or Federal Government, for the purpose of the Federation (not being Military, Naval or Air Force works), but as regards property situate in the Gilgit-Baltistan, subject always to law made by the Assembly, save in so far as Federal law otherwise provides.
33. Census.
34. Establishment of standards of weights and measures.
35. Extension of the powers and jurisdiction of members of a police force belonging to the Gilgit-Baltistan or any Province of Pakistan to any area in such Province or the Gilgit-Baltistan, but not so as to enable the police of the Gilgit-Baltistan or such province to exercise powers and jurisdiction in such Province or the Gilgit-Baltistan without the consent of the Government of that Province or the Gilgit-Baltistan; extension of the powers and jurisdiction of members of a police force belonging the Gilgit-Baltistan or a Province of Pakistan to railway areas outside the Gilgit-Baltistan or that Province.
36. Duties of Customs, including export duties.
37. Duties of excise, including duties on salt but not including duties on alcoholic liquors, opium and other narcotics.
38. Railways.
39. Mineral oil natural gas; liquids substances declared by Federal law to be dangerously inflammable.
40. Development of industries, where development under Federal control is declared by Federal law to be expedient in the public interest; institutions, establishments,

bodies and corporations administered or managed by the Federal Government immediately before the commencing day of this Order
41. Electricity and bulk water storage.
42. Major ports, that is to say the declaration and delimitation of such ports, and the constitution and powers of port authorities therein
43. All regulatory authorities established under Federal laws.
44. Supervision and management of public debt.
45. Legal, medical and other professions.
46. Standards in institutions for higher education and research, scientific and technical institutions.
47. Terminal taxes on goods or passengers carried by railway or air, taxes on their fares and freights.
48. Fees in respect of any of the matter enumerated in this list.
49. Fees in respect of any of the matters enumerated in this list, but not including fees taken in any court.
50. National Planning and national economic coordination including planning and coordination of scientific and technological research.
51. Inter-provincial matters and co-ordination
52. Jurisdiction and powers of all courts with respect to any of the matters enumerated in this list.
53. Offences against laws with respect to any of the matters enumerated in this list.
54. Inquiries and statistics for the purpose of any of the matters enumerated in this list.
55. Matters which under the law are within the legislative competence of the Council or relates to the Chairman of the Council.
56. Taxes on income other than agricultural income.
57. Taxes on corporations.
58. Taxes on the sale and purchases of goods and services imported, exported, produced, manufactured or consumed.
59. Taxes on the capital value of the assets, not including taxes on capital gains on immovable property.
60. Taxes and duties on the production capacity of any plant, machinery, under taking, establishment or installation in lieu of the taxes and duties specified in entries 56 and 57 or in lieu of either or both of them.
61. Election to the Council
62. The salaries, allowances and privileges of the Members of the Council and Advisors.
63. Matter incidental or ancillary to any of the matters enumerated in this list.

****

FOURTH SCHEDULE SERVICES
[See Article 93(3)]

POSITION OR VACANCY SHARING FORMULA BETWEEN THE GOVERNMENT OF PAKISTAN AND THE GOVERNMENT OF GILGIT-BALTISTAN.

Government of Gilgit-Baltistan	PAS/PSP/APS	BS-17	BS-18	BS-19	BS-20	BS-21
		25%	40%	50%	60%	65%

N.B.: Percentage showing the share earmarked for PAS/PSP/APS, out of total number of vacancies in Gilgit-Baltistan (on the pattern of Federal Government and Provinces of Pakistan).

F.No. 13 (2)/2018-Admn (GBC)

(Hamid Mahmood Rana)
Deputy Secretary

APPENDIX

A. **In the proposed Article 82**:
   (i) In clause (5), for sub-clause (a), substitute the following:
   (a) has been, or is qualified to be, a judge of the Supreme Court of Pakistan; or
   (ii) In clause (7), replace the full stop with a colon, and add the following proviso at the end:
   Provided that if the Chief Judge or a Judge is a person who has been a Judge of the Supreme Court of Pakistan, he/she shall hold office until he/she attains the age of 70 years, or unless he/she sooner resigns or is removed from office in accordance with law.

B. **For the proposed Article 103, substitute the following**:
   103. Supreme Court of Pakistan. –
   (1) The Supreme Court of Pakistan shall, to the exclusion of every other court including the Supreme Appellate Court and the Chief Court, have original jurisdiction in respect of:
      (i) any dispute between the Government, the Federation or the Government of a Province of Pakistan;
      (ii) any challenge to, or dispute raising any issue regarding, the *vires* or validity of this Order or any amendment hereto or modification herein, including an Order repealing, replacing or substituting this Order, and clause (2) of Article 126 hereof shall apply accordingly.
   (2) Any aggrieved person may, subject to clause (3), appeal to the Supreme Court of Pakistan against any judgment, order or decree of the Supreme Appellate Court or the Chief Court made in any proceedings where the subject matter of the dispute or the matter in issue is not exclusively in relation to or under this Order or any law made hereunder or Gilgit-Baltistan.
   (3) An appeal under clause (2) shall lie only if the Supreme Court of Pakistan grants leave to appeal.
   (4) A decision of the Supreme Court of Pakistan, whether made under any of the foregoing clauses or otherwise, shall be as binding on all courts established by or under this Order as it is in terms of Article 189 of the Constitution on all courts in Pakistan, and Article 86 and Article 96 hereof shall apply accordingly.

C. **For the proposed Article 124, substitute the following**:
   124. Power to amend. – (1) The President on advice of the Federal Government may, by notified Order, amend the provisions of this Order:
   Provided that no amendment shall be made or take effect unless it has been placed before the Supreme Court of Pakistan under application moved by the

Federal Government, which shall be treated as a petition under clause (3) of Article 184 of the Constitution, and the Supreme Court has not disapproved of the amendment.

(2) For purposes of this Article, any Order proposing or seeking to repeal or replace this Order shall be deemed to be a measure to amend it.

PRESS SUMMARY

17th January 2019

CIVIL AVIATION AUTHORITY VS. SUPREME APPELLATE COURT GILGIT BALTISTAN, ETC. (CONSTITUTION PETITION NO.50/2018, ETC.)

JUSTICES

Chief Justice Mian Saqib Nisar, Justice Sh. Azmat Saeed, Justice Umar Ata Bandial, Justice Faisal Arab, Justice Ijaz Ul Ahsan, Justice Sajjad Ali Shah and Justice Munib Akhtar

BACKGROUND

The instant matters pertain to an important historical and constitutional issue involving the status, authority and powers for Gilgit-Baltistan, including the judiciary and the rights available to its people. The following issues were presented in the various petitions and considered by the Court:

i. Would granting fundamental rights and a status, role and recognition of Gilgit-Baltistan in the constitutional scheme of Pakistan prejudice Pakistan's cause for the resolution of the Kashmir dispute by such appropriate means as may be acceptable to Pakistan (which could, for example, be a United Nations sanctioned and supervised plebiscite)?
ii. What rights can be granted to the people of Gilgit-Baltistan?
iii. Is the Gilgit-Baltistan Supreme Appellate Court a constitutional court?

JUDGMENT

The Supreme Court disposes of the matters according to the details contained in the judgment, save those petitions in which a specific order or judgment, of either the Gilgit-Baltistan Supreme Appellate Court or the Chief Court, has been challenged. Such petitions shall be deemed pending and be treated and disposed of as the leave petitions envisaged under Article 103 of the Proposed Order (as described in the judgment), when promulgated.

REASONS FOR JUDGMENT

Nothing this Court recommends or orders should affect the nature and status of the Kashmir issue. It must be emphasized that all the measures and directions taken and given must be predicated by the caveat that these are subject to the result of the plebiscite, which is duly recognized in Article 257 of the Constitution of the Islamic Republic of Pakistan, 1973 ("Constitution"). As a responsible member of the comity of nations Pakistan remains aware of its obligations in such terms. As and when the promised plebiscite is organized by the parties to the dispute, it will be up to the people of all of Jammu and Kashmir, and of Gilgit-Baltistan, to make their choice. Till then, it is surely incumbent upon both India as well as Pakistan to ensure that the people of this region enjoy maximum rights for areas within each country's control. Therefore, till such time that the plebiscite is held, a proper arrangement must be provided for by Pakistan for the people of Gilgit-Baltistan for purposes of governance within a framework of a constitutional nature, including most importantly the enjoyment of fundamental rights. (See paragraph 20 of the judgment)

In 1999, this Court in the case of *Al-Jehad Trust* (1999 SCMR 1379) directed the Pakistan Government to extend fundamental freedoms to the Northern Areas (now referred to as Gilgit-Baltistan) within six months. The judgment declared that Pakistan exercised both de facto and de jure administrative control over the Northern Areas. This Court ruled in the *Al-Jehad Trust* case that the people of the region were *"citizens of Pakistan for all intents and purposes…and could invoke constitutionally guaranteed fundamental rights."* It also emphasized that the people of the Northern Areas were *"entitled to participate in the governance of their area and to have an independent judiciary to enforce…Fundamental Rights."* (See paragraph 16 of the judgment)

In the judgment, the Court has considered what would be the position (i.e., status, powers and jurisdiction) of the judicial, legislative and executive organs established by an instrument of the nature of the Gilgit Baltistan Order, 2018. In accordance with well-established principles of law, the Gilgit-Baltistan legislature would only have such powers as are conferred upon it by the Federation through the Proposed Order. The courts created by such Order shall have the power to judicially review the laws enacted by such legislature. Of course, the organs created by the Proposed Order (or any previous or subsequent such Order), and especially any legislative body, would be bound not merely by the Order, but also by the Constitution. The jurisdiction of a Gilgit-Baltistan court established by or under the Proposed Order is confined to the territory of Gilgit-Baltistan. Therefore, it is concluded that the intention was, and is, to give the Gilgit-Baltistan Supreme Appellate Court and the Chief Court the status of a "constitutional" court within the ambit of Gilgit-Baltistan and the Proposed Order. The Gilgit-Baltistan Courts do not, and will not, sit as courts having the power of judicial review in respect of the territory of Pakistan, nor can they declare Orders made or legislation passed by the President or the Parliament as ultra vires, nor can they initiate judicial review of departments working outside of Gilgit-Baltistan. Instead, the Proposed Order (or any previous or subsequent such Order) can be challenged by, inter alia, the people of Gilgit-Baltistan, but only before this Court, either under Article 184 of the Constitution or in the manner herein after provided. (See paragraphs 24 and 25 of the judgment)

DIRECTIONS

Accordingly, by the judgment, this Court directs and orders as follows:

i. The Proposed Order (modified in the manner as noted in the judgment), and annexed to the judgment, shall be forthwith promulgated by the President on the advice of the Federal Government, and in any case within a fortnight hereof;

ii. No amendment shall be made to the Order as so promulgated except in terms of the procedure provided in Article 124 of the same, nor shall it be repealed or substituted, without the instrument amending, repealing or substituting (as the case may be) the same being placed before this Court by the Federation through an application that will be treated as a petition under Article 184(3) of the Constitution. Nothing in the judgment shall be construed to limit the jurisdiction conferred on this Court by the Proposed Order itself; and

iii. If the Order so promulgated is repealed or substituted by an Act of Parliament the validity thereof, if challenged, shall be examined on the touchstone of the Constitution.

(See paragraph 29 of the judgment)

NOTE: This summary is provided to assist in understanding the Court's decision. It does not form part of the reasons for the decision. The full judgment of the Court is the only authoritative document. The judgment is a public document and available at http://www.supremecourt.gov.pk.

Maps

Maps

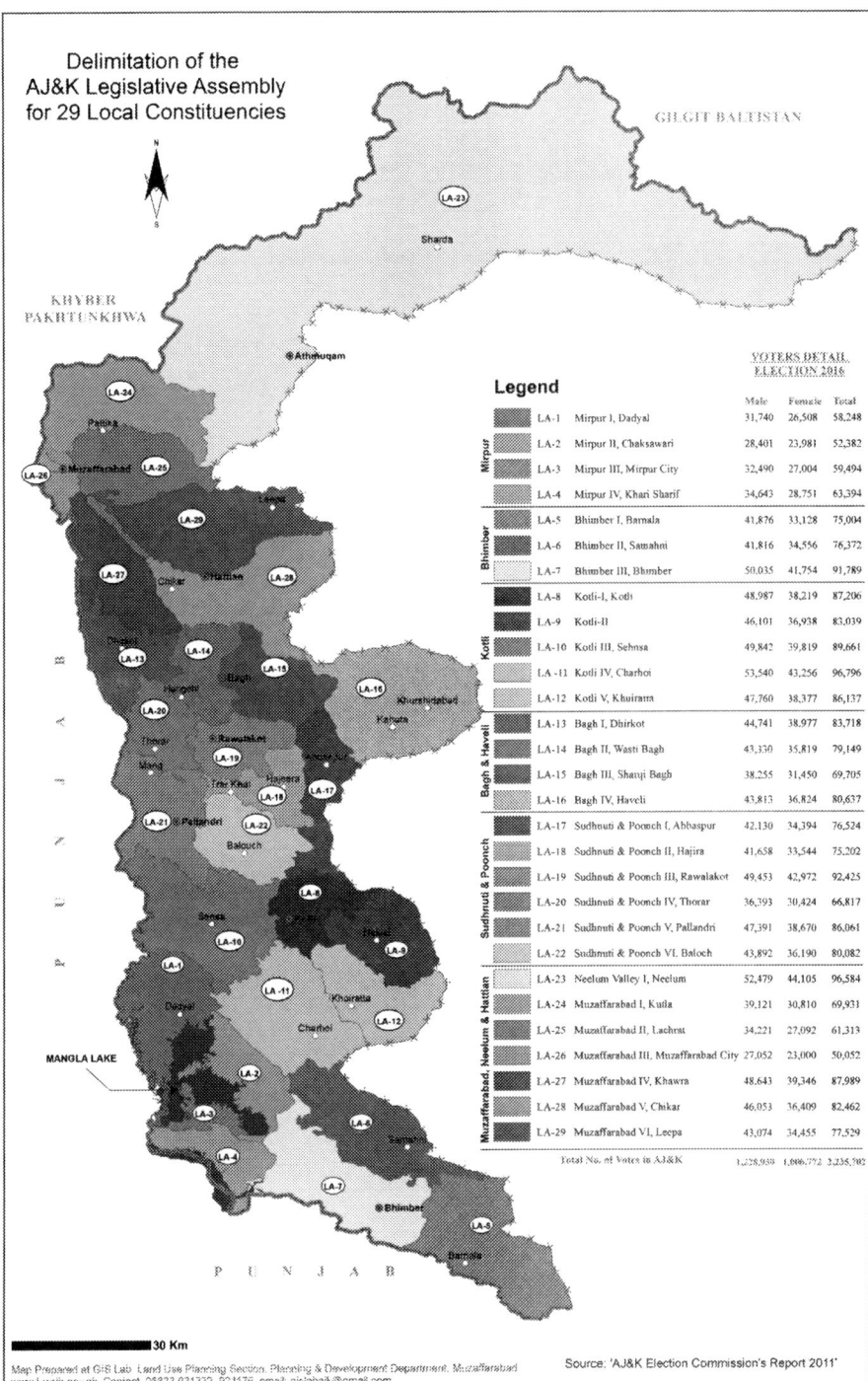

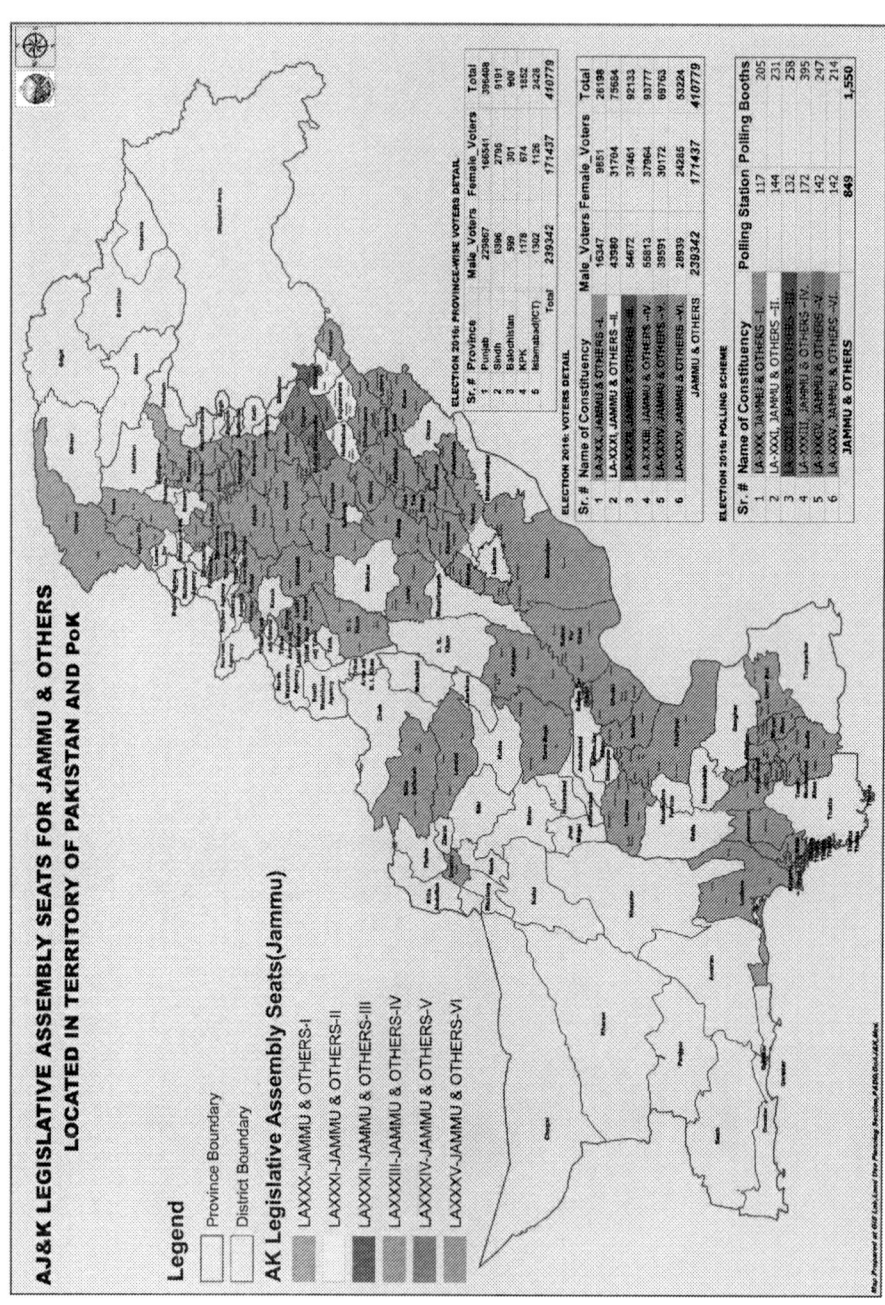

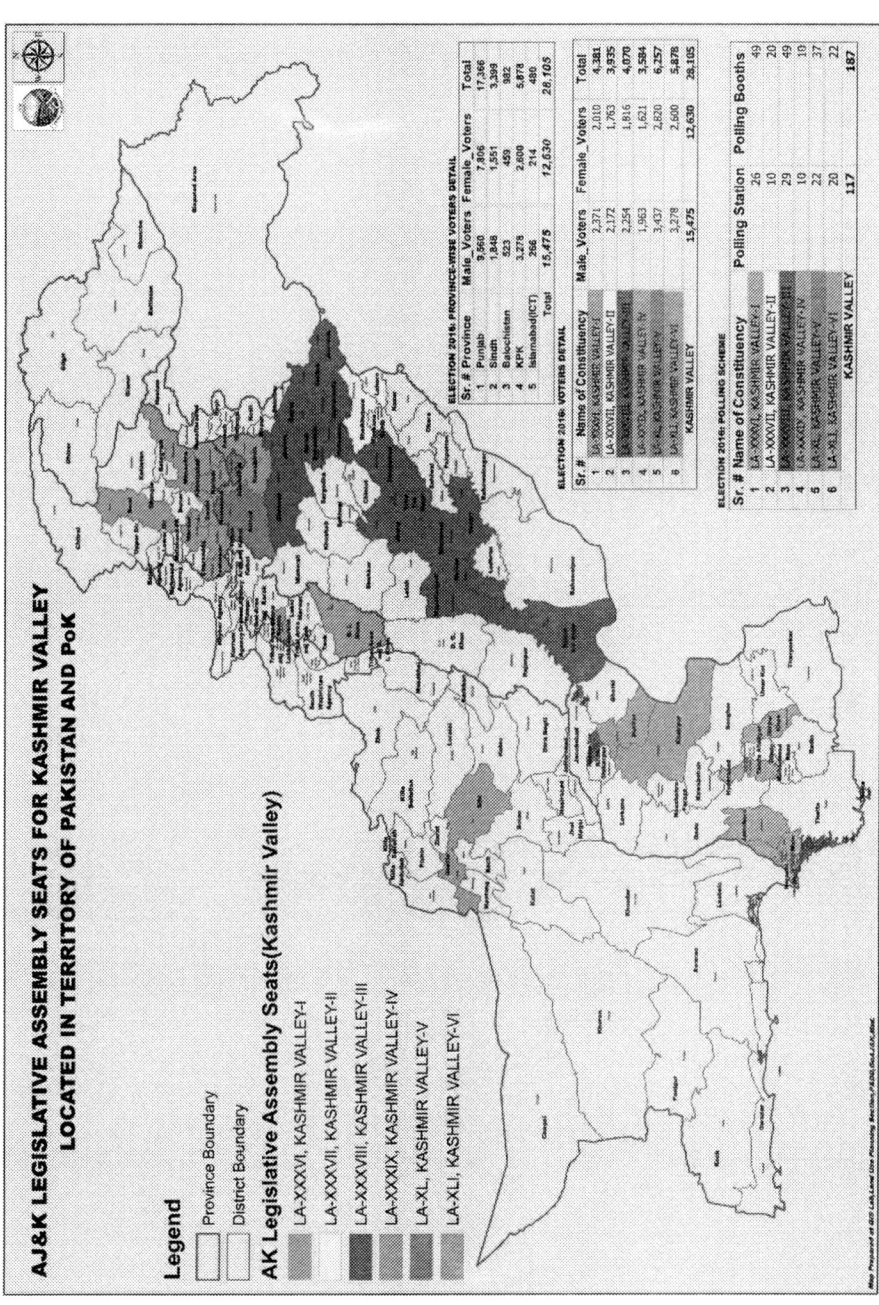

Bibliography

Akhtar, Jamna Das, "Involvement in Jammu & Kashmir", *Strategic Analysis*, Vol. 16, No. 8, Nov 1993, pp. 1051-1068.

Alam, Mohammad Monir & Bali, Ajeet Kumar: *Pakistan occupied Kashmir [constitutional status and political reality]*, New Delhi. Lancer's Books, 2012.

Ankit, Rakesh, "Britain and Kashmir, 1948: the arena of the UN", *Diplomacy and Statecraft*, Vol. 24, No.2, Jun 2013, pp.273-29.

Arya, Shailender, "UNMOGIP: a subcontinental relic", *USI Journal*, Vol. 143, No.591, Jan-Mar 2013, pp.115-122.

Ashraf, Fahmida, "Models of conflict resolution and the Kashmir issue", *Pakistan Horizon*, Vol. 56, No.2, April 2003, 119-133.

Bahadur, Kalim, "Politics of the POK", *World Focus*, Vol. 28, No.1, Jan 2007, pp.3-8.

Baid, Samuel, "Self-Determination for Kashmiris: a camouflage for Pak's own claim", *Strategic Analysis*, Vol. 13, No. 3, Jun 1990, pp.327-356.

Bakshi, Gagandeep, "Paradigm shift in the situation in J&K", *Aakrosh* Vol. 15, No.56, Jul 2012, pp.34-44.

Baweja Harinder, "Pakistan occupied Kashmir: prisoners of propaganda", *India Today*, Vol. 19, No 9, May 15, 1994, 79-83.

Behuria, Ashok K., "Pakistan's Approach to Kashmir Since the Lahore Agreement: Is There Any Change?", *Strategic Analysis*, Vol. 33, No.3, May 2009, pp.433-449.

Behuria, Ashok K., "Playing Chinese checkers in Gilgit – Baltistan", *Journal of Peace Studies* Vol. 20, No. 1, Oct 2012 – Mar 2013, pp. 18-26.

Bennett-Jones, Owen, "Musarraf's Kashmir Policy", *Asian Affairs*, Vol. 38, No.3, Nov 2007, pp.305-317.

Bhandari, M.C., *Solving Kashmir*, New Delhi. Lancer Publishers & Distributors, 2006.

Blank, Jonah, "Kashmir: all tactics, no strategy", *India Review*, Vol. 2, No.31, Jul 2003, pp. 181-202.

Bloeria, Sudhir S, "Kashmir: summers of disruption", *USI Journal*, Vol. 141, No. 583, Jan-Mar 2011, pp.22-38.

Bloeria, Sudhir S., *Pakistan's Insurgency Vs India's security* [tacking military in Kashmir], New Delhi. Manas Publications, 2000.

Chakravartty, Nikhil, *India-Pakistan [themes beyond borders]*, Delhi. Konark Publishers, 2004.

Chandran, Suba, "Pakistan's endgame in Kashmir: India's options", *Indian Foreign Affairs Journal*, Vol. 1, No. 3, Jul-Sep 2006, pp.85-103.

Chaudhury, Dipanjan Roy, "POK and Northern Areas: unwilling partners", *World Focus*, Vol. 27, No. 7, Jul 2006, pp.12-15.

Chibber, M.L., *Pakistan's Criminal Folly in Kashmir [the drama of accession and rescue of Ladakh]*, New Delhi. Manas Pub., 1998.

Chopra, Pran, *Scene changes in Kashmir*, India and Pakistan, New Delhi, Gyan Publishing House, 2003.

Chopra, V.D., *Genesis of Indo-Pakistan conflict on Kashmir*, New Delhi. Patriot Publishers, 1990.

Commuri, Gitika, *Indian identity narratives and the politics of security*, New Delhi, Sage Publications, 2010.

D P Kumar, *Kashmir: Pakistan's proxy war*. New Delhi. Har Anand Pub., 1992, 81.

Dani, Ahmad Hasan, *History of the Northern Areas of Pakistan*, Sang-e-Meel Publication, Lahore, 2001

Dawson, Pauline, *Peacekeepers of Kashmir [UN military observer group in India and Pakistan]*, Bombay. Popular Prakashan, 1995.

Dhar, M K, "An itinerant's journey through POK", *World Focus*, Vol. 28, No.1, Jan 2007, pp.9-18.

Dixit, J.N., *India's foreign policy challenge of terrorism.* [fashioning new interstate equations], New Delhi. Gyan Publishing House, 2002.

Douie, James, *Punjab, north-west frontier province and Kashmir*. Delhi. Low Price Publications, 1994.

Ganguly, Sumit, "Will Kashmir stop India's rise?", *Foreign Affairs*, Vol. 85, No. 4, Jul/Aug 2006, pp.45-56.

Gulati, M.N., *Pakistan's downfall in Kashmir [the three Indo-Pak wars]*, New Delhi. Manas Publication, 2001.

Gupta, K.R. (ed.), *India-Pakistan relations with special reference to Kashmir*, New Delhi, Atlantic Publishers and Distributors, 2003.

Gupta, Sisir, *Kashmir [study in India Pakistan relations]*, Bombay, Asia Publisher, 1966.

Gupta, Virendra & Bansal, Alok (eds), *Pakistan occupied Kashmir. [the untold story]*, New Delhi, Institute for Defence Studies and Analyses, 2007.

Haqqani, Husain, "Pakistan's endgame in Kashmir", *India Review*, Vol. 2, No.3, Jul 2003, pp.34-54.

Hussain, Syed Tassadque, *Contemporary Pakistan and Kashmir Politics [Pakistan elections 2008 critically analysed]*, Srinagar, Gulshan Books, 2008.

IDSA, *Pakistan occupied Kashmir [changing the discourse]*, New Delhi. IDSA, 2011.

Institute of Strategic Studies, *Kashmir dispute in the context of Pakistan-India dialogue*, Islamabad, Institute of Strategic Studies, 2005.

Jalalzai, Musa Khan, *Foreign policy of Pakistan [Kashmir, Afghanistan and internal security threats (1947-2004)]*, Lahore, Ariana Publications, 2003.

Jha, D.C. & All India Seminar on Foreign Policies of South Asian Studies: *Kashmir as a factor in the foreign policies of India and Pakistan*, Jaipur, South Asia Studies Centre, 1968.

Jha, Nalini Kant Jha, Gaurav Kumar, "India-Russia ties from tempest to tranquility", *World Focus*, Vol. 32, No.11-12, Nov-Dec 2011, pp.830-834.

Kanwal, Gurmeet, *Pakistan's proxy war*, New Delhi, Lancer Publishers, 2002.

Karim, Afsir, "Pakistan's aggression in Kashmir 1999," *Aakrosh*, Vol. 2 No 4, Jul 1999, pp.3-21.

Hassnain, F.M., *Gilgit: The Northern Gate of India*, Sterling Publishers, India, 1978.

Kennedy, Charles H. (ed), *Pakistan. [1992]*, Lahore, Pak. Book Corporation, 1993.

Khajooria, M M, "Jammu and Kashmir tangle: prospects of resolution through Indo-Pak peace process?", *Security and Society*, Vol. 2, No. 2, Summer 2006, pp.39-48.

Khan, Hafeez R, "Kashmir intifada and 9/11", *Pakistan Horizon*, Vol. 56, No. 2, April 2003, 97-118.

Khanna, D.D. & Kishore Kumar, *Dialogue of the deaf [India-Pakistan divide]*, Delhi. Konark Publishers, 1992.

Hussain, Altaf, "The Gilgit-Baltistan Reforms 2009", Forum of Federations Project, Pakistan, funded by the *German Ministry of Foreign Affairs*, December 2009 pp. 1-19.Rana Muhammad Amir and Rathore, Mujtaba, *Northern Areas: Crisis and Prospects*, Pakistan Institute for Peace Studies, Lahore, 2007,

Kasuri, Khurshid Mahmud, *Neither a Hawk nor a Dove*, Penguin, India, 2015,

Khan, F.M., *The Story of Gilgit, Baltistan and Chitral: A Short History of Two Millenniums: 1 AD -1999*, Eejaz, Gilgit, 2002.

Kumar, Sumita, "Human rights issue in Pakistan's Kashmir strategy", *Strategic Analysis*, Vol. 17, No. 7, Oct 1994, pp.825-846.

Leather, Kaia, *Kashmiri separatists [origins, competing ideologies and prospects for resolution of the conflict]*, New York, Novinka Books, 2003.

Madan, Vijay, "Pakistan's strategic thrust into Afghanistan and Kashmir", *Aakrosh*, Vol. 2, No 5, Oct 1999, pp.58-74.

Mahapatra, D.A., "Earthquake in J & K: a report", *Himalayan and Central Asian Studies*, Vol. 9, No. 4, Oct-Dec 2005, pp.38-46.

Malhotra, Adit, "Red shadow in Pakistan occupied Kashmir", *CLAWS Journal*, Vol., No.1, Autumn 2011, pp. 74-79.

Malick, Nasir, Third option will create divisions in azad Kashmir: an interview with Sardar Abdul Qayyum", *Herald* Vol. 23, No 3, Mar 1992, pp. 48b-51.

Mattoo, Amitabh, Kak, Kapil & Jacob, Happymon (eds.), *India and Pakistan. [pathways ahead]*, New Delhi, KW Publishers, 2007.

Mazari, Shireen M, "Critical new moves on Kashmir" *Strategic Studies*, Vol. 25, No.4, Winter 2005, pp.1-6.

Mohan, Surinder, "Azad Jammu and Kashmir and Gilgit-Baltistan: a tale of economic exploitation", *Journal of Peace Studies*, Vol. 17, No. 1, Jan-Mar 2010, pp.31-44.

Mohan, Surinder, "Democracy in Jammu and Kashmir 1947-2008", *World Affairs*, Vol. 16, No.3, Jul-Sep 2012, pp.88-116.

Nanda, Ravi, *Kargil a wake-up call*, New Delhi, Lancers Books, 1999.

Nanda, Ravi, *Kashmir and Indo-Pak relations*, New Delhi, Lancer's Books, 2001.

Noor, Sanam, "Kashmir bus service" *Pakistan Horizon*, Vol. 58, No.3, Jul 2005, pp.35-43.

Pattanaik, Smruti S, "Pakistan's Kashmir policy: Objectives and approaches", *Strategic Analysis*, Vol. 26, No. 2, April-June 2002, 199-225.

Prabha, Kshitij, *Terrorism [an instrument of foreign policy]*, New Delhi, South Asian Publication, 2000.

Prasad, Bimal, *March to Pakistan 1937-1947*, New Delhi, Manohar Publication, 2009.

Punjabi, Riyaz, "Conflict transformation in Kashmir IV", *Journal of Peace Studies*, Vol. 13, No.1, Jan-Mar 2006, pp.3-8.

Qazi Shakil ahmad, "Partition plan, Indian design and the Kashmir issue", *Pakistan Horizon*, Vol. 56, No. 2, April 2003, 17-35.

R.K. Bhat, *Changing attitudes of the Kashmir is towards India and Pakistan*, Jaipur, University of Rajasthan, 1968.

Rahman, Mushtaqur, *Divided Kashmir [old problems, new oppurtunities for India, Pakistan, and the Kashmiri people]*, New Delhi, Lynne Rienner Publishers, 1996.

Rammohan, E N, "India, Pakistan and the recalcitrant Kashmir problem", *Agni*, Vol. 9, No. 3, Jul-Sep 2006, pp.32-53.

Raza, Maroof, "Pakistan-Sponsored insurgency in Kashmir: a case study", *Aakrosh*, Vol. 2, No 4, Jul 1999: pp.31-56.

Rifaat Hussain, "Pakistan's relations with Azad Kashmir", Autumn 2003, *Regional Studies*, Vol. 21, No.4 (Autumn 2003) 82-97.

Roy, J N, "Indo-Pak relations: grandstanding on Kashmir alone will not do", *Dialogue*, Vol. 8, No.2, Oct-Dec 2006, pp.102-107.

S.V. Balasubramaniyan, "Terrorism in India – cross-border support structures in India's neighborhood Raghavan", *Agni*, Vol. 14, No.3, Apr 2012, pp.65-78.

Sahni, Sati, *Kashmir underground*, Delhi, Har-Anand Publications, 1999.

Sardar Qayyum, "Kashmir and Pakistan's security: text of an interview", *Defence Journal*, Vol. 18, No. 5-6, June-July 1992, 11-25.

Sawhney, Pravin Wahab, Ghazala, "Military matters: both for peace and Kashmir resolution, India needs to talk with general Kayan", *Force*, Vol. 9, No. 4, Dec 2011, pp.26-29.

Schofield, Victoria, *Kashmir in conflict* [*India, Pakistan and the unending war*], London. I.B. Tauris, 2003.

Sen, L.P., *Slender was the thread* [*Kashmir confrontation 1947-48*], Bombay. Orient Longmans, 1969.

Shekhawat, Seema, "Electoral politics in Pakistan-Occupied Kashmir", *India Quarterly*, Vol. 63, No.3, Jul-Sep 2007, pp.145-167.

Sibal, Kanwal, "Tracking talks: India continues to fumble in its engagement with Pakistan" *Force*, Vol. 10, No.3, Nov 2012, pp.14-20.

Sidhu, Ravel Singh, "Operation riddle: 7 Sikh action – Poonch sector (Aug-Sep 1965)", *USI Journal* Vol. 143, No.591, Jan-Mar 2013, pp.141-149.

Singh, Indu & Saksena, Ajay, *Human Rights in India and Pakistan*, New Delhi, Deep & Deep Publications, 2004.

Singh, Jasjit (ed), *Pakistan occupied Kashmir* [*under the jackboot*], New Delhi, Siddhi Books, 1995.

Singh, Jasjit (ed.), *Kargil 1999* [*Pakistan's fourth war for Kashmir*], New Delhi. Knowledge World, 1999.

Singh, Mandip, "Pakistan-occupied Kashmir-a buffer state in the making?" *Strategic Analysis*, Vol. 37, No.1, Jan-Feb 2013, pp.1-7.

Sinha, J K, "Kashmir imbroglio", *Indian Defence Review*, Vol. 21, No.1, Jan-Mar 2006, pp.70-74.

Snedden Christopher, *The Untold Story of the People of Azad Kashmir*, London, Hurst & Company, 2012.

Sood, Vikram, "Vicious war: under Al Qaeda's protective umbrella, terrorism expands beyond Kashmir", *Force*, Vol. 4, No. 1, Sep 2006, pp.48-49.

Subrahmanyam, K., "Kashmir", *Strategic Analysis*, Vol. 13, No. 2, May 1990, pp.111-198.

Swami, Praveen, "Terrorism in Jammu and Kashmir in theory and practice", *India Review*, Vol. 2, No.3, Jul 2003, pp.55-88.

Swami, Praveen, *India, Pakistan and the secret Jihad* [*the covert war in Kashmir, 1947-2004*], London, Routledge, 2007.

Tehmina Mahmood, "Peaceful resolution of Kashmir dispute: India's avoidance", *Pakistan Horizon*, Vol. 54, No 4, Oct 2001, 7-24.

Vaish, Varu, "Negotiating the India-Pakistan conflict in relation to Kashmir", *International Journal on World Peace*, Vol. 28, No. 3, Sep 2011, pp.53-80.

Warikoo K. (ed.), *The Other Kashmir: Society, Culture and Politics in the Karakoram Himalayas*, Pentagon, New Delhi, 2014.

Wirsing, Robert G., *India, Pakistan and the Kashmir dispute on regional conflict and its resolution*. Houndmills. Macmillan, 1994.

Yusuf, Moeed Najam, Adil, "Kashmir: ripe for resolution", *Third World Quarterly*, Vol. 30, No. 8, 2009, pp.1503-1528.

Zeb, Rizwan & Chandran, Suba, *Indo-Pak conflicts ripe to resolve*, New Delhi. Manohar, 2005.

Index

Abbas, Chaudhry Ghulam, 3, 5-8, 13, 37-38, 167, 217, 238
Abdullah, Sheikh
 Aatish-e-Chinar, 36-37
Abpara Chowk, 179
Adviser, means, 300
Advocate, Amjad Hussain, 136, 155, 206, 227
Afghanistan, 123
Agha Khan Development Network, 146
Agha Khan Educational Services (AKES), 118
Ahmed, Bashir, 224
AJK Muttahida Quami Movement (AJKMQM), 84
AJK Pakistan Muslim League-Nawaz (AJKPML-N), 77
AJK Pakistan People's Party (AJKPPP), 70
AJK Pakistan People's Party Shaheed Bhutto (AJKPPPSB), 76
Akbar, Chaudhry Latif, 24, 74-75, 220
Akhtar, Muhammad Ali, 228
al Qaeda, 92, 172
Al-Hussaini, Agha Rahat Hussain, 226
Ali, Agha Muhammad, 228
All Jammu and Kashmir Muslim Conference (AJKMC), 34
All Jammu and Kashmir National Conference (AJKNC), 36
All Pakistan Muslim League (APML), 161, 198
All Parties Conference (APC), 204
All Parties Hurriyat Conference (APHC), 54, 61
All Parties National Alliance (APNA), 66
All Party National Alliance (APNA), 42, 52, 66-70, 180, 215
Altaf Bhai, 89
Anglo-Afghan war, 124
Anjuman Sipah-i-Sahaba Pakistan (ASSP), 167
Ansari, Amina, 161, 228
Asian Development Bank (ADB), 26, 143
Asif Ali Zardari, 23, 71, 74, 91, 177, 231
Assembly, means, 325, 408
Astore Supreme Council, 119
Australian Agency for International Development (AUAID), 120
Awami Watan Party, 64
Awami Workers Party (AWP), 178-79, 225
Azad Jammu & Kashmir Pakistan Muslim League-Nawaz (AJKPML-N), 23-24, 44-45, 58, 77, 94, 214, 216-17
Azad Jammu and Kashmir (AJK), 1-29, 33, 37-46, 48-69, 71-72, 74-77, 81-85, 87-90, 92-93, 95-100, 121, 127-30, 136, 138, 165, 183, 190-92, 194-98, 211-23, 230-31, 235, 240-41, 247
 Interim Constitution (13th Amendment) Act, 2018, 266-87
 Members Legislative Assembly 2016, 297-98
 Political Parties in, 288-94
 Presidents/Prime Ministers of, 295-96
Azad Jammu and Kashmir Election Commission (AJKEC), 33
Azad Jammu and Kashmir Muslim Conference (AJKMC), 3, 7, 15-17, 19-24, 33-34, 42-46, 53, 72, 76, 77, 81, 85, 97, 100, 212-14, 216, 219
Azad Kashmiris, 38

Baba Jan, 64, 176, 179, 225-26
Baid, Samuel, 117
Baig, Haji Shah, 165, 225
Balawaristan National Front (BNF), 67, 168-73, 177-78, 199, 205, 223, 226-27, 373-74

Balawaristan National Front, 373-75
Balawaristan Students' National Organisation (BSNO), 171-72, 176
Balochistan Liberation Army, 91
Balor Research Forum (BRF), 175
Ban Ki Moon, 169
Bang-e-Sahar, 174
Belgium, 64
Belt and Road Initiative (BRI), 203
Bhasha Dam, 51, 63, 141-46
Bhutto, Begum Nusrat, 40
Bhutto, Benazir, 17, 19, 40-41, 71, 77, 91, 127, 138, 220
Bhutto, Bilawal Zardari, 74, 76
Bhutto, Zulfiqar Ali, 9, 15-16, 39-40, 65, 70, 77, 79, 91, 126, 153-54, 190-91, 214, 218-19, 231
Birmingham (UK), 173
Blor, Afaq, 228
Boloristan Labour Party (BLP), 175, 177
Brig. Samson Simon Sharaf (Retd.), 136

Canada, 64, 74, 97
Ceasefire Line (CFL), 25
Central Intelligence Agency (CIA), 140
Centre for Peace, Development and Reforms (CPDR), 196
Chairman, means, 326, 408
Chaudhry, Sultan Mahmood, 13, 18, 20, 41, 54, 59, 61, 72, 75, 93-94, 96, 98, 214
Chenab formula, 67
Chief Executive, means, 300
China, 62, 74, 116, 120-21, 143, 145, 173, 177, 180, 182, 198, 202-8, 231-32
China and Pakistan, Boundary Agreement Between, 1963, 255-58
China-Pakistan Economic Corridor (CPEC), 64, 119, 133, 143, 169, 173, 198, 202-8, 231, 235, 249
Choudhry, Dr. Shabir, 69, 134, 216, 235
Citizen means, 330, 408
Col. Imtiaz-ul-Haque, 197
Commissioner, means, 300
Council for Human Rights in Kashmir, 52
Council, means, 300, 326, 408
Creutzmann, Jurgen, 181

Daily Jang, 48
Dawn, 118, 199
Deputy Chief Executive, means, 300

Deputy Speaker, means, 300
Deutsche Bank, 146
Dignified and Honourable, 104
Dixit, J.N., 191
Dogra Sabha, 34

East Pakistan, 9, 71, 78-79, 191
Economic Times, 120
Election Bodies Disqualification Ordinance (EBDO), 79
Election Commission of Pakistan (ECP), 97
Electoral Rolls, means, 300
Emir, 101
Empowerment for All, 86
Europe, 97
Express Tribune, 195

Federation, means, 408
Financial year, means, 326, 408
Force Command Northern Areas (FCNA), 129
Four Point Formula, 45
France, 179
Free Trade Agreements (FTAs), 204
Frontier Crimes Regulation (FCR), 1, 124, 126, 137, 153, 191, 237, 397-98

Gen. Zia-ul-Haq, 16-17, 39-40, 71, 79-80, 99, 126, 140, 218, 222, 231, 240
Geological Survey of Pakistan (GSP), 144
Ghaffar, Khawaja Abdul, 218
Gharib Qaumi Movement (GQM), 184
Ghulam Muhammad, 158, 228
Gilgit-Baltistan (GB), 1-2, 7, 10, 49-52, 55, 62-64, 66, 68, 74, 88-90, 99, 116-19, 121-22, 126-27, 129-43, 145-46, 153-85, 190-208, 213-14, 221-27, 229-35, 326
  Area, 116
  Challenges, 144
  Demography, 116
  Economic Conditions, 118
  Electoral Rolls, Election 2015, 378
  India's Response, 136
  Karakoram Highway, 120
  Land Scam, 145
  Legislative Assembly Elections, 132
  Local Government Act 2014, 139
  Members of Assembly, 379-80
  Political Developments, 137
  Political History, 122
  Population, 116

Registered Political Parties, Election Symbols, 376-77
Religion 116
Sectarianism in, 139
Threat to Buddhist Heritage, 146
Tourism Industry, 121
Gilgit Baltistan Democratic Alliance (GBDA), 67, 175, 199, 373
Gilgit-Baltistan Legislative Assembly (GBLA), 131-32, 134, 139, 222, 226-27, 248
Gilgit Baltistan National Alliance (GBNA), 178
Gilgit Baltistan United Alliance (GBUA), 177
Gilgit Baltistan United Movement (GBUM), 175-76, 199
Gilgit-Baltistan Bar Council (GBBC), 182
Gilgit-Baltistan Council (GBC), 131, 139
Gilgit-Baltistan Council Income Tax (Adaptation) Act, 2012, 119
Gilgit-Baltistan Empowerment and Self-Governance Order (GBESGO), 116, 130-32, 134-37, 153, 178, 242
Gilgit-Baltistan (Empowerment and Self-Governance) Order, 2009, 325-72
Gilgit-Baltistan Ladakh Democratic Movement (GBLDM), 175
Gilgit-Baltistan Metals Minerals and Gem Association (GBMMGA), 220
Gilgit-Baltistan National Congress (GBNC), 180-81
Gilgit-Baltistan National Movement (GBNM), 180
Gilgit-Baltistan Thinker's Forum (GBTF), 181
Gilgit-Baltistan United Movement (GBUM), 67, 175-77, 205, 223
Gilgit-Baltistan, means, 326, 409
Glancy Commission report, 34
Government of Gilgit-Baltistan Order, 2018, 116
Government, means, 326, 409
Governor, means, 326, 409
Grare, Frederic, 102

Hashmatullah, 227
Hayat, Javid, 28
Hizbul Mujahideen (HM), 51, 103
Human Rights Commission of Pakistan (HRCP), 194, 200
Human Rights Watch Report 2012, 13, 129
Hunzai, Izhar, 141, 225, 228
Hussain, Dr. Akmal, 73
Hussain, Mirza, 155, 161, 170, 228

Hydroelectric Power Generation Projects, 26-27, 88, 144

Inayatullah, Qazi, 165, 224
Indian Express, 63
Industrial and Commercial Bank of China, 146
Inqalabi, Shafqat, 223
Interim Constitution Act 1974, 9, 11, 63
International Crisis Group (ICG), 129, 140, 154
International Food Policy Research Institute (IFPRI), 144
International Monetary Fund (IMF), 101, 178
Inter-Services Intelligence (ISI), 48-49, 51, 90, 98, 182, 213, 373
Iqbal, Zafar, 155, 225, 228
Islami Tehreek Pakistan (ITP), 164
Islami-Jamhoori-Ittehad (IJI), 80
Islamiyat, 141
Ismail, 117, 122, 154, 169, 185
Ismail, Engineer Muhammad, 227
Italy, 64

Jafar, Muhammad, 228
Jamaat-e-Islami (JI), 93, 97-103, 165, 190, 221
Jamaat-e-Islami AJK (JIAJK), 98
Jamaat-ud-Dawa, 51
Jamiat Ulema-e-Islam-Fazl (JUI-F), 154-55, 164, 198, 225
Jammu and Kashmir (J&K), 1, 3, 5-6, 12, 48, 215, 218, 247
Jammu and Kashmir Liberation Front (JKLF), 17, 29, 33, 41-42, 48-52, 54, 64, 67, 69, 103, 138, 173, 194, 211, 246
Jammu and Kashmir Liberation League (JKLL), 7, 33, 52-58, 64
Jammu and Kashmir National Awami Party (JKNAP), 65
Jammu and Kashmir National Students Federation (JKNSF), 28, 65
Jammu and Kashmir People's Muslim League (JKPML), 59-61
Jinnah, Muhammad Ali, 7, 36-37, 53, 94, 219
Jammu Kashmir Council For Human Rights, 52
Jehnzaib, Raja, 228
Jinnah Model Town Housing Scheme, 23
Jinnah-Abdullah conflict, 36
Joint Sitting, means, 326, 409
Judge, 326, 409

K-2, 121

Karachi Agreement, 4, 259-62
Karachi-based Jammu Kashmir Welfare Association, 52
Karakoram Highway (KKH), 120-21, 203, 205
Karakorum National Movement (KNM), 67, 174-75, 177-78, 199
Karakorum Students Organisation (KSO), 174, 223
Kargil International, magazine, 177
Karim Khan (aka) KK, 228
Kashmir American Council, 52
Kashmir and Northern Areas (KANA), 1, 238, 297
Kashmir Azad *banega*, 13
Kashmir Canadian Council, 52
Kashmir Council for Human Rights, 52
Kashmir Liberation Cell, 58
Kashmir Voice International (KVI), 104
Kashmir Watch, 52
Kashmir Welfare Association (Kashmir Relief Fund), 52
Kashmiri, Sardar Shaukat Ali, 184, 213-14
Kasuri, Khurshid Mahmud
   Neither a Hawk or a Dove, 137
Khan, Abdul Hamid, 39, 168-69, 172-73, 177, 184, 227
Khan, Ali Ashraf, 134
Khan, Amanullah, 48-49, 57, 69, 135, 173, 211
   Jehad-e-Musalsal, 48, 138
Khan, Col. Mirza Hasan
   Shamsher se Zanjir Tak, 137
Khan, Dr. Imran Ahmad, 144
Khan, F.M.,
   The Story of Gilgit, Baltistan and Chitral, 122
Khan, Gen. Ayub, 7, 14, 70, 78-79, 137
Khan, Gen. Yahya, 8-9, 53
Khan, Haji Jaffar Ullah, 225
Khan, Haji Janbaz, 228
Khan, Imran, 23-24, 93, 96-98, 162-63, 214, 232-33
Khan, M Ismail, 208
Khan, Maj. Gen. Sardar Muhammad Anwar, 220, 296
Khan, Mir Ghazanfar Ali, 133, 161, 222, 248
Khan, Raja Farooq Haider, 72, 83, 216-17, 288, 296, 298
Khan, Raja Zulqarnain, 21, 72, 212
Khan, Sardar Attique Ahmed, 47, 212, 288, 296-97
Khan, Sardar Ghulam Sadiq, 219

Khan, Sardar Muhammad Abdul Qayyum, 8, 20, 42, 53, 100, 214, 295-96
Khan, Sardar Muhammad Yaqoob, 23, 44, 216, 296
Khan, Sardar Muhammad Ibrahim, 218, 295-96
Khan, Sardar Sikandar Hayat, 17, 19-20, 41, 213, 295-96
Khidmat-e-Khalq Foundation, 90
Khyber Pakhtunkhwa (KP), 126, 174, 184, 204
Khyber Pakhtunkhwa Assembly, 93
Khyber-Pakhtunkhwa Valley, 82
Khurshid, K.H., 7-8, 15-16, 21, 37, 39-40, 43, 53-54, 57-59, 212, 218-19
Knight, E.F., 125

Lail-o-Nihar, Lahore Weekly 191
Lashkar-e-Jhangvi, 91
Lashkar-i-Taiba, 91
Legal Framework Order (LFO), 127
Liaquat Ali Khan, 38
Line of Control (LoC), 9-10, 25, 50, 59, 63, 68, 177, 191, 194-95
Lord Lytton, 123

Mahmood, Dr. Khalid, 102, 166, 221
Mahmud, Ershad, 6, 72, 75, 100, 156-57, 193, 195, 197
Majid, Chaudhry Abdul, 74, 195, 215
Majlis-e-Shura, 102, 126, 191
Majlis-e-Wahadat Muslimeen Gilgit-Baltistan (MWM-GB), 132-33, 166-67, 198, 225
Malik, Bashir A., 145
Malik, Justice Abdul Majid, 59
Malik, Yasin, 29, 48, 69-70, 194, 246
Mangla Dam Raising Project, 88
Maqpoon, Raja Jalal Hussain, 133, 227
Martial Law Zone, 126
Member, means, 300
Minhas, Raja Muhammad Mushtaq, 82, 221-22
Ministry of Kashmir Affairs (MKA), 3-4, 6-8, 18, 25
Mirpur Development Authority, 23
Mirpur Greater Water Scheme, 23
Mirpur University of Engineering and Technology, 23
Mirza Wajahat Hasan, 67
Miskeen, Malik, 228
Mohajir Rabita Command (MRC), 90
Moqaddam, Sobia, 160, 224
Most Favoured Nation status (MFN), 103

Movement for Justice, 93
Movement for the Restoration of Democracy (MRD), 40
MQM-London (MQM-L), 92
MQM-Pakistan (MQM-P), 92
Muhajir Ittehad Tehriq (MIT), 90
Murder of Traders, 119
Musharraf, Gen. Pervez, 41-45, 50, 59, 61, 80-81, 85, 130, 143, 157-58, 161, 177, 184, 198, 222
Muslim Conference, 4-6, 12, 14, 17, 21, 34-42, 45, 47, 53-54, 57, 61, 75, 81-82, 126, 138, 214, 217-18
Muttahida Majlis-e-Amal (MMA), 43, 100
Muttahida Qaumi Movement (MQM), 21-22, 75, 84-93, 154-55, 166, 247

Naji, Nawaz Khan, 134, 168-71, 226, 379
Nanga Parbat, 121
Naqvi, Syed Ghulam Raza, 217, 290
Naseer, Muhammad, 228
Nashad, Haji Fida Muhammad, 224-25, 227
National Economic Council (ECNEC) of Pakistan, 144
National Press Club, 68
Nawa-i-Waqt, 191
Naya Azad Kashmir, 97
Naya Pakistan, 93
New Anti-capitalist Party (NPA), 179
No Objection Certificate (NOC), 143
Non-Governmental Organisations (NGOs), 52
Noorbakshi, 117, 122
Northern Areas Council (NAC), 126
Legal Framework Order (LFO), 138
Northern Areas Legislative Council (NALC), 127-28, 130, 138, 157, 191-92, 242, 300, 398
Northern Areas Rules of Business, 138
North-West Frontier Province (NWFP), 125-26, 140, 174

Obama, Barack, 84
One Belt One Road (OBOR), 202

Pakistan, 1-5, 7-29, 33-34, 37-38, 40-48, 50-52, 54-55, 58-59, 61-72, 76-83, 86-88, 90-94, 96-104, 116, 118-21, 125-42, 144-46, 153-54, 160, 164, 166, 168-78, 182-83, 190-200, 202-4, 206-8, 215, 218, 220-21, 232-35

Pakistan Economic Survey 2014-15, 204
Pakistan International Airlines (PIA), 40
Pakistan Mineral Development Corporation (PMDC), 120
Pakistan Muslim League-Nawaz (PML-N), 14, 17, 20, 22-24, 29, 42, 44, 46, 75-77, 80-84, 96-98, 103, 116, 119, 133, 139, 144, 156, 159-60, 162, 166, 190, 198, 204, 207, 213, 217, 221-22, 224-25, 250
Pakistan Muslim League-Quaid-e-Azam (PML-Q), 154-55, 160-61
Pakistan Occupied Kashmir (PoK), 1-3, 34, 49, 51-52, 63, 93, 126, 190, 193, 197, 213, 230, 232
Pakistan People's Party Azad Jammu & Kashmir (PPPAJK), 94
Pakistan People's Party Gilgit-Baltistan (PPP-GB), 131, 153, 155, 157, 161, 165, 178, 206-7
Pakistan People's Party Shaheed Bhutto (PPPSB), 156
Pakistan Supreme Court Order on Gilgit Baltistan, 385-465
Pakistan Tehreek-i-Insaf (PTI), 23-24, 44, 46, 76, 82, 92-98, 162-64, 198, 200, 205, 214, 221, 225, 227, 234, 247
Pakistan Today, 134
Pakistan-based Kashmir Action Committee, 52
Parwana, Manzoor Hussain, 176-77, 205, 223
Person, means, 326, 409
Pir Sahib, 90
Plebiscite Front, 48
Political Parties Act (PPA), 79
Prescribed, means, 326, 409
President, means, 409
Prevention of Terrorism Act (POTA), 60
Progressive Youth Front (PYF), 175
Property, means, 326, 409
Provincial Government, means, 300

Raja Zulqarnain, 23
Rathore, Faisal Mumtaz, 17, 41, 220-21
Rathore, Raja Mumtaz Hussain, 72, 219-20, 296
Rehman, Hafiz Hafeezur, 133, 157, 160, 222
Remuneration, means, 326, 409
Research and Analysis Wing (RAW), 92
Rizvi, Syed Raziuddin, 227
Rules of Business, means, 6, 300
Rules of Procedure, means, 300

Sami, Maulana Abdul, 228

Secretary of the Council, means, 300
Secular thinking, 36
Sering, Sange Hasnain, 181
Service of Council, means, 409
Service of Gilgit-Baltistan, means, 326, 409
Service, means, 409
Shah, Muhammad Ayub, 228
Shah, Syed Jaffar, 223-24
Shah, Syed Mehdi, 132, 156, 226
Shah, Syed Pir Karam Ali, 227
Shahid, Sardar Arif, 68, 70, 215
Shamilat-e-Deh Act, 206
Sharia state, 98
Sharif, Nawaz, 17-21, 23-24, 40-41, 71, 80-84, 97, 157, 16, 183, 197, 203-4, 207, 221-22
Sheikh Abdullah, 5, 8, 34-37, 217
Shia, 117, 140, 164
Silk Road Economic Belt, 203
Simla Agreement, 263-65
Singh, Maharaja Hari, 13, 34, 124-25
Singh, Pratap, 124
Singh, Raja Ranbir, 123
Sipah-i-Sahaba Pakistan, 91
Snedden, Christopher, 36, 135
South Africa, 120
Speaker, means, 300, 326, 409
Special Economic Zones (SEZs), 203-5
Sultan Madad, 228
Sunni, 117, 165
Supreme Court of Pakistan, means, 409
Switzerland, 64

Taban, Haji Akbar, 158, 160, 225
Taliban, 51, 97
Tanzeem Ahl-e-Sunnat Wal Jamaat, 167
Terrorist and Disruptive Activities (Prevention) Act (TADA), 60
The Express Tribune, 173
The Nation, 119, 136
The News, 195

The Northern Areas Council Legal Frame Work Order, 1994, 299-324
Thinkers Forum (TF), 175, 199
Three Gorges, 144
Tiezzi, Shannon, 203

UK, 52, 64, 126
UK-based Tehreek-e-Kashmir, 52
UN Security Council, 171
United Arab Emirates (UAE), 50, 52
United Kashmir Peoples' National Party (UKPNP), 61-64, 67, 179, 213-14, 216
United Nations (UN), 38, 73, 85, 101, 144
United Nations Commission for India and Pakistan (UNCIP), 3, 126, 173, 394
United Nations General Assembly, 83
United Nations Human Rights Council, 181
United States of Kashmir, 61
Unrepresented Nations and Peoples Organisation (UNPO), 168, 175
US, 52, 64, 74, 97, 143

Vice Chairman of the Council, means, 326, 409

Wajahat Mirza, 182
War Council, 5
Wazarat, 122, 125
West Pakistan, 9, 79
World Bank (WB), 142-44, 146, 178
World Kashmir Freedom Movement, 52
World Kashmiri Freedom Federation, 52

Xi Jinping, 144
Xinjiang, 143

Yasin Malik and Nawaz Sharif Letters Exchanged Between, 381-84

Zaman, Muhammad, 228
Zarb-i-Azb, 97